The Broadview Reader

Second Edition

The
Broadview Reader

Second Edition

edited by

Herbert Rosengarten and Jane Flick

broadview press

Canadian Cataloguing in Publication Data

Main entry under title:

The Broadview Reader

2nd ed. rev.
ISBN 0-921149-88-3

1. English essays.   2. College readers.
3. English language – Rhetoric.   I. Rosengarten,
Herbert.   II. Flick, Jane, 1944-   .

PE1417.B76   1992   814.08   C92-093424-2

broadview press
P.O. Box 1243
Peterborough, Canada, K9J 7H5

Printed and bound in Canada by
Gagné Ltd.

Preface to the Second Edition

For this new edition we are pleased to have been able to preserve much of the first. We have kept representative pieces by such writers as George Orwell, Virginia Woolf, E.B. White and E.M. Forster, not only because they are recognized as "classics" that are touchstones of style and substance, but also because they can be relied on to offer something fresh and exciting to each new set of readers. As teachers, we turn to such pieces as to old friends. Many of the other essays included in the first edition have also become old friends; consequently, fewer than a dozen items from that edition have been cut.

At the same time, we have sought to include a selection of new essays from the recent past. In particular, we wanted to reflect in the book some of the stimulating and often controversial changes that have spread through society — and enlivened the study of English — over the past five years. A new section, "Ethnicity and Culture," signals the inclusion of a variety of essays on such topics as appropriation of voice, the conflict of cultures, and the representation of First Nations' peoples in art, history, and the cinema. Elsewhere, the reader will find a range of materials on other issues of current concern, including animal rights, "political correctness," and questions of race and gender.

We have retained the format of the first edition, including a thematic table of contents, a set of questions following each selection, and a glossary of terms used in the analysis of prose discourse.

HJR
JMF

Preface to the First Edition

Like many anthologies, *The Broadview Reader* was born out of a conviction that most other collections of this kind failed in one way or another to meet students' needs, and that it would not be difficult to improve on the efforts of our predecessors. In the event, the experience proved to be a humbling one. What began as an almost casual enterprise, to be completed in a short time, turned into a year-long search through books, magazines, newspapers, indexes, and catalogues. The process of selection became more and more complicated as we proceeded; many of the essays we had first chosen were edged out by later discoveries; categories formed and reformed with bewildering frequency; firm favorites suddenly lost their appeal and found their way into an ever-growing discard file. But for the exigencies of publishers' deadlines, *The Broadview Reader* might still be gestating in a hundred dog-eared yellow folders.

In making our final choices, we were guided by three considerations: would the essay be interesting to a variety of readers? would it lend itself to discussion and analysis? would it demonstrate some of the techniques and strategies of effective writing? We have not sought to present a history of the prose essay; though a few of our examples have been drawn from earlier periods, the emphasis is very much on twentieth-century writing. Nor have we attempted to assemble a "manual of styles" of the kind sometimes offered to students as models for their own writing. Our hope is rather that student writers will be stimulated by the ideas and issues presented in the essays, and be encouraged to search for ways of articulating their own ideas effectively.

The essays are grouped by subject to facilitate a thematic focus and a comparison of writers, attitudes, and approaches. Each essay is followed by a list of questions intended to help the reader identify the main lines of thought, and recognize some of the writer's strategies of language and organization. The questions are not comprehensive, or chosen with some particular rhetorical prescription in mind; rather, their function is to prepare the reader for more detailed discussion and analysis in the classroom, and to suggest writing exercises that might form a natural culmination of the critical process.

To help the reader focus on salient aspects of technique, we have also provided a "Guide to Rhetorical Patterns and Devices," and a glossary of terms commonly used in the critical analysis of prose discourse.

HJR
JMF

Table of Contents

Guide to Rhetorical Patterns and Devices

Essays which employ analogy

Frye	The Motive for Metaphor
Crean	Taking the Missionary Position
Hoban	Thoughts on a Shirtless Cyclist, Robin Hood and One or Two Other Things
Swift	A Modest Proposal
Trefil	Unexpected Vistas
Woolf	How Should One Read a Book?

Essays which employ analysis

Bettelheim	The Art of Moving Pictures
Castillo	*Dances With Wolves*: Review
Dryden	The Game
Ingram	The Science of Walking
Lurie	Women's Clothes — Towards Emancipation
Orwell	Politics and the English Language
Rafferty	True Believers
Richler	An Unquiet Awakening
Rybczynski	Nostalgia
Salutin	Loose Canons
Steinem	Marilyn Monroe: The Woman Who Died Too Soon
Walker	Westward Oh!

Essays which employ argumentation and persuasion

Atwood	The Writer's Responsibility
Awiakta	Red Alert! A Meditation on *Dances With Wolves*
Bronowski	The Real Responsibilities of the Scientist
Carson	The Obligation to Endure
Dryden	The Game
Farr	Dangerous Determination
Giangrande	Allowing the Mind to Wander
Gould	Let's Ban Applause!
Haldane	Some Enemies of Mankind
Hoggart	The Case Against Advertising
Keeshig-Tobias	Stop Stealing Native Stories
Kennedy	Who Killed King Kong?
Sillitoe	Sport and Nationalism
Suzuki	The Pain of Animals
Swift	A Modest Proposal
Thomas	Humanities and Science
Woodcock	The Tyranny of the Clock

Essays which employ cause and effect

Essays which employ classification

Essays which employ comparison and contrast

Essays which employ definition

Leacock   Roughing it in the Bush (My Plans for Moose-Hunting
                 in the Canadian Wilderness)
MacLennan   Confessions of a Wood-Chopping Man
O'Connor   Writing Short Stories
Salutin   Loose Canons
Stegner   Specifications for a Hero
Tuchman   The Historian's Opportunity

Essays which employ description

Brody   A Hearing
Dobbs   Matata
Graham   Life and Death in Ontario County
Iglauer   Bella Coola
Laurence   Where the World Began
Lurie   Women's Clothes — Towards Emancipation
Morris   St. John's
Mowat   The Nature of the North
Twain   A River Pilot Looks at the Mississippi
Wilson   Storm Over the Amazon

Essays which employ example and illustration

Allen   Slang Origins
Arkin   At the Movies
Avis   Canadian Spoken Here
Bettelheim   The Art of Moving Pictures
Bissoondath   I'm Not Racist But …
Cowley   Sociological Habit Patterns in Linguistic
                 Transmogrification
Fulford   Paperback Mentors
Giangrande   Allowing the Mind to Wander
Hoban   Thoughts on a Shirtless Cyclist, Robin Hood and One or
                 Two Other Things
Johnson   The Abuses of Advertising
Johnston   Is That All There Is? Tribal Culture
Lurie   Women's Clothes — Towards Emancipation
O'Connor   Writing Short Stories
Orwell   Politics and the English Language
Salutin   Loose Canons
Suzuki   The Pain of Animals
Thomas   Humanities and Science
Thurber   Courtship Through the Ages
Tuchman   The Historian's Opportunity
Visser   Taking Our Places
Walker   Westward Oh!

Essays which employ induction and deduction

Essays which employ narration

Essays which employ humour and satire

Chronological Table of Contents

Acknowledgements

Woody Allen, 'Slang Origins,' from *Without Feathers* © 1975 by Woody Allen. Reprinted by permission of Random House Inc.

Margaret Atwood, 'The Writer's Responsibility,' published as 'Amnesty International: An Address' in *Second Words: Selected Critical Prose* (Toronto: House of Auansi Press, 1982).

Walter Avis, 'Canadian Spoken Here,' from *Looking at Language*, M.H. Scargill and P.G. Penner (eds.). Copyright © W.J. Gage Limited 1966. Reprinted by permission of Gage Educational Publishing Company.

Marilou Awiakta, 'Red Alert! A Meditation on *Dances With Wolves*.' *Ms.* Magazine, March-April 1991, 70-71.

Russell Baker, 'Little Red Riding Hood Revisited,' Copyright © 1980 by The New York Times Company. Reprinted by permission.

Bruno Bettelheim, 'The Art of Moving Pictures,' reprinted by permission of the author and his agents. This article originally appeared in *Harper's Magazine*. Copyright © 1981 by Bruno Bettelheim.

Geoffrey Bibby, 'The Body in the Bog,' from the Winter 1968 issue of *Horizon*. Reprinted with permission from *Horizon*, Volume X, Number 1. Copyright 1968 by American Heritage, a division of Forbes Inc.

Neil Bissoondath, 'I'm Not Racist But...' by Neil BissoondathCopyright 1989. Reprinted by permission of the author.

Hugh Brody, 'A Hearing,' from *Maps and Dreams* by Hugh Brody. Copyright © 1981 Douglas & McIntyre Ltd. Reprinted by permission.

Jacob Bronowski, 'The Real Responsibilities of the Scientist,' reprinted by permission of the *Bulletin of Atomic Scientists*, a magazine of science and world affairs. Copyright © 1956 by the Educational Foundation for Nuclear Sciences, 6042 South Kimbark, Chicago, IL 60637.

Rachel Carson, 'The Obligation to Endure,' from *Silent Spring* by Rachel Carson. Copyright © 1962 by Rachel L. Carson. Copyright © renewed 1990 by Roger Christie. Reprinted by permission of Houghton Mifflin Company. All rights reserved.

Edward D. Castillo, '*Dances With Wolves*: Review.' *Film Quarterly* 44.4 (Summer 1991): 14-23. Reprinted by permission.

Simone Collier, 'At War with the Army.' *Ryerson Review of Journalism*, April 1991, 16-23. Reprinted by permission.

Malcolm Cowley, 'Sociological Habit Patterns in Linguistic Transmogrification,' from *The Reporter*, Sept. 20, 1956.

Susan Crean, 'Taking the Missionary Position.' *This Magazine* 24.6 (February 1991): 23-28. Reprinted by permission.

Richard Hoggart, 'The Case Against Advertising,' from *Speaking to Each Other* by Richard Hoggart © 1970. Reprinted by permission of the author and of Chatto & Windus.

Edith Iglauer, 'Bella Coola.' *The Strangers Next Door.* Madeira Park, B.C.: Harbour, 1991. 276-284. Reprinted by permission of Sterling Lord Literistic, Inc.

Jay Ingram, 'The Science of Walking.' From *The Science of Everyday Life.* © Jay Ingram, 1989. Reprinted by permission of Penguin Books Canada Limited.

Basil H. Johnston, 'Is That All There Is? Tribal Literature.' *Canadian Literature* 128 (Spring 1991): 54-62. Reprinted by permission.

Pauline Kael, 'New Age Daydreams' From *Movie Love: Complete Reviews* by Pauline Kael. Copyright © 1988, 1989, 1990, 1991 by Pauline Kael. Originally appealed in *The New Yorker.* Used by permission of the publisher, Dutton, an imprint of New American Library, a division of Penguin Books USA Inc.

Lenore Keeshig-Tobias, 'Stop Stealing Native Stories.' *The Globe and Mail*, 26 January 1990. Reprinted by permission.

X.J. Kennedy, 'Who Killed King Kong?' originally published in *Dissent, 1960.* Copyright © Dissent; reprinted by permission.

Margaret Laurence, 'Where the World Began,' from *The Heart of a Stranger,* reprinted by permission of The Canadian Publishers, McClelland and Stewart.

Stephen Leacock, 'Roughing it in the Bush,' reprinted by permission of Dodd Mead & Company, Inc. from *Over the Footlights* by Stephen Leacock. Copyright © 1923 by Dodd Mead & Company Inc. Copyright renewed 1950 by George Leacock.

Alison Lurie, 'Women's Clothes: Towards Emancipation,' from *The Language of Clothes* by Alison Lurie, Copyright © 1981 by Alison Lurie. Reprinted by permission of Melanie Jackson Agency.

Hugh MacLennan, 'The Shadow of Captain Bligh,' from *The Other Side of Hugh MacLennan* (ed. Elspeth Cameron), © 1978. Reprinted by permission of Macmillan of Canada, A Division of Canada Publishing Corporation.

Jan Morris, 'St John's.' *City to City.* Toronto: MacFarlane Walter and Ross, 1990. 1-17. [Originally in *Saturday Night.*] Reprinted by permission.

Farley Mowat, 'The Nature of the North,' excerpts from *Canada North (Toronto:* McClelland and Stewart, 1967), reprinted by permission of the author.

Flannery O'Connor, 'Writing Short Stories,' from *Mystery and Manners* by Flannery O'Connor. Copyright © 1957, 1961, 1963, 1964, 1966, 1967, 1969 by the Estate of Mary Flannery O'Connor. Copyright © 1962 by Flannery O'Connor. Reprinted by permission of Farrar, Straus and Giroux, Inc.

George Orwell, 'Shooting an Elephant,' from *Shooting an Elephant and Other Essays.* Reprinted by permission of the estate of Sonia Brownell Orwell and of Secker & Warburg Ltd.

Language and Communication

Slang Origins

by Woody Allen

How many of you have ever wondered where certain slang expressions 1
come from? Like "She's the cat's pajamas," or to "take it on the lam."
Neither have I. And yet for those who are interested in this sort of thing
I have provided a brief guide to a few of the more interesting origins.

Unfortunately, time did not permit consulting any of the established 2
works on the subject, and I was forced to either obtain the information
from friends or fill in certain gaps by using my own common sense.

Take, for instance, the expression "to eat humble pie." During the 3
reign of Louis the Fat, the culinary arts flourished in France to a degree
unequaled anywhere. So obese was the French monarch that he had
to be lowered onto the throne with a winch and packed into the seat
itself with a large spatula. A typical dinner (according to DeRochet)
consisted of a thin crêpe appetizer, some parsley, an ox, and custard.
Food became the court obsession, and no other subject could be discussed
under penalty of death. Members of a decadent aristocracy consumed
incredible meals and even dressed as foods. DeRochet tells us that M.
Monsant showed up at the coronation as a weiner, and Étienne Tisserant
received papal dispensation to wed his favorite codfish. Desserts grew
more and more elaborate and pies grew larger and larger until the
minister of justice suffocated trying to eat a seven-foot "Jumbo pie."
Jumbo pie soon became *jumble* pie and "to eat a jumble pie" referred
to any kind of humiliating act. When the Spanish seamen heard the word
jumble, they pronounced it "humble," although many preferred to say
nothing and simply grin.

Now, while "humble pie" goes back to the French, "take it on the 4 lam" is English in origin. Years ago, in England, "lamming" was a game played with dice and a large tube of ointment. Each player in turn threw dice and then skipped around the room until he hemorrhaged. If a person threw seven or under he would say the word "quintz" and proceed to twirl in a frenzy. If he threw over seven, he was forced to give every player a portion of his feathers and was given a good "lamming." Three "lammings" and a player was "kwirled" or declared a moral bankrupt. Gradually any game with feathers was called "lamming" and feathers became "lams." To "take it on the lam" meant to put on feathers and later, to escape, although the transition is unclear.

5   Incidentally, if two of the players disagreed on the rules, we might say they "got into a beef." This term goes back to the Renaissance when a man would court a woman by stroking the side of her head with a slab of meat. If she pulled away, it meant she was spoken for. If, however, she assisted by clamping the meat to her face and pushing it all over her head, it meant she would marry him. The meat was kept by the bride's parents and worn as a hat on special occasions. If, however, the husband took another lover, the wife could dissolve the marriage by running with the meat to the town square and yelling, "With thine own beef, I do reject thee. Aroo! Aroo!" If a couple "took to the beef" or "had a beef" it meant they were quarreling.

6   Another marital custom gives us that eloquent and colorful expression of disdain, "to look down one's nose." In Persia it was considered a mark of great beauty for a woman to have a long nose. In fact, the longer the nose, the more desirable the female, up to a certain point. Then it became funny. When a man proposed to a beautiful woman he awaited her decision on bended knee as she "looked down her nose at him." If her nostrils twitched, he was accepted, but if she sharpened her nose with pumice and began pecking him on the neck and shoulders, it meant she loved another.

7   Now, we all know when someone is very dressed up, we say he looks "spiffy." The term owes its origin to Sir Oswald Spiffy, perhaps the most renowned fop of Victorian England. Heir to treacle millions, Spiffy squandered his money on clothes. It was said that at one time he owned enough handkerchiefs for all the men, women and children in Asia to blow their noses for seven years without stopping. Spiffy's sartorial innovations were legend, and he was the first man ever to wear gloves on his head. Because of extra-sensitive skin, Spiffy's underwear had to be made of the finest Nova Scotia salmon, carefully sliced by one particular tailor. His libertine attitudes involved him in several notorious

scandals, and he eventually sued the government over the right to wear earmuffs while fondling a dwarf. In the end, Spiffy died a broken man in Chichester, his total wardrobe reduced to kneepads and a sombrero.

Looking "spiffy," then, is quite a compliment, and one who does is **8** liable to be dressed "to beat the band," a turn-of-the-century expression that originated from the custom of attacking with clubs any symphony orchestra whose conductor smiled during Berlioz. "Beating the band" soon became a popular evening out, and people dressed up in their finest clothes, carrying with them sticks and rocks. The practice was finally abandoned during a performance of the *Symphonie Fantastique* in New York when the entire string section suddenly stopped playing and exchanged gun-fire with the first ten rows. Police ended the melee but not before a relative of J.P. Morgan's was wounded in the soft palate. After that, for a while at least, nobody dressed "to beat the band."

If you think some of the above derivations questionable, you might **9** throw up your hands and say, "Fiddlesticks." This marvelous expression originated in Austria many years ago. Whenever a man in the banking profession announced his marriage to a circus pinhead, it was the custom for friends to present him with a bellows and a three-year supply of wax fruit. Legend has it that when Leo Rothschild made known his betrothal, a box of cello bows was delivered to him by mistake. When it was opened and found not to contain the traditional gift, he exclaimed, "What are these? Where are my bellows and fruit? Eh? All I rate is fiddlesticks!" The term "fiddlesticks" became a joke overnight in the taverns amongst the lower classes, who hated Leo Rothschild for never removing the comb from his hair after combing it. Eventually "fiddlesticks" meant any foolishness.

Well, I hope you've enjoyed some of these slang origins and that they **10** stimulate you to investigate some on your own. And in case you were wondering about the term used to open this study, "the cat's pajamas," it goes back to an old burlesque routine of Chase and Rowe's, the two nutsy German professors. Dressed in oversized tails, Bill Rowe stole some poor victim's pajamas. Dave Chase, who got great mileage out of his "hard of hearing" specialty, would ask him:

Chase: Ach, Herr Professor. Vot is dot bulge under your pocket?
Rowe: Dot? Dot's de chap's pajamas.
Chase: The cat's pajamas? Ut mein Gott?

Audiences were convulsed by this sort of repartee and only a premature **11** death of the team by strangulation kept them from stardom.

(1975)

The Writer's Subject

1. Allen's essay is an example of literary burlesque. What form of writing is Allen burlesquing in this essay?

2. The essay depends for its effect upon inventing incredible etymologies for well-known phrases such as "to eat humble pie" or "to look down one's nose." With the help of a dictionary of etymology, choose any of the words or phrases that Allen pretends to explain, and trace its real origin.

The Writer's Style and Strategy

1. What assumptions does Allen make about his audience in paragraph 1?

2. What methods associated with sociology does Allen pretend to employ in his study of word origins?

3. Allen uses a variety of techniques to achieve his humorous effects, such as inflating the trivial, reversing the reader's expectations, juxtaposing sense and nonsense, mixing real names (Morgan, Rothschild) with invented ones (Sir Oswald Spiffy), or combining objects or ideas in unexpected ways. Take one of Allen's explanations (e.g., "to eat humble pie" in para. 3), and try to pinpoint the means by which he creates humour.

4. Allen imposes an apparent order on his material by means of transitions. Examine some of these transitions and comment on their logic.

Suggested Topics for Writing and Discussion

1. Allen pokes fun at odd customs, as well as at essays on the curiosities of language. For example, the "custom" he describes in paragraph 5 concerning the use of a slab of meat in courtship and marriage during the Renaissance is not significantly more ridiculous than such real customs as a girl's putting a slice of wedding cake under her pillow, or having baby shoes coated in bronze. Discuss one or two odd or peculiar customs you are familiar with, and trace their origins as far as you can.

2. Choose one of the following slang expressions, and make up your own derivation in the style of Allen's essay: off his rocker; round the bend; dressed fit to kill.

3. Give a description of a group of slang terms which you or your friends currently use. Write explanations of these terms for a member of the older generation.

Canadian Spoken Here

by Walter S. Avis

Fifteen years ago a writer in a Canadian magazine complained that the
word *snye* was not defined in any dictionary in spite of the fact that
the Canadian Board on Geographical Names had certified it as "a lawful
and proper generic term." A few years later another writer, in another
journal, complained that none of his dictionaries included the word
mukluk. Nor have these been the only voices raised in frustration because
so many terms met with in Canada were ignored by dictionaries. Until
quite recently, however, all were voices crying in the wilderness; for
few Canadians were interested enough in their speech to undertake the
gigantic task of finding out about it. Consequently, there were no Canadian dictionaries worthy of the name; and our imported dictionaries virtually ignored Canadian usage. After all, British dictionaries are primarily intended for Britons and American dictionaries for Americans; no
reputable editor claims anything more.

To say that British and American dictionaries do not reflect Canadian usage is to say that Canadian English is neither British nor
American, that the English spoken in Canada is distinct in many ways
from that spoken in the United Kingdom and from that spoken in the
United States. It should be observed that this distinctive variety of speech
is referred to as "Canadian English" and not as the "Canadian language,"
for Canadians share one language with Britons, Americans, and a host of
other people both inside the Commonwealth and beyond it. To claim
that there is a Canadian language, or, as many Americans do, an
American language, is to distort the meaning of the word *language* for
nationalistic purposes. On the other hand, it is a form of blindness to

insist, as many do, that "English is English" and that it is folly to dignify the "slang and dialect" of Canada by discussing it as if it merited serious attention.

3   Any Canadian who has spent some time in both the United Kingdom and the United States knows that his English is recognized as non-British by Britons and (perhaps less often) as non-American by Americans. While it is true that the uninformed in Britain may identify us with Americans and the uninformed in the United States may identify us with Englishmen, people in both countries who are familiar with Canadians recognize speech habits that are unlike their own. An American, for example, may point to our way of using *blind* where he would use *shade*, *tap* where he would use *faucet*, *serviette* where he would use *napkin*, *braces* where he would use *suspenders*, and *porridge* where he would use *oatmeal*; or he might point to our way of pronouncing *been* to rhyme with "bean" instead of "bin," *ration* to rhyme with "fashion" instead of "nation," *lever* to rhyme with "beaver" instead of "never," and Z to rhyme with "bed" instead of "knee." He will certainly notice that most of us pronounce *lout* with a different sounding vowel from that of *loud*. He will, in fact, wrongly insist that we pronounce *out* to rhyme with "shoot," just as speakers of Scots dialect do.

4   The Britisher, on the other hand, will observe that we pronounce *aunt, glass, path, clerk, war,* and *tomato* in a way quite different from his; he may also note that most of us make no distinction between the vowel of *caught* and that of *cot*, whereas for him the vowels are very different indeed. He observes, too, that many of the words he uses every day in England are simply not understood by his Canadian friends. Suppose he gets into a conversation about cars. Says he, "I think a car should have a roomy boot." Communication will come to a halt until someone rescues him by pointing out that Canadians call a *boot* a "trunk." Before this chat is over, he will learn that Canadians use *hood* for his *bonnet*, *muffler* for *silencer, bumper* for *fender*, and (egad, sir!) *fender* for *wing*. These few examples illustrate the point that Canadian patterns of speech are neither British nor American, though they are in some degree a blend of both.

5   Canadian English, then, is a dialect which resembles American English in some respects and British English in others and includes, at the same time, a great deal that is significantly Canadian. The explanation of this mixed character lies in the settlement history of the country. As the eastern regions of British North America were opened for settlement, before, during, and after the Revolutionary War, Americans were promi-

nent among the settlers. New Englanders began moving into Nova Scotia several decades before the Revolution and the Loyalist influx of 1790 brought thousands more. Today, as in the days of Judge Haliburton's *Sam Slick, the Clockmaker,* the New England origin of large numbers of Bluenoses is evident in the speech and customs of the province. Both New Brunswick and the Eastern Townships of Quebec were first colonized by American Loyalists and, in both areas, post-Loyalist settlers added to the preponderance of American stock.

In Upper Canada the early influx of American settlers was especial- 6 ly significant, for Ontario was to become the populous heart of English-speaking Canada. By 1795 there were some 10,000 Loyalists settled around Kingston and Niagara, at opposite ends of Lake Ontario. When the War of 1812 began, the population of Upper Canada had grown to some 50,000, almost entirely made up of former Americans, both Loyalist and post-Loyalist, none of whom were any less American in language and manners than their former compatriots to the south. This American preponderance is evident from the composition of the legislative assembly in 1828, there being four members born in Ireland, six in Scotland, seven in England, three in other British colonies, thirteen in Canada, and fifteen in the United States.

In Ontario, there is no doubt, American speech habits have been en- 7 trenched from the beginning. The settlers from south of the line introduced their system of education along with their system of municipal government. The public elementary school was always the normal thing in Upper Canada, many of the textbooks being imported from the United States or adapted from American models. This state of affairs did not pass unnoticed, as is made clear in the following observations made by a British doctor travelling through the province in 1832:

It is really melancholy to traverse the province and go into many of the common schools; you find a herd of children instructed by some anti-British adventurer, instilling into the young and tender mind sentiments hostile to the parent state [that is, American geography and history with a republican bias]; and American spelling books, dictionaries and grammars, teaching them anti-British dialect and idiom.

Later in the century the conditions which so irritated the doctor were 8 somewhat moderated by the mildly pro-British reforms of Egerton Ryerson, a second-generation Loyalist from New York, who was superintendent of education in Ontario from 1844 to 1876. One of the reforms is alluded to in the following quotation from a contemporary issue of *The Voice of the Fugitive* (Oct. 23, 1851) published in Sandwich, Canada West:

> We are also in great need of reading books, slates, and some 6 or 7 dozen of Webster's spelling book (only American spelling book allowed in Government schools) for the use of poor scholars.

Ryerson's success in eliminating American influence from the schools was far from complete; yet his efforts and those of others with similar views have doubtless had a significant effect on the English of Canadians, for the practice of "teaching British" has a long history in this country. It must be remembered that the prestige of British English has always exerted a strong influence on Canadian patterns of speech, especially among the educated. Nevertheless, it seems clear that the American idiom was already implanted deep in Upper Canada when the great stream of British immigrants began to flow into the country during the later stages of settlement.

9   Population movements between the United States and Canada have never ceased to be an important factor in the settlement of the Dominion of the North. When hard times struck Upper Canada in the 1830's, many Canadians joined the American settlers, who, freed from the Indian menace in Illinois and Indiana, were moving into the Middle West. The exodus of Canadians to the States during this period brought about the opening up of the old Northwest. The transcontinental railway was undertaken by the Canadian government and attractive land grants were made available to prospective homesteaders. The forty-ninth parallel during this period was little more than a geographical abstraction; the tax collector was, as one historian has said, the only important indication that a boundary existed.

10   In the 1870's and the 1880's many farmers in Upper Canada contracted "Manitoba fever" and hastened to take advantage of the opportunities Manitoba had to offer. These settlers, many of them of Loyalist background, reached their new homes by way of the United States, being joined en route by many landhungry Americans. Immigrants from the Old Country were very much in the minority and generally settled in their own communities, as did the Red River Scots of Lord Selkirk.

11   Twenty years later, Saskatchewan and Alberta were opened up, at a time when the American Northwest had been largely settled. The C.P.R., completed in 1885, carried great numbers of Eastern Canadians and some Britishers to the new territories. But the greatest number

of settlers came from the south, where the frontier was fast disappearing, almost a million Americans entering southern Alberta and Saskatchewan from 1900 to 1915. Thus, the North American character of the English spoken on the Prairies was entrenched through the domination of Canadians (mostly Ontarians but a substantial number of Maritimers) and Americans among the English-speaking settlers. The thousands of non-English-speaking Scandinavians and Central Europeans who immigrated to the Prairie Provinces learned the kind of English spoken by their neighbors, most of whom, as we have seen, spoke the North American variety. Latter-day American arrivals, particularly in oil-rich Alberta, have reinforced this North American pattern.

Fewer Americans were drawn to British Columbia, largely because 12 the type of farming land was not to their liking. As a result, the Pacific-coast province was settled, in large measure, by emigrants from the British Isles, although Canadians from both Ontario and the Maritimes were well represented. This British predominance has had a noticeable but as yet undefined effect on the nature of British Columbia English, especially in certain areas — as the Okanagan Valley and southern Vancouver Island — and among people at the higher social levels, who traditionally send their children to private schools conducted more or less on the British pattern. On the other hand, British Columbia has strong lines of north-south communication with the United States, lines which have in many ways been more active than those running eastward through the Rockies. This close bond with the United States has also had its effect on the English of British Columbia, perhaps most noticeably in Vancouver and its areas of influence.

This summary of population movements, oversimplified as it obviously 13 is, should serve to emphasize the significance of the American element in Canadian settlement history. Influence from the United States has been constant and strong from the beginning. Canadians are often taught from American textbooks; they listen to American radio programs, watch American television and movies, read American novels; in large numbers they are constantly moving back and forth across the border, as immigrants, as tourists, as students, and as bargain hunters. Finally, as a North American country, Canada quite naturally shares a large vocabulary with the United States, a vocabulary made up of words designating all manner of things indigenous to this continent. One need only leaf through the *Dictionary of Canadianisms* or the *Dictionary of Americanisms* to appreciate this fact. There is nothing very surprising about the closeness of Canadian and American English.

14   It must be understood that the United Kingdom has also made an enormous contribution to the settlement of English-speaking Canada. For
more than a century an almost continuous stream of Britishers, speaking various dialects, have emigrated to Canada. In most communities,
especially those along the Canada-United States border (where Canada's
population is still concentrated), these newcomers came into contact
with already established Canadians and, as might be expected, their
children adopted the speech habits of the communities they settled in.
Only in certain areas, where relatively homogeneous Old Country groups
established themselves, did markedly British dialectal features survive
through several generations. Such communities can be found in Newfoundland, northern Nova Scotia, the Ottawa Valley, the Red River
region, and the parts of British Columbia already mentioned. It might
be added that the English-speaking natives of Montreal and Quebec have
an English and Scots heritage going back nearly two centuries, a fact
that is often evident in their speech, which is, nevertheless, obviously
Canadian. British immigrants have unquestionably made substantial contributions to every department of the language, none perhaps in greater
degree than the Scots and Scots-Irish, who have from earliest times been
prominent in Canada's affairs, the Scots schoolteacher, or dominie, being
a part of the community scene in so many areas in colonial times. To
a great extent, what is not American about Canadian English has been
brought directly from the Old Country, such features often competing
with American variants already current in Canada, and even gradually
displacing them. Just such a process seems to be taking place at present with respect to the pronunciation of *schedule:* the British (shej ül),
though apparently used by a minority, might well be displacing the
characteristically American (skej ül), very probably influenced by the
practice of CBC announcers.

15   With the passing years, the speech habits of educated Canadians have
become remarkably homogeneous, though by no means free of regional
variety. Taken as a whole, the language of this country is neither British
nor American; it is distinctively Canadian. This distinctiveness is most
easily demonstrated with reference to the vocabulary, for there are
hundreds of words which are native to Canada or which have meaning
peculiar to this country. All of these words, which may be called Canadianisms, and many more, are defined in Canadian dictionaries already
available or soon to be published; many, indeed, will be found in Canadian editions of foreign dictionaries, especially of the larger size, for
foreign dictionary-makers are at last aware that Canadians, who form

an important part of their market, are nowadays expecting dictionaries to give information about Canadian words, pronunciations, and spellings.

There is a surprisingly large number of Canadianisms, some of national 16 currency, others largely regional; still others are confined mainly to special fields of activity, such as logging, fishing, or athletics. Most are terms coined in this country from English-language resources, or words borrowed here from the several other-language groups encountered by English-speaking Canadians. Others are native English words which have taken on specialized or transferred meanings here in Canada.

Prominent among Canadianisms are proper nouns, such as names of 17 regions: *French Shore, Cariboo;* of natives of certain regions: *Herring Chokers, Spud Islanders;* of things associated with persons or places: *Calgary redeye, Digby chicken.* Needless to say, many terms referring to things political are peculiarly Canadian: *Grit, Socred, reeve, rural municipality, police village.* Moreover, various institutions of a social character have Canadian names, most of them being Canadian institutions: *collegiate institute, separate school.* A great many words are loanwords from other languages: French, *aboideau, shanty;* Eskimo, *komatik, oomiak;* Amerindian languages, *chipmunk, pemmican.* Sometimes the origin of such loanwords is obscured in the process of adoption: *chowder, shanty, mush, shivaree, snye,* for example, are all borrowings from Canadian French, the original forms being *chaudière, chantier, marche, charivari,* and *chenail.*

Many Canadianisms seem more or less limited to certain regions: 18 to Newfoundland, *jinkers, glitter;* Maritimes, *gaspereau, Cape Island Boat;* Ontario, *fire-reels, Aurora trout;* Prairies, *pothole trout, grid road;* British Columbia, *salt chuck, kokanee;* Northland, *cat-swing, cheechako.*

The field of sports has made its contributions as well, for hockey and 19 lacrosse, and probably broomball, were born and developed here, while a native variety of rugby, that is, football, has developed among us. Furthermore, curling, introduced from Scotland, has flourished so remarkably in Canada that many of the terms our curlers use came into being in this country. From hockey and lacrosse we get *blueline, rover, spearing, crosse;* from rugby-football, *rouge, flying-wing;* from curling, *spieler, knockout game.* And in the area of sport, needless to say, numerous slang terms have made their appearance: *import, homebrew, rink rat, deke.* In other areas, too, slang has been born: *suitcase farmer, screech, Spam medal, pogey,* although most slang heard in Canada is imported from south of the border.

20   Sometimes names for a commonly encountered thing will be numerous
indeed. The perky little Canada jay, familiar to all who frequent the
Canadian bush, has been called many names over the years and across
the country; here are a number (28) that have been met with by readers
for the *Dictionary of Canadianisms* (not all, of course, are in current
use; some are highly regional; and a few may well have been used in
error by early travellers unfamiliar with the country and its creatures):
*blue pie, butcher bird, camp bird, camp robber, Canada jay, Cana-
dian jay, Canadian wood jay, caribou bird, carrion bird, cinerous crow,
grease bird, gray jay, Hudson Bay bird, Johnnie, Labrador jay, lumber-
jack, meat bird, meat hawk, meatjay, moose bird, moose jay, Oregon
jay, Rocky Mountain jay, Rupert's bird, venison bird, whisky-jack,
whisky-jay, whisky-john.*

21   The proliferation of names for the Canada jay is, obviously, an exceptional case; it is much more usual for a word to become popular
and take on a wide range of meanings over a period of time, often in
a relatively limited geographical region. Take for example, the word
Siwash, which came into English from the Chinook Jargon, a once widely
used trade-language on the Pacific Coast. In Chinook Jargon the word
meant "Indian" and was derived from French *sauvage,* as Indians were
called by the coureurs de bois and voyageurs in the days of exploration. Our earliest evidence of the word in a normal English context is
in a trader's journal dated 1851 at Kamloops Fort. It may be that the
word originally referred to the Salish Indians of Southwestern British
Columbia and adjacent parts of Washington, but in due course it came
to mean any Indian. The term spread into the Yukon and the Northwest
Territories during the late nineteenth century, probably by way of the
fur traders and later by way of the sourdoughs, many of whom had
worked in the Cariboo gold diggings before moving on to the Klon-
dike. As the years passed, *Siwash* took on additional meanings, one
of them being "any Indian language" and still another "the Chinook
Jargon." Some persons appear to have used the word to mean "male
Indian" only, using *klooch* or *kloochman* for "woman" or "wife"; still
others used the word to refer to a person camping on the trail Indian-
style, that is with no shelter other than that provided by nature. For
the word had by now taken on verbal meanings, one of these being "to
travel light, establishing *Siwash camps"* (an Indian-style camp using
natural resources for protection from the elements). Another verbal
meaning, this one at the slang level, is "prohibit from obtaining liquor;
place on the Indian list," a meaning developing out of the fact that it

was illegal in British Columbia and the Northwest (as in other provinces) to sell liquor or beer to Indians.

Although the word had no apparent derogatory connotations in the 22 beginning, it certainly developed them in the nineteenth century, at least in the senses having to do with people. It first came to be used of Indians in a derogatory way, and later of any person as a term of contempt. It was a "fighting word," so to speak, and as such fell out of decent use. Indeed, such names as *Siwash sweater,* a long-established term for the warm pullover of gray, unbleached wool made by the native Indians of southern Vancouver Island, became unusable, being displaced in recent years by *Indian sweater* or *Cowichan sweater.* Thus when a word loses prestige in one area of its use, the unfavorable connotations invariably spread to other areas, causing an avoidance of the term by sensitive persons and creating a need for new words having favorable or neutral connotations.

This word *Siwash* has been especially prolific in compounds over the 23 past century; in addition to *Siwash camp* and *Siwash sweater,* already mentioned, the *Dictionary of Canadianisms* lists *Siwash berry* (the saskatoon), *Siwash blanket* (a low cloud ceiling), *Siwash dog* (a hybrid sled dog in the Northwest), *Siwash goose* (the western grebe), *Siwash house* (the Indian hall at a trading post), *Siwash logger* (a no-account beachcomber), *Siwash pudding* (a pudding made with saskatoon berries), *Siwash rhubarb* (a kind of plant; Indian rhubarb), *Siwash slipper* (a mocassin), *Siwash sock* (a puttee-like duffel sock worn inside mocassins), *Siwash tongue* (the Chinook Jargon), *Siwash wapatoo* (an edible tuber; Indian potato), *Siwash wind* (a brisk wind). When to this impressive list we add such derivatives as *Siwashing, Siwashdom, Siwash fashion,* and *Siwash style,* it can be seen that this term has been uncommonly productive.

Another word of great interest is *snye,* which comes into Canadian 24 English from Canadian French, the source being the dialectal *chenail* (as opposed to Mod.F *chenal* channel). We encounter this word first in the 1820's during the building of the Rideau Canal between Ottawa (then Bytown) and Kingston. As among the voyageurs, it referred to a side-channel, especially one which by-passed a rapids or falls, creating a kind of island. Such snyes, often shallow and sometimes dry, were deepened and widened to serve as channels for the Ottawa lumbermen to run their timber rafts through in by-passing obstructions in the river. During the height of the lumbering period in this neck of the woods, *snye* was a widely used word, occurring in such compounds as *dry snye,*

snye dam, and *timber snye,* and in numerous place names, as *Gloucester Snye* and *Mississippi Snye.* It is as a place name that the word is best known today in the Ottawa Valley.

25   Later in the century the word *snye* makes its appearance in the Northwest. Here too it was taken into English from the French of the voyageur, but here it has continued to flourish. In the Northwest *snye* refers primarily to a narrow, meandering, sluggish side-channel of a river, usually shallow and often coming to a dead end (also called a *blind snye* or *blind slough).* It does, however, seem to have developed some secondary meanings in recent years: (a) a stream connecting two rivers some distance away from their confluence, thus creating an island (a meaning apparently developing out of the familiarity many persons had with "the Snigh," a water-course of just this description at Fort McMurray on the Mackenzie River); (b) a channel, or other adequate stretch of water, utilized as a landing place for bush planes (also called a *landing snye*); and (c) any small tributary stream. Over the years this borrowing from Canadian French has had many spellings, including *schny, she-ny, shnay, snie,* and *snigh,* several of them revealing early stages in the process of anglicization, *sh* representing the pronunciation of French *ch.* The currently accepted pronunciation is (sni), although older (shni) is said to be heard in places still; the usual spelling is *snye,* the older *sny* also being met occasionally. The plural, it seems, may be either *snyes* or *snies.*

26   This process of borrowing and the continuing development of meanings within the language is one of the most intriguing aspects of English, or any other language, for that matter. Canadian English provides numerous examples of just such proliferation, as in the case of *bateau, cariole, cache, shanty,* and many more. Often words which are not themselves of Canadian origin develop meanings or become elements in compounds which are, and here we might cite such words as *beaver, bush, Indian, lumber, slough, timber,* and *wood.* Of course, many of the words which we call Canadian are now to be classed as "historical" or "obsolete." But the meanings of such no-longer-used words are important to people who read earlier writings for whatever reason and, of course, to those who read historical novels about the early days of life in Canada. For this reason as well as for their intrinsic interest, such terms as *York boat, Red River cart, Montreal canoe, buffalo runner, home-guard Indian, pork-eater, Eastmain, Rupert's Land, New Caledonia,* and a host of others have their claim to the attention of the student of Canadian English.

Of course, the field of Canadian English involves much more than 27 the searching out and defining of words and expressions. One must be concerned with the study of regional speech, called "dialect geography," a thoroughly fascinating area of study; one must also be concerned with pronunciation patterns, not only from a regional point of view but from a social point of view as well. And, finally, although this is a rather special area of language that is purely visual, one must be concerned with practices of spelling, for here perhaps more than anywhere else inadequately informed critics of language focus their attention. Such problems can be understood only after an extensive and thorough examination of the language as it is spoken in Canada and after an intelligent assessment of the practices of educated Candians in these matters. The worker in the vineyard is sometimes frustrated by the very complexity of the evidence, but the irritations are more than balanced by the utterly thrilling discoveries one makes and by the pleasure that comes with deepening one's knowledge of man's most precious possession — his language.

(1966)

The Writer's Subject

1. What distinctions does the writer draw between the phrases "Canadian English" and "the American language"? (para. 2)

2. What, according to Avis, are the principal elements that make up Canadian English? (paras. 3-5)

3. Explain the importance of patterns of immigration to Canada in the development of Canadian English. (paras. 6-13)

4. What reasons does Avis give for the greater influence of British English in British Columbia than in other areas of Canada? (para. 12)

5. What, according to Avis, constitutes a Canadianism? (para. 15)

6. What are the chief categories which Avis identifies in his account of the development of Canadianisms?

7. In what ways has the development of Canadian English been influenced by other languages?

8. Using an example provided by Avis, show how a word can change in meaning over a period of time.

The Writer's Style and Strategy

1. This essay is primarily expository in nature, its main function being to define and illustrate Canadian English. What methods does Avis use to make an otherwise dry subject interesting?

2. Avis presents a variety of materials in this essay. How does he organize these materials?

3. In what way does the title throw light on Avis's purposes in writing this essay?

Suggested Topics for Writing and Discussion

1. Avis points to spelling differences between Canadian and British English, and between Canadian and American English. Using your college library, consult three or four handbooks of English designed for use by Canadian students. Show the points upon which these agree and the points upon which they differ with regard to spelling.

2. Avis mentions dialect geography in his closing paragraph. Using your college library, find out what you can about dialect geography and discuss striking features of the English dialect of a particular area of North America (e.g., Newfoundland, Texas, Cape Breton Island, North Carolina).

3. Do you think that those who speak the dialect of a particular region should be encouraged to preserve that dialect or to adopt the standard forms and pronunciation of "received" English?

4. Examine your own "dialect." Explain, for a speaker of English from another region or another country, the features of your dialect which make it distinctive.

Little Red Riding Hood
Revisited

by Russell Baker

In an effort to make the classics accessible to contemporary readers, 1
I am translating them into the modern American language. Here is the
translation of *Little Red Riding Hood:*

Once upon a point in time, a small person named Little Red Riding 2
Hood initiated plans for the preparation, delivery and transportation of
foodstuffs to her grandmother, a senior citizen residing at a place of
residence in a wooded area of indeterminate dimension.

In the process of implementing this program, her incursion into the 3
area was in mid-transportation process when it attained interface with
an alleged perpetrator. This individual, a wolf, made inquiry as to the
whereabouts of Little Red Riding Hood's goal, as well as inferring that
he was desirous of ascertaining the contents of Little Red Riding Hood's
foodstuffs basket, and all that.

"It would be inappropriate to lie to me," the wolf said, displaying 4
his huge jaw capability. Sensing that he was a mass of repressed hostility
intertwined with acute alienation, she indicated.

"I see you indicating," the wolf said, "but what I don't see is whatever 5
it is you're indicating at, you dig?"

Little Red Riding Hood indicated more fully, making one thing perfect- 6
ly clear — to wit, that it was to her grandmother's residence and with
a consignment of foodstuffs that her mission consisted of taking her
to and with.

At this point in time the wolf moderated his rhetoric and proceeded 7
to grandmother's residence. The elderly person was then subjected to

the disadvantages of total consumption and transferred to residence in the perpetrator's stomach.

8   "That will raise the old woman's consciousness," the wolf said to himself. He was not a bad wolf, but only a victim of an oppressive society, a society that not only denied wolves' rights, but actually boasted of its capacity for keeping the wolf from the door. An interior malaise made itself manifest inside the wolf.

9   "Is that the national malaise I sense within my digestive tract?" wondered the wolf. "Or is it the old person seeking to retaliate for her consumption by telling wolf jokes to my duodenum?" It was time to make a judgment. The time was now, the hour had struck, the body lupine cried out for decision. The wolf was up to the challenge. He took two stomach powders right away and got into bed.

10   The wolf had adopted the abdominal distress recovery posture when Little Red Riding Hood achieved his presence.

11   "Grandmother," she said, "your ocular implements are of an extraordinary order of magnitude."

12   "The purpose of this enlarged viewing capability," said the wolf, "is to enable your image to register a more precise impression upon my sight systems."

13   "In reference to your ears," said Little Red Riding Hood, "it is noted with the deepest respect that far from being underprivileged, their elongation and enlargement appear to qualify you for unparalleled distinction."

14   "I hear you loud and clear, kid," said the wolf, "but what about these new choppers?"

15   "If it is not inappropriate," said Little Red Riding Hood, "it might be observed that with your new miracle masticating products you may even be able to chew taffy again."

16   This observation was followed by the adoption of an aggressive posture on the part of the wolf and the assertion that it was also possible for him, due to the high efficiency ratio of his jaw, to consume little persons, plus, as he stated, his firm determination to do so at once without delay and with all due process and propriety, notwithstanding the fact that the ingestion of one entire grandmother had already provided twice his daily recommended cholesterol intake.

17   There ensued flight by Little Red Riding Hood accompanied by pursuit in respect to the wolf and a subsequent intervention on the part of a third party, heretofore unnoted in the record.

18   Due to the firmness of the intervention, the wolf's stomach underwent ax-assisted aperture with the result that Little Red Riding Hood's

grandmother was enabled to be removed with only minor discomfort.

The wolf's indigestion was immediately alleviated with such effec- 19
tiveness that he signed a contract with the intervening third party to
perform with grandmother in a television commercial demonstrating
the swiftness of this dramatic relief for stomach discontent.

"I'm going to be on television," cried grandmother.   20

And they all joined her happily in crying, "What a phenomena!"   21

(1979)

The Writer's Subject

1. Baker takes the traditional folktale of "Little Red Riding Hood" and "translates" it into an inflated jargon-ridden English. What is his purpose in doing this?

2. What are the objects of Baker's satire in his opening sentence?

3. In the original story, the wolf was clearly the villain, but in Baker's version he is described as "a victim of an oppressive society" (para. 8). What is Baker making fun of through this change?

4. The traditional story ends with the death of the wolf at the hands of a woodsman. What is the point Baker makes through the changed ending?

5. What comment on modern American values is Baker making in this essay?

The Writer's Style and Strategy

1. Why does Russell Baker use the phrase "the modern American Language" in paragraph 1? (In this connection, see Avis's "Canadian Spoken Here," paragraph 2.)

2. The inflated language of this essay draws attention to the abuse of English by writers who use jargon, euphemism, and needlessly elaborate diction. Pick out examples of each of these abuses as they are mimicked by Baker, and suggest what areas they might be drawn from (e.g., politics, law, psychology, advertising).

3. At what kind of audience is Baker aiming his essay?

4. What effect is created by the sudden injection of slang in paragraphs 5 and 14?

5. Comment on Baker's use of clichés in this essay.

6. "Translate" one of the paragraphs of the essay (e.g., paras. 2,3,7,16) into plain English, and compare the number of words you require with the number in the original.

7. Baker uses many passive constructions (e.g., "it is noted that . . ."; "it might be observed that . . ."; "this observation was followed by . . ."). What is Baker's purpose?

8. Comment on the closing sentence of the essay.

Suggested Topics for Writing and Discussion

1. Choose a well known folktale or fairy tale, and "translate it for a modern reader" in the way that Baker has done with "Little Red Riding Hood."

2. Discuss the ways in which Baker's essay is similar to Orwell's "Politics and the English Language" or Malcolm Cowley's "Sociological Habit Patterns in Linguistic Transmogrification" in its attitude to the uses and abuses of language.

3. Choose a well known folktale or fairy tale and write a satirical modern ending of the kind which Baker has provided in "Little Red Riding Hood Revisited." Explain why you have changed the ending.

4. Baker's treatment of "Little Red Riding Hood" suggests that he does not think such classics need "updating." One area in which "updating" is taking place is in literature for children. What is your view of the current trend to update classic children's stories, notably to remove elements now thought to be sexist or violent? Consult your local library for information on this movement.

Bullshit wording

Sociological Habit Patterns in Linguistic Transmogrification

by Malcolm Cowley

I have a friend who started as a poet and then decided to take a 1
postgraduate degree in sociology. For his doctoral dissertation he combined his two interests by writing on the social psychology of poets.
He had visited poets by the dozen, asking each of them a graded series
of questions, and his conclusions from the interviews were modest and
useful, though reported in what seemed to me a barbarous jargon. After
reading the dissertation I wrote and scolded him. "You have such a fine
sense of the poet's craft," I said, "that you shouldn't have allowed the
sociologists to seduce you into writing their professional slang — or
at least that's my judgmental response to your role selection."

My friend didn't write to defend himself; he waited until we met again. 2
Then dropping his voice, he said: "I knew my dissertation was badly
written, but I had to get my degree. If I had written it in English, professor Blank" — he mentioned a rather distinguished name — "would
have rejected it. He would have said it was merely belletristic."

From that time I began to study the verbal folkways of the sociologists. 3
I read what they call "the literature." A few sociologists write the best
English they are capable of writing, and I suspect that they are the best
men in the field. There is no mystery about them. If they go wrong,
their mistakes can be seen and corrected. Others, however — and a
vast majority — write in a language that has to be learned almost like
Esperanto. It has a private vocabulary which, in addition to strictly
sociological terms, includes new words for the commonest actions, feelings, and circumstances. It has the beginnings of a new grammar and

syntax, much inferior to English grammar in force and precision. So far as it has an effect on standard English, the effect is largely pernicious.

4   Sometimes it misleads the sociologists themselves, by making them think they are profoundly scientific at points where they are merely being verbose. I can illustrate by trying a simple exercise in translation, that is, by expressing an idea first in English and then seeing what it looks like in the language of sociology.

5   An example that comes to hand is the central idea of an article by Norman E. Green, printed in the February, 1956, issue of the *American Sociological Review.* In English his argument might read as follows:

6   "Rich people live in big houses set farther apart than those of poor people. By looking at an aerial photograph of any American city, we can distinguish the richer from the poorer neighborhoods."

7   I won't have to labor over a sociological expression of the same idea, because Mr. Green has saved me the trouble. Here is part of his contribution to comparative linguistics. "In effect, it was hypothesized," he says — a sociologist must never say "I assumed," much less "I guessed" — "that certain physical data categories including housing types and densities, land use characteristics, and ecological location" — not just "location" mind you, but "ecological location," which is almost equivalent to locational location — "constitute a scalable content area. This could be called a continuum of residential desirability. Likewise, it was hypothesized that several social data categories, describing the same census tracts, and referring generally to the social stratification system of the city, would also be scalable. This scale could be called a continuum of socio-economic status. Thirdly, it was hypothesized that there would be a high positive correlation between the scale types on each continuum."

8   Here, after ninety-four words, Mr. Green is stating, or concealing, an assumption with which most laymen would have started, that rich people live in good neighborhoods. He is now almost ready for his deduction, or snapper:

9   "This relationship would define certain linkages between the social and physical structure of the city. It would also provide a precise definition of the commonalities among several spatial distributions. By the same token, the correlation between the residential desirability scale and the continuum of socio-economic status would provide an estimate of the predictive value of aerial photographic data relative to the social ecology of the city."

Mr. Green has used 160 words — counting "socio-economic" as only 10
one — to express an idea that a layman would have stated in thirty-
three. As a matter of fact, he has used many more than 160 words,
since the whole article is an elaboration of this one thesis. Whatever
may be the virtues of the sociological style — or Soc-speak, as George
Orwell might have called it — it is not specifically designed to save
ink and paper. Let us briefly examine some of its other characteristics.

Fuzzing Up the Obvious

A layman's first impression of sociological prose, as compared with 11
English prose, is that it contains a very large proportion of abstract
words, most of them built on Greek or Latin roots. Often — as in the
example just quoted — they are used to inflate or transmogrify a meaning that could be clearly expressed in shorter words surviving from King
Alfred's time.

These Old English or Anglo-Saxon words are in number less than 12
one-tenth of the entries in the largest dictionaries. But they are the names
of everyday objects, attributes, and actions, and they are also the pronouns, the auxiliary verbs, and most of the prepositions and conjunctions, so that they form the grammatical structure of the language. The
result is that most novelists use six Anglo-Saxon words for every one
derived from French, Latin, or Greek, and that is probably close to
the percentage that would be found in spoken English.

For comparison or contrast, I counted derivations in the passage quoted 13
from the *American Sociological Review,* which is a typical example of
"the literature." No less than forty-nine per cent of Mr. Green's prose
consists of words from foreign or classical languages. By this standard
of measurement, his article is more abstruse than most textbooks of
advanced chemistry and higher mathematics, which are said to contain
only forty per cent of such words.

In addition to being abstruse, the language of the sociologists is also 14
rich in neologisms. Apparently they like nothing better than inventing
a word, deforming a word, or using a technical word in a strange context. Among their favorite nouns are "ambit," "extensity" (for "extent"),
"scapegoating," "socializee," "ethnicity," "directionality," "cathexis," "affect" (for "feeling"), "maturation" (for both "maturing" and "maturity"),
and "commonalities" (for "points in common"). Among their favorite
adjectives are "processual," "prestigeful," and "insightful" — which last
is insightful to murder — and perhaps their favorite adverb is "minimal-

making up their
own words.

ly," which seems to mean "in some measure." Their maximal pleasure seems to lie in making new combinations of nouns and adjectives and nouns used as adjectives, until the reader feels that he is picking his way through a field of huge boulders, lost among "universalistic-specific achievement patterns" and "complementary role-expectation-sanction systems," as he struggles vainly toward "ego-integrative action orientation," guided only by "orientation to improvement of the gratification deprivation balance of the actor" — which last is Professor Talcott Parsons's rather involved way of saying "the pleasure principle."

15   But Professor Parsons, head of the Sociology Department at Harvard, is not the only delinquent recidivist, convicted time and again of corrupting the language. Among sociologists in general there is a criminal fondness for using complicated terms when there are simple ones available. A child says "Do it again," a teacher says "Repeat the exercise," but the sociologist says "It was determined to replicate the investigation." Instead of saying two things are alike or similar, as a layman would do, the sociologist describes them as being either isomorphic or homologous. Instead of saying that they are different, he calls them allotropic. Every form of leadership or influence is called a hegemony.

16   A sociologist never cuts anything in half or divides it in two like a layman. Instead he dichotomizes it, bifurcates it, subjects it to a process of binary fission, or restructures it in a dyadic conformation — around polar foci. .

The New Grammar

17   So far I have been dealing with the vocabulary of sociologists, but their private language has a grammar too, and one that should be the subject of intensive research by the staff of a very well-endowed foundation. I have space to mention only a few of its more striking features.

18   The first of these is the preponderance of nouns over all the other parts of speech. Nouns are used in hyphenated pairs or dyads, and sometimes in triads, tetrads, and pentads. Nouns are used as adjectives without change of form, and they are often used as verbs, with or without the suffix "ize." The sociological language is gritty with nouns, like sanded sugar.

19   On the other hand, it is poor in pronouns. The singular pronoun of the first person has entirely disappeared, except in case histories, for the sociologist never comes forward as "I." Sometimes he refers to himself as "the author" or "the investigator," or as "many sociologists,"

or even as "the best sociologists," when he is advancing a debatable opinion. On rare occasions he calls himself "we," like Queen Elizabeth speaking from the throne, but he usually avoids any personal form and writes as if he were a force of nature.

The second-personal pronoun has also disappeared, for the sociologist 20 pretends to be speaking not to living persons but merely for the record. Masculine and feminine pronouns of the third person are used with parsimony, and most sociologists prefer to say "the subject," or "X —," or "the interviewee," where a layman would use the simple "he" or "she." As for the neuter pronoun of the third person, it survives chiefly as the impersonal subject of a passive verb. "It was hypothesized," we read, or "It was found to be the case." Found by *whom?*

The neglect and debasement of the verb is another striking feature 21 of "the literature." The sociologist likes to reduce a transitive verb to an intransitive, so that he speaks of people's adapting, adjusting, transferring, relating, and identifying, with no more of a grammatical object than if they were coming or going. He seldom uses transitive verbs of action, like "break," "injure," "help," and "adore." Instead he uses verbs of relation, verbs which imply that one series of nouns and adjectives, used as the compound subject of a sentence, is larger or smaller than, dominant over, subordinate to, causative of, or resultant from another series of nouns and adjectives.

Considering this degradation of the verb, I have wondered how one 22 of Julius Caesar's boasts could be translated into Soc-speak. What Caesar wrote was "*Veni, vidi, vici*" — only three words, all of them verbs. The English translation is in six words: "I came, I saw, I conquered," and three of the words are first personal pronouns, which the sociologist is taught to avoid. I suspect that he would have to write: "Upon the advent of the investigator, his hegemony became minimally coextensive with the areal unit rendered visible by his successive displacements in space."

The whole sad situation leads me to dream of a vast allegorical paint- 23 ing called "The Triumph of the Nouns." It would depict a chariot of victory drawn by the other conquered parts of speech — the adverbs and adjectives still robust, if yoked and harnessed; the prepositions bloated and pale; the conjunctions tortured; the pronouns reduced to sexless skeletons; the verbs dichotomized and feebly tottering — while behind them, arrogant, overfed, roseate, spilling over the triumphal car, would be the company of nouns in Roman togas and Greek chitons, adorned with laurel branches and flowering hegemonies.

(1956)

The Writer's Subject

1. Why did Cowley's friend fear that his dissertation might be rejected if it were well written? (paras. 1-2)

2. What point is Cowley making by his quotation of an excerpt from the article by Norman E. Green? (paras. 4-10)

3. What are the chief characteristics of the sociological style as identified by Cowley?

4. Why, in Cowley's view, does Norman Green's use of words from foreign or classical languages produce an article "more abstruse than most textbooks of advanced chemistry and higher mathematics"? (para. 13)

5. Summarize Cowley's principal criticisms of the vocabulary of sociologists. (paras. 14-16)

6. Why is Cowley so critical of the sociologists' neglect of first and second-person pronouns? (paras. 19-20)

The Writer's Style and Strategy

1. Discuss the appropriateness of Cowley's title.

2. What is the function of the anecdote with which Cowley begins his essay? Where does he first state his thesis?

3. What methods does Cowley use to demonstrate the bad writing of sociologists?

4. How does Cowley convey his attitude to the vocabulary of sociology in paragraph 14?

5. Show how Cowley uses metaphor and simile as means of strengthening his argument in paragraphs 15, 18, and 19.

6. Discuss the effectiveness of the essay's conclusion. How does it sum up the principal elements of Cowley's argument?

7. Compare this essay to Orwell's "Politics and the English Language." What are the differences in their purposes? How are these differences reflected in the tone of each essay?

Suggested Topics for Writing and Discussion

1. Cowley's article is an attack on the language used by sociologists. Choose a book or journal in a different field (e.g., education, economics, political science). Basing your views on a sample passage from your source, indicate whether the writer is guilty of any of the sins with which Cowley charges sociologists.

2. What measures do you think should be taken by colleges and universities to ensure that *all* their graduates, whether in Arts or the Sciences, write good, clear English? What changes or improvements would you make in the writing requirements at your own institution?

3. Cowley takes an article from the February 1956 issue of the *American Sociological Review* to illustrate his criticism of the language of sociology. Choose a recent article from this or a similar journal, or a chapter from a book on the social sciences, and offer your own views on the current state of sociological writing as reflected in your source.

The Case Against Advertising
by Richard Hoggart

1 By turns hurt, defiant, apologetic and self-justifying, advertising men seem particularly sensitive to criticism just now. Criticism has certainly been heavy in the last few years, perhaps because the number of reasonably well-informed people is somewhat greater than it used to be. You need a fairly widespread critical public opinion to get the Consumers' Association, the Advertising Inquiry Council and similar organizations started. Yet few people in advertising have taken the measure of this development. Some have seen its superficial aspects and made their advertising more self-conscious and sophisticated; but the moderate widening of critical opinion has so far escaped almost all of them.

2   I will try to sum up as directly as I can the case against advertising. Even so, I do not expect to have much, if any, effect. None of us likes our profession to be attacked, and we fight back when it is. But usually someone somewhere in a profession steps out of line and says that he does see some justice in the criticisms, that some things in his particular house do need to be put in order. This can be seen in the quite fierce arguments about the function and financing of universities today. But I have not heard any spokesman of the advertising (or public relations) industry admit to other than minor faults (that claims are sometimes a bit exaggerated, say, or not strictly truthful); I have not heard any spokesman of the industry take the full measure of the case against advertising, let alone answer it.

3   Why is this? Is it because a profession which lives by manipulating reality, by weaving attractive but deceptive verbal links between products and potential consumers, gets taken in by its own sleight-of-hand?

And that, by-and-large, such a trade gets the servants it needs, who fit its demands and are suited by them? For such men, when they find themselves criticized, the temptation to sell themselves a rationalization, like an outfitter clothing himself from stock, must be strong. Still, if the case against advertising is going to be seen (not necessarily accepted, but at least seen), then people in advertising have to make a harder effort than they have made so far. The time for easy rides, especially for the big public spokesman of advertising, is past.

To get a few red herrings out of the way first. There can be some 4
unexceptionable advertising (and it need not be dull). It has not been proved that advertising in its present form (the kind of advertising that is being criticized) is essential to the economy, or reduces costs. It is true that the industry has done some self-policing; but only at an innocuous, true-or-false level. Last, no one in his senses is proposing censorship; anyway, the important problems could not be touched by censorship.

The really serious questions raised by advertising are much wider 5
than advertising itself. If critics spend a lot of time attacking advertising this is not because advertising is a peculiar kind of vice, but because it is a symptom, because it exhibits more plainly and persistently than anything else the issues raised by mass persuasion. At bottom the case against advertising is the same as that against political propaganda, much religious proselytizing and any other form of emotional blackmail.

The case is this:/that advertising tries to achieve its ends by emo- 6
tionally abusing its audiences. Recognizing that we all have fears, hopes, anxieties, aspirations, insecurities, advertisers seek not to increase our understanding of these feelings and so perhaps our command of them, but to use their existence to increase the sales of whatever product they happen to have been paid to sell at any particular time. They exploit human inadequacy, and we have the right to say to them what Hamlet said to Guildenstern: "Why look you now, how unworthy a thing you make of me; you would play upon me; you would seem to know my stops; you would pluck out the heart of my mystery; you would sound me from my lowest note, to the top of my compass. . . . Why do you think that I am easier to be played on, than a pipe?"

There is no point in illustrating, since illustrations are all around, 7
nor in elaborating on the occasional exceptions. The basic charge is indisputable, unless you adopt a purely predatory — every man for himself — attitude; in which case there is no basis for argument. But if you accept some responsibility in your conduct towards others then

you have problems, in advertising, which verbal manoeuvres can only evade, not solve.

8   Some apologists seek to rebut all this by taking up the Stance of the Licensed Pantaloon. You are too solemn, they argue. No one really believes what we say. The ordinary chap is much more subtle than you give him credit for. He recognizes that we add to the amusement and colour of his life — and that's all there is to it.

9   Coming from anyone who has read the research literature this is disingenuous. The evidence shows, and a reasonably close acquaintance with 'ordinary people' will tell you anyway, that a lot of people do literally believe what they read in the ads. A surprising number, when you think of the effort which goes into training in literacy. Still, that effort has been long delayed and is still small in proportion to the need. Most men in advertising are, of course, more effectively trained, more articulate and mentally quicker than their audiences — which doesn't make the business any pleasanter. What usually passes for sophisticated advertising (e.g. in the Sunday glossies) is at bottom as simple in its appeals as the stuff in the mass circulation papers; its stage-properties and snobberies are different, that's all. Outside that range there is, I suppose, a small core of self-aware intellectuals who do enjoy, or claim to enjoy, advertisements as aesthetic objects, as sources of verbal, sociological or psychological fun. Most talk of this kind strikes me as disingenuous; but men in advertising are grateful for it. It confirms their status as harmless amusers and pays tribute to their verbal inventiveness. Since there is a poet or novelist manqué inside many a copywriter, this is a benison. And an outsider may feel that, though it is a sad little claim they are making, at least it isn't portentous.

10   It is easy to appreciate the excitement, even the glamour, which advertising can have. Playing with words, making them do tricks for you within narrowly prescribed rules (this product, this target audience, this number of words), is obviously fascinating and in some ways similar to working within the rules of a simple literary form. I once passed hours, on a sticky hot journey by troop-train from Italy, inventing copy (with a man who is now a very popular columnist) for 'Critch', a mythical powder which would eliminate the awful persistent itch in our crutches. Still, how long can that sort of fun satisfy a man? A long time, I suppose, if the rewards are good, and if you find something cathartic for your spare time. But it's a shabby business.

11   Which is why the least attractive people in the whole advertising business are the front men with the public relations voices — the men

who cheer up conferences with fighting keynote speeches about the public-service element in advertising and make prepared palliative statements on all other suitable occasions. Their routine is usually predictable. They assert that advertising is the linch-pin or lubricant of a modern progressive economy. They use words like 'creative', 'dedicated' and 'sincere', so much that you remember Hemingway's *A Farewell to Arms*: "I was always embarrassed by the words. There were many words that you could not stand to hear and finally only the names of places had dignity. Abstract words were obscene. . . ." They take a few cheering-up-the-troops swipes at critics (this is a fairly recent development), and offer the services of advertising to promote any good cause the community can name — citizenship, education, religion.

With people like that you are really up against it. They seem to have **12** no sense of the difficulty of truth and of the need to respect other people's effort after it: "There's no limit to the wonderful things advertising can be made to sell . . . religion, social conscience, racial tolerance, education. . . ." How do you explain that if religion is to mean anything it must be founded on personal commitment, arrived at with any help others can disinterestedly give, but in the end arrived at personally and in the fullest possible emotional clarity? Or how do you explain that illicit manoeuvres (associating religion with togetherness or smartness) cannot really convert anyone and only prepare the ground for equally illicit manoeuvres with more questionable ends. As 'professionals', Goebbels' ad men were very efficient indeed.

There is, of course, good persuasion as well as bad persuasion; and **13** advertisers keep the debate murkier than it should be by sliding between the two types. In one sense, any good book is an act of persuasion. But the gap between that and the persuasion of advertisers is so large as to make virtually a difference of kind. Good persuasion, whether in dispassionate argument or in a powerfully moving novel, has two root qualities: respect for the reality of the subject, and respect for the listener's right to judge for himself his attitude to the subject. This definition does not rule out emotional engagement; any important commitment is a mixture of emotion and intellect. But it insists on emotional relevance — that the emotion, in both its nature and its intensity, fit the theme.

Naturally, the line between this and illicit emotional persuasion is **14** a continuous one, and it is difficult to decide just where the watershed comes. But look at each end of the line and you see the distinction at once, and see its importance; and this makes it all the more important not to blur distinctions in the large middle area (which is where most of the battles about persuasion are fought), but to try to make them clearer.

15   It is important for outside critics not to use advertisers as scapegoats for bigger social problems; they reflect more than they affect in society. There are a lot of reasons why a society such as this throws up so much persuasion, and so to many people in advertising theirs seems as respectable a trade as many others.

16   That much can be granted. But it is just as important not to make easy accommodations. The overriding fact is that much of the work of this profession, as it is at present practised, consists of exploiting weakness, through language. Anyone who thinks it is better to try to understand one's weaknesses than to indulge them, anyone who thinks that language (the articulation of our thoughts and feelings in communicable form) can help in that better grasp, anyone with these two premises must regard most modern advertising as, at the best, a waste of good human resources and, at the worst, a misuse of other people.

(1970)

The Writer's Subject

1. Why, in Hoggart's view, have advertisers failed to criticize themselves? (paras. 2-3)

2. How, according to Hoggart, do advertisers emotionally abuse their audiences? (para. 6)

3. What kind of apology for advertising does Hoggart discuss in paragraph 8? How does he regard such an apology?

4. What is Hoggart's view of "sophisticated advertising"? (para. 9)

5. Why, in speaking of the apparently limitless possibilities of advertising, does Hoggart end his paragraph with a reference to Goebbels? (para. 12)

6. How does Hoggart distinguish between good persuasion and bad persuasion in paragraphs 12-14?

The Writer's Style and Strategy

1. What kind of audience is implied in this essay? (See, for example, paragraphs 7 and 16.)

2. A way of dealing with opponents to an argument is to denigrate their views by making them seem trivial, irrelevant, or absurd. Find instances in this essay of Hoggart's use of this strategy.

3. Do you think Hoggart presents his "case" fairly and objectively?

4. Comment on Hoggart's use of the two literary references to works by Shakespeare and Hemingway. (paras. 6, 11)

5. What use does Hoggart make of personal anecdote to support his case against advertising?

Suggested Topics for Writing and Discussion

1. Write an argument in defense of advertising.

2. Hoggart sees advertising as merely one example of the workings of mass persuasion in our society. (para. 5) Discuss another example of mass persuasion (e.g., election campaigns, religious broadcasting), showing how it makes use of the techniques commonly used to sell products.

3. Hoggart says a few individuals "claim to enjoy advertisements as aesthetic objects." Can a serious claim be made for advertising as an art form? Give examples to support your view.

4. Describe an advertisement which has wide currency (i.e., on television, in national magazines) as "a source of verbal, sociological or psychological fun" and discuss the nature of its appeal.

The Abuses of Advertising

by Samuel Johnson

The Idler No. 40 — Saturday, 20 January 1759

1 The practice of appending to the narratives of public transactions, more minute and domestic intelligence, and filling the news-papers with advertisements, has grown up by slow degrees to its present state.

2 Genius is shewn only by invention. The man who first took advantage of the general curiosity that was excited by a siege or battle, to betray the readers of news into the knowledge of the shop where the best puffs and powder were to be sold, was undoubtedly a man of great sagacity, and profound skill in the nature of man. But when he had once shewn the way, it was easy to follow him; and every man now knows a ready method of informing the publick of all that he desires to buy or sell, whether his wares be material or intellectual; whether he makes cloaths, or teaches the mathematics; whether he be a tutor that wants a pupil, or a pupil that wants a tutor.

3 Whatever is common is despised. Advertisements are now so numerous that they are very negligently perused, and it is therefore become necessary to gain attention by magnificence of promises, and by eloquence sometimes sublime and sometimes pathetic.

4 Promise, large promise, is the soul of an advertisement. I remember a "wash-ball" that had a quality truly wonderful, it gave "an exquisite edge to the razor." And there are now to be sold "for ready money only," some "duvets for bed-coverings, of down, beyond comparison superior to what is called otter down," and indeed such, that its "many excellencies cannot be here set forth." With one excellence we are made acquainted, "it is warmer than four or five blankets, and lighter than one."

5 There are some, however, that know the prejudice of mankind in

favour of modest sincerity. The vendor of the "Beautifying Fluid" sells a lotion that repels pimples, washes away freckles, smooths the skin, and plumps the flesh; and yet, with a generous abhorrence of ostentation, confesses, that it will not "restore the bloom of fifteen to a lady of fifty."

The true pathos of advertisements must have sunk deep into the heart **6** of every man that remembers the zeal shewn by the seller of the anodyne necklace, for the ease and safety "of poor toothing infants," and the affection with which he warned every mother, that "she would never forgive herself" if her infant should perish without a necklace.

I cannot but remark to the celebrated author who gave, in his notifica- **7** tions of the camel and dromedary, so many specimens of the genuine sublime, that there is now arrived another subject yet more worthy of his pen. "A famous Mohawk Indian warrior, who took Dieskaw the French general prisoner, dressed in the same manner with the native Indians when they go to war, with his face and body painted, with his scalping knife, tom-ax, and all other implements of war: a sight worthy the curiosity of every true Briton!" This is a very powerful description; but a critic of great refinement would say that it conveys rather "horror" than "terror." An Indian, dressed as he goes to war, may bring company together; but if he carries the scalping knife and tom-ax, there are many true Britons that will never be persuaded to see him but through a grate.

It has been remarked by the severer judges, that the salutary sorrow **8** of tragick scenes is too soon effaced by the merriment of the epilogue; the same inconvenience arises from the improper disposition of advertisements. The noblest objects may be so associated as to be made ridiculous. The camel and dromedary themselves might have lost much of their dignity between "The True Flower of Mustard" and "The Original Daffy's Elixir"; and I could not but feel some indignation when I found this illustrious Indian warrior immediately succeeded by "A Fresh Parcel of Dublin Butter."

The trade of advertising is now so near to perfection, that it is not **9** easy to propose any improvement. But as every art ought to be exercised in due subordination to the publick good, I cannot but propose it as a moral question to these masters of the publick ear, whether they do not sometimes play too wantonly with our passions, as when the register of lottery tickets invites us to his shop by an account of the prize which he sold last year; and whether the advertising controvertists do not indulge asperity of language without any adequate provocation; as in the dispute about "straps for razors," now happily subsided, and in the altercation which at present subsists concerning *Eau de Luce*.

10   In an advertisement it is allowed to every man to speak well of himself, but I know not why he should assume the privilege of censuring his neighbour. He may proclaim his own virtue or skill, but ought not to exclude others from the same pretensions.

11   Every man that advertises his own excellence, should write with some consciousness of a character which dares to call the attention of the publick. He should remember that his name is to stand in the same paper with those of the King of Prussia, and the Emperor of Germany, and endeavour to make himself worthy of such association.

12   Some regard is likewise to be paid to posterity. There are men of diligence and curiosity who treasure up the papers of the day merely because others neglect them, and in time they will be scarce. When these collections shall be read in another century, how will numberless contradictions be reconciled, and how shall fame be possibly distributed among the tailors and boddice-makers of the present age.

13   Surely these things deserve consideration. It is enough for me to have hinted my desire that these abuses may be rectified; but such is the state of nature, that what all have the right of doing, many will attempt without sufficient care or due qualifications.

(1759)

The Writer's Subject

1. What are Johnson's speculations on how advertising began?

2. Explain what Johnson means by "Genius is shewn only by invention." (para. 2)

3. According to Johnson, what means do advertisers employ to attract attention to their products? (paras. 3-7)

4. In paragraphs 5 and 6, what styles or techniques of advertising does Johnson illustrate?

5. In paragraphs 7 and 8 Johnson describes an advertisement for the public exhibition of a Mohawk Indian Warrior. What aspects of advertising does he comment on through reference to this example?

6. In paragraphs 9 and 10, what faults of advertisers does Johnson point to?

7. Why, according to Johnson, should advertisers be concerned about "posterity"? (para. 12)

The Writer's Style and Strategy

1. Find an example of parallel structure in paragraph 2.

2. Johnson, it is often said, is excessively fond of lengthy, complex structures, yet in this essay he makes pointed use of the short simple sentence. Find several short sentences and comment upon their effectiveness.

3. What is the tone of the first sentence of paragraph 9?

4. How does Johnson structure the long sentence that makes up most of paragraph 9?

5. How does Johnson use sentence structure to present opposing views in paragraph 10?

6. What clues in paragraph 12 suggest that Johnson's concerns about posterity may not be entirely serious?

Suggested Topics for Writing and Discussion

1. Johnson complains of the state of advertising in his day — the mid-eighteenth century. In what ways are advertisements of today similar to those which Johnson discusses? Provide specific examples to support your view.

2. Johnson states that "Promise, large promise, is the soul of an advertisement." Choose one or two advertisements in which you feel the "promise" of the advertisement is a false one. Discuss the way in which language either exaggerates, distorts, or misrepresents the product being sold.

3. Johnson talks about the advertisers' unfair appeals to emotion in selling their products. Discuss one or two advertisements that seem to you to indulge in this same reprehensible practice. Identify the nature of these appeals to emotion.

Politics and the English Language
by George Orwell

1   Most people who bother with the matter at all would admit that the English language is in a bad way, but it is generally assumed that we cannot by conscious action do anything about it. Our civilization is decadent and our language — so the argument runs — must inevitably share in the general collapse. It follows that any struggle against the abuse of language is a sentimental archaism, like preferring candles to electric light or hansom cabs to aeroplanes. Underneath this lies the half-conscious belief that language is a natural growth and not an instrument which we shape for our own purposes.

2   Now, it is clear that the decline of a language must ultimately have political and economic causes: it is not due simply to the bad influence of this or that individual writer. But an effect can become a cause, reinforcing the original cause and producing the same effect in an intensified form, and so on indefinitely. A man may take to drink because he feels himself to be a failure, and then fail all the more completely because he drinks. It is rather the same thing that is happening to the English language. It becomes ugly and inaccurate because our thoughts are foolish, but the slovenliness of our language makes it easier for us to have foolish thoughts. The point is that the process is reversible. Modern English, especially written English, is full of bad habits which spread by imitation and which can be avoided if one is willing to take the necessary trouble. If one gets rid of these habits one can think more clearly, and to think clearly is a necessary first step towards political regeneration: so that the fight against bad English is not frivolous and is not the exclusive concern of professional writers. I will come back to this presently, and I hope that by that time the meaning of what I

have said here will have become clearer. Meanwhile, here are five specimens of the English language as it is now habitually written.

These five passages have not been picked out because they are especially bad — I could have quoted far worse if I had chosen — but because they illustrate various of the mental vices from which we now suffer. They are a little below the average, but are fairly representative samples. I number them so that I can refer back to them when necessary: **3**

"(1) I am not, indeed, sure whether it is not true to say that the Milton who once seemed not unlike a seventeenth-century Shelley had not become, out of an experience ever more bitter in each year, more alien [*sic*] to the founder of that Jesuit sect which nothing could induce him to tolerate."

Professor Harold Laski (Essay in *Freedom of Expression*).

"(2) Above all, we cannot play ducks and drakes with a native battery of idioms which prescribes such egregious collocations of vocables as the Basic *put up with* for *tolerate* or *put at a loss* for *bewilder*."

Professor Lancelot Hogben *(Interglossa)*.

"(3) On the one side we have the free personality: by definition it is not neurotic, for it has neither conflict nor dream. Its desires, such as they are, are transparent, for they are just what institutional approval keeps in the forefront of consciousness; another institutional pattern would alter their number and intensity; there is little in them that is natural, irreducible, or culturally dangerous. But *on the other side,* the social bond itself is nothing but the mutual reflection of these self-secure integrities. Recall the definition of love. Is not this the very picture of a small academic? Where is there a place in this hall of mirrors for either personality or fraternity?"

Essay on psychology in *Politics* (New York).

"(4) All the 'best people' from the gentlemen's clubs, and all the frantic fascist captains, united in common hatred of Socialism and bestial horror of the rising tide of the mass revolutionary movement, have turned to acts of provocation, to foul incendiarism, to medieval legends of poisoned wells, to legalize their own destruction of proletarian organizations, and rouse the agitated petty-bourgeoisie to chauvinistic fervour on behalf of the fight against the revolutionary way out of the crisis."

Communist pamphlet.

"(5) If a new spirit *is* to be infused into this old country, there is one thorny and contentious reform which must be tackled, and that is the humanization and galvanization of the B.B.C. Timidity here will bespeak canker and atrophy of the soul. The heart of Britain may be sound and of strong beat, for instance, but the British lion's roar at present is like that of Bottom in Shakespeare's *Midsummer Night's Dream* — as gentle as any sucking dove. A virile new Britain cannot continue indefinitely to be traduced in the eyes or rather ears, of the world by the effete languors of Langham Place, brazenly masquerading as 'standard English'. When the Voice of Britain is heard at nine o'clock, better far and infinitely less ludicrous to hear aitches honestly dropped than the present priggish, inflated, inhibited, school-ma'amish arch braying of blameless bashful mewing maidens!"

Letter in *Tribune*.

4   Each of these passages has faults of its own, but, quite apart from avoidable ugliness, two qualities are common to all of them. The first is staleness of imagery: the other is lack of precision. The writer either has a meaning and cannot express it, or he inadvertently says something else, or he is almost indifferent as to whether his words mean anything or not. This mixture of vagueness and sheer incompetence is the most marked characteristic of modern English prose, and especially of any kind of political writing. As soon as certain topics are raised, the concrete melts into the abstract and no one seems able to think of turns of speech that are not hackneyed: prose consists less and less of *words* chosen for the sake of their meaning, and more and more of *phrases* tacked together like the sections of a prefabricated hen-house. I list below, with notes and examples, various of the tricks by means of which the work of prose-construction is habitually dodged:

5   *Dying Metaphors.* A newly invented metaphor assists thought by evoking a visual image, while on the other hand a metaphor which is technically "dead" (e.g. *iron resolution*) has in effect reverted to being an ordinary word and can generally be used without loss of vividness. But in between these two classes there is a huge dump of worn-out metaphors which have lost all evocative power and are merely used because they save people the trouble of inventing phrases for themselves. Examples are: *Ring the changes on, take up the cudgels for, toe the line, ride roughshod over, stand shoulder to shoulder with, play into the hands of, no axe to grind, grist to the mill, fishing in troubled waters, on the order of the day, Achilles' heel, swan song, hotbed.* Many of these are used without knowledge of their meaning (what is a "rift", for instance?), and incompatible metaphors are frequently mixed, a sure sign that the writer is not interested in what he is saying. Some metaphors now current have been twisted out of their original meaning without those who

use them even being aware of the fact. For example, *toe the line* is sometimes written *tow the line*. Another example is *the hammer and the anvil*, now always used with the implication that the anvil gets the worst of it. In real life it is always the anvil that breaks the hammer, never the other way about: a writer who stopped to think what he was saying would be aware of this, and would avoid perverting the original phrase.

   Operators or verbal false limbs. These save the trouble of picking **6** out appropriate verbs and nouns, and at the same time pad each sentence with extra syllables which give it an appearance of symmetry. Characteristic phrases are: *render inoperative, militate against, make contact with, be subjected to, give rise to, give grounds for, have the effect of, play a leading part (role) in, make itself felt, take effect, exhibit a tendency to, serve the purpose of, etc., etc.* The keynote is the elimination of simple verbs. Instead of being a single word, such as *break, stop, spoil, mend, kill,* a verb becomes a *phrase,* made up of a noun or adjective tacked on to some general-purposes verb such as *prove, serve, form, play, render.* In addition, the passive voice is wherever possible used in preference to the active, and noun constructions are used instead of gerunds *(by examination of* instead of *by examining).* The range of verbs is further cut down by means of the *-ize* and *de-* formations, and the banal statements are given an appearance of profundity by means of the *not un-* formation. Simple conjunctions and prepositions are replaced by such phrases as *with respect to, having regard to, the fact that, by dint of, in view of, in the interests of, on the hypothesis that;* and the ends of sentences are saved from anticlimax by such resounding commonplaces as *greatly to be desired, cannot be left out of account, a development to be expected in the near future, deserving of serious consideration, brought to a satisfactory conclusion,* and so on and so forth. ← FAULTY WORDING

Pretentious diction. Words like *phenomenon, element, individual* (as **7** noun), *objective, categorical, effective, virtual, basic, primary, promote, constitute, exhibit, exploit, utilize, eliminate, liquidate,* are used to dress up simple statements and give an air of scientific impartiality to biased judgments. Adjectives like *epoch-making, epic, historic, unforgettable, triumphant, age-old, inevitable, inexorable, veritable,* are used to dignify the sordid processes of international politics, while writing that aims at glorifying war usually takes on an archaic colour, its characteristic words being: *realm, throne, chariot, mailed fist, trident, sword, shield, buckler, banner, jackboot, clarion.* Foreign words and expressions such as *cul de sac, ancien régime, deus ex machina, mutatis mutan-*

dis, status quo, gleichschaltung, weltanschauung, are used to give an air of culture and elegance. Except for the useful abbreviations *i.e., e.g.,* and *etc.,* there is no real need for any of the hundreds of foreign phrases now current in English. Bad writers, and especially scientific, political and sociological writers, are nearly always haunted by the notion that Latin or Greek words are grander than Saxon ones, and unnecessary words like *expedite, ameliorate, predict, extraneous, deracinated, clandestine, subaqueous* and hundreds of others constantly gain ground from their Anglo-Saxon opposite numbers.[1] The jargon peculiar to Marxist writing (*hyena, hangman, cannibal, petty bourgeois, these gentry, lacquey, flunkey, mad dog, White Guard,* etc.) consists largely of words and phrases translated from Russian, German or French; but the normal way of coining a new word is to use a Latin or Greek root with the appropriate affix and, where necessary, the -ize formation. It is often easier to make up words of this kind (*deregionalize, impermissible, extramarital, non-fragmentatory* and so forth) than to think up the English words that will cover one's meaning. The result, in general, is an increase in slovenliness and vagueness.

8   *Meaningless words.* In certain kinds of writing, particularly in art criticism and literary criticism, it is normal to come across long passages which are almost completely lacking in meaning.[2] Words like *romantic, plastic, values, human, dead, sentimental, natural, vitality,* as used in art criticism, are strictly meaningless, in the sense that they not only do not point to any discoverable object, but are hardly ever expected to do so by the reader. When one critic writes, "The outstanding feature of Mr. X's work is its living quality", while another writes, "The immediately striking thing about Mr. X's work is its peculiar deadness", the reader accepts this as a simple difference of opinion. If words like *black* and *white* were involved, instead of the jargon words *dead* and *living,* he would see at once that language was being used in an improper way. Many political words are similarly abused. The word *Fascism* has now no meaning except in so far as it signifies "something not desirable". The words *democracy, socialism, freedom, patriotic, realistic, justice,* have each of them several different meanings which cannot be reconciled with one another. In the case of a word like *democracy,* not only is there no agreed definition, but the attempt to make one is resisted from all sides. It is almost universally felt that when we call a country democratic we are praising it: consequently the defenders of every kind of régime claim that it is a democracy, and fear that they might have to stop using the word if it were tied down

to any one meaning. Words of this kind are often used in a consciously dishonest way. That is, the person who uses them has his own private definition, but allows his hearer to think he means something quite different. Statements like *Marshal Pétain was a true patriot, The Soviet Press is the freest in the world, The Catholic Church is opposed to persecution,* are almost always made with intent to deceive. Other words used in variable meanings, in most cases more or less dishonestly, are: *class, totalitarian, science, progressive, reactionary, bourgeois, equality.*

Now that I have made this catalogue of swindles and perversions,   **9** let me give another example of the kind of writing that they lead to. This time it must of its nature be an imaginary one. I am going to translate a passage of good English into modern English of the worst sort. Here is a well-known verse from *Ecclesiastes:*

"I returned and saw under the sun, that the race is not to the swift, nor the battle to the strong, neither yet bread to the wise, nor yet riches to men of understanding, nor yet favour to men of skill; but time and chance happeneth to them all."

Here it is in modern English: **10**

"Objective consideration of contemporary phenomena compels the conclusion that success or failure in competitive activities exhibits no tendency to be commensurate with innate capacity, but that a considerable element of the unpredictable must invariably be taken into account."

This is a parody, but not a very gross one. Exhibit (3), above, for   **11** instance, contains several patches of the same kind of English. It will be seen that I have not made a full translation. The beginning and ending of the sentence follow the original meaning fairly closely, but in the middle the concrete illustrations – race, battle, bread – dissolve into the vague phrase "success or failure in competitive activities". This had to be so, because no modern writer of the kind I am discussing – no one capable of using phrases like "objective consideration of contemporary phenomena" – would ever tabulate his thoughts in that precise and detailed way. The whole tendency of modern prose is away from concreteness. Now analyse these two sentences a little more closely. The first contains forty-nine words but only sixty syllables, and all its words are those of everyday life. The second contains thirty-eight words of ninety syllables: eighteen of its words are from Latin roots, and one from Greek. The first sentence contains six vivid images, and only one phrase ("time and chance") that could be called vague. The second contains not a single fresh, arresting phrase, and in spite of its ninety syllables it gives only a shortened version of the meaning contained in the first.

Yet without a doubt it is the second kind of sentence that is gaining ground in modern English. I do not want to exaggerate. This kind of writing is not yet universal, and outcrops of simplicity will occur here and there in the worst-written page. Still, if you or I were told to write a few lines on the uncertainty of human fortunes, we should probably come much nearer to my imaginary sentence than to the one from *Ecclesiastes*.

12   As I have tried to show, modern writing at its worst does not consist in picking out words for the sake of their meaning and inventing images in order to make the meaning clearer. It consists in gumming together long strips of words which have already been set in order by someone else, and making the results presentable by sheer humbug. The attraction of this way of writing is that it is easy. It is easier — even quicker, once you have the habit — to say *In my opinion it is a not unjustifiable assumption that* than to say *I think*. If you use ready-made phrases, you not only don't have to hunt about for words; you also don't have to bother with the rhythms of your sentences, since these phrases are generally so arranged as to be more or less euphonious. When you are composing in a hurry — when you are dictating to a stenographer, for instance, or making a public speech — it is natural to fall into a pretentious, Latinized style. Tags like *a consideration which we should do well to bear in mind* or *a conclusion to which all of us would readily assent* will save many a sentence from coming down with a bump. By using stale metaphors, similes and idioms, you save much mental effort, at the cost of leaving your meaning vague, not only for your reader but for yourself. This is the significance of mixed metaphors. The sole aim of a metaphor is to call up a visual image. When these images clash — as in *The Fascist octopus has sung its swan song, the jackboot is thrown into the melting pot* — it can be taken as certain that the writer is not seeing a mental image of the objects he is naming; in other words he is not really thinking. Look again at the examples I gave at the beginning of this essay. Professor Laski (1) uses five negatives in fifty-three words. One of these is superfluous, making nonsense of the whole passage, and in addition there is the slip *alien* for akin, making further nonsense, and several avoidable pieces of clumsiness which increase the general vagueness. Professor Hogben (2) plays ducks and drakes with a battery which is able to write prescriptions, and, while disapproving of the everyday phrase *put up with,* is unwilling to look *egregious* up in the dictionary and see what it means. (3), if one takes an uncharitable attitude towards it, is simply meaningless: probably one could

work out its intended meaning by reading the whole of the article in which it occurs. In (4), the writer knows more or less what he wants to say, but an accumulation of stale phrases chokes him like tea leaves blocking a sink. In (5), words and meaning have almost parted company. People who write in this manner usually have a general emotional meaning — they dislike one thing and want to express solidarity with another — but they are not interested in the detail of what they are saying. A scrupulous writer, in every sentence that he writes, will ask himself at least four questions, thus: What am I trying to say? What words will express it? What image or idiom will make it clearer? Is this image fresh enough to have an effect? And he will probably ask himself two more: Could I put it more shortly? Have I said anything that is avoidably ugly? But you are not obliged to go to all this trouble. You can shirk it by simply throwing your mind open and letting the ready-made phrases come crowding in. They will construct your sentences for you — even think your thoughts for you, to a certain extent — and at need they will perform the important service of partially concealing your meaning even from yourself. It is at this point that the special connection between politics and the debasement of language becomes clear.

In our time it is broadly true that political writing is bad writing. Where **13** it is not true, it will generally be found that the writer is some kind of rebel, expressing his private opinions and not a "party line". Orthodoxy, of whatever colour, seems to demand a lifeless, imitative style. The political dialects to be found in pamphlets, leading articles, manifestos, White Papers and the speeches of under-secretaries do, of course, vary from party to party, but they are all alike in that one almost never finds in them a fresh, vivid, home-made turn of speech. When one watches some tired hack on the platform mechanically repeating the familiar phrases — *bestial atrocities, iron heel, bloodstained tyranny, free peoples of the world, stand shoulder to shoulder* — one often has a curious feeling that one is not watching a live human being but some kind of dummy: a feeling which suddenly becomes stronger at moments when the light catches the speaker's spectacles and turns them into blank discs which seem to have no eyes behind them. And this is not altogether fanciful. A speaker who uses that kind of phraseology has gone some distance towards turning himself into a machine. The appropriate noises are coming out of his larynx, but his brain is not involved as it would be if he were choosing his words for himself. If the speech he is making is one that he is accustomed to make over and over again, he may be almost unconscious of what he is saying, as one is when one utters the responses in church. And this reduced state of consciousness, if not indispensable, is at any rate favourable to political conformity.

14   In our time, political speech and writing are largely the defence of the indefensible. Things like the continuance of British rule in India, the Russian purges and deportations, the dropping of the atom bombs on Japan, can indeed be defended, but only by arguments which are too brutal for most people to face, and which do not square with the professed aims of political parties. Thus political language has to consist largely of euphemism, question-begging and sheer cloudy vagueness. Defenceless villages are bombarded from the air, the inhabitants driven out into the countryside, the cattle machine-gunned, the huts set on fire with incendiary bullets: this is called *pacification*. Millions of peasants are robbed of their farms and sent trudging along the roads with no more than they can carry: this is called *transfer of population* or *rectification of frontiers*. People are imprisoned for years without trial, or shot in the back of the neck or sent to die of scurvy in Arctic lumber camps: this is called *elimination of unreliable elements*. Such phraseology is needed if one wants to name things without calling up mental pictures of them. Consider for instance some comfortable English professor defending Russian totalitarianism. He cannot say outright, "I believe in killing off your opponents when you can get good results by doing so". Probably, therefore, he will say something like this:

"While freely conceding that the Soviet régime exhibits certain features which the humanitarian may be inclined to deplore, we must, I think, agree that a certain curtailment of the right to political opposition is an unavoidable concomitant of transitional periods, and that the rigours which the Russian people have been called upon to undergo have been amply justified in the sphere of concrete achievement."

15   The inflated style is itself a kind of euphemism. A mass of Latin words falls upon the facts like soft snow, blurring the outlines and covering up all the details. The great enemy of clear language is insincerity. When there is a gap between one's real and one's declared aims, one turns as it were instinctively to long words and exhausted idioms, like a cuttlefish squirting out ink. In our age there is no such thing as "keeping out of politics". All issues are political issues, and politics itself is a mass of lies, evasions, folly, hatred and schizophrenia. When the general atmosphere is bad, language must suffer. I should expect to find — this is a guess which I have not sufficient knowledge to verify — that the German, Russian and Italian languages have all deteriorated in the last

ten or fifteen years, as a result of dictatorship.

But if thought corrupts language, language can also corrupt thought. **16**
A bad usage can spread by tradition and imitation, even among people
who should and do know better. The debased language that I have been
discussing is in some ways very convenient. Phrases like *a not unjustifiable assumption, leave much to be desired, would serve no good
purpose, a consideration which we should do well to bear in mind,* are
a continuous temptation, a packet of aspirins always at one's elbow.
Look back through this essay, and for certain you will find that I have
again and again committed the very faults I am protesting against. By
this morning's post I have received a pamphlet dealing with conditions
in Germany. The author tells me that he "felt impelled" to write it. I
open it at random, and here is almost the first sentence that I see: "(The
Allies) have an opportunity not only of achieving a radical transformation of Germany's social and political structure in such a way as to avoid
a nationalistic reaction in Germany itself, but at the same time of laying the foundations of a co-operative and unified Europe." You see,
he "feels impelled" to write — feels, presumably, that he has something
new to say — and yet his words, like cavalry horses answering the bugle,
group themselves automatically into the familiar dreary pattern. This
invasion of one's mind by ready-made phrases *(lay the foundations,
achieve a radical transformation)* can only be prevented if one is constantly on guard against them, and every such phrase anaesthetizes a
portion of one's brain.

I said earlier that the decadence of our language is probably curable. **17**
Those who deny this would argue, if they produced an argument at all,
that language merely reflects existing social conditions, and that we cannot influence its development by any direct tinkering with words and
constructions. So far as the general tone or spirit of a language goes,
this may be true, but it is not true in detail. Silly words and expressions
have often disappeared, not through any evolutionary process but owing to the conscious action of a minority. Two recent examples were
explore every avenue and *leave no stone unturned,* which were killed
by the jeers of a few journalists. There is a long list of flyblown
metaphors which could similarly be got rid of if enough people would
interest themselves in the job; and it should also be possible to laugh
the *not un-* formation out of existence,[3] to reduce the amount of Latin
and Greek in the average sentence, to drive out foreign phrases and
strayed scientific words, and, in general, to make pretentiousness unfashionable. But all these are minor points. The defence of the English

language implies more than this, and perhaps it is best to start by saying what it does *not* imply.

18   To begin with it has nothing to do with archaism, with the salvaging
of obsolete words and turns of speech, or with the setting up of a "standard English" which must never be departed from. On the contrary,
it is especially concerned with the scrapping of every word or idiom
which has outworn its usefulness. It has nothing to do with correct grammar and syntax, which are of no importance so long as one makes one's
meaning clear, or with the avoidance of Americanisms, or with having
what is called a "good prose style". On the other hand it is not concerned with fake simplicity and the attempt to make written English
colloquial. Nor does it even imply in every case preferring the Saxon
word to the Latin one, though it does imply using the fewest and shortest
words that will cover one's meaning. What is above all needed is to
let the meaning choose the word, and not the other way about. In prose,
the worst thing one can do with words is to surrender to them. When
you think of a concrete object, you think wordlessly, and then, if you
want to describe the thing you have been visualizing you probably hunt
about till you find the exact words that seem to fit it. When you think
of something abstract you are more inclined to use words from the start,
and unless you make a conscious effort to prevent it, the existing dialect
will come rushing in and do the job for you, at the expense of blurring
or even changing your meaning. Probably it is better to put off using
words as long as possible and get one's meaning as clear as one can
through pictures or sensations. Afterwards one can choose — not simply
accept — the phrases that will best cover the meaning, and then switch
round and decide what impression one's words are likely to make on
another person. This last effort of the mind cuts out all stale or mixed
images, all prefabricated phrases, needless repetitions, and humbug and
vagueness generally. But one can often be in doubt about the effect of
a word or a phrase, and one needs rules that one can rely on when instinct fails. I think the following rules will cover most cases:

 (i)   Never use a metaphor, simile or other figure of speech which
       you are used to seeing in print.
 (ii) Never use a long word where a short one will do.
 (iii) If it is possible to cut a word out, always cut it out.
 (iv) Never use the passive where you can use the active.
 (v)   Never use a foreign phrase, a scientific word or a jargon word
       if you can think of an everyday English equivalent.

(vi) Break any of these rules sooner than say anything outright barbarous.

These rules sound elementary, and so they are, but they demand a deep change of attitude in anyone who has grown used to writing in the style now fashionable. One could keep all of them and still write bad English, but one could not write the kind of stuff that I quoted in those five specimens at the beginning of this article.

I have not here been considering the literary use of language, but merely language as an instrument for expressing and not for concealing or preventing thought. Stuart Chase and others have come near to claiming that all abstract words are meaningless, and have used this as a pretext for advocating a kind of political quietism. Since you don't know what Fascism is, how can you struggle against Fascism? One need not swallow such absurdities as this, but one ought to recognize that the present political chaos is connected with the decay of language, and that one can probably bring about some improvement by starting at the verbal end. If you simplify your English, you are freed from the worst follies of orthodoxy. You cannot speak any of the necessary dialects, and when you make a stupid remark its stupidity will be obvious, even to yourself. Political language — and with variations this is true of all political parties, from Conservatives to Anarchists — is designed to make lies sound truthful and murder respectable, and to give an appearance of solidity to pure wind. One cannot change this all in a moment, but one can at least change one's own habits, and from time to time one can even, if one jeers loudly enough, send some worn-out and useless phrase — some *jackboot, Achilles' heel, hotbed, melting pot, acid test, veritable inferno* or other lump of verbal refuse — into the dustbin where it belongs.

(1946)

1. An interesting illustration of this is the way in which the English flower names which were in use till very recently are being ousted by Greek ones, *snapdragon* becoming *antirrhinum, forget-me-not* becoming *myosotis*, etc. It is hard to see any practical reason for this change of fashion; it is probably due to an instinctive turning-away from the more homely word and a vague feeling that the Greek word is scientific.

2. Example: "Comfort's catholicity of perception and image, strangely Whitmanesque in range, almost the exact opposite in aesthetic compulsion, continues to evoke that trembling atmospheric accumulative hinting at a cruel, an inexorably serene timelessness . . . Wrey Gardiner scores by aiming at simple bull's-eyes with precision. Only they are not so simple, and through this contented sadness runs more than the surface bitter-sweet of resignation." *(Poetry Quarterly)*

3. One can cure oneself of the *not un-* formation by memorizing this sentence: *A not unblack dog was chasing a not unsmall rabbit across a not ungreen field.*

The Writer's Subject

1. What cause and effect relationship does Orwell perceive between language and thought? (paras. 2, 16)

2. What vices of bad writing does Orwell illustrate in citing the five passages given in paragraph 3? (See paras. 4, 12)

3. Why is Orwell so critical of "dying metaphors"? (para. 5)

4. What is Orwell's objection to the use in English writing of foreign words and phrases? (para. 7)

5. Why, according to Orwell, are words like "democracy," "freedom," and "patriotic" used dishonestly? (para. 8)

6. What is Orwell's point in comparing a political speaker with a dummy or a machine? (para. 13)

7. Why, according to Orwell, is it necessary for modern political language to consist largely of "euphemism, question-begging, and sheer cloudy vagueness"? (para. 14)

8. What connection does Orwell see between the decline of language and the rise of modern dictatorships? (para. 15)

9. Why, in Orwell's view, must one be on guard against the ready-made phrases found in political writing? (para. 16)

The Writer's Style and Strategy

1. What purposes are served by the first two paragraphs of the essay?

2. In paragraph 16, Orwell invites the reader to "look back through this essay, and for certain you will find that I have again and again committed the very faults I am protesting against." Why does Orwell make this statement?

3. Orwell constantly emphasizes the need for concrete images in place of vague abstractions or ready-made phrases. Does his own writing exemplify this principle? Find examples of Orwell's attempt to give concrete expression to his ideas.

4. In paragraph 9 and again in paragraph 22 Orwell demonstrates the misuse of language by modern writers. How does he do this?

5. What is the tone of Orwell's essay? Does it change in any way as he moves from a consideration of language to a discussion of politics?

6. How effectively does the final paragraph sum up the main points of Orwell's argument? Why, in the last sentence, does Orwell use the words "verbal refuse" and "dustbin"?

Suggested Topics for Writing and Discussion

1. Find a printed version of a political speech, and analyze it along the lines of Orwell's comments about political writing. Is it guilty of any of the sins he attributes to political speakers or writers, such as stale images, imprecision, ready-made phrases, meaningless words, or euphemisms?

2. Choose an issue that has aroused controversy, such as abortion, capital punishment, or sex education, and write a speech that might be delivered on the subject by a politician hoping to win votes. Then offer an analysis of the speech, showing where you have used the kind of language attacked by Orwell.

3. Read Russell Baker's "Little Red Riding Hood Revisited" in this reader. Write an essay in which you demonstrate how much Baker's "translation" of the traditional tale owes to the bad habits discussed by Orwell.

Literature and Audience

Of Studies

by Francis Bacon

Studies serve for delight, for ornament, and for ability. Their chief use
for delight is in privateness and retiring; for ornament, is in discourse;
and for ability, is in the judgement and disposition of business. For expert men can execute and perhaps judge of particulars, one by one; but
the general counsels and the plots and marshalling of affairs come best
from those that are learned. To spend too much time in studies is sloth;
to use them too much for ornament is affectation; to make judgement
wholly by their rules is the humour of a scholar. They perfect Nature
and are perfected by experience. For natural abilities are like natural
plants, that need pruning by study; and studies themselves do give forth
directions too much at large, except they be bounded in by experience.
Crafty men condemn studies; simple men admire them; and wise men
use them; for they teach not their own use, but that is a wisdom without
them and above them, won by observation. Read not to contradict and
confute, nor to believe and take for granted, nor to find talk and discourse,
but to weigh and consider. Some books are to be tasted, others to be
swallowed, and some few to be chewed and digested: that is, some books
are to be read only in parts; others to be read but not curiously; and
some few to be read wholly and with diligence and attention. Some books
also may be read by deputy, and extracts made of them by others, but
that would be only in the less important arguments and the meaner sort
of books; else distilled books are like common distilled waters, flashy
things. Reading maketh a full man; conference a ready man, and writing
an exact man. And therefore if a man write little, he had need have
a great memory; if he confer little, he had need have a present wit;

and if he read little, he had need have much cunning to seem to know that he doth not. Histories make men wise; poets, witty; the mathematics, subtle; natural philosophy, deep; moral, grave; logic and rhetoric, able to contend. *Abuent studia in mores.*[1] Nay there is no stond or impediment in the wit but may be wrought out by fit studies, like as diseases of the body may have appropriate exercises. Bowling is good for the stone and reins; shooting for the lungs and breast; gentle walking for the stomach; riding for the head; and the like. So if a man's wit be wandering, let him study the mathematics, for in demonstrations, if his wit be called away never so little, he must begin again. If his wit be not apt to distinguish or find differences, let him study the schoolmen, for they are *Cymini sectores.*[2] If he be not apt to beat over matters and to call up one thing to prove and illustrate another, let him study the lawyers' cases. So every defect of the mind may have a special receipt.

(1613)

1. Studies are transformed into behaviour.
2. hair-splitters. "Schoolmen" in this context refers to medieval scholars such as Thomas Aquinas and John Duns Scotus, who spent much time arguing very subtle theological distinctions.

The Writer's Subject

1. What is the difference between a learned man and an expert, according to Bacon?

2. In Bacon's view, what are the possible evils of study?

3. Why do "Crafty men condemn studies, simple men admire them, and wise men use them"?

4. What uses of reading does Bacon warn against?

5. What does Bacon mean when he says "some books may be read by deputy"?

6. What particular virtues does Bacon see in specific types of reading?

7. What "prescriptions" for reading does Bacon provide?

The Writer's Style and Strategy

1. How does Bacon develop his opening assertion?

2. What figure of speech does Bacon employ when he writes, "for natural abilities are like natural plants, that need pruning by study"? How is this figure of speech "explained" by Bacon?

3. How does Bacon develop the analogy between "diseases" of the wit and those of the body?

4. Consider Bacon's sentence style. Find instances of parallel structures and balanced structures. What rhetorical effects are gained by using these sentence strategies?

Suggested Topics for Writing and Discussion

1. In "Of Studies" Bacon says, "Reading maketh a full man." What do you understand by this statement? Use specific details to explain your view.

2. Bacon says, "Some books are to be tasted, others to be swallowed, and some few to be chewed and digested." Write an essay in which you develop Bacon's classification by means of reference to and discussion of particular books.

The Motive for Metaphor

by Northrop Frye

1   For the past twenty-five years I have been teaching and studying English
literature in a university. As in any other job, certain questions stick
in one's mind, not because people keep asking them, but because they're
the questions inspired by the very fact of being in such a place. What
good is the study of literature? Does it help us to think more clearly,
or feel more sensitively, or live a better life than we could without it?
What is the function of the teacher and scholar, or of the person who
calls himself, as I do, a literary critic? What difference does the study
of literature make in our social or political or religious attitude? In my
early days I thought very little about such questions, not because I had
any of the answers, but because I assumed that anybody who asked them
was naïve. I think now that the simplest questions are not only the hardest
to answer, but the most important to ask, so I'm going to raise them
and try to suggest what my present answers are. I say try to suggest,
because there are only more or less inadequate answers to such questions – there aren't any right answers. The kind of problem that literature
raises is not the kind that you ever 'solve'. Whether my answers are
any good or not, they represent a fair amount of thinking about the questions. As I can't see my audience, I have to choose my rhetorical style
in the dark, and I'm taking the classroom style, because an audience
of students is the one I feel easiest with.

2   There are two things in particular that I want to discuss with you.
In school, and in university, there's a subject called 'English' in English-
speaking countries. English means, in the first place, the mother tongue.
As that, it's the most practical subject in the world: you can't under-

stand anything or take any part in your society without it. Wherever illiteracy is a problem, it's as fundamental a problem as getting enough to eat or a place to sleep. The native language takes precedence over every other subject of study: nothing else can compare with it in usefulness. But then you find that every mother tongue, in any developed or civilized society, turns into something called literature. If you keep on studying 'English', you find yourself trying to read Shakespeare and Milton. Literature, we're told, is one of the arts, along with painting and music, and, after you've looked up all the hard words and the Classical allusions and learned what words like imagery and diction are supposed to mean, what you use in understanding it, or so you're told, is your imagination. Here you don't seem to be in quite the same practical and useful area: Shakespeare and Milton, whatever their merits, are not the kind of thing you must know to hold any place in society at all. A person who knows nothing about literature may be an ignoramus, but many people don't mind being that. Every child realizes that literature is taking him in a different direction from the immediately useful, and a good many children complain loudly about this. Two questions I want to deal with, then, are, first: what is the relation of English as the mother tongue to English as a literature? Second: what is the social value of the study of literature, and what is the place of the imagination that literature addresses itself to, in the learning process?

Let's start with the different ways there are of dealing with the world   3
we're living in. Suppose you're shipwrecked on an uninhabited island in the South Seas. The first thing you do is to take a long look at the world around you, a world of sky and sea and earth and stars and trees and hills. You see this world as objective, as something set over against you and not yourself or related to you in any way. And you notice two things about this objective world. In the first place, it doesn't have any conversation. It's full of animals and plants and insects going on with their own business, but there's nothing that responds to you: it has no morals and no intelligence, or at least none that you can grasp. It may have a shape and a meaning, but it doesn't seem to be a human shape or a human meaning. Even if there's enough to eat and no dangerous animals, you feel lonely and frightened and unwanted in such a world.

In the second place, you find that looking at the world, as something   4
set over against you, splits your mind in two. You have an intellect that feels curious about it and wants to study it, and you have feelings or emotions that see it as beautiful or austere or terrible. You know that both these attitudes have some reality, at least for you. If the ship

you were wrecked in was a Western ship, you'd probably feel that your intellect tells you more about what's really there in the outer world, and that your emotions tell you more about what's going on inside you. If your background were Oriental, you'd be more likely to reverse this and say that the beauty or terror was what was really there, and that your instinct to count and classify and measure and pull to pieces was what was inside your mind. But whether your point of view is Western or Eastern, intellect and emotion never get together in your mind as long as you're simply looking at the world. They alternate, and keep you divided between them.

5   The language you use on this level of the mind is the language of consciousness or awareness. It's largely a language of nouns and adjectives. You have to have names for things, and you need qualities like 'wet' or 'green' or 'beautiful' to describe how things seem to you. This is the speculative or contemplative position of the mind, the position in which the arts and sciences begin, although they don't stay there very long. The sciences begin by accepting the facts and the evidence about an outside world without trying to alter them. Science proceeds by accurate measurement and description, and follows the demands of the reason rather than the emotions. What it deals with is there, whether we like it or not. The emotions are unreasonable: for them it's what they like and don't like that comes first. We'd be naturally inclined to think that the arts follow the path of emotion, in contrast to the sciences. Up to a point they do, but there's a complicating factor.

6   That complicating factor is the contrast between 'I like this' and 'I don't like this'. In this Robinson Crusoe life I've assigned you, you may have moods of complete peacefulness and joy, moods when you accept your island and everything around you. You wouldn't have such moods very often, and when you had them, they'd be moods of identification, when you felt that the island was a part of you and you a part of it. That is not the feeling of consciousness or awareness, where you feel split off from everything that's not your perceiving self. Your habitual state of mind is the feeling of separation which goes with being conscious, and the feeling 'this is not a part of me' soon becomes 'this is not what I want'. Notice the word 'want': we'll be coming back to it.

7   So you soon realize that there's a difference between the world you're living in and the world you want to live in. The world you want to live in is a human world, not an objective one: it's not an environment but a home; it's not the world you see but the world you build out of what you see. You go to work to build a shelter or plant a garden, and as

soon as you start to work you've moved into a different level of human life. You're not separating only yourself from nature now, but constructing a human world and separating it from the rest of the world. Your intellect and emotions are now both engaged in the same activity, so there's no longer any real distinction between them. As soon as you plant a garden or a crop, you develop the conception of a 'weed', the plant you don't want in there. But you can't say that 'weed' is either an intellectual or an emotional conception, because it's both at once. Further, you go to work because you feel you have to, and because you want something at the end of the work. That means that the important categories of your life are no longer the subject and the object, the watcher and the things being watched: the important categories are what you have to do and what you want to do — in other words, necessity and freedom.

One person by himself is not a complete human being, so I'll provide   8
you with another shipwrecked refugee of the opposite sex and an eventual family. Now you're a member of a human society. This human society after a while will transform the island into something with a human shape. What that human shape is, is revealed in the shape of the work you do: the buildings, such as they are, the paths through the woods, the planted crops fenced off against whatever animals want to eat them. These things, these rudiments of city, highway, garden and farm, are the human form of nature, or the form of human nature, whichever you like. This is the area of the applied arts and sciences, and it appears in our society as engineering and agriculture and medicine and architecture. In this area we can never say clearly where the art stops and the science begins, or vice versa.

The language you use on this level is the language of practical sense,   9
a language of verbs or words of action and movement. The practical world, however, is a world where actions speak louder than words. In some ways it's a higher level of existence than the speculative level, because it's doing something about the world instead of just looking at it, but in itself it's a much more primitive level. It's the process of adapting to the environment, or rather of transforming the environment in the interests of one species, that goes on among animals and plants as well as human beings. The animals have a good many of our practical skills: some insects make pretty fair architects, and beavers know quite a lot about engineering. In this island, probably, and certainly if you were alone, you'd have about the ranking of a second-rate animal. What makes our practical life really human is a third level of the mind,

a level where consciousness and practical skill come together.

10   This third level is a vision or model in your mind of what you want
to construct. There's that word 'want' again. The actions of man are
prompted by desire, and some of these desires are needs, like food and
warmth and shelter. One of these needs is sexual, the desire to reproduce
and bring more human beings into existence. But there's also a desire
to bring a social human form into existence: the form of cities and
gardens and farms that we call civilization. Many animals and insects
have this social form too, but man knows that he has it: he can compare what he does with what he can imagine being done. So we begin
to see where the imagination belongs in the scheme of human affairs.
It's the power of constructing possible models of human experience.
In the world of the imagination, anything goes that's imaginatively possible, but nothing really happens. If it did happen, it would move out
of the world of imagination into the world of action.

11   We have three levels of the mind now, and a language for each of
them, which in English-speaking societies means an English for each
of them. There's the level of consciousness and awareness, where the
most important thing is the difference between me and everything else.
The English of this level is the English of ordinary conversation, which
is mostly monologue, as you'll soon realize if you do a bit of eavesdrop-
ping, or listening to yourself. We can call it the language of self-
expression. Then there's the level of social participation, the working
or technological language of teachers and preachers and politicians and
advertisers and lawyers and journalists and scientists. We've already
called this the language of practical sense. Then there's the level of imagination, which produces the literary language of poems and plays and
novels. They're not really different languages, of course, but three different reasons for using words.

12   On this basis, perhaps, we can distinguish the arts from the sciences.
Science begins with the world we have to live in, accepting its data
and trying to explain its laws. From there, it moves towards the imagination: it becomes a mental construct, a model of a possible way
of interpreting experience. The further it goes in this direction, the more
it tends to speak the language of mathematics, which is really one of
the languages of the imagination, along with literature and music. Art,
on the other hand, begins with the world we construct, not with the
world we see. It starts with the imagination, and then works towards
ordinary experience: that is, it tries to make itself as convincing and
recognizable as it can. You can see why we tend to think of the sciences

as intellectual and the arts as emotional: one starts with the world as it is, the other with the world we want to have. Up to a point it is true that science gives an intellectual view of reality, and that the arts try to make the emotions as precise and disciplined as sciences do the intellect. But of course it's nonsense to think of the scientist as a cold unemotional reasoner and the artist as somebody who's in a perpetual emotional tizzy. You can't distinguish the arts from the sciences by the mental processes the people in them use: they both operate on a mixture of hunch and common sense. A highly developed science and a highly developed art are very close together, psychologically and otherwise.

Still, the fact that they start from opposite ends, even if they do meet **13** in the middle, makes for one important difference between them. Science learns more and more about the world as it goes on: it evolves and improves. A physicist today knows more physics than Newton did, even if he's not as great a scientist. But literature begins with the possible model of experience, and what it produces is the literary model we call the classic. Literature doesn't evolve or improve or progress. We may have dramatists in the future who will write plays as good as *King Lear,* though they'll be very different ones, but drama as a whole will never get better than *King Lear. King Lear* is it, as far as drama is concerned; so is *Oedipus Rex,* written two thousand years earlier than that, and both will be models of dramatic writing as long as the human race endures. Social conditions may improve: most of us would rather live in nineteenth-century United States than in thirteenth-century Italy, and for most of us Whitman's celebration of democracy makes a lot more sense than Dante's Inferno. But it doesn't follow that Whitman is a better poet than Dante: literature won't line up with that kind of improvement.

So we find that everything that does improve, including science, leaves **14** the literary artist out in the cold. Writers don't seem to benefit much by the advance of science, although they thrive on superstitions of all kinds. And you certainly wouldn't turn to contemporary poets for guidance or leadership in the twentieth-century world. You'd hardly go to Ezra Pound, with his fascism and social credit and Confucianism and anti-semitism. Or to Yeats, with his spiritualism and fairies and astrology. Or to D.H. Lawrence, who'll tell you that it's a good thing for servants to be flogged because that restores the precious current of blood-reciprocity between servant and master. Or to T.S. Eliot, who'll tell you that to have a flourishing culture we should educate an élite, keep most people living in the same spot, and never disestablish the

Church of England. The novelists seem to be a little closer to the world they're living in, but not much. When Communists talk about the decadence of bourgeois culture, this is the kind of thing they always bring up. Their own writers don't seem to be any better, though; just duller. So the real question is a bigger one. Is it possible that literature, especially poetry, is something that a scientific civilization like ours will eventually outgrow? Man has always wanted to fly, and thousands of years ago he was making sculptures of winged bulls and telling stories about people who flew so high on artificial wings that the sun melted them off. In an Indian play fifteen hundred years ago, *Sakuntala,* there's a god who flies around in a chariot that to a modern reader sounds very much like a private aeroplane. Interesting that the writer had so much imagination, but do we need such stories now that we have private aeroplanes?

15   This is not a new question: it was raised a hundred and fifty years ago by Thomas Love Peacock, who was a poet and novelist himself, and a very brilliant one. He wrote an essay called *Four Ages of Poetry,* with his tongue of course in his cheek, in which he said that poetry was the mental rattle that awakened the imagination of mankind in its infancy, but that now, in an age of science and technology, the poet has outlived his social function. 'A poet in our times,' said Peacock, 'is a semi-barbarian in a civilized community. He lives in the days that are past. His ideas, thoughts, feelings, associations, are all with barbarous manners, obsolete customs, and exploded superstitions. The march of his intellect is like that of a crab, backwards.' Peacock's essay annoyed his friend Shelley, who wrote another essay called *A Defence of Poetry* to refute it. Shelley's essay is a wonderful piece of writing, but it's not likely to convince anyone who needs convincing. I shall be spending a good deal of my time on this question of the relevance of literature in the world of today, and I can only indicate the general lines my answer will take. There are two points I can make now, one simple, the other more difficult.

16   The simple point is that literature belongs to the world man constructs, not to the world he sees; to his home, not his environment. Literature's world is a concrete human world of immediate experience. The poet uses images and objects and sensations much more than he uses abstract ideas; the novelist is concerned with telling stories, not with working out arguments. The world of literature is human in shape, a world where the sun rises in the east and sets in the west over the edge of a flat earth in three dimensions, where the primary realities are not atoms or elec-

trons but bodies, and the primary forces not energy or gravitation but love and death and passion and joy. It's not surprising if writers are often rather simple people, not always what we think of as intellectuals, and certainly not always any freer of silliness or perversity than anyone else. What concerns us is what they produce, not what they are, and poetry, according to Milton, who ought to have known, is 'more simple, sensuous and passionate' than philosophy or science.

The more difficult point takes us back to what we said when we were 17 on that South Sea island. Our emotional reaction to the world varies from 'I like this' to 'I don't like this'. The first, we said, was a state of identity, a feeling that everything around us was part of us, and the second is the ordinary state of consciousness, or separation, where art and science begin. Art begins as soon as 'I don't like this' turns into 'this is not the way I could imagine it'. We notice in passing that the creative and the neurotic minds have a lot in common. They're both dissatisfied with what they see; they both believe that something else ought to be there, and they try to pretend it is there or to make it be there. The differences are more important, but we're not ready for them yet.

At the level of ordinary consciousness the individual man is the cen- 18 tre of everything, surrounded on all sides by what he isn't. At the level of practical sense, or civilization, there's a human circumference, a little cultivated world with a human shape, fenced off from the jungle and inside the sea and the sky. But in the imagination anything goes that can be imagined, and the limit of the imagination is a totally human world. Here we recapture, in full consciousness, that original lost sense of identity with our surroundings, where there is nothing outside the mind of man, or something identical with the mind of man. Religions present us with visions of eternal and infinite heavens or paradises which have the form of the cities and gardens of human civilization, like the Jerusalem and Eden of the Bible, completely separated from the state of frustration and misery that bulks so large in ordinary life. We're not concerned with these visions as religion, but they indicate what the limits of the imagination are. They indicate too that in the human world the imagination has no limits, if you follow me. We said that the desire to fly produced the aeroplane. But people don't get into planes because they want to fly; they get into planes because they want to get somewhere else faster. What's produced the aeroplane is not so much a desire to fly as a rebellion against the tyranny of time and space. And that's a process that can never stop, no matter how high our Titovs and Glenns may go.

19   For each of these six talks I've taken a title from some work of
literature, and my title for this one is 'The Motive for Metaphor', from
a poem of Wallace Stevens. Here's the poem:

You like it under the trees in autumn,
Because everything is half dead.
The wind moves like a cripple among the leaves
And repeats words without meaning.

In the same way, you were happy in spring,
With the half colors of quarter-things,
The slightly brighter sky, the melting clouds,
The single bird, the obscure moon —

The obscure moon lighting an obscure world
Of things that would never be quite expressed,
Where you yourself were never quite yourself
And did not want nor have to be,

Desiring the exhilarations of changes:
The motive for metaphor, shrinking from
The weight of primary noon,
The A B C of being,

The ruddy temper, the hammer
Of red and blue, the hard sound —
Steel against intimation — the sharp flash,
The vital, arrogant, fatal, dominant X.

What Stevens calls the weight of primary noon, the A B C of being,
and the dominant X is the objective world, the world set over against
us. Outside literature, the main motive for writing is to describe this
world. But literature itself uses language in a way which associates our
minds with it. As soon as you use associative language, you begin using
figures of speech. If you say this talk is dry and dull, you're using figures
associating it with bread and breadknives. There are two main kinds
of association, analogy and identity, two things that are like each other
and two things that are each other. You can say with Burns, 'My love's
like a red, red rose', or you can say with Shakespeare:

Thou that art now the world's fresh ornament
And only herald to the gaudy spring.

One produces the figure of speech called the simile; the other produces
the figure called metaphor.

20   In descriptive writing you have to be careful of associative language.
You'll find that analogy, or likeness to something else, is very tricky

to handle in description, because the differences are as important as the resemblances. As for metaphor, where you're really saying 'this *is* that', you're turning your back on logic and reason completely, because logically two things can never be the same thing and still remain two things. The poet, however, uses these two crude, primitive archaic forms of thought in the most uninhibited way, because his job is not to describe nature, but to show you a world completely absorbed and possessed by the human mind. So he produces what Baudelaire called a "suggestive magic including at the same time object and subject, the world outside the artist and the artist himself". The motive for metaphor, according to Wallace Stevens, is a desire to associate, and finally to identify, the human mind with what goes on outside it, because the only genuine joy you can have is in those rare moments when you feel that although we may know in part, as Paul says, we are also a part of what we know.

The Writer's Subject

1. What does the title of this essay mean?

2. In paragraph 2, Frye distinguishes between English as "the mother tongue, the most practical subject in the world," and "English as a literature." How does he illustrate this distinction in the paragraphs that follow?

3. What is the distinction Frye draws between the intellectual response and the emotional response to the world? (para. 4) How does he think these responses might be shaped by a Western or an Oriental view?

4. Frye uses an extended analogy of life on a desert island as a model to discuss levels of thought and language. What are the stages of human development that Frye identifies through use of this analogy? (paras. 3-11)

5. Frye identifies three levels of the mind and, correspondingly, three levels of language. What are these? (paras. 4-11)

6. According to Frye, how do the sciences deal with the external world differently than do the arts? (para. 5)

7. What turns the external objective world into a human world? What gives the human world its "human shape"? (paras. 7-8)

8. What processes of thought distinguish the artist's approach from the scientist's? (para. 12)

9. In paragraph 14 Frye asks the question, "Is it possible that literature, especially poetry, is something that a scientific civilization like ours will eventually outgrow?" How does he answer this question in paragraphs 16-18?

10. Why, according to Frye, does the poet make use of metaphor and simile? (paras. 19-20)

The Writer's Style and Strategy

1. This essay is the first of six published lectures. How does Frye establish the context for his discussion? Where, in the essay, are you aware that this essay is an introduction to the series?

2. Frye says, "I'm taking the classroom style." How is the classroom style demonstrated in the tone, structure, and diction of the essay?

3. Analyze the structure of Frye's essay as a whole. Indicate the major stages of the essay. How does Frye effect the transitions from one part to another?

4. What is the function of paragraph 11?

5. What means does Frye use to demonstrate his point that literary artists don't serve as useful social guides? (para. 14)

6. How does the lengthy reference to Thomas Love Peacock in paragraph 15 contribute to Frye's arguments at this point?

7. What is Frye's purpose in including the poem by Wallace Stevens?

Suggested Topics for Writing and Discussion

1. In an age of science and technology, does the poet have a role to play?

2. Frye talks about the imaginative processes involved in scientific thinking. Do you think that scientific advances depend upon the imagination as much as upon the analytical process of thought? Provide an example to support your point of view.

3. Many students going on to college feel they already "know" enough English to get on in the world without studying more — especially literature. What are your views on the place of literature courses in colleges and universities?

4. Choose an article from a popular magazine (e.g., *Time, Maclean's, Saturday Night, Science Digest*) and analyze the article to determine the extent to which the writer uses metaphorical language.

Let's Ban Applause!
by Glenn Gould

1   The good citizens of Toronto, my hometown, received last spring their annual visit from the Metropolitan Opera Company. This is an occasion much looked forward to by all of us, and this season was the subject of special attention, since it involved the transfer of that splendid ensemble from the regal expanse of a hockey arena to the more confined proscenium of a new theatre constructed in our behalf through the generosity, civic vision, and tax advantage of a local brewing firm. The Metropolitan, with its accustomed tact and diplomacy, wisely declined to present to us the alcoholic dissipations of Sir John Falstaff or the aphrodisiac delusions of Master Tristan or, indeed, any other tableaus which might compromise the corporate image of its host. But, despite these courtesies, the visit was attended by a most disagreeable correspondence in the local press. This emanated from the displeasure which several writers voiced with the relatively restricted capacity of the new salon and from sympathy with those of our less affluent fellow citizens who found the consequent raise in admission prohibitive.

2   It was not these modest, though justified, complaints that arrested my attention, however, but the grave alarms raised by several of our more worldly-wise columnists (those who have attended concerts as far afield as Buffalo) that what we had lost with the reduced attendance at the Metropolitan was not money — a concept which all Torontonians could readily grasp — but was, rather, that intangible spirit of theatrical excitement generated by those whose native customs permit the unabashed display of enthusiasm or displeasure. We had, we were told, callously excluded the services of that indispensable component of grand

opera — the upper-balcony jeer leader. This view, disseminated in the local press, caused much consternation among my fellow citizens, an effect it would surely not have achieved in any other city. This is, of course, because Toronto is one of the last bastions of puritan influence in North America, and, despite the encroachment of science, Henry Miller, and immigration, we have managed to hold firm those convictions upon which the faith of our fathers was founded.

We do not regard the theatre as an intrinsically wicked institution;   **3**
we do consider it in need of careful and constant scrutiny.   But once we have satisfied ourselves as to the moral discernment of its productions, we proceed to it with a total humility born of reverence for that which we do not wholly understand. It would never have occurred to us to demand for ourselves the right to proclaim our approbation demonstratively by rudely punctuating a work of musical theatre. Even less would we presume, by forwarding uncomplimentary noises from the stalls, to express our distaste for the message of a composer which we found difficult or the hapless screechings of an ill-advised soprano.

This is not to say that we would withhold a measure of encourage-   **4**
ment from an artist whose work and whose private life are beyond reproach. I have seen elderly ladies remove their gloves to render their tribute to the symphonies of Mr. Elgar — after all, he was well received at court, wasn't he? — and certainly our pleasure with Dr. Mendelssohn knows no bounds. And I can attest from personal experience that Torontonians are well able to convey their consternation at the beeps and groans of Mr. Anton Webern by a silence as timeless as those within that gentleman's music itself.

But now we were being told by this racy contingent of high-living   **5**
newspapermen that we must surrender our right to the genteel response of our cultural tradition and look for leadership to those whose heritage does not consider musical theatre an adjunct of the church (as ours does) but rather as a comfortably upholstered extension of the Roman Colosseum. This has given me occasion to ponder the relationship of applause to musical culture, and I have come to the conclusion, most seriously, that the most efficacious step which could be taken in our culture today would be the gradual but total elimination of audience response.

I am disposed toward this view because I believe that the justifica-   **6**
tion of art is the internal combustion it ignites in the hearts of men and not its shallow, externalized, public manifestations. The purpose of art is not the release of a momentary ejection of adrenaline but is, rather, the gradual, life-long construction of a state of wonder and serenity.

Through the ministrations of radio and the phonograph, we are rapidly and quite properly learning to appreciate the elements of aesthetic narcissism — and I use that word in its best sense — and are awakening to the challenge that each man contemplatively create his own divinity.

7   The effect of this newly acquired introspection has been salutary upon our culture as a whole. Never before have Ockeghem and Costeley invaded our drawing room in the company of Chopin and Liszt. Never before has Gesualdo competed with Schubert for our attention. Never before has a composer been able to render electronically the exact specifications of his intention without resorting to the self-centered affectations of a performing middleman. If, then, it has been possible to achieve within one generation this degree of conditioned listening, surely the next generation will find it no mighty task to carry this quality of introspection one step further — into the concert hall and theatre themselves.

8   There are those, of course, who counsel that only in the theatre, only with the direct communion of artist to listener, can we experience the high drama of human communication. The answer to this, it seems to me, is that art on its loftiest mission is scarcely human at all.

9   "But surely," some may counter, "applauding after a performance is as natural to a listener as sneezing at the sun on a windy day." I reply that one may listen to a recording of a Beethoven symphony alone or in the company of friends and, though deeply moved at its conclusion, experience no more urgent need than a quick trip to the icebox for a soda water. And if we concede, then, that it is the law of the heard that governs the response of an audience to a performer, can this response be further justified?

10   "Democracy, the rule of Majority," someone argues. "Why should the paying customer be deprived of the right to voice his opinion?" Well, apart from the fact that the other paying customers did not subscribe to hear his opinion, one must take into account the peculiar laws of acoustical psychology, whereby a strategically placed rooter or detractor may, by applying the proper vocal leverage at a judicious moment, enlist the bellowing echo of many hundreds of his fellows.

11   "But what harmful effect can it have?" someone asks. "Everybody knows that artists are incredibly conceited and quite able to survive the taunts of an impolite laity." Ah, are they indeed? I ask. Or are the absurdly competitive extravaganzas of our operatic colleagues not the product of, or maybe the antidote to, the vulgar artistic hostility of those sun-baked societies who have built an operatic tradition in which their

primal instinct for gladiatorial combat has found a more gracious but thinly disguised sublimation?

"All right," our disputant allows, "granted that a few of the less sturdy 12 vocalists must concede in the fray, but what about the composers? Let's not forget that many of our great composers became famous by having more disorderly premieres than their colleagues were able to muster. Let's not forget Stravinsky and the riots at the *Rite* or Schoenberg and the pummelings at *Pierrot.*" True, I retort, they did become famous, and they deserved to become famous, but not because of the riots and not even, I would venture to suggest, because of those particular works. A more just citation, if you will allow me, would be an incident at one of our own Toronto premieres – an incident which deeply shocked all true Torontonians. It happened several years ago, at the first performance of a new concerto by a Canadian composer, a lady of considerable gift, though perhaps of less resilient spirit than a Stravinsky or a Schoenberg. Preceding the performance, an introductory speaker (non-Torontonian) spoke harshly to us on the subject of apathy toward contemporary composition. He urged us, as only a non-Torontonian would, to express our approval of the works we enjoyed, or, if we were so inclined, our disapproval. Now, this adjuration would certainly have gone for naught but for the unlucky chance that in the audience that night there sat another non-Torontonian, a historian by profession and an intelligent chap, but a fellow whose musical sympathies stop somewhere short of Josquin des Prés. Well, as you can imagine, the new concerto did not fall upon receptive ears, and so our friend the historian, having been encouraged to voice his estimation, did so. Regrettably, he was being closely scrutinized at the time by some eager members of his graduate class (non-Torontonians all), who were seated nearby. And so "Hoot," said the professor, and "Hoot, hoot," said the students, while visions of better grades danced in their heads. I wish I could relate that the concerto and its composer became infamous that night, but such was not to be the case, and it has not been rendered since. There is, however, a sequel to the story. The lady composer had another premiere in Toronto quite recently – a new symphony. Our historian was not present, but nonetheless the new work was shown the same intolerance as its elder brother – the only work in our concert season to be so honored. Clearly, the herd is breeding.

"Aha," says the disputant in a final effort to demolish my case, "this 13 fellow Gould speaks with a singular passion. Perhaps he, too, has been put to his heels to escape the wrath of an outraged public!" Yes, I admit candidly, there was such an occasion. It was in Florence, or, as we international men prefer to say, Firenze. I had just concluded a performance of the Schoenberg Suite, Op. 25, which, although it was at the time thirty-five years old, had not yet been admitted to the vocabulary of the Florentines. I arose from the instrument to be greeted by a most disagreeable chant from the upper balcony, which was at once contradicted by feverish encouragements from the lower levels. Although I was new to this experience, I instinctively realized that no harm could come to me so long as I permitted the spectators to vent their fury upon each other. Therefore, I cunningly milked the applause for six curtain calls (an exceptional acclaim for Op. 25), and, thereafter, the exhausted audience sat back in a liverish somnolence to attend the "Goldberg" Variations.

14   I feel that I have now presented my case with true candor, and so it only remains to suggest ways and means to implement my proposal that the audience of the future should be seen but not heard. To this end, and for the assistance of any concert manager who may care to make use of it, I have drawn up the Gould Plan for the Abolition of Applause and Demonstrations of All Kinds, hereinafter referred to as GPAADAK. Needless to say, GPAADAK in its early stages will require, in addition to an active promotional campaign, a measure of goodwill on the part of artist, audience, and management alike.

15   The first step in instituting GPAADAK will be the scheduling of applauseless concerts on each Friday, Saturday, and Sunday. These three days, with their inherent liturgical connotations, are best able to evoke a suitably reverent state of mind. Concerts during the balance of the week, Monday to Thursday, could be billed as Family Excursion Events, if I may beg a term from the airlines. Reduced prices would apply, and, of course, applause would be permitted. Children would be encouraged to attend during the week, and the duty to guide them there would provide a convenient excuse for those of the older generation who found the conversion difficult. The performers, naturally, would be strictly second-team. At the prestige weekend concerts, the most serious problem in the early stage of GPAADAK will be the selection of appropriate repertoire — works which will most contribute to the overall solemnity. I would suggest that large-scale oratorios be tried first, followed, perhaps, by a series consisting of music composed by members of royal houses. There is a wide field here, and works such as the Piano Concerto in A by Louis Ferdinand of Prussia or the *Pastorale Cantata for Lady Augusta's Birthday* by Frederick Louis, Prince of Wales (and father,

incidentally, of George III), deserve a firm place in our musical life. There might, of course, be certain judicious exclusions. Perhaps a composition by the Maharaja of Porbandar would not be appropriate for a Sunday concert in Karachi.

The next area of repertoire to be included in GPAADAK should be the presentation of ninth symphonies — anybody's Ninth Symphony, really, although Shostakovitch's might be a little flip — but, after exploring the Beethoven-Bruckner-Mahler parallel, it would be wise to conclude with Schubert's Ninth, since, being really his Seventh, it would introduce an appropriate note of secularism into the numerical piety of the series. I think that these few suggestions already indicate that the concert managers of the future will be under pressure to display an unaccustomed initiative in programming. Indeed, under the aegis of GPAADAK, many of these gentlemen may well advance from their present status as bookers and become worthy of the old and noble title of impresario.   16

In the early stages of GPAADAK, the performers may feel a moment of unaccustomed tension at the conclusion of their selection, when they must withdraw to the wings unescorted by the homage of their auditors. For orchestral players this should provide no hazard: a platoon of cellists smartly goose-stepping offstage is an inspiring sight. For the solo pianist, however, I would suggest a sort of lazy-Susan device which would transport him and his instrument to the wings without his having to rise. This would encourage performance of those sonatas which end on a note of serene reminiscence, and in which the lazy Susan could be set gently in motion some moments before the conclusion. I foresee a heavy run on Op. 109, which could almost be staged, provided there were a clear understanding between the soloist and the commissionaire backstage.   17

As the founder and chronicler of GPAADAK, I feel that it behooves me to be among the first to put it into practice. Needless to say, I have given this responsibility much consideration. Regrettably, Toronto does not provide the ideal site, since, apart from the fact that it needs GPAADAK less urgently than almost any other center, I personally would be confronted with the age-old civic antagonism for the local boy with a vision. It has occurred to me as a codirector of the Stratford Music Festival that the unique intimacy of our beautiful stage there might be especially appropriate for applauseless concerts, but then, those actors are such a wild, unpredictable bunch. Perhaps my chance will come at Mr. Tom Patterson's recently announced Dawson City Festival of   18

1962. Here indeed is virgin territory. Here is an audience without prejudice, without preconception. I wonder how Diamond Lil would react
to the Maharaja of Porbandar?

(1962)

The Writer's Subject

1. According to Gould, how did Torontonians receive the visit of the
   Metropolitan Opera to their new theatre? (para. 1)

2. What was the "grave alarm" sounded in the local press? (para. 2)

3. What attitudes to theatre, especially musical theatre, does Gould attribute
   to Torontonians? (paras. 3, 5)

4. Why does Gould suggest "total elimination of audience response"? (paras.
   5-6)

5. How, according to Gould, has listening to music changed as a consequence
   of the development of the radio and the phonograph? (para. 7)

6. What objections does Gould anticipate from those who would not share
   his desire to ban applause? How does he answer these objections? (paras.
   8-13)

7. What steps does Gould say are necessary if the "Gould Plan for the Abolition of Applause and Demonstrations of All Kinds" is to be implemented?
   (paras. 15-16)

8. Gould rejects Toronto as the place for the introduction of his Plan. Why?
   (para. 18)

9. How serious do you think Gould is in making this proposal?

The Writer's Style and Strategy

1. What is Gould's tone?

2. What features of the essay suggest that it was originally written for a music
   magazine?

3. How does Gould lead up to the presentation of his "Plan"?

4. What persona does Gould create for himself as the proposer of a plan to
   ban applause? At several points in the essay he draws attention to himself
   as a performing musician. What is his purpose in doing so?

5. What use does Gould make of the Toronto audience throughout his essay? How does he create the "character" of this audience?

6. What use does Gould make of relatively unpopular composers (e.g., Webern, Stravinsky, Schoenberg) or little-known early composers (e.g., Ockeghem, Costeley, Gesualdo, Josquin des Prés)? (paras. 4, 7, 12)

7. Choose two or three examples of inflated and ornate diction in this essay. What purposes are served by Gould's choices of words and phrasing?

8. Gould uses parallel structures for a variety of purposes. Choose one or two sentences with parallelism and explain the effects Gould achieves (e.g., "constructed in our behalf through the generosity, civic vision, and tax advantage of a local brewing firm," in paragraph 1; "despite the encroachment of science, Henry Miller, and immigration," in paragraph 2).

9. In what way is Gould's closing strategy like that of the projector in Swift's "A Modest Proposal"?

Suggested Topics for Writing and Discussion

1. Write a proposal (serious or otherwise) to ban some activity or behaviour which you find objectionable (e.g., dogs on public beaches, traffic in a congested area, "ghetto-blasters" in public places).

2. Gould suggests that the pleasure in listening to recorded music is possibly greater than that experienced in listening to music performed live. Do you agree?

3. Gould suggests that certain kinds of music are unlikely to elicit much applause from an audience (e.g., large-scale oratorios, music composed by members of royal houses). Write your own proposal for a programme of music you think would be boring or unlikely to please an audience. (Explain the audience you have in mind and the type of music least likely to please that audience.)

Where the World Began

by Margaret Laurence

1   A strange place it was, that place where the world began. A place of
incredible happenings, splendours and revelations, despairs like
multitudinous pits of isolated hells. A place of shadow-spookiness, inhabited by the unknowable dead. A place of jubilation and of mourning, horrible and beautiful.

2   It was, in fact, a small prairie town.

3   Because that settlement and that land were my first and for many years
only real knowledge of this planet, in some profound way they remain
my world, my way of viewing. My eyes were formed there. Towns
like ours, set in a sea of land, have been described thousands of times
as dull, bleak, flat, uninteresting. I have had it said to me that the railway
trip across Canada is spectacular, except for the prairies, when it would
be desirable to go to sleep for several days, until the ordeal is over.
I am always unable to argue this point effectively. All I can say is —
well, you really have to live there to know that country. The town of
my childhood could be called bizarre, agonizingly repressive or cruel
at times, and the land in which it grew could be called harsh in the
violence of its seasonal changes. But never merely flat or uninteresting.
Never dull.

4   In winter, we used to hitch rides on the back of the milk sleigh, our
moccasins squeaking and slithering on the hard rutted snow of the roads,
our hands in ice-bubbled mitts hanging onto the box edge of the sleigh
for dear life, while Bert grinned at us through his great frosted moustache
and shouted the horses into speed, daring us to stay put. Those mornings, rising, there would be the perpetual fascination of the frost feathers

on windows, the ferns and flowers and eerie faces traced there during
the night by unseen artists of the wind. Evenings, coming back from
skating, the sky would be black but not dark, for you could see a cold
glitter of stars from one side of the earth's rim to the other. And then
the sometime astonishment when you saw the Nothern Lights flaring
across the sky, like the scrawled signature of God. After a blizzard,
when the snowploughs hadn't yet got through, school would be closed
for the day, the assumption being that the town's young could not possibly
flounder through five feet of snow in the pursuit of education. We would
then gaily don snowshoes and flounder for miles out into the white dazzl-
ing deserts, in pursuit of a different kind of knowing. If you came back
too close to night, through the woods at the foot of the town hill, the
thin black branches of poplar and chokecherry now meringued with frost,
sometimes you heard coyotes. Or maybe the banshee wolf-voices were
really only inside your head.

Summers were scorching, and when no rain came and the wheat   5
became bleached and dried before it headed, the faces of farmers and
townsfolk would not smile much, and you took for granted, because
it never seemed to have been any different, the frequent knocking at
the back door and the young men standing there, mumbling or thrusting
defiantly their request for a drink of water and a sandwich if you could
spare it. They were riding the freights, and you never knew where they
had come from, or where they might end up, if anywhere. The Drought
and Depression were like evil deities which had been there always. You
understood and did not understand.

Yet the outside world had its continuing marvels. The poplar bluffs   6
and the small river were filled and surrounded with a zillion different
grasses, stones, and weed flowers. The meadowlarks sang undaunted
from the twanging telephone wires along the gravel highway. Once we
found an old flat-bottomed scow, and launched her, poling along the
shallow brown waters, mending her with wodges of hastily chewed
Spearmint, grounding her among the tangles of soft yellow marsh
marigolds that grew succulently along the banks of the shrunken river,
while the sun made our skins smell dusty-warm.

My best friend lived in an apartment above some stores on Main Street   7
(its real name was Mountain Avenue, goodness knows why), an elegant
apartment with royal-blue velvet curtains. The back roof, scarcely sloping at all, was corrugated tin, of a furnace-like warmth on a July afternoon, and we would sit there drinking lemonade and looking across
the back lane at the Fire Hall. Sometimes our vigil would be rewarded.

Oh joy! Somebody's house burning down! We had an almost-perfect callousness in some ways. Then the wooden tower's bronze bell would clonk and toll like a thousand speeded funerals in a time of plague, and in a few minutes the team of giant black horses would cannon forth, pulling the fire wagon like some scarlet chariot of the Goths, while the firemen clung with one hand, adjusting their helmets as they went.

8   The oddities of the place were endless. An elderly lady used to serve, as her afternoon tea offering to other ladies, soda biscuits spread with peanut butter and topped with a whole marshmallow. Some considered this slightly eccentric, when compared with chopped egg sandwiches, and admittedly talked about her behind her back, but no one ever refused these delicacies or indicated to her that they thought she had slipped a cog. Another lady dyed her hair a bright and cheery orange, by strangers often mistaken at twenty paces for a feather hat. My own beloved stepmother wore a silver fox neckpiece, a whole pelt, *with the embalmed (?) head still on.* My Ontario Irish grandfather said, "sparrow grass," a more interesting term than asparagus. The town dump was known as "the nuisance grounds," a phrase fraught with weird connotations, as though the effluvia of our lives was beneath contempt but at the same time was subtly threatening to the determined and sometimes hysterical propriety of our ways.

9   Some oddities were, as idiom had it, "funny ha ha"; others were "funny peculiar." Some were not so very funny at all. An old man lived, deranged, in a shack in the valley. Perhaps he wasn't even all that old, but to us he seemed a wild Methuselah figure, shambling among the underbrush and the tall couchgrass, muttering indecipherable curses or blessings, a prophet who had forgotten his prophesies. Everyone in town knew him, but no one knew him. He lived among us as though only occasionally and momentarily visible. The kids called him Andy Gump, and feared him. Some sought to prove their bravery by tormenting him. They were the medieval bear baiters, and he the lumbering bewildered bear, half blind, only rarely turning to snarl. Everything is to be found in a town like mine. Belsen, writ small but with the same ink.

10   All of us cast stones in one shape or another. In grade school, among the vulnerable and violet girls we were, the feared and despised were those few older girls from what was charmingly termed "the wrong side of the tracks." Tough in talk and tougher in muscle, they were said to be whores already. And may have been, that being about the only profession readily available to them.

11   The dead lived in that place, too. Not only the grandparents who had,

in local parlance, "passed on" and who gloomed, bearded or bonneted, from the sepia photographs in old albums, but also the uncles, forever eighteen or nineteen, whose names were carved on the granite family stones in the cemetery, but whose bones lay in France. My own young mother lay in that graveyard, beside other dead of our kin, and when I was ten, my father, too, only forty, left the living town for the dead dwelling on the hill.

When I was eighteen, I couldn't wait to get out of that town, away 12 from the prairies. I did not know then that I would carry the land and town all my life within my skull, that they would form the mainspring and source of the writing I was to do, wherever and however far away I might live.

This was my territory in the time of my youth, and in a sense my 13 life since then has been an attempt to look at it, to come to terms with it. Stultifying to the mind it certainly could be, and sometimes was, but not to the imagination. It was many things, but it was never dull.

The same, I now see, could be said for Canada in general. Why on 14 earth did generations of Canadians pretend to believe this country dull? We knew perfectly well it wasn't. Yet for so long we did not proclaim what we knew. If our upsurge of so-called nationalism seems odd or irrelevant to outsiders, and even to some of our own people *(what's all the fuss about?)*, they might try to understand that for many years we valued ourselves insufficiently, living as we did under the huge shadows of those two dominating figures, Uncle Sam and Britannia. We have only just begun to value ourselves, our land, our abilities. We have only just begun to recognize our legends and to give shape to our myths.

There are, God knows, enough aspects to deplore about this coun- 15 try. When I see the killing of our lakes and rivers with industrial wastes, I feel rage and despair. When I see our industries and natural resources increasingly taken over by America, I feel an overwhelming discouragement, especially as I cannot simply say "damn Yankees." It should never be forgotten that it is we ourselves who have sold such a large amount of our birthright for a mess of plastic Progress. When I saw the War Measures Act being invoked in 1970, I lost forever the vestigial remains of the naive wish-belief that repression could not happen here, or would not. And yet, of course, I had known all along in the deepest and often hidden caves of the heart that anything can happen anywhere, for the seed of both man's freedom and his captivity are found everywhere, even in the microcosm of a prairie town. But in raging against our injustices, our stupidities, I do so *as family*, as I did, and still do in writing, about those aspects of my town which I hated and which are always in some ways aspects of myself.

16   The land still draws me more than other lands. I have lived in Africa and in England, but splendid as both can be, they do not have the power to move me in the same way as, for example, that part of southern Ontario where I spent four months last summer in a cedar cabin beside a river. "Scratch a Canadian, and you find a phony pioneer," I used to say to myself in warning. But all the same it is true, I think, that we are not yet totally alienated from physical earth, and let us only pray we do not become so. I once thought that my lifelong fear and mistrust of cities made me a kind of old-fashioned freak; now I see it differently.

17   The cabin has a long window across its front western wall, and sitting at the oak table there in the mornings, I used to look out at the river and at the tall trees beyond, green-gold in the early light. The river was bronze; the sun caught it strangely, reflecting upon its surface the near-shore sand ripples underneath. Suddenly, the crescenting of a fish, gone before the eye could clearly give image to it. The old man next door said these leaping fish were carp. Himself, he preferred muskie, for he was a real fisherman and the muskie gave him a fight. The wind most often blew from the south, and the river flowed toward the south, so when the water was wind-riffled, and the current was strong, the river seemed to be flowing both ways. I liked this, and interpreted it as an omen, a natural symbol.

18   A few years ago, when I was back in Winnipeg, I gave a talk at my old college. It was open to the public, and afterward a very old man came up to me and asked me if my maiden name had been Wemyss. I said yes, thinking he might have known my father or my grandfather. But no. "When I was a young lad," he said, "I once worked for your great-grandfather, Robert Wemyss, when he had the sheep ranch at Raeburn." I think that was a moment when I realized all over again something of great importance to me. My long-ago families came from Scotland and Ireland, but in a sense that no longer mattered so much. My true roots were here.

19   I am not very patriotic, in the usual meaning of that word. I cannot say "My country right or wrong" in any political, social or literary context. But one thing is inalterable, for better or worse, for life.

20   This is where my world began. A world which includes the ancestors — both my own and other people's ancestors who became mine. A world which formed me, and continues to do so, even while I fought it in some of its aspects, and continue to do so. A world which gave me

my own lifework to do, because it was here that I learned the sight of my own particular eyes.

(1971)

The Writer's Subject

1. On what grounds does Laurence reject the stereotypical description of the prairie as "dull, bleak, flat, uninteresting"?

2. In referring to the child's response to the Depression, Laurence says, "You understood and did not understand" (para. 5). Explain what she means by this statement.

3. What is revealed about small-town attitudes in Laurence's description of the town dump? (para. 8)

4. Why does Laurence say that she would carry the land and town within her all her life? (paras. 12-13)

5. What connections does Laurence perceive between small town prairie life and Canadian life on the national scale? (paras. 14-15)

6. Why is Laurence drawn so strongly to "the land"?

7. Suggest possible interpretations of what Laurence calls "a natural symbol," the river's flowing both ways. (para. 17)

8. What does Laurence mean by "patriotic, in the usual meaning of that word"? (para. 19)

9. Why is the essay entitled "Where the World Began" (and not "Where My World Began," for example)?

The Writer's Style and Strategy

1. Why does Laurence begin her description of a small prairie town with a series of fragments?

2. The second paragraph consists of only one sentence. Why?

3. How does Laurence make the reader see the prairie winter through a child's eyes? (para. 4)

4. How does Laurence recreate the romantic excitement the child felt at the prospect of a fire? Where is the consciousness of the writer as adult apparent? (para. 7)

5. Discuss the shift in tone at the end of paragraph 9. How is this shift achieved? What is its purpose?

6. How does Laurence achieve the transition from a discussion of mistaken perceptions of the prairie town and the land to a discussion of perceptions of Canada?

7. Why does Laurence describe the small prairie town as a microcosm? (para. 15)

8. There are obvious similarities between the opening and concluding paragraphs. What are these similarities? What are the differences?

Suggestions for Writing and Discussion

1. Where did your world begin? Write an essay introducing and explaining what you believe to be the beginnings of your particular world.

2. Margaret Laurence writes about a very personal place that carries special significance for her. Describe a place that has particular significance for you and explain its importance.

3. Laurence suggests that Canada is commonly viewed as dull. Defend Canada — or your region — against this common view.

4. Laurence writes with obvious pleasure of the adventures of childhood in winter and in summer. If you could return to childhood, what season would you choose, and why?

Writing Short Stories
by Flannery O'Connor

I have heard people say that the short story was one of the most dif- **1**
ficult literary forms, and I've always tried to decide why people feel
this way about what seems to me to be one of the most natural and fundamental ways of human expression. After all, you begin to hear and
tell stories when you're a child, and there doesn't seem to be anything
very complicated about it. I suspect that most of you have been telling
stories all your lives, and yet here you sit — come to find out how to
do it.

Then last week, after I had written down some of these serene thoughts **2**
to use here today, my calm was shattered when I was sent seven of
your manuscripts to read.

After this experience, I found myself ready to admit, if not that the **3**
short story is one of the most difficult literary forms, at least that it
is more difficult for some than for others.

I still suspect that most people start out with some kind of ability to **4**
tell a story but that it gets lost along the way. Of course, the ability
to create life with words is essentially a gift. If you have it in the first
place, you can develop it; if you don't have it, you might as well forget it.

But I have found that the people who don't have it are frequently the **5**
ones hell-bent on writing stories. I'm sure anyway that they are the ones
who write the books and the magazine articles on how-to-write-short-
stories. I have a friend who is taking a correspondence course in this
subject, and she has passed a few of the chapter headings on to me -
such as, "The Story Formula for Writers," "How to Create Characters,"
"Let's Plot!" This form of corruption is costing her twenty-seven dollars.

6   I feel that discussing story-writing in terms of plot, character, and theme is like trying to describe the expression on a face by saying where the eyes, nose, and mouth are. I've heard students say, "I'm very good with plot, but I can't do a thing with character," or, "I have this theme but I don't have a plot for it," and once I heard one say, "I've got the story but I don't have any technique."

7   Technique is a word they all trot out. I talked to a writers' club once, and during the question time, one good soul said, "Will you give me the technique for the frame-within-a-frame short story?" I had to admit I was so ignorant I didn't even know what that was, but she assured me there was such a thing because she had entered a contest to write one and the prize was fifty dollars.

8   But setting aside the people who have no talent for it, there are others who do have the talent but who flounder around because they don't really know what a story is.

9   I suppose that obvious things are the hardest to define. Everybody thinks he knows what a story is. But if you ask a beginning student to write a story, you're liable to get almost anything — a reminiscence, an episode, an opinion, an anecdote, anything under the sun but a story. A story is a complete dramatic action — and in good stories, the characters are shown through the action and the action is controlled through the characters, and the result of this is meaning that derives from the whole presented experience. I myself prefer to say that a story is a dramatic event that involves a person because he is a person, and a particular person — that is, because he shares in the general human condition and in some specific human situation. A story always involves, in a dramatic way, the mystery of personality. I lent some stories to a country lady who lives down the road from me, and when she returned them, she said, "Well, them stories just gone and shown you how some folks *would* do," and I thought to myself that that was right; when you write stories, you have to be content to start exactly there — showing how some specific folks *will* do, *will* do in spite of everything.

10   Now this is a very humble level to have to begin on, and most people who think they want to write stories are not willing to start there. They want to write about problems, not people; or about abstract issues, not concrete situations. They have an idea, or a feeling, or an overflowing ego, or they want to Be A Writer, or they want to give their wisdom to the world in a simple-enough way for the world to be able to absorb it. In any case, they don't have a story and they wouldn't be willing to write it if they did; and in the absence of a story, they set out to

find a theory or a formula or a technique.

Now none of this is to say that when you write a story, you are sup- 11
posed to forget or give up any moral position that you hold. Your beliefs
will be the light by which you see, but they will not be what you see
and they will not be a substitute for seeing. For the writer of fiction,
everything has its testing point in the eye, and the eye is an organ that
eventually involves the whole personality, and as much of the world
as can be got into it. It involves judgment. Judgment is something that
begins in the act of vision, and when it does not, or when it becomes
separated from vision, then a confusion exists in the mind which transfers
itself to the story.

Fiction operates through the senses, and I think one reason that people 12
find it so difficult to write stories is that they forget how much time
and patience is required to convince through the senses. No reader who
doesn't actually experience, who isn't made to feel the story is going
to believe anything the fiction writer merely tells him. The first and
most obvious characteristic of fiction is that it deals with reality through
what can be seen, heard, smelt, tasted, and touched.

Now this is something that can't be learned only in the head; it has 13
to be learned in the habits. It has to become a way that you habitually
look at things. The fiction writer has to realize that he can't create compassion with compassion, or emotion with emotion, or thought with
thought. He has to provide all these things with a body; he has to create
a world with weight and extension.

I have found that the stories of beginning writers usually bristle with 14
emotion, but *whose* emotion is often very hard to determine. Dialogue
frequently proceeds without the assistance of any characters that you
can actually see, and uncontained thought leaks out of every corner of
the story. The reason is usually that the student is wholly interested
in his thoughts and his emotions and not in his dramatic action, and
that he is too lazy or highfalutin to descend to the concrete where fiction operates. He thinks that judgment exists in one place and sense-
impression in another. But for the fiction writer, judgment begins in
the details he sees and how he sees them.

Fiction writers who are not concerned with these concrete details are 15
guilty of what Henry James called "weak specification." The eye will
glide over their words while the attention goes to sleep. Ford Madox
Ford taught that you couldn't have a man appear long enough to sell
a newspaper in a story unless you put him there with enough detail to
make the reader see him.

16   I have a friend who is taking acting classes in New York from a Russian lady who is supposed to be very good at teaching actors. My friend
wrote me that the first month they didn't speak a line, they only learned
to see. Now learning to see is the basis for learning all the arts except
music. I know a good many fiction writers who paint, not because they're
any good at painting, but because it helps their writing. It forces them
to look at things. Fiction writing is very seldom a matter of saying things;
it is a matter of showing things.

17   However, to say that fiction proceeds by use of detail does not mean
the simple, mechanical piling-up of detail. Detail has to be controlled
by some overall purpose, and every detail has to be put to work for
you. Art is selective. What is there is essential and creates movement.

18   Now all this requires time. A good short story should not have less
meaning than a novel, nor should its action be less complete. Nothing
essential to the main experience can be left out of a short story. All
the action has to be satisfactorily accounted for in terms of motivation,
and there has to be a beginning, a middle, and an end, though not
necessarily in that order. I think many people decide that they want
to write short stories because they're short, and by short, they mean
short in every way. They think that a short story is an incomplete action
in which a very little is shown and a great deal suggested, and they
think you suggest something by leaving it out. It's very hard to disabuse
a student of this notion, because he thinks that when he leaves something
out, he's being subtle; and when you tell him that he has to put something
in before anything can be there, he thinks you're an insensitive idiot.

19   Perhaps the central question to be considered in any discussion of
the short story is what do we mean by short. Being short does not mean
being slight. A short story should be long in depth and should give us
an experience of meaning. I have an aunt who thinks that nothing happens in a story unless somebody gets married or shot at the end of it.
I wrote a story about a tramp who marries an old woman's idiot daughter
in order to acquire the old woman's automobile. After the marriage,
he takes the daughter off on a wedding trip in the automobile and aban-
dons her in an eating place and drives on by himself. Now that is a
complete story. There is nothing more relating to the mystery of that
man's personality that could be shown through that particular dramatization. But I've never been able to convince my aunt that it's a complete
story. She wants to know what happened to the idiot daughter after that.

20   Not long ago that story was adapted for a television play, and the
adapter, knowing his business, had the tramp have a change of heart

and go back and pick up the idiot daughter and the two of them ride away, grinning madly. My aunt believes that the story is complete at last, but I have other sentiments about it — which are not suitable for public utterance. When you write a story, you only have to write one story, but there will always be people who will refuse to read the story you have written.

And this naturally brings up the awful question of what kind of a reader   21 you are writing for when you write fiction. Perhaps we each think we have a personal solution for this problem. For my own part, I have a very high opinion of the art of fiction and a very low opinion of what is called the "average" reader. I tell myself that I can't escape him, that this is the personality I am supposed to keep awake, but that at the same time, I am also supposed to provide the intelligent reader with the deeper experience that he looks for in fiction. Now actually, both of these readers are just aspects of the writer's own personality, and in the last analysis, the only reader he can know anything about is himself. We all write at our own level of understanding, but it is the peculiar characteristic of fiction that its literal surface can be made to yield enter- tainment on an obvious physical plane to one sort of reader while the selfsame surface can be made to yield meaning to the person equipped to experience it there.

Meaning is what keeps the short story from being short. I prefer to   22 talk about the meaning in a story rather than the theme of a story. People talk about the theme of a story as if the theme were like the string that a sack of chicken feed is tied with. They think that if you can pick out the theme, the way you pick the right thread in the chicken-feed sack, you can rip the story open and feed the chickens. But this is not the way meaning works in fiction.

When you can state the theme of a story, when you can separate it   23 from the story itself, then you can be sure the story is not a very good one. The meaning of a story has to be embodied in it, has to be made concrete in it. A story is a way to say something that can't be said any other way, and it takes every word in the story to say what the meaning is. You tell a story because a statement would be inadequate. When anybody asks what a story is about, the only proper thing is to tell him to read the story. The meaning of fiction is not abstract meaning but experienced meaning, and the purpose of making statements about the meaning of a story is only to help you to experience that meaning more fully.

Fiction is an art that calls for the strictest attention to the real — whether   24 the writer is writing a naturalistic story or a fantasy. I mean that we always begin with what is or with what has an eminent possibility of truth about it. Even when one writes a fantasy, reality is the proper basis of it. A thing is fantastic because it is so real, so real that it is fantastic. Graham Greene has said that he can't write, "I stood over a bottomless pit," because that couldn't be true, or "Running down the stairs I jumped into a taxi," because that couldn't be true either. But Elizabeth Bowen can write about one of her characters that "she snatched at her hair as if she heard something in it," because that is eminently possible.

25   I would even go so far as to say that the person writing a fantasy has to be even more strictly attentive to the concrete detail than someone writing in a naturalistic vein — because the greater the story's strain on the credulity, the more convincing the properties in it have to be.

26   A good example of this is a story called "The Metamorphosis" by Franz Kafka. This is a story about a man who wakes up one morning to find that he has turned into a cockroach overnight, while not discarding his human nature. The rest of the story concerns his life and feelings and eventual death as an insect with human nature, and this situation is accepted by the reader because the concrete detail of the story is absolutely convincing. The fact is that this story describes the dual nature of man in such a realistic fashion that it is almost unbearable. The truth is not distorted here, but rather, a certain distortion is used to get at the truth. If we admit, as we must, that appearance is not the same thing as reality, then we must give the artist the liberty to make certain rearrangements of nature if these will lead to greater depths of vision. The artist himself always has to remember that what he is re-arranging *is* nature, and that he has to know it and be able to describe it accurately in order to have the authority to rearrange it at all.

27   The peculiar problem of the short-story writer is how to make the action he describes reveal as much of the mystery of existence as possible. He has only a short space to do it in and he can't do it by statement. He has to do it by showing, not by saying, and by showing the concrete — so that his problem is really how to make the concrete work double time for him.

28   In good fiction, certain of the details will tend to accumulate meaning from the action of the story itself, and when this happens they become symbolic in the way they work. I once wrote a story called "Good Country People," in which a lady Ph.D. has her wooden leg stolen by a Bible salesman whom she has tried to seduce. Now I'll admit that, paraphrased

in this way, the situation is simply a low joke. The average reader is pleased to observe anybody's wooden leg being stolen. But without ceasing to appeal to him and without making any statements of high intention, this story does manage to operate at another level of experience, by letting the wooden leg accumulate meaning. Early in the story, we're presented with the fact that the Ph.D. is spiritually as well as physically crippled. She believes in nothing but her own belief in nothing, and we perceive that there is a wooden part of her soul that corresponds to her wooden leg. Now of course this is never stated. The fiction writer states as little as possible. The reader makes this connection from things he is shown. He may not even know that he makes the connection, but the connection is there nevertheless and it has its effect on him. As the story goes on, the wooden leg continues to accumulate meaning. The reader learns how the girl feels about her leg, how her mother feels about it, and how the country woman on the place feels about it; and finally, by the time the Bible salesman comes along, the leg has accumulated so much meaning that it is, as the saying goes, loaded. And when the Bible salesman steals it, the reader realizes that he has taken away part of the girl's personality and has revealed her deeper affliction to her for the first time.

If you want to say that the wooden leg is a symbol, you can say that. **29** But it is a wooden leg first, and as a wooden leg it is absolutely necessary to the story. It has its place on the literal level of the story, but it operates in depth as well as on the surface. It increases the story in every direction, and this is essentially the way a story escapes being short.

Now a little might be said about the way in which this happens. I **30** wouldn't want you to think that in that story I sat down and said, "I am now going to write a story about a Ph.D. with a wooden leg, using the wooden leg as a symbol for another kind of affliction." I doubt myself if many writers know what they are going to do when they start out. When I started writing that story, I didn't know there was going to be a Ph.D. with a wooden leg. As the story progressed, I brought in the Bible salesman, but I had no idea what I was going to do with him. I didn't know he was going to steal that wooden leg until ten or twelve lines before he did it, but when I found out that this was what was going to happen, I realized that it was inevitable. This is a story that produces a shock for the reader, and I think one reason for this is that it produced a shock for the writer.

Now despite the fact that this story came about in this seemingly **31** mindless fashion, it is a story that almost no rewriting was done on. It is a story that was under control throughout the writing of it, and it might be asked how this kind of control comes about, since it is not entirely conscious.

32   I think the answer to this is what Maritain calls "the habit of art." It is a fact that fiction writing is something in which the whole personality takes part — the conscious as well as the unconscious mind. Art is the habit of the artist; and habits have to be rooted deep in the whole personality. They have to be cultivated like any other habit, over a long period of time, by experience; and teaching any kind of writing is largely a matter of helping the student develop the habit of art. I think this is more than just discipline, although it is that; I think it is a way of looking at the created world and of using the senses so as to make them find as much meaning as possible in things.

33   Now I am not so naive as to suppose that most people come to writers' conferences in order to hear what kind of vision is necessary to write stories that will become a permanent part of our literature. Even if you do wish to hear this, your greatest concerns are immediately practical. You want to know how you can actually write a good story, and further, how you can tell when you've done it; and so want to know what the form of a short story is, as if the form were something that existed outside of each story and could be applied or imposed on the material. Of course, the more you write, the more you will realize that the form is organic, that it is something that grows out of the material, that the form of each story is unique. A story that is any good can't be reduced, it can only be expanded. A story is good when you continue to see more and more in it, and when it continues to escape you. In fiction two and two is always more than four.

34   The only way, I think, to learn to write short stories is to write them, and then to try to discover what you have done. The time to think of technique is when you've actually got the story in front of you. The teacher can help the student by looking at his individual work and trying to help him decide if he has written a complete story, one in which the action fully illuminates the meaning.

35   Perhaps the most profitable thing I can do is to tell you about some of the general observations I made about these seven stories I read of yours. All of these observations will not fit any one of the stories exactly, but they are points nevertheless that it won't hurt anyone interested in writing to think about.

36   The first thing that any professional writer is conscious of in reading anything is, naturally, the use of language. Now the use of language

in these stories was such that, with one exception, it would be difficult to distinguish one story from another. While I can recall running into several clichés, I can't remember one image or one metaphor from the seven stories. I don't mean there weren't images in them; I just mean that there weren't any that were effective enough to take away with you.

In connection with this, I made another observation that startled me 37 considerably. With the exception of one story, there was practically no use made of the local idiom. Now this is a Southern Writers' Conference. All the addresses on these stories were from Georgia or Tennessee, yet there was no distinctive sense of Southern life in them. A few place-names were dropped, Savannah or Atlanta or Jacksonville, but these could just as easily have been changed to Pittsburgh or Passaic without calling for any other alteration in the story. The characters spoke as if they had never heard any kind of language except what came out of a television set. This indicates that something is way out of focus.

There are two qualities that make fiction. One is the sense of mystery 38 and the other is the sense of manners. You get manners from the texture of existence that surrounds you. The great advantage of being a Southern writer is that we don't have to go anywhere to look for manners; bad or good, we've got them in abundance. We in the South live in a society that is rich in contradiction, rich in irony, rich in contrast, and particularly rich in its speech. And yet here are six stories by Southerners in which almost no use is made of the gifts of the region.

Of course the reason for this may be that you have seen these gifts 39 abused so often that you have become self-conscious about using them. There is nothing worse than the writer who doesn't *use* the gifts of the region, but wallows in them. Everything becomes so Southern that it's sickening, so local that it is unintelligible, so literally reproduced that it conveys nothing. The general gets lost in the particular instead of being shown through it.

However, when the life that actually surrounds us is totally ignored, 40 when our patterns of speech are absolutely overlooked, then something is out of kilter. The writer should then ask himself if he is not reaching out for a kind of life that is artificial to him.

An idiom characterizes a society, and when you ignore the idiom, 41 you are very likely ignoring the whole social fabric that could make a meaningful character. You can't cut characters off from their society and say much about them as individuals. You can't say anything meaningful about the mystery of a personality unless you put that personality in a believable and significant social context. And the best way to do this is through the character's own language. When the old lady in one of Andrew Lytle's stories says contemptuously that she has a mule that is older than Birmingham, we get in that one sentence a sense of a society, and its history. A great deal of the Southern writer's work is done for him before he begins, because our history lives in our talk. In one of Eudora Welty's stories a character says, "Where I come from, we use fox for yard dogs and owls for chickens, but we sing true." Now there is a whole book in that one sentence; and when the people of your section can talk like that, and you ignore it, you're just not taking advantage of what's yours. The sound of our talk is too definite to be discarded with impunity, and if the writer tries to get rid of it, he is liable to destroy the better part of his creative power.

42   Another thing I observed about these stories is that most of them don't go very far inside a character, don't reveal very much of the character. I don't mean that they don't enter the character's mind, but they simply don't show that he has a personality. Again this goes back partly to speech. These characters have no distinctive speech to reveal themselves with; and sometimes you feel in the end that no personality is revealed because no personality is there. In most good stories it is the character's personality that creates the action of the story. In most of these stories, I feel that the writer has thought of some action and then scrounged up a character to perform it. You will usually be more successful if you start the other way around. If you start with a real personality, a real character, then something is bound to happen; and you don't have to know what before you begin. In fact it may be better if you don't know what before you begin. You ought to be able to discover something from your stories. If you don't, probably nobody else will.

(1957)

The Writer's Subject

1. What is O'Connor's view of books or courses on the techniques of writing short stories? (paras. 5-7)

2. What does O'Connor mean by the statement that a story involves "the mystery of personality"? (para. 9) (Note her use of this phrase in paras. 19 and 41.)

3. What does O'Connor mean by saying that the writer must "create a world with weight and extension"? (para. 13) How does she show that this is to be accomplished? (paras. 12-16).

4. In paragraphs 19-20 O'Connor describes one of her stories which was adapted for television. What disturbed her about the adaptation? What did the adapter fail to recognize?

5. What distinction does O'Connor draw between "meaning" and "theme" in the discussion of short stories? (paras. 22-23)

6. Why, according to O'Connor, must the writer pay "the strictest attention to the real" even if the story is a fantasy? How does she illustrate this assertion? (paras. 24-26)

7. Summarize O'Connor's explanation in paragraphs 28 and 29 of the creation and function of symbols in a short story.

8. What does O'Connor mean by the statement, "In fiction two and two is always more than four"? (para. 33)

9. What importance does O'Connor attach to the use of local idioms by fictional characters? How does she illustrate her point by reference to the stories submitted to her? (paras. 36-41)

10. What, finally, are O'Connor's criteria for a good short story?

The Writer's Style and Strategy

1. O'Connor's essay was written to be delivered as an address to a Southern Writers' Conference. Pick out details that reflect O'Connor's awareness of her audience, and show how she adapts her material to the interests of that audience. Pay particular attention to diction, sentence patterns, and the use of personal pronouns.

2. Discuss O'Connor's use of anecdote and personal detail as a means of developing her ideas.

3. A definition may be arrived at through negation. Where does O'Connor use negation as well as positive assertion to explain what constitutes a good short story? Discuss some of the ways in which she offers her definition.

4. Discuss the opening and the closing of this essay. At what point does the writer move from her introduction to the body of her discussion? What is she attempting to do in the introduction? Does the last paragraph form a fitting conclusion to the essay?

Topics for Writing and Discussion

1. Choose a good short story, preferably one discussed in your class, and discuss whether it meets O'Connor's criteria for the successful depiction of character.

2. O'Connor maintains that the writer of fantasy must be "even more attentive to the concrete detail than someone writing in a naturalistic vein — because the greater the story's strain on the credulity, the more convincing the properties in it have to be." (para. 25) Choose a work of science fiction or fantasy, and discuss the writer's use of concrete details.

3. Use your college or local library to find a book intended to teach would-be authors how to write fiction. Discuss the organization and content of the book in light of O'Connor's criticism in paragraphs 5-7.

4. Using O'Connor's suggestions about creating character, write a character sketch of a close friend or a member of your family.

An Unquiet Awakening
by Mordecai Richler

Reading was not one of my boyhood passions. Girls, or rather the 1
absence of girls, drove me to it. When I was 13 years old, short for
my age, more than somewhat pimply, I was terrified of girls. They made
me feel sadly inadequate.

Retreating into high seriousness, I acquired a pipe, which I chewed 2
on ostentatiously, and made it my business to be seen everywhere, even
at school basketball games, absorbed by books of daunting significance.
The two women who ran the lending library, possibly amused by my
pretensions, tried to interest me in fiction.

"I want fact. I can't be bothered with stories," I protested, waving 3
my pipe at them affronted, "I just haven't got the time for such nonsense."

Novels, I knew, were mere romantic make-believe, not as bad as 4
poetry, to be fair, but bad enough.

I fell ill with a childhood disease, I no longer remember which, but 5
obviously I meant it as a rebuke to those girls in tight sweaters who
continued to ignore me. Never mind, they would mourn at my funeral,
burying me with my pipe. Too late, they would say, "Boy, was he ever
an intellectual."

The women from the lending library, concerned, dropped off books 6
for me at our house. The real stuff. Fact-filled. Providing me with the
inside dope on Theodore Herzl's childhood and *Brazil Yesterday, Today,
and Tomorrow.*

One day they brought me a novel: *All Quiet on the Western Front* 7
by Erich Maria Remarque. The painting on the jacket that was taped
to the book showed a soldier wearing what was unmistakably a Ger-

man Army helmet. What was this, I wondered, some sort of bad joke?

8   Nineteen forty-four that was, and I devoutly wished every German left on the face of the earth an excruciating death. The Allied invasion of France had not yet begun, but I cheered every Russian counterattack, each German city bombed, and − with the help of a map tacked to my bedroom wall − followed the progress of the Canadian troops fighting their way up the Italian boot. Boys from our street had already been among the fallen. Izzy Draper's uncle. Harvey Kegelmass' older brother. The boy who was supposed to marry Gita Holtzman.

9   *All Quiet on the Western Front* lay unopened on my bed for two days. Finally, I was driven to picking it up out of boredom. I never expected that a mere novel, a stranger's tale, could actually be dangerous, creating such turbulence in my life, obliging me to question so many received ideas. About Germans. About my own monumental ignorance of the world. About what novels were.

10   At the age of 13 in 1944, happily as yet untainted by English 104, I couldn't tell you whether Remarque's novel was
    a. a slice of life
    b. symbolic
    c. psychological
    d. seminal.

I couldn't even say if it was well or badly written. In fact, as I recall, it didn't seem to be "written" at all. Instead, it just flowed. Now, of course, I understand that writing that doesn't advertise itself is art of a very high order. It doesn't come easily. But at the time I wasn't capable of making such distinctions. I also had no notion of how *All Quiet on the Western Front* rated critically as a war novel. I hadn't read Stendhal or Tolstoy or Crane or Hemingway. I hadn't even heard of them. I didn't know that Thomas Mann, whoever he was, had praised the novel highly. Neither did I know that in 1929 the judges at some outfit called the Book-of-the-Month Club had made it their May selection.

11   But what I did know is that, hating Germans with a passion, I had read only 20, maybe 30, pages before the author had seduced me into identifying with my enemy, 19-year-old Paul Baumer, thrust into the bloody trenches of the First World War with his schoolmates: Muller, Kemmerich and the reluctant Joseph Behm, one of the first to fall. As if that weren't sufficiently unsettling in itself, the author, having won my love for Paul, my enormous concern for his survival, then betrayed me in the last dreadful paragraphs of his book:

12   "He fell in October 1918, on a day that was so quiet and still on the

whole front, that the army report confined itself to the single sentence: All Quiet on the Western Front.

"He had fallen forward and lay on the earth as though sleeping. Turn- 13 ing him over one saw that he could not have suffered long; his face had an expression of calm, as though almost glad the end had come."

The movies, I knew from experience, never risked letting you down 14 like that. No matter how bloody the battle, how long the odds, Errol Flynn, Robert Taylor, even Humphrey Bogart could be counted on to survive and come home to Ann Sheridan, Lana Turner or − if they were sensitive types − Loretta Young. Only character actors, usually Brooklyn Dodger fans, say George Tobias or William Bendix, were expendable.

Obviously, having waded into the pool of serious fiction by accident, 15 I was not sure I liked or trusted the water. It was too deep. Anything could happen.

There was something else, a minor incident in *All Quiet on the Western* 16 *Front* that would not have troubled an adult reader but, I'm embarrassed to say, certainly distressed that 13-year-old boy colliding with his first serious novel:

Sent out to guard a village that has been abandoned because it is being 17 shelled too heavily, Katczinsky, the incomparable scrounger, surfaces with suckling pigs and potatoes and carrots for his comrades, a group of eight altogether:

"The suckling pigs are slaughtered, Kat sees to them. We want to 18 make potato cakes to go with the roast. But we cannot find a grater for the potatoes. However, that difficulty is soon over. With a nail we punch a lot of holes in a pot lid and there we have a grater. Three fellows put on thick gloves to protect their fingers against the grater, two others peel the potatoes, and business gets going."

The business, I realized, alarmed − not affronted − was the making 19 of potato latkes, a favorite of mine as well as Paul Baumer's, a dish I had always taken to be Jewish, certainly not a German concoction.

What did I know? Nothing. Or, looked at another way, my real educa- 20 tion, my life-long addiction to fiction, began with the trifling discovery that the potato latke was not of Jewish origin, but something borrowed from the German and now a taste that Jew and German shared in spite of everything.

I felt easier about my affection for the German soldier Paul Baumer 21 once I was told by the women from the lending library that when Hitler came to power in 1933 he had burned all of Erich Maria Remarque's books and in 1938 he took away his German citizenship. Obviously Hitler had grasped that novels could be dangerous, something I learned when I was only 13 years old. He burned them; I began to devour them. I started to read at the breakfast table and on streetcars, often missing my stop, and in bed with benefit of a flashlight. It got me into trouble.

22   I grasped, for the first time, that I didn't live in the centre of the world but had been born into a working-class family in an unimportant country far from the cities of light: London, Paris, New York. Of course this wasn't my fault, it was my inconsiderate parents who were to blame. But there was, I now realized, a larger world out there beyond St. Urbain Street in Montreal.

23   Preparing myself for the Rive Gauche, I bought a blue beret, but I didn't wear it outside, or even in the house if anybody else was at home. I looked at but lacked the courage to buy a cigarette holder.

24   As my parents bickered at the supper table, trapped in concerns now far too mundane for the likes of me — what to do if Dworkin raised the rent again, how to manage my brother's college fees — I sat with but actually apart from them in the kitchen, enthralled, reading for he first time, "All happy families are alike but an unhappy family is unhappy after its own fashion."[1]

25   Erich Maria Remarque, born in Westphalia in 1897, went off to war, directly from school, at the age of 18. He was wounded five times. He lost all his friends. After the war he worked briefly as a schoolteacher, a stonecutter, a test driver for a tire company and an editor of Sport-bild magazine. His first novel, *Im Westen Nichts Neues,* was turned down by several publishers before it was brought out by the Ullstein Press in Berlin in 1928. *All Quiet on the Western Front* sold 1.2 million copies in Germany and was translated in 29 languages, selling some four million copies throughout the world. The novel has been filmed three times; the first time, memorably by Lewis Milestone in 1930. The Milestone version, with Lew Ayres playing Paul Baumer, won Academy Awards for best picture and best direction.

26   Since *All Quiet on the Western Front* once meant so much to me, I picked it up again with a certain anxiety. After all this time, I find it difficult to be objective about the novel. Its pages still evoke for me a back bedroom with a cracked ceiling and a sizzling radiator on St. Urbain Street: mice scrabbling in the walls, and a window looking out on the sheets frozen stiff on the laundry line.

27   Over the years the novel has lost something in shock value. The original jacket copy of the 1929 Little, Brown & Company edition of

1.   The opening sentence of *Anna Karenina* by Leo Tolstoy.

All Quiet on the Western Front warns the reader that it is "at times crude" and "will shock the supersensitive by its outspokenness." Contemporary readers, far from being shocked, will be amused by the novel's discretion, the absence of explicit sex scenes, the unbelievably polite dialogue of the men in the trenches.

The novel also has its poignant moments, both in the trenches and when Paul Baumer goes home on leave, an old man of 19, only to find insufferably pompous schoolmasters still recruiting the young with mindless prattle about the fatherland and the glory of battle. Strong characters are deftly sketched. Himmelstoss, the postman who becomes a crazed drillmaster. Tjaden, the peasant soldier. Kantorek, the schoolmaster. **28**

On the front line the enemy is never the Frogs or the Limeys, but the insanity of the war itself. It is the war, in fact, and not even Paul Baumer, that is the novel's true protagonist. In a brief introduction to the novel Remarque wrote: "This book is to be neither an accusation nor a confession, and least of all an adventure, for death is not an adventure to those who stand face to face with it. It will try simply to tell of a generation of men who, even though they may have escaped its shells, were destroyed by the war." **29**

Since the First World War we have become altogether too familiar with larger horrors. The Holocaust, Hiroshima, the threat of a nuclear winter. Death by numbers, cities obliterated by decree. At peace, as it were, we live the daily dread of the missiles in their silos, ours pointed at them, theirs pointed at us. None of this, however, diminishes the power of *All Quiet on the Western Front,* a novel that will endure because of its humanity, its honor and its refusal to lapse into sentimentality or strike a false note. **30**

(1986)

The Writer's Subject

1. What was Richler's attitude to novels before he had read *All Quiet on the Western Front*? What *did* he read, and why? (paras. 1-6)

2. Why did the young Richler react with anger when Remarque's novel was first lent to him? (paras. 7-8)

3. Why did Richler feel betrayed by "the last dreadful paragraphs" of the novel? Why had he expected a different ending? (paras. 11-15)

4. Why was Richler so distressed by the episode describing the making of potato cakes? (paras. 18-21)

5. Why does Richler twice use the word "dangerous" in connection with the reading of novels? (paras. 9, 21)

6. How did his reading of *All Quiet on the Western Front* change Richler's view of his own life? Why did he prepare himself for the "Rive Gauche" (the Left Bank, an area in Paris associated with the bohemian life)? (paras. 22-24)

7. Why, in Richler's view, has the novel lost something of its original "shock value"? What makes it, nevertheless, a work that will endure? (paras. 27-30)

The Writer's Style and Strategy

1. Discuss the appropriateness of the essay's title.

2. The essay was adapted from an introduction to a new edition of *All Quiet on the Western Front*. What elements of the essay reflect that function? What might the reader expect to find in the introduction to a reprinted novel?

3. Spending the first six paragraphs on his own conduct, Richler does not mention Remarque's novel until the seventh paragraph. What is Richler's purpose in adopting this strategy?

4. What is Richler burlesqueing in paragraph 10? What is the function of the paragraph in its context?

5. Discuss Richler's use of direct quotation from the novel and from its author's introduction. Why did he choose the passages he quotes?

6. What differences in tone are evident between the essay's opening section and its conclusion? Relate the shift in tone to the shape of Richler's essay.

Suggested Topics for Writing and Discussion

1. *All Quiet on the Western Front,* both as a novel and as a film, presents a powerful indictment of the waste and insanity of war. Choose another novel or film that seems to you to have a similar intention, and assess its treatment of the subject.

2. Richler feels that Remarque's novel may have lost some of its "shock value" for modern readers. Do you agree with his view that events in modern history may have hardened us to horror? Have film, literature, and the media made us more aware of the horrors of war and violence, or have they somehow dulled our moral and emotional responses?

3. Richler claims that Remarque's novel began the process of his "real education." From your own reading experience, select a work of literature that you found memorable, and attempt to account for its impact on you.

4. Richler was deeply affected by the ending of Remarque's novel, noting that it had shown him a picture of reality very different from what he had previously encountered in war movies. How faithfully, in your view, does the modern war movie reflect the reality of war?

The Historian's Opportunity
by Barbara Tuchman

1 Given the current decline of the novel and the parallel decline of poetry and the drama, public interest has turned toward the literature of actuality. It may be that in a time of widening uncertainty and chronic stress the historian's voice is the most needed, the more so as others seem inadequate, often absurd. While the reasons may be argued, the opportunity, I think, is plain for the historian to become the major interpreter in literary experience of man's role in society. The task is his to provide both the matter to satisfy the public interest and those insights into the human condition without which any reading matter is vapid.

2   Historians have performed this role before. Although we have no figures on readership in classical Greece and Rome, it is evident from their continuers and imitators and from later references that Herodotus, Thucydides and Xenophon, Tacitus, Polybius, Josephus, Plutarch, Livy, and the others were significant voices to their contemporaries. Since the outbreak of World War II the statistics of the book trade reflect the growing appetite of the public for biography, autobiography, science, sociology, and history — especially contemporary history.

3   The last category, as we have lately been made rather tiresomely aware, has its special problems, although in the long tradition of authorized biography a subject's family has usually found quieter means than legal recourse for retaining control over personal matters. The simple way to keep private affairs private is not to talk about them — to the authorized, or even the "hired," writer.

4   I do not cite as evidence of the public interest in the literature of ac-

tuality the fact that since 1964 nonfiction, so called, has outsold fiction by two to one, because that merely reflects the mass buying of cookbooks and peace-of-mind books (the two front runners), plus voyeur books — that is, the sex life of everybody else — cartoon books, and how-to books on baby care, home decorating, curing arthritis, counting calories, golf, etiquette, and that recent sleeper, avoiding probate. Non-books aside, by whatever criterion you use — number of titles published and book-club choices, hardcovers and paperbacks, new titles and reprints — the categories concerned with reality all show greater increases than fiction.

People are turning to the books of reality for a truer image of man 5 and society than is offered by contemporary novels. To look for the reason why fictional truth has gone askew is part of the historian's task. The novelists' failure is a consequence, I believe, of the historical experience of the twentieth century, which since the First World War has been one of man's cumulative disillusionment in himself. The idea of progress was the greatest casualty of that war, and its aftermath was cynicism, confirmed by a second round of world conflict and by the implications of the Nazis' gas chambers. Then the advent into man's hands of unlimited lethal power has been topped by the frightening pressure of overpopulation, so that now we live under the weight of a weird paradox which threatens us simultaneously with too many people in the world and too much power to destroy them. Finally, we are faced with mounting evidence — in pollution of air and water, in destruction of the balance of nature, in the coming ear-shattering boom of supersonic flight — that we cannot refrain from despoiling our environment.

The experience has been enough to destroy in many of our genera- 6 tion their inherited belief in human goodness. Gilbert Murray found the same despair of the world overtaking the Greeks after their own period of prolonged internecine warfare and ascribed it to a sense of "the pressure of forces that man could not control or understand."

Man in the twentieth century is not a creature to be envied. Former- 7 ly he believed himself created by the divine spark. Now, bereft of that proud confidence, and contemplating his recent record and present problems, he can no longer, like the Psalmist, respect himself as "a little lower than the angels." He cannot picture himself today, as Michelangelo did on the Sistine ceiling, in the calm and noble image of Adam receiving the spark from the finger of God. Overtaken by doubt of human purpose and divine purpose, he doubts his capacity to be good or even to survive. He has lost certainty, including moral and ethical certainty, and is left with a sense of footloose purposelessness and self-disgust which literature naturally reflects. The result is what the *Times Literary Supplement* has named the "Ugh" school of fiction.

8   Writers who dislike their fellow men have taken over the literary world. The mainstream of their work is epitomized by the recent novel advertised as an "engrossing" treatment of "more or less random adventures touching on thievery, homosexuality, pimping, sadism, voyeurism, a gang bang." Unaccountably, drug addiction was missing. As we all know, this is not exceptional, but run-of-the-mill, and the drama, in the dreary examples that reach the stage today, does its best to keep pace. The preferred characters of current fiction are the drifters and derelicts of life in whose affairs or ultimate fate it is impossible to sustain interest. They do not excite the question that is the heart of narrative — "What happens next?" — because one cannot care what happens to them.

9   Perhaps the fault is not in the novelists but in the times that their characters are underlings; anti-heroes who reflect a general sense of man as victim. Perhaps the novelist today cannot honestly create a protagonist who is master of his fate and captain of his soul because man in the image of Henley seems obsolete. That man belonged to the self-confident nineteenth century, whereas the twentieth finds its exponent in losers, "beautiful losers" according to the title of a recent novel, although few seem to deserve the adjective. Oedipus was a loser and so was King Lear, but their losing was universal and profound, not pointless.

10   Since fiction and drama no longer present a true balance of human activity and motive, it is not to be wondered that they are losing their audience. According to a recent report from the capital, "Official Washington does not read contemporary novels" for the reason given by a sub-Cabinet officer in these words: "I try to read them and give up. Why should I spend my time on [books] . . . where the central character spends 350 pages quivering about whether to cross the street or go to the toilet?"

11   He has a point. Reading, which is to say writing, is the greatest gift with which man has endowed himself, by whose means we may soar on unlimited voyages. Are we to spend it picking through the garbage of humanity? Certainly the squalid and worthless, the mean and depraved are part of the human story just as dregs are part of wine, but the wine is what counts. Sexual perversion and hallucinatory drugs, as Eliot Fremont-Smith said of a recent novel, "are not what drives us, not what

human history is about."

The task then devolves upon historians to tell what human history **12**
is about and what are the forces that *do* drive us. That is not to say
that history excludes the squalid and depraved, but, being concerned
as it is with reality and subject as it is to certain disciplines, it deals
with these in proportion to the whole.

Historians start with a great advantage over fiction in that our **13**
characters, being public, are invested with power to affect destiny. They
are the captain and kings, saints and fanatics, traitors, rogues and villains,
pathfinders and explorers, thinkers and creators, even, occasionally,
heroes. They are significant − if not necessarily admirable. They may
be evil or corrupt or mad or stupid or even stuffed shirts, but at least,
by virtue of circumstance or chance or office or character, they *matter*.
They are the actors, not the acted upon, and are consequently that much
more interesting.

Readers want to see man shaping his destiny or, at least, struggling **14**
with it, and this is the stuff of history. They want to know how things
happened, why they happened, and particularly what they themselves
have lived through, just as after a record heat or heavy snow the first
thing one turns to in the morning paper is the account of yesterday's
weather. And now more than ever, when man's place in the world has
never been so subject to question, when "alienation" is the prevailing
word, the public also hopes to find some guidelines to destiny, some
pattern or meaning to our presence on this whirling globe. Whether
or not, as individuals, historians believe in one pattern or another, or
some of us in none, the evidence we have to present provides reassurance
in showing that man has gone through his dark ages before.

When I was a young parent a series of books appeared on child **15**
behavior by Dr. Arnold Gesell and his associates of the Yale Clinic
in which one discovered that the most aberrant, disturbing, or apparently
psychotic behavior of one's own child turned out to be the common age
pattern of the group innocently disporting itself behind Dr. Gesell's one-
way observation screen. Nothing was ever so comforting. Historians
provide a one-way screen on the past through which one can see man,
at one time or another, committing every horror, indecency, or idiocy
that he is capable of today. It is all already on his record, in kind if
not in degree. I do not suggest that history can be as comforting as Gesell
because the difference in degree that we face today is so great − in
the speed and impact of the mechanisms we have created − that problems and dangers multiply faster than we can devise solutions. Henry

Adams' law of acceleration is proving perilously true. Nevertheless, Adams' law is one of those guidelines historians have to offer. The story and study of the past, both recent and distant, will not reveal the future, but it flashes beacon lights along the way and it is a useful nostrum against despair.

16   Historians cannot expect to take over the leading role in literature without competition. Last summer Albert Rosenfeld, science editor of *Life*, wrote in an editorial that creative writers must turn to science to revive literature because "That is where the action is." There is a relevant and challenging truth in his statement. Science is formidably relevant and dynamic. "Great writing in any age," Rosenfeld continued, "casts some illumination on the major contemporary dilemmas." That is equally cogent. If science can evoke great creative writers who will do for space aeronautics or genetics or nuclear energy what Rachel Carson, for example, did for the sea around us, they will certainly win a large share of the public interest. The chief obstacle is language. Great writing in science must come from inside the discipline, and everything will depend on the rare talent which can break through the meshes of a technical vocabulary and express itself in words of common usage.

17   Here, too, we have a head start. Historians can — though not all do — make themselves understood in everyday English, the language in use from Chaucer to Churchill. Let us beware of the plight of our colleagues, the behavioral scientists, who by use of a prolifering jargon have painted themselves into a corner — or isolation ward — of unintelligibility. *They* know what they mean, but no one else does. Psychologists and sociologists are the farthest gone in the disease and probably incurable. Their condition might be pitied if one did not suspect it was deliberate. Their retreat into the arcane is meant to set them apart from the great unlearned, to mark their possession of some unshared, unsharable expertise. No matter how illuminating their discoveries, if the behavioral scientists write only to be understood by one another, they must come to the end of the Mandarins.

18   Communication, after all, is what language was invented for. If history is to share its insights with a public in need of them, it must practice communication as an art, as Gibbon did, or Parkman. History has, of course, other parts; like that other famous property, it is divisible into three: the investigative or research, the didactic or theory, and the narrated or communication. The elements that enter into communication are what I want to discuss, because history, it seems to me, is nothing if not communicated. Research provides the material, and theory a pat-

tern of thought, but it is through communication that history is heard and understood.

At the risk of stating the obvious, it is worth remarking that success of **19** communication depends upon the charm (I use the word in its most serious sense) of the narrative. "Writings are useless," declared Theodore Roosevelt, speaking as president of the American Historical Association in 1912, "unless they are read, and they cannot be read unless they are readable."

The history most successfully communicated, as far as the public is **20** concerned, can in one sense be determined by the annual lists of the top best-sellers. Up to 1960 the all-time best-seller in history was H. G. Wells's *Outline of History,* first published in 1921, which stayed among the top ten for three years in a row and reappeared on the list in a cheaper edition in 1930. It is the only book of history up to 1960 to have sold more than two million copies – more, oddly enough, than *The Kinsey Report.* Since then the leading work in history has been William L. Shirer's *Rise and Fall of the Third Reich*, which has sold, at last report, close to three million copies in the United States alone.

These names suggest what the evidence confirms: During the 1920s **21** and 1930s, when serious books had a better chance of reaching the top ten, the best-sellers in historical biography and straight history (as distinct from personal history and current events) included four academics, James Harvey Robinson, Charles Beard, Carl Van Doren, and James Truslow Adams three times over; and twelve non-academics, Emil Ludwig with four books, Hendrik van Loon with three, Lytton Strachey, Claude Bowers, Van Wyck Brooks, Andre Maurois, Francis Hackett, Stefan Zweig with two each, Will Durant, Frederick Lewis Allen, Margaret Leech, and Douglas Southall Freeman with one each. During the 1940s, when the war books took over, one academic, Arnold Toynbee (with his one-volume condensation) and one non-academic, Catherine Drinker Bowen, made the top ten. After that, except for Shirer and Frederic Morton's *The Rothchilds*, the swamping effect of the non-books begins and one has to look just beneath the top ten to the books which have been best-sellers during the course of the year without making the final list. Taking only the 1960s, these included three academics, Garrett Mattingly, Samuel Eliot Morison, Arthur Schlesinger, Jr., and nine independent writers, Winston Churchill, Bruce Catton, Alan Moorehead, Thomas Costain, Walter Lord, Cecil Woodham-Smith, and myself with two or more books each, Stewart Holbrook and George Kennan each with one.

22   To be a best-seller is not necessarily a measure of quality, but it *is* a measure of communication. That the independent writers have done better is hardly surprising, since communicating is their business; they know how. To capture and hold the interest of an audience is their object, as it has been that of every storyteller since Homer. Perhaps the academic historian suffers from having a captive audience, first in the supervisor of his dissertation, then in the lecture hall. Keeping the reader turning the page has not been his primary concern.

23   My intention is not to exacerbate the distinction between the professional historian and the so-called amateur but to clarify its terms. "Professional" — meaning someone who has had graduate training leading to a professional degree and who practices within a university — is a valid term, but "amateur" — used to mean someone outside the university without a graduate degree — is a misnomer. Graduate training certainly establishes a difference of which I, who did not have it, am deeply aware, sometimes regretfully, sometimes thankfully. But I would prefer to recognize the difference by distinguishing between academics and independents, or between scholars and writers, rather than between professionals and amateurs, because the question is not one of degree of professionalism but which profession. The faculty people are professional historians, we outside are professional writers. Insofar as they borrow our function and we borrow their subject, each of us has a great deal to learn from the other.

24   An objection often made to the independents is that they are insufficiently acquainted or careless with the facts. An extreme case is the Cortez of Keats, staring at the Pacific with a wild surmise, silent upon a peak in Darien. Keats, of course, got the name wrong but the idea right. Through the power of marvelous phrasing and the exercise of a poet's imagination he immortalized a historic moment. It is possible that his vision of the man on the peak is more important, for conveying history, than the name of the man. Poets aside, historians of course should offer both. There is no need to choose between accuracy and beauty; one should be clothed in the other.

25   In pockets of survival there may be some historians who still retain the old notion imposed by scientific history that, as another president of the American Historical Association, Walter Prescott Webb, put it, "There is something historically naughty about good writing," that "a great gulf exists between truth and beauty and the scholar who attempts to bridge it deserves to fall in and drown," and that "the real scholar must choose truth and somehow it is better if it is made so ugly that

nobody could doubt its virginity." If some still believe this, communication is not for them.

For the first element in communication, Webb gave the perfect triple 26 criterion: a writer's belief that he has something to say, that it is worth saying, and that he can say it better than anyone else — and, he added, "not for the few but for the many." For coupled with compulsion to write must go desire to be read. No writing comes alive unless the writer sees across his desk a reader, and searches constantly for the word or phrase which will carry the image he wants the reader to see and arouse the emotion he wants him to feel. Without consciousness of a live reader, what a man writes will die on his page. Macaulay was a master of this contact with the reader. His sister Hannah cried when he read the *History of England* aloud to her. What writer could ask for more?

When it comes to content, inspiration, what Webb calls the moment 27 of synthesis — the revealing flash of a synthesizing idea — is obviously a help. Webb describes his own moment of insight when the idea came to him that the emergence of Americans from the life of the forests to the life of the plains was of dramatic significance. Admiral Mahan had his moment when, from the study of Hannibal's failure to control sea communication with Carthage, the idea flashed on him of the influence of sea power on history. The moment is exciting but not, I think, essential. A theme may do as well to begin with as a thesis and does not involve, like the overriding theory, a creeping temptation to adjust the facts. The integrating idea or insight then evolves from the internal logic of the material, in the course of putting it together. From the gathering of the particulars one arrives at the general, at that shining grail we are all in search of, the historical generalization. To state it in advance does not seem necessary to me. The process is more persuasive and the integrating idea more convincing if the reader discovers it for himself out of the evidence laid before him.

All theses run the risk of obsolescence. The pathways of history, said 28 the great historian of the frontier, Frederick Jackson Turner, are "strewn with the wrecks" of once known and acknowledged truths, discarded by a later generation. Revision and counter-revision roll against the shores of history as rhythmically as waves. Even so, a true inspiration or integrating idea such as Mahan's or Turner's will be valid and enlightening for its time, regardless of subsequent fortune.

29 Though some will debate it, intuition, too, is an aid. The intuitive historian can reach an understanding of long-past circumstance in much the same way as Democritus, the predecessor of Aristotle, arrived at

the idea of the atom. His mind, mulling over observed phenomena, worked out a theory of matter as composed of an infinite number of mobile
particles. The process may have been cerebral, but its impetus was intuitive. Strict disciples of history as a science may scorn the intuitive
process, but that attitude comes from being more Catholic than the Pope.
True scientists know its value. It is an arrow shot into the air, which
will often pierce the same target that the scientific historian with his
nose on the ground will take months to reach on foot.

30   Of all the historian's instruments, belief in the grandeur of his theme
is the most compelling. Parkman, in his preface to *Montcalm and Wolfe*,
describes his subject, the Seven Years' War in the American theater,
as "the most momentous and far-reaching question ever brought to issue
on this continent." Its outcome determined that there would be an
American Revolution. "With it began a new chapter in the annals of
the world." That is the way an author should feel about his subject.
It ensures that no reader can put the book down.

31   Enthusiasm, which is not quite the same thing, has a no less leaven-
ing effect. It was recognized by Admiral Mahan, who, in the course
of studying Britain's contest with Napoleon, developed a particular admiration for Pitt. "His steadfast nature," Mahan wrote, "aroused in me
an enthusiasm which I did not seek to check; for I believe enthusiasm
no bad spirit in which to realize history to yourself and to others."

32   Mahan's prescription disposes of the myth of "pure objectivity" when
used to mean "without bias." As John Gunther once said of journalism,
"A reporter with no bias at all would be a vegetable." If such a thing
as a "purely objective" historian could exist, his work would be
unreadable — like eating sawdust. Bias is only misleading when it is
concealed. After reading *The Proud Tower*, a onetime member of the
Asquith government scolded me in a letter for misrepresenting as he
thought, his party. "Your bias against the Liberals sticks out," he wrote.
I replied that it was better to have it stick out than be hidden. It can
then be taken into account. I cannot deny that I acquired a distaste for
Mr. Asquith as, for other reasons, I did for Henry Adams. There are
some people in history one simply dislikes, and as long as they are not
around to have their feelings hurt, I see no reason to conceal it. To
take no sides in history would be as false as to take no sides in life.

33   A historian tries to be objective in the sense of learning as much as
possible, and presenting as sympathetically as possible the motives and
conditions of both sides, because to do so makes the drama more intense — and more believable. But let us not pretend that this is being

without bias — as if historians were mere recorders who have given up the exercise of judgment. Bias means a *leaning* which *is* the exercise of judgment as well as a source of insight. Admittedly, it is usually helped by emotional conditioning, but that is what makes for commitment. The great historians more often than not have been passionately committed to a cause or a protagonist, as Mommsen was to Julius Caesar or Michelet to the glorious power of the people.

How commitment can generate insight and heighten communication 34 is nowhere better shown than in G.M. Trevelyan's *Garibaldi and the Thousand*, one of the finest works of history, I think, both for investigation and narrative, produced in this century. Trevelyan's commitment to his hero is explicit. Describing the foot track from the Villa Spinola down to the embarkation point in Genoa, he writes in a footnote, "I had the honor of going down it" with a veteran of the Thousand. There is no doubt where he stands. His feeling of personal involvement led Trevelyan to visit every place connected with the Garibaldini, to walk in their footsteps, to interview those still living, until he knew the persons, terrain, view, sounds, smells, sights, distances, weather — in short, the feel — of every scene of action he was to write about.

As the Thousand marched to the Battle of Calatafimi, Trevelyan writes, 35 "Their hearts were light with the sense that they were enviable above all Italians, that their unique campaign was poetry made real." The quality of emotion here is not, as so often, created out of the historian's feelings and foisted onto his characters, but drawn from the evidence. A footnote gives the original from a letter of one of the Garibaldini to his mother telling her, "*Questa spedizione è così poetica.*" ("This expedition is a poetical thing.") Approaching the battle, they pass through a green valley at early morning. "In the bloom of the early Sicilian summer," Trevelyan writes, "the vale fresh from last night's rain, and sung over by the nightingale at dawn, lay ready to exhale its odors to the rising sun. Nature seemed in tune with the hearts of Garibaldi and his men." Here, too he worked from evidence in diaries and letters that it had rained the night before and that the nightingale had sung. In these two passages he has conveyed the sense of miraculous freshness and noble enterprise which the Garibaldi expedition signalized for the liberal spirit of the nineteenth century. He could accomplish this, first, because of his quick sensitivity to source material, and second, because he himself was in tune with the hearts of Garibaldi and his men.

Again, when Garibaldi's bugler blew reveille, "the unexpected music 36 rang through the noonday stillness like a summons to the soul of Italy."

In the verb of sound, "rang," the reader hears the bugle and in the phrase "like the summons to the soul of Italy" feels the emotion of the listener. Without knowing that he is being told, he has learned the meaning to history of the expedition.

37   To visit the scene before writing, even the scene of long-dead adventures, is, as it were, to start business with money in the bank. It was said of Arthur Waley, the great Orientalist who died a few months ago, that he had never visited Asia, explaining that he was content with the ideal image of the East in his imagination. For a historian that would be a risky position. On the terrain motives become clear, reasons and explanations and origins of things emerge that might otherwise have remained obscure. As a source of understanding, not to mention as a corrective for fixed ideas and mistaken notions, nothing is more valuable than knowing the scene in person, and, even more so, living the life that belongs to it, Without that intimacy Francis Parkman would not have been the master he was.

38   Parkman's hero was really the forest. Through experience he learned passion for it, and fear, and understood both its savagery and beauty. In those long days of intermittent blindness when he was not allowed to write, his mind must have worked over remembered visions of the forest so that they come through on the page with extra clarity. As a scout paddles across the lake in autumn, "the mossed rocks double in the watery mirror" and sumachs on the shore glow like rubies against the dark green spruce. Or the frontier settler, returning at evening, sees a "column of blue smoke rising quietly in the still evening air" and runs to find the smoldering logs of his cabin and the scalped bodies of his murdered wife and children.

39   Vision, knowledge, experience will not make a great writer without that extra command of language which becomes their voice. This, too, was Parkman's. When the English are about to descend the rapids of the upper St. Lawrence, they look on the river whose "reckless surges dashed and bounded in the sun, beautiful and terrible as young tigers at play." In choice of verbs and nouns and images that is a masterpiece. It is only physical description, to be sure, not a great thought, but it takes perfect command of words to express great thoughts in the event one has them.

40   Steeped in the documents he spent his life collecting, as he was steeped in the forest, Parkman understood the hardship and endurance, grim energy, and implacable combat that underlay the founding of the American nation. He knew the different groups of combatants as if he

had lived with each, and could write with equal sympathy of French or Indians, English or colonials. Consider his seventeenth-century French courtiers, "the butterflies of Versailles...facing death with careless gallantry, in their small three-cornered hats, powdered perukes, embroidered coats, and lace ruffles. Their valets served them with ices in the trenches, under the cannon of besieged towns." In this case the ices in the trenches is a specimen of the historian's selective insight at work. He has chosen a vivid item to represent a larger whole. It distills an era and a culture in a detail.

Distillation is selection, and selection, as I am hardly the first to af- **41** firm, is the essence of writing history. It is the cardinal process of composition, the most difficult, the most delicate, the most fraught with error as well as art. Ability to distinguish what is significant from what is insignificant is *sine qua non.*[1] Failure to do so means that the point of the story, not to mention the reader's interest, becomes lost in a morass of undifferentiated matter. What it requires is simply the courage and self-confidence to make choices and, above all, to leave things out.

In history as in painting, wrote the great stylist Macaulay, to put in **42** everything achieves a less, rather than a more, truthful result. The best picture and best history, he said, are those "which exhibit such parts of the truth as most nearly produce the effect of the whole." This is such an obvious rule that it is puzzling why so many historians today seem to practice a reverse trend toward total inclusion. Perhaps the reason is timidity: fear of being criticized for having left something out, or, by injudicious selection, of not conforming to the dominant thesis of the moment. Here the independent writer has an advantage over the professional historian: He need not be afraid of the outstuck neck.

Finally, the historian cannot do without imagination. Parkman, in- **43** tense as always in his effort to make the reader "feel the situation," chose to picture the land between the Hudson and Montreal as it would look to a wild goose flying northward in spring. He sees the blue line of the river, the dark mass of forests and shimmer of lakes, the geometric lines and mounds of man-made forts, "with the flag of the Bourbons like a flickering white speck" marking Ticonderoga, and the "mountain wilderness of the Adirondacks like a stormy sea congealed." On reading that passage I feel the excitement of the Count of Monte Cristo when he opened the treasure chest. It would not be remarkable for one of us who has traveled in airplanes to think of the device of the bird's-eye view, but Parkman had never been off the ground. It was a pure effort of imagination to put himself behind the eye of the goose, to see

---

1. sine qua non: "without which, nothing"

the flag as a flickering white speck and the mountains, in that perfect phrase, as "a stormy sea congealed."

44   Great as this is, the more necessary use of imagination is in application to human behavior and to the action of circumstance on motive. It becomes a deliberate effort at empathy, essential if one is to understand and interpret the actions of historical figures. With antipathetic characters it is all the more necessary. The historian must put himself inside them, as Parkman put himself inside the wild goose, or as I tried to do inside Sir John French in an effort to understand the draining away of his will to fight. As soon as the effort was made, the explanation offered itself. I could feel the oppression, the weight of responsibility, the consciousness of the absence of any trained reserves to take the place of the BEF if it were lost.[2] The effort to get inside is, obviously enough, a path to insight. It is the *Einfühlung* that Herder demanded of historians: the effort to "feel oneself into everything." The interpreter of the Hebrew scriptures, as he put it, must be "a shepherd with shepherds, a peasant in the midst of an agricultural people, an oriental with the primitive dwellers of the East."

45   To describe the historian's task today in terms of narrative history and two romantic practitioners, Parkman and Trevelyan, will seem old-fashioned at a time when interdisciplinary techniques, and horizontal subjects such as demography, and the computerized mechanics of quantification are the areas of fresh endeavor. These are methods of research, not of communication, for one reason because the people who use them tend to lose contact with ordinary language; they have caught the jargon disease. Their efforts are directed, I take it, toward uncovering underlying patterns in history and human behavior which presumably might help in understanding the past and managing the future, or even the present. Whether quantification will reveal anything which could not have been discerned by deduction is not yet clear. What seems to be missing in the studies that I have seen is a certain element of common sense.

46   The new techniques will, I am sure, turn up suggestive material and open avenues of thought, but they will not, I think, transform history into a science, and they can never make it literature. Events happen: but to become history they must be communicated and understood. For that, history needs writers — preferably great writers — a Trevelyan who can find and understand the *cosi poetica* in a soldier's letter and make the right use of it, a Parkman who can see and feel, and report with Shakespeare's gift of words; both, I need not add, assemblers of

2. BEF – British Expeditionary Force of World War I, headed in 1914 by Sir John French. Tuchman is referring in this paragraph to her Pulizer prize winning book, *The Guns of August*.

their own primary material. To be a really great historian, Macaulay said, "is the rarest of intellectual distinctions." For all who try, the opportunity is now and the audience awaits.

(1967)

The Writer's Subject

1. What does Tuchman mean by "the literature of actuality"? (paras. 1-4)

2. What cause and effect relation does Tuchman draw between "man's cumulative disillusionment in himself" (para. 5) and the state of contemporary fiction and drama? Why, in her view, are fiction and drama losing their audience? (paras. 5-11)

3. How, according to Tuchman, does the historian take account of "the squalid and worthless" differently from the contemporary novelist? (paras. 11-12)

4. How may the historian, in Tuchman's view, offer reassurance to the modern reader disturbed by the problems of contemporary life? (paras. 14-15)

5. What contrast does Tuchman draw between the writing of historians and that of behavioural scientists? (para. 17)

6. Why, in Tuchman's view, have the independent, non-academic historical writers been more successful with the reading public than the professional, academic historians? (paras. 20-24)

7. What are the most important attributes for a good historian, according to Tuchman? (paras. 26-44)

8. What is Tuchman's response to the idea that a historian should be completely objective and without bias? (paras. 32-33)

9. What qualities does Tuchman admire in the historians G.M. Trevelyan and Francis Parkman? (paras. 34-40)

10. What does Tuchman mean in asserting that "selection . . . is the essence of writing history"? (paras. 41-42)

11. What importance does Tuchman ascribe to the historian's ability to empathize with historical figures? (para. 44)

12. Of what value are computers and statistical approaches to the study of history, in Tuchman's view? (para. 45)

The Writer's Style and Strategy

1. How does Tuchman's title reflect her purposes in this essay?

2. What is Tuchman's thesis, and where is it most clearly stated?

3. What evidence does the essay provide of its origin as an address to the American Historical Association? What assumptions does Tuchman make about her audience?

4. Tuchman observes that the study of the past can throw light upon the present. Where does she exemplify this principle in the course of her discussion?

5. Show how Tuchman uses the works of other historians to illustrate the principles of good historical writing.

6. Tuchman alludes to W.E. Henley's poem "Invictus" (para. 9) and Keats's poem "On First Looking into Chapman's Homer" (para. 24). Look up the poems, and discuss the appropriateness of Tuchman's references to them for her argumentative purposes.

7. Tuchman believes that historians should "make themselves understood in everyday English" (para. 17). What qualities of "everyday English" does Tuchman's own writing display? Choose one or two paragraphs for the purpose of your analysis.

Suggested Topics for Writing and Discussion

1. Find a work of history by a noted historian of the nineteenth or twentieth century. Choose two or three pages for analysis and indicate whether the writer, in your opinion, exhibits the qualities that Tuchman maintains are needed for good historical writing.

2. Tuchman, writing this essay in 1967, says that most works of literature of the time were characterized by "the squalid and the worthless, the mean and depraved." Choose any well-known work of imaginative literature written in the last twenty years and indicate whether the work fits the generalized pattern described by Tuchman.

3. Tuchman says: "To be a best-seller is not necessarily a measure of quality, but it *is* a measure of communication." Consult a bestseller list in a national magazine or newspaper to locate a work of non-fiction which has been on the list for several months. Find two or three reviews of the book and report on its capacity to "communicate" its subject.

Influences

by Guy Vanderhaeghe

1 It was only after I published a book that I was forced to consider the
question of influence on my writing. Until that point I had merely written.
But reviewers made me aware of the problem of influence, drawing
as they did convincing parallels between my short stories and the work
of writers I had never read. Interviewers, too, were keen to unearth
literary debts. Which writers and books, they asked, had most influenced
me?

2   It was a question I wanted to answer honestly. But I was not sure
I could. For one thing I had the impression I was really being asked
which books and writers I admired most, asked that in the certainty
that the answer to both questions was the same. That might be so, but
isn't necessarily. *Ulysses,* for instance, is one of those universally admired works which has influenced writers less than one would think.
Remembrance of Things Past is another.

3   What I was coming to suspect was that literary influences are more
various and varied than I had imagined. In my case, the threads of these
influences resolved themselves into a Gordian knot which stubbornly
resisted all my efforts to untangle it. For instance, when asked to produce a list of those authors whom I particularly admired I was inevitably
struck by the heterogeneity of the list I compiled. I could not but help
imagine these authors incongruously yoked in conversation at literary
cocktail parties. Flannery O'Connor and Anthony Powell? Christopher
Isherwood and Rudy Wiebe? Alice Munro and Evelyn Waugh?

    I could not see how these converging vectors of probable influence   4
had shaped my writing. Worse, I felt I was suppressing another, perhaps

equally important list of names. Names such as Zane Grey, Walter Scott, John Buchan, and Robert Louis Stevenson came immediately to mind. Yet I was afraid of being thought facetious if I gave these writers the nod of acknowledgement.

It was only when I read Vladimir Nabokov's autobiography *Speak, Memory* that I seriously began to define and elaborate a dim suspicion I had been harbouring: that "bad" writing is as influential in the development of a writer as "good" writing. A brief reference of Nabokov's to an article he had read as a child in the *Boy's Own Paper* strengthened that suspicion because it helped carry me back, back beyond my first acquaintance with Zane Grey, Stevenson, Buchan, and Scott, back to my earliest reading, to my introduction to the *Boy's Own Annual.*

During Nabokov's Edwardian childhood the *Boy's Own Paper* was one of those bellicose boys' magazines which tub-thumped for the British Empire and the "right little, tight little Island!" It may seem strange that such a paper found its way into the Nabokov home, but Vladimir Nabokov's father was a wealthy anglophile who insisted on English governesses, governesses who, in turn, insisted that their little Russian charges read and write English before they read and write Russian. Thus the *Boy's Own Paper.*

All this smacks a bit of Alice in Wonderland. There is surely something absurd in the notion of a young Russian aristocrat, citizen of a xenophobe empire, reading, in English, the rival claims to glory of a competing xenophobe empire. The only thing possibly more absurd is that almost exactly fifty years later, in 1957 or thereabouts, I was poring over a like-minded publication, the *Boy's Own Annual.* My volume too was Edwardian, an issue that Nabokov might conceivably have read on dark St. Petersburg winter evenings, a book that had lost its covers and was coming apart in my hands and which I, at the age of six, took to be a reasonably accurate account of the world outside my bailiwick. No one told me that the fabulous world described in its pages had expired in the mud of Flanders more than forty years before.

Or perhaps it was just that I refused not to believe in what I was reading. In any case, I held on to the illusion for something like three years before it evaporated. During that time I confined my reading basically to two books (aside from the insipid things assigned in school) and those books were an old school text of my mother's, *A History of the World,* and the previously mentioned volume of the *Boy's Own Annual.* In the beginning I found *A History of the World* the more intriguing because of its illustrations: photographs of antiquities such as

Mycenaean daggers and Etruscan coins, and reproductions of "historical" paintings which showed Egyptian charioteers dramatically dying, transfixed by Hittite arrows. The *Boy's Own Annual* supplanted the *History* in my affections only as my ability to read improved. Only then did it become the staple nourishment of my imagination. I never read, or had read to me, for instance, any of the chlldren's classics such as *Winnie the Pooh, The Jungle Book,* or *The Wind in the Willows.* In retrospect I can say it would have been a good thing if I had read other books, but at the time I certainly didn't suffer from these omissions. My pre-World War I issue of the *Boy's Own Annual* kept me entranced. I needed no other books. I was like a fundamentalist with his Bible.

9   The *Boy's Own Annual* fell into my hands by way of an elderly English lady who was cleaning out her attic. This lady was typically English — or at least what North American readers of Agatha Christie mysteries might imagine as typically English. A widow, she lived for her huge garden, her budgerigars, and a cocker spaniel named Rusty. She presented me the tattered copy with the assurance that it was "just the thing for a lively young fellow." Against all odds it was.

10   The contents of the *Boy's Own,* as I remember it, divided fairly evenly into three broad categories. Practical knowledge; historical yarns which even I recognized as historical; and "contemporary" tales which were, at the time I read them, already more than forty years old. The latter I insisted on thinking of as accurate reflections of life in the British Isles and Empire. With hindsight I conclude that this misconception of mine probably continued to flourish primarily because my parents didn't own a television. A TV set would have rubbed my nose in the grit of reality. But I also must have practised self-delusion on a grand scale, some part of my mind censoring all evidence that contradicted the *Boy's Own* picture of the world. Still, in my defence I can say that this was the age of Tarzan movies.

11   Anyway, who wouldn't wish to keep alive such magnificent delusions? How well I recall the *Boy's Own* article on self-defence. Here was practical knowledge indeed, a step by step, blow by blow account of the proper use of one's walking stick in repulsing assailants. The reader was enjoined to strike *glancing* blows off threatening blackguards because glancing blows foil any attempts at seizing one's walking stick, wresting it from one's grasp, and turning it against one. (It being understood that blackguards were clearly not the kind of fellows to carry walking sticks of their own.) Recommended targets for such glancing blows were elbows, shins, and, of course, the crown of the head. As

a bonus several policeman's grips were described and illustrated. When applied these grips promised to bring about the instant submission of felons. Young readers were reminded to use minimum force when practising such grips on their chums.

The article incited in me a powerful longing. I knew that there were 12 no interesting blackguards stalking the streets of Esterhazy, Saskatchewan, of the type depicted in *Boy's Own*. Nor did I own an ashplant. However, that didn't mean I oughtn't to study the article very closely. Particularly since I had, on the spot, determined to go to England where there apparently was an abundance of blackguards, villains, and ruffians. All suitable for thrashing.

The rest of *Boy's Own* was, if possible, even better, stuffed plum- 13 full to bursting with plucky youths. There were the plucky youths of the past: a ferreter-out of the Gunpowder Plot, an alarm-raiser at the Great Fire of London, an aider and abettor of the escape of Bonny Prince Charlie to France. Then there were the plucky youths I mistook for my contemporaries. My favourite among these was a lad who had stained his skin with berry juice, wrapped his head in a turban, and embarked on a steamer ferrying pilgrims to Mecca. His mission? To uncover a ring of Arab slavers dealing in British subjects. After making fog-bound London streets safe for respectable strollers I thought I might lend this chap a hand tidying up the Red Sea. My future bloomed.

If it was Nabokov's perfunctory comment about the *Boy's Own Paper* 14 that resurrected memories which had lain mute under the dead weight of all the books that followed this one volume, books deposited year by year, strata upon strata, it was something else in *Speak, Memory* that made me consider whether my writing hadn't been flavoured by this early infatuation of mine with the *Boy's Own Annual*.

Reading Nabokov's autobiography I was struck by a curious thing. 15 I noted that although Nabokov makes frequent reference to the authors of the great European and Russian masterpieces, he devotes more space to a man called Captain Mayne Reid than he does to either Blok, Pushkin, Tolstoy, Gogol, Kafka, Flaubert, Dostoevsky, or for that matter, any other writer.

Who was Captain Mayne Reid? Captain Mayne Reid (1818-83), 16 Nabokov informs us, was a writer of Wild West romances. At the turn of the century translations of his work were enormously popular with Russian schoolchildren. Young Vladimir Nabokov was, however, because of the diligence of his governesses, fluent enough in English to have the privilege of reading them in the original language. His favourite, he tells his readers, was *Headless Horseman.*

17   From what Nabokov has to say in *Speak, Memory* it is possible to deduce that Mayne Reid completely captivated his young reader. Nabokov even admits to re-reading *Headless Horseman* as an adult, and he maintains that the book has its points. It is instructive to note what these points are.

18   First of all Nabokov takes delight in the artificiality and intricacy of Captain Mayne Reid's plots. Second, several passages of prose are quoted with approval. There is the Whiskey decanter behind a Texan barman which looks like "an iris sparkling behind his shoulder," and the barman himself is improbably graced with "an aureole surrounding his perfumed head." Now it is true that in all this Nabokovian applause there is more than a trace of the familiar Nabokovian mockery. But two things came to my mind also: Nabokov's own prose, touched as it is with the fantastic and a tincture of the archaic, and his own taste for studied melodrama and gloriously coincidental plots. One has, after all, only to think of how improbably the nymphet's mother was despatched in *Lolita* to leave the field free for Humbert Humbert.

19   On such slender, even feeble evidence it would be foolhardy to argue a connection between Reid and Nabokov, to see the romancer's taste, filtered and purified by Nabokov's genius, later making a bow in the shadows of Nabokov's novels. But I sensed that, if clearly unprovable, it was still possible. Nabokov himself is frank in admitting that many of the books he later read resonated with Reidian echoes. Dwelling on Louise Pointdexter, a young lady equipped with lorgnette that he discovered in *Headless Horseman,* Nabokov writes,

> That lorgnette I found afterward in the hands of Madame Bovary, and later Anna Karenin had it, and then it passed into the possession of Chekhov's Lady with the Lapdog and was lost by her on the pier at Yalta. When Louise held it, it was directed toward the speckled shadows under the mesquites, where the horseman of her choice was having an innocent conversation with the daughter of a wealthy haciendado, Doña Isidora Covarubio de los Llanos (whose 'head of hair in luxuriance rivalled the tail of a wild steed').

In just this manner the turbaned heads of Moslem pilgrims that I had met in the *Boy's Own Annual* sprang into view when I read *Lord Jim*, and walking sticks in the hands of Henry James' characters were suddenly transformed from the innocent appurtenances of dandies into menacing clubs.

There was something else, too. I had come to wonder if I had not 20 begun the process of learning to write long ago with the *Boy's Own*. The one problem with the magazine was that it was a serial, and I possessed only a single volume. Some of the stories had no beginning. Worse, some had no end. Several of the more harrowing tales had appended to their last page a cruel joke: To be continued. My favourite character, the berry-stained boy, I had to leave manacled in the bottom of an Arab dhow on the point of being pitched overboard to sharks. What, I asked myself in torments of anxiety, had happened to him?

I like to think now that he would have remained forever frozen in 21 that queer limbo of near death if I hadn't assumed the responsibility of rescuing him. Because at some point in my childhood I came to realize that what I was reading was fiction, a structure created by the imagination. If I were daring enough I might collaborate in the making of it. Or as I saw it then: the boy can be saved. So at about the age of seven or eight I set about saving him, manufacturing ploys and desperate acts of desperate courage that would deliver him from implacable fate. In other words, I began an apprenticeship. I was learning to write.

Perhaps all my subsequent fiction has been marked by this experience, 22 this revelation. Certain reviewers have remarked on my "traditionalism." Others have gently chided me for my interest in plot and "story." Is the *Boy's Own Annual* the obscure root of these tendencies? Have the stratagems concocted to elude the wicked slavers become, in some sense, second nature?

I don't know. The only testimony I can offer is the confession that 23 when I sit down to write it is only with the greatest effort of will I manage to force the turbaned heads down, out of sight below the bulwarks of the dhows, or manage to master the violent and intoxicating urge to conclude every chapter with a clear suggestion of imminent peril.

It is, I suppose, only a matter of time before the will weakens and 24 the long serialization begun twenty-five years ago resumes under a slightly different guise. I find that once acquired the taste is hard to lose.

(1984)

The Writer's Subject

1. What difficulties did Vanderhaeghe encounter when he first considered the question of influences on his writing? (paras. 1-4)

2. Explain the meaning and relevance of Vanderhaeghe's allusion to a "Gordian knot." (para. 3)

3. In paragraphs 3 and 4 Vanderhaeghe describes two lists he made up, of writers he admired. Why was he "afraid of being thought facetious" if he acknowledged the writers on the second list?

4. What parallels does Vanderhaeghe draw between Nabokov's childhood reading and his own? Why does he find something absurd about their respective experiences? (paras. 5-7)

5. How does Vanderhaeghe's reference to "the mud of Flanders" reinforce his point about the vision of the world conveyed in the *Boy's Own Annual*? (para. 7)

6. Why, in speaking of his "self-delusion," does Vanderhaeghe say that "in my defence I can say that this was the age of Tarzan movies" (para. 10)?

7. Vanderhaeghe draws attention to the frequent references in Nabokov's autobiography to Captain Mayne Reid, a minor English writer of Wild West romances. What influence did Mayne Reid's work have on Nabokov? What parallel does Vanderhaeghe draw between Nabokov's reading experience and his own? (paras. 14-19)

8. How does Vanderhaeghe conclude that his own writing may have been shaped to some extent by his childhood reading of the single volume of the *Boy's Own Annual* in his possession? (paras. 20-24)

The Writer's Style and Strategy

1. What is Vanderhaeghe's thesis? How does he introduce it, and at what point does he make his thesis explicit? (paras. 1-5)

2. How does Vanderhaeghe convey the chauvinistic nature of the *Boy's Own Paper*? (paras. 6 and 7) What does the repeated phrase "xenophobe empire" tell you about the values of the *Boy's Own Paper*?

3. Why does Vanderhaeghe use the word "fabulous" to describe the world in the pages of the *Boy's Own Annual*? (para. 7)

4. How does Vanderhaeghe convey the flavour of the articles in the *Boy's Own Annual*? (para. 11) How does he create a sense of the romantic excitement he felt as a youthful reader of such articles? (paras. 12 and 13)

5.   Vanderhaeghe begins his essay by saying that he wants to answer honest-
     ly the questions of interviewers concerning which writers and books most
     influenced him. What is the connection between Vanderhaeghe's statement
     of purpose and the essay's conclusion?

Suggested Topics for Writing and Discussion

1.   Vanderhaeghe observes that "bad" writing may be as influential in the
     development of a writer as "good" writing. Drawing from your own reading
     experience, offer your views of what constitutes "bad" literature. Does
     "bad" literature have any redeeming qualities?

2.   In discussing his misconceptions about reality derived from the *Boy's Own
     Annual*, Vanderhaeghe observes that these flourished in part because his
     parents did not own a TV set: "A TV set would have rubbed my nose
     in the grit of reality." To what extent, in your view, does television pre-
     sent us with a true picture of the real world?

3.   Vanderhaeghe notes that as a child he did not read such children's classics
     as *Winnie the Pooh, The Jungle Book,* or *Wind in the Willows.* Choose
     one of these works, or another acknowledged children's classic, and offer
     your views about its possible appeal for young readers today.

4.   Choose a contemporary magazine intended for children or teenagers, and
     analyze its contents. What assumptions does it make about its audience?
     What "picture of the world" does it create? How accurately does it reflect
     the values or circumstances of our society? In your assessment, you might
     consider whether the contents are likely to excite a young reader's curiosity
     and imagination.

How Should One Read a Book?
by Virginia Woolf

1   In the first place, I want to emphasize the note of interrogation at the
end of my title. Even if I could answer the question for myself, the
answer would apply only to me and not to you. The only advice, indeed, that one person can give another about reading is to take no advice, to follow your own instincts, to use your own reason, to come
to your own conclusions. If this is agreed between us, then I feel at
liberty to put forward a few ideas and suggestions because you will not
allow them to fetter that independence which is the most important quality
that a reader can possess. After all, what laws can be laid down about
books? The battle of Waterloo was certainly fought on a certain day;
but is *Hamlet* a better play than *Lear*? Nobody can say. Each must decide
that question for himself. To admit authorities, however heavily furred
and gowned, into our libraries and let them tell us how to read, what
to read, what value to place upon what we read, is to destroy the spirit
of freedom which is the breath of those sanctuaries. Everywhere else
we may be bound by laws and conventions − there we have none.

2   But to enjoy freedom, if the platitude is pardonable, we have of course
to control ourselves. We must not squander our powers, helplessly and
ignorantly, squirting half the house in order to water a single rose-bush;
we must train them, exactly and powerfully, here on the very spot. This,
it may be, is one of the first difficulties that faces us in a library. What
is "the very spot"? There may well seem to be nothing but a conglomera-
tion and huddle of confusion. Poems and novels, histories and memoirs,
dictionaries and blue-books; books written in all languages by men and
women of all tempers, races, and ages jostle each other on the shelf.

And outside the donkey brays, the women gossip at the pump, the colts gallop across the fields. Where are we to begin? How are we to bring order into this multitudinous chaos and so get the deepest and widest pleasure from what we read?

It is simple enough to say that since books have classes — fiction, 3 biography, poetry — we should separate them and take from each what it is right that each should give us. Yet few people ask from books what books can give us. Most commonly we come to books with blurred and divided minds, asking of fiction that it shall be true, of poetry that it shall be false, of biography that it shall be flattering, of history that it shall enforce our own prejudices. If we could banish all such preconceptions when we read, that would be an admirable beginning. Do not dictate to your author; try to become him. Be his fellow-worker and accomplice. If you hang back, and reserve and criticise at first, you are preventing yourself from getting the fullest possible value from what you read. But if you open your mind as widely as possible, then signs and hints of almost imperceptible fineness, from the twist and turn of the first sentences, will bring you into the presence of a human being unlike any other. Steep yourself in this, acquaint yourself with this, and soon you will find that your author is giving you, or attempting to give you, something far more definite. The thirty-two chapters of a novel — if we consider how to read a novel first — are an attempt to make something as formed and controlled as a building: but words are more impalpable than bricks; reading is a longer and more complicated process than seeing. Perhaps the quickest way to understand the elements of what a novelist is doing is not to read, but to write; to make your own experiment with the dangers and difficulties of words. Recall, then, some event that has left a distinct impression on you — how at the corner of the street, perhaps, you passed two people talking. A tree shook; an electric light danced; the tone of the talk was comic, but also tragic; a whole vision, an entire conception, seemed contained in that moment.

But when you attempt to reconstruct it in words, you will find that 4 it breaks into a thousand conflicting impressions. Some must be subdued; others emphasized; in the process you will lose, probably, all grasp upon the emotion itself. Then turn from your blurred and littered pages to the opening pages of some great novelist — Defoe, Jane Austen, Hardy. Now you will be better able to appreciate their mastery. It is not merely that we are in the presence of a different person — Defoe, Jane Austen, or Thomas Hardy — but that we are living in a different world. Here, in *Robinson Crusoe*, we are trudging a plain high road; one thing happens after another; the fact and the order of the fact is enough. But if the open air and adventure mean everything to Defoe they mean nothing to Jane Austen. Hers is the drawing-room, and people talking, and by the many mirrors of their talk revealing their characters. And if, when we have accustomed ourselves to the drawing-room and its reflections, we turn to Hardy, we are once more spun round. The moors are round us and the stars are above our heads. The other side of the mind is now exposed — the dark side that comes uppermost in solitude, not the light side that shows in company. Our relations are not towards people, but towards Nature and destiny. Yet different as these worlds are, each is consistent with itself. The maker of each is careful to observe the laws of his own perspective, and however great a strain they may put upon us they will never confuse us, as lesser writers so frequently do, by introducing two different kinds of reality into the same book. Thus to go from one great novelist to another — from Jane Austen to Hardy, from Peacock to Trollope, from Scott to Meredith — is to be wrenched and uprooted; to be thrown this way and then that. To read a novel is a difficult and complex art. You must be capable not only of great fineness of perception, but of great boldness of imagination if you are going to make use of all that the novelist — the great artist — gives you.

5   But a glance at the heterogeneous company on the shelf will show you that writers are very seldom "great artists"; far more often a book makes no claim to be a work of art at all. These biographies and autobiographies, for example, lives of great men, of men long dead and forgotten, that stand cheek by jowl with the novels and poems, are we to refuse to read them because they are not "art"? Or shall we read them, but read them in a different way, with a different aim? Shall we read them in the first place to satisfy that curiosity which possesses us sometimes when in the evening we linger in front of a house where the lights are lit and the blinds not yet drawn, and each floor of the house shows us a different section of human life in being? Then we are consumed with curiosity about the lives of these people — the servants gossiping, the gentlemen dining, the girl dressing for a party, the old woman at the window with her knitting. Who are they, what are they, what are their names, their occupations, their thoughts, and adventures?

6   Biographies and memoirs answer such questions, light up innumerable such houses; they show us people going about their daily affairs, toil-

ing, failing, succeeding, eating, hating, loving, until they die. And sometimes as we watch, the house fades and the iron railings vanish and we are out at sea; we are hunting, sailing, fighting; we are among savages and soldiers; we are taking part in great campaigns. Or if we like to stay here in England, in London, still the scene changes; the street narrows; the house becomes small, cramped, diamond-paned, and malodorous. We see a poet, Donne, driven from such a house because the walls were so thin that when the children cried their voices cut through them. We can follow him, through the paths that lie in the pages of books, to Twickenham; to Lady Bedford's Park, a famous meeting-ground for nobles and poets; and then turn our steps to Wilton, the great house under the downs, and hear Sidney read the *Arcadia* to his sister; and ramble among the very marshes and see the very herons that figure in that famous romance; and then again travel north with that other Lady Pembroke, Anne Clifford, to her wild moors, or plunge into the city and control our merriment at the sight of Gabriel Harvey in his black velvet suit arguing about poetry with Spenser. Nothing is more fascinating than to grope and stumble in the alternate darkness and splendour of Elizabethan London. But there is no staying there. The Temples and the Swifts, the Harleys and the St. Johns beckon us on; hour upon hour can be spent disentangling their quarrels and deciphering their characters; and when we tire of them we can stroll on, past a lady in black wearing diamonds, to Samuel Johnson and Goldsmith and Garrick; or cross the channel, if we like, and meet Voltaire and Diderot, Madame du Deffand; and so back to England and Twickenham − how certain places repeat themselves and certain names! − where Lady Bedford had her Park once and Pope lived later, to Walpole's home at Strawberry Hill. But Walpole introduces us to such a swarm of new acquaintances, there are so many houses to visit and bells to ring that we may well hesitate for a moment, on the Miss Berrys' doorstep, for example, when behold, up comes Thackeray; he is the friend of the woman whom Walpole loved; so that merely by going from friend to friend, from garden to garden, from house to house, we have passed from one end of English literature to another and wake to find ourselves here again in the present, if we can so differentiate this moment from all that have gone before. This, then, is one of the ways in which we can read these lives and letters; we can make them light up the many windows of the past; we can watch the famous dead in their familiar habits and fancy sometimes that we are very close and can surprise their secrets, and sometimes we may pull out a play or a poem that they have written

and see whether it reads differently in the presence of the author. But
this again rouses other questions. How far, we must ask ourselves, is
a book influenced by its writer's life — how far is it safe to let the man
interpret the writer? How far shall we resist or give way to the sympathies and antipathies that the man himself rouses in us — so sensitive
are words, so receptive of the character of the author? These are questions that press upon us when we read lives and letters, and we must
answer them for ourselves, for nothing can be more fatal than to be
guided by the preferences of others in a matter so personal.

7   But also we can read such books with another aim, not to throw light
on literature, not to become familiar with famous people, but to refresh
and exercise our own creative powers. Is there not an open window
on the right hand of the bookcase? How delightful to stop reading and
look out! How stimulating the scene is, in its unconsciousness, its ir-
relevance, its perpetual movement — the colts galloping round the field,
the woman filling her pail at the well, the donkey throwing back his
head and emitting his long, acrid moan. The greater part of any library
is nothing but the record of such fleeting moments in the lives of men,
women, and donkeys. Every literature, as it grows old, has its rubbish-
heap, its record of vanished moments and forgotten lives told in filter-
ing and feeble accents that have perished. But if you give yourself up
to the delight of rubbish-reading you will be surprised, indeed you will
be overcome, by the relics of human life that have been cast out to
moulder. It may be one letter — but what a vision it gives! It may be
a few sentences — but what vistas they suggest! Sometimes a whole
story will come together with such beautiful humour and pathos and
completeness that it seems as if a great novelist had been at work, yet
it is only an old actor, Tate Wilkinson, remembering the strange story
of Captain Jones; it is only a young subaltern serving under Arthur
Wellesley and falling in love with a pretty girl at Lisbon; it is only Maria
Allen letting fall her sewing in the empty drawing-room and sighing
how she wishes she had taken Dr. Burney's good advice and had never
eloped with her Rishy. None of this has any value; it is negligible in
the extreme; yet how absorbing it is now and again to go through the
rubbish-heaps and find rings and scissors and broken noses buried in
the huge past and try to piece them together while the colt gallops round
the field, the woman fills her pail at the well, and the donkey brays.

But we tire of rubbish-reading in the long run. We tire of searching
for what is needed to complete the half-truth which is all that the Wilkin-
sons, the Bunburys, and the Maria Allens are able to offer us. They

had not the artist's power of mastering and eliminating; they could not
tell the whole truth even about their own lives; they have disfigured
the story that might have been so shapely. Facts are all that they can
offer us, and facts are a very inferior form of fiction. Thus the desire
grows upon us to have done with half-statements and approximations;
to cease from searching out the minute shades of human character, to
enjoy the greater abstractness, the purer truth of fiction. Thus we create
the mood, intense and generalised, unaware of detail, but stressed by
some regular, recurrent beat, whose natural expression is poetry; and
that is the time to read poetry — when we are almost able to write it.

> Western wind, when wilt thou blow?
> The small rain down can rain.
> Christ, if my love were in my arms,
> And I in my bed again!

The impact of poetry is so hard and direct that for the moment there 9
is no other sensation except that of the poem itself. What profound depths
we visit then — how sudden and complete is our immersion! There is
nothing here to catch hold of; nothing to stay us in our flight. The illusion of fiction is gradual; its effects are prepared; but who when they
read these four lines stops to ask who wrote them, or conjures up the
thought of Donne's house or Sidney's secretary; or enmeshes them in
the intricacy of the past and the succession of generations? The poet
is always our contemporary. Our being for the moment is centred and
constricted, as in any violent shock of personal emotion. Afterwards,
it is true, the sensation begins to spread in wider rings through our minds;
remoter senses are reached; these begin to sound and to comment and
we are aware of echoes and reflections. The intensity of poetry covers
an immense range of emotion. We have only to compare the force and
directness of

> I shall fall like a tree, and find my grave,
>   Only remembering that I grieve,

with the wavering modulation of

> Minutes are numbered by the fall of sands,
> As by an hour glass; the span of time
> Doth waste us to our graves, and we look on it;
> An age of pleasure, revelled out, comes home
> At last, and ends in sorrow; but the life,
> Weary of riot, numbers every sand,

> Wailing in sighs, until the last drop down,
> So to conclude calamity in rest,

or place the meditative calm of

> whether we be young or old,
> Our destiny, our being's heart and home,
> Is with infinitude, and only there;
> With hope it is, hope that can never die,
> Effort, and expectation, and desire,
> And something evermore about to be,

beside the complete and inexhaustible loveliness of

> The moving Moon went up the sky,
> And no where did abide:
> Softly she was going up,
> And a star or two beside —

or the splendid fantasy of

> And the woodland haunter
> Shall not cease to saunter
>   When, far down some glade,
> Of the great world's burning,
> One soft flame upturning
> Seems, to his discerning,
>   Crocus in the shade.

to bethink us of the varied art of the poet; his power to make us at once actors and spectators; his power to run his hand into character as if it were a glove, and be Falstaff or Lear; his power to condense, to widen, to state, once and for ever.

10   "We have only to compare" — with those words the cat is out of the bag, and the true complexity of reading is admitted. The first process, to receive impressions with the utmost understanding, is only half the process of reading; it must be completed, if we are to get the whole pleasure from a book, by another. We must pass judgment upon these multitudinous impressions; we must make of these fleeting shapes one that is hard and lasting. But not directly. Wait for the dust of reading to settle; for the conflict and the questioning to die down; walk, talk, pull the dead petals from a rose, or fall asleep. Then suddenly without our willing it, for it is thus that Nature undertakes these transitions, the book will return, but differently. It will float to the top of the mind as a whole. And the book as a whole is different from the book re-

ceived currently in separate phrases. Details now fit themselves into their places. We see the shape from start to finish; it is a barn, a pigsty, or a cathedral. Now then we can compare book with book as we compare building with building. But this act of comparison means that our attitude has changed; we are no longer the friends of the writer, but his judges; and just as we cannot be too sympathetic as friends, so as judges we cannot be too severe. Are they not criminals, books that have wasted our time and sympathy; are they not the most insidious enemies of society, corrupters, defilers, the writers of false books, faked books, books that fill the air with decay and disease? Let us then be severe in our judgments; let us compare each book with the greatest of its kind. There they hang in the mind, the shapes of the books we have read solidified by the judgments we have passed on them – *Robinson Crusoe, Emma, The Return of the Native.* Compare the novels with these – even the latest and least of novels has a right to be judged with the best. And so with poetry – when the intoxication of rhythm has died down and the splendour of words has faded, a visionary shape will return to us and this must be compared with *Lear*, with *Phèdre*, with *The Prelude*; or if not with these, with whatever is the best or seems to us to be the best in its own kind. And we may be sure that the newness of new poetry and fiction is its most superficial quality and that we have only to alter slightly, not to recast, the standards by which we have judged the old.

It would be foolish, then, to pretend that the second part of reading, to judge, to compare, is as simple as the first – to open the mind wide to the fast flocking of innumerable impressions. To continue reading without the book before you, to hold one shadow-shape against another, to have read widely enough and with enough understanding to make such comparisons alive and illuminating – that is difficult; it is still more difficult to press further and to say, "Not only is the book of this sort, but it is of this value; here it fails; here it succeeds; this is bad; that is good." To carry out this part of a reader's duty needs such imagination, insight, and learning that it is hard to conceive any one mind sufficiently endowed; impossible for the most self-confident to find more than the seeds of such powers in himself. Would it not be wiser, then, to remit this part of reading and to allow the critics, the gowned and furred authorities of the library, to decide the question of the book's absolute value for us? Yet how impossible! We may stress the value of sympathy; we may try to sink our own identity as we read. But we know that we cannot sympathise wholly or immerse ourselves wholly;

there is always a demon in us who whispers, "I hate, I love," and we cannot silence him. Indeed, it is precisely because we hate and we love that our relation with the poets and novelists is so intimate that we find the presence of another person intolerable. And even if the results are abhorrent and our judgments are wrong, still our taste, the nerve of sensation that sends shocks through us, is our chief illuminant; we learn through feeling; we cannot suppress our own idiosyncrasy without impoverishing it. But as time goes on perhaps we can train our taste; perhaps we can make it submit to some control. When it has fed greedily and lavishly upon books of all sorts — poetry, fiction, history, biography — and has stopped reading and looked for long spaces upon the variety, the incongruity of the living world, we shall find that it is changing a little; it is not so greedy, it is more reflective. It will begin to bring us not merely judgments on particular books, but it will tell us that there is a quality common to certain books. Listen, it will say, what shall we call *this*? And it will read us perhaps *Lear* and then perhaps the *Agamemnon* in order to bring out that common quality. Thus, with our taste to guide us, we shall venture beyond the particular book in search of qualities that group books together; we shall give them names and thus frame a rule that brings order into our perceptions. We shall gain a further and a rarer pleasure from that discrimination. But as a rule only lives when it is perpetually broken by contact with the books themselves — nothing is easier and more stultifying than to make rules which exist out of touch with facts, in a vacuum — now at last, in order to steady ourselves in this difficult attempt, it may be well to turn to the very rare writers who are able to enlighten us upon literature as an art. Coleridge and Dryden and Johnson, in their considered criticism, the poets and novelists themselves in their unconsidered sayings, are often surprisingly relevant; they light up and solidify the vague ideas that have been tumbling in the misty depths of our minds. But they are only able to help us if we come to them laden with questions and suggestions won honestly in the course of our own reading. They can do nothing for us if we herd ourselves under their authority and lie down like sheep in the shade of a hedge. We can only understand their ruling when it comes in conflict with our own and vanquishes it.

12   If this is so, if to read a book as it should be read calls for the rarest qualities of imagination, insight, and judgment, you may perhaps conclude that literature is a very complex art and that it is unlikely that we shall be able, even after a lifetime of reading, to make any valuable contribution to its criticism. We must remain readers; we shall not put

on the further glory that belongs to those rare beings who are also critics. But still we have our responsibilities as readers and even our importance. The standards we raise and the judgments we pass steal into the air and become part of the atmosphere which writers breathe as they work. An influence is created which tells upon them even if it never finds its way into print. And that influence, if it were well instructed, vigorous and individual and sincere, might be of great value now when criticism is necessarily in abeyance; when books pass in review like the procession of animals in a shooting gallery, and the critic has only one second in which to load and aim and shoot and may well be pardoned if he mistakes rabbits for tigers, eagles for barndoor fowls, or misses altogether and wastes his shot upon some peaceful cow grazing in a further field. If behind the erratic gunfire of the press the author felt that there was another kind of criticism, the opinion of people reading for the love of reading, slowly and unprofessionally, and judging with great sympathy and yet with great severity, might this not improve the quality of his work? And if by our means books were to become stronger, richer, and more varied, that would be an end worth reaching.

Yet who reads to bring about an end, however desirable? Are there **13** not some pursuits that we practise because they are good in themselves, and some pleasures that are final? And is not this among them? I have sometimes dreamt, at least, that when the Day of Judgment dawns and the great conquerors and lawyers and statesmen come to receive their rewards — their crowns, their laurels, their names carved indelibly upon imperishable marble — the Almighty will turn to Peter and will say, not without a certain envy when He sees us coming with our books under our arms, "Look, these need no reward. We have nothing to give them here. They have loved reading."

(1932)

The Writer's Subject

1. Why does Woolf put her title in the form of a question?

2. What is the difficulty facing a reader in a library? (para. 2)

3. What, according to Woolf, should be the reader's attitude to the author whose work one is reading? (para. 3)

4. What, according to Woolf, is "the quickest way to begin to understand the elements of what a novelist is doing"? (paras. 3-4)

5. What accounts for the interest most readers have in works of biography and autobiography? (paras. 5-6)

6. What does Woolf mean by "the delight of rubbish-reading"? What is missing from such reading? (paras. 7-8)

7. What does Woolf mean by the statement, "The poet is always our contemporary"? (para. 9)

8. What are the two halves of the process of reading, as Woolf sees it? (para. 10) How does the second half of the process alter the reader's relationship with the writer which she describes in paragraph 3?

9. What importance does Woolf attach to individual taste? How is this taste formed? (para. 11)

10. At what stage in reading may the reader wish "to turn to the very rare writers who are able to enlighten us upon literature as an art"? (para. 11)

11. In what way may readers have an effect upon writers? (para. 12)

12. What, finally, is the reward of reading? (para. 13)

The Writer's Style and Strategy

1. How does Woolf organize her ideas in this essay? How does she divide and sub-divide her materials? What are the stages by which Woolf moves from her opening rejection of critical advice and judgment to her eventual assertion of their importance?

2. In paragraph 2, Woolf introduces the donkey, the women, and the colts outside the library window. What is her purpose, and what use does she make of them elsewhere in her essay?

3. What is Woolf's purpose in beginning over a third of her paragraphs with the word "But"?

4. What extended analogies does Woolf use to clarify her ideas about the appeal of biography? (paras. 5-6)

5. Discuss the ways in which Woolf makes use of example. What purposes do the examples serve in paragraph 4? in paragraph 6? in paragraph 7?

6. Discuss the effectiveness of Woolf's use of poetic quotation in paragraph 9.

7. Comment on Woolf's use of metaphorical language in paragraph 10. How does the writer's use of images here enhance her ideas?

8. Although Woolf's paragraphs are unusually long, they are all highly unified. Choose one paragraph and show how Woolf achieves this unity.

Suggested Topics for Writing and Discussion

1. Woolf speaks of the delight of "rubbish-reading." Choose two or three books that you think might be placed in such a category, and explain what pleasure a reader might derive from them.

2. Woolf says, "The poet is always our contemporary." Using the work of one poet not alive today, write an essay supporting this view.

3. Woolf says that books "return" to us at unexpected moments. Is there a book which has returned to you in this way? Try to account for its power over you.

4. Woolf ends her essay by saying that reading is its own reward. Do you agree?

The Media

The Art of Moving Pictures
by Bruno Bettelheim

Whether we like it or not — and many may disagree with my thesis 1
because painting, or music, or some other art is more important to them
— the art of the moving image is the only art truly of our time, whether
it is in the form of the film or television. The moving picture is our
universal art, which comprises all others, literature and acting, stage
design and music, dance and the beauty of nature, and, most of all,
the use of light and of color.

It is always about us, because the medium is truly part of the message 2
and the medium of the moving image is uniquely modern. Everybody
can understand it, as everyone once understood religious art in church.
And as people used to go to church on Sundays (and still do), so the
majority today go to the movies on weekends. But while in the past
most went to church only on some days, now everybody watches moving
images every day.

All age groups watch moving pictures, and they watch them for many 3
more hours than people have ever spent in churches. Children and adults
watch them separately or together; in many ways and for many people,
it is the only experience common to parents and children. It is the only
art today that appeals to all social and economic classes, in short, that
appeals to everybody, as did religious art in times past. The moving
picture is thus by far the most popular art of our time, and it is also
the most authentically American of arts.

When I speak here of the moving picture as the authentic American 4
art of our time, I do not think of art with a capital *A*, nor of "high"
art. Putting art on a pedestal robs it of its vitality. When the great

medieval and Renaissance cathedrals were erected, and decorated outside and in with art, these were popular works, that meant something
to everybody.

5   Some were great works of art, others not, but every piece was significant and all took pride in each of them. Some gain their spiritual experience from the masterpiece, but many more gain it from the mediocre
works that express the same vision as the masterpiece but in a more
accessible form. This is as true for church music or the church itself
as for paintings and sculptures. This diversity of art objects achieves
a unity, and differences in quality are important, provided they all represent, each in its own way, the overarching vision and experience of
a larger, important cosmos. Such a vision confers meaning and dignity
on our existence, and is what forms the essence of art.

6   So among the worst detriments to the healthy development of the art
of the moving image are efforts by aesthetes and critics to isolate the
art of film from popular movies and television. Nothing could be more
contrary to the true spirit of art. Whenever art was vital, it was always
equally popular with the ordinary man and the most refined person.
Had Greek drama and comedy meant nothing to most citizens, the
majority of the population would not have sat all day long entranced
on hard stone slabs, watching the events on the stage; nor would the
entire population have conferred prizes on the winning dramatist. The
medieval pageants and mystery plays out of which modern drama grew
were popular entertainments, as were the plays of Shakespeare.
Michelangelo's David stood at the most public place in Florence, em-
bodying the people's vision that tyranny must be overthrown, while it
also related to their religious vision, as it represented the myth of
David and Goliath. Everybody admired the statue; it was simultaneously
popular and great art but one did not think of it in such disparate terms.
Neither should we. To live well we need both: visions that lift us up,
and entertainment that is down to earth, provided both art and entertainment, each in its different form and way, are embodiments of the
same visions of man. If art does not speak to all of us, common men
and elites alike, it fails to address itself to that true humanity that is
common to all of us. A different art for the elites and another one for
average man tears society apart; it offends what we most need: visions
that bind us together in common experiences that make life worth living.

7   When I speak of an affirmation of man, I do not mean the presentation of fake images of life as wonderfully pleasant. Life is best celebrated
in the form of battle against its inequities, of struggles, of dignity in

defeat, of the greatness of discovering oneself and the other.

Quite a few moving pictures have conveyed such visions. In **8** *Kagemusha,* the great beauty of the historical costumes, the cloak-and-dagger story with its beguiling Oriental settings, the stately proceedings, the pageantry of marching and fighting armies, the magnificent rendering of nature, the consummate acting — all these entrance us and convince us of the correctness of the vision here: the greatness of the most ordinary of men. The hero, a petty thief who turns impostor, grows before our eyes into greatness, although it costs him his life. The story takes place in sixteenth-century Japan, but the hero is of all times and places: he accepts a destiny into which he is projected by chance and turns a false existence into a real one. At the end, only because he wants to be true to his new self, he sacrifices his life and thus achieves the acme of suffering and human greatness. Nobody wants him to do so. Nobody but he will ever know that he did it. Nobody but the audience observes it. He does it only for himself; it has no consequences whatsoever for anybody or anything else. He does it out of conviction; this is his greatness. Life that permits the lowest of men to achieve such dignity is life worth living, even if in the end it defeats him, as it will defeat all who are mortal.

Two other films, very different, render parallel visions that celebrate **9** life, a celebration in which we, as viewers, vicariously participate although we are saddened by the hero's defeat. The first was known in the United States by its English name, *The Last Laugh,* although its original title, *The Last Man,* was more appropriate. It is the story of the doorman of a hotel who is demoted to cleaning washrooms. The other movie is *Patton.* In one of these films the hero stands on the lowest rung of society and existence; in the other, he is on society's highest level. In both pictures we are led to admire a man's struggle to discover who he really is, for, in doing so, he achieves tragic greatness. These three films, as do many others, affirm man and life, and so inspire in us visions that can sustain us.

My choice of these three films out of many is arbitrary. What I want **10** to illustrate is their celebration of life in forms appropriate to an age in which self-discovery may exact the highest possible price. Only through incorporating such visions can we achieve satisfaction with our own life, and defeat and transcend existential despair.

What our society suffers from most today is the absence of consen- **11** sus about what it and life in it ought to be. Such consensus cannot be gained from society's present stage, or from fantasies about what it ought to be. For that the present is too close and too diversified, and the future too uncertain, to make believable claims about it. A consensus in the present hence can be achieved only through a shared understanding of the past, as Homer's epics informed those who lived centuries later what it meant to be Greek, and by what images and ideals they were to live their lives and organize their societies.

12   Most societies derive consensus from a long history, a language all their own, a common religion, common ancestry. The myths by which they live are based on all of these. But the United States is a country of immigrants, coming from a great variety of nations. Lately, it has been emphasized that an asocial, narcissistic personality has become characteristic of Americans, and that it is this type of personality that makes for the malaise, because it prevents us from achieving a consensus that would counteract a tendency to withdraw into private worlds. In his study of narcissism, Christopher Lasch says that modern man, "tortured by self-consciousness, turns to new cults and therapies not to free himself of his personal obsessions but to find meaning and purpose in life, to find something to live for." There is wide-spread distress because national morale has declined, and we have lost an earlier sense of national vision and purpose.

13   Contrary to rigid religions or political beliefs, as are found in totalitarian societies, our culture is one of great individual differences, at least in principle and in theory. But this leads to disunity, even chaos. Americans believe in the value of diversity, but just because ours is a society based on individual diversity, it needs consensus about some overarching ideas more than societies based on the uniform origin of their citizens. Hence, if we are to have consensus, it must be based on a myth — a vision — about a common experience, a conquest that made us Americans, as the myth about the conquest of Troy formed the Greeks. Only a common myth can offer relief from the fear that life is without meaning or purpose. Myths permit us to examine our place in the world by comparing it to a shared idea. Myths are shared fantasies that form the tie that binds the individual to other members of his group. Such myths help to ward off feelings of isolation, guilt, anxiety, and purposelessness — in short, they combat isolation and anomie.

14   We used to have a myth that bound us together; in *The American Adam*, R.W.B. Lewis summarizes the myth by which Americans used to live:

God decided to give man another chance by opening up a new world across the sea. Practically vacant, this glorious land had almost inexhaustible natural resources. Many people came to this new world. They were people of special energy, self-reliance, intuitive intelligence, and purity of heart. . . This nation's special mission in the world would be to serve as the moral guide for all other nations.

The movies used to transmit this myth, particularly the westerns, which 15 presented the challenge of bringing civilization to places where before there was none. The same movies also suggested the danger of that chaos; the wagon train symbolized the community men must form on such a perilous journey into the untamed wilderness, which in turn became a symbol for all that is untamed within ourselves. Thus the western gave us a vision of the need for cooperation and civilization, because without it man would perish. Another symbol often used in these westerns was the railroad, which formed the link between wilderness and civilization. The railroad was the symbol of man's role as civilizer.

Robert Warshow delineates in *The Immediate Experience* how the 16 hero of the western − the gunfighter − symbolizes man's potential: to become either an outlaw or a sheriff. In the latter role, the gunfighter was the hero of the past, and his opening of the West was our mythos, our equivalent of the Trojan War. Like all such heroes, the sheriff experienced victories and defeats, but, through these experiences, he grew wiser and learned to accept the limitations that civilization imposes.

This was a wonderful vision of man − or the United States − in 17 the New World; it was a myth by which one could live and grow, and it served as a consensus about what it meant to be an American. But although most of us continue to enjoy this myth, by now it has lost most of its vitality. We have become too aware of the destruction of nature and of the American Indian − part of the reality of opening the West − to be able to savor this myth fully; and, just as important, it is based on an open frontier that no longer exists. But the nostalgic infatuation with the western suggests how much we are in need of a myth about the past that cannot be invalidated by the realities of today. We want to share a vision, one that would enlighten us about what it means to be an American today, so that we can be proud not only of our heritage but also of the world we are building together.

Unfortunately, we have no such myth, nor, by extension, any that 18 reflects what is involved in growing up. The child, like the society, needs such myths to provide him with ideas of what difficulties are involved in maturation. Fairy tales used to fill this need, and they would still do so, if we would take them seriously. But sugar-sweet movies of the Disney variety fail to take seriously the world of the child — the immense problems with which the child has to struggle as he grows up, to make himself free from the bonds that tie him to his parents, and to test his own strength. Instead of helping the child, who wants to understand the difficulties ahead, these shows talk down to him, insult his intelligence, and lower his aspirations.

19   While most of the popular shows for children fall short of what the child needs most, others at least provide him with some of the fantasies that relieve pressing anxieties, and this is the reason for their popularity. Superman, Wonder Woman, and the Bionic Woman stimulate the child's fantasies about being strong and invulnerable, and this offers some relief from being overwhelmed by the powerful adults who control his existence. The Incredible Hulk affords a confrontation with destructive anger. Watching the Hulk on one of his rampages permits a vicarious experience of anger without having to feel guilty about it or anxious about the consequences, because the Hulk attacks only bad people. As food for fantasies that offer temporary relief, such shows have a certain value, but they do not provide material leading to higher integration, as myths do.

20   Science-fiction movies can serve as myths about the future and thus give us some assurance about it. Whether the film is *2001* or *Star Wars,* such movies tell about progress that will expand man's powers and his experiences beyond anything now believed possible, while they assure us that all these advances will not obliterate man or life as we now know it. Thus one great anxiety about the future — that it will have no place for us as we now are — is allayed by such myths. They also promise that even in the most distant future, and despite the progress that will have occurred in the material world, man's basic concerns will be the same, and the struggle of good against evil — the central moral problem of our time — will not have lost its importance.

21   Past and future are the lasting dimensions of our lives; the present is but a fleeting moment. So these visions about the future also contain our past; in *Star Wars,* battles are fought around issues that also motivated man in the past. There is good reason that Yoda appears in George Lucas's film: he is but a reincarnation of the teddy bear of infancy, to which we turn for solace; and the Yedi Knight is the wise old man, or the helpful animal, of the fairy tale, the promise from our

distant past that we shall be able to rise to meet the most difficult tasks life can present us with. Thus any vision about the future is really based on visions of the past, because that is all we can know for certain.

As our religious myths about the future never went beyond Judgment 22 Day, so our modern myths about the future cannot go beyond the search for life's deeper meaning. The reason is that only as long as the choice between good and evil remains man's paramount moral problem does life retain that special dignity that derives from our ability to choose between the two. A world in which this conflict has been permanently resolved eliminates man as we know him. It might be a universe peopled by angels, but it has no place for man.

What Americans need most is a consensus that includes the idea of 23 individual freedom, as well as acceptance of the plurality of ethnic backgrounds and religious beliefs inherent in the population. Such consensus must rest on convictions about moral values and the validity of overarching ideas. Art can do this because a basic ingredient of the aesthetic experience is that it binds together diverse elements. But only the ruling art of a period is apt to provide such unity: for the Greeks, it was classical art; for the British, Elizabethan art; for the many petty German states, it was their classical art. Today, for the United States, it has to be the moving picture, the central art of our time, because no other art experience is so open and accessible to everyone.

The moving picture is a visual art, based on sight. Speaking to our 24 vision, it ought to provide us with the visions enabling us to live the good life; it ought to give us insight into ourselves. About a hundred years ago, Tolstoy wrote, "Art is a human activity having for its purpose the transmission to others of the highest and best feelings to which men have risen." Later, Robert Frost defined poetry as "beginning in delight and ending in wisdom." Thus it might be said that the state of the art of the moving image can be assessed by the degree to which it meets the mythopoetic task of giving us myths suitable to live by in our time — visions that transmit to us the highest and best feelings to which men have risen — and by how well the moving images give us that delight which leads to wisdom. Let us hope that the art of the moving image, this most authentic American art, will soon meet the challenge of becoming truly the great art of our age.

(1981)

The Writer's Subject

1. Why does Bettelheim regard the moving picture as the "only art truly of our time" (paras. 1-4)?

2. What is the point of the analogy between going to the movies and going to church? (para. 2)

3. Why does Bettelheim insist that mediocre works of art are as important as masterpieces in conferring "meaning and dignity on our existence" (para. 5)? Why does Bettelheim argue against an art for the élite?

4. What common qualities of heroes does Bettelheim identify in the movies *Kagemusha, The Last Laugh,* and *Patton*? Why does he attach such importance to movies of this kind? (paras. 8 and 9)

5. Why, according to Bettelheim, does a society need common myths? (paras. 10-14)

6. Bettelheim says that Americans used to be bound together by a myth. What was this myth? In what ways was this myth expressed in the Western movie? Why has the Western lost its vitality as myth? (paras. 15-17)

7. What mythic qualities are embodied in science fiction movies, according to Bettelheim? (paras. 20-21)

8. Why does Bettelheim compare the art of the moving picture in the United States to classical art in Greece and Elizabethan art in Britain? (para. 23)

The Writer's Style and Strategy

1. Bettelheim asserts that the efforts of aesthetes and critics to distinguish the art of film from popular movies and television are "contrary to the true spirit of art" (para. 6). What method does he use to support his argument?

2. "Vision" is a key word in this essay. Examine Bettelheim's use of this word, and show its importance to his central argument.

3. What use does Bettelheim make of examples to demonstrate his point that, for modern audiences, science fiction films have taken over the role of myth?

4. Show the relationship between the opening and closing sentences of the essay, and comment on their different emphases.

Suggested Topics for Writing and Discussion

1. Choose a science fiction film with which you are familiar and argue for it as myth.

2. According to Bettelheim, the American myth focused on a new world, a myth often embodied in Westerns. What myth do you think characterizes the Canadian experience? In what form has this myth found expression?

3. Do you agree with Bettelheim's assertion that movies of the Disney variety "talk down to [the child], insult his intelligence, and lower his aspirations"? Use specific examples to explain your view.

4. The heroes of television programs, films and books can tell us a great deal about the values and attitudes of our society. Choose one hero from a contemporary television program, film or book and explain what that hero tells us about our values and attitudes. Be specific and detailed in your response.

At War with the Army
by Simone Collier

1   It all starts with the pelt-pelt-pelt of pebbles against tarpaulin. That's when
    everything gets surreal. It is the evening of September 6, 1990, almost six
    months since Mohawk Warriors mounted their barricade at Kanesatake,
    30 kilometres west of Montreal, in a dramatic bid to keep a golf course from
    spreading onto their ancestral land. Tensions between the Mohawks and
    the army, which has been called in to disperse them, increase with each
    day that passes. Tonight they are extreme. Five days ago the army ad-
    vanced, squeezing the Warriors back onto their last couple of acres. Three
    days ago the soldiers sealed them in with massive rolls of razor wire. And
    now the soldiers are aiming pebbles at the tarpaulin the Mohawks erected
    to shield themselves from the glare of army searchlights. Pelt-pelt-pelt-pelt.
2   A Mohawk woman walks out from behind the plastic covering. The
    soldiers (whom Prime Minister Brian Mulroney will later congratulate for
    their "forbearance") shout obscenities at her, the mildest of them being
    "bitch" and "squaw." Infuriated, the Warriors shout back. One lunges out
    and pounds the razor wire with a baseball bat.
3   The soldiers raise their rifles and run back and forth, taunting the
    Mohawks. Then the Warrior throws the bat, with a bedroom mirror (used
    to deflect the army's searchlights), across to the soldiers' side of the wire.
4   From behind the tarpaulin, Mohawks — and a band of renegade jour-
    nalists who have ignored army pressure to clear out — watch the shadows
    of soldiers fixing their bayonets for the first time since they replaced the
    Sûreté du Québec (the provincial police) 17 days ago. Major Alain
    Tremblay, commander of C Company of the Royal 22nd Regiment, yells,
    "I'm not going to fuck around here. I have a military job to do, and I'm going
    to do it," and orders his men to "lock and load," a euphemism for "prepare
    to fire." Harry Oakes, an Akwesasne Mohawk known as Beekeeper, orders
    the Warriors to do the same.
5   Then, as quickly as it starts, the confrontation stops. Robert Skidders,

a 53-year-old American Mohawk known as Mad Jap, tells the Warriors to cool it. And they do.

This incident erupted less than 24 hours after the retreat — on orders from **6** the army — of a couple of dozen reporters, photographers and camera operators to a vantage point behind a shoulder-high wall of sandbags half a kilometre from the firing line. Lieutenant-Colonel Pierre Daigle explained that journalists "were simply getting in the way." But the journalists behind the wire stayed there in defiance both of the army and the example set by their more compliant colleagues. They were determined to provide an independent version of events in the Mohawk camp. Without them, as it turns out, the Canadian public would never have known what really happened the night the Oka standoff nearly became a shooting war — the time that came to be called the Night of the Bayonets.

Was either side more (or less) restrained because journalists were **7** standing witness? No one really knows. But there's no doubt that without The Insiders — at least one of whom now faces five criminal charges related to her coverage of the events — the media would have failed miserably in their obligation to provide Canadians with balanced coverage of the Oka crisis. Without the stories filed by The Insiders, media reports — and therefore public sympathy — would have weighed even more heavily in favor of the "official reports" supplied by the army. Which, of course, was exactly what the army was attempting to engineer.

From the moment the army got involved, the outcome of the siege was **8** never in question. At the height of the crisis the army deployed as many as 4,000 soldiers to quell the "uprising" at Oka. When the operation came to an end on September 26, 50 Mohawk men, women and children walked out, along with The Insiders, to face 300 armed soldiers backed up by more than 2,000 others. Quebec Premier Robert Bourassa made the unprecedented decision to call in the army under the National Defence Act — to use the Canadian army against Canadian citizens — in August when he yielded to pressure to replace the Sûreté du Québec. In July, an SQ officer had been shot and killed during an assault on the Mohawks by 100 SQ officers bearing rifles, concussion grenades and tear gas. To date no one has been charged, but negative media coverage of the SQ on this occasion and throughout the crisis was so intense that the army seemed the only answer.

Much more sophisticated than the SQ, the army understood that the **9** standoff was as much a media battle as a military one. It quickly took the PR offensive, smoothly and efficiently maneuvering to control the flow of information to largely acquiescent journalists.

For starters, the army deployed a contingent of 20 public relations **10** personnel to analyze media coverage and prepare its strategists for managing the media. And what that meant, in part, was managing its own image — portraying the soldiers as cool-headed peacekeepers struggling against stereotypical hot-tempered adversaries. The army readily admits that part of its strategy was to get The Insiders, the journalists behind the wire, out of there. "From our perspective, one of the reasons it [the standoff] was dragging on so long was because the journalists were there," says Commodore David Cogden, director general of public affairs for the Department of National Defence. "That's why we decided to tighten up." When The Insiders resisted, the army fought back by tapping telephones, providing self-serving reports of incidents and attempting to discredit journalists reporting from behind the wire. "Their PR people are as good at manipulating the media as the soldiers are at strategic maneuvers," says Julian Sher, president of the Canadian Association of Journalists. Insider and *Globe and Mail* parliamentary correspondent Geoffrey York wrote on September 20: "They say the truth is the first casualty of war. When I see the nightly TV news, heavily influenced by the army's regular briefings to the outside media, I realize how difficult it will be to keep the truth alive."

11   Holed up in the basement of Mohawk headquarters — a two-storey drug and alcohol treatment centre — The Insiders had their next powerful opportunity to bear independent witness to events just 36 hours after the Night of the Bayonets. On the morning of September 8, the army sent four soldiers behind the wire on a reconnaissance mission. Randy Horne, 41, a Warrior known as Spudwrench, was sleeping in a bunker close to the barricade along with a few other older Warriors. They were stationed near the frontlines to prevent confrontations between aggressive young Warriors and soldiers. At 4:30 a.m., following an early morning campfire, Leroy Gabriel, a 22-year-old construction worker nicknamed Splinter, was heading back to his bunker when he spotted two soldiers dragging the badly beaten Spudwrench toward the army side of the wire. Splinter shone his flashlight on the soldiers. They dropped Spudwrench and fled. Spudwrench was in shock, needed 25 stitches to close the gashes in his head, and suffered a concussion.

12   Later that morning the army told reporters outside the barricade (The Outsiders) that the soldiers, two of whom received minor stab wounds, were defending themselves against a Mohawk who had attacked them with a knife. The Insiders told a different story, and by the end of the day the army admitted that the soldiers came upon Spudwrench accidentally and had to "restrain" him from alerting the other Warriors. "I think that is a good example of what would have been reported without the journalists in the

treatment centre," says Outsider Ian Barrett, a photographer working for Reuters. "The army was saying the Mohawks were the aggressors. It was the journalists on the inside who set the record straight."

The Insiders dutifully chronicled all the army's acts of aggression. "There 13 were a lot of instances of abuses when the cameras were not there," says the *Globe*'s York. "The army told the public they would not be crossing the barrier, yet when the cameras were not around, they did." Incidents ranged from the petty — trying to steal the Mohawk flag and a mirror used to deflect searchlights — to the provocative: the day they assaulted Spudwrench they also taunted the Mohawks with a sign that read, "Lazagne [sic] your [sic] dead meat," and was signed "2R22R," short for the 2nd Battalion of The Royal 22nd Regiment. (Lasagna was the nickname of Warrior Ronald Cross.) Insider Ted Cash, who was freelancing for the *Montreal Mirror* and CFCF TV, recalls a particularly chilling encounter of his own. He was peering through a small slit in the tarpaulin one day when a soldier on the other side looked him straight in the eye and said, "You'll be dead tomorrow." Cash walked around to the front of the tarpaulin and asked the soldier what he meant. "He took a few steps back when he realized it was a journalist he had been speaking to," says Cash. "Two other soldiers came up immediately, stood in front of him and said, 'No, no, he didn't say anything.'"

Tension had been mounting ever since September 3 when the razor wire 14 sealed the journalists in along with the Warriors. Until then, they had been free to come and go. But if they left for any reason now, the army would prevent them from returning. Matters were made worse five days later, the day of the Spudwrench beating, when the CBC radio and TV networks pulled five remaining staffers and all the video cameras out from behind the barricade.

News reports of the CBC withdrawal outraged Albert Nerenberg, a 15 freelance columnist for Montreal's *The Gazette,* and freelance photographer Robert Galbraith. "I felt that the CBC had chickened out," says Nerenberg. Galbraith agreed. "The CBC is funded by my money and your money, and those bastards pulled their reporters out. They should have been the last people to leave that place."

The next afternoon Nerenberg, armed with a Sony Camcorder, and 16 Galbraith, with his bag of cameras and lenses, snuck through the barricade while the army was engaged in one of its two daily press briefings. They edged past distracted guards and crawled through a pine forest toward the treatment centre, working their way carefully past trip wires that, if activated, would send up flares. After three tense and tedious hours, they finally reached the centre and joined the other journalists in the filthy, semifinished basement.

17   "It looked like some sort of refugee camp," says Galbraith. Pieces of foam
insulation were spread on the concrete floor and covered with sleeping bags
and blankets. There was one television, one fridge, one sink and one toilet
in a 30 foot by 20 foot area. (Journalists were occasionally permitted to
take a shower, usually cold, in an upstairs washroom.) The room stank of
perspiration and stale cigarettes.

18   But the atmosphere was electric. Since the army turned up the pressure
on the Night of the Bayonets, the journalists were increasingly afraid that
a gun battle was a very real possibility. Some Insiders felt that Nerenberg
and Galbraith had failed to recognize the seriousness of the situation. "There
was a definite risk that sneaking in could have touched off gunfire and put
everyone's lives in danger," says York. "They didn't realize how close it
had come to shooting already." The Insiders were pleased, however, that
once again a video camera was at the scene.

19   Whenever the news came on they rushed to the TV to find out what was
happening outside. And they were horrified to hear the army dismissing
them as "Mohawk sympathizers." That certainly wasn't how The Insiders
saw themselves — or their role in the conflict. They figured other reporters
were covering the other angles — the perspectives of the army, the politicians, the native community, the negotiators. In order for coverage to be
well-rounded and fair, it was essential to get the story from behind the wire
as well. "We never said we had the whole story," says Nerenberg. "We just
said we were talking to the Mohawks. If we had been the only source of
information, that would have been biased. But we were not."

20   According to The Insiders, neither they nor the Mohawks lost sight of
the fact that they were not comrades-in-arms. They did not eat or socialize
together. The journalists initiated most conversations — in the pursuit of
their stories. They kept their own campfire burning. As darkness fell, they
gathered close to the fire for warmth and conversation. It was there that
they discussed group issues, particularly ways and means of maintaining
their impartiality. "We were very aware that we were being seen as a
group," says photographer Shaney Komulainen.

21   The Insiders understood that the standoff was a publicity coup for the
Mohawks. By creating a "media event," the Warriors had made great strides
in generating public support for their cause. But journalists found that the
Mohawks' attempts at media manipulation were not as sophisticated and
premeditated as the army's. The Mohawks tried — usually unsuccessfully — to ban reporters whose stories seemed critical of their actions. As well,
they asked camera crews not to film Warriors without their face masks for
fear of army reprisals. "The Mohawks never told us what to write or what

to shoot," says Insider Ian MacLeod, an *Ottawa Citizen* reporter. "They only pressured us on identification issues." Their attempts at manipulation were mostly staged, face-to-face staredowns with soldiers when cameras were running. Native spokesperson Georges Erasmus, national chief of the Assembly of First Nations, says that the Mohawks were more concerned with being run over by the army on any given day than they were with manipulating the media. "The main thing the Mohawks wanted," he says, "was to get their story out."

On September 14, eight days after the Night of the Bayonets, the army 22 made its next major move against the media. It cut off Insiders' access to all personal supplies — food, film, batteries, clothing and cigarettes. "The army was trying to freeze the journalists out," says Charles Bury, chairman of the Canadian Association of Journalists. "They did everything they could to scare them into leaving." The Insiders were forced to share the rations sent in by the army. "The fact that we sent food in one bunch instead of a journalists' bunch and a native bunch — to us it didn't make any difference," says Commodore Cogden. Sensitive to army accusations of being Mohawk sympathizers, journalists did what they could, short of starving, to remain unbeholden to the Mohawks; they paid for the food they consumed.

The issue of food — both quantity and quality — remains a contentious 23 one. Major Tim Dunne of the Department of National Defence wrote in a letter to *The Ottawa Citizen* last January 10 that "the army provided the 50 Mohawks at the treatment centre with enough food to feed 250 people." "No way," says Insider Ann McLaughlin, a staff reporter for Montreal's *The Gazette*. "It was not enough food to feed 60 people three meals a day." Ian MacLeod agrees: "The food I saw coming in to the Mohawks was not enough to feed 250 people unless each person took only one bite."

At the time, however, the conflicting stories focused on the condition 24 of the food that did arrive. The Insiders reported that the food was frequently inedible because it had been pierced by bayonets and covered with dirt. "On the news," recalls Nerenberg, "the army said it must have happened in the Warrior camp, but we saw the army hand over boxes with cooking oil dripping from them because bottles had been punctured." Ted Cash also saw the food arriving bayoneted and messed up. "From the point of view of security, I would say it was inedible because you didn't know what they put in it. It would have been in the army's interests to put something in the food to make people very ill."

If The Insiders came across as paranoid at times, it was not without good 25 reason. They were, in fact, targets of psychological warfare. Army personnel telephoned journalists individually to "warn" them that the army could "no longer guarantee" their safety. Soldiers offered the same warnings over the razor wire. This was as unnerving as the sleep deprivation tactics that the journalists were forced to endure along with the Mohawks. Many of The Insiders slept outside in sleeping bags until it got too cold. At night, low-flying army helicopters passed eerily overhead, making a peaceful night's sleep difficult. "It was a wonder that we did get to sleep," says Galbraith. "It was sort of like the movie *Apocalypse Now,* that's how it felt. Choppers, flares, taunts every night — it really played a head trip on you." To make matters worse, a septic tank broke down and journalists were driven inside by the stench from the growing cesspool. "The smell would overpower me," recalls Ian MacLeod, "if the wind blew in my direction."

26   Arguably the most powerful psychological weapon in the army's arsenal turned out to be the simple withholding of cigarettes. Half The Insiders were nicotine addicts, and their reactions to abrupt withdrawal caused already taut nerves to fray. Some tried smoking cedar bark or peeled off the paper around old butts and hand-rolled new ones. But quarrels and petty disputes sometimes escalated into physical confrontations. "When supplies and food were cut off," says Shaney Komulainen, "you could feel the tension rise. One of the journalists physically lost his temper a few times. I think that went a bit far, and I think it had a lot to do with the nicotine."

27   The army's next and most aggressive move to restrict freedom of the press was its attempt to totally cut off independent communication with the outside. On the same day it cut off the supplies, the army, through the SQ, obtained a court order to cut off 30 cellular telephones — the only route that remained for journalists to transmit stories. The army claimed the journalists were lending their phones to Warriors who used them to incite acts of sabotage. "They pulled the accusations out of nowhere," says Ann McLaughlin. "If the Warriors were inciting other natives on the outside to create acts of sabotage, they would not do it in front of a bunch of reporters." Adds Ian MacLeod: "It seemed ridiculous to suggest that the Warriors were using our cellular phones to plan acts of sabotage knowing full well that our phones were tapped." (The reporters' suspicions about phone tapping were confirmed when the SQ released the evidence used to obtain the court order.) "It was clearly wrong when the journalists' phones were cut off," says Joe David, a Mohawk artist known as Stonecarver. "Yet there seemed to be a silent acceptance that this was okay. I think the outside journalists took the position that the army was right."

28   Ironically, the army's list of cellular phones was incomplete. Five numbers remained intact, and these phones were shared by journalists. They went to an area they called the phone booth, the only location in the compound where the cellular phones were not affected by the army's

jamming of transmission lines.

The result of all the army's maneuvers against the media was a harden- **29**
ing of The Insiders' resolve. Nerenberg says the soldiers could have and
should have made an effort to treat the journalists in a neutral way. "When
the army put the screws on us," says his colleague Galbraith, "it made us
more determined to stay there and get more reports out. How dare they
try to suppress us like that? We were the eyes of the nation, we were there
telling Canadians what was going on. We did not want to let the army come
in and do their dirty work and come out and tell their own version of the
story."

While the army was tightening the noose on The Insiders, its media **30**
managers were smothering The Outsiders with self-serving generosity.
They conducted helicopter tours and offered rides aboard armored
personnel carriers. They provided background papers, aerial photographs,
camera-ready maps and diagrams, a list of alleged Warrior armaments and
a videotape that made it look like the army would have to use considerable
force to "neutralize" the situation.

The army even conducted walking tours to allow journalists to see their **31**
colleagues — and then forbade them to speak with them. "There we were
behind the razor wire," says MacLeod, "having our pictures taken from
across the road. Some of us were calling out and we were getting no
response. I got the feeling I was in some sort of zoo. This was Canada, and
they were not allowed to talk to me because the army said so." The army
insisted that the touring journalists wear army-issue flak jackets for protection. "I don't find anything unusual about that," says Outsider and Reuters
photographer Ian Barrett. "We were under the army's care and they didn't
want to take any chances that we would get hurt." The army did not,
however, think it necessary to provide jackets for the construction workers
who were assembling searchlight scaffolding just a few feet from the tour
site.

"What really struck me," says Ted Cash, "was that we were taking all **32**
the criticism for being too close to the Mohawks, but that criticism was not
levelled at the journalists who were on organized tours run by the army.
Those journalists were subjected to the most evident limitations that you
can imagine, and yet they did not say anything. They went along with it
all, and nobody criticized them."

The first army-orchestrated media tour came as a surprise to The **33**
Insiders. By the second tour later on the same day, they were better
prepared. *Gazette* photographer John Kenney shot a picture of fellow
Gazetter Ann McLaughlin tying a story to a rock. Kenney took the film
out and wrapped it, along with three other film canisters, with masking

tape. Then McLaughlin and Kenney signalled to *Gazette* reporter Jeff Heinrich to come a bit closer. And they began throwing. A barrage of film canisters and stories from other journalists soon followed, and reporters and soldiers scrambled after them. "I think it showed how ridiculous the army's restrictions on the media were," says the *Globe*'s York. "It drama- tized the fact that the army was censoring the media by preventing them from doing their job." The army cancelled further tours.

34   Journalists behind the wire were surprised — and dismayed — by the readiness with which the outside journalists obeyed the commands of the army. "A lot of the reporters just stood there and obediently took their pictures from far away," says Nerenberg. "Some people say it was because they were Canadians and there is no tradition here of aggressive, get-the- story journalism. It is a very obedient press."

35   The coverage recalls the October Crisis in 1970 when self-censorship ran rampant and few journalists were willing to challenge the government line. "I suspect that is what happened this time," says McLaughlin. "I think people were afraid to write what we were telling them because they were afraid of contradicting the army. We listen to authority. It is scary that the army has so much power."

36   An unrepentant Commodore Cogden says that if the army were ever in a similar position, he would like to see the media cut off much sooner. "And that," says Sher of the Canadian Association of Journalists, "is one of the most significant statements made since the Oka crisis. If the military had their druthers, they would do what the Americans did in Grenada, what the South Africans did in Soweto. They would get the cameras and the journalists out of there."

37   Canadian journalists tend to view media censorship in other countries as the oppressive tactic of a tyrannical government — an offence against democracy. But when the same restrictions were imposed in Canada, most journalists didn't even question them, much less fight them. The *Globe*'s York says outside journalists should have fought harder in the courts, "lobbying or using any pressure tactics they could to have our rights rein- stated. They could have written more stories about censorship. These things would have made a difference." The Mohawk artist Stonecarver asks the larger question: "Is the press supposed to be the conscience of the country or a tool of the state?"

38   Foreign journalists were also surprised at Canadian acquiescence to authority. Rafael Abramovitz, senior correspondent with a US television newsmagazine, *Hard Copy,* tried to find out what was going on behind the barricade. He walked across a gap in the army's sandbag perimeter and over the metal spikes designed to puncture tires. "I thought the rest of the

press would follow my lead, but they all just stood there. They were shocked that I walked over." Abramovitz kept walking toward the treatment centre until a soldier blocked him from going further. "The soldier was doing his job," says Abramovitz, "and I was doing mine. My job was to witness events and try to report what I saw. I take that responsibility very seriously. I did not consider myself one of the sheep that stood where the army told me to stand."

Julian Sher has a kinder perspective: he thinks the reporters caved in **39** largely because they didn't know any better. "Very few journalists cover wars," says Sher, "and I think the army was able to play up to that. The Armed Forces did what they were supposed to do, but it does not mean we have to accept that."

In light of events in the months that have followed, the most contempt- **40** ible army strategy was its campaign to discredit The Insiders. For the army went further than accusing them of being Mohawk sympathizers; on September 16, Brigadier-General Armand Roy labelled them victims of Stockholm syndrome — a characterization that was reported in the media.

The term Stockholm syndrome was coined in 1973 when hostages in that **41** city were trapped in a vault with their captor and became very attached and sympathetic to him. By definition, however, hostages are held involuntarily. The journalists at Oka were free to leave, and restrictions on their movements and communications were enforced by the army, not their alleged captors.

Unfortunately, the inaccuracy of the analogy did not stop the poisonous **42** assault on the journalists' credibility. Once the premise of Stockholm syndrome was accepted, anything the journalists reported that appeared to support the Mohawk position or criticize the army's could be interpreted as symptoms of the disorder. "Even the editors were concerned about Stockholm syndrome," says McLaughlin. "They would ask us if we really knew for a fact that the food was destroyed before it crossed the wire — and we knew because we saw it ourselves."

The Stockholm syndrome label continues to be used against Insiders **43** who, since leaving Oka, attempt to set the record straight. A case in point: On November 16, 1990, the Armed Forces held a Post-Oka Communications Symposium in Ottawa. The object was to review how the army and the media handled the crisis. Joe Scanlon, director of the Emergency Communications Research Unit at Carleton University's school of journalism and an expert on terrorist and hostage-taking incidents called the Mohawk activities "an act of terrorism" and the Warriors' control of the Mercier Bridge "a hostage-taking." The bridge, he explained, was the hostage. "I don't buy that nonsense," says native spokesperson Georges

Erasmus, who had no opportunity to speak at the symposium because no native representatives were invited. "There was an attempt by the Armed Forces to call it an act of terrorism to legitimize everything that they did." While Scanlon acknowledged that journalists who chose to be behind the wire were not held hostage by the Mohawks, he too accused them of suffering from Stockholm syndrome. When Insider Geoffrey York of the *Globe* challenged Scanlon's analysis, he replied: "It would be impossible for you to perceive these events except in the light of your own psychological damage." End of discussion.

44   How do The Insiders feel now that they've put some distance between themselves and the events at Oka? Ann McLaughlin: "It has given me a strong distrust of authority. I will not believe something the army or a policeman says to me ever again without double-checking. I often wonder if my phone is tapped. I have found myself looking over my shoulder to see if anyone is following me." Geoffrey York: "Oka changed my opinion of the army because I thought they were professional and calm and disciplined and so on, and certainly they were not.... Also, I have to assume now that any phone I am using is tapped because the police are still trying to lay charges." Ted Cash: "Oka made it perfectly clear to me that this country is not run in the interests of the people who live here and it shows how willing the government is to use massive military force to respond to anything that threatens its authority."

45   It would be easy for the rest of us to dismiss The Insiders' comments as nothing more than paranoia. Too easy. And completely inaccurate. As it turned out, freelance photographer Shaney Komulainen was the first of The Insiders to have her worst fears confirmed. When it all ended on September 26, Komulainen was arrested by the SQ along with Nerenberg. She was handcuffed, strip-searched and detained for five hours. Last January, while she was in hospital recovering from a car accident that left her with a broken arm and two broken legs, she learned that the SQ had laid charges related to her time at Oka, including possession of a weapon or an imitation of a weapon, threatening and interfering with the work of a peace agent, and participating in a riot. The other Insiders believe that, as a freelancer, she is an easy target. "Are they making an example of her — that you do not defy the army or charges will be laid?" asks McLaughlin.

46   Whatever the outcome of this and perhaps other criminal proceedings, Shaney Komulainen and the rest of The Insiders can take comfort from the sure knowledge that the standoff at Oka ended peacefully, at least in part due to their determination and guts in the face of considerable pressure on all fronts. It has been proven time and again in other countries that when freedom of the press is curtailed, so are human rights. "The Oka crisis

completely changed my opinion of Canada," says Albert Nerenberg, who crawled on his hands and knees for three hours to get behind the wire and was detained, punched, kicked and spit on by an SQ officer when he left. "Canada stopped being a friendly, decent place where nobody gets hurt for no reason. It has turned into a place where anything can happen. They can cut off press freedoms, they can beat people up because it is a 'crisis.' To me, Canada seems frightening now."

(1991)

The Writer's Subject

1. Who were the "Insiders," and why were they in the Mohawk camp at Oka?

2. How, according to Collier, did the Army manipulate the media coverage of the crisis? What evidence does she provide to support her accusation?

3. What was the nature of the relationship between the Insiders and the Mohawks?

4. Were there any attempts at media manipulation by the Mohawks?

5. In what ways, according to Collier, were the Insiders "targets of psychological warfare"? (para. 25)

6. How did the Insiders regard their colleagues on the outside of the wire?

7. Why did the Army call the Insiders victims of the "Stockholm syndrome"? (paras. 40-43)

The Writer's Style and Strategy

1. What is Collier's purpose in this article? Where is it made explicit?

2. Where do Collier's sympathies lie? How is her position made apparent to the reader?

3. Why does Collier put the word "uprising" in quotation marks? (para. 8)

4. Are the two sides facing one another at Oka described differently in the article? How are members of the Army described, in comparison to the Mohawks or the Insiders?

5.   Why does Collier write the opening section of the essay in the present tense?

6.   How does Collier describe the journalists on the outside? What is her attitude towards them?

7.   Is there, in your opinion, any slanting in the way Collier presents her account, or is she fair to both sides?

Suggested Topics for Writing and Discussion

1.   Find and compare two or three accounts by different reporters of the events during the crisis at Oka. Can you detect differences in the presentation of the facts, or in the selection of the facts being reported?

2.   Do you believe that there should be any limits on press freedom? Does the state ever have the right to censor or otherwise control the news media?

3.   Some members of the press went to extraordinary lengths at Oka to make sure that the "inside" story was told. Do you think reporters are justified in using whatever means they can to get their story, even at the risk of their own or other people's lives?

4.   Find out what you can about the use of the media in totalitarian regimes such as Hitler's Germany or the former Soviet Union. How did such regimes employ the press to further their own political ends? Is there any evidence that the press is used to serve such purposes in democratic countries like Canada or the U.S.?

The Grand Illusion
by Robert Fulford

There is something slightly inhuman and robotic about the reporters   1
who deliver the news to us on television. As a class they do not represent humanity. TV news people are never ugly. They are never old and
seldom middle-aged. They are rarely overweight or bald and they do
not wear striking or ungainly clothing. They are never unhappy or ill
at ease. They are, without exception, middle class: no national TV
reporter speaks with a regional or working-class accent, or for that matter
a Rosedale honk or a Westmount whine. Whatever eccentricities they
may have are suppressed. They are chosen not to reflect the audience
but to reflect the way producers believe − perhaps with good reason
− that we want to see our society represented. They appear to be picked as carefully as actors in a play − except that directors of plays often
look for striking or anomalous characteristics and TV news producers
never do.

The script for television news varies only slightly from performance   2
to performance and from actor to actor. As interviewers, TV reporters
ask roughly the same questions of successful politicians and grief stricken
widows ("How do you feel?"). When they address the audience they
maintain an even, cool tone and a direct, noncommittal gaze. They are
affable but never effusive. Their intonation betrays neither delight nor
anger. They are surprised by nothing. They are apparently never excited. Someone being interviewed may shout or burst into tears − that
makes "good television" − but the reporter will remain calm. In general
TV reporters take their subjects, particularly politicians, less seriously
than the subjects take themselves. Often they speak of the people they
cover with a certain easy disdain. Sometimes, as with Peter Trueman

of Global or Roger Mudd of NBC, this reflects the cynicism of long experience; sometimes it appears to be nothing more than a mannerism picked up from other reporters, an attitudinal twitch.

3   The standard TV news item begins brightly, perhaps a bit urgently: the reporter has something important to tell us. Then, in ninety seconds or less, the material is packaged and put in its place and the item ends tidily — always in the same way. Covering a routine fire or the most terrifying hostage-taking, the reporter never fails to conclude with the same earnest glance into the camera, the same dying fall ("Mike Duffy, CBC News, Ottawa"). The reporter is saying: no matter what happens, we are in control.

4   Long ago Marshall McLuhan argued that the facts and ideas we absorb through a medium of communication matter less than the nature of the medium itself. What counts is the form, because the form will determine how we see the world. If we read two or three newspapers a day, then the newspapers — whether we like it or not - shape our way of thinking; if we are confirmed magazine readers, then our minds are influenced by the specific approach of magazines to their subjects. In McLuhan's famous phrase, the medium is the message. Not all of us, of course, read either newspapers or magazines, but nearly all of us watch the news on television and some of us see TV news three or four times a day. Arguably, the TV newscast is the most influential form of mass communication. In Canada it may be even more influential than in the United States, because Canadians have about twice as much news to watch as Americans — we can see theirs as well as ours — and this summer a viewer in Vancouver or Montreal may be equally sophisticated about the Democratic primaries and the Liberal leadership campaign. In Canada, TV news provides one set of facts (American) overlaid on another (Canadian). Perhaps in no other country is so much TV news available, and so much consumed. But when we watch TV news, what do we experience? Aside from the facts themselves, and the occasional idea or overt opinion, what message does television news deliver to us? What attitude does it pass on?

5   One obvious fact about TV reporters is that they convey information much more skilfully than newspaper reporters. The daily newspaper is centuries old, but newspaper reporters — as opposed to editorial writers, columnists, and feature writers — have still not worked out an adequate and convincing way to present data. In the nineteenth century, newspapers developed the "inverted pyramid" news story, in which the crucial facts appear in the heading and the first paragraph. The

material grows less and less consequential until, in the last few paragraphs, when many readers have stopped reading, the least interesting facts are finally dropped in.

That form was set in the early years of the telegraph system, so that 6 if a message were interrupted in the middle the essential facts would still be conveyed. It was maintained through the days when newspapers published many editions; inverted-pyramid news stories could be changed several times through the day and could be hastily cut from the bottom up without the loss of the most essential details. In recent decades newspapers have eliminated many of their editions and there's now much more time to prepare a news page; but such is the atavism of newspaper editors that the inverted pyramid has persisted and still dominates most news pages. It remains, as it was in the beginning, a clumsy and unsatisfactory form of communication. It makes daily newspapers much more boring than they need to be.

By contrast, the TV news report — no more than about three decades 7 old — is a work of art. It has a beginning, a middle, and an end. Its practitioners appear to know instinctively that they must present a thesis, allow for an antithesis, then make a stab at a synthesis. The result is a structured and carefully crafted little drama, without unexplained facts or unanswered questions. Television news stories are much more persuasive than their newspaper equivalents because they appear to make good sense and the reporters appear to be completely in control of their material. The style of TV reporting makes us believe that the whole story has been told, whereas the style of newspaper reporting - with its loose ends and incomplete thoughts — makes us believe we are receiving only a partial account. The effect is partly subconscious but no less real for that.

In structure, TV news stories are closer to the reports in *Time* magazine 8 than to newspaper stories. TV news stories also borrow from commercials: they have some of the same urgency and pacing. In fact, the news people and the producers of commercials appear to learn from each other. In the most professional TV news operations, each report is polished to the point of apparent perfection. Even when an item must be drastically cut — for instance, when items from *The National* are trimmed to fit into the news roundup at 11 p.m. — the style persists. In their most truncated state, TV news stories retain their format; only the most careful viewer will notice the seams.

The superiority of TV news is, of course, purely aesthetic. Newspapers 9 are much more useful. The people who put them out are more knowledgeable than TV reporters, spend more time on research, and earn more respect from the people they write about. TV gets on the air with the news faster than newspapers and displays it more convincingly; but, paradoxically, newspaper editors make society's decisions about what is important. In the United States *The Washington Post* and *The New York Times*, rather than ABC or CBS, decide which public officials must be pilloried, which issue must be pursued; in Canada *The Globe and Mail* fills a similar office.

10   After watching the media for some years from his perch in the prime minister's office, Jim Coutts declared that "Print in Canada still sets the basic day-to-day news and public-affairs agenda for the electronic media — and not the other way around. How often in Ottawa you see the circle operate. A story begins at *The Globe and Mail*. It goes out overnight on the Canadian Press wire, hits radio and television by morning, and re-appears as a question in the House of Commons at two p.m. It goes from there via television cameras to the local and national prime time evening TV news - while the *Globe* and other print media are already launching Round II."

11   Newspapers of course provide far more information than TV, and readers use that information more selectively. Each of us functions privately as an editor. We re-edit the newspaper by passing over stories or whole sections we don't want to read and concentrating on those items that matter to us. Increasingly, newspapers are edited for specialists — those who urgently need many facts on certain subjects. The Montreal *Gazette*, for example, will include far more about local politics than any television station would consider worth carrying; presumably there are people who need to know the details of local government and the *Gazette* may be valuable to them for that alone. Sometimes a newspaper story — on a zoning issue, for example, or a long-running royal commission — will be comprehensible only to those who have followed previous stories.

12   On television everything must be understood by everyone, even those who have not seen previous broadcasts. In a sense TV is the most democratic of media because it assumes that we can all understand whatever subject it decides to cover and implies that those subjects it doesn't cover aren't worth worrying about. It involves all of us in the ritual of finding form and order in disparate and otherwise baffling facts. The central myth of TV news is the breathtakingly audacious idea that *everything* can be understood.

13   Television reporters don't get above themselves, don't exceed their

authority. They never claim superior knowledge — in fact, they don't even hint that they know anything except the facts they are delivering. They are aware, and perhaps the audience is too, that all but very few TV reporters are innocent children when set beside knowledgeable newspaper reporters.

What the TV people have in place of knowledge or wisdom is techni- **14** que and an unerring sense of ritual. They can fit the world together, make sense of it, in a way that other journalists cannot. They make life a dramatic pageant, a series of interesting and satisfying vignettes. They never bore us with the more cumbersome details of reality or the awkward corners of events. The underlying message of their broad- casts is that one plausibly described little event is very much like another.

In this way television news responds to one of our most profound **15** needs: it reduces the chaos of the day to something approaching order. The anthropologist Clifford Geertz has explained that human beings are "symbolizing, conceptualizing, meaning-seeking" animals who wish to "make sense out of our experience, to give it form and order." It is this form that the TV reporter is reaching for as he fits his film and his commentary into a carefully organized "story". Geertz's studies of various primitive tribes convince him that humanity's need for order and explanation is "evidently as real and as pressing as the more familiar biological needs," sustenance and sex. There was a time when many of us routinely satisfied this pattern-seeking need through religion; for people from whose lives religious belief has departed, the manipula- tion of information about the world provides a kind of substitute. TV manipulates information better than any other medium, and however sceptical we are in most other ways we tend to believe in TV news dur- ing the time we are watching it. Indeed, I think we badly want to believe in it.

Those people who appear on our television sets every night, show- **16** ing us their film and explaining what it means, occupy a unique place where the history of technology and the history of culture come together. Technology has made their work possible. Culture — which now acknowledges that almost everything in the universe is uncertain - has made their work extremely important to us, perhaps even necessary. Their central function is to make an incomprehensible world seem, for a few minutes, comprehensible.

(1984)

The Writer's Subject

1. On what grounds does Fulford maintain that "There is something slightly inhuman and robotic" about news reporters? (para. 1)

2. Why is "form" such an important element in the communication of facts and ideas? What is meant by McLuhan's famous phrase, "the medium is the message" (para 4)?

3. Discuss the contrast Fulford draws between the structure and style of news reports prepared for television and the approach taken in newspaper articles. What essential differences does he perceive?

4. "The superiority of TV news is, of course, purely aesthetic. Newspapers are much more useful." What does Fulford mean by "aesthetic" here? What evidence does he bring in support of the second of these contentions? (paras. 7-12)

5. In what way, according to Fulford, has television news become a "kind of substitute" for religion? What human needs does it appear to satisfy? (para. 15)

The Writer's Style and Strategy

1. Fulford writes from the perspective of a print journalist rather than a television journalist. How is his bias revealed?

2. Discuss the diction and the tone of paragraph 3. How does Fulford slant his argument?

3. How does Fulford develop his comparison of news reports on television with those in the print media? (paras. 6-8)

4. Paragraph 10 consists almost entirely of a quotation from Jim Coutts, an aide in the Prime Minister's Office. What is Fulford's purpose in quoting such a highly placed government official?

5. How does the phrase "the myth of TV news" in paragraph 12 convey Fulford's attitude?

Suggested Topics for Writing and Discussion

1. "In Canada, TV news provides one set of facts (American) overlaid on another (Canadian)." Using broadcasts of the evening news on one or two Canadian networks, explain whether you agree with Fulford's assessment of TV news in Canada.

2. Choose one news item of current national or international importance being reported in the press and on television. Compare the ways in which each medium presents the information, and offer your view about their respective strengths and weaknesses.

3. According to Fulford, TV displays news more convincingly than newspapers, "but, paradoxically, newspaper editors make society's decisions about what is important." Choose one or two controversial issues (e.g., an international issue, such as terrorism; an environmental issue, such as acid rain; or a local issue, such as cutbacks in educational funding). Discuss the part that television news or printed news has played in shaping your opinions of these issues.

Who Killed King Kong?

by X.J. Kennedy

1   The ordeal and spectacular death of *King Kong*, the giant ape, undoubtedly has been witnessed by more Americans than have ever seen a performance of *Hamlet, Iphigenia at Aulis,* or even *Tobacco Road.* Since RKO-
Radio Pictures first released *King Kong,* a quarter-century has gone by; yet
year after year, from prints that grow more rain-beaten, from sound
tracks that grow more tinny, ticket-buyers by thousands still pursue
Kong's luckless fight against the forces of technology, tabloid journalism
and the DAR. They see him chloroformed to sleep, see him whisked
from his jungle isle to New York and placed on show, see him burst
his chains to roam the city (lugging a frightened blonde), at last to plunge
from the spire of the Empire State Building, machine gunned by model
airplanes.

2   Though Kong may die, one begins to think his legend unkillable. No
clearer proof of his hold upon the popular imagination may be seen
than what emerged one catastrophic week in March 1955, when New
York WOR-TV programmed Kong for seven evenings in a row (a total
of sixteen showings). Many a rival network vice-president must have
scowled when surveys showed that Kong — the 1933 B-picture — had
lured away fat segments of the viewing populace from such powerful
competitors as Ed Sullivan, Groucho Marx and Bishop Sheen.

3   But even television has failed to run *King Kong* into oblivion. Coffee-
in-the-lobby cinemas still show the old hunk of hokum, with the apology
that in its use of composite shots and animated models the film remains
technically interesting. And no other monster in movie history has won
so devoted a popular audience. None of the plodding mummies, the

stultified draculas, the whitecoated Lugosis with their shiny pinball-machine laboratories, none of the invisible stranglers, berserk robots, or menaces from Mars has ever enjoyed so many resurrections.

Why does the American public refuse to let *King Kong* rest in peace? 4 It is true, I'll admit, that Kong outdid every monster movie before or since in sheer carnage. Producers Cooper and Schoedsack crammed into it dinosaurs, headhunters, riots, aerial battles, bullets, bombs, bloodletting. Heroine Fay Wray, whose function is mainly to scream, shuts her mouth for hardly one uninterrupted minute from first reel to last. It is also true that Kong is larded with good healthy sadism, for those whose joy it is to see the frantic girl dangled from cliffs and harried by pterodactyls. But it seems to me that the abiding appeal of the giant ape rests on other foundations.

Kong has, first of all, the attraction of being manlike. His simian nature 5 gives him one huge advantage over giant ants and walking vegetables in that an audience may conceivably identify with him. Kong's appeal has the quality that established the Tarzan series as American myth — for what man doesn't secretly imagine himself a huge hairy howler against whom no other monster has a chance? If Tarzan recalls the ape in us, then Kong may well appeal to that great-granddaddy primordial brute from whose tribe we have all deteriorated.

Intentionally or not, the producers of *King Kong* encourage this iden- 6 tification by etching the character of Kong with keen sympathy. For the ape is a figure in a tradition familiar to moviegoers: the tradition of the pitiable monster. We think of Lon Chaney in the role of Quasimodo, of Karloff in the original *Frankenstein*. As we watch the Frankenstein monster's fumbling and disastrous attempts to befriend a flower-picking child, our sympathies are enlisted with the monster in his impenetrable loneliness. And so with Kong. As he roars in his chains, while barkers sell tickets to boobs who gape at him, we perhaps feel something more deep than pathos. We begin to sense something of the problem that engaged Eugene O'Neill in *The Hairy Ape*: the dilemma of a displaced animal spirit forced to live in a jungle built by machines.

King Kong, it is true, had special relevance in 1933. Landscapes of 7 the depression are glimpsed early in the film when an impresario, seeking some desperate pretty girl to play the lead in a jungle movie, visits souplines and a Woman's Home Mission. In Fay Wray — who's been caught snitching an apple from a fruitstand — his search is ended. When he gives her a big feed and a movie contract, the girl is magic-carpeted out of the world of the National Recovery Act. And when, in the film's climax, Kong smashes that very Third Avenue landscape in which Fay had wandered hungry, audiences of 1933 may well have felt a personal satisfaction.

What is curious is that audiences of 1960 remain hooked. For in the heart of urban man, one suspects, lurks the impulse to fling a bomb. Though machines speed him to the scene of his daily grind, though IBM comptometers ("freeing the human mind from drudgery") enable him to drudge more efficiently once he arrives, there comes a moment when he wishes to turn upon his machines and kick hell out of them. He wants to hurl his combination radioalarmclock out the bedroom window and listen to its smash. What subway commuter wouldn't love − just for once − to see the downtown express smack head-on into the uptown local? Such a wish is gratified in that memorable scene in Kong that opens with a wideangle shot: interior of a railway car on the Third Avenue El. Straphangers are nodding, the literate refold their newspapers. Unknown to them, Kong has torn away a section of trestle toward which the train now speeds. The motorman spies Kong up ahead, jams on the brakes. Passengers hurtle together like so many peas in a pail. In a window of the car appear Kong's bloodshot eyes. Women shriek. Kong picks up the railway car as if it were a rat, flips it to the street and ties knots in it, or something. To any commuter the scene must appear one of the most satisfactory pieces of celluloid ever exposed.

9   Yet however violent his acts, Kong remains a gentleman. Remarkable is his sense of chivalry. Whenever a fresh boa constrictor threatens Fay, Kong first sees that the lady is safely parked, then manfully thrashes her attacker. (And she, the ingrate, runs away every time his back is turned.) Atop the Empire State Building, ignoring his pursuers, Kong places Fay on a ledge as tenderly as if she were a dozen eggs. He fondles her, then turns to face the Army Air Force. And Kong is perhaps the most disinterested lover since Cyrano: his attentions to the lady are utterly without hope of reward. After all, between a five-foot blonde and a fifty-foot ape, love can hardly be more than an intellectual flirtation. In his simian way King Kong is the hopelessly yearning lover of Petrarchan convention. His forced exit from his jungle, in chains, results directly from his single-minded pursuit of Fay. He smashes a Broadway theater when the notion enters his dull brain that the flashbulbs of photographers somehow endanger the lady. His perilous shinnying up a skyscraper to pluck Fay from her boudoir is an act of the kindliest of hearts. He's impossible to discourage even though the love of his life can't lay eyes on him without shrieking murder.

The tragedy of King Kong then, is to be the beast who at the end   10
of the fable fails to turn into the handsome prince. This is the conviction that the scriptwriters would leave with us in the film's closing line.
As Kong's corpse lies blocking traffic in the street, the entrepreneur
who brought Kong to New York turns to the assembled reporters and
proclaims: "That's your story, boys — it was Beauty killed the Beast!"
But greater forces than those of the screaming Lady have combined
to lay Kong low, if you ask me. Kong lives for a time as one of those
persecuted near-animal souls bewildered in the middle of an industrial
order, whose simple desires are thwarted at every turn. He climbs the
Empire State Building because in all New York it's the closest thing
he can find to the clifftop of his jungle isle. He dies, a pitiful dolt, and
the army brass and publicity men cackle over him. His death is the only
possible outcome to as neat a tragic dilemma as you can ask for. The
machine guns do him in, while the manicured human hero (a nice clean
Dartmouth boy) carries away Kong's sweetheart to the altar. O, the
misery of it all. There's far more truth about upper-middle-class
American life in *King Kong* than in the last seven dozen novels of John
P. Marquand.

A Negro friend from Atlanta tells me that in movie houses in colored   11
neighborhoods throughout the South, Kong does a constant business.
They show the thing in Atlanta at least every year, presumably to the
same audiences. Perhaps this popularity may simply be due to the fact
that Kong is one of the most watchable movies ever constructed, but
I wonder whether Negro audiences may not find some archetypical appeal in this serio-comic tale of a huge black powerful free spirit whom
all the hardworking white policemen are out to kill.

Every day in the week on a screen somewhere in the world, King   12
Kong relives his agony. Again and again he expires on the Empire State
Building, as audiences of the devout assist his sacrifice. We watch him
die, and by extension kill the ape within our bones, but these little deaths
of ours occur in prosaic surroundings. We do not die on a tower, New
York before our feet, nor do we give our lives to smash a few flying
machines. It is not for us to bring to a momentary standstill the civilization in which we move. King Kong does this for us. And so we kill
him again and again, in much-spliced celluloid, while the ape in us
expires from day to day, obscure, in desperation.

(1960)

The Writer's Subject

1. What evidence does Kennedy bring in support of his contention that "no other monster in movie history has won so devoted a popular audience" as Kong? (paras. 1-3)

2. Summarize what Kennedy believes to be the reasons for "the abiding appeal of the giant ape."

3. Why does Kennedy refer to the Tarzan series as an American myth? What connection does this myth have with *King Kong*? (para. 5)

4. What does Kennedy mean by "the tradition of the pitiable monster"? (para. 6)

5. Why, in Kennedy's view, did the film have particular appeal to audiences during the Depression? (para. 7)

6. Why does Kennedy believe that the violent episode he describes in paragraph 8 would be satisfying to audiences in modern cities?

7. What use does Kennedy make of the well known fairytale, "Beauty and the Beast"? (para. 10)

8. What larger social significance does Kennedy perceive in the ordeal and the inevitable death of Kong? (para. 10)

9. To what does Kennedy attribute the popularity of King Kong with black audiences? (para. 11)

10. What does Kennedy mean when he says, in paragraph 12, that Kong's celluloid death is a "sacrifice"? Relate his comment to his choice of title.

The Writer's Style and Strategy

1. What details of phrasing and diction in the first four paragraphs reveal Kennedy's attitude to *King Kong* as film?

2. In paragraph 3 Kennedy compares Kong to other movie monsters. How does his description of Kong's rivals convey his sense of their inferiority?

3. What use does Kennedy make of analogy in paragraph 6 to convey Kong's "pitiable" qualities?

4. Discuss the organization of paragraph 8. How does Kennedy relate his assertion about modern urban man to the scene he describes from *King Kong*?

5. What is the tone of paragraph 9, and how is it established? Why does Kennedy describe Kong as "a gentleman" with a "sense of chivalry," and as "the hopelessly yearning lover of Petrarchan convention"?

6. The tone and language of this essay are informal, even colloquial, for the most part, but they change dramatically in the closing paragraphs (compare, for example, paragraphs 4 and 12). Why does Kennedy adopt this strategy?

7. Identify the major stages of Kennedy's discussion. At what point does he move from his introduction to his principal arguments? How is the reader prepared for the conclusion?

Suggested Topics for Writing and Discussion

1. Kennedy points to a number of reasons for the success of *King Kong,* including psychological, political and social. Choose a popular movie and discuss those elements which might claim for the film a deeper significance.

2. Choose a genre other than monster movies (e.g., Westerns, science fiction movies, spy thrillers, ninja and kung-fu movies) and account for the genre's popularity.

3. Many of the modern equivalents of *King Kong* are notable for their realistic violence and brutality, aided by the use of special effects. Do you think there is a case for the censoring of such films?

4. Locate reviews of the "remake" of *King Kong* which appeared in 1980 and the "sequel," *King Kong Lives!* which appeared in 1986. What do these reviews suggest about the continuing popularity of *King Kong*?

Loose Canons
by Rick Salutin

1   *The first time I heard the phrase was in a Chinese restaurant during the late 1960s, after a political meeting or protest march. Those things built an appetite. Someone always has to take charge when you're ordering Chinese food, and someone did. She listed a number of dishes and asked if it sounded okay. "I don't know," somebody else said, "whether that's a politically correct order." It got a little laugh, as a touch of slightly self-conscious left-wing humour. But it worked because the cuisine was Chinese, and Maoism was then the most popular fare on the left's ideological menu.*

2   *Around the same time, a comic strip called Korrect Line Komix appeared in the alternative press along with the Fabulous Furry Freak Brothers. A chubby little Mao face in the corner of each panel said things like, "Where do correct ideas come from?" Next panel he'd ask, "Do they fall from the sky?" Then some guy would get bonked on the head by a falling idea and Mao would chirp, "Nope!" A nice send-up. It's a shame really: people on the left concoct a phrase that pokes fun at themselves – a healthy instinct – and more than twenty years later every mass medium in the triumphant capitalist West is using it to pummel whatever spirit of opposition remains in the post-Cold War world.*

3   The media frenzy over political correctness, or PC, has consumed most of 1991. It started before the Gulf War and outlasted it. It must be trying to tell us something. To me the best way to treat the subject is to start with that media reaction before going back to have a look at the thing itself. I'm

not saying the object of all the attention doesn't exist; it does, and I'll get to it. But the reality of political correctness is minuscule compared to the orgy of media attention — the overkill — launched in its name. I mean, how big should a story be to rate cover or feature treatment in *Newsweek, New York, Time, The Atlantic, The New Republic,* and (wait for it, because you had to) *Maclean's*? We're talking about World War III or the fall of the Berlin Wall. At least you'd think so.

The first cover story showed up like a grim Christmas present in the 4 December 24, 1990, issue of *Newsweek,* wrapped in the words, "Watch What You Say: THOUGHT POLICE." The story centred on universities, where, as *Time* later put it, "a troubling number of teachers, at all levels, regard the bulk of American history and heritage as racist, sexist, and classist and believe their purpose is to bring about social change." The evidence was mainly anecdotal. Check that: entirely anecdotal. In fact, *all* the coverage has revealed nothing more than a batch of scary tales: some students or professors being criticized or harassed for using certain language; some changes in curriculum to de-emphasize certain authors and stress others. No statistics to show how widespread the phenomenon is, no studies or surveys, no coherent theory to explain the thing and put it in perspective. (One of the few stats I did find said 100 to 200 U.S. colleges and universities — out of 3,600 — had tried to restrict speech on PC grounds, and a number of those restrictions had now been withdrawn.) Even the anecdotes were often feeble. "If I was at lunch [in the dorm]," a Stanford student told *Newsweek,* "and we started talking about something like civil rights, I'd get up and leave.... I knew they didn't want to hear what I had to say." Now, into each life a little rain must fall, but for these stories, newsmagazine correspondents all over America are asked to submit reports, which are exhaustively culled by editors at head office — and *this* tale made the cut?

There was also some light analysis in *Newsweek.* Like: "PC is, strictly 5 speaking, a totalitarian philosophy." Huh? Where is it taught? Name a single thinker or book that expounds this philosophy. Elsewhere, PC was called a "movement." So what are its organizational structures or publications or membership? For Pete's sake, "Star Trek" is more of a movement than PC. It makes better sense to call racism a movement or philosophy; you could name spokesmen, institutions, guiding thoughts, and thinkers. *Newsweek* also struggled to uncloak the obscure literary technique called deconstruction, seen as a deadly weapon in the PC armament, and expose its threat to, gasp, The Canon. Some of this gets pretty unreal. The foes of PC are furious over challenges to the list of literary and philosophical classics taught as the Western "canon" and the attempts to add on, say, "testimonials written by oppressed Guatemalan women" — as Ray Conlogue of *The Globe and Mail* put it in a fine show of Western open-mindedness. They're terrified that Shakespeare and, of all things, Rabelais will be tossed out with the morning garbage. Yet even the notion of canonization in its original sense — establishing the text of the Bible — is controversial: the Catholic canon differs from the Protestant, which differs from the Jewish. The revered canon of Western literature wasn't even set until the 1930s, in the case of its British component; and until the 1950s, for the American. I don't mean there's not a lot of good stuff in there — I'm partial to Shakespeare myself, though I doubt he'd be peeing his pants over whether he made the canon — but there's mediocrity, too: did you ever try reading *The Pilgrim's Progress*?

6   The whole investigation by *Newsweek* had a thumb-sucking quality, a sulky sense of grievance that anyone would dare challenge the prevailing value system in the West, and especially "the single most compelling idea in human history, individual liberty, which as it happens is just now sweeping the entire world." *Hey, we're number one, our product is wiping the competition, how come they're raining on our parade?* Still, *Newsweek* wasn't entirely one-sided. It ran an interview with a prof who supported curriculum change, and an account from someone who'd worked on a campus program to combat traditional prejudices. In retrospect, *Newsweek* starts to look good.

7   *New York* magazine's January 21, 1991, cover showed a bespectacled white fellow tortured by the question "Are you Politically Correct?" There were photographs of Hitler Youths burning books in the 1930s, along with student guidelines handed out by Smith University, and washroom graffiti at Brown. Imagine how swamped you'd be if you decided to go after racism or sexism on the basis of such "evidence?" *Time*'s long essay on April 1 agreed that universities should be "centers for the critical examination of Western beliefs," but said this had now taken a "strident turn" — as if upping the volume were cause for declaring a national emergency. It singled out an assistant professor who teaches a course on white male writers; she argues that since there are courses on women writers and black writers, why not one on white men? Personally, I don't see the fallacy. In *The New Republic,* historian Eugene Genovese called the PC people "storm troopers" and demanded counterterror in response. Others referred to PC as "fascism of the left" and "the new McCarthyism." A little overstated, perhaps, since, unlike German, Italian, or Japanese fascism, or the original McCarthyism, the PC movement has no government representing it, no money behind it, no mass media or propaganda presence, no paramilitary forces. What would fascism have amounted to with so little support? Something like the

PC "movement" — maybe. The *Atlantic's* March cover story, by a former
Reagan staffer, Dinesh D'Souza, quoted a teacher at Duke University who
hopes "to create a Marxist culture in this country, to make Marxism an
unavoidable presence in American social, cultural and intellectual life."
A man and his dream, to be sure, but enough to make an entire society
tremble? At a time when even the Soviet Communist Party had ditched
Uncle Karl? The worst, though, was yet to come.

In late May, "Canada's Weekly Newsmagazine" became the last on its   8
block to get a PC cover. It showed a young white couple in graduation garb
with gags over their mouths and hurt expressions. The title was "The
Silencers." In his note to readers, *Maclean's* editor, Kevin Doyle, condemned the "vociferous intolerance" of what he called "the Nons." Though
he found many practices they were protesting (racism, sexism, fascism)
"distasteful" — "in the extreme," actually — he said their own actions
represented "a far more insidious evil." Doyle relied for backup, as did the
cover story, on what he called "a recent, little noticed speech" by George
Bush. The speech was about as little noticed as the heart scare Bush had
later the same day he gave it. It was valuable in one way though: it summed
up the shallowness and hypocrisy of much of the assault against PC.

Bush criticized political correctness for declaring off limits certain topics,   9
expressions, "and even certain gestures." Yet he himself had run against
Michael Dukakis on the issue of the pledge of allegiance, and had tried to
introduce a constitutional amendment forbidding gestures demeaning the
U.S. flag. Bush attacked those who'd set "citizens against one another on
the basis of their class or race" — after using mug shots of the convicted
black killer Willie Horton to create white anxiety about Dukakis. He
denounced "the temptation to assign bad motives to people who disagree
with us," yet had called Saddam Hussein *worse* than Hitler and the war
against him a simple case of good versus evil. Bush warned of "the growing tendency to use intimidation rather than reason in settling disputes,"
but rejected sanctions against Iraq despite evidence that they were working.
And he praised the freedom to speak one's mind as "the most fundamental and deeply revered of all liberties," after attacking Dukakis as a "card-
carrying member" of the American Civil Liberties Union. Bush, just like
Kevin Doyle, found the desire to combat racism and sexism "laudable,"
apparently forgetting that after his 1988 television debate with Geraldine
Ferraro he had told the world that he'd "kicked some feminist ass." Bush's
speech was normal political pap. What's remarkable is the deference with
which Doyle and *Maclean's* — alone in all of journalism — treated it. Two
weeks later, even *Maclean's* own American columnist, Fred Bruning,
ridiculed the speech.

10   The text of the *Maclean's* cover story was mostly a rehash, larded with
weasel words ("many academics," "some feminists," "some social
commentators," "critics say," "lots of people") to hide the absence of
specifics. A psychology prof at the University of Western Ontario
grumbled "I have to measure my words carefully" — which doesn't sound
like such a horrid burden for a teacher and scholar. Besides Bush, the piece
peddled one other U.S. authority, an employee of the National Association of Scholars, which is an anti-PC organization funded by several
seriously right-wing American foundations. *Maclean's* quoted him seven
times in two pages, and included his photo. Speaking of pictures, one could
do a little deconstruction of the juxtaposition of George and Barbara Bush
at a graduation, waving and smiling with open hands, set across the page
from a sea of mostly black graduates raising clenched fists. Then, there
was one of those joyous generalizations only *Maclean's* has the staff to
research: "From Vancouver to Miami, people say that they are constantly being harangued or induced to change." I'd love to see the transcripts.
Historian Michael Bliss lamented that, these days, "You're not allowed to
sin against gender equality." Pity. But as the mag assured us, in another
breathtaking *aperçu,* "off-color and ethnic jokes are now as rare in mixed
company as the three-martini lunch." If you think you've heard the odd such
joke lately, well, you probably just drank too much at lunch.

11   What's a touch hard to take is how distressed Doyle and his employees
get about "The Silencers" when they've been known to practise some, let's
say, restraint themselves. Merely on the level of editing, *Maclean's,* as
Robert Fulford has said, "is the most rigidly edited magazine in Canadian
history." Or have you never wondered why all those reporters write in
exactly the same style? One former correspondent says any time he proudly
reported anything that hadn't appeared elsewhere, the editors would say,
"Good. We'll cut that." Or there was the time *Maclean's* airbrushed the
genitals out of a painting by Attila Richard Lukacs, after Doyle had warned
the art department to stay alert for "objectionable details." In fact, *Maclean's*
own employees have formed an "Editorial Integrity Committee" evincing
a certain lack of confidence in their leader. A survey taken in-house by that
committee showed widespread alarm over "lack of balance" in the political-
correctness cover story itself. For another case of "Stifling," as the subhead
on the cover put it, consider Kevin Doyle's own, ah, alteration to an
exclusive interview with President Bush himself in the summer of 1990.
Bush referred to a dinner he'd had with Brian Mulroney, "and a couple of
drinks, I might add" — an interesting reference since there'd been much
speculation at that time about whether Mulroney had returned to his old
drinking habits because of Meech and Oka. Then Bush added, "Oh, I hope

I'm not getting the prime minister into trouble," or words to that effect. It showed an impressive awareness of Mulroney's medical and political problems, but Doyle cut the line from the story.

And for a sample of political correctness of a different sort, just glance 12 at *Maclean's* cover two weeks later. "The Private Prime Minister" featured seven pages of exclusive photos of a day in the life of Brian. It came in the wake of this year's spate of rumours and reports about the PM, which centred on marital breakdown. Strangely enough, nine of the twenty-eight pictures included Mila or the kids — with lots of kissyface and popping in unexpectedly on hubby at the office. The shots were taken by a *Maclean's* photo editor who happened to have been Mulroney's official photographer during his first year in office.

There's been some other Canadian comment on PC. "How long might 13 it take to repair the damage wrought by the PC movement?" fretted Conlogue in *The Globe and Mail,* neatly assuming a devastation of the campuses that had nowhere been established. On CTV's "W5," the regular political panel also grumped about the subject. The New Democrats' Gerry Caplan was sure they all regretted that everybody on their panel was a white man in a suit, but no one volunteered to step down and improve the balance. In an impassioned column, Dalton Camp said he could remember "when it was considered politically correct for anyone to say anything that came to mind and when outrageous opinion was not only indulged, but encouraged." Funny, I don't. He never said when that happened, but you got the impression he was thinking of the *fifties.*

All those poor fellows in suits with columns and tenure are twitching 14 frantically about a lost golden age that never was, except maybe for them; and about a new McCarthyism, or worse, for which there's only meagre evidence. Sure there are some students and profs making demands. Ranged against them are the entire mass media, most of the academic establishment, and politicians starting at the level of the president of the U.S. You get the idea the anti-PCs might manage to hold their own. Could that really be what it's all about: a bunch of guys sitting there in their bastions of privilege, at the *Globe* or the university, with tenure or a by-line they've worked and schemed to acquire, and feeling so incredibly insecure they go wild to protect that privilege against — not even a threat but a mild and fairly marginal challenge?

You don't hear much from these same people about a different threat to 15 university independence: the invasion of business influence, for which there's lots of evidence — joint academic-corporate councils and forums, grants to encourage research that will increase profits, "joint-venture discovery parks" on campus just like the industrial parks cities build to

compete for business, deals profs negotiate with companies on patents and
discoveries, university-business liaison, and real-estate officers alongside
the deans and registrars. You could say there are signs of a threat to
academic independence there — but no magazine covers.

16   And finally, there's the mainstream media's own version of PC, though
they never call it that. As Thomas Walkom of the *Toronto Star* wrote, "This
year's most telling examples of political correctness come not from the dispossessed but from the powerful: the media jingos who treated any criticism
of the Gulf War as treasonous; and the business lobbies that — regardless
of the circumstances — rail against government deficits."

17   So, having established that the entire media offensive against the so-
called PC movement is overblown, dishonest, and hypocritical, I'd like
to turn to the phenomenon itself. Personally and politically, I find it a pain
in the ass.

18   It can be irksome and picky, for starters, especially concerning language:
doing search-and-destroy missions on phrases like "a nip in the air," or "a
chink in the armour," or words like "blackmail." And I can't get comfortable with the phrase "people of colour." It sounds prissy and self-
congratulatory to me. I feel like the San Francisco writer who was up-
braided for dumping on the term, and said he didn't want to discuss it until
he'd had his coffee of morning.

19   It gets more serious though. People or groups with rigid, "politically
correct" attitudes and demands on matters like racism and sexism really
can be a threat — but *not* to pillars of the establishment like *Newsweek,
Maclean's,* and George Bush, who've been responding to them with the
equivalent of the war against Iraq. The politically correct people are
generally pretty marginal and powerless, striving for a toehold in the
curriculum or hiring policy, or just to be noticed. They pose no serious
danger to the right, or the establishment; but they can be a real problem
for the left, and for efforts actually to combat forces like racism and sexism.
They muddy the water, set people of goodwill against each other, create
disunity, and present a version of their causes that alienates potential allies
and provides a big fat target for their enemies.

20   This is an old story. It happened even to Maoism, to go back to where
we started. Just twenty years ago, it didn't look all that implausible, in China
or elsewhere. But the mindless and parodic versions of it mouthed by
students and others during the Cultural Revolution made it impossible to
ever take seriously again. Mao himself, who had a sense of humour — just
read some of his unofficial speeches — wondered if there wasn't a plot to
make his ideas look ridiculous.

21   The PC mind-set is just a phoney nuisance for the establishment, but it

can make real trouble for serious movements of social change. Consider, for instance, the battle of the Women's Press, a small feminist publisher painstakingly created over a period of sixteen years. A few years ago it nearly died in a virtual blood bath of political correctness about who was racist. There were demands for public confessions, stacked meetings, and the lock on the door got changed. In the end eight women who'd put their life's effort into building a useful feminist institution were driven out, and the bitterness and infighting are still going on. Not exactly the way you build an alternative movement to challenge the status quo.

Then there's the case of June Callwood, who until the end of 1989 was   22 a rare voice of social conscience at the new, Darwinian *Globe and Mail.* Publisher Roy Megarry had been trying to ditch her for years, unsuccessfully. Then, outside a writers' convention, the black author Marlene Nourbese Philip harangued Callwood for racism — a ludicrous charge. In frustration, Callwood told Philip to "fuck off," which was duly reported, re-reported, and editorialized about in our newspaper of record. The upshot was that Callwood left the paper, not really a great victory for the cause of reform — though Marlene Philip was the subject of a flattering profile in the paper a few days after Callwood departed.

Or take even the case of the playwright Joanna Glass, a person of talent   23 and goodwill, but little experience of political action, who attended a Women Playwrights Conference in Toronto recently. She was so alienated by the posturing and bullying that went on concerning colour, and men, and the "correct" views on women in the arts that she "came away from it deploring (for a change) not man's inhumanity to man, but women's inhumanity to women." My own feeling is that so much needs changing in this society — and the larger world society too — and the forces in power are so cocky and entrenched that it's sheer idiocy to drive away potential supporters like Joanna Glass, while creating deep divisions among those already committed.

The scariest part of all is who you find yourself agreeing or disagree-   24 ing with — for instance, when the well-meaning advisers to York University on the status of women, and race and ethnic relations, write, in the style of an encyclical, "White males cannot be victims of racism or sexism. Discrimination results from systemic oppression." Sorry, but racism and sexism are more flexible than that, which is what makes them hard to eradicate. Oppression can be practised by victims; in fact, victims are powerfully motivated to victimize others in turn — if they can get away with it. On the other hand, I reluctantly nod my head to Lorrie Goldstein, in the odious (and often racist and sexist) *Toronto Sun,* when he says, "Political correctness isn't just good liberal intentions run amok.... It is

racism and, for that matter, sexism.... Accept that only blacks can teach
African history or that only men can be sexist and you are not very far from
accepting that blacks have rhythm, that women make lousy drivers, and
that Jews are good with money." Ouch. The *Toronto Sun* gets it right?

25   So a pox on both their houses, both the media hysterics of the mainstream
and the self-righteous crusaders of PC. It will, however, require a considerably larger pox to deal with the former than with the latter.

                                                                    (1991)

The Writer's Subject

1. What is the nature of "political correctness," as it is described in Salutin's
    article?

2. What deficiencies does Salutin point to in the coverage of "political correct-
    ness" by such magazines as *Newsweek, Time, The New Republic,* and the
    Atlantic?

3. What fears are expressed by the foes of political correctness concerning the
    possible fate of the classics of Western literature? (para. 5)Does Salutin think
    this fear is justified?

4. On what grounds does Salutin attack *Maclean's* handling of the political
    correctness issue?

5. What does Salutin mean by his reference to "political correctness of a different
    sort" in the pages of *Maclean's*? (para. 12)

6. What in Salutin's view is a greater threat than "political correctness" to the
    independence of thought at universities?

7. What dangers do "the politically correct people" pose to our society, in
    Salutin's view?

The Writer's Style and Strategy

1. Discuss the play on words in Salutin's title.

2. "Loose Canons" first appeared in the weekly magazine *Saturday Night*. What
    aspects of its style indicate its journalistic origins?

3. How does Salutin's vocabulary in paragraph 3 reflect his attitude towards the
    handling of political correctness by the press?

4. Why does Salutin give such prominence to a speech by George Bush, reported in detail by *Maclean's*? (paras. 8-9)

5. Why does Salutin spend so long criticizing the various media assaults on political correctness before he turns to examine the phenomenon itself?

6. Discuss the way in which Salutin mocks the excessive concerns about "politically correct" language in paragraph 18.

Suggested Topics for Writing and Discussion

1. Examine some of the magazine articles cited by Salutin, and say whether his summary of them is a fair representation of their content.

2. Has any aspect of "political correctness," as described in Salutin's article, had an effect on you, your circle of acquaintance, or your community?

3. Examine the essays in this book by Susan Crean, Moira Farr, or Lenore Keeshig-Tobias. Do you see in their arguments anything of what might be called "political correctness"?

4. Salutin speaks of "frenzy" and "hysterics" in media treatments of the issue of political correctness. Discuss another example of frenzied or hysterical reporting of an issue of public interest (e.g., the private life of political candidates; drug abuse in professional sport; royal marriages or divorces). Point to instances of distortion, exaggeration, or sensationalism.

Films at Issue

Black Robe: Copyright 1991 Alliance Communications Corporation

Red Alert! A Meditation on "Dances With Wolves"

by Marilou Awiakta

What does *Dances With Wolves* mean — in itself and for the future? For 1
weeks I've thought about this question — and also about a Lakota woman
whose face I glimpsed only once in the movie. She is Pretty Shield, wife
of the elder and chief, Ten Bears. Gathered with friends around their home
fire, she is sitting by Ten Bears and leans over to make a humorous
comment. Her countenance is strong, weathered with adversity — yet
calm, joyful, and *capable*. The face of a Mother of the Nation. Her spirit
has helped keep my thoughts centered on what is essential in *Dances With
Wolves*.

It recounts Lieutenant John Dunbar's experience with a peaceable band 2
of Lakota (Sioux) in Dakota Territory in 1863 — just before the federal
army sweeps in to clear the land of "hostile savages." For the first time,
a highly commercial film portrays Native Americans as individuals —
intelligent, complex, humorous. *Civilized*. True, Dunbar tells the story,
and men are primary. But the Lakota tradition of strength and tenderness
for both sexes is evident. I understand with regret that some scenes of
Lakota women were cut. Nevertheless, Black Shawl, the wife of Kicking
Bird, and their adopted daughter, Stands With A Fist — a European
American who has been raised Lakota — powerfully represent the women.

The essential point is: the Lakota themselves endorse the integrity of 3
Kevin Costner and the film he produced.

So, yes, I listen to Dunbar's story with a positive mind. I'm glad when 4
he finds among the Lakota the harmony he's been seeking and becomes one

of them, accepting the name they give him, Dances With Wolves. But my greatest pleasure is being with the Lakota in their daily round of family, councils, hunts, and ceremonies. I had read that their life was "softened by a great equality," with mutual respect between women and men and complementarity in their roles. I see this equality at work, especially between Kicking Bird and Black Shawl. Clearly, the people translate their guiding principle of reverence for life into a cooperative social pattern (albeit with human ups and downs). Most important for viewers to remember is that *Lakota scholars and advisers shaped this film portrayal of their people.*

5   What does *Dances With Wolves* mean? It is appropriate that the two tribal scholars who translated the script into Lakota speak first. (The quotes are from an article by Thomas S. McAnally, in the *United Methodist Reporter,* January 4, 1991.) Both come from the Sinte Gleska College on the Rosebud Reservation in South Dakota. Doris Leader Charge teaches arts and language. Albert White Hat is professor of Lakota medicine and philosophy. Looking at the picture of Doris Leader Charge, I recognize the face of the "Mother of the Nation" in the movie! And from an insider on the set I hear that she helped cast and crew keep centered.

6   During the summer of 1989, Leader Charge coached the actors in Lakota, which was used with subtitles when Indians spoke, or when either Dunbar or Stands With A Fist spoke to them. Leader Charge said she was "deeply impressed" with the script and added that the film "showed the mutual care and support, the sense of humor that characterizes our people.... I hope it teaches our young people that they have something to be proud of. That is why I worked so hard on it."

7   Albert White Hat said, "I hope the movie will change attitudes toward who we were and who we are." He expressed amazement that Native American spirituality has survived. For nearly 100 years (until 1978), the U.S. Government effectively banned our religious ceremonies, while the churches and the schools sought to destroy our language and traditions. "But we are still here," he said, "... our spirituality is just as strong as it ever was."

8   This spirituality speaks in and through *Dances With Wolves.* It moved director/producer/actor Kevin Costner to make the film, moved the cast and crew, and is reaching out to people across the country. The Lakota and Costner have established a "trailhead" — an opportunity for a new beginning of truth. The crucial question is: What trail will we — Indians and non-Indians, and the film industry itself — lay from this point? Will we just rework the old ethnocentric, patriarchal trail? Or forge a new one that leads deeper into Indian Country?

Those sincere in their response to Native American spirituality and 9
Native concerns will set to work immediately on the new trail, beginning
with our own thoughts. This meditation is my spadeful of earth turned in
that direction. The earth is red. Red for the Indian People. Red for courage
and honor. Red for the moon blood of women, which most Native traditions teach is clean and powerful, a sign of the sacred life force.

Red also signals danger/caution. From the Lakota perspective, it is clear 10
in *Dances With Wolves* that gender balance is central to their harmony. But
Dunbar (and the non-Indian viewer) may see the harmony without fully
understanding the spiritual base that undergirds it, and so it appears as
enlightened patriarchy. (Obviously next in order is a film story written *by*
the Lakota.) Anthropologist Ella Deloria, who is Sioux, identifies the
problems and prejudices of observers of Indian life:

"Outsiders seeing women keep to themselves have frequently expressed 11
a snap judgment that they were regarded as inferior to the noble male; the
simple fact is that woman had her own place and man his. They were not
the same and neither inferior nor superior."

Deloria's cautionary words appear in *Oglala Women: Myth, Ritual, and* 12
Reality, by anthropologist Marla N. Powers. This study, written from the
Indian perspective, has Oglala women speaking for themselves whenever
possible. (The Oglala are a major constituent of the Lakota.) Read it. Self-
education is essential spadework in laying the new trail of understanding,
and in the dominant culture even many feminists have been reluctant to
do it.

We must all insist that — in film and other media — the positive portrayal 13
of Native Americans be deepened and enlarged and that the People have
the opportunity *to speak for ourselves.* The financial success of this movie
is both a danger and a hope. Historically, the discovery of "gold" in Indian
Country has meant doom for the People. Being deeply sexist and ethnocentric, Hollywood will try to make a string of films in which the white
man and the red man become so dominant that the red woman is erased —
and the balanced wisdom of traditional Native American spirituality will
be erased with her. This is a setup for Indian men and women to become
adversarial, a modern version of the old patriarchal trick of "divide and
conquer" that has been played on Native people since white contact. By
being alert, we can turn the financial success of *Dances With Wolves* to
advantage and use it to open the way to Native producers, directors, actors,
and scriptwriters. They will guide the public further along the trail of
authentic understanding.

The American Indian Registry for the Performing Arts is leading in that 14 direction, while the ATLATL Native Arts Network leads a similar movement for all the arts. The energy that *Dances With Wolves* is generating should be focused to support these movements and others that benefit Native Americans. Most important, it should be used to engender respect for the People.

15   What does *Dances With Wolves* mean? Contemplate with me the face of Doris Leader Charge, and take her words to heart. "I hope it teaches our young people that they have something to be proud of." This pride is the birthright of the young. They shall not be robbed of it. Never again.

(1991)

The Writer's Subject

1. What is the significance for the writer of this essay of the movie *Dances With Wolves*?

2. Why does the writer attach such importance to the fact that "Lakota scholars and advisers shaped this film portrayal of their people"? (para. 4)

3. What is the role of Indian women, as understood by Awiakta in this essay?

4. What dangers does the writer see in the success of *Dances With Wolves*?

The Writer's Style and Strategy

1. Discuss the implications of Awiakta's title.

2. Awiakta writes from the perspective of a Native American woman. What impact does that have on her handling of the material, and on her conclusions?

3. Awiakta's article first appeared in *Ms.* magazine. What assumptions does Awiakta make about her audience?

4. What use does Awiakta make of supporting authorities?

5. Why does Awiakta twice repeat the question she asks at the beginning of the essay, "What does *Dances With Wolves* mean?"

Suggested Topics for Writing and Discussion

1. The movie *Dances With Wolves* invites us to take a new look at the Native peoples of North America. Discuss some of the literary and cinematic stereotypes that have been challenged by recent films about North American Indians.

2. In your experience, how are Native North American women portrayed in the movies? You may wish to compare a recent film such as *Dances With Wolves* or *Black Robe* with older films such as *The Man Who Loved Cat Dancing* or *Cheyenne Autumn*.

3. Awiakta asserts that Hollywood is "deeply sexist and ethnocentric." Do you agree?

Dances With Wolves: Review

by Edward D. Castillo

1   *Dances With Wolves* is not only a well-crafted film by a first-time director, but it also touches on a number of important spiritual, social, and
environmental issues vital to all Americans at the end of this century.
American Indian historians have long been well aware of many important
stories that resulted from the encounters between native peoples and Euro-
Americans in the last century. Hope, fear, hatred, dread, humor, guilt,
and loathing can be found in nearly every such encounter. From a native
point of view, we have long been mystified as to why this rich mine of
human experience has been studiously avoided by Hollywood film-makers.
Within the Indian world, Costner's powerful directing debut is for certain
the most talked about mainstream Hollywood Indian film in two decades.
Despite some negative reviews by jaded Eurocentric urbanites, Costner's
vision of an alternate Lakota encounter with Americans has captured the
imagination of Americans from a variety of social, economic, and racial
backgrounds.

2   From a native viewpoint, the film's primary virtue is its sensitive exploration of a native culture. The screenplay, without preaching, engenders
understanding, acceptance, and sympathy for Lakota culture. I am thinking
especially here of small scenes, as when Kicking Bird and his wife get into
bed and we sense concern and confusion in his face; then he pulls out one
of his children's dolls that he has lain upon. This vignette tells us in purely
cinematic terms of the humanity of this family, and rings warmly familiar
to all parents in the audience. With such small touches the director achieved

his goal of demonstrating the most important aspect of the picture was "... the sentiment, the humanity, not the politics."[1]

As non-Indian archaeologists, ethnographers, and historians have been 3 painfully reminded over the last 20 years, all contemporary endeavors to interpret Indian history and culture have the dual potential of possibly hurting or helping contemporary Indians. In this respect most native peoples seem pleased with Costner in this most recent portrayal of our people in the last century. However, those expecting immediate reform in the social, economic, and political fortunes of the Sioux or any other tribe are sure to be disappointed. This film may help bring about much-needed reform in our nation and our tribes, but true reform will always require more than Hollywood can offer. Nevertheless, to minimize the power of the mass media to generate sympathy, concerns, and demands for reform is to ignore reality. For that reason alone it seems worthwhile to devote some thoughtful reflection to the shadows of the Indians whom Costner and screenwriter Michael Blake have lyrically dance upon the screen, thrusting us backward in time for a fleeting moment.

The characters portrayed are both engaging and varied. Kicking Bird 4 is of course the most sympathetic of the Lakotas, the father figure who rescues and raises the small white girl (Christine/Stands With Fists) who had escaped a Pawnee raiding party, and eventually opens communication between Dunbar and the Lakota. He is a shaman/warrior whose poised and convincing portrayal by Canadian-born Oneida Indian Graham Greene rivals Costner's, and gained him an Academy Award nomination. The archetype Lakota warrior in the story is Wind In His Hair, played by Omaha Indian Rodney Grant. His commanding presence is sexually charged, with an aura of danger just beneath his angry bluster. Early on in the film his character is dramatically revealed in a confrontation with Dunbar: he charges on horseback directly toward Dunbar, stopping only feet from the soldier, shouts his defiance and lack of fear of this strange white man, and disdainfully turns his back on a cocked pistol to demonstrate his contempt for Dunbar — who promptly faints.

The most familiar Native American actor is folk singer/activist Floyd 5 Red Crow Westerman, a Lakota Indian. He plays Ten Bears, chief of the film's Lakota band. His understated performance is in sharp contrast to his real character: for those who know him, he is nearly always smiling and a performer with an easygoing demeanor. Perhaps reflecting the growing dominance of warriors in Lakota society as the crisis of the frontier enveloped the plains Indian societies, the film offers few prominent parts for Indian women. The most important Indian female part is Canadian Cree/Chippewa Tantoo Cardinal as Black Shawl, wife of Kicking Bird.

It is a small part which she performs skillfully. She delivers one of the best one-liners in the film: when Kicking Bird declares that his crying step-daughter, Stands With Fists, is being difficult, Black Shawl observes sardonically that it is perhaps Kicking Bird who is being difficult, since Stands With Fists is the one who is crying. While women in the audience will find this an appropriate rejoinder, it offers little comfort for the curious lack of strong females or for that matter, any young Indian women/children roles in the remainder of the screenplay. On the other hand, young viewers will be especially pleased with the trio of pre-pubescent Lakota boys led by Lakota Indian Nathan Lee Chasing His Horse (Smiles A Lot), who appropriately displays the independence, foolishness, and self-sacrificing courage typical of Indian youth both then and today. The other Lakota characters inhabiting Ten Bears's village, while undeniably likeable, are rather conventional and lack the delightfully quirky characters found in *Little Big Man*'s Cheyenne camp — a saucy berdache (homosexual) and the frustrated contrary warrior.

6   The "enemy" Pawnee portrayal has generated a good deal of discussion among Indians. Some viewers have decried the one-dimensional and negative portrait of Pawnee so badly maligned earlier in *Little Big Man* (1970). Despite a largely negative image, careful viewers will note the Pawnee war party that attacks the mule skinner Timmons is led by the unidentified actor and character I call "Violent Leader" who seeks both to humiliate and drive his hesitant followers into attacking the yet unseen whites. Later we see the Pawnee scouts helping the soldiers track down Ten Bears' people. One recalls Jack Crabbe's acerbic declaration, "Pawnees always were sucking up to whites," from *Little Big Man*. In reality much of Indian frontier history is characterized by a native survival response that varied between fight, flight, and accommodation. Earlier, the Pawnee offered considerable armed resistance to white encroachment upon their territory while later they assisted the US government in pursuing their traditional enemies, the Sioux. These unfortunate people were sub-jected to the purposeful introduction of smallpox by traders along the Santa Fe trail in 1831.[2] The film makes it too easy to dismiss these much maligned Indians as stereotypical "bad Indians." Their kind of imprudent judgment is today often chided by those living comfortably with full bellies and not faced with the horrible leadership decisions that could spell violent death or starvation for their men, women, and children. In the last quarter of the nineteenth century various bands of Sioux faced these terrible choices too and ultimately cooperated with federal authorities, riding with the blue coats as scouts, auxiliaries, and even as U.S. soldiers.[3] Thoughtful viewers wishing to know more about the tortuous history of the Pawnee can find

the works of Pawnee authors James Murie and Gene Weltfish in a recently published Pawnee bibliography.[4]

The non-Indian characters present some striking contrasts as well. I've [7] discussed this film with some colleagues who claim the whites in it were negatively portrayed throughout its three-hour running time. That type of generalization does not do justice to Michael Blake's subtly textured screenplay. In fact, the film is really about the transformation of the white soldier Lt. John Dunbar into the Lakota warrior Dances With Wolves. Kevin Costner's sensitive and convincing character transformation earned him an Oscar. What Blake has done with Dunbar's character is to assume that, as in the race- and class-conscious nineteenth-century James Fenimore Cooper leatherstocking tales, largely white American audiences will not endure a story centered around Indians only. Therefore a white central character is mandatory to capture audience sympathy. However, unlike Cooper's protagonist Natty Bumppo, a white frontiersman of common social origin, Blake at first sight provides us with another type of frontier hero, the "military aristocrat" — a hero who combines high status and potential leadership in Eastern society with the ability to both survive and triumph in the wilderness. This traditional type of frontier hero has a future in a post-frontier America beginning to evolve into a rather rigid system divided by class and race, based on land ownership and wealth. He has the resourcefulness and skills to fight and conquer Indians as well as the wilderness. He is supposed to be able to do this without developing savage traits nor forgetting that he is the agent of progress and order in the wild. But that is precisely what Costner's character ultimately rejects. Dunbar does the unthinkable: he breaks out of the rigid confines of the Frontier Aristocrat prototype. The widespread abhorrence of Indians and their wilderness empire shared by all classes of frontier whites is slyly demonstrated by Blake's screenplay that has the illiterate and sadistic Private Spivey (Tony Pierce) stealing Dances With Wolves/Dunbar's journal of his gradual evolution into a Lakota Warrior and using it for toilet paper![5]

Stands With Fists is of course the other major non-Indian character in [8] the story. However, it could be argued that she is in fact "Lakota," her family having been killed by marauding Pawnee (again!) and rather completely assimilated into Ten Bears' band as a mourning widow of a recently killed Lakota warrior. It is to the film-maker's credit that such a skilled and mature actress as Mary McDonnell was cast in this pivotal role. Costner recently revealed his reasoning in selecting McDonnell: "The key word in characterizing Stands With Fists was woman not girl. I wanted someone with lines on her face. That's not an easy thing to explain to a studio."[6] While the character is inherently likeable, McDonnell's skillful performance adds immeasurably to her appeal; strong yet vulnerable, possessing beauty without vanity. Especially noteworthy is the actress's authentic Lakota cadence and accent throughout the film. Her scenes where she relearns English are skillfully executed with pathos and conviction. For all of the above reasons she has gained the respect and acknowledgement of her peers who nominated her for the Academy's Best Supporting Actress category.

9   Other white characters in the film also show a great deal of variety. The flatulent mule skinner Timmons (Robert Pastorelli), despite limited screen time, manages to steal scenes from Costner. His role evokes humor, disgust, and ultimately pathos. One can only suppose it was someone of Timmons's character that prompted Thomas Jefferson to observe that when the Indians encountered the typical frontiersman in the wilderness it was hardly an elevating experience for the Indians. Screenwriter Blake juxtaposes Timmons's painfully detailed violent death with his unexpected plea that his killers not hurt his mules. Just when the audience is ready to see the dirty, disgusting, crude, and racist Timmons killed, Blake introduces us to an unexpectedly compassionate side of the character and leaves the audience the disquieting reflection on our eagerness to see this low-lifer killed. That scene also clearly shows us that in the Pawnee "Violent Leader" scalping of Timmons, there is no honor.

10   Even among the soldiers we find all types − good, bad, insane, and brutal. The enlisted men at the beginning of the film are shown to be tired, disgusted, and demoralized by the indecisiveness of their leaders. While we are witness to General Tide's personal pledge to save the "hero" of St. David's Field, the majority of the military leaders are shown to be cruel, brutal, or alcoholic. The suicidal Major Fambrough is quickly shown to be an isolated and insane alcoholic; he perhaps serves as a warning to Dunbar that the same fate awaits him at Fort Sedgewick. Blake perhaps went over the top with having his pathetic individual announce he had wet his pants! However, we can be reasonably sure that the audience clearly recognizes Fambrough's alcoholic insanity. Unquestionably the most brutal soldiers were to be found near the end of the film at the regarrisoned Fort Sedgewick. The film-makers leave no question in our minds that this is a particularly unsavory and dangerous bunch. This group kills Dances With Wolves' magnificent buckskin Cisco. They repeatedly brutalize Dances With Wolves, and threaten to hang him if he does not lead them to the "hostiles." Finally, they kill the partly domesticated wolf Two Sox. The film-makers show us by this senseless act the all too familiar fear and hatred in the American psyche of the natural world. Yet even among this motley crew, careful observers will find Lt. Elgin (Charles Rocket). Perhaps out

of military respect for a fellow officer of equal rank, or sense of common decency, he repeatedly acts to curb the excesses of enlisted men as well as the indifferent Major in command.

While the characters in Blake's screenplay are satisfactorily varied, some 11 violence has been done to the historical realities in which this story is set. Blake's original novel centered on the Comanche of the Southern Plains, not the Lakota. According to producer Jim Wilson, the change of tribes occurred because the production company gained access to a 3,500-strong herd of buffalo available on the private ranch of former Lieutenant Governor Roy Houck of South Dakota. Yet we are still presented with a Lakota chief called Ten Bears. In fact the real Ten Bears (Par-Roowah Sermehno) was a Southern Plains Yapparika Comanche chief and signer of the Medicine Lodge Treaty of 1867.[7] One rather obvious overlooked transitional casualty of the relocation of the story to the Northern Plains is revealed when Ten Bears shows Dances With Wolves and Kicking Bird an aged Spanish morion and explains, "The men who wore this came in the time of my grandfather's grandfather. Eventually we drove them out. Then came the Mexicans. They do not come here anymore. In my own time, the Texans...." The Lakota could never have encountered this assemblage of Southern colonists on the Northern Plains. The real Kicking Bird was a principal chief (not shaman) of the Kiowas, yet another Southern Plains tribe. Blake is said to have fashioned the film's Kicking Bird after the Kiowa chief because he favored peace with whites. Ironically the real Kicking Bird was believed to have been poisoned by a rival Kiowa shaman/ warrior called Ma Man-ti (Skywalker) for his role in imprisoning resisting tribesmen in 1875.[8] Perhaps the film's most glaring factual inaccuracy is the depiction of a winter military campaign by soldiers hunting for Dances With Wolves and Ten Bears' band in the winter of 1864. In fact no U.S. Army winter campaign was undertaken on the Plains until November of 1868. Interestingly enough, this was Lieutenant Colonel George A. Custer's 7th Cavalry massacre of Cheyenne at Washita Creek on Thanksgiving Day. That massacre, which killed 38 warriors and 67 women and children of the luckless Chief Black Kettle's people (earlier subjected to yet another massacre at Sand Creek, 1864) was portrayed with chilling authenticity in *Little Big Man*.[9]

In addition to factual errors, the film contains a number of unlikely 12 absurdities. Audiences are asked to believe that the Confederate infantry at the St. David's battlefield in 1863 could not hit a lone Union officer at a slow gallop within 50 feet of its picket lines. Viewers literate in Civil War battlefield history will have difficulty reconciling the known Confederate accuracy in small arms fire with the film's myopic troopers. We are also asked to believe that an Eastern neophyte would need to inform a highly skilled, hungry, and presumably alert band of Indians that a thunderously noisy herd of buffalo was in their neighbourhood.

13   The costumes have received wide praise and were beautifully executed by Kathy Smith and Larry Belitz. Costume designer Elso Zamparelli has received a much deserved Academy Award nomination as well. Indeed they appear to have sprung to life from the works of nineteenth-century painters Karl Bodmer and George Catlin. And that may be precisely the problem: all of the Indian characters appear to be wearing their finest ceremonial regalia all the time, everyday! While it makes for colorful and picturesque village life, it certainly would have been impractical. In a similar vein we witness the marriage of Stands With Fists to Dances With Wolves taking place in the middle of the day, and in a white buckskin dress. The latter is certainly outside of acknowledged Lakota culture norms. Finally we are asked to believe that Army rifles buried in the ground for weeks and soaked from a fierce storm could be used functionally by Lakota who within hours of an impending attack had only used war clubs, bows and arrows, and lances. It makes for great drama but presses the limits of our willing suspension of disbelief.

14   A little acknowledged aspect of the appeal this film has for both Indian and non-Indian audiences is its sly sense of humor. A good part of that humor is at the expense of non-Indians. Nervous chuckles are heard among audiences as the mad Major Fambrough scavenges through his bottle-laden "files" and disjointedly converses with a bewildered and shocked Lt. Dunbar. We are disgustingly amused by the ill-mannered ignorance of the mule skinner Timmons and his bizarre behaviour. Costner himself provides a good many laughs. Audiences are delighted with Dunbar's buffalo pantomime and coffee-grinding antics as he desperately attempts to communicate with an incredulous Lakota visiting party. Indians in the audience are especially amused by Dunbar's perplexed reaction to the Lakota ritual of eating the raw buffalo liver following Dunbar's kill.

15   Perhaps director Costner's best remembered amusing visuals are a series of delightful sight jokes centered around the many Lakota attempts to steal Dunbar's magnificent buckskin mare Cisco. Much of the humor here is in fact at the expense of the Indians. A naked Lt. Dunbar confronts a startled Kicking Bird and causes him to flee. A trio of Lakota youth led by Smiles A Lot gallops away leading Cisco and boasting of their soon-to-be-acknowledged warrior status when abruptly their dreams of glory are literally yanked out of their hands and instead of acclaim, they consequently

face a whipping. Even Wind In His Hair has Cisco's persistent loyalty to Lt. Dunbar thwart his best efforts to capture the prized mount. Yet the best belly laugh of this running gag is the delayed realization that during one of the attempts to steal Cisco, Dunbar has knocked himself unconscious on the low door jamb of his Fort Sedgewick sod house.

Perhaps in the same vein, although in this instance made ironically 16 poignant, is Wind In His Hair's boastful soliloquy, "When I heard that more whites are coming, more than can be counted, I wanted to laugh. We took 100 horses from those people, there was no honor in it. They don't ride well, they don't shoot well, they're dirty. They have no women, no children. They could not even make it through one winter in our country. And these people are said to flourish? I think they will be dead in ten years." These moments of humor relieve the tension of early contact and eventual hunted lives that the Indians, we all know, were inevitably subjected to.

The film's phenomenal popularity can be attributed to a number of 17 factors. Thoughtful viewers are conscious of the film's powerfully evocative images of our country in the mid-nineteenth century, including the struggle with the persistent issue of slavery and the ubiquitous "Indian Problem." Those problems have unrelentingly dogged the American psyche for over 100 years and remain largely unresolved to this day. But perhaps more to the point, the character of Lt. Dunbar is very appealing to today's audience precisely because he is a 1990s man, not an 1860s white man. Dunbar is for the Baby Boomer generation the disillusioned soldier seeking personal redemption in a wilderness experience. In the process he is literally transformed before our eyes from an Army officer to a Lakota warrior. He tells the quietly deranged Major Fambrough that he wants to be stationed in the west to "see the frontier ... before it's gone." That simple childlike desire touches an unspoken yearning in many Americans, young and old. Who can blame Dunbar for wanting to escape the mass killing of the Civil War battlefields?

Confronting the solitude of Fort Sedgewick we are only provided with 18 a presumption that the military post had been abandoned, not plundered by Indians. Actually the film-makers reportedly filmed a segment showing the nearly starving and desertion-ridden garrison abandoning the fort. Nevertheless, as Dunbar surveys his post we are treated to an elevated back panning shot revealing a disturbing foregound scene of the former soldiers' hovels burrowed in the hill, a fouled water source littered with trash and partially devoured animal carcasses. It is clear the white men from the East have been reduced to a condition that is truly barbaric by their attempt to attempt to conquer the Indians and their natural world. We witness Lt.

Dunbar cleaning up the animal carcasses and the trash and filling in the burrow holes, just as sensible Americans everywhere work to heal the ecological mess the first wave of Euro-Americans have left in their frenzy to possess the American landscape. Still, Lt. Dunbar's growth in ecological consciousness and personal transformation into a "native" is gradual and incremental. First his beard, then his jacket, his hat, and then his moustache is exchanged for Lakota breastplate armor, knife, and long hair with feathers. His journal entries speak of his awe and love of this new territory, though he habitually longs for company. Done entirely on location, Dean Semler's stunning cinematography effectively captures the unspoiled plains biosphere. It becomes apparent to Dunbar and the audience that he can find an unexpected satisfaction in relationships with animals (Two Sox and Cisco) as well as the natural world around him. His first instinct upon seeing the wolf later called "Two Sox" is to raise his rifle and kill it. Only as he pauses do we begin to realize he is truly changing, perhaps driven by loneliness to allow the magnificent predator to live.

19   The pivotal event in Dunbar's transformation is just prior to the magnificently photographed buffalo hunt. As Ten Bears' band approaches the herd they come upon two dozen buffalo carcasses, shot for their hides with the bodies left to rot upon the plains. Although the mass slaughter of buffalo became rampant a few years later, the scene evokes strong emotions – we know this is only the beginning. Dunbar notes in his journal, "Who would do such a thing? The field was proof enough that it was a people without value and without soul, with no regard for Sioux rights. The wagon tracks leading away left little doubt, and my heart sank as I knew it could only be white hunters." Not seen in the theatrical release is a scene of Dunbar coming upon Ten Bears' hunting camp as a scalp dance is in progress. Fresh white scalps are seen and the suggestion is that the white buffalo hunters have been discovered and killed.

20   In the buffalo hunt audiences are treated to a sight not witnessed for over 120 years. To be sure it was for Native Americans the high point of the movie. Bareback Lakota hunters are shown charging among a thunderous avalanche of large and dangerous bison. Non-Indians are shown that this too is a part of the natural order, a world of predator and game animals. In the feasting and celebrations that follow, we see Dunbar begin to exchange his uniform for native attire. When Dunbar returns to Fort Sedgewick he builds a fire and dances around it alone. Powerful drumbeats rhythmically signal a deeper transformation of Dunbar as he joins in the rhythm of the earth and perhaps harks back to a race memory of his own neolithic ancestors.

21   It is the next day that Kicking Bird gives Dunbar his Indian name, Dances

With Wolves, after the Indians witness his extraordinary relationship with the wolf Two Sox. Interestingly enough, it is the white captive Stands With Fists who mentors and entices Dances With Wolves deeper into Lakota culture, teaching him the language and thus opening up communication between the Indians and this newcomer to their land. The significance of this should not be underestimated. Those who wish to physically and spiritually embrace the land must first learn how from its native people. When Dances With Wolves and Stands With Fists first embrace near a stream we cannot ignore the cattail pollen that fills the air around them — symbolizing germination of their new love for one another and also a new ecological consciousness among the Euro-Americans who have embraced the Indians. Their marriage follows and represents not only the union of the white woman who had preceded Dunbar in her own transformation into an "Indian woman," but also a final rite of passage of Dances With Wolves into a tribal citizen.

Yet another scene missing from the theatrical release occurred after the 22 marriage. In this instance, Kicking Bird and Dances With Wolves encounter a sacred forested area that whites had recently despoiled. The bloated bodies of dozens of small animals killed for target practice swarming with flies, half-consumed deer, and empty whisky bottles littered the landscape. It was this senseless carnage that ultimately prompts Dances With Wolves to tell Kicking Bird that whites will be coming, "more than can be counted, ... like the stars." When this frightening specter is revealed to Ten Bears he seems unable to grasp the terrible physical and ecological carnage that we know will eventually envelop the Lakota and all other Indians.

Perhaps because that scene was excised from the print of the film the 23 public saw, the shock value of the capture of Dances With Wolves by the regarrisoned Fort soldiers is more powerful. As if to underscore the ominous hints of the impending campaigns to ruthlessly exploit or destroy the winged creatures, those that crawled, the two-legged, and the four-legged, we witness the recently metamorphized Dances With Wolves/ Dunbar captured after the soldiers heartlessly kill his beloved buckskin Cisco. In the brutal interrogation that follows, despite kicks, punches, and clubbing with a rifle Dances With Wolves refuses to cooperate in "hunting hostiles and returning white captives." We know Dances With Wolves has completely assumed his Lakota persona when he refuses to speak English to his captors. As he is being transported back to Fort Hays his brutal escorts stop long enough to kill his companion Two Sox. In a shot that cinematically tells us all we need to know, as this scene progresses the camera reveals that just behind the ridge on which Two Sox is killed a Lakota rescue party is tracking the soldiers. Naturally the brutal despoilers of Lakota territory are summarily dispatched in stylish Hollywood fashion. This is a very satisfying scene for 1990s audiences. The Indians on an ecologically moral high ground become a kind of environmental SWAT team for the future Americans.

24   If there is any lingering question about the meaning of all this personal transformation and evolution of ecological ethos among this new white man and woman who have internalized Lakota culture, it is confirmed in the film's final scene. Deciding his presence will only further endanger his Lakota brothers, Dances With Wolves and Stands With Fists sadly leave their mentors to their inevitable fate and strike off on their own, perhaps to search for an America where they can live in peace and flourish with a new ecological ethos. While exchanging parting gifts, Dances With Wolves tells Kicking Bird, "You were the first man I ever wanted to be like. I will not forget you." Indians know that no white man or woman can become Indian, but many of us hope those who have learned of our cultures and appreciate their unique humanity will be our friends and allies in protecting the earth and all of her children. An interesting postscript to this tale of personal transformation and rebirth of an ecologically sound ethos for the Plains has a parallel in real life. Currently efforts are underway to create a "buffalo commons" amid the failed federal-subsidized farming that replaced the great Plains buffalo range. Imagine, a huge area where buffalo could again roam free! Perhaps the Ghost Dance prophets were right: the buffalo may be returning after all.

25   While Hollywood has a dismal record of employing Indian actors and technical staff, *Dances With Wolves* has clearly demonstrated that an American Indian presence in a film can make it work. The Native American actors naturally lent an air of authenticity to the work. This viewer, like thousands of other Native Americans, remains mystified as to why Hollywood still continues to employ non-Indian actors in red-face to play major speaking parts (e.g. Trevor Howard in *Windwalker*). Many of us had hoped that Dan George's endearing performance of "Old Lodgeskins" in Arthur Penn's *Little Big Man* would throw open the doors of opportunity for Indian actors. It didn't happen then, but happily today we again have a major film with a number of important and significant roles for Native Americans. Certainly Tantoo Cardinal, Nathan Lee Chasing His Horse, Graham Greene, Rodney Grant, and Floyd Red Crow Westerman created memorable performances and demonstrated there is a significant pool of talented Native American actors out there. Responsible for a good deal of the authenticity of the Indian roles was South Dakota's Sinte Gleska Indian College Linguist, Doris Leader Charge. She is the Lakota linguist who

translated Michael Blake's screenplay into Lakota, coached the actors in the language, and played a small role in the film. This was no small feat, since none of the actors spoke Lakota fluently. However, the Indian grapevine reports that among the Plains Indians it was the 24 Native American bareback stunt riders who charged in among a 3500-strong herd of buffalo (a feat that had not been accomplished in more than a century) who were the true heroes of the film. My Cheyenne and Comanche friends tell me the buffalo hunt alone was worth the price of admission. No doubt about it, Costner counted coup (gained honor by taking risks) on all Hollywood Indian movies and touched something deeply significant in the Plains Indian cultures with that magnificent buffalo hunt.

Some audiences and critics have commented on the violence in the film 26 and called it excessive. Especially disturbing and painful to watch is the Pawnee killing of the mule skinner Timmons. In Stands With Fists's childhood flashback, we witness a hatchet murder of a white farmer. When Pretty Shield (Doris Leader Charge) crushes a Pawnee skull with a burning log and Stands With Fists shoots another Pawnee during an attack, we clearly see these women are not to be messed with. The soldiers at the end of the film are particularly sadistic and themselves meet a brutal end. Even youth get in the act; after being pistol-whipped Smiles A Lot kills the sadistic Sgt. Bauer by burying a hatchet into his chest to the hilt. As awful as these and other violent acts are, they hardly compare to the violence of the real American frontier. Despite a highly romantic and mythologized popular view of the American past, the American Indian frontier was an incredibly heartless, sordid, violent, and chaotic scramble by Euro-Americans to get something (Indian land and resources) for nothing. For viewers upset over this cinematic tip of an iceberg of violence that Costner reveals for the popcorn-eating masses, I suggest they stick to Roy Rogers westerns or similar pablum. Costner has reminded all popular culture consumers of the violent underpinnings of the American Indian policy.

I suppose it is inevitable and perhaps *de rigueur* that comparisons will 27 be made between Costner's epic and other recent films that prominently feature Indian culture and actors or themes. Thematically perhaps *Windwalker* (1973) makes the best comparison. That film also featured a mythological death and rebirth. Furthermore it also took pains to show Indian society in a positive light, where grandparents, children, and families dominate the portrait of Cheyenne society just prior to sustained colonial contact. While *Windwalker* does feature a touching love story, it is somewhat troublesome to Indians that its most important leads are played by non-Indians. Many writers have commented on the extensive use of the Lakota language in Costner's film, but it was not the first such use in Indian films; in fact *Windwalker* holds that distinction. (*Little Big Man* began using Cheyenne but soon switched over to English.) However, it is probably the brooding and melancholy American Playhouse epic *Roanoak* (1986) that best utilized an Indian language effectively to demonstrate communication problems between whites and America's native people.

28   A film that may not be considered by critics as an Indian film but nevertheless shows some important links to mainstream Indian films is Clint Eastwood's *The Outlaw Josey Wales* (1975). This last great American Western was adapted from Cherokee writer Forrest Carter's novel *Gone to Texas*. On the surface it is about an embittered and extremely violent Civil War guerilla's attempt to escape the madness of the Reconstruction South. It could be interpreted as another attempt to retell the familiar story of a lone white man on the Indian frontier who ultimately attracts an ethnically diverse following, ultimately makes peace with local Indians, and finds physical and spiritual refuge in that diverse milieu. Especially memorable in the Phillip Kaufman-Sonia Chernuss adaptation of Carter's story is the charming performance of Dan George as Confederate Cherokee Lone Watie and Will Sampsom in a powerful and menacing role as the Comanche chief Ten Bears.

29   One can almost feel sorry for the "creative talents" that recently completed the four-hour miniseries adaptation of Evan S. Connell's *Son of Morning Star* (1991). This utterly boring, dramaless, flat, one-dimensional, and totally humorless attempt to tell the story of Lt. Col. George Armstrong Custer's career and his fateful encounter at Little Big Horn is a lesson for film-makers everywhere. While it was laudable for its conscientious attempt to give an even-handed account of the clash of Americans and Plains Indians, its Indians were not allowed to speak. All native reactions and motivations are relegated to a voice-over narration (Buffy St. Marie) that instead of providing insights further isolates the Indians by denying them a voice in history. It is perhaps symptomatic of the contempt network moguls hold for their audiences. In contrast, PBS programmers offered the haunting *Roanoak* where more than two-thirds of the film is in the Chippewa dialect.

30   Unquestionably the film that invites most comparison is Arthur Penn's 1970 classic *Little Big Man*. Again we find the theme of a white man encountering the Indians and discovering their humanity. Yet that bawdy parody of the American frontier only focused on Indians for less than one-third of its screen time. The real similarities of the two films lie in their unusual juxtaposition of humor and drama. Jack Crabbe's humorous sexual encounter with his wife's three sisters is immediately followed by Custer's

murderous attack upon the Cheyenne camp at Washita River where his wife and newborn child are massacred along with many others. In a similar vein, *Dances With Wolves* invites us to laugh both with and at the ignorant mule skinner Timmons only to shortly witness his frightening murder by Pawnee. Both films featured an elaborate and memorable set piece; for Costner it was the buffalo hunt, in Arthur Penn's film it was the re-enactment of the Battle of Greasy Grass (Custer's Last Stand). However, significant differences exist. Penn's film was made at the height of the Vietnam War and emphasized the military assault on America's native peoples. Costner's film on the other hand is concerned with the re-establishment of a spiritual and ecologically sound American ethic with which Euro-Americans can enter the twenty-first century. Costner has been widely quoted as calling his film his personal love letter to the past. It also seems to offer one artist's optimistic blueprint for a new America, where a spiritually based and ecologically sound future awaits those willing to learn from this land's first children.

(1991)

Notes

1. Costner, Kevin et al., *Dances With Wolves, The Illustrated Story of the Epic Film.* New York: New Market Press, 1990.

2. Miles, William. "Enamored with Civilization: Isaac McCoy's Plan for Indian Reform." *Kansas Historian* Vol. 38, 1972: 268-286.

3. Dunlay, Thomas W. *Wolves for the Blue Soldiers, Indian Scouts and Auxiliaries with the United States Army, 1860-90.* Lincoln: University of Nebraska Press, 1987.

4. Blaine, Martha Royce. *The Pawnees: A Critical Bibliography.* Bloomington: Indiana University Press, 1979.

5. Drinnon, Richard. *Facing West: The Metaphysics of Indian Hating and Empire Building.* New York: New American Library, 1980.

6. Costner, ibid., 44.

7. Utley, Robert M. *Frontier Regulars, The United States Army and the Indian, 1866-1891.* New York: Macmillan, 1973.

8. Nye, Wilber S. *Bad Medicine and Good, Tales of the Kiowas.* Norman: University of Oklahoma Press, 1962.

9. Utley, Ibid., 150-156.

The Writer's Subject

1. *Dances With Wolves* is set in the 1860s. Why then does Castillo see the film as important to Americans at the end of the 20th century?

2. How does Castillo deal with the film's depiction of the Pawnee Indians who attack the Lakotas? Does he offer any defence of their conduct?

3. Explain what Castillo means by the "military aristocrat" type of frontier hero. (para. 7)

4. How does Castillo deal with the charge that all the white characters in the film are negatively portrayed throughout? (para. 7)

5. What are some of the film's factual inaccuracies and "unlikely absurdities"?

6. In what ways, according to Castillo, does the principal white character, Lieutenant Dunbar, represent Americans of the 1990s?

7. What significance does the reviewer attach to the film's depiction of the buffalo hunt?

8. How, according to Castillo, does the film convey a sense of a "new ecological ethos"? (para. 24)

9. In what respects, in Castillo's opinion, does the film offer an "optimistic blueprint for a new America"? (para. 30)

The Writer's Style and Subject

1. In what ways, if any, is the review affected by the fact that the writer is himself a native North American?

2. What is meant by the phrase "jaded Eurocentric urbanites" (para. 1), and what does it convey about the writer's attitude?

3. What use does Castillo make of other films about North American Indians?

4. Castillo's review of *Dances With Wolves* first appeared in *Film Quarterly*. In what respects does it go beyond the usual bounds of a movie review?

Suggested Topics for Writing and Discussion

1. Compare Castillo's review of *Dances With Wolves* with the comments by Pauline Kael and by Marilou Awiakta elsewhere in this anthology.

2. Castillo notes that in *Dances With Wolves* the main white character breaks out of the rigid confines of the "Frontier Aristocrat" type of hero. Compare this or other recent films about native North American life to earlier films in this genre, and indicate what differences you see in the portrayal of white characters.

3. Castillo believes that *Dances With Wolves* reflects the emergence of a "new ecological order" in our time. What evidence is there of such an order in other recent films, such as *The Emerald Forest* or *Medicine Man*?

4. What in your view is gained by having native North American characters in films speak in their own languages?

New Age Daydreams
by Pauline Kael

1 A friend of mine broke up with his woman friend after they went to see *Field of Dreams*: she liked it. As soon as I got home from *Dances With Wolves*, I ran to the phone and warned him not to go to it with his new woman friend. Set during the Civil War, this new big Indians-versus-Cavalry epic is about how the white men drove the Native Americans from their land. But Kevin Costner, who directed *Dances With Wolves* and stars in it, is not a man who lets himself be ripped apart by the violent cruelty of what happened. He's no extremist: it's a middle-of-the-road epic. Lieutenant Dunbar (Costner), a Union officer, sees that the Sioux have a superior culture — they're held up as models for the rest of us — and he changes sides. Costner must have heard Joseph Campbell on PBS advising people to "follow your bliss." This is a nature-boy movie, a kid's daydream of being an Indian. When Dunbar has become a Sioux named Dances With Wolves, he writes in his journal that he knows for the first time who he really is. Costner has feathers in his hair and feathers in his head.

2   Once our hero has become an Indian, we don't have to feel torn or divided. We can see that the white men are foulmouthed, dirty louts. The movie — Costner's début as a director — is childishly naïve. When Lieutenant Dunbar is alone with his pet wolf, he's like Robinson Crusoe on Mars. When he tries to get to know the Sioux, and he and they are feeling each other out, it's like a sci-fi film that has the hero trying to communicate with an alien race. But in this movie it's the white men who are the aliens: the smelly brutes are even killing each other, in the war between the North

and the South. Luckily, we Indians are part of a harmonious community. 3
Dances With Wolves has never seen people "so dedicated to their families."
And he loves their humor.

At the beginning, there's a bizarre Civil War battle sequence with the 4
wounded Lieutenant Dunbar riding on horseback between rows of Union
and Confederate soldiers, his arms outstretched, welcoming bullets in a
Christlike embrace, and throughout the movie he is brutalized, seems dead,
but rises again. (Does getting beaten give Costner a self-righteous feeling? Even when it's as unconvincingly staged as it is here?) There's nothing
really campy or shamelessly flamboyant after the opening. There isn't even
anything with narrative power or bite to it. This Western is like a New Age
social-studies lesson. It isn't really revisionist; it's the old stuff toned down
and sensitized.

Costner and his friend Michael Blake, who worked up the material with 5
him in mind and then wrote the novel and the screenplay, are full of good
will. They're trying to show the last years of the Sioux as an independent
nation from the Sioux point of view. And it's that sympathy for the Indians
that (I think) the audience is responding to. But Costner and Blake are
moviemaking novices. Instead of helping us understand the Sioux, they
simply make the Sioux like genial versions of us. The film provides the
groovy wisdom of the Sioux on the subjects of peace and togetherness: you
never fight among yourselves – you negotiate. Each of the Indian
characters is given a trait or two; they all come across as simple-minded,
but so does the hero. Even the villains are endearingly dumb, the way they
are in stories children write.

There's nothing affected about Costner's acting or directing. You hear 6
his laid-back, surfer accent; you see his deliberate goofy faints and falls,
and all the close-ups of his handsomeness. This epic was made by a bland
megalomaniac. (The Indians should have named him Plays with Camera.)
You look at that untroubled face and know he can make everything light-
weight. How is he as a director? Well, he has moments of competence.
And the movie has an authentic vastness. The wide-screen cinematography,
by Dean Semler, features the ridges, horizons, and golden sunsets of South
Dakota; it is pictorial rather than emotionally expressive, but it is spacious
and open at times, and there are fine images of buffalo pounding by.

Mostly, the action is sluggish and the scenes are poorly shaped. Crowds 7
of moviegoers love the movie, though – maybe partly because the issues
have been made so simple. As soon as you see the Indians, amused, watch
the hero frolicking with his wolf, you know that the white men will kill it.
Maybe, also, crowds love this epic because it is so innocent: Costner shows
us his bare ass like a kid at camp feeling one with the great outdoors. He

is the boyish man of the hour: the Sioux onscreen revere him, because he
is heroic and modest, too. TV interviewers acclaim him for the same
qualities. He is the Orson Welles that everybody wants — Orson Welles
with no belly.

(1990)

The Writer's Subject

1. What does Kael mean by calling *Dances With Wolves* "a middle-of-the-road
    epic"? (para. 1)

2. Why is the movie, in Kael's opinion, "childishly naive"? (para. 2)

3. What is the writer's principal criticism of the movie's depiction of the Sioux?

4. Given that she herself is so critical in her estimate, why does Kael think that
    the movie is so popular?

The Writer's Style and Strategy

1. Why does Kael begin her review of *Dances With Wolves* with an anecdote
    about a friend?

2. Clearly, the reviewer did not like *Dances With Wolves*. How does she seek
    to persuade the reader to share her point of view?

3. What is the predominant tone of the review? How is it established?

4. Discuss the intended effect of the following phrases: "like Robinson Crusoe
    on Mars" (para. 2); "a New Age social-studies lesson" (para. 3); "the groovy
    wisdom of the Sioux" (para. 4).

5. A favourite device of critics is to "damn with faint praise." Where does Kael
    make use of this technique?

Suggested Topics for Writing and Discussion

1. Compare Kael's views about *Dances With Wolves* with those of Awiakta and
    Castillo. Are there any points of agreement?

2. Find other examples of hostile or critical film reviews, and discuss the
    methods by which the writers convey their unfavourable response.

3. Write your own review of a film you have seen recently.

4. Choose a film that has been widely reviewed, and compare the styles of the
    reviewers in a number of different magazines or newspapers.

Going Native

by Don Gillmor

On the shores of Lake Ha! Ha!, fifty kilometres south of Chicoutimi, a man   1
in a black leather jacket is constructing an authentic Algonkin wigwam with
a power drill in the bleak cold of late autumn. A dozen natives in traditional
dress are sitting in cedar and fibreglass canoes painted to masquerade as
birchbark. Men with portable smoke machines move hunched through the
trees, creating the dissolving mist of a seventeenth-century dawn. It is raining, a late fall drizzle that feels like English winter. Overlooking a sandy
spit, a crew member holds an umbrella over Mestigoit, a three-foot man
whose face is painted yellow, the skulls of small game tied into his hair.
He is wrapped in furs, holding a cane, an Algonkin sorcerer waiting for
his cue.

The set of *Black Robe,* a film based on Brian Moore's 1985 novel, is   2
authentically cold, echoing the weather in the book. The winter of 1634
is approaching when Father Laforgue, a Jesuit priest, is summoned to a
Huron outpost. Champlain persuades a group of Algonkins to take
Laforgue to the Huron village above the Great Rapids where he can bring
enlightenment, baptism, and misery to the natives. Moore's book
chronicles the clash of cultures, the impact of the Europeans upon the
natives, and the reciprocal effect of the Algonkins on Laforgue's wavering
faith. It is a timely subject, months after the blockade at Oka and the government's renewed commitment to inaction on native issues. In the context
of recent events, *Black Robe* is a creation myth, the story of First Contact.

It is a Canadian/Australian co-production, the set a melange of accents   3
and haircuts; native actors; French-Canadian technicians; a crew of

Australians and English Canadians. At the centre of this historical swirl and immediate chaos is the Australian director Bruce Beresford (*Driving Miss Daisy, Mr. Johnson, Tender Mercies*). Beresford is dressed in winter gear, fur-lined boots and a green toque that a ten year old would instinctively have hidden in his pocket a block from home. He is a relaxed director; there is none of the legendary bombast of De Mille, the devious authority of Hitchcock. He approaches a canoe full of natives who are waiting in the icy drizzle. "For this next scene," he says, joking with them, "I want to see lust, envy, greed, and regret. At the same time, see if you can give me disgust and disgrace." His Australian accent makes it *disgrice*. He walks to a place behind the camera and the assistant director says into the microphone, "Okay, clear the frame. *Attention*. Stand by." This is the scene: Father Laforgue, played by Lothaire Bluteau (*Jesus of Montreal*), and Daniel, a young French carpenter (played by Australian actor Aden Young), are being deserted by the Algonkins who have been guiding them. There are terse words spoken in Cree, then Laforgue says in English, "Where are paddlers? You promised." The Algonkin chief tells Laforgue that he is on his own and turns away to his canoe.

4   "Cut. *Coupez*."

5   Aden Young walks over to Helen Atkinson, a Cree woman who is working as a linguistic coach and extra, and asks how his Cree speech was. She smiles and nods politely. Much of the film's dialogue is spoken in Cree and Mohawk and subtitled. Language has been a tricky thing in *Black Robe*. A rigorous reading of history would have Laforgue speaking French, the Algonkins speaking Algonkin, and the Hurons speaking Huron. Hollywood canons would dictate that the natives speak accented pidgin English and the parts be played by Italians. A historically acceptable compromise has been struck, with the Cree language, which is still in use, substituting for Algonkin, and Laforgue speaking English. Natives have been cast in native roles, breaking with the tradition that has given us the noble L.A. savages Charles Bronson (*Chato's Land*) and Rock Hudson (*Taza, Son of Cochise* in 3D).

6   "This is where it all started," said Billy Two Rivers, a Mohawk actor and a Kahnawake spokesman who spent part of the summer explaining why his people had blockaded the Mercier Bridge in a gesture of solidarity with the Oka Mohawks. Two Rivers is fifty-five, a former wrestler with the weathered face of a benevolent Ernest Borgnine. The front part of his head has been shaved except for a loony-sized circle of hair that is grown long and tied with beads. He is dressed in buckskins, fur, and a pair of rubber galoshes. We are standing on the shore of Lake Ha! Ha! and Two Rivers is pointing to a scene being shot, Laforgue mixing with his Algonkin guides.

"This is where the two cultures first started to bump into one another," he says. "The Jesuits wanted to change us, we didn't want to change them. We wanted to coexist."

The 360-odd years of coexistence have been, for the most part, exploitive 7 and uneasy. As part of the Iroquois League, the Mohawks distrusted the Europeans immediately, but they adapted to the changing frontier. They worked as guides for the French, then as trappers when the fur trade expanded.

"After the fur trade diminished," Two Rivers says, "we became lumber- 8 jacks and river pilots. With our knowledge of the rapids, we brought the log booms down and delivered them to Montreal Harbour where the oak could be shipped to England. In the 1850s, when the Victoria Bridge was built, our people were delivering a lot of the materials, the stone came from Kahnawake, and we went and walked the narrow beams of the bridges as if it were a street. That was the beginning of high-steel work for the Mohawk people." Some of the Mohawks opted for the theatre, creating the image of warlike savages for Buffalo Bill's Wild West Show.

The Mohawks have since expanded into bingo and cigarette sales and 9 the assorted weaponry the new warrior tradition demands: AK-47s, shotguns, deer rifles. Last summer Two Rivers was a regular presence in the news; after explaining the native position, he would go to Montreal for make-up tests for the part of Ougebemat in *Black Robe*. Army helicopters hovered as the cast took canoe lessons on Lake St. Louis.

The first Europeans brought the lasting allure of a consumer society, an 10 ethic that was reluctantly embraced by the Iroquois. "When Champlain shot an Iroquois chief at the headwaters of the St. Lawrence," Two Rivers says, "that is when we began trading for muskets." In the *Jesuit Relations,* a record of missionary work from 1632 to 1673, and a source for *Black Robe,* an ironic Montagnais chief was quoted as saying, "The Beaver does everything perfectly well, it makes kettles, hatchets, swords, knives, bread; and, in short, it makes everything." The careful ecological balance sustained by the native hunters for hundreds of years was quickly upset by this new approach; trapping for survival was replaced by trapping for profit.

Helen Atkinson, the Cree adviser, is from Chisasibi in the James Bay 11 region. When the hydroelectric project began in 1971, the local Cree were still a traditional hunting society, their religion a holistic cultural continuum that invested the air, water, trees, fish, and game with spirits. Some of the hunting grounds were flooded by the dam and the game moved away. The fish are contaminated with mercury. The Cree could see that the project was inevitable; they cut the best deal they could and took a twenty-year,

$225-million settlement, the spirit world suddenly hammered by the fiscal.

12   "My father used to say the white man is insatiable in his quest for power, land, and destruction," Billy Two Rivers says. "We drink the same water, eat the same food, walk on the same land, and neither of us has much time."

13   "There is a moment in a person's life when what they believe in is taken away from them," Brian Moore said in a 1988 interview. "I am interested in what happens then." In *Black Robe,* Laforgue is faced with the disquieting irony that the natives may be better Christians than he himself. They share everything with genuine happiness while Laforgue hoards tobacco, wine, his seed, and his few possessions. They are tireless and forgiving; Laforgue worries that he is an exalted salesman: what can he offer these people? He offers them salvation in the form of eternal life. The natives interpret the offer literally: they believe they will live forever. It is the first misunderstood treaty, the first deception.

14   On a hillside near Lake Eternité, forty kilometres east of Chicoutimi, the native cast is assembled for a shot that has Daniel, the young Frenchman, coming up over a rise to see an Algonkin warrior facing him with a drawn bow. Aden Young comes up the steep path, stops, and staggers down the hill under the weight of his pack. "Jesus."

15   "One more time, same thing," the assistant director says into his mike.

16   "You should be *wye* in the beckground," Beresford says, arranging the cast. "You weren't chewing, were you, Annie?" An actress who is chewing gum is caught out like a schoolgirl. A vaguely Indian chant descends into a doo-wop chorus of "The Lion Sleeps Tonight." It's getting cold, the wind coming off the lake in damp gusts. "It reminds me of Boy Scouts," Beresford says of shooting in northern Quebec. "I finally had to give it up. I realized I *hited* it."

17   "Lose the spear, Billy," a microphoned voice calls out. Beresford gets the shot and they break for lunch.

18   Beresford sits at a picnic table in the lunch cabin with Jake Eberts, one of the executive producers. Eberts grew up in the Saguenay-Lac-St-Jean area nearby, a chemical engineer by training who went on to produce *Gandhi, The Killing Fields, Driving Miss Daisy, Chariots of Fire,* and *Dances With Wolves. Black Robe,* like most of the films made by Eberts and/or Beresford, is an independent production, made without the financial backing of a major studio. The $14-million budget was raised by Samson Productions in Australia and Alliance Communications in Canada, with Eberts making up the $6-million shortfall.

19   "If you go to a studio for financing," Eberts says over lunch, "you are in bed with them creatively." Eberts doesn't look like a producer; he is tall, slim, without a cigar, dressed like a chemical engineer on a hiking vacation.

"The studios may like *Black Robe,* but they will support it only if Richard Gere or Bruce Willis plays Laforgue. If you tell them Lothaire Bluteau looks the part, that he is a fine actor, it won't matter, they'll still want Richard Gere. You have to film it with Lothaire and then show it to them. Then they'll say, 'That guy who's playing Laforgue is perfect for the part.'"

Beresford cast Bluteau after seeing him play a psychotic male prostitute 20
on the London stage in *Being at Home with Claude.* "We'd been looking around for a long time for an actor to play Laforgue," Beresford says between mouthfuls of pasta. "We'd discussed and rejected all sorts of possibilities. I saw *Being at Home with Claude* advertised week after week in London and I saw Lothaire's name get bigger in the ads and I thought, what *is* it with this guy? So I went and saw him and thought, this guy's fantastic. So I called Robert Lantos at Alliance and said, 'You don't have to go searching around for Laforgue, you have the actor in Canada.' Robert said, 'He doesn't speak a word of English.' I said, 'He did pretty well in this play last night.'"

Beresford read *Black Robe* the day it was published in 1985. He had come 21
to Brian Moore with *The Lonely Passion of Judith Hearne,* a book he read while working as a film editor in Africa. "When I read *Black Robe,*" Beresford says, "the strength of the Indians, the bravery of the Jesuits, the period, the physical conditions, the snow, it was all a revelation. I didn't know it had all happened. I thought, what an extraordinary period of North American history."

He inquired after the film rights, which had been presold to ICC, a Cana- 22
dian production company, before the book's publication. ICC later merged with Alliance Communications and the project ended up in the hands of Robert Lantos. *Black Robe* went through the standard gyrations of film properties, bouncing by various directors, ricocheting among prospective backers. Beresford had heard that David Cronenberg (*Dead Ringers*) was going to direct, then read that he wasn't, and talked to Lantos in 1988. Beresford had a three-film commitment to fulfil first; among those projects was *Driving Miss Daisy,* which won the Oscar for best picture.

Despite Beresford's currency in the film world, there was little 23
Hollywood interest in a movie shot partly in Cree about French Jesuits meeting native Indians in Canada. If *Black Robe* follows *Dances With Wolves* as a box-office and critical success, Hollywood may grind out a rush of native films, but it is unlikely that they will be subtitled explorations into cultural dissonance. Perhaps we'll see Tom Hanks as a wacky Cherokee real-estate developer (*Take My Land, Please*). Or Sylvester Stallone as a lone Iroquois determined to reclaim New York with an Uzi (*I'll Take Manhattan*).

24   Robert Lantos, when I interviewed him earlier in Toronto, outlined the blunt priorities of the major studios. "It doesn't matter if the film is brilliant. The only thing that is important is money. Oscars are important, but only because Oscars mean money." Unlike Eberts, Lantos does look like a producer; he is swarthy, cigar-smoking, one foot pumping madly in a caffeine jig. He looks like a money man, the bad cop in his and Eberts' good cop/bad cop production team. "It is important that this film succeed," Lantos said. "It shows we can make films this size in Canada and bring in foreign money. Most Canadian films cost $3-million or less." I asked Lantos whether recent events at Oka and Kahnawake would help lend *Black Robe* box-office appeal. A satisfied smile moved his heavy features upward. "I didn't have anything to do with what happened at Oka," he said, his palms facing outward in the universal gesture of innocence.

25   Some of the *Black Robe* crew are staying in La Baie, an industrial city of 24,000 that is twenty kilometres closer to the set than Chicoutimi. The town is situated at the edge of a bay formed by the Saguenay River. An Alcan plant sits loudly at the vertex of the semicircle described by the shoreline, a pulp plant nearby. There is a walking path built along the water, a grey-stone Catholic church at the centre of town, and fine industrial grit in the air. Aluminum has been recently linked to Alzheimer's and various environmental misfortunes. A local group is suing Alcan, the company that provides both blight and sustenance for the area. In the grim relief of early morning, La Baie has the whipped look of a company town.

26   Thirty kilometres south, the film set has the pristine air of the northern woods, the cold lending a sense of purity that may no longer be supported by fact. They are shooting in the forest today, a campfire scene. A short track has been built for the camera to run on; two tepees stand in a small clearing. The native extras move around the site with bundles of birchbark, the principals in the foreground.

27   "Everyone moves on 'action,'" the assistant director says into the mike. "Clear the frame."

28   "It's too busy, much too busy," Beresford says of the scene, and they make compositional adjustments. During the break, a make-up woman refers to a Polaroid to touch up a scar on Lothaire's mournful face. A special-effects man holding a coffee cup full of fake blood discusses the realism of his latest wound. The crew compare the merits of various boot brands and remark on the efficiency of wool when it's wet.

29   "Can we give the camera more energy?" the Australian cameraman asks.

30   Someone pours water on the campfire and the smoke is too dense, the cast disappearing through the lens. A religious point is raised and Beresford says, "Okay, let's bring on the spiritual adviser." The cameraman moves

off his seat and wanders into the smoke. "The cameraman is a staunch Catholic so he's become our spiritual adviser," Beresford says. "He's very handy."

It's getting close to lunch and the union goes into overtime at noon. "Do 31 you want the shot?" the assistant director asks Beresford. "Do we go into penalty?"

Beresford nods and the assistant calls into the mike, "Okay, we go into 32 penalty, let's go. Ready."

"*Vas-y, vas-y*," Beresford says, exercising most of his French vocabu- 33 lary. "Am I being a bit familiar?"

It starts to snow an hour later, wispy flakes that circle in the winds. The 34 set designer is walking around with a plastic bag full of crushed potato flakes to use as snow should they need it to match shots. There is a canoeing scene to shoot and the native paddlers are fitted with wet suits under their buckskins should a canoe tip into the freezing water. The canoes move expertly in tight formation. One of the leads in the film gets accidentally swatted in the nose with a paddle and everyone takes a break.

"Look up there," Beresford says, pointing to the snow that has collected 35 in descending patches along the small mountains around the lake.

"It won't be long." 36

"It won't be long before *what*?" 37

"Before the snow covers everything down here too." 38

"Oh God." 39

In Moore's book, Laforgue and the Algonkins are racing against the 40 coming winter, trying to get upriver before the cold and snow make it impossible. The cast and crew are engaged in the same race. Winter will arrive soon.

In the lunch cabin, the young native boy who is playing the son of 41 Chomina, an Algonkin chief, is gleefully anticipating his death at the hands of the Iroquois. "Okay, say you're Sandrine, and he just goes *aaaagh*," the boy says, making the motion of slitting his own throat. "All those kids are going to see me die," he says, pointing happily to a group of extras in the corner.

"It's an interesting experience," Helen Atkinson says of working on the 42 set of *Black Robe*. "But it isn't the native perspective, it's a Jesuit perspective, a white film." She and Tantoo Cardinal (who plays Chomina's wife) have talked of making a film that would show some of the matriarchal elements of native culture. The native sentiment on the set is that the Jesuit version of First Contact is biased. But the Jesuits kept rigorous records; the natives' oral culture is viewed by whites as unreliable history, stories descended through generations, gathering momentum and mythology. The happiest nations have no history, George Eliot wrote. With three histories currently in competition — French, native, and English — is it any surprise that we are un unhappy nation? The native version is slightly at odds with the Jesuit account, but then history is written by the winners.

43   The afternoon snow is light but steady, a taste of northern winter. The paddlers in the film are standing on the shore of Lake Ha! Ha! posing for a group photograph, twenty men and women in native dress preparing their smiles. "Where's Lothaire?" someone asks. "Where is Laforgue?" A cry goes up for Lothaire Bluteau, who is standing on the beach 200 metres away. He begins to run along the crescent of sand, his woollen Jesuit robes flapping, his feet slipping in the sand, his smoker's lungs aching. The natives cheer his arrival as he rounds the point breathlessly. "Jesus, I'm going to die," he says into the north wind.

                                                                  (1991)

The Writer's Subject

1. Gillmor calls the film *Black Robe* "a creation myth, the story of First Contact" (para. 2). Since the story of the film is set in 1634, in what sense are we to understand the phrase "creation myth"?

2. What connection does Gillmor draw between the subject of *Black Robe* and the Oka crisis that occurred near Montreal in 1990?

3. According to this article, what have been the principal effects of "contact" on the Mohawk and the Cree?

4. How, according to Gillmor, does the film deal with the differences between white and native cultures?

5. What are the problems of making a film without the backing of a major studio?

6. What does Gillmor mean by describing the cold weather as "lending a sense of purity that may no longer be supported by fact"? (para. 26)

7. How does Gillmor deal with the conflicting historical perspectives on the events dramatized by the film?

The Writer's Style and Strategy

1. "Going Native" presents us with an account of the story of *Black Robe,* a description of its filming, and an outline of the historical background. How does the writer organize his essay so that these different elements cohere?

2. Discuss the portrait that emerges of the film's director, Bruce Beresford. Is the portrait neutral and objective?

3. How and where does the writer allow his own views to become apparent?

4. What picture emerges of the Native Indian actors and advisers?

5. Explain the point of Gillmor's references to Hollywood stars in paragraph 5, 19, and 23. What is the predominant tone of these paragraphs?

6. In your view, is the final paragrah an effective conclusion to Gillmor's article?

Suggested Topics for Writing and Discussion

1. Gillmor writes about a film that dramatizes the turmoil of "cultural dissonance." Choose another film or a book that deals directly or indirectly with this subject and show how "dissonance" is depicted in the work concerned.

2. In recent years, scholars and educators have realized the need to revise many of the history books long used in schools. Find and compare the treatments of Canada's Native peoples in two works of history, one published pre-1950 and one issued in the last five years.

3. "History is written by the winners," says Gillmor. Perhaps this is nowhere better illustrated than in the many accounts of the "discovery" of America by Christopher Columbus in 1492. Find out what you can about recent revaluations of Columbus's achievements, and about the attempts to view those achievements from the perspective of Native peoples.

4. Gillmor alludes to the early Jesuit missionaries who arrived in Canada in the sixteenth century, and to the *Jesuit Relations* in which they described their activities. Find a translation of the *Relations,* and examine the attitudes revealed there to the Native Indian inhabitants of the country.

True Believers

by Terrence Rafferty

1   The title of Bruce Beresford's unusual and absorbing new film, "Black
Robe," refers to the long cassocks worn by Jesuit missionaries in North
America in the seventeenth century. The zealous priests were part of the
early days of French exploration in the New World; while explorers like
Champlain plunged into the wilderness, claimed land, and established
settlements, the Jesuits who travelled alongside them were out to claim the
souls of the Algonquian, Huron, and Iroquois Indians who inhabited that
wilderness. The priests considered these people savage and godless, and
the Indians called the missionaries "Blackrobes" — an ominous, mythic-
sounding name for figures who were of all the white intruders surely the
most disturbing and the least comprehensible. "Black Robe," which is based
on Brian Moore's 1985 novel of that name (Moore himself did the
screenplay), is a culture-clash drama in which the most important conflicts
take place in the realm of the spirit. The hero is a pale and excruciatingly
pious young Jesuit called Father Laforgue (Lothaire Bluteau), who sets
out from the Quebec settlement on a journey up the St. Lawrence and
Ottawa rivers. His destination is a remote mission among the Hurons.
Father Jerome, the Jesuit in charge there, hasn't been heard from for too
long, and his superiors in Quebec are worried. Laforgue is to find out what's
going on; it's understood that he will take over the mission if Father Jerome
is dead.

2   As Laforgue heads upriver with a reluctant escort of Algonquians, we
begin to understand why the Indians and the priests are so fearful and
suspicious of each other. The differences between Laforgue and the Algon-

quian chief, Chomina (August Schellenberg), aren't matters of social organization of moral codes. The world views of Laforgue and Chomina are so radically opposed that at times the two men seem unable even to acknowledge each other as human. The priest and the Indian, making their way together to the distant mission, are sharing experience in only the most literal, limited sense. We feel at every moment that Laforgue and Chomina aren't seeing or hearing the same things — that they aren't living the same history. These characters don't engage in philosophical debates; there's nothing to talk about. Most stories of this sort are framed so that the characters can "learn" from each other: people from different cultures wind up looking into each other's eyes and thinking, These people have something good. Often, though, this cross-cultural understanding seems to have been accomplished in a facile way — by treating the features of complex, integrated cultures as if they were merely life-style choices. "Black Robe" offers no easy way out of the spiritual impasse between the Jesuits and the Indians, and the characters are presented without concessions to twentieth-century sensibilities. Laforgue and Chomina are as alien to us as they are to each other.

Laforgue is the strangest, most difficult hero in recent movies. Looking at him, you do not think of a modern Jesuit — not the fiendishly ingenious intellectuals who befuddle students in American high schools and universities, and not the liberation-theology activists who work in the Third World. The Jesuit in "Black Robe" is an old-fashioned true believer. He prays, he reads Scripture, he struggles to resist fleshly temptations; he lives only to serve the one true God of Catholicism. For him, the material world is nothing, an illusion: all nature is just the antechamber to Heaven, and the body is the cell in which the soul counts the days until its release. Aspiring to a state of pure, incorporeal spirituality, Laforgue often seems inhuman, lifeless, spectral. He's a spooky guy, and it's easy to see why the Indians he means to convert find his values so resistible; many of them think he's a demon. Laforgue, the Father from another planet, is so bizarre that any other world view should, by contrast, look pretty attractive. Chomina and the rest of the Algonquians do at least live by a philosophy that allows for sensual pleasure; they don't deny the reality of the physical world or reduce day-to-day existence to the status of diligent, joyless preparation for a blissful afterlife. Their vision of nature is animistic — the spirits of the dead speak through birds and animals and rivers and trees — and they believe in the truth of dreams. The movie's portrayal of the Indians' mysticism is straightforward, unromanticized; it has an anthropological detachment. The signs and portents that come to Chomina are always ambiguous and often unreliable: disturbed by dream images, he consults

his wife and his friends and a shaman (a nasty-spirited dwarf) for their interpretations, and the ideas that they give him are confusing and contradic-
tory. He's never quite sure how he should act on his visions. If the priest's
world seems thin and insubstantial, the Indian's is perhaps too rich;
Chomina often appears to be wandering uncertainly through a blizzard of
meanings.

4   Moore and Beresford show extraordinary respect for the stubborn,
almost impenetrable otherness of their historical characters. "Black Robe"
dares to build a story around people whom contemporary audiences
couldn't possibly identify with. This is a movie we have to feel our way
into − tentatively, gradually − and it accumulates emotional force as it
goes along. It's an adventure story in the truest sense: the filmmakers lead
us into unknown territory, and keep pushing us farther and farther on, until,
by the end, we find ourselves deep in the wilderness of the seventeenth-
century consciousness. We're not entirely at home there, but at least we're
able to figure out where we are − to recognize some of the moral and
philosophical coordinates of this strange new world. Despite the movie's
rigor, it never feels austere or merely academic. The story has plenty of
action, in the James Fenimore Cooper manner − ambushes, escapes, tense
confrontations. Even when nothing dramatic is happening, the movie is
suspenseful: we're constantly aware of danger − and aware, too, that the
Huron mission at the end of the journey might be the scene of an appalling
catastrophe. And the late-autumn and winter landscapes in which the action
is set are piercingly lovely: the river is broad and sinuous, and it cuts
through tree-covered mountains; the skies have the mysterious dull-gray
beauty of pewter; and the snow, when it comes, gives a kind of radiance
to everything. Beresford and his cinematographer, Peter James, have
provided "Black Robe" with a voluptuous surface, and the movie's visual
splendor is more than decoration. These views of natural phenomena have
a clarity that's almost unreal: paradoxically, they seem to justify both the
Indians' pantheism and the Jesuits' sense of the world as illusion. Beresford
("Driving Miss Daisy," "Mister Johnson") puts his characteristic pictorialism to good use here. "Black Robe" has real sweep, and its beauties
are expressive; this is the best filmmaking he has ever done.

5   By the end of the picture, Moore and Beresford have accustomed us to
the peculiar terms in which the characters understand their lives. Without
ever feeling that Laforgue or Chomina or any of the other people on the
screen are "just like us," we begin, nonetheless, to respond to their struggles
wholeheartedly. The intensity of their beliefs becomes very moving, and
the irreconcilable disparity between the Blackrobes' philosophy and the
Indians' becomes unbearably sad. In the movie's greatest scene, near the

end, Laforgue stands over a dying Algonquian and searches for something to say to him. The priest tries to bless the old Indian, to tell him "My God loves you," and the dying man's daughter is outraged. It's a complex, disorienting moment. In a sense, the blessing is obscenely irrelevant: it's no solace to the Algonquian, who doesn't believe in the Jesuit's God and, for that matter, isn't entirely sure that Laforgue isn't some kind of sorcerer. The gesture can be seen, too, as a confirmation of the spiritual colonialism of missionary activity — the impulse to collect souls the way trappers bag pelts. (The Jesuits were keen on baptizing dying Indian babies and sending their souls straight to Heaven.) And yet Laforgue's awkward words are touching; we sense that they come from a genuine desire to do good and a real affection for the dying man. The priest has no choice but to speak, and no other way of expressing himself fully, and his absurd invocation of his God is somehow an act of bravery: he has to trust that the Algonquian will hear honest feelings rather than meaningless words.

"Black Robe" moves on a steady, powerful flow of ideas and emotions. 6 Moore's superbly intelligent script and Beresford's confident direction carry us past the movie's one serious weakness, which is Lothaire Bluteau's enervated performance as Laforgue. Fortunately, August Schellenberg's Chomina is magnificent, and the movie is so strongly conceived that its themes come through despite Bluteau's passivity. (Repressed characters should look as if they might once have had some impulse vital enough to be worth repressing.) In every other respect, the picture is a triumph. "Black Robe" isn't about anything so simple as lost innocence, but its freshness gives us an intimation of how audiences must have responded when movies were a new world: it stirs in us a sense of discovery.

(1991)

The Writer's Subject

1. How, according to Rafferty's account, does *Black Robe* dramatize the clash of cultures between Native Indians and whites?

2. What is meant by the statement, "... the characters are presented without concessions to twentieth-century sensibilities"? (para. 2)

3. What contrast does the reviewer draw between the beliefs of the priest and those of the Indians? (para. 3)

4. What does the review tell us about the "spiritual colonialism" of the Jesuit missionaries who accompanied the early explorers into Canada?

5. In what way has the director put his "characteristic pictorialism" to good use in *Black Robe,* according to Rafferty? (para. 4)

The Writer's Style and Strategy

1. How effectively does Rafferty blend the elements of description, analysis, and evaluation that are generally found in movie or drama reviews? Pick out those passages in which the reviewer's own opinions are most clearly evident.

2. The film is about a journey, both in the literal and in the spiritual sense. How does the reviewer apply the metaphor of a journey of exploration to the experience of the viewer?

3. How does Rafferty use comparison and contrast to set forth the film's central conflict?

4. What does the writer mean by calling Laforgue "the Father from another planet"? (para. 3)

Suggested Topics for Writing and Discussion

1. Find other reviews of *Black Robe* for comparison with that by Rafferty.

2. Compare Rafferty's discussion of *Black Robe*'s treatment of Native Indians with the account given by Don Gillmor ("Going Native," above).

3. Rafferty says of *Black Robe,* "it stirs in us a sense of discovery" (para. 6). Write about another movie that provided you with "a sense of discovery" about some aspect of culture, society, or human nature.

Nature and Humankind

The Obligation to Endure
by Rachel Carson

The history of life on earth has been a history of interaction between   1
living things and their surroundings. To a large extent, the physical form
and the habits of the earth's vegetation and its animal life have been
moulded by the environment. Considering the whole span of earthly
time, the opposite effect, in which life actually modifies its surroundings, has been relatively slight. Only within the moment of time
represented by the present century has one species — man — acquired
significant power to alter the nature of his world.

During the past quarter century this power has not only increased   2
to one of disturbing magnitude but it has changed in character. The most
alarming of all man's assaults upon the environment is the contamination of air, earth, rivers, and sea with dangerous and even lethal
materials. This pollution is for the most part irrecoverable; the chain
of evil it initiates not only in the world that must support life but in
living tissues is for the most part irreversible. In this now universal
contamination of the environment, chemicals are the sinister and little
recognized partners of radiation in changing the very nature of the world
— the very nature of its life. Strontium 90, released through nuclear
explosions into the air, comes to earth in rain or drifts down as fallout,
lodges in soil, enters into the grass or corn or wheat grown there, and
in time takes up its abode in the bones of a human being, there to remain until his death. Similarly, chemicals sprayed on croplands or forests
or gardens lie long in soil, entering into living organisms, passing from
one to another in a chain of poisoning and death. Or they pass mysteriously by underground streams until they emerge and, through the alchemy

of air and sunlight, combine into new forms that kill vegetation, sicken cattle, and work unknown harm on those who drink from once pure wells. As Albert Schweitzer has said, "Man can hardly even recognize the devils of his own creation."

3   It took hundreds of millions of years to produce the life that now inhabits the earth — eons of time in which that developing and evolving and diversifying life reached a state of adjustment and balance with its surroundings. The environment, rigorously shaping and directing the life it supported, contained elements that were hostile as well as supporting. Certain rocks gave out dangerous radiation; even within the light of the sun, from which all life draws its energy, there were short-wave radiations with power to injure. Given time — time not in years but in millennia — life adjusts, and a balance has been reached. For time is the essential ingredient; but in the modern world there is no time.

4   The rapidity of change and the speed with which new situations are created follow the impetuous and heedless pace of man rather than the deliberate pace of nature. Radiation is no longer merely the background radiation of rocks, the bombardment of cosmic rays, the ultraviolet of the sun that have existed before there was any life on earth; radiation is now the unnatural creation of man's tampering with the atom. The chemicals to which life is asked to make its adjustment are no longer merely the calcium and silica and copper and all the rest of the minerals washed out of the rocks and carried in rivers to the sea; they are the synthetic creations of man's inventive mind, brewed in his laboratories, and having no counterparts in nature.

5   To adjust to these chemicals would require time on the scale that is nature's; it would require not merely the years of a man's life but the life of generations. And even this, were it by some miracle possible, would be futile, for the new chemicals come from our laboratories in an endless stream; almost five hundred annually find their way into actual use in the United States alone. The figure is staggering and its implications are not easily grasped — 500 new chemicals to which the bodies of men and animals are required somehow to adapt each year, chemicals totally outside the limits of biologic experience.

6   Among them are many that are used in man's war against nature. Since the mid-1940's over 200 basic chemicals have been created for use in killing insects, weeds, rodents, and other organisms described in the modern vernacular as "pests": and they are sold under several thousand different brand names.

7   These sprays, dusts, and aerosols are now applied almost universal-

ly to farms, gardens, forests, and homes — nonselective chemicals that have the power to kill every insect, the "good" and the "bad," to still the song of birds and the leaping of fish in the streams, to coat the leaves with a deadly film, and to linger on in soil — all this though the intended target may be only a few weeds or insects. Can anyone believe it is possible to lay down such a barrage of poisons on the surface of earth without making it unfit for all life? They should not be called "insecticides," but "biocides."

The whole process of spraying seems caught up in an endless spiral. **8** Since DDT was released for civilian use, a process of escalation has been going on in which ever more toxic materials must be found. This has happened because insects, in a triumphant vindication of Darwin's principle of the survival of the fittest, have evolved super races immune to the particular insecticide used. Hence a deadlier one has always to be developed — and then a deadlier one than that. It has happened also because, for reasons to be described later, destructive insects often undergo a "flareback," or resurgence, after spraying, in numbers greater than before. Thus the chemical war is never won, and all life is caught in its violent crossfire.

Along with the possibility of the extinction of mankind by nuclear **9** war, the central problem of our age has therefore become the contamination of man's total environment with such substances of incredible potential for harm — substances that accumulate in the tissues of plants and animals and even penetrate the germ cells to shatter or alter the very material of heredity upon which the shape of the future depends.

Some would-be architects of our future look toward a time when it **10** will be possible to alter the human germ plasm by design. But we may easily be doing so now by inadvertence, for many chemicals, like radiation, bring about gene mutations. It is ironic to think that man might determine his own future by something so seemingly trivial as the choice of an insect spray.

All this has been risked — for what? Future historians may well be **11** amazed by our distorted sense of proportion. How could intelligent beings seek to control a few unwanted species by a method that contaminated the entire environment and brought the threat of disease and death even to their own kind? Yet this is precisely what we have done. We have done it, moreover, for reasons that collapse the moment we examine them. We are told that the enormous and expanding use of pesticides is necessary to maintain farm production. Yet is our real problem not one of *overproduction*? Our farms, despite measures to remove acreages from production and to pay farmers *not* to produce, have yielded such a staggering excess of crops that the American taxpayer in 1962 is paying out more than one billion dollars a year as the total carrying cost of the surplus-food storage program. And is the situation helped when one branch of the Agriculture Department tries to reduce production while another states, as it did in 1958, "It is believed generally that reduction of crop acreages under provisions of the Soil Bank will stimulate interest in use of chemicals to obtain maximum production on the land retained in crops." ?

12   All this is not to say there is no insect problem and no need of control. I am saying, rather, that control must be geared to realities, not to mythical situations, and that the methods employed must be such that they do not destroy us along with the insects.

13   The problem whose attempted solution has brought such a train of disaster in its wake is an accompaniment of our modern way of life. Long before the age of man, insects inhabited the earth — a group of extraordinarily varied and adaptable beings. Over the course of time since man's advent, a small percentage of the more that half a million species of insects have come into conflict with human welfare in two principal ways: as competitors for the food supply and as carriers of human disease.

14   Disease-carrying insects become important where human beings are crowded together, especially under conditions where sanitation is poor, as in time of natural disaster or war or in situations of extreme poverty and deprivation. Then control of some sort becomes necessary. It is a sobering fact, however, as we shall presently see, that the method of massive chemical control has had only limited success, and also threatens to worsen the very conditions it is intended to curb.

15   Under primitive agricultural conditions the farmer had few insect problems. These arose with the intensification of agriculture — the devotion of immense acreages to a single crop. Such a system set the stage for explosive increases in specific insect populations. Single-crop farming does not take advantage of the principles by which nature works; it is agriculture as an engineer might conceive it to be. Nature has introduced great variety into the landscape, but man has displayed a passion for simplifying it. Thus he undoes the built-in checks and balances by which nature holds the species within bounds. One important natural check is a limit on the amount of suitable habitat for each species. Obviously then, an insect that lives on wheat can build up its population

to much higher levels on a farm devoted to wheat than on one in which wheat is intermingled with other crops to which the insect is not adapted.

The same thing happens in other situations. A generation or more 16 ago, the towns of large areas of the United States lined their streets with the noble elm tree. Now the beauty they hopefully created is threatened with complete destruction as disease sweeps through the elms, carried by a beetle that would have only limited chance to build up large populations and to spread from tree to tree if the elms were only occasional trees in a richly diversified planting.

Another factor in the modern insect problem is one that must be viewed 17 against a background of geologic and human history: the spreading of thousands of different kinds of organisms from their native homes to invade new territories. This worldwide migration has been studied and graphically described by the British ecologist Charles Elton in his recent book *The Ecology of Invasions*. During the Cretaceous Period, some hundred million years ago, flooding seas cut many land bridges between continents and living things found themselves confined in what Elton calls "colossal separate nature reserves." There, isolated from others of their kind, they developed many new species. When some of the land masses were joined again, about 15 million years ago, these species began to move out into new territories — a movement that is not only still in progress but is now receiving considerable assistance from man.

The importation of plants is the primary agent in the modern spread 18 of species, for animals have almost invariably gone along with the plants, quarantine being a comparatively recent and not completely effective innovation. The United States Office of Plant Introduction alone has introduced almost 200,000 species and varieties of plants from all over the world. Nearly half of the 180 or so major insect enemies of plants in the United States are accidental imports from abroad, and most of them have come as hitchhikers on plants.

In new territory, out of reach of the restraining hand of the natural 19 enemies that kept down its numbers in its native land, an invading plant or animal is able to become enormously abundant. Thus it is no accident that our most troublesome insects are introduced species.

These invasions, both the naturally occurring and those dependent 20 on human assistance, are likely to continue indefinitely. Quarantine and massive chemical campaigns are only extremely expensive ways of buying time. We are faced, according to Dr. Elton, "with a life-and-death need not just to find new technological means of suppressing this plant or that animal"; instead we need the basic knowledge of animal populations and their relations to their surroundings that will "promote an even balance and damp down the explosive power of outbreaks and new invasions."

21   Much of the necessary knowledge is now available but we do not use it. We train ecologists in our universities and even employ them in our governmental agencies but we seldom take their advice. We allow the chemical death rain to fall as though there were no alternative, whereas in fact there are many, and our ingenuity could soon discover many more if given opportunity.

22   Have we fallen into a mesmerized state that makes us accept as inevitable that which is inferior or detrimental, as though having lost the will or the vision to demand that which is good? Such thinking, in the words of the ecologist Paul Shepard, "idealizes life with only its head out of water, inches above the limits of toleration of the corruption of its own environment. . . . Why should we tolerate a diet of weak poisons, a home in insipid surroundings, a circle of acquaintances who are not quite our enemies, the noise of motors with just enough relief to prevent insanity? Who would want to live in a world which is just not quite fatal?"

23   Yet such a world is pressed upon us. The crusade to create a chemically sterile, insect-free world seems to have engendered a fanatic zeal on the part of many specialists and most of the so-called control agencies. On every hand there is evidence that those engaged in spraying operations exercise a ruthless power. "The regulatory entomologists . . . function as prosecutor, judge and jury, tax assessor and collector and sheriff to enforce their own orders," said Connecticut entomologist Neely Turner. The most flagrant abuses go unchecked in both state and federal agencies.

24   It is not my contention that chemical insecticides must never be used. I do contend that we have put poisonous and biologically potent chemicals indiscriminately into the hands of persons largely or wholly ignorant of their potentials for harm. We have subjected enormous numbers of people to contact with these poisons, without their consent and often without their knowledge. If the Bill of Rights contains no guarantee that a citizen shall be secure against lethal poisons distributed either by private individuals or public officials, it is surely only because our forefathers, despite their considerable wisdom and foresight, could conceive of no such problem.

25   I contend, furthermore, that we have allowed these chemicals to be used with little or no advance investigation of their effect on soil, water,

wildlife, and man himself. Future generations are unlikely to condone our lack of prudent concern for the integrity of the natural world that supports all life.

There is still very limited awareness of the nature of the threat. This 26 is an era of specialists, each of whom sees his own problem and is unaware of or intolerant of the larger frame into which it fits. It is also an era dominated by industry, in which the right to make a dollar at whatever cost is seldom challenged. When the public protests, confronted with some obvious evidence of damaging results of pesticide applications, it is fed little tranquilizing pills of half truth. We urgently need an end to these false assurances, to the sugar coating of unpalatable facts. It is the public that is being asked to assume the risks that the insect controllers calculate. The public must decide whether it wishes to continue on the present road, and it can do so only when in full possession of the facts. In the words of Jean Rostand, "The obligation to endure gives us the right to know."

(1962)

The Writer's Subject

1. What does Carson mean by "the chain of evil" initiated by chemical pollution? (para. 2) How does she illustrate her point?

2. Why does Carson believe that modern man cannot adjust to the various chemicals he has introduced into the environment? (paras. 3-5)

3. Why does Carson say that insecticides should be called "biocides"? (para. 7)

4. Why does Carson believe that the chemical war against insects may never be won? (para. 8)

5. What does Carson mean by saying that "control must be geared to realities, not to mythical situations" (para. 12)?

6. How do modern agricultural practices help to increase specific insect populations rather than curb them? (para. 15)

7. Carson says that man has the knowledge necessary to control troublesome insects without polluting the environment. Why, in her view, has man not used this knowledge?

8. What changes in attitudes and government policies does Carson imply must take place if the dangers of chemical pollution are to be checked?

The Writer's Style and Strategy

1. What is the tone of this essay? How is it established?

2. The essay is both an exposition of the effects of chemicals and an argument against their uncontrolled use. Identify those elements which are primarily expository and those which are particularly calculated to appeal to the reader's emotions.

3. Carson makes use of a number of devices to lend weight and add emphasis to her argument: rhetorical questions, the citing of authorities, references to statistical information. Find an example of each of these and comment on its effectiveness.

Suggested Topics for Writing and Discussion

1. This essay is taken from Rachel Carson's book *Silent Spring*, published in 1962. In what respects are we still threatened by the dangers which Carson pointed out 30 years ago?

2. We are a society accustomed to the free use of chemicals in the home as well as in industry and agriculture. Drawing on your own experience, show how chemical products play a part in our daily lives. To what extent do any of these products constitute a threat to human life or the natural environment?

3. Compare the concerns of Carson in "The Obligation to Endure" with those of Bronowski in "The Real Responsibilities of the Scientist." Both are concerned with the need to keep the public well informed about scientific research. How might this be accomplished?

4. Carson says that ours is "an era dominated by industry, in which the right to make a dollar at whatever cost is seldom challenged." Do you agree with Carson's assessment?

The Bird and the Machine
by Loren Eiseley

I suppose their little bones have years ago been lost among the stones   1
and wind of those high glacial pastures. I suppose their feathers blew
eventually into the piles of tumbleweed beneath the straggling cattle
fences and rotted there in the mountain snows, along with dead steers
and all the other things that drift to an end in the corners of the wire.
I do not quite know why I should be thinking of birds over the *New
York Times* at breakfast, particularly the birds of my youth half a continent away. It is a funny thing what the brain will do with memories
and how it will treasure them and finally bring them into odd juxtapositions with other things, as though it wanted to make a design, or get
some meaning out of them, whether you want it or not, or even see it.

It used to seem marvelous to me, but I read now that there are machines   2
that can do these things in a small way, machines that can crawl about
like animals, and that it may not be long now until they do more things
— maybe even make themselves — I saw that piece in the *Times* just
now. And then they will, maybe — well, who knows — but you read
about it more and more with no one making any protest, and already
they can add better than we and reach up and hear things through the
dark and finger the guns over the night sky.

This is the new world that I read about at breakfast. This is the world   3
that confronts me in my biological books and journals, until there are
times when I sit quietly in my chair and try to hear the little purr of
the cogs in my head and the tubes flaring and dying as the messages
go through them and the circuits snap shut or open. This is the great
age, make no mistake about it; the robot has been born somewhat ap-

propriately along with the atom bomb, and the brain they say now is just another type of more complicated feedback system. The engineers have its basic principles worked out; it's mechanical, you know; nothing to get superstitious about; and man can always improve on nature once he gets the idea. Well, he's got it all right and that's why, I guess, I sit here in my chair, with the article crunched in my hand, remembering those two birds and that blue mountain sunlight. There is another magazine article on my desk that reads "Machines Are Getting Smarter Every Day." I don't deny it, but I'll stick with the birds. It's life I believe in, not machines.

4   Maybe you don't believe there is any difference. A skeleton is all joints and pulleys, I'll admit. And when man was in his simpler stages of machine building in the eighteenth century, he quickly saw the resemblances. "What," wrote Hobbes, "is the heart but a spring, and the nerves but so many strings, and the joints but so many wheels, giving motion to the whole body?" Tinkering about in their shops it was inevitable in the end that men would see the world as a huge machine "subdivided into an infinite number of lesser machines."

5   The idea took on with a vengeance. Little automatons toured the country – dolls controlled by clockwork. Clocks described as little worlds were taken on tours by their designers. They were made up of moving figures, shifting scenes, and other remarkable devices. The life of the cell was unknown. Man, whether he was conceived as possessing a soul or not, moved and jerked about like these tiny puppets. A human being thought of himself in terms of his own tools and implements. He had been fashioned like the puppets he produced and was only a more clever model made by a greater designer.

6   Then in the nineteenth century, the cell was discovered, and the single machine in its turn was found to be the product of millions of infinitesimal machines – the cells. Now, finally, the cell itself dissolves away into an abstract chemical machine, and that into some intangible, inexpressible flow of energy. The secret seems to lurk all about, the wheels get smaller and smaller, and they turn more rapidly, but when you try to seize it the life is gone – and so, by popular definition, some would say that life was never there in the first place. The wheels and the cogs are the secret and we can make them better in time – machines that will run faster and more accurately than real mice to real cheese.

7   I have no doubt it can be done, though a mouse harvesting seeds on an autumn thistle is to me a fine sight and more complicated, I think, in his multiform activity than a machine "mouse" running a maze. Also,

I like to think of the possible shape of the future brooding in mice, just as it brooded once in a rather ordinary mousy insectivore who became man. It leaves a nice fine indeterminate sense of wonder that even an electronic brain hasn't got, because you know perfectly well that if the electronic brain changes, it will be because of something man has done to it. But what man will do to himself he doesn't really know. A certain scale of time and a ghostly intangible thing called change are ticking in him. Powers and potentialities like the oak in the seed, or a red and awful ruin. Either way, it's impressive; and the mouse has it, too. Or those birds, I'll never forget those birds — yet before I measured their significance, I learned the lesson of time first of all. I was young then and left alone in a great desert — part of an expedition that had scattered its men over several hundred miles in order to carry on research more effectively. I learned there that time is a series of planes existing superficially in the same universe. The tempo is a human illusion, a subjective clock ticking in our own kind of protoplasm.

As the long months passed, I began to live on the slower planes and 8 to observe more readily what passed for life there. I sauntered, I passed more and more slowly up and down the canyons in the dry baking heat of midsummer. I slumbered for long hours in the shade of huge brown boulders that had gathered in tilted companies out on flats. I had forgotten the world of men and the world had forgotten me. Now and then I found a skull in the canyons, and these justified my remaining there. I took a serene cold interest in these discoveries. I had come, like many naturalists before me, to view life with a wary and subdued attention. I had grown to take pleasure in the divested bone.

I sat once on a high ridge that fell away before me into a waste of 9 sand dunes. I sat through hours of a long afternoon. Finally, as I glanced beside my boot an indistinct configuration caught my eye. It was a coiled rattlesnake, a big one. How long he had sat with me I do not know. I had not frightened him. We were both locked in the sleep-walking tempo of the earlier world, baking in the same high air and sunshine. Perhaps he had been there when I came. He slept on as I left, his coils, so ill-discerned by me, dissolving once more among the stones and gravel from which I had barely made him out.

Another time I got on a higher ridge, among some tough little wind- 10 warped pines half covered over with sand in a basinlike depression that caught everything carried by the air up to those heights. There were a few thin bones of birds, some cracked shells of indeterminable age, and the knotty fingers of pine roots bulged out of shape from their long and agonizing grasp upon the crevices of the rock. I lay under the pines in the sparse shade and went to sleep once more.

11   It grew cold finally, for autumn was in the air by then, and the few things that lived thereabouts were sinking down into an even chillier scale of time. In the moments between sleeping and waking I saw the roots about me and slowly, slowly, a foot in what seemed many centuries, I moved my sleep-stiffened hands over the scaling bark and lifted my numbed face after the vanishing sun. I was a great awkward thing of knots and aching limbs, trapped up there in some long, patient endurance that involved the necessity of putting living fingers into rock and by slow, aching expansion bursting those rocks asunder. I suppose, so thin and slow was the time of my pulse by then, that I might have stayed on to drift still deeper into the lower cadences of the frost, or the crystalline life that glistens pebbles, or shines in a snowflake, or dreams in the meteoric iron between the worlds.

12   It was a dim descent, but time was present in it. Somewhere far down in that scale the notion struck me that one might come the other way. Not many months thereafter I joined some colleagues heading higher into a remoter windy tableland where huge bones were reputed to protrude like boulders from the turf. I had drowsed with reptiles and moved with the century-long pulse of trees; now, lethargically, I was climbing up some invisible ladder of quickening hours. There had been talk of birds in connection with my duties. Birds are intense, fast-living creatures — reptiles, I suppose one might say, that have escaped out of the heavy sleep of time, transformed fairy creatures dancing over sunlit meadows. It is a youthful fancy, no doubt, but because of something that happened up there among the escarpments of that range, it remains with me a lifelong impression. I can never bear to see a bird imprisoned.

13   We came into that valley through the trailing mists of a spring night. It was a place that looked as though it might never have known the foot of man, but our scouts had been ahead of us and we knew all about the abandoned cabin of stone that lay far up on one hillside. It had been built in the land rush of the last century and then lost to the cattlemen again as the marginal soils failed to take to the plow.

14   There were spots like this all over that country. Lost graves marked by unlettered stones and old corroding rim-fire cartridge cases lying where somebody had made a stand among the boulders that rimmed the valley. They are all that remain of the range wars; the men are under the stones now. I could see our cavalcade winding in and out through

the mist below us: torches, the reflection of the truck lights on our collecting tins, and the far-off bumping of a loose dinosaur thigh bone in the bottom of a trailer. I stood on a rock a moment looking down and thinking what it cost in money and equipment to capture the past.

We had, in addition, instructions to lay hands on the present. The 15 word had come through to get them alive — birds, reptiles, anything. A zoo somewhere abroad needed restocking. It was one of those reciprocal matters in which science involves itself. Maybe our museum needed a stray ostrich egg and this was the payoff. Anyhow, my job was to help capture some birds and that was why I was there before the trucks.

The cabin had not been occupied for years. We intended to clean it 16 out and live in it, but there were holes in the roof and the birds had come in and were roosting in the rafters. You could depend on it in a place like this where everything blew away, and even a bird needed some place out of the weather and away from coyotes. A cabin going back to nature in a wild place draws them till they come in, listening at the eaves, I imagine, pecking softly among the shingles till they find a hole, and then suddenly the place is theirs and man is forgotten.

Sometimes of late years I find myself thinking the most beautiful sight 17 in the world might be the birds taking over New York after the last man has run away to the hills. I will never live to see it, of course, but I know just how it will sound because I've lived up high and I know the sort of watch birds keep on us. I've listened to sparrows tapping tentatively on the outside of air conditioners when they thought no one was listening, and I know how other birds test the vibrations that come up to them through the television aerials.

"Is he gone?" they ask, and the vibrations come up from below, "Not 18 yet, not yet."

Well, to come back, I got the door open softly and I had the spotlight 19 all ready to turn on and blind whatever birds there were so they couldn't see to get out through the roof. I had a short piece of ladder to put against the far wall where there was a shelf on which I expected to make the biggest haul. I had all the information I needed, just like any skilled assassin. I pushed the door open, the hinges squeaking only a little. A bird or two stirred — I could hear them — but nothing flew and there was a faint starlight through the holes in the roof.

I padded across the floor, got the ladder up and the light ready, and 20 slithered up the ladder till my head and arms were over the shelf. Everything was dark as pitch except for the starlight at the little place back of the shelf near the eaves. With the light to blind them, they'd never make it. I had them, I reached my arm carefully over in order to be ready to seize whatever was there and I put the flash on the edge of the shelf where it would stand by itself when I turned it on. That way I'd be able to use both hands.

21   Everything worked perfectly except for one detail — I didn't know what kind of birds were there. I never thought about it at all, and it wouldn't have mattered if I had. My orders were to get something interesting. I snapped on the flash and sure enough there was a great beating and feathers flying, but instead of my having them, they, or rather he, had me. He had my hand, that is, and for a small hawk not much bigger than my fist he was doing all right. I heard him give one short metallic cry when the light went on and my hand descended on the bird beside him; after that he was busy with his claws and his beak was sunk in my thumb. In the struggle I knocked the lamp over on the shelf, and his mate got her sight back and whisked neatly through the hole in the roof and off among the stars outside. It all happened in fifteen seconds and you might think I would have fallen down the ladder, but no, I had a professional assassin's reputation to keep up, and the bird, of course, made the mistake of thinking the hand was the enemy and not the eyes behind it. He chewed my thumb up pretty effectively and lacerated my hand with his claws, but in the end I got him, having two hands to work with.

22   He was a sparrow hawk and a fine young male in the prime of life. I was sorry not to catch the pair of them, but as I dripped blood and folded his wings carefully, holding him by the back so that he couldn't strike again, I had to admit the two of them might have been more than I could have handled under the circumstances. The little fellow had saved his mate by diverting me, and that was that. He was born to it and made no outcry now, resting in my hand hopelessly but peering toward me in the shadows behind the lamp with a fierce, almost indifferent glance. He neither gave nor expected mercy and something out of the high air passed from him to me, stirring a faint embarrassment.

23   I quit looking into that eye and managed to get my huge carcass with its fist full of prey back down the ladder. I put the bird in a box too small to allow him to injure himself by struggle and walked out to welcome the arriving trucks. It had been a long day, and camp still to make in the darkness. In the morning that bird would be just another episode. He would go back with the bones in the truck to a small cage in a city where he would spend the rest of his life. And a good thing,

too. I sucked my aching thumb and spat out some blood. An assassin has to get used to these things. I had a professional reputation to keep up.

In the morning, with the change that comes on suddenly in that high 24 country, the mist that had hovered below us in the valley was gone. The sky was a deep blue, and one could see for miles over the high outcroppings of stone. I was up early and brought the box in which the little hawk was imprisoned out on to the grass where I was building a cage. A wind as cool as a mountain spring ran over the grass and stirred my hair. It was a fine day to be alive. I looked up and all around and at the hole in the cabin roof out of which the other little hawk had fled. There was no sign of her anywhere that I could see.

"Probably in the next county by now," I thought cynically, but before 25 beginning work I decided I'd have a look at my last night's capture.

Secretively, I looked again all around the camp and up and down and 26 opened the box. I got him right out in my hand with his wings folded properly and I was careful not to startle him. He lay limp in my grasp and I could feel his heart pound under the feathers but he only looked beyond me and up.

I saw him look that last look away beyond me into a sky so full of 27 light that I could not follow his gaze. The little breeze flowed over me again, and nearby a mountain aspen shook all its tiny leaves. I suppose I must have had an idea then of what I was going to do, but I never let it come up into consciousness. I just reached over and laid the hawk on the grass.

He lay there a long minute without hope, unmoving, his eyes still 28 fixed on that blue vault above him. It must have been that he was already so far away in heart that he never felt the release from my hand. He never even stood. He just lay with his breast against the grass.

In the next second after that long minute he was gone. Like a flicker 29 of light, he had vanished with my eyes full on him but without actually seeing a premonitory wing beat. He was gone straight into that towering emptiness of light and crystal that my eyes could scarcely bear to penetrate. For another long moment there was silence. I could not see him. The light was too intense. Then from far up somewhere a cry came ringing down.

I was young then and had seen little of the world, but when I heard 30 that cry my heart turned over. It was not the cry of the hawk I had captured; for, by shifting my position against the sun I was now seeing farther up. Straight out of the sun's eye, where she must have been soaring restlessly above us for untold hours, hurtled his mate. And from far up, ringing from peak to peak of the summits over us, came a cry of such unutterable and ecstatic joy that it sounds down across the years and tingles among the cups on my quiet breakfast table.

31   I saw them both now. He was rising fast to meet her. They met in a great soaring gyre that turned to a whirling circle and a dance of wings. Once more, just once, their two voices, joined in a harsh wild medley of question and response, struck and echoed against the pinnacles of the valley. Then they were gone forever somewhere into those upper regions beyond the eyes of men.

32   I am older now, and sleep less, and have seen most of what there is to see and am not very much impressed any more, I suppose, by anything. "What Next in the Attributes of Machines?" my morning headline runs. "It Might Be the Power to Reproduce Themselves."

33   I lay the paper down and across my a mind a phrase floats insinuating-ly: "It does not seem that there is anything in the construction, consti-tuents, or behavior of the human being which it is essentially impossi-ble for science to duplicate and synthesize. On the other hand. . . ."

34   All over the city the cogs in the hard, bright mechanisms have begun to turn. Figures move through computers, names are spelled out, a thoughtful machine selects the fingerprints of a wanted criminal from an array of thousands. In the laboratory an electronic mouse runs swiftly through a maze toward the cheese it can neither taste nor enjoy. On the second run it does better than a living mouse.

35   "On the other hand. . . ." Ah, my mind takes up, on the other hand the machine does not bleed, ache, hang for hours in the empty sky in a torment of hope to learn the fate of another machine, nor does it cry out with joy nor dance in the air with the fierce passion of a bird. Far off, over a distance greater than space, that remote cry from the heart of heaven makes a faint buzzing among my breakfast dishes and passes on and away.

(1955)

The Writer's Subject

1. What fears about the "new world" does Eiseley express in the first three paragraphs?

2. Eiseley says that man has come to see himself as a mechanism. What, in Eiseley's opinion, are the limitations of this view? (paras. 4-7)

3. Eiseley describes time as "a series of planes existing superficially in the same universe" and speaks of his own experience in the desert where he "began to live on the slower planes." How did Eiseley become aware of these "slower planes of time" (para. 7-11)?

4. In speaking of time at the beginning of paragraph 12, what does Eiseley mean by "one might come the other way"?

5. What feelings are stirred in Eiseley by the resistance of the male sparrow hawk? (paras. 22-23)

6. Why did Eiseley let the bird go?

7. In his description of the release of the sparrow hawk, Eiseley gives special prominence to the sky. Why? (paras. 24-31)

8. Why does Eiseley place his reflections in the mundane setting of his breakfast table?

The Writer's Style and Strategy

1. Eiseley treats the machine age in ironic terms. How is this irony conveyed? (paras. 2-3)

2. How does Eiseley move from general observations about men and machines to the more personal element of his narrative?

3. How does Eiseley's use of co-ordinated clauses in paragraph 11 help to convey his experience of the slowing down of time?

4. What is Eiseley's attitude to the expedition's secondary task, that the researchers "lay hands on the present" (para. 15)? How is this attitude conveyed?

5. Why does Eiseley refer to himself at several points as a skilled assassin with a professional reputation to keep up (paras. 19, 21, and 23)? What is the significance of his description of himself as a "huge carcass with a fistful of prey" (para. 23)?

6. Discuss the tone and language of the final paragraph. What makes the paragraph a fitting conclusion to Eiseley's reflections?

7. Comment on Eiseley's title. What emphasis does he gain by using the definite article?

Suggested Topics for Writing and Discussion

1. Eiseley seems disturbed at the notion that he must send the sparrow hawk to the city, to spend the rest of its life in a zoo. What is your own attitude to zoos? Do you think they serve a useful function?

2. Eiseley expresses concern at scientists' attempts to duplicate life forms. Do you believe that scientists should be given unrestricted freedom to pursue their experiments in genetic engineering and artificial intelligence?

3. Relate an incident which led to a change in your perspective. Use specific details of the experience to develop your narrative.

4. Eiseley is not enamoured of man's achievements in the modern age. Do you share his view? Choose one achievement of modern technology and show whether its benefits outweigh its drawbacks.

Roughing It in the Bush

My Plans for Moose Hunting in the Canadian Wilderness

by Stephen Leacock

The season is now opening when all those who have a manly streak 1
in them like to get out into the bush and "rough it" for a week or two
of hunting and fishing. For myself, I never feel that the autumn has
been well spent unless I can get out after the moose. And when I go
I like to go right into the bush and "rough it" — get clear away from
civilization, out in the open, and take fatigue or hardship just as it comes.

So this year I am making all my plans to get away for a couple of 2
weeks of moose hunting along with my brother George and my friend
Tom Gass. We generally go together because we are all of us men who
like the rough stuff and are tough enough to stand the hardship of living in the open. The place we go to is right in the heart of the primitive
Canadian forest, among big timber, broken with lakes as still as glass,
just the very ground for moose.

We have a kind of lodge up there. It's just a rough place that we put 3
up, the three of us, the year before last, built out of tamarack logs faced
with a broad axe. The flies, while we were building it, were something
awful. Two of the men that we sent in there to build it were so badly
bitten that we had to bring them out a hundred miles to a hospital. None
of us saw the place while we were building it, — we were all busy at
the time, — but the teamsters who took in our stuff said it was the worst
season for the black flies that they ever remembered.

Still we hung to it, in spite of the flies, and stuck at it till we got 4
it built. It is, as I say, only a plain place but good enough to rough

it in. We have one big room with a stone fireplace, and bedrooms round the sides, with a wide verandah, properly screened, all along the front. The verandah has a row of upright tamaracks for its posts and doesn't look altogether bad. In the back part we have quarters where our man sleeps. We had an ice-house knocked up while they were building and water laid on in pipes from a stream. So that on the whole the place has a kind of rough comfort about it, — good enough anyway for fellows hunting moose all day.

5   The place, nowadays, is not hard to get at. The government has just built a colonization highway, quite all right for motors, that happens to go within a hundred yards of our lodge.

6   We can get the railway for a hundred miles, and then the highway for forty, and the last hundred yards we can walk. But this season we are going to cut out the railway and go the whole way from the city in George's car with our kit with us.

7   George has one of those great big cars with a roof and thick glass sides. Personally none of the three of us would have preferred to ride in a luxurious darned thing like that. Tom says that as far as he is concerned he'd much sooner go into the bush over a rough trail in a buckboard, and for my own part a team of oxen would be more the kind of thing that I'd wish.

8   However the car is there, so we might as well use the thing especially as the provincial government has built the fool highway right into the wilderness. By taking the big car also we can not only carry all the hunting outfit that we need but we can also, if we like, shove in a couple of small trunks with a few clothes. This may be necessary as it seems that somebody has gone and slapped a great big frame hotel right there in the wilderness, not half a mile from the place we go to. The hotel we find a regular nuisance. It gave us the advantage of electric light for our lodge (a thing none of us care about), but it means more fuss about clothes. Clothes, of course, don't really matter when a fellow is roughing it in the bush, but Tom says that we might find it necessary to go over to the hotel in the evenings to borrow coal oil or a side of bacon or any rough stuff that we need; and they do such a lot of dressing up at these fool hotels now that if we do go over for bacon or anything in the evening we might just as well slip on our evening clothes, as we could chuck them off the minute we get back. George thinks it might not be a bad idea, — just as a way of saving all our energy for getting after the moose, — to dine each evening at the hotel itself. He knew some men who did that last year and they told him that

the time saved for moose hunting in that way is extraordinary. George's idea is that we could come in each night with our moose, — such and such a number as the case might be — either bringing them with us or burying them where they die, — change our things, slide over to the hotel and get dinner and then beat it back into the bush by moonlight and fetch in the moose. It seems they have a regular two dollar table d'hôte dinner at the hotel, — just rough stuff of course but after all, as we all admit, we don't propose to go out into the wilds to pamper ourselves with high feeding: a plain hotel meal in a home-like style at two dollars a plate is better than cooking up a lot of rich stuff over a camp fire.

If we *do* dine at the hotel we could take our choice each evening be- 9
tween going back into the bush by moonlight to fetch in the dead moose from the different caches where we had hidden them, or sticking round the hotel itself for a while. It seems that there is dancing there. Nowadays such a lot of women and girls get the open air craze for the life in the bush that these big wilderness hotels are crowded with them. There is something about living in the open that attracts modern women and they like to get right away from everybody and everything; and of course hotels of this type in the open are nowadays always well closed in with screens so that there are no flies or anything of that sort.

So it seems that there is dancing at the hotel every evening, — nothing 10
on a large scale or pretentious, — just an ordinary hardwood floor, — they may wax it a little for all I know — and some sort of plain, rough Italian orchestra that they fetch up from the city. Not that any of us care for dancing. It's a thing that personally we wouldn't bother with. But it happens that there are a couple of young girls that Tom knows that are going to be staying at the hotel and of course naturally he wants to give them a good time. They are only eighteen and twenty (sisters) and that's really younger than we care for, but with young girls like that, — practically kids, — any man wants to give them a good time. So Tom says, and I think quite rightly, that as the kids are going to be there we may as well put in an appearance at the hotel and see that they are having a good time. Their mother is going to be with them too, and of course we want to give her a good time as well; in fact I think I will lend her my moose rifle and let her go out and shoot a moose. One thing we are all agreed upon in the arrangement of our hunting trip, is in not taking along anything to drink. Drinking spoils a trip of that sort. We all remember how in the old days we'd go out into a camp in the bush (I mean before there used to be any highway

or any hotel) and carry in rye whiskey in demijohns (two dollars a gallon it was) and sit around the camp fire drinking it in the evenings.

11   But there's nothing in it. We all agree that the law being what it is, it is better to stick to it. It makes a fellow feel better. So we shall carry nothing in. I don't say that one might not have a flask or something in one's pocket in the car; but only as a precaution against accident or cold. And when we get to our lodge we all feel that we are a darned sight better without it. If we *should* need anything, — though it isn't likely, — there are still three cases of old Scotch whiskey, kicking around the lodge somewhere; I think they are kicking round in a little cement cellar with a locked door that we had made so as to use it for butter or anything of that sort. Anyway there are three, possibly four, or maybe, five, cases of Scotch there and if we should for any reason want it, there it is. But we are hardly likely to touch it, — unless we hit a cold snap, or a wet spell; — then we might; or if we strike hot dry weather. Tom says he thinks there are a couple of cases of champagne still in the cellar; some stuff that one of us must have shot in there just before prohibition came in. But we'll hardly use it. When a man is out moose hunting from dawn to dusk he hasn't much use for champagne, not till he gets home anyway. The only thing that Tom says the champagne might come in useful for would be if we cared to ask the two kids over to some sort of dinner; it would be just a rough kind of camp dinner (we could hardly ask their mother to it) but we think we could manage it. The man we keep there used to be a butler in England, or something of the sort, and he could manage some kind of rough meal where the champagne might fit in.

12   There's only one trouble about our plans for our fall camp that bothers us just a little. The moose are getting damn scarce about that place. There used, so they say, to be any quantity of them. There's an old settler up there that our man buys all our cream from who says that he remembers when the moose were so thick that they would come up and drink whiskey out of his dipper. But somehow they seem to have quit the place. Last year we sent our man out again and again looking for them and he never saw any. Three years ago a boy that works at the hotel said he saw a moose in the cow pasture back of the hotel and there were the tracks of a moose seen last year at the place not ten miles from the hotel where it had come to drink. But apart from these two exceptions the moose hunting has been poor.

13   Still, what does it matter? What we want is the *life*, the rough life just as I have described it. If any moose comes to our lodge we'll shoot

him, or tell the butler to. But if not, — well, we've got along without
for ten years, I don't suppose we shall worry.

1923

The Writer's Subject

1. What image of himself does the narrator create in the first two paragraphs?

2. At what point in the essay does the reader see that the narrator is not all
   that he professes to be?

3. What are the "rough comforts" that the narrator reluctantly feels that he
   and his companions must take advantage of?

4. Under what conditions does the narrator indicate that he and his companions
   might partake of a little alcohol? (paras. 10-11)

5. How important to the narrator and his friends is the prospect of shooting
   a moose?

The Writer's Style and Strategy

1. This is clearly a humorous essay. What seems to you to be its chief
   humorous effect? How is this effect achieved?

2. What expectations are set up by the title of the essay? Comment on the
   subtitle.

3. In paragraphs 3 and 4, the narrator uses such phrases as "a kind of lodge,"
   "just a rough place," "only a plain place," and "a kind of rough comfort."
   Why does the narrator use such vague phrases? Find other examples.

4. What effect does the narrator wish to create by his references to "the fool
   highway" and "these fool hotels" (para. 8)?

5. How does the narrator suggest again and again that the unfortunate luxuries of life in the bush are not of his choosing? How does Leacock's use
   of expletive constructions (i.e., "it is," "there are," "it seems that") convey
   the narrator's apparent reluctance?

6. Discuss the appropriateness to the essay as a whole of the concluding
   paragraph.

Suggested Topics for Writing and Discussion

1. Though Leacock's essay is humorous, it touches on the serious subject of man's encroachment on the wilderness. Discuss one form of man's encroachment (e.g., tourism, hunting, logging) and show how it threatens a particular wilderness area.

2. The myth of "the great outdoors" as an important part of North American life is still kept alive in films and on television. Discuss one TV programme or movie and show how it perpetuates this myth.

3. Camping has come a long way from the original idea of "getting away from it all" with a tent and a campfire. Write an essay showing the extent to which modern camping equipment and supplies have taken the "roughing it" element out of camping.

4. Write a humorous account of a camping or holiday experience.

The Nature of the North
by Farley Mowat

Somewhere far to the north of Newfoundland, the St. Lawrence Seaway, 1
Place Ville Marie, the Macdonald-Cartier Freeway, the bald-headed
prairie and Stanley Park lies an unreal world conceived in the mind's
eye, born out of fantasy and cauled in myth. It is a weird and terrible
land where nothing is as it may seem. Home of the ice worm and the
igloo, of mad trappers and mushing Mounties, of pingos and polar bears,
of the legions of the damned that were conjured into being by Robert
Service, its voice is the baleful whisper of the aurora borealis, the eerie
howl of Jack London's malemutes and the whining dirge of C.B.C. wind
machines. It is a "white hell", "the ultimate desolation", a "howling
wasteland", "the Land that God Forgot" and "the Land God Gave to
Cain." It is a region almost wholly of our contriving, and we have made
of it so inimical a world that the truly alien moon, even as seen on television screens and in picture magazines, seems to have more reality.

This North, this Arctic of the mind, this frigid concept of a flat and 2
formless void of ice and snow congealed beneath the impenetrable
blackness of the polar night, is pure illusion. Behind it lies a lost world
obscured in drifts of literary drivel, obliterated by blizzards of bravado
and buried under an icy weight of obsessive misconceptions. The magnificent reality behind the myth has been consistently rejected by Canadians since the day of our national birth and is rejected still. Through
almost a century the Far North has meant to Canadians either a
nightmarish limbo or an oppressive polar presence looming darkly over
southern Canada and breathing icily down our necks. During most of
that century the handful of people who called themselves Canadians

were engrossed in the occupation of the apparently limitless spaces on the southern fringes of the country. When that space was finally circumscribed and its limits reached, Canadians did not look northward to the challenge of the unknown half of their share of the continent. The northern myth seemed more than they could face, even as it had in the past. They shunned it then – they shun it still. With the exception of a very few outstanding individuals, most of them employed by the Geological Survey of Canada, the exploration of the High North was accomplished, not by Canadians, but by British, French, Scandinavian, German, American and even Portuguese adventurers – men who mastered the myth, faced the reality, and took their knowledge home with them to their native lands. Those who followed in the paths of the explorers and made use of their discoveries, the traders and merchant exploiters, were English, Scotch, French and American, and the companies that employed them (such as the Hudson's Bay Company, Revillon Frères, Canalaska Trading Company) operated out of London, Paris, New York and Seattle. Even the missionaries, coming in time-honoured manner in the wake of trade, were aliens. Moravians from Germany, and Grenfell from England, worked the Labrador coast; throughout the rest of the North, Oblate priests from Belgium and France competed for souls with Anglican priests straight out from England. Meanwhile the seas of the Canadian North were being exploited by Scotch and American whalers. In the Yukon the placer gold fields were overrun by men of half a hundred lands – and there were precious few Canadians among them. White trappers, moving in on the Eskimos and Indians, were almost exclusively northern Europeans. Even Canada's standard-bearers of a token sovereignty in the Arctic, the North West (later the Royal Canadian) Mounted Police, got most of their first recruits from England, Scotland, Newfoundland and even farther afield.

3   The pattern is old and well established. A century after the nation's birth, about three-quarters of the exploration and exploitation of the Canadian North is being carried out by consortiums controlled by American, European and Japanese companies. Military occupation of the North, while nominally a joint undertaking, remains effectively American. Until the middle of the twentieth century almost the only Canadians in the Arctic were Indians and Eskimos; but they were people born to the reality and in any case were, and are, "Canadians" only by courtesy.

4   Only since the early 1950's have southern Canadians begun to glance over their shoulders northward. As yet only a handful have made the effort to penetrate to the reality behind the myth and to actually go north,

not to make a quick buck and then flee south as if the very hounds of hell were on their heels, but to attempt to make themselves integral parts of a gigantic and exciting world spurned by the nation that pretends to own it.

They are very few indeed. Apart from government employees and similar transients employed by mines and military installations, there are not more than a few thousand Canadians of other than Eskimo or Indian ancestry living in a land that is larger than the ten provinces. And most of these few are concentrated in southern Yukon Territory and around Great Slave Lake. In the central and eastern reaches, themselves ten times as vast as Texas, only a few hundred southern Canadians make the North their abiding home.

These are the true pioneers in a nation that is fond of boasting about her pioneering spirits. Men like Bob Williamson at Rankin Inlet, Terry Ryan at Cape Dorset, Ross Peyton at Pangnirtung, Ernie Lyall at Spence Bay, Fred Ross at Cambridge Bay, Tom Butters at Inuvik, Allan Innis-Taylor at Dawson, Bob Engles at Yellowknife, Don Stuart at Hay River — these are of the few, the dedicated ones, who have committed their lives to a land the rest of us reject. They are trying desperately to neutralize the apathy and ignorance of southern Canda, to destroy the suffocating myth so that we others may come to know the North for what it really is. So that we may come to recognize it as a part of our nation.

Men like these believe that la dolce vita is the way of death for any country. They would have us face resolutely north to a world that offers us — if we are men and women enough to recognize and grasp the opportunity — not only the material wealth we crave, but a fighting chance of finding the greatness of spirit that Canada so signally lacks.

* * *

The first difficulty that must be mastered in coming to grips with the Far North is to decide just where "north" begins and to ascertain its boundaries. Modern man has tried to evade the issue by separating the northern regions into sections, like a layer cake, so that he can deal with each part as a separate entity. Ask a scientist for a definition of "north" and you are instantly ears deep in boreal, subarctic and arctic zones, in isotherms, degree-days and permafrost limits. The truth is that the region has no arbitrary southern boundary except insofar as one exists in us as a state of mind. The situation is akin to that of an astronaut shot up in a rocket. At what point does he enter space? At no point, but only when he has become aware that he has entered an alien environment.

9   Since Canadians generally regard the Far North as an alien environment, they enter it when they leave their familiar world of the South behind them. The entry takes place in the upper reaches of the broad band of sombre coniferous forest that stretches across the entire breadth of Canada. Beginning near the Yukon — British Columbia border, this transition region slopes southeastward to Hudson Bay near Churchill where it swings sharply south, paralleling the coast around James Bay. It then angles northeastward across Ungava to reach the Atlantic in the general vicinity of Nain on the Labrador coast. At its southernmost point (the top of James Bay) there are polar bears, seals, tundra, and caribou. The North embraces the arctic zone but it is not limited to that region, nor to the Yukon and the Northwest Territories. It includes a sliver of northern Alberta, rather more of northern Saskatchewan, a goodly bite of northern Manitoba, a nibble of Ontario, a large part of Quebec, and the upper portion of Labrador.

10   It comprises a huge section of the earth's surface. Measuring from the north tip of Ellesmere Island (less than five hundred miles from the North Pole), the northern land mass strikes southward nearly two thousand miles to Cape Henrietta Maria on Hudson Bay — roughly the distance between Montreal and Calgary! And from the Alaska-Yukon border to Cape Dyer on the coast of Baffin Bay it stretches about the same distance east and west. It encompasses about one million, seven hundred thousand square miles — nearly half the total area of Canada.

11   The Canadian North reaches from Atlantic to Pacific but, more important, it extends almost to the heart of the Arctic Ocean. Canada fronts on this third ocean, which is a true mediterranean sea, in exactly the same way that North Africa fronts on the European Mediterranean. This is a startling idea but one we would be well advised to get used to since Asia, Europe and North America all face each other across the almost land-locked polar sea and it is here that the three continents lie closest together. The orientation we get from looking at standard maps that show the North Pole at the top of beyond is arbitrary and wrong. This is not the way the world really is. The polar region is actually the centre of the northern hemisphere, and the geographic centre of Canada is in the Keewatin tundra 250 miles north-northwest of Churchill. Consequently when we turn our back on the North in the belief that there isn't much of interest in that direction, we are turning our backs on Europe and Asia, as well as on a great part of our own country. So far only the military men, preoccupied with death and destruction, have

grasped this vital fact. When and if Canadians have the sense to appreciate its peaceful significance we may become a nation at the centre, instead of remaining a sycophantic satellite at the back door of the United States.

One of the particularly cockeyed misconceptions we have about our 12 North is that it is all of a piece — or, at the most, of two pieces: a bleak expanse of frozen sea and a dreary wilderness of frozen plain. The truth is that the Arctic displays as much variety as any other great natural realm on earth. Stretching from central Labrador to Baffin Island, the up-tilted eastern edge of the Canadian Shield forms a shaggy range of glacier-encrusted mountains that are as formidable, as massively overwhelming in appearance, as anything in the Rockies. There is nothing to match them in eastern North America; yet they are almost unknown to us. They form the eastern wall of the North. Far to the westward, beyond the Mackenzie River, rise range after range of mountains that culminate in the St. Elias Range whose glacier-shrouded peaks soar to nearly twenty thousand feet in Canada and twenty-four thousand in Alaska. This is the western wall. Between these walls sprawls the worn and pitted face of the Canadian Shield composed of some of the oldest rocks on earth and so eroded by the work of the eons that only the time-smoothed stubs of its once-mighty mountains remain as undulating hills, giving relief to the naked, ancient rock. Here, in the shield country, lies the greatest assemblage of lakes upon our planet. Between the western edge of the Shield and the risers of the Yukon Cordillera lies a broad tongue of lowlands that extends north from the Great Central Plains of North America, and down it one of the world's greatest rivers, the Mackenzie, carries the waters of the Peace, the Liard, and many lesser rivers to the Arctic Ocean.

North of the mainland lies the Arctic Archipelago, some nine hun- 13 dred thousand square miles of lands constituting the largest island group in the world. These islands, too, have their variety. Some are mountainous, others are low and grassy plains, still others are bald stone and gravel deserts. Surrounding them lies a complex of sounds and channels as intricate as the most sophisticated maze.

Contained within the arctic lands of Canada is the vast inland sea of 14 Hudson Bay, in which the British Isles could be sunk without a trace. East of the main northern land mass a tremendous river carried on the Labrador Current flows down through Baffin Bay and Davis Strait, stretching an arctic tentacle as far south as Nova Scotia. The polar ocean is itself a species of "land", for it is perpetually ice covered and, though the ice moves, men can and do travel over it, and four-engine aircraft can land upon it.

15   Although the bone structure of most of the North, the Canadian Shield, is perhaps five million years old, much of the land looks raw and new. This is because a mere ten thousand years ago the entire region, except for the northwestern corner, lay buried beneath a gigantic ice sheet. The dome of the Keewatin District ice sheet was two miles thick. Its own titanic weight made the ice sheet plastic and it flowed implacably in all directions outwards from several high-domed centers. It scoured and gouged the ancient rocks, shearing off the surface soil layers and leaving behind an incredibly intricate pattern of water-filled valleys, basins, and deep coastal fiords. When the ice eventually melted it left the land littered with debris that ranged from barn-sized boulders to vast fields of shattered rock, and it embossed the naked bones of the country with a complex design of morainic ridges, drumlins, and long sinuous eskers of sand and gravel.

16   The ice had another, unseen effect. It deep-froze the rock beneath it, producing what we call permafrost. In the extreme northern islands permafrost penetrates fifteen hundred feet into the primeval rock. Even as far south as northern Manitoba the ancient frost remains, unyielding, only a few feet below the shallow surface layers that thaw in summer.

17   Remnants of the ice sheet itself also survive. In the wall of the eastern mountains some sixty thousand square miles of ice crown the heights and fill great valleys. Other remnants of ice persist in the mountains of the west.

18   Another generally held misconception about the North is that its climate is so hostile that only polar bears and Eskimos can endure it. Yet winter blizzards on the western prairies can match, in ferocity if not in intensity, the worst weather the North produces. Northern residents who have subsequently endured a winter at Saskatoon or Winnipeg have been heard to refer with nostalgia to the North as "the banana belt". Surprisingly, it is a dry world with very little rain or snowfall. Winter snows often lie deeper in Toronto or Montreal than in most parts of the North. Although not even the Yellowknife Chamber of Commerce would call northern winters balmy, summers can be lovely. There are only two true seasons: winter and summer, the transitions between them being so brief as to be negligible. Near and north of the Arctic Circle the midsummer sun never sets and temperatures sometimes persist in the comfortable sixties and higher for days on end. In winter above the Arctic Circle the sun vanishes for weeks or months, but this "long

night" is seldom really dark. The Northern Lights often give a pervading luminosity and the glitter of the stars in a lucid atmosphere combined with bright moonlight provides enough light for almost normal activity, including hunting.

The concept of the Far North as a lifeless land is another of our more 19 grotesque illusions. Its southern fringes include the upper reaches of the taiga forests — mainly black and white spruce, larch, birch and poplar. The northward-marching trees of the taiga grow sparser and more stunted until they fade out in the vast open plains called tundra. There is no absolute line of demarcation between taiga and tundra — no real "timberline". The two regions interpenetrate like the clasped fingers of gigantic hands. There are pockets of tundra deep inside the forest, and oases of trees far out on the sweep of the tundra. Nor is the tundra all of a kind. There is alpine tundra high on mountain slopes, shrub tundra close to the taiga region, sedge tundra to the north, moss-and-lichen tundra still farther north and, on the extreme northern islands, fell-field tundra where vegetation finally gives up its stubborn attempt to occupy the remote lands that lie surrounded by unyielding polar ice. But in summertime most tundra regions boast an array of flowering plants of infinite number and delight. Although they are small, they mass in such profusion that they suffuse hundreds of square miles with shifting colour. They form a Lilliputian jungle where hunting spiders, bumblebees, small and delicate moths and butterflies abound. Black flies and mosquitoes abound too, alas, and there is no evading the fact that they are the bane of summer in the North.

Birds breed almost everywhere. Mammals of many species, ranging 20 from squat, rotund lemmings to massive muskox occupy the lands. The seas are home to whales, seals, obese walrus and sinuous white bears. The seas are also rich in fishes as are the numberless inland lakes. For those with eyes to see, the North is vitally and vividly alive. Long, long ago, men of other races out of another time recognized this truth and learned to call the northern regions "home".

(1967)

The Writer's Subject

1. What does Mowat mean by his assertion that the North is "a region almost wholly of our contriving" (para. 1)?

2. Why, in Mowat's view, have Canadians consistently rejected "the magnificent reality behind the myth" of the North? (para. 2)

3. Mowat outlines the pattern of early exploration and development of the Canadian North, pointing out how little was the contribution made by Canadians themselves. What, in his view, is the current situation?

4. What contrast does Mowat draw in paragraphs 4-7 between southern Canadians and those who live and work in the North? Why does he believe that southern Canadians must "face resolutely north"?

5. What analogy does Mowat use in paragraph 8 to show the difficulty of establishing where the North begins?

6. What is the "vital fact" about the Canadian North that is so far understood only by the military?

7. What are the principal misconceptions about the North that Mowat addresses from paragraph 12 onwards? What evidence does he produce to dispose of these misconceptions?

The Writer's Style and Strategy

1. Why does Mowat begin the essay with a list of the various images associated with the North?

2. What effect is he seeking by using such phrases as "mad trappers and mushing Mounties" or "the whining dirge of C.B.C. wind machines"? What is the point Mowat is making with the five phrases in quotation marks? (para. 1)

3. What is the tone of the first two sentences of paragraph 2? What figure of speech does Mowat use in the second sentence of paragraph 2? What response does Mowat hope to arouse in the reader by this strategy?

4. What words or phrases convey most clearly Mowat's critical attitudes to southern Canadians?

5. What audience has Mowat in mind for this essay? Provide specific evidence for your point of view.

6. Much of this essay is devoted to a description of the North. How does the descriptive element of this essay serve Mowat's argumentative purpose?

7. Discuss the means by which Mowat establishes the size and magnificence of the Arctic landscape in paragraphs 12-15. Comment on his use of adjectives, particularly superlatives.

8. How does Mowat convey the rich variety of plant life on the tundra in paragraph 19? Identify instances of personification, simile, and metaphor in this paragraph, and comment on the description of the flowering plants as "a Lilliputian jungle."

Suggested Topics for Writing and Discussion

1. Find a recent newspaper or magazine article about Canada's North and discuss how it confirms or contradicts Mowat's thesis that Southern Canadians have constructed a false myth about the North.

2. Mowat says somewhat bitterly that Canada lacks greatness of spirit. Do you agree?

3. Choose a nation, national group or geographic region (e.g., China, the Russians, the Sahara) and discuss the stereotypical images and myths associated with it. Can you, as Mowat has done, account for the formation of such myths and offer an opposing view?

4. In paragraph 4, Mowat says that it is only since the 1950s that southern Canadians have "begun to glance over their shoulders northward"; he implies that Canadians habitually face south. Indeed, he goes on to condemn Canada as a "sycophantic satellite" of the United States. Has the situation changed since Mowat wrote this essay in 1967? Does the North figure more prominently in our national consciousness, or is our orientation still primarily to the south?

A River Pilot Looks at the Mississippi
by Mark Twain

1 The face of the water, in time, became a wonderful book — a book that was a dead language to the uneducated passenger, but which told its mind to me without reserve, delivering its most cherished secrets as clearly as if it uttered them with a voice. And it was not a book to be read once and thrown aside, for it had a new story to tell every day. Throughout the long twelve hundred miles there was never a page that was void of interest, never one that you could leave unread without loss, never one that you would want to skip, thinking you could find higher enjoyment in some other thing. There never was so wonderful a book written by man; never one whose interest was so absorbing, so unflagging, so sparklingly renewed with every re-perusal. The passenger who could not read it was charmed with a peculiar sort of faint dimple on its surface (on the rare occasions when he did not overlook it altogether); but to the pilot that was an *italicized* passage; indeed, it was more than that, it was a legend of the largest capitals, with a string of shouting exclamation-points at the end of it, for it meant that a wreck or a rock was buried there that could tear the life out of the strongest vessel that ever floated. It is the faintest and simplest expression the water ever makes, and the most hideous to a pilot's eye. In truth, the passenger who could not read this book saw nothing but all manner of pretty pictures in it, painted by the sun and shaded by the clouds, whereas to the trained eye these were not pictures at all, but the grimmest and most dead-earnest of reading-matter.

2 Now when I had mastered the language of this water, and had come

to know every trifling feature that bordered the great river as familiarly as I knew the letters of the alphabet, I had made a valuable acquisition. But I had lost something, too. I had lost something which could never be restored to me while I lived. All the grace, the beauty, the poetry, had gone out of the majestic river! I still keep in mind a certain wonderful sunset which I witnessed when steamboating was new to me. A broad expanse of the river was turned to blood; in the middle distance the red hue brightened into gold, through which a solitary log came floating, black and conspicuous; in one place a long, slanting mark lay sparkling upon the water; in another the surface was broken by boiling, tumbling rings, that were as many-tinted as an opal; where the ruddy flush was faintest, was a smooth spot that was covered with graceful circles and radiating lines, ever so delicately traced; the shore on our left was densely wooded, and the somber shadow that fell from this forest was broken in one place by a long, ruffled trail that shone like silver; and high above the forest wall a clean-stemmed dead tree waved a single leafy bough that glowed like a flame in the unobstructed splendor that was flowing from the sun. There were graceful curves, reflected images, woody heights, soft distances; and over the whole scene, far and near, the dissolving lights drifted steadily, enriching it every passing moment with new marvels of coloring.

I stood like one bewitched. I drank it in, in a speechless rapture. The world was new to me, and I had never seen anything like this at home. But as I have said, a day came when I began to cease from noting the glories and the charms which the moon and the sun and the twilight wrought upon the river's face; another day came when I ceased altogether to note them. Then, if that sunset scene had been repeated, I should have looked upon it without rapture, and should have commented upon it, inwardly, after this fashion: "This sun means that we are going to have wind tomorrow; that floating log means that the river is rising, small thanks to it; that slanting mark on the water refers to a bluff reef which is going to kill somebody's steamboat one of these nights, if it keeps on stretching out like that; those tumbling 'boils' show a dissolving bar and a changing channel there; the lines and circles in the slick water over yonder are a warning that that troublesome place is shoaling up dangerously; that silver streak in the shadow of the forest is the 'break' from a new snag, and he has located himself in the very best place he could have found to fish for steamboats; that tall dead tree, with a single living branch, is not going to last long, and then how is a body ever going to get through this blind place at night without the friendly old landmark?"

4   No, the romance and beauty were all gone from the river. All the value any feature of it had for me now was the amount of usefulness it could furnish toward compassing the safe piloting of a steamboat. Since those days, I have pitied doctors from my heart. What does the lovely flush in a beauty's cheek mean to a doctor but a "break" that ripples above some deadly disease? Are not all her visible charms sown thick with what are to him the signs and symbols of hidden decay? Does he ever see her beauty at all, or doesn't he simply view her professionally, and comment upon her unwholesome condition all to himself? And doesn't he sometimes wonder whether he has gained most or lost most by learning his trade?

(1875)

The Writer's Subject

1. Why did Twain find the river so absorbing and interesting? (para. 1)

2. What contrast does Twain draw between the perceptions of a passenger and those of a river pilot? (para. 1)

3. What does Twain feel he lost when he had "mastered the language of this water"? (para. 2)

4. How did Twain respond to a beautiful sunset on the river when steamboating was still a new experience? How did his response change with experience? (paras. 3-4)

5. Why does Twain say that he pities doctors? (para. 4) What is the relation between this observation and his account of his river-boat experiences?

The Writer's Style and Strategy

1. How does Twain use an extended metaphor in paragraph 1 to describe the features of the river?

2. How does Twain effect a transition from paragraph 1 to paragraph 2?

3. Paragraphs 2 and 3 present two different views of the river. How does Twain organize the details of the contrast?

4. How does the language of paragraph 2 convey the sense of "rapture" that Twain first felt about the river at sunset? What details in paragraph 3 convey a change of tone?

5. Discuss the function of the concluding paragraph. By what means does Twain reinforce the connection between this paragraph and what has preceded it?

Suggested Topics for Writing and Discussion

1. Twain shows how a writer may convey his feelings about a landscape by a careful selection of detail and descriptive words. Describe a place or landscape in such a way as to help the reader share your feelings about the scene (e.g., a city seen from an airplane; a mountain range; a building).

2. Twain's closing comment suggests that professional training and education involve losses as well as gains. Choose a career or profession that interests you, and speculate what gains and losses it may entail.

3. Choose a place or a person that impressed you in childhood, and write an essay contrasting your early impressions with those you hold now.

Death of a Pig

by E.B. White

1 I spent several days and nights in mid-September with an ailing pig and I feel driven to account for this stretch of time, more particularly since the pig died at last, and I lived, and things might easily have gone the other way round and none left to do the accounting. Even now, so close to the event, I cannot recall the hours sharply and am not ready to say whether death came on the third night or the fourth night. This uncertainty afflicts me with a sense of personal deterioration; if I were in decent health I would know how many nights I had sat up with a pig.

2 The scheme of buying a spring pig in blossomtime, feeding it through summer and fall, and butchering it when the solid cold weather arrives, is a familiar scheme to me and follows an antique pattern. It is a tragedy enacted on most farms with perfect fidelity to the original script. The murder, being premeditated, is in the first degree but is quick and skillful, and the smoked bacon and ham provide a ceremonial ending whose fitness is seldom questioned.

3 Once in a while something slips — one of the actors goes up in his lines and the whole performance stumbles and halts. My pig simply failed to show up for a meal. The alarm spread rapidly. The classic outline of the tragedy was lost. I found myself cast suddenly in the role of pig's friend and physician — a farcical character with an enema bag for a prop. I had a presentiment, the very first afternoon, that the play would never regain its balance and that my sympathies were now wholly with the pig. This was slapstick — the sort of dramatic treatment that instantly appealed to my old dachshund, Fred, who joined the vigil, held the bag, and, when all was over, presided at the interment. When

we slid the body into the grave, we both were shaken to the core. The
loss we felt was not the loss of ham but the loss of pig. He had evident- •
ly become precious to me, not that he represented a distant nourishment in a hungry time, but that he had suffered in a suffering world.
But I'm running ahead of my story and shall have to go back.

My pigpen is at the bottom of an old orchard below the house. The   4
pigs I have raised have lived in a faded building that once was an ice-
house. There is a pleasant yard to move about in, shaded by an apple
tree that overhangs the low rail fence. A pig couldn't ask for anything
better - or none has, at any rate. The sawdust in the icehouse makes
a comfortable bottom in which to root, and a warm bed. This sawdust,
however, came under suspicion when the pig took sick. One of my
neighbors said he thought the pig would have done better on new ground
— the same principle that applies in planting potatoes. He said there
might be something unhealthy about that sawdust, that he never thought
well of sawdust.

It was about four o'clock in the afternoon when I first noticed that   5
there was something wrong with the pig. He failed to appear at the trough
for his supper, and when a pig (or a child) refuses supper a chill wave
of fear runs through any household, or ice-household. After examining my pig, who was stretched out in the sawdust inside the building,
I went to the phone and cranked it four times. Mr Dameron answered.
"What's good for a sick pig?" I asked (There is never any identification
needed on a country phone; the person on the other end knows who
is talking by the sound of the voice and by the character of the question.)

"I don't know, I never had a sick pig," said Mr. Dameron, "but I can   6
find out quick enough. You hang up and I'll call Henry."

Mr. Dameron was back on the line again in five minutes. "Henry   7
says roll him over on his back and give him two ounces of castor oil
or sweet oil, and if that doesn't do the trick give him an injection of
soapy water. He says he's almost sure the pig's plugged up, and even
if he's wrong, it can't do any harm."

I thanked Mr. Dameron. I didn't go right to the pig, though. I sank   8
into a chair and sat still for a few minutes to think about my troubles,
and then I got up and went to the barn, catching up on some odds and
ends that needed tending to. Unconsciously I held off, for an hour, the
deed by which I would officially recognize the collapse of the performance of raising a pig; I wanted no interruption in the regularity of
feeding, the steadiness of growth, the even succession of days. I wanted
no interruption, wanted no oil, no deviation. I just wanted to keep on

raising a pig, full meal after full meal, spring into summer into fall. I didn't even know whether there were two ounces of castor oil in the place.

9   Shortly after five o'clock I remembered that we had been invited out to dinner that night and realized that if I were to dose a pig there was no time to lose. The dinner date seemed a familiar conflict: I move in a desultory society and often a week or two will roll by without my going to anybody's house to dinner or anyone's coming to mine, but when an occasion does arise, and I am summoned, something usually turns up (an hour or two in advance) to make all human intercourse seem vastly inappropriate. I have come to believe that there is in hostesses a special power of divination, and that they deliberately arrange dinners to coincide with pig failure or some other sort of failure. At any rate, it was after five o'clock and I knew I could put off no longer the evil hour.

10   When my son and I arrived at the pigyard, armed with a small bottle of castor oil and a length of clothesline, the pig had emerged from his house and was standing in the middle of his yard, listlessly. He gave us slim greeting. I could see that he felt uncomfortable and uncertain. I had brought the clothesline thinking I'd have to tie him (the pig weighed more than a hundred pounds) but we never used it. My son reached down, grabbed both front legs, upset him quickly, and when he opened his mouth to scream I turned the oil into his throat — a pink, corrugated area I had never seen before. I had just time to read the label while the neck of the bottle was in his mouth. It said Puretest. The screams, slightly muffled by oil, were pitched in the hysterically high range of pig-sound, as though torture were being carried out, but they didn't last long: it was all over rather suddenly, and, his legs released, the pig righted himself.

11   In the upset position the corners of his mouth had been turned down, giving him a frowning expression. Back on his feet again, he regained the set smile that a pig wears even in sickness. He stood his ground, sucking slightly at the residue of oil; a few drops leaked out of his lips while his wicked eyes, shaded by their coy little lashes, turned on me in disgust and hatred. I scratched him gently with oily fingers and he remained quiet, as though trying to recall the satisfaction of being scratched when in health, and seeming to rehearse in his mind the indignity to which he had just been subjected. I noticed, as I stood there, four or five small dark spots on his back near the tail end, reddish brown in color, each about the size of a housefly. I could not make out what

they were. They did not look troublesome but at the same time they did not look like mere surface bruises or chafe marks. Rather they seemed blemishes of internal origin. His stiff white bristles almost completely hid them and I had to part the bristles with my fingers to get a good look.

Several hours later, a few minutes before midnight, having dined well 12 and at someone else's expense, I returned to the pighouse with a flashlight. The patient was asleep. Kneeling, I felt his ears (as you might put your hand on the forehead of a child) and they seemed cool, and then with the light made a careful examination of the yard and the house for signs that the oil had worked. I found none and went to bed.

We had been having an unseasonable spell of weather — hot, close 13 days, with the fog shutting in every night, scaling for a few hours in midday, then creeping back again at dark, drifting in first over the trees on the point, then suddenly blowing across the fields, blotting out the world and taking possession of houses, men, and animals. Everyone kept hoping for a break, but the break failed to come. Next day was another hot one. I visited the pig before breakfast and tried to tempt him with a little milk in his trough. He just stared at it, while I made a sucking sound through my teeth to remind him of past pleasures of the feast. With very small, timid pigs, weanlings, this ruse is often quite successful and will encourage them to eat; but with a large, sick pig the ruse is senseless and the sound I made must have made him feel, if anything, more miserable. He not only did not crave food, he felt a positive revulsion to it. I found a place under the apple tree where he had vomited in the night.

At this point, although a depression had settled over me, I didn't sup- 14 pose that I was going to lose my pig. From the lustiness of a healthy pig a man derives a feeling of personal lustiness; the stuff that goes into the trough and is received with such enthusiasm is an earnest of some later feast of his own, and when this suddenly comes to an end and the food lies stale and untouched, souring in the sun, the pig's imbalance becomes the man's, vicariously, and life seems insecure, displaced, transitory.

As my own spirits declined, along with the pig's, the spirits of my 15 vile old dachshund rose. The frequency of our trips down the footpath through the orchard to the pigyard delighted him, although he suffers greatly from arthritis, moves with difficulty, and would be bedridden if he could find anyone willing to serve him meals on a tray.

He never missed a chance to visit the pig with me, and he made many 16 professional calls on his own. You could see him down there at all hours, his white face parting the grass along the fence as he wobbled and stumbled about, his stethoscope dangling — a happy quack, writing his villainous prescriptions and grinning his corrosive grin. When the enema bag appeared, and the bucket of warm suds, his happiness was complete, and he managed to squeeze his enormous body between the two lowest rails of the yard and then assumed full charge of the irrigation. Once, when I lowered the bag to check the flow, he reached in and hurriedly drank a few mouthfuls of the suds to test their potency. I have noticed that Fred will feverishly consume any substance that is associated with trouble — bitter flavor is to his liking. When the bag was above reach, he concentrated on the pig and was everywhere at once, a tower of strength and inconvenience. The pig, curiously enough, stood rather quietly through this colonic carnival, and the enema, though ineffective, was not as difficult as I had anticipated.

17   I discovered, though, that once having given a pig an enema there is no turning back, no chance of resuming one of life's more stereotyped roles. The pig's lot and mine were inextricably bound now, as though the rubber tube were the silver cord. From then until the time of his death I held the pig steadily in the bowl of my mind; the task of trying to deliver him from his misery became a strong obsession. His suffering soon became the embodiment of all earthly wretchedness. Along toward the end of the afternoon, defeated in physicking, I phoned the veterinary twenty miles away and placed the case formally in his hands. He was full of questions, and when I casually mentioned the dark spots on the pig's back, his voice changed its tone.

18   "I don't want to scare you," he said, "but when there are spots, erysipelas has to be considered."

19   Together we considered erysipelas, with frequent interruptions from the telephone operator, who wasn't sure the connection had been established.

20   "If a pig has erysipelas can he give it to a person?" I asked.

21   "Yes, he can," replied the vet.

22   "Have they answered?" asked the operator.

23   "Yes, they have," I said. Then I addressed the vet again. "You better come over here and examine the pig right away."

24   "I can't come myself," said the vet, "but McFarland can come this evening if that's all right. Mac knows more about pigs than I do anyway. You needn't worry too much about the spots. To indicate erysipelas they would have to be deep hemorrhagic infarcts."

"Deep hemorrhagic what?" I asked.   25

"Infarcts," said the vet.   26

"Have they answered?" asked the operator.   27

"Well," I said, "I don't know what you'd call these spots, except they're   28
about the size of a housefly. If the pig has erysipelas I guess I have
it, too, by this time, because we've been very close lately."

"McFarland will be over," said the vet.   29

I hung up. My throat felt dry and I went to the cupboard and got   30
a bottle of whiskey. Deep hemorrhagic infarcts — the phrase began
fastening its hooks in my head. I had assumed that there could be nothing
much wrong with a pig during the months it was being groomed for
murder; my confidence in the essential health and endurance of pigs
had been strong and deep, particularly in the health of pigs that belonged
to me and that were part of my proud scheme. The awakening had been
violent and I minded it all the more because I knew that what could
be true of my pig could be true also of the rest of my tidy world. I
tried to put this distasteful idea from me, but it kept recurring. I took
a short drink of the whiskey and then, although I wanted to go down
to the yard and look for fresh signs, I was scared to. I was certain I
had erysipelas.

It was long after dark and the supper dishes had been put away when   31
a car drove in and McFarland got out. He had a girl with him. I could
just make her out in the darkness — she seemed young and pretty. "This
is Miss Owen," he said. "We've been having a picnic supper on the shore,
that's why I'm late."

McFarland stood in the driveway and stripped off his jacket, then   32
his shirt. His stocky arms and capable hands showed up in my flashlight's
gleam as I helped him find his coverall and get zipped up. The rear
seat of his car contained an astonishing amount of paraphernalia, which
he soon overhauled, selecting a chain, a syringe, a bottle of oil, a rubber tube, and some other things I couldn't identify. Miss Owen said
she'd go along with us and see the pig. I led the way down the warm
slope of the orchard, my light picking out the path for them, and we
all three climbed the fence, entered the pighouse, and squatted by the
pig while McFarland took a rectal reading. My flashlight picked up
the glitter of an engagement ring on the girl's hand.

"No elevation," said McFarland, twisting the thermometer in the light.   33
"You needn't worry about erysipelas." He ran his hand slowly over the
pig's stomach and at one point the pig cried out in pain.

"Poor piggledy-wiggledy!" said Miss Owen.   34

35   The treatment I had been giving the pig for two days was then repeated,
somewhat more expertly, by the doctor, Miss Owen and I handing him
things as he needed them — holding the chain that he had looped around
the pig's upper jaw, holding the syringe, holding the bottle stopper, the
end of the tube, all of us working in darkness and in comfort, working
with the instinctive teamwork induced by emergency conditions, the
pig unprotesting, the house shadowy, protecting, intimate. I went to
bed tired but with a feeling of relief that I had turned over part of the
responsibility of the case to a licensed doctor. I was beginning to think,
though, that the pig was not going to live.

36   He died twenty-four hours later, or it might have been forty-eight
— there is a blur in time here, and I may have lost or picked up a day
in the telling and the pig one in the dying. At intervals during the last
day I took cool fresh water down to him and at such times as he found
the strength to get to his feet he would stand with head in the pail and
snuffle his snout around. He drank a few sips but no more; yet it seemed
to comfort him to dip his nose in water and bobble it about, sucking
in and blowing out through his teeth. Much of the time, now, he lay
indoors half buried in sawdust. Once, near the last, while I was attend-
ing him I saw him try to make a bed for himself but he lacked the
strength, and when he set his snout into the dust he was unable to plow
even the little furrow he needed to lie down in.

37   He came out of the house to die. When I went down, before going
to bed, he lay stretched in the yard a few feet from the door. I knelt,
saw that he was dead, and left him there: his face had a mild look, expressive neither of deep peace nor of deep suffering, although I think
he had suffered a good deal. I went back up to the house and to bed,
and cried internally — deep hemorrhagic intears. I didn't wake till nearly
eight the next morning, and when I looked out the open window the
grave was already being dug, down beyond the dump under a wild apple. I could hear the spade strike against the small rocks that blocked
the way. Never send to know for whom the grave is dug, I said to myself,
it's dug for thee. Fred, I well knew, was supervising the work of digging, so I ate breakfast slowly.

38   It was Saturday morning. The thicket in which I found the gravedig-
gers at work was dark and warm, the sky overcast. Here, among alders
and young hackmatacks, at the foot of the apple tree, Lennie had dug
a beautiful hole, five feet long, three feet wide, three feet deep. He
was standing in it, removing the last spadefuls of earth while Fred patroll-

ed the brink in simple but impressive circles, disturbing the loose earth of the mound so that it trickled back in. There had been no rain in weeks and the soil, even three feet down, was dry and powdery. As I stood and stared, an enormous earthworm which had been partially exposed by the spade at the bottom dug itself deeper and made a slow withdrawal, seeking even remoter moistures at even lonelier depths. And just as Lennie stepped out and rested his spade against the tree and lit a cigarette, a small green apple separated itself from a branch overhead and fell into the hole. Everything about this last scene seemed overwritten — the dismal sky, the shabby woods, the imminence of rain, the worm (legendary bedfellow of the dead), the apple (conventional garnish of a pig).

But even so, there was a directness and dispatch about animal burial, **39** I thought, that made it a more decent affair than human burial: there was no stopover in the undertaker's foul parlor, no wreath nor spray; and when we hitched a line to the pig's hind legs and dragged him swiftly from his yard, throwing our weight into the harness and leaving a wake of crushed grass and smoothed rubble over the dump, ours was a business-like procession, with Fred, the dishonorable pallbearer, staggering along in the rear, his perverse bereavement showing in every seam in his face; and the post-mortem performed handily and swiftly right at the edge of the grave. so that the inwards that had caused the pig's death preceded him into the ground and he lay at last resting squarely on the cause of his own undoing.

I threw in the first shovelful, and then we worked rapidly and without **40** talk, until the job was complete. I picked up the rope, made it fast to Fred's collar (he is a notorious ghoul), and we all three fled back up the path to the house, Fred bringing up the rear and holding back every inch of the way, feigning unusual stiffness. I noticed that although he weighed far less than the pig, he was harder to drag, being possessed of the vital spark.

The news of the death of my pig traveled fast and far, and I received **41** many expressions of sympathy from friends and neighbors, for no one took the event lightly, and the premature expiration of a pig is, I soon discovered, a departure which the community marks solemnly on its calendar, a sorrow in which it feels fully involved. I have written this account in penitence and in grief, as a man who failed to raise his pig, and to explain my deviation from the classic course of so many raised pigs. The grave in the woods is unmarked, but Fred can direct the mourner to it unerringly and with immense good will, and I know he and I shall often revisit it, singly and together, in seasons of reflection and despair, on flagless memorial days of our own choosing.

(1947)

The Writer's Subject

1. From White's reference to "the pigs I have raised" (para. 4), it is clear that he was no novice in the business of fattening up and slaughtering pigs. Why, then, is he so affected by the illness and death of the pig described in this essay?

2. Why did the pig's illness mean that "the classic outline of the tragedy was lost" (para. 3)? What "tragedy" is White referring to here?

3. Explain the importance of White's statement that "the loss we felt was not the loss of ham but the loss of pig" (para. 3).

4. What is revealed by White's reluctance to administer the castor oil? (para. 8)

5. Discuss the role of Fred the dachshund. Why did he seem to enjoy the pig's illness and death? Why does White call him "a happy quack"? (para. 16)

6. Why did White become obsessed with the task of saving the pig from its misery? (para. 17)

7. Why was White so disturbed by the preliminary diagnosis of erysipelas? In what way did this news affect his attitude to life? (paras. 18-30)

8. Why did everything about the pig's burial seem "overwritten" in White's eyes? (para. 38)

9. White states that he is writing his account of the pig's death "in penitence and in grief" (para. 41). Why should he feel penitent? Do you think he means this statement to be taken seriously?

The Writer's Style and Strategy

1. White's essay is a subtle blend of humour, irony, and pathos. Find examples of these differing tones in the essay, and explain their appropriateness.

2. Why does White "run ahead of his story" in the first three paragraphs? What function is performed by these paragraphs?

3. Discuss White's use of analogy in paragraphs 2 and 3. How does the analogy contribute to our understanding of White's feelings about the death of his pig?

4. Discuss the terms in which White describes the pig. What is conveyed by the use of the pronoun "he" rather than "it" in White's references to the animal? Why does he twice draw analogies between the pig and a child? (paras. 5, 12)

5. Examine the effect of each of the following statements in their respective contexts:
    (a) "I found myself cast suddenly in the role of pig's friend and physician — a farcical character with an enema bag for a prop" (para. 3).
    (b) "A pig couldn't ask for anything better — or none has, at any rate" (para. 4).
    (c) "I went back up to the house and to bed, and cried internally — deep hemorrhagic intears" (para. 37).
    (d) "'Poor piggledly-wiggledy!' said Miss Owen" (para. 34).
    (e) "Never send to know for whom the grave is dug, I said to myself, it's dug for thee" (para. 37).

6. In the concluding paragraph, White states that the whole community feels sorrow at "the premature expiration of a pig." How does he create a sense of that community in the course of his essay?

7. Discuss the essay's final paragraph. What makes it a fitting conclusion to the account that has preceded it?

Suggested Topics for Writing and Discussion

1. Most people have at one time or another suffered the loss of a pet. Working from a real or an imaginary experience, describe your own response to such an event.

2. As White explains in his essay, the breeding and butchering of animals for food is a commonplace feature of life on a farm. In recent years, however, animal activists have questioned our right to exploit animals, even in this way. Do you believe that we have the right to use animals as we see fit?

3. As White presents him, Fred the dachshund is more than a dog; he is a character in the drama of the pig's death. Describe an animal you have known that might be regarded as "a character."

Storm Over the Amazon
by Edward O. Wilson

1   The Amazonian forest of Brazil whipsaws the imagination. After two or three days there I grow familiar with the earthy smell and vegetation as though in a Massachusetts woodlot, so that what was recently new and wonderful starts to fade from my senses. Then some small event occurs to shift my conceptual framework, and the mystery comes back in its original force. One night I walked into the forest north of Manaus with a headlamp to study the ground surface and everywhere I saw — diamonds! At regular intervals of several yards, intense pinpoints of white light flashed on and off with each turning of the lamp. They were reflections from the eyes of wolf spiders on the prowl. When the spiders were spotlighted they froze into stillness, allowing me to peer at them from inches away. I could distinguish a wide variety of species by size, color, and hairiness. Where did they all come from? What was their prey, and how could so many kinds exist there in these numbers? By morning they would retreat into the leaf litter and soil, yielding the microterrain to a new set of predators. Because I had come for other purposes, I abandoned their study to the arachnologists who would surely follow.

2   Each evening after dinner I carried a folding chair to a clearing to escape the noise and stink of the camp I shared with Brazilian field hands. The forest around us was in the process of being clearcut northward along an east-west line, mostly to create short-lived pastures. Even so, what remained was and is one of the few great wildernesses of the world, stretching almost unbroken from where I sat across five hundred miles to the Venezuelan savannas.

Just knowing I was on the edge of that immensity deepened the sense of   3
my own purpose. I stared straight into the dark for hours at a time, thinking in spurts about the ecological research that had attracted me there,
dreaming pleasantly about the forest as a reservoir of the unknown, so complicated that its measure will not be taken in my lifetime. I was a would-
be conquistador of sorts, searching not for Amazonian gold but for great
discoveries to be made in the interior. I fantasized about new phenomena
and unborn insights. I confess this without embarrassment, because science
is built on fantasies that can be proved true. For me the rainforest is the
greatest of fantasy lands, a place of hope still unchained by exact
knowledge.

And I strained to catch any trace of sound or light. The rainforest at night   4
is an experience in sensory deprivation, black and silent as a tomb. Life
is moving out there all right, but the organisms communicate chiefly by
faint chemical trails laid over the surface, puffs of odor released into the
air, and body scents detected downwind. Most animals are geniuses in this
chemical channel where we are idiots. On the other hand, we are masters
of the audiovisual channel, matched in that category only by a few odd
groups like birds and lizards. At the risk of oversimplification, I can say
that this is why we wait for the dawn while they wait for the fall of darkness.

So I welcomed every meteorite's streak and distant mating flash from   5
luminescent beetles. Even the passage of a jetliner five miles up was
exciting, having been transformed from the familiar urban irritant to a rare
sign of the continuance of my own species.

Then one August night in the dry season, with the moon down and   6
starlight etching the tops of the trees, everything changed with wrenching
suddenness. A great storm came up from the west and moved quickly
toward where I sat. It began as a flickering of light on the horizon and a
faint roll of thunder. In the course of an hour the lightning grew like a
menacing organism into flashes that spread across the sky and illuminated
the thunderhead section by section. The sound expanded into focused claps
to my left, front, and right. Now the rain came walking through the forest
with a hiss made oddly soothing by its evenness of pitch. At this moment
the clouds rose straight up and even seemed to tilt a little toward me, like
a gigantic cliff about to topple over. The brilliance of the flashes was
intimidating. Here, I knew, was the greatest havoc that inanimate nature
can inflict in a short span of time: 10,000 volts dropping down an ioniz-
ing path at 500 miles an hour and a countersurge in excess of 30,000
amperes back up the path at ten times that speed, then additional back-and-
forth surges faster than the eye can follow, all perceived as a single flash
and crack of sound.

7   In the midst of the clamour something distracted my attention off to the side. The lightning bolts were acting like photoflashes to illuminate the wall of the rainforest. In glimpses I studied its superb triple-tiered structure: top canopy a hundred feet off the ground, middle tree layer below that, and a scattering of lowest trees and shrubs. At least 800 kinds of trees had been found along a short transect eastward from the camp, more than occur natively in all of North America. A hundred thousand or more species of insects and other small animals were thought to live in the same area, many of which lack scientific names and are otherwise wholly unstudied. The symmetry was complete: the Amazonian rainforest is the most that life has been able to accomplish within the constraints of this stormy planet.

8   Large splashing drops turned into sheets of water driven by gusts of wind. I retreated into the camp and waited with my *mateiros* friends under the dripping canvas roof. In a short time leptodactylid frogs began to honk their territorial calls in the forest nearby. To me they seemed to be saying rejoice! rejoice! The powers of nature are within our compass.

9   For that is the way it is in the nonhuman world. The greatest powers of the physical environment slam into the resilient forces of life and nothing much happens. The next morning the forest is still there, and although a few old trees have fallen to create clearings and the way to new plant growth, the profile stays the same. For a very long time, approximately 150 million years, the species of the rainforest evolved to absorb precisely this form and magnitude of violence. They even coded its frequent occurrence into their genes. Organisms use heavy rain and floods to time their mating and other episodes of the life cycle.

10   Awe is what I am talking about here. It is the most peculiar human response, an overwhelming feeling of reverence or fear produced by that which is sublime or extremely powerful, sometimes changing perception in a basic way. I had experienced it by seeing a living system in a dramatic and newly symbolic fashion. Far larger storms occur on Venus and Jupiter, but they disclose no life underneath. Nothing like the forest wall exists anywhere else we will ever visit. To drop onto another planet would be a journey into death.

11   A few days later the grinding of gears announced the approach of the truck sent to return me and two workers to Manaus. We watched it coming across the pastureland, a terrain strewn with fire-blackened stumps and logs, the battlefield the rainforest finally lost. On the ride back I tried not to look at it. No awe there, only defeat and decay. I think that the ultimate irony of organic evolution is that in the instant of achieving self-understanding through the mind of man, it doomed its most beautiful creations.

(1986)

The Writer's Subject

1. Why is the Brazilian rain forest of such importance to the writer?

2. In what respect are animals "geniuses" and humans "idiots"? (para. 4)

3. What aroused the writer's awe during his experience of the storm? (para. 10)

4. What is "the ultimate irony of organic evolution" to which Wilson refers to in the last paragraph of the essay?

The Writer's Style and Strategy

1. Explain the meaning of the opening sentence of Wilson's essay. In what sense does he use "whipsaw" here?

2. Why does Wilson call himself "a would-be conquistador of sorts"? (para. 3) Who were the conquistadors?

3. What details in Wilson's account give readers a sense of the power of the storm? Why does he place such emphasis on that power?

4. Why does Wilson describe the frogs' honking in the forest during the storm?

5. What words or phrases in the essay best convey the writer's feelings about the Amazonian forest?

6. What is the tone of the concluding paragraph? How is it created?

Suggested Topics for Writing and Discussion

1. Find out what you can about the ecological importance of the Amazonian forest, and show what is being lost through the process of its destruction.

2. The destruction of the Amazonian forest is an issue that has raised world-wide concern. However, similar concerns about the need to protect and enhance our natural environment are evident on a more local scale. Examine a conservation issue that has aroused debate in your community (e.g., the preservation of a park or marshland, the felling of old trees, the use of aerial sprays), and outline the principal arguments presented by both sides.

3. At some time in their lives, most people have been moved, frightened, or excited by an experience in nature. Describe one such experience in your life.

Patterns of Social Behaviour

Of Marriage and Single Life
by Francis Bacon

He that hath wife and children hath given hostages to Fortune, for they are impediments to great enterprises either of virtue or mischief. Certainly the best works and of greatest merit for the public have proceeded from the unmarried or childless men, which both in affection and means have married and endowed the public. Yet it were great reason that those that have children should have greatest care of future times, unto which they know they must transmit their dearest pledges. Some there are who though they lead a single life, yet their thoughts do end with themselves and account future times impertinences. Nay, there are some other that account wife and children but as bills of charges. Nay more, there are some foolish rich covetous men that take a pride in having no children, because they may be thought so much the richer. For perhaps they have heard some talk, "Such an one is a great rich man," and another except to it, "Yea, but he hath a great charge of children," as if it were an abatement to his riches. But the most ordinary cause of a single life is liberty, especially in certain self-pleasing and humorous minds which are so sensible of every restraint as they will go near to think their girdles and garters to be bonds and shackles. Unmarried men are best friends, best masters, best servants, but not always best subjects, for they are light to run away, and almost all fugitives are of that condition. A single life doth well with Church men, for charity will hardly water the ground where it must first fill a pool. It is indifferent for judges and magistrates, for if they be facile and corrupt, you shall have a servant five times worse than a wife. For soldiers I find the generals, commonly in their hortatives, put men in mind of their wives and children. And I think the despising of marriage amongst the Turks maketh the vulgar soldier more base. Certainly wife and children are a kind of discipline of humanity; and single men, though they be many times more charitable, because their means are less exhaust, yet, on the other side, they are more cruel and hard hearted, (good to make severe inquisitors) because their tenderness is not so oft called upon. Grave natures, led by custom and therefore constant, are commonly loving husbands; as was said of Ulysses, *"Vetulam suam praetulit immortalitati."*[1] Chaste women are often proud and forward, as presuming upon the merit of their chastity. It is one of the best bonds, both of chastity and obedience, in the wife if she think her husband wise, which she will never do if she find him jealous. Wives are young men's mistresses, companions for middle age, and old men's nurses. So as a man may have a quarrel to marry when he will. But yet he was reputed one of the wise men, that made answer to the question, When a man should marry? "A young man not yet, an elder man not at all." It is often seen that bad husbands have very good wives; whether it be that it raiseth the price of their husbands' kindness when it comes, or that the wives take a pride in their patience. But this never fails, if the bad husbands were of their own choosing, against their friends' consent; for then they will be sure to make good their own folly.

(1613)

---

1. "He preferred his old wife to immortality."

The Writer's Subject

1. At the beginning of this essay, Bacon seems to give the advantage to the single life. How does he go on to qualify this view?

2. What is the single man's view of marriage and family, according to Bacon?

3. Why are unmarried men "not always best subjects"?

4. Why does Bacon think that churchmen should be single, whereas soldiers should be married?

5. Why, in Bacon's view, do single men make good inquisitors?

6. What qualities does Bacon suggest are necessary in a good wife?

7. What advice does Bacon offer about the best time for a man to marry?

The Writer's Style and Strategy

1. Explain the metaphor in the first sentence.

2. This essay is a loosely constructed contrast between marriage and the single life. In what ways does Bacon impose order on what might otherwise seem a series of unconnected observations?

3. What does Bacon's comment about single men's views of "their girdles and garters" reveal about his attitude to the single life? (In the Renaissance, "girdles and garters" were belts and stocking fasteners worn by men.)

4. The sentence beginning, "grave natures, led by custom . . ." acts as a transition between Bacon's discussion of married or single men and his observations on good husbands and good wives. What is the function of the allusion to the Homeric story of Ulysses and Penelope in this sentence?

Suggested Topics for Writing and Discussion

1. Write a brief essay on marriage versus the single life, twentieth-century style.

2. In "Of Marriage and Single Life," Bacon writes about marriage and the single life, but only as it affects men. Write an essay in which you explain why a woman should or should not get married. Use appropriate examples to support your arguments in favour of marriage or the single life for women.

3. Is there, in your view, any "best time" to marry?

A Hearing

by Hugh Brody

1   In June, Joseph and his family set up their summer camp on the Reserve.
Four small households camped together in a patch of woodland only
a few hundred yards from Joseph's house. There Atsin and David
stretched a small tarpaulin between the trees and a sloping ridge pole.
This provided shelter from rain, but, being open-sided, was cool. Sam
Crown and Jimmy Wolf, Joseph and Liza, and Reza, Shirley and Tommy
all pitched tents around a central fireplace. Atsin had a fire in front
of his camp, but he and David − along with everyone else who lived
or visited there − spent much of their time sitting, chatting, and eating
by Joseph's fire.

2   The hot days of summer had their own special mood. Every morning one or two of the younger men went to find the horses, following
their tracks along the riverside or into the hay and oat fields where they
liked to feed. Once they had chased them back to camp, the hunters
tethered the ones they thought they might need during the day. But it
was often too hot to hunt; days slipped by without much activity. The
men lay for hours, a short distance from the fires, half asleep, getting
up to eat, visit a neighbour, or play cards. Liza, Reza, and Shirley fried
bannock on the campfire above which they carefully hung meat to smoke
and to protect it from flies. On very still days they also built smoke
fires to keep away the flies and wasps that persistently bit the horses.
Children roamed the hillsides and river banks looking for berries, swimming, or hunting rabbits and grouse.

3   Thomas and Abe Fellow worked almost every day on the Reserve
ranch, riding off to herd cattle, move a bull from one meadow to another,

or look for horses that had strayed into the surrounding woods. Some days Sam and Atsin suggested a hunt, and then we would ride down the Midden River valley or drive to promising areas within fifteen miles of the Reserve. In summer, bull moose and buck mule deer are in prime condition, and hunting spots were chosen with them in mind. But tracking in great heat and through thick undergrowth and clouds of mosquitoes is hard work. Although enough kills were made to maintain an adequate supply of fresh meat, we spent most days dozing in the shade of the campsite.

In early August, almost everyone on the Reserve went to the Fort St. John rodeo. In mid-August, Joseph's brother and sister-in-law visited for two weeks, camping with us in the small wood by Joseph's house. At this time berries were ripening in abundance — first strawberries, then gooseberries, blueberries, and saskatoon berries. Everyone picked them as they found them, the children sometimes returning to camp with hats or plastic bags full of blueberries. Thomas's sister-in-law stewed panfuls of them in fat; that way, everyone said, you can eat as much as you want without any risk of diarrhoea.

In August, the heat was often intense. During the middle of the day even the mosquitoes kept to the cool shade of the undergrowth. The stillness was broken only by groups of children who walked and rode to a deep swimming hole a mile from camp. There they splashed and swam, sometimes riding into the water until their horses were out of their depth and then clinging on as the animal swam, or plunging off when a horse lunged and bucked in protest. A few older men and women at times came and watched these games, but many people spent their days in almost total inactivity. Summer is a time for resting.

So July and August passed quickly, quietly, and pleasantly. We twice moved camp from one part of the woodland to another. A porcupine, one or two mule deer, and grouse contributed to the excellence of our diet. From time to time someone went fishing within a half mile of the camp and returned with a sucker or a few rainbow trout. But there were also mishaps. Joseph was stung on the face by a wasp and spent two days with a painfully swollen cheek. Jimmy Wolf cut himself on the leg when angrily swatting at a bee with his hunting knife. One of the horses developed sores on its back and could not be ridden. These and similar events lent small features to a hazy, undifferentiated passage of time.

Then, in early September, thoughts turned yet again to Quarry and Bluestone, and the need to build up stocks of meat. Joseph spoke of the marmot that would be easy to shoot as they basked, fat from a summer of feeding, on rocks high in the foot hills. He also said they might now find caribou in the mountains. It was at this time that the Blueberry Reserve was evacuated. A pipe in a nearby gas-cleaning plant had fractured and the reserve had been enveloped in the middle of the night in a cloud of hydrogen-sulphide gas. Thanks to haste, nobody was killed; but the community was forced to live temporarily in summer tents a few miles east of the Alaska Highway. This alarming event caused much discussion. Joseph and others at the Reserve had relatives who lived at Blueberry, and there had long been rumours of impending drilling for oil or gas on the Reserve itself.

8   But as summer turned to another autumn, the events at Blueberry were overshadowed by talk of the Alaska Highway Pipeline, and about a plan to hold hearings in each of the communities that might suffer some of the consequences of this enormous project. An employee of the Northern Pipeline Agency (an office set up by the federal government to prepare social and environmental conditions as well as to facilitate pipeline construction) visited the Reserve. He left a sheaf of papers at the house of the Chief. Then, some weeks later, a long and difficult document was also left, which set out, in provisional form, the terms and conditions that might govern the pipeline's construction. Finally, a notice was fixed to the door of the meeting hall that announced a date on which a public hearing into these terms and conditions would be held.

9   It is possible that a few people on the Reserve saw, or even tried to read, the documents, although no one did at Joseph's camp. If they had tried, they would have made little sense of the tortured bureaucratese by which every idea in the documents was obscured. Perhaps agency officials had attempted to discuss the ideas that they were advancing. If so, the people's interest or understanding was too slight for such ideas to become topics of conversation in our camp. The Alaska Highway Pipeline was seen as a vast, unwelcome, and perplexing menace. But no one knew quite where it was supposed to go; few knew what it would carry; no one knew if its possible dangers had been considered. The construction project that developers had hailed, and environmentalists bewailed, as the largest and most significant in the history of free enterprise was little more than a vague and distant enigma to the people who were supposedly to be its first and absolute victims.

10   Some chiefs and other representatives of the Indians of northeast British Columbia had visited Ottawa the year before to appear before a parliamentary subcommittee, where they had spoken out against the

pipeline. But the connection between that visit and the papers left in the Chief's home was not clear. White officials were always saying that bits of paper were of special importance, but right now there were other important matters at hand: the beginning of the autumn hunt, marmot, caribou. . . .

In September, Joseph's household, along with several others, return- 11 ed to Quarry for the first autumn hunt; but the weather broke and for two weeks the hunters endured almost continuous rain, eventually returning to the Reserve. By this time the hearing had become a more pressing issue. Northern Pipeline Agency officials had drawn up a provisional timetable, and political anxieties about how the whole process was to be effected were becoming intense. Yet the many meetings and disputes about the hearing took place in offices in Vancouver, Calgary, and Ottawa, and did not bear in any direct way upon the people. In early October, however, the Indians were told that representatives of the company planning to construct the pipeline, officials of the Northern Pipeline Agency, political and legal workers from the Union of British Columbia Indian Chiefs, along with an independent presiding chairman, and the press would converge upon the Reserve in November. Then, they said, they would listen to the people. A schedule set out the dates on which a hearing would take place at each of the reserves and at several of the towns and white communities throughout the region.

These community hearings were characterized by the Northern 12 Pipeline Agency as an opportunity for the Indians and others to respond to the terms and conditions which they, at the agency, had already drafted. This limitation would not be rigidly enforced, since it was bound to result either in endless misunderstandings or a reduction of the hearings to discussion that, for many people, might well be unintelligible. The preparation of terms and conditions − the rules that were supposed to reflect the Indian interest − had also taken place before any close attention had been given to the Indian point of view.

The people at the Reserve nonetheless anticipated their hearing with 13 great interest. Doubts may have arisen in the minds of their political representatives. Reports and papers left in the reserves by various officials may have gone unread. But the people themselves insisted that the coming meeting was of great importance. There was an ever-growing sense of occasion. No one had taken much trouble to ask the Indians what they thought about pipelines or any other frontier activity, and a hearing seemed to many like the first real chance to express their long-neglected points of view. As the event came nearer, the Fort St. John radio station repeatedly announced the days and times of different hearings. Everyone at the Reserve including Joseph began to look forward to the occasion.

14   The morning of the hearing was sunny and cold. No one was quite sure when it was supposed to begin. The notice on the door of the Hall gave the time as 10 A.M., but some people insisted that nothing much was going to happen before noon. At Joseph's house there was some excitement. On the previous afternoon, Atsin and Sam had discovered the freshly prepared den of a black bear. Branches and earth had been piled up around the den's entrance: the bear was about to bed down for the winter. The way the branches had been pulled and heaped left the men sure that they would be able to force the animal from its den and kill it in the entranceway, where it could easily be dragged out. The sooner they went back to the new den, said Atsin, the better. At this time of year, after a whole summer of feeding and the early autumn cold, the meat and fur should both be in excellent condition and there would be plenty of fat. Joseph added that he could use some bear grease, the best thing for softening and protecting the leather of his saddles and bridles.

15   Joseph, Atsin, and Sam were adamant: we should go and get the bear right away. Maybe we would be able to get back in time for the meeting; maybe the meeting should wait until later in the day; or maybe we could get the talking over with quickly, and be on our way to the den by early afternoon. It was a perfect day for hunting. Who could possibly want to spend it listening to talk? What was there to say about the pipeline anyway? After a long discussion, we finally agreed that the bear hunt could wait until first thing the following morning. Joseph and Atsin decided to stay for the hearing. Sam Wolf, however, said he would never listen to talk when he could be out hunting. He pointedly prepared his equipment and set off on foot to look for moose. Brian Akattah and I went to the hall to put up the maps the people of the Reserve had drawn to show the extent of their hunting and trapping territories. Everyone else patiently waited at home for the hearing to begin.

16   It was a long wait. The chairman came early, to be shown the Reserve, but it was midday before a busload of officials drove up to the hall. Specialists on social and economic impacts, a secretary to oversee proceedings, people whose job it was to record every word that was spoken, all climbed out and began to assemble their equipment. In separate cars came the men from West Coast Transmission — the company that would build the British Columbian section of the line — with their diagrams

of the pipeline, the press, and representatives of the Union of Chiefs.

Inside the hall, chairs and tables were arranged, maps pinned on the 17
walls. In the kitchen, beside the main meeting room, the women of the
Reserve were cooking. They had prepared two kinds of moose stew,
venison steaks, and a bountiful supply of bannock. Rich aromas filled
the hall and indicated that however numerous and alien the outsiders
and their technology might be, the Reserve was going to do its best
to turn the hearing into its own kind of occasion.

By the time the hall was finally ready for the hearing to begin, there 18
were at least as many outsiders to listen, report, or observe as there
were Indians prepared to speak. The visitors were talkative and jovial
and quickly chose their seats. The Indians were quiet and reluctant even
to enter the room. The chairman took his place at the altar-table on
which, just over a year ago, Stan had drawn his hunting map. The two
transcribers sat among a tangle of equipment. The Reserve women stayed
in the kitchen, out of sight and busy with their work, but able to see
and hear through a hatch and doorway which opened into the hall.
Joseph, Jimmy Wolf, Abe Fellow, Robert Fellow, and Clare Akattah,
with other community elders and leaders, had been urged into sitting
at a table to one side of the chairman. They looked uncomfortable. No
doubt they were wondering what was expected of them and were puzzled
by the microphones an official kept rearranging in front of them —
technology that hardly seemed necessary in so small a room.

In this unpromising way, the meeting at length began. The chairman 19
started by trying to explain its purpose. He spoke about the Alaska
Highway Pipeline and sought to give some rudimentary history of the
litigation by which it was being facilitated. Nervously, in an attempt
to overcome the problems of language and culture, and conscious of
the extreme lack of background information among the people who sat
there trying to make sense of it all, he laid out the reason for the hearing. He talked about terms and conditions and explained what kinds
of rules there would be. He tried, also, to describe the differences between the roles of the governments, agencies, and construction companies. And he emphasized his wish to hear all that the people of the
Reserve might have to say about the pipeline, or any of the other
developments to which it related.

The elders at the table watched and listened. They quickly felt some 20
sympathy for the chairman, an elderly man with a quiet voice and gentle
manner, who was wearing beaded moccasins. By keeping their focus
on him, they lessened the disturbing effects of the other strangers and

could feel that they were able to talk and be listened to in a personal, human way.

21   But it was not easy for them. The chairman was followed by the Northern Pipeline Agency's secretary and a representative of West Coast Transmission who introduced their colleagues and said what each of them did. The introductions were not translated into Beaver. At this time, in any case, only a small number of the people had come to sit in the hall. They continued to stand in the doorway, in the kitchen, or to wait outside. When the chairman did at last ask the Indians to offer their points of view, Joseph began to talk. His clarity and confidence filled the hall and transformed its atmosphere. He spoke in Beaver, with an interpreter. The unfamiliarity of the sounds and the richness of his tone cast a spell over the proceedings. The absurdities and awkwardness of the event faded away. Here, at last, was an Indian voice. After every few sentences, Joseph paused and let the interpreter translate. In English, the words were not easy to grasp, and its being rendered in the third person made the sense no clearer. But the points were not lost:

> He was saying in our country there was no such thing as money before the white man came; our only way to make a living is to hunt and there is no such thing as money to get from one another and big bulldozers that come over, go across our country.

> He is saying as long as there is the sun that goes over, that he shall never stop hunting in this country and wherever he likes to do, as long as the sun is still there.

> He is saying that the white man pushed his way into our country, that he stakes up all the land and a long time ago there was no people and then now there is so many. . . .

> He is saying if the pipeline goes through, the game will never be here and is there no way that we can stop this pipeline from going through and when the game goes away how would the people make their survival for meat?

> He says if the white man makes more roads, what if they get on my trapline and if they cut all the trees down, where would I go for hunting and where would I get the fur?

Then another of the elders made his statement. Again the Beaver language filled the room. Again the translation was uncertain, but the hesitant and broken English combined with the resonance of the Beaver to powerful effect.

One after the other the people spoke. Atsin tried to convey the im- 22 portance of Quarry and, determined to speak in English, made a cryptic, struggling, but moving statement. Robert Fellow spoke in a mixture of Beaver and English about the progressive destruction of the timber on his trapline and tried to explain how this is driving away the squirrel, marten, and lynx. Clare Akattah talked about her ten-year-old son and the happiness he gets from trapping. Brian Akattah explained the significance of the people's hunting maps and pointed out that his family — like others on the Reserve — needed to have their trapline. His mother spoke in support of him and, in one sentence, encapsulated what everyone had been trying to say: "There is no way you can make paper into moccasins."

After the Reserve people had spoken, the representatives of West Coast 23 Transmission explained their project. With the use of a pipeline map, they gave numbers, routes and scraps of history: 444 miles of 56-inch diameter pipe along a 125-foot right-of-way; nine construction camps at 50-mile intervals; four compressor stations, the nearest to be 46 miles away; at Mile 92 of the Highway there is already a compressor station. West Coast Transmission's other pipelines were built in the area in 1956, 1961, and 1964. Several gathering lines have been built around Fort St. John and Fort Nelson to connect the main lines with scattered gas fields. The proposed Alaska Highway pipeline, permissions granted, will be started in 1982 or 1983; the section on muskeg would be built in winter, the other parts in summer and fall; pipe would be brought into the area by the British Columbia Railroad, and off-loaded at Fort St. John, Beatton River, or Fort Nelson; this would be done in winter and the pipe then stored at compressor station sites to be distributed to construction points along the line.

Then the Northern Pipeline Agency representative spoke. Pipelines 24 cause problems. There must be rules; the people here, and in all the other communities in the region, must say what rules they think they need. West Coast Transmission will have to follow the rules. Problems with traplines or any other issues can now be voiced. The job is to finalize rules, but there can be more discussion. "Our purpose in being here," he said, "is to listen to you so that we can set the best rules possible, but at the same time, recognizing that those rules have to be reasonable."

These men did not speak for long. Perhaps they sensed the impossi- 25 bility of their task. Their statements were not translated. They may have been untranslatable. The divide between the details they offered and the people's voices was too enormous. West Coast Transmission and the Northern Pipeline Agency men came as employees of remote organizations to discuss a pipeline. They were on a business trip, doing a job. The men and women of the Reserve spoke of their homes, their lives and, moved to do so by profound apprehensions about the future,

26   they struggled against language barriers and nervousness.

By 2 P.M. everyone had spoken. Joseph and Abe Fellow made final statements. The chairman expressed his thanks and admiration and adjourned the meeting. The West Coast Transmission men began packing up their map. Agency officials bantered cheerfully with one another. The transcribers coiled up their wires and packed away their machines. The Union of British Columbia Indian Chiefs' representatives and organizers exchanged the happy opinion that the hearing had been a success. Meanwhile, work in the kitchen continued. A few individuals had slipped in there to eat. Children crowded around their mothers, curious to glimpse the proceedings in the hall without being caught by the strangers' eyes. When the hearing adjourned, everyone was urged to help themselves to steaming dishes of stews, steaks, bannock. It was a lavish welcome, an invitation to share. If speeches and explanations had not captured the attention of the visitors, or had caused them to be at all uneasy, here was a feast to reassure everyone and, in its way, to give special emphasis to the importance of what the Indians had said.

27   It was all very convivial. The chairman and his associates, however, were eager to be on their way. Tired and satisfied, they regarded the hearing as ended. Once the social niceties were over and done with, the visitors could return to their homes and hotels in town satisfied that a job had been well done. Another hearing was scheduled for the next day. The formal business of making statements and placing them on the record was over. Children now ran in and out, and the two worlds of kitchen and hall had become the combined setting for a feast.

28   But the people had more to say. The Whites may have completed their work, but now that everyone was eating the Indians' food and talking to one another without agonizing and distorting formality, the hearing could get under way on the Indians' terms. Relaxed and scattered around the hall and kitchen in small groups, the visitors and officials failed to notice when Jimmy Wolf's brother Aggan and Aggan's wife Annie brought a moosehide bundle into the hall. Neither Aggan nor Annie had spoken earlier in the day, but they went directly to the table at which the elders had sat. There they untied the bundle's thongs and began very carefully to pull back the cover. At first sight the contents seemed to be a thick layer of hide, pressed tightly together. With great care, Aggan

took this hide from its cover and began to open the layers. It was a magnificent dream map.

The dream map was as large as the table top, and had been folded 29
tightly for many years. It was covered with thousands of short, firm, and variously coloured markings. The people urged the chairman and other white visitors to gather round the table. Abe Fellow and Aggan Wolf explained. Up here is heaven; this is the trail that must be followed; here is a wrong direction; this is where it would be worst of all to go; and over there are all the animals. They explained that all of this had been discovered in dreams.

Aggan also said that it was wrong to unpack a dream map except 30
for very special reasons. But the Indians' needs had to be recognized; the hearing was important. Everyone must look at the map now. Those who wanted to might even take photographs. They should realize, however, that intricate routes and meanings of a dream map are not easy to follow. There was not time to explain them all. The visitors crowded around the table, amazed and confused. The centre of gravity had suddenly shifted away from procedural concerns, pipelines and terms and conditions, to the Indians' world.

A corner of the map was missing and one of the officials asked how 31
it had come to be damaged. Aggan answered: someone had died who would not easily find his way to heaven, so the owner of the map had cut a piece of it and buried it with the body. With the aid of even a fragment, said Aggan, the dead man would probably find the correct trail, and when the owner of the map died, it would all be buried with him. His dreams of the trail to heaven would then serve him well.

Prompted by the map, the elders spoke again about the way their life 32
is changing, and the extent to which frontier developments have damaged their lands. They complained, too, about the weakness of dreamers to-day: would the young people be able to use these essential skills? Some of these thoughts had been spoken into the microphones and, in inchoate form, had become part of the official record. But now there was no recording, nothing that made the words official. The people now spoke in their own ways, and with real confidence. Most important of all, they said what they wanted and needed. The officials and visitors expressed delight and interest, but it is difficult to know how much they understood. Did the dream map come from too remote a cultural domain? Did the fractured and hesitant English in which the Beaver people spoke too completely obscure their points? Or, taking place after the hearing had been adjourned, off the record, was the conversation around the

map seen as no more than a further display of agreeable hospitality? It is never easy to judge the political significance of informal events. Evoking a strange and distant world, the Indians who showed the dream map could have failed to make their point simply because they were now using their own, very unfamiliar idioms.

33   All the men and women who spoke, whether at the microphones, in seemingly sociable conversations over plates of food, or while the dream map was being shown, said that their lives depended on traplines. They said that logging should be carried out in such a way as to leave enough habitat for squirrels and marten. They said that sports hunters must be kept out of the Indians' hunting territories. Many also insisted that the Alaska Highway pipeline either should not be built at all, or should somehow be built in a way that would not drive away the region's moose. They spoke of oppression in the past and disregard for their interests in the present. The substance of their remarks, along with the gentle tones they used, made it clear that the people had not given up hope, either of being listened to or of leading the kind of life that strengthens their economy and culture. They had tried to explain their concerns in many different ways. They took part in the outsiders' hearing and used it to explain their point of view, but they also prepared moose meat stew and showed a dream map. Despite a century of experience that might urge them to do otherwise, the Indians took the hearing seriously.

34   Many of the Whites who spent the day in the Reserve hall said they were deeply moved. The chairman repeatedly thanked the people for their words and generosity, and thanked the elders for sharing their wisdom. Yet discussion of the dream map soon petered out, and the officials hurried into their bus, anxious to drive back to town. The people of the Reserve were puzzled. Where had their visitors gone? The meeting was just getting under way. Thinking that there must be some misunderstanding, they asked everyone to come back into the hall, though representatives of the pipeline construction company had long since driven away.

35   Inside the hall, the elders explained that whenever a dream map is taken out, someone must play a drum and chant. The visitors would, of course, want to share in this. And one of the elders made the room echo with the soft but insistent rhythm of the drum, and sang. No one understood the words, and the singer was too shy to explain. He sat in a corner and relied on the power of the rhythm to hold everyone's attention. At the end of the first song he stopped and looked up. Perhaps

someone else would now drum? The evening was just beginning.

But as soon as the drumming stopped the officials expressed their 36
thanks and escaped again to their bus. They were tired, they said, and
it really was time they were back in town. From their point of view
the meeting had ended more than an hour before. The people in the
hall let them go. Perhaps they were no longer surprised by this
demonstration of the white man's haste and incomprehension. No one
criticized or complained. The drummer began another song. The sound
of the bus driving away broke into the music, but soon the noise of
its engine faded into the distance. When the second song ended, the
men said that it was a pity there had been no time to play the stick game.
They had looked forward to it.

People lingered in the hall. A young man visiting from another village 37
drummed and sang for a while. Others ate. The elders talked about
dreams and dreaming, and the maps of the Indians' hunting territories
were taken from the wall. The hall began to seem very empty. It was
still early. Outside a group of men talked about the meeting and the
weather. "Tomorrow will be fine and cold," said Joseph. "We'll go and
look for the bear early."

By the next morning it was hard to remember all that had happened 38
at the hearing. Atsin led us to the bear's den. He and Sam Crown judged
the lie of its interior by the shapes and textures of the ground, and then
they dug and pounded until the animal appeared at the entrance. Sam
shot it. Joseph and Robert Fellow skinned and butchered the bear while
the others set off on a moose hunt. The sports-hunting season was over.
The people again had the woods to themselves. No one said whether
or not they felt they had gained anything by all the talk of the previous
day. It is difficult to mix hunting with politics. But when they discovered
a sports hunter's equipment cache and old campsite a few miles from
the bear kill, their expressions of indignation were nothing if not political.
As he uncovered cans of fuel, ropes, and tarpaulins, and looked around
to see if a kill had been made, Atsin declared over and over again that
white men had no right to hunt there, on the Indians' land. When Joseph
heard about the cache he said: "Pretty soon we'll fix it all up. We've
made maps and everyone will see where we have our land."

(1981)

The Writer's Subject

1. Brody quotes Clare Akhata as saying "There is no way you can make paper into moccasins" (para. 22). How does this statement "encapsulate" what everyone had been trying to say at the hearing?

2. Brody describes what both the Indians and the white men say at the hearing. What differences are apparent in their ways of presenting their respective positions?

3. What details in the account show that the Indians take the hearing seriously?

4. What is the importance of the fractured pipe incident in Brody's narrative? (para. 7)

5. What details in the essay help us understand the Indians' sense of time? The white man's sense of time?

6. What is the importance of the Indians' debate about whether to attend the hearing or kill the bear? (paras. 14-15)

7. This essay is taken from a book entitled *Maps and Dreams*, and maps play an important part in this essay itself. What different significances do the Indians and the white men attach to maps at the hearing? What is the force of the concluding sentence of the essay?

The Writer's Style and Strategy

1. Why does Brody spend the first few pages of this essay giving a detailed account of Indian life in the summer months?

2. How does Brody make the reader aware of where his sympathies lie?

3. What use does Brody make of the *verbatim* rendering of the translation of Joseph's words at the hearing? Compare this translation with the explanation of their project by the representatives from West Coast Transmission.

4. What details of the hearing emphasize the contrasting attitudes and behaviours of the white men and the Indians?

Suggested Topics for Writing and Discussion

1. This essay centres on a clash of cultures. Discuss examples or instances of cultural conflicts that may exist within your own community.

2. Using your college library, find out what you can about the Alaska Pipeline Hearings and the outcome of the project.

3. Brody's essay is, in part, about the impact of technological change on a traditional way of life, a situation also common in other areas of the world (e.g., mining and logging operations in the Amazon, and hydroelectric projects such as the James Bay project in Quebec or the Aswan Dam project in Egypt). Choose an example of this kind of technological impact and discuss its effect on the way of life of a specific cultural group.

4. In his essay, "Tyranny of the Clock," George Woodcock discusses modern industrial man's view of time as a "commodity." Compare this view of time with that of the Indians as described by Brody.

Murder Among the Lovebirds
by Janet Flanner

1   Maybe our grandmothers were right and female standards are, on all sides, not so high as they used to be. Certainly an eclectic comparison between the mediocre murder recently committed by the nineteen-year-old Parisian flapper Mlle. Violette Nozière and the stylish assassination achieved by the consummate Mme. Germaine d'Anglemont, aged forty-eight, indicates a deplorable decline in the younger generation. Mme. d'Anglemont shot her lover like a lady, because she was jealous; Violette Nozière killed her father like a cannibal, because she wanted to eat and drink up the savings that were his French life and blood.

2   Even in their private lives − or as private as could be, considering that both females lived on love for sale − Germaine d'Anglemont cut the grander figure, since, though an uneducated foundling, in her long life she had learned to dine with royalty, own a smart house, accept diamonds, and take such an intelligent interest in politics that senators and deputies had been her slaves. And even the gentleman she finally shot was a chief magistrate.

3   Though her doting parents had educated her over their heads and means in a Paris private school, in her brief career Violette Nozière had learned merely how to drink bad cocktails with penniless collegiates, was at home only on the Boul' Mich', gave her mother's engagement ring to a lover rather than received any gem from him, and certainly never met any member of the government until, on trial for parricide, she made the acquaintance of her judge.

4   Germain d'Anglemont was the last of the silk-ruffled, scented, hard-lipped, handsome prewar courtesans, and she made a fortune. Violette

was, one fears, not the last of the fake-silver-foxed, hard-toothed, modern young monsters of mediocre looks and without any sense of the business of life. Being up to date, her crime cruelly lacked the grand manner.

Since she was faintly intellectual, Violette Nozière characteristically 5 chose poison and patience as her weapons. Though she did not succeed till August 1934 in putting her father into his grave and her mother into the hospital, she practised up on murdering them in March by giving them, "as a nice new tonic" with their evening coffee, six and three tablets of veronal, respectively, which they hungrily swallowed, since both were passionate patent-medicine gourmets.

At shortly past midnight after the March evening, contented with their 6 coma, their daughter set fire to the flat's modest parlor curtains, walked across the hall, roused a neighbor with a scream of "Fire!" and a brainy afterscream of, "I think the electricity must have short-circuited." The local fire brigade was called, and the next day M. and Mme. Nozière made the second page of the Parisian newspapers for the first and last time − thereafter they were unfortunately to be front-page stuff − for being unconscious from suffocation in what was called "A Bizarre Conflagration." Murder in an odd form was on its way to the Rue de Madagascar, where the three Nozières dwelt till they started on their separate paths toward cemetery, clinic and prison.

In the five months which followed, the immodest Violette did nothing 7 unusual − for her. She continued her afternoon and evening life on the large sidewalks and in the small hotels of the Boulevard Saint-Michel where, from the age of fifteen, she had been playing hooky from the costly female seminary for which her parents had scrimped so that she might star in mathematics. But though majoring in geometry, Vi knew less about Euclid than about a lot of other men. At her trial, it was brought out that she was not only a nympho − but also a mythomaniac − or a natural tart plus a born liar.

On the Café d'Harcourt terrace, she picked up men with a dual pur- 8 pose, the second being to tell them fantastic fibs − that she was an heiress, that her grandmother owned a château, that an aunt had millions, an uncle billions, that she herself was noble, that she was a trigonometry professor, and that her father was a director in the French railways. He was, in a way. He was the locomotive engineer on the Paris-Vichy fast train; her grandmother's country place was a cottage where, after her granddaughter's arrest, the old peasant humbly died of shame among her cabbages. Indeed, only two things unusual were performed by Vi during those fatal five months. She continued to try to kill her mother occasionally: at any rate, whenever the girl prepared breakfast for her, *maman* was deathly sick after, so Vi must have been putting something into the coffee — besides the chicory, that is. (Her father, having just fallen out of his engine cab onto his head, was momentarily in the hospital and so drank his bad coffee without ill results.)

9   Violette's second odd act was to fall in love: the emotion was great, since she eventually killed for it; the object was slight — an eighteen-year-old gigolo law student with sleek hair, slack morals, and American horn-rimmed spectacles, worn like a foolish foreign trade-mark on his French phiz. His name was Jean Dabin; his father, in Vi's mythology, was also probably a railway director — i.e., in reality, a whistle-blowing petty station-master on the Paris belt railroad.

10   Violette's love for Jean was the only true passion in her life, except that for murder. To him she gave all she had — herself plus one hundred francs a day, which she got from other men by night. She also promised to give him a secondhand Bugatti and a first-rate September holiday, for, as she said, she was shortly expecting to inherit one hundred and eighty thousand francs, or the exact sum her father had saved up from a lifetime of driving the Paris-Vichy express.

11   On August 23, her patience and poison and passion finally focused. Violette Nozière repeated what she had tried out in March, except that she increased her father's dose to twenty powdered veronal tablets and her mother's to six. This time she also gave herself a small dose of milk of magnesia, as she was feeling liverish. Then she curled up in a chair for a nap by her parent's couch while they died — she hoped. At two a.m. when she called the same neighbor, she this time screamed — since she had turned on the kitchen range without lighting it — "Gas!" and, as a new addition, "I think the pipe has burst."

12   The neighbor was, of all men to call in twice, an electrician and gas fitter by trades. Whatever he had failed to smell in March, this time he smelled not only gas but a rat. So did Vi, at dawn in the city hospital, sitting tenderly by her mother's bedside; the authorities had refused to let her sit tenderly by her father's slabside in the morgue. Sensing danger, she calmly rose and walked out into the new Paris day and what for one week seemed limbo, since no one could find her. By dinner, her news photo as "Wanted for Parricide" was posted all over Paris. Police hunted her everywhere, except at the Bal Tabarin (where she spent the first night after her crime gracefully waltzing) and on the Boulevard de la Madeleine, where a white-faced, neurotic, not very pretty young creature plied her trade while whispering crazily to her customers that

her father was a railway director, her grandmother owned a château, and that she herself was an heiress . . . to one hundred and eighty thousand francs . . . oh, yes, she was surely an heiress by now. . . . On the sixth day she was trapped into a second rendezvous by a gallant young male who had recognized her face on the pillow from the newspaper he'd tossed on the chair. Arrested, she told the truth, probably for the first time in her life. At any rate she said she was glad she'd killed her father, who, she claimed, was a satyr, though her relief at hearing that her mother was yawning back from the jaws of death may have been a lie.

Her trial for murder in the autumn of 1934 was melodramatic. It 13 opened in the Paris Assizes with a five-minute silence for King Alexander of Yugoslavia, who had also just been murdered in Marseilles. In the three days which followed, Violette fainted frequently, was occasionally nearly lynched by angry crowds, and was constantly hectored in court by her mother, who was sentimentally suing her for damages for having robbed her of the sweetest husband woman ever knew.

In addition to other details, the jury was swayed by the fact that Violette 14 had also robbed what she thought was her mother's corpse of a thousand francs pinned to the maternal corset. With lust for money to spend on her lover in cafés (for bad Martinis) accredited as her miserable motive, the jury judged her guilty of the uncivilized crime of parricide, whereupon the judge read what remains the most medieval death sentence preserved in modern French law: "She is to have her head cut off in death upon a public place in Paris. She shall be taken there barefooted, clad only in her chemise and with her head covered by a black veil. Before the execution shall be done, let the clerk in a clear voice read aloud this Judgment." Though women are no longer guillotined in France, and if they were, no matter whom they had killed, they would be allowed to die dressed and with their boots on, the rare sentence was followed by unusual silence in court, suddenly broken by Violette's vulgarly shouting, "Curse my father, curse my mother!"

To the outraged gendarme who dragged her away, she shouted in 15 one of her illuminating afterthoughts, "Fetch my handbag with my powder, rouge, money. I must have dropped it in the prisoner's box." What was most precious she had clearly left behind her in court. Thus passed from youth into lifelong imprisonment the best-educated, worst-mannered young murderess in French annals. But it was the fact of the girl's having rudely slept in the intimate presence of the dead and dying that caused the French jury to cut her off from civilized society as long as she might live.

16   The jury in the same Paris court which had just tried Germaine d'Anglemont for having shot her late love, Causeret, had only cut her off from civilized society for eleven months. And even that period of sequestration was a cultivated *passetemps*, since she spent it as prison librarian; both before and after murdering, dear Germaine was ever the bookworm. Her crime, trial, sentence, were all as cynical and sociable as her origin. Born a love child humbly named Huot, whose father only made her acquaintance when she was aged eleven, at twelve Germaine had won the catechism prize in her orphan asylum, at fourteen had her first flirtation, at fifteen her first carriage and pair and the stylish name of D'Anglemont, which she picked out of a dime novel. The week before Mlle. Huot became Mme. d'Anglemont, she had been noted − pretty and shabby − in the then famous Jardin de Paris Café, the noting being done by a tableful which included Catulle Mendès, the poet; Henry Bernstein, the playwright: Prince Fouad, now King of Egypt: and other gentlemen of the 1905 *belle époque*, one of whom asked her how she got there.

17   She said she had run away from home penniless and had got into the café by pawning her umbrella for three francs with the *vestiaire*. The gentlemen handed her five hundred francs (one hundred dollars in those lovely days) to get some decent clothes, three francs to get her umbrella, and invited her to dine. Her second lover, according to the list the Paris judge indelicately read out at her murder trial thirty-four years later, was a Dutch millionaire named Van Horschoot; the third was an Argentine tutor the Dutchman had hired to complete the girl's education − though she seemed to know a great deal already; the fourth love was the Prince Franz Josef of the royal house of Bavaria, who died of a broken heart because she wouldn't marry him.

18   Among the innumerable others she did not marry were the Polish Count Wielsinski, who, instead of a wedding ring, could give her only diamonds and pearls; the Agha Khan, who merely gave her a diamond (though it was eighteen karats); Camille Picard, today Deputy from the Vosges; a M. France, who was seventy and in sugar; a M. Astruc, at whom she once threw an expensive Gothic statue of the Virgin; and a Dr. Morgilewski (whom she never saw again for thirteen years, till the fatal day when she telephoned him to come round professionally as she seemed to have shot one of his successors). The mass of Parliamentarians she also enmeshed finally dwindled down, in her

forties, to the late-lamented Chief Magistrate Causeret, young, promising politician, fickle, married, father of children — and what was worse, son of the prime Rector Causeret of Clermont University.

"If I've omitted any of your lovers, pray excuse me, Madame," the 19 Judge said ironically at her trial. "The list is already so long, You were a *courtisane de haut vol* — a highflier; you are also, alas, a good shot." It was her custom to practise in the shooting gallery near the Rond-Point where Ivar Kreuger bought his fatal suicide gun: she kept two pistols in her boudoir alongside the statue of Sainte Thérèse — all three useful as weapons to a woman in a jealous rage. For it was for jealousy that she murdered Causeret. She had him followed through the streets of Paris by a hunchback female detective (a masseuse, when spying was scarce), who reported that he had gone to a department store to buy suspicious silk pajamas, instead of going, as he had announced, to talk politics with an old gentleman.

At noon, five minutes after Causeret had returned to her smart Place 20 Beauvais flat to lunch, there was still nothing to eat on the dining-room table, but there was a corpse with only a bullet in its stomach in the boudoir. As Germaine later admitted to the jury, she'd been a little hasty — the handsomest apology a murderess ever made.

At her trial the jury also was hasty; in one minute they saw it would 21 be useless to condemn her, since they also saw, all around the court, the visiting politicos who would demand and obtain her pardon. The jury therefore judged her guilty but with a cynically strong recommendation for mercy, which to the judge's mind meant a sentence of eleven months. Thus the quality of mercy was for once strained, since six years is a normal clement "stretch" for French female killers. Along with her eleven months, Germaine d'Anglemont also got bouquets of flowers in court, and her male friends shook hands, kissing hers.

In her trial, justice was not done. Yet injustice would have been ac- 22 complished had not a D'Anglemont's punishment been infinitely less than a Nozière's. For in a way these two were test cases, illustrating the modern French attitude toward murder, which can be summed up thus: the manner of killing is as important as the manner of living.

(1936)

The Writer's Subject

1. What were the principal differences in character and background of the two women described by Flanner? (paras. 1-4)

2. Why, according to Flanner, did Violette Nozière want to murder her parents? (paras. 7-10)

3. How was Violette eventually captured? (para. 12)

4. What was Germaine d'Anglemont's motive for murdering her lover? (para. 19)

5. Why was Germaine's sentence so much lighter than Violette's, even though both women were convicted of murder? (para. 21)

6. Why does Flanner believe that an injustice would have been done "had not a D'Anglemont's punishment been infinitely less than a Nozière's" (para. 22)?

The Writer's Style and Strategy

1. A writer, particularly a journalist, will often choose an "angle" from which to approach a subject. What "angle" is established in the opening paragraph? How does it determine the shape of the account that follows?

2. Flanner's essay first appeared in the *New Yorker*, a weekly magazine. Judging by Flanner's treatment of her subject, what conclusions might you draw about the *New Yorker*'s readership?

3. The tone of Flanner's essay is ironic throughout. What does the tone reveal about Flanner's attitude to the two women she describes, and to the society which condemned them?

4. Why does Flanner refer to Violette as "Vi" at many points in her essay? (paras. 7-12)

5. Flanner uses a variety of devices in her prose, including parallel or contrasting sentence elements, nouns or noun clauses in series, parenthetical comments, unexpected juxtapositions, colloquialisms, and alliteration. Pick out examples of each of these in paragraphs 6-11, and indicate how their use contributes to the ironic effect sought by Flanner.

6. Why does Flanner describe some of Germaine d'Anglemont's innumerable lovers? (paras. 17-18) How does that description prepare the reader for the essay's concluding paragraphs?

7. How does Flanner's title reflect the tone of the essay as a whole?

Suggested Topics for Writing and Discussion

1. Germaine d'Anglemont served a sentence of only eleven months before she was released. Today in North America, though murderers must generally serve much longer sentences, many become eligible for early release through parole. Do you think that a murderer should ever be released from jail?

2. Find two or three published accounts of a recent murder trial in local newspapers and national magazines. What differences are apparent in the various accounts of the proceedings? How is the character of the murderer drawn in each of your sources?

3. In discussing the sentencing of two murderers, Flanner demonstrates the application, a rather extreme one, of a double standard. Using an instance from public or private life, discuss another situation in which a double standard seems to apply.

Women's Clothes — Towards Emancipation

by Alison Lurie

The Superficially Liberated Woman

1   The more conventional late-Victorian and Edwardian woman, though she was no longer supposed to be childish and frail, was far from liberated by modern standards. Though her appearance was queenly, like most queens of recent years her freedom was hedged round with duties and restrictions. She was often called "divine" — and, as is the custom with goddesses, stood on a pedestal, which is an inconvenient place to stand if you want to do anything other than be worshipped. If you move at all, you are in danger of falling off — of becoming, in the popular phrase of the time, a "fallen woman."

2   The first wave of feminism, as historians of costume have pointed out, did not liberate most women from the bulky and elaborate clothes of the period. Indeed in many ways the female fashions of the time were more oppressive than those of midcentury. The corset had previously ended at or just below the waist, accommodating the many pregnancies of the early-Victorian woman. Now advances in medical science had decreased infant mortality, and it was no longer necessary or fashionable to have many children. The late-Victorian corset lengthened to midthigh, severely restricting locomotion. Gradually it began to push the chest forward and the hips back, creating the S-bend figure with its low-slung monobosom and protruding monorump. Over the corset were worn a corset cover, a camisole, several petticoats, and dresses with trailing skirts and trains. All these garments were richly trimmed with lace, ruffles, tucks, ribbons and embroidery; they were in constant danger of being rumpled or soiled, often giving a literal meaning

to the current euphemism "soiled dove."

The ordinary woman who held a job or emancipated opinions might   3
wear, instead of a lace-trimmed gown, a more plainly cut wool or linen
suit (the "tailor-made") with a shirtwaist, tie and straw boater that imitated those of men. But this imitation was superficial. Beneath her clothes
her corset was as uncomfortable and confining as ever, and when she
lifted her heavy floor-length skirt she showed a froth of delicate petticoats and lacy stockings. The message of this costume was clear: the
masculine efficiency or intellectual force were only external; underneath
she was still a member of the frailer sex. To wear such clothes, however,
did not necessarily mean acceptance of the status quo. Some feminists
wore them deliberately in order to confuse or disarm their opponents:
indeed, several of the leaders of the Emancipation Movement were
famous for their stylishness. This stratagem was also used during the
second wave of women's liberation, by Gloria Steinem among others.

The Modern Girl

In the early twentieth century substantial gains in dress reform were   4
achieved. Slowly, women began to liberate themselves from the duty
of acting as walking advertisements of their own helplessness and their
male relatives' wealth. (The struggle was an uphill one, however, and
it is by no means over.) There was also a gradual relaxation of the corset and a rise in the skirt, which cleared the ground by 1905, and by
1912 was above the ankle. Once women could breathe a little more easily
and had no trains to trip over they were better able to take part in sports.
Some, though to our eyes still absurdly handicapped, joined in professional competition. By the end of World War I women's clothes had
become relatively unconfining, but they were still sex-typed, and by
no means as comfortable as those of men. Various counterrevolutionary
efforts were made – notably, the introduction of the hobble skirt in
1910 – but these were generally unsuccessful. As in all transitional
periods, however, they provided a useful guide to the political and social
views of the women who wore them.

The clothes of the 1920s were thought at the time to represent an   5
extreme of freedom for women, and certainly they were a relief to anyone
old enough to have worn the styles of twenty years earlier. For one
thing, they drastically reduced the time spent in washing, ironing and
mending, and also in simply getting dressed and undressed. The woman
who bobbed her waist-length hair, for instance, saved several hours
a week that had previously been employed in brushing it out, washing

Portrait of Mr. and Mrs. I.N. Phelps-Stokes, John Singer Sargent, 1897
Reprinted by permission of the Metropolitan Museum of Art,
Bequest of Edith Mintern Phelps Stokes, 1938

and drying it, braiding it at night and putting it up in a pompadour over pads of wire mesh and false hair every morning.

Twenties' dresses often had little-boy collars or ties, but these were 6 no more than piquant additions to a recognizably feminine costume; they declared that their wearer was charmingly boyish, but not that she was a boy. The fulminations of contemporary critics against mannish women and womanish men seem exaggerated today. In photographs of the twenties men and women do look more alike; but this is because they both look more like children, and the difference between the sexes is less pronounced in childhood. Even in her Buster Brown or Peter Pan collar the flapper of the 1920s (like the Gibson Girl of a generation earlier in her mannish shirt and tie) is only male from the waist up. Below it, her skirt, silk stockings and pumps proclaim that basically she is a female.

Wearing the Pants

Reform of the bottom half of women's costume got seriously underway 7 in the 1890s, when the introduction of the bicycle was followed by the introduction of the divided skirt for female bicyclists. Though at first it was called unfeminine and even shocking, the divided skirt was in fact voluminously modest. Eventually it was generally accepted — possibly because no one could mistake it for masculine dress.

Real trousers took much longer to become standard female wear. It 8 was not until the 1920s that women and girls began to wear slacks and even shorts for sports and lounging. The new style was greeted with disapproval and ridicule. Women were told that they looked very ugly in trousers, and that wanting to wear The Pants — in our culture, for centuries, the symbolic badge of male authority — was unnatural and sexually unattractive. Nevertheless the fashion spread, and by the mid-1930s a woman could go on a picnic, play tennis or dig in the garden in clothes that did not handicap her. This freedom, however, was limited to the private and informal side of life. Wearing slacks to the office or to a party was out of the question, and any female who appeared on a formal occasion in a trouser suit was assumed to be a bohemian eccentric and probably a lesbian. Most schools and colleges insisted on skirts for classes and in the library until the 1960s; and even today this custom occasionally survives. At the Frick Collection Library in New York women may not be admitted unless they are wearing skirts; a particularly ancient and unattractive skirt is kept at the desk for the use of readers ignorant of this rule.

9   The woman who wore slacks or shorts before 1960, too, was only outwardly liberated. Underneath her clothes she was more pinched and squeezed and trussed-up than she had been in the twenties. Her bra hauled her breasts up toward the shoulders and forced them into the currently fashionable shape, often with the help of wires or deceptive padding. The straps of this bra usually cut into the flesh, leaving sore red lines on her shoulders and around her body to match the sore red lines left lower down by her tight elastic girdle. Even slim women wore girdles, since the fashionable figure had almost no hips or derrière, and a bouncy rear end was thought vulgar. There was also no other decent way to hold up the obligatory stockings: unless your skirt was very full, any garter belt would show an embarrassing outline beneath it.

To Freedom and Partway Back

10   The fifties and early sixties were the years of the baby boom, togetherness and the feminine mystique; and, as usually happens in patriarchal periods, female and male clothes were sharply distinguished. The New Look Woman and the Man in the Gray Flannel Suit were almost as distinct in silhouette as their grandparents. Nevertheless it was in this period that trousers for women began to edge their way into respectability. At first they took rather peculiar and unbecoming forms. The popular "toreador" or "Capri" pants, for instance, came in odd, glaring colors and ended a tight, awkward six inches above the ankle as if they had shrunk in the wash. They were often worn under maternity or mock-maternity smocks, producing a costume that resembled that of a medieval page. It was accompanied by shoes as narrow and sharply pointed — and no doubt as uncomfortable — as those fashionable in the fourteenth and fifteenth centuries. This outfit was appropriate, since the harassed, untrained middle-class mother of the baby-boom years — unlike her own parents — had no servants, and was reduced to waiting hand and foot on her husband and too many children.

11   In the late 1960s trousers for women finally became elegant as well as respectable, and underwear vanished or mutated into harmless forms. Even before the second wave of women's liberation got underway, the long struggle for comfort and freedom in female dress seemed to have been won at last. The introduction of panty hose freed women from the ugly and often painful rubber and metal and plastic hardwear they had been using to hold up their stockings. It was again permissible to have curves below the waist as well as above; and millions of girdles went into the trash can, where they were soon joined by millions of

padded and wired bras. During the 1970s pants suits and slacks were worn to work, to parties, to the theater, in elegant restaurants and on international planes, by women of all ages. They were usually accompanied by comfortable low-heeled shoes or boots. Fashion editors asserted, and women believed, that the bad old days were over forever.

In the last few years, however, there have been ominous signs of **12** retrenchment and a counterrevolutionary movement seems to be gaining force. If one is pessimistic it is possible to see the sixties and seventies as merely a period of temporary victory. Indeed, the entire history of female fashion from 1910 to the present can be viewed as a series of more or less successful campaigns to force, flatter or bribe women back into uncomfortable and awkward styles, not only for purposes of Vicarious Ostentation and security of sexual ownership, but also and increasingly in order to handicap them in professional competition with men. The hobble skirt, the girdle, the top-heavy hats of the teens and the forties, the embarrassingly short dresses of the twenties and the sixties, all have aided this war effort. Today its most effective strategic devices are fashionable footwear and the demand for slimness.

The Shoe as a Strategic Weapon

Attempts to limit female mobility by hampering locomotion are ancient **13** and almost universal. The foot-binding of upper-class Chinese girls and the Nigerian custom of loading women's legs with pounds of heavy brass wire are extreme examples, but all over the world similar stratagems have been employed to make sure that once you have caught a woman she cannot run away, and even if she stays around she cannot keep up with you. What seems odd is that all these devices have been perceived as beautiful, not only by men but by women. The lotus foot, which seems to us a deformity, was passionately admired in China for centuries, and today most people in Western society see nothing ugly in the severely compressed toes produced by modern footwear. The high-heeled, narrow-toed shoes that for most of this century have been an essential part of woman's costume are considered sexually attractive, partly because they make the legs look longer — an extended leg is the biological sign of sexual availability in several animal species — and because they produce what anthropologists call a "courtship strut." They also make standing for any length of time painful, walking exhausting and running impossible. The halting, tiptoe gait they produce is thought provocative — perhaps because it guarantees that no woman wearing them can outrun a man who is chasing her. Worst of all, if they are worn continually from adolescence on, they deform the muscles of the feet and legs so that it becomes even more painful and difficult to walk in flat soles.

14   Literally as well as figuratively modern women's shoes are what keep Samantha from running as fast as Sammy. As anyone who has worn them can testify, it is hard to concentrate on your job when your feet are killing you — especially if you are faint with hunger because you had only half a grapefruit and coffee for breakfast so as to stay a glamorous ten pounds below your natural healthy weight. For a while in the sixties and seventies it was not necessary to be handicapped in this way unless you chose to be. During the last few years, however, women have begun wearing tight high-heeled shoes again, even with pants, and the most fashionable styles are those that, like clogs and ankle-strap sandals, give least support to the feet and make walking most difficult.

Counterrevolution and Ambiguity

15   There have been other signs recently that all is not well with the in-dependent woman. One is the gradual demotion of the pants suit for both daytime and evening wear. By now it has become a low-status indicator, especially when made of polyester, and is seldom seen in middle-class circumstances. It has been replaced by the "skirted suit" recommended as the proper costume for white-collar success, which must of course be worn with panty hose and heels. Another ominous sign is the narrowing of the skirt to the point where ordinary gestures like sitting on a low sofa or stepping over a puddle become difficult.

16   Prudence Glynn, a former fashion editor of the London *Times,* was one of the first to point out the internal contradictions of much post-feminist fashion. The platform shoes and clogs that became popular during the seventies, for instance, are usually made on a wide last which does not compress the foot; however, they produce a clumping, awkward gait and are not only hard to manage but dangerous, often leading to serious injury. As Prudence Glynn puts it, "By their height they cater to an instinct in women to be taller and thus of more consequence vis-à-vis men. By their construction, which makes walking extremely dif-ficult, they cater to an instinct to remain vulnerable."

17   Another popular style of the time, known as the Annie Hall Look after the clothes worn by Diane Keaton in the film of the same name, was ambiguous in a more complex way. Essentially it involved the wear-ing of actual men's clothing: elegant three-piece suits, vests, shirts, ties

and hats in pale colors — beige, off-white, tan and gray — often with a twenties look. Everything was worn very large and loose — collars open, shirts ballooning out, sleeves and trouser legs rolled up. These clothes were accompanied by huge handbags and kooky, childish costume jewelry: ceramic and wood and painted-tin ice cream cones and rainbows and Mickey Mice.

The wearing of men's clothes can mean many different things. In the **18** thirties, sophisticated actresses such as Marlene Dietrich in top hat and tails and elegantly cut suits projected sophistication, power and a dangerous eroticism. The slacks and sweaters of the war period, and the jeans and pants outfits of the sixties and early seventies, were serious gestures toward sexual equality.

The Annie Hall style is a double message. It announces that its wearer **19** is a good sport, a pal: not mysteriously and delicately female, but an easy-going, ready-for-anything tomboy type, almost like one of the guys. She will not demand to be protected from the rain or make a fuss about having to stand up at a football game. She probably enjoys active sports and is good at them (though not annoyingly, competitively good). Besides, you can see from her Snoopy pin that she has a sense of humor and is just a kid at heart.

At the same time, however, these clothes convey an ironic antifeminist **20** message. Because they are worn several sizes too large, they suggest a child dressed up in her daddy's or older brother's things for fun, and imply "I'm only playing; I'm not really big enough to wear a man's pants, or do a man's job." This is a look of helpless cuteness, not one of authority; it invites the man to take charge, even when he is as incompetent himself as the characters played by Woody Allen.

(1981)

The Writer's Subject

1. What connection does Lurie make between women's clothes and the degree of female emancipation in late-Victorian society? (paras. 1-3)

2. To what extent did dress reform in the 1920s close the gap between the sexes? (paras. 4-6)

3. What, according to Lurie, was the early reaction to the wearing of slacks or shorts by women? (paras. 7-9) How far did this trend in women's clothes really represent liberation?

4. Lurie notes that in the sixties women's trousers were often worn with smocks, "producing a costume that resembled that of a medieval page" (para. 10). Why does she call such an outfit "appropriate"?

5. Why, according to Lurie, was the introduction of pantyhose so important to women's clothing styles? (para. 11)

6. What contrast does Lurie draw between the fashions of the sixties and seventies, and those of the last few years? What does she mean by the statement that "a counterrevolutionary movement seems to be gaining force" (para. 12)?

7. How does Lurie interpret the styles of footwear customarily worn by women? Why is she disturbed by the modern fashion for high-heeled shoes? (paras. 13-14)

8. In the last four paragraphs of the essay, Lurie discusses the wearing of men's clothes by women. Why does this fashion seem to her to "convey an ironic antifeminist message"?

The Writer's Style and Strategy

1. Lurie's account is a mixture of social history, sociological commentary, and polemic. Where does Lurie move away from history and analysis to make her own position clear? How does she do so?

2. Discuss the language of paragraph 12. What is the extended metaphor through which Lurie presents the history of changes in women's fashions?

3. Discuss the structure and development of Lurie's paragraphs. Where does she usually place the topic sentence? (See, for example, paras. 8-11.)

4. From time to time Lurie shifts from the impersonality of the third person to "you." Discuss the purpose and effectiveness of this shift in point of view in paragraphs 13 and 14.

5. How does Lurie demonstrate that women have been handicapped by fashion? (paras. 13-15)

6. Examine Lurie's description of the "Annie Hall look" in paragraphs 17-20. What is Lurie's attitude to this fashion, and how is it conveyed?

Suggested Topics for Writing and Discussion

1. Lurie sees a direct connection between women's clothes and the degree of women's independence in a male-dominated society. To what extent do you agree with her findings? Are the current fashions, as were those in 1981 when this essay was written, a sign that "all is not well with the independent woman"?

2. Lurie's analysis focuses on women's fashions. What might a similar study of men's clothes tell us about the status of men in modern society?

3. Lurie discusses ways in which women's clothing "sex-types" them. Discuss other ways in which society encourages boys or girls (or both) to fix their sexual identities.

4. When *Dress for Success,* a book on women's clothing, appeared in 1976, it soon established a "dress code" for professional women. A spate of such books followed and, in fact, even became a target for satire — as in 1984's collection of Gary Trudeau's cartoons entitled *Dressed for Failure, I See. Dressing Thin* (1981), *Dressing Rich: A Guide to Classic Chic for Women with More Taste than Money* (1984), and *Dressing Up: How to Look and Feel Absolutely Perfect for Any Social Occasion* (1984) were included in the books for women; *Dressing Right* (1976) and *Dressing to Win: How to Have More Money, Romance, and Power in Your Life* (1984) were among those for men. Using your local library or bookstore, locate one such book and analyze its appeal. Write an essay outlining the book's assumptions about the audience's interests.

De Mortuis
by J.H. Plumb

1   The British have hilarious fun over the quaint funerary habits of the
Americans. The death of Hubert Eaton, the world's greatest entrepreneur
of death, and the recent discovery of a funeral home for pets, by a
wandering British journalist, released another gale of satirical laughter
in the English press. The mockery was hearty and sustained; yet was
it deserved? Well, certainly much of Mr. Eaton's Forest Lawn is hard
to take — the wet, nursery language for the hard facts of dying ("the
loved one" for the corpse, "leave taking" for burying, and "slumber"
for death), the cosmetic treatment (the contortions of death waxed away,
replaced by rouge and mascara and fashionably set hair) — all of this
is good for a gruesome joke. The place names of Forest Lawn appall
— Lullabyland, Babyland. The piped guff, the music that flows like
oil, and the coy fig-leaved art give one goose flesh.

2   One turns, almost with relief, to a harsh fifteenth-century representation of the dance of death — livid corpses, jangling bones, and skulls
that haunt. How wholesome, after Hubert Eaton, seem the savage depic-
tions by Bonfigli of the ravages of plague, or even the nightmares of
death painted by Hieronymus Bosch. And how salutary in our own age
to turn from Forest Lawn to the screaming, dissolving bodies of a Francis
Bacon painting, for surely this is how life ends for most of us, in pain,
in agony.

3   And if Forest Lawn nauseates, what of the Pets Parlor? "Blackie"
combed and brushed, stretched out on the hearth rug before a log fire,
waits for his sorrowing owners. The budgerigar is wired to its perch.
The Ming Room houses the Siamese cats, and if you want to do your

kitty proud, you can spend three hundred dollars or so on a stately laying out, a goodly coffin (if you're worried about its fun in the afterlife,
you can put an outsize rubber mouse in with it), and naturally a special
plot in Bide-A-Wee, the memorial park for pets. President Nixon's dog,
Checkers, had the treatment: he lies among the immortals in Bide-A-
Wee, like Hubert in Forest Lawn.

However, this will become a mere second-class death if deep-freezing   4
really catches on, as it shows every sign of doing. The Life Extension
Society is spreading, and the entrepreneurs have smelled the profit in
immortality. As soon as the breath goes, get yourself encapsulated in
liquid nitrogen and stored in one of the specially constructed freezers
that are springing up all over America from Phoenix to New York. And
so wait for the day when they can cure what you died of, or replace
what gave way — the heart, the brain, the liver, or the guts — or re-
juvenate your cells.

None of this is cheap: the capsule costs four thousand dollars, and   5
then there are the freezing costs and who knows what they may be in
fifty years, so it would be imprudent not to make ample provision. Forest
Lawn may be death for the rich; this is death for the richer, death for
the Big Time. But in America there are a lot of very rich, so maybe
soon now, outside all the large cities, there will be refrigerators as huge
as pyramids, full of the frozen dead. This surely must be a growth
industry.

Perhaps by the year 2000 Hubert Eaton will seem but a modest pioneer   6
of the death industry, for who does not crave to escape oblivion? The
rich have always tried to domesticate death, to make death seem like
life. The American way of death is not novel: seen in proper historical
perspective it reaches back not only down the centuries but down the
millennia, for it is a response to a deep human need.

Some of the earliest graves of men, dating from paleolithic times,   7
contained corpses decked out with bits of personal finery and sprinkled
with red ocher, perhaps the symbol of blood and life, done in the hope
of a future resurrection. After the neolithic revolution, which created
much greater resources and considerable surplus wealth, men went in
for death in a very big way. Doubtless the poor were thrown away,
burned or exposed or pushed into obscurity, back to the anonymous
mind from which they came.

The rich and the powerful, high priests and kings, could not die; they   8
merely passed from one life to another. Because the life hereafter was
but a mirror image of life on earth, they took with them everything

they needed — jewels, furniture, food, and, of course, servants. In the Royal Graves at Ur, some of the earliest and most sumptuous of tombs ever found, a row of handmaidens had been slaughtered at the burial — death's necessities were life's. No one, of course, carried this elaboration of funerary activity further than the Egyptians. And the tombs of Pharaohs and the high officials of the Egyptian kingdom make Forest Lawn seem like a cheap cemetery for the nation's down-and-outs.

9   What should we think of vast stone mausoleums outside Washington, stuffed with personal jewelry from Winston's, furniture from Sloane's, glassware by Steuben, food from Le Pavillon, etc., etc., and in the midst of it all the embalmed corpse of a Coolidge or a Dulles? We should roar with laughter. We should regard it as vulgar, ridiculous, absurd. Pushed back three millennia, such habits acquire not only decorum but also majesty, grandeur, awe.

10   The Egyptians were as portentous in death as in life, and their grave goods only occasionally give off the breath of life, unlike the Etruscans who domesticated death more completely and more joyously than any other society. A rich caste of princes built tombs of singular magnificence, filling them with amphorae, jewels, and silver. And they adorned their walls with all the gaiety that they had enjoyed alive. There was nothing solemn about their attitude to death. In their tombs they hunted, played games, performed acrobatics, danced, feasted; their amorous dalliance was both wanton and guiltless. Deliberately they banished death with the recollected gusto of life. No society has brought such eroticism, such open and natural behavior, to the charnel house. But in the annals of death, Etruscans are rare birds.

11   How different the grandiose tombs of medieval barons, with their splendid alabaster or marble effigies. There they lie, larger than life, grave, portentous, frozen in death, a wife, sometimes two, rigidly posed beside them, and beneath, sorrowing children, kneeling in filial piety, the whole structure made more pompous with heraldic quarterings. Yet these are but another attempt to cheat death, to keep alive in stone what was decaying and crumbling below. And even here a breath of life sometimes creeps in. The Earl and Countess of Arundel lie side by side, dogs beneath the feet, pillows under the head, he in armor, she in her long woolen gown. But, movingly enough, they are holding hands. The sons of Lord Teynham cannot be parted, even in death, with their hawk and hound. Nor were these tombs so cold, so marmoreal, when they were first built. They were painted, the faces as alive with color as the corpses in the parlors of Forest Lawn.

Seen in the context of history, Forest Lawn is neither very vulgar 12
nor very remarkable, and the refrigerators at Phoenix are no more surprising than a pyramid in Palenque or Cairo. If life has been good, we,
like the rich Etruscans, want it to go on and on and on, or at the very
least to be remembered. Only a few civilizations have evaded expensive funerary habits for their illustrious rich, and these usually poverty
stricken ones. For all their austerity, the Hindus, burning bodies and
throwing the ashes into the Ganges, have maintained distinction in their
pyres. Not only were widows coaxed or thrown onto the flames, but
rare and perfumed woods were burned to sweeten the spirit of the rich
Brahman as it escaped from its corrupt carapace. Cremation à la Chanel!

What is tasteless and vulgar in one age becomes tender and moving 13
in another. What should we say if we decorated our tombs with scenes
from baseball games, cocktail bars, and the circus, or boasted on the
side of our coffins of our amatory prowess, as erect and as unashamed
in death as in life. And yet when the Etruscans do just these things,
we are moved to a sense of delight that the force of life could be so
strong that men and women reveled in it in their graves.

So the next time you stroll through Forest Lawn, mildly repelled by 14
its silly sentimentality, think of those Etruscans; you will understand
far more easily why seven thousand marriages a year take place in this
California graveyard. After all, like those Arundels, Eros and Death
have gone hand in hand down the ages. The urge to obliterate death
is the urge to extend life, and what more natural than that the rich should
expect renewal. How right, how proper, that Checkers should be waiting
in Slumberland.

(1967)

The Writer's Subject

1. What is Plumb's thesis, and where is it most clearly stated?

2. What aspects of American funerary practice provoked "satirical laughter" in the British press?

3. What is suggested about American attitudes to death in the first five paragraphs of the essay?

4. Why does Plumb seem to find the grim paintings of death described in paragraph 2 "wholesome" or "salutary" in comparison with the practices of Forest Lawn?

5. What parallels does Plumb draw between American burial practices and those of earlier civilizations? To what conclusions do these comparisons lead him, with respect to the apparent vulgarity of places like Forest Lawn?

6. How did the Etruscans banish death "with the recollected gusto of life" (para. 10)? What connection does Plumb draw between Etruscan burial practices in particular and those found in Forest Lawn? (paras. 13-14)

7. Why is Plumb not surprised that "seven thousand marriages a year take place in this California graveyard" (para. 1)?

The Writer's Style and Strategy

1. What examples of euphemism does Plumb include in the first paragraph?

2. What tone is established in the opening paragraph of the essay? Where is there a clear shift in tone, and what occasions that shift?

3. What is conveyed of the writer's attitude to American funerary practices by such statements as "the entrepreneurs have smelled the profit in immortality" (para. 4), or "This surely must be a growth industry" (para. 5)?

4. How does Plumb convey his sense of the absurdities involved in the burial of pets? (para. 3)

5. Show what use Plumb makes of comparison and contrast as a strategy to structure his argument. In this connection, what function is performed by paragraph 6?

6. In his use of historical evidence, Plumb alludes to the tombs of medieval barons and gives several examples. (para. 11) Discuss how the use of examples and descriptive details at this point develops Plumb's thesis.

7. Discuss the effectiveness of the essay's conclusion. How well does it round off Plumb's discussion? What does its tone reveal about his attitude?

8. Why does Plumb use a Latin title for this essay?

Suggested Topics for Writing and Discussion

1. Plumb describes some of the methods by which modern Americans try to "domesticate death." What aspects of funerary practice in your own community seem to you to have the same purpose?

2. Plumb treats cryogenics (a term to describe the deep-freezing of the dead, taken over from the branch of physics dealing with very low temperatures) somewhat sardonically; he focusses almost exclusively on its high costs. What is your own view of this process? Do you think that any ethical or religious considerations may be involved?

3. Many cemeteries in North America now forbid the erection of funerary monuments; they require instead that graves be marked only with a horizontal stone so that the effect of a park is achieved. What is your view of this practice? Do you think cemeteries should be showplaces? Parks? Quiet places for the dead and their surviving family and friends?

4. Cemeteries are often fascinating places, especially as tourist attractions. Using travel guides from your local library or bookstore, find out what you can about some of the famous cemeteries of Europe and prepare your own "mini-guide to the best resting places." You may want to look up some of the following: Père-Lachaise in Paris — burial place of Frederick Chopin, Oscar Wilde, Jim Morrison and many other celebrated figures; the Protestant Cemetery in Rome — burial place of John Keats and Percy Bysshe Shelley's ashes; the Central Cemetery in Vienna — burial place of Mozart, Beethoven, Brahms, and Schubert; Highgate Cemetery in London — burial place of Karl Marx and George Eliot.

Nostalgia

by Witold Rybczynski

*However, insofar as there is such reference to a historic
past, the peculiarity of "invented" traditions is that the
continuity with it is largely factitious.*

Eric Hobsbawm
The Invention of Tradition

1   We've all seen this comfortable man; his face looks out from the advertising pages of magazines. His graying hair, which is close-cropped,
belies his age — he is only forty-three — just as his frayed shirt and
faded Levi's belie his eight-figure income. The latter is barely hinted
at by the silver Rolex discreetly half-hidden by the jacket sleeve, and
by the hand-made cowboy boots. What he does for a living is not immediately clear. Well, we do know that despite his worn work clothes
he doesn't pick lettuce; migrant workers don't wear muted wool-and-
mohair sport jackets. He could be a professional athlete — a purveyor
of light beer and deodorant — but his clothes are too low-key, and in
any case he lacks a mustache. Still, whatever he does do, it seems to
agree with him — a half-smile crosses his tanned face. But his glance
is neither the vacuous stare of the professional clotheshorse nor the self-
satisfied grin of the celebrity; this man looks content. "Look at me,"
he is saying, "I could dress any way I want, but I don't need to impress
anyone, not even you. I feel good just like this." Since all ads, whether
for cigarettes or for cancer research, are selling something, we can only
conclude that what this man is selling is comfort.

2   Of course, this man is comfortable. Why shouldn't he be? He owns
90 percent of a business whose annual sales total a billion dollars. His
personal after-tax income in 1982 was said to be fifteen million dollars.
He has all the perks that success of this kind brings: an upper Fifth
Avenue duplex (more about that later), an estate in Westchester, another
on Jamaica, a beach house on Long Island, a ten-thousand-acre ranch
in Colorado, and a private jet to travel among them.

3   What does he do, this business mogul, this multimillionaire, this com-

fortable man? He thinks up ways for people to dress. Fifty years ago he might have been a tailor or a dressmaker; if he had lived in France he would have been called a couturier. But to call Ralph Lauren a tailor is like calling the Bechtel Corporation a builder. The word does not convey the sheer size or the international scale of the operation. A tailor makes clothes; Lauren's corporation franchises manufacturers on four continents who turn out products that are sold in more than three hundred shops carrying his name, as well as in specialty boutiques in department stores in the United States, Canada, England, Italy, Switzerland, Scandinavia, Mexico, and Hong Kong. As it has grown, his business has also diversified. It started modestly, with neckties, but soon expanded to men's wear, then clothes for women, lately a special line for children. Now perfumes, soaps, cosmetics, shoes, luggage, belts, wallets, and eyeglasses all bear his imprimatur. Lauren's is that most modern of professions: he is the total fashion designer.

The first thing that strikes us about Lauren's clothes is how American 4 they look. They are based on recognizable homegrown images: the western ranch, the prairie farm, the Newport mansion, the Ivy League college. The feeling of déjà vu is intentional: Lauren is an orchestrator of images. Although his clothes are not faithful replicas of period dress, their appearance does reflect popular ideas about various romantic periods of American history. We have seen them all before, in paintings, in photographs, on television, and, especially, in films.

Lauren understands films. One of his early designs for men's even- 5 ing wear consisted of a black dinner suit, wing-collared shirt, white gloves, and a white silk muffler. Reporting on the show, *The New York Times* described this outfit as having "stepped out of a Leslie Howard movie"; Lauren himself appeared in black pinstripes and reminded the reporter of Douglas Fairbanks. The cinematic simile was appropriate, since Lauren had just designed the men's costumes for a film version of *The Great Gatsby*. For a brief time, Twenties-influenced fashion became popular; dress-for-success, Lauren called it. A few years later, many of his designs were featured in the film *Annie Hall*; the comfortable, relaxed clothes worn by its stars, Woody Allen and Diane Keaton, became the look of the year. This inclination to be a costumer, along with a career built as much on advertising as on fashion shows and *Vogue* magazine, has not assured Lauren a secure position in the fashion world. It is unlikely that there will ever be a Ralph Lauren retrospective of the Metropolitan Museum, as there was in 1984 for Yves Saint Laurent.

Whether or not fashion design is an art is arguable, but there is no 6 doubt that today it is a very big business. It all started in 1967, when Yves Saint Laurent, the boy wonder of haute couture who had succeeded Christian Dior as Paris's leading dressmaker, opened Rive Gauche, a chain of shops that sold expensive but mass-produced clothes with the now-famous YSL label. Rive Gauche proved to be a great success (there are now more than 170 outlets around the world), and soon other couturiers such as Courrèges and Givenchy were lending — that is, selling — their talents to the *prêt à porter* trade. Even the conservative Chanel succumbed to this trend, although the house did so only after the death of its founder.

7   Haute couture had provided the fashion industry with glamour, but ready-to-wear clothing now became its bread and butter.* In the process many designers acquired a distinctly commercial relationship to the products that they endorsed; if you've seen athletes peddling golf clothes or tennis shoes you get the idea. It is difficult to believe that Pierre Cardin, for instance, would ever be caught dead wearing much of the perfume or the clothing (made in a Bombay sweatshop) that carries his cachet. It is obvious that the fashion pates often have little, if anything, to do with the design of "their" products; in any case, their reputations, like those of Arnold Palmer or Bjorn Borg, are made elsewhere. In that sense, at least, mass marketing, lucrative though it may be, is only a sideline.

8   Unlike Cardin and Saint Laurent, whose careers were founded in the exclusive dress salons, Lauren was never a couturier; from the beginning he was concerned with mass-produced clothing, and so he acquired an understanding of popular instead of elite tastes. His renown as a designer has been the result of his commercial success, not vice versa. His influence on the way that Americans dress is often overlooked, precisely because it has been indirect. Most of the women who copied Diane Keaton's loose tweed jackets or oversized men's shirts in 1977 were unaware that they were imitating Lauren originals. The 1980s fashion for Ivy League clothes — the so-called preppy look — was also Lauren-inspired.

9   What does this have to do with domestic comfort? In 1984, Ralph Lauren announced that he was entering the home furnishings field. The only surprise is that it took him so long. The relationship between clothing and interior decoration is venerable. Look at a Hogarth paint-

*The dressmaker Charles Frédéric Worth invented the term "haute couture" in 1858. For a long time it could only be used by fashion houses that were recognized by the French government Office pour Art et Création. Curiously, haute couture was *not* the highest accreditation; the work of the most select fashion houses was referred to as "couture création."

ing of an early Georgian interior. The soft curves of the carved furniture were a counterpart to the rich costumes of the time and complemented the voluminous gowns of the women and the lace fronts and elaborate wigs of the men. The slightly pompous interiors of the nineteenth century also reflected clothing fashions; skirted chairs and gathered draperies imitated the details of how cloth was used in skirts and gowns, and wallpaper copied the designs used in fabrics. The richness of Art Deco furniture mirrored its owners' luxurious costumes.

And how does Ralph Lauren intend to dress the modern home? The   10
line of furnishings — it is called a Collection — provides everything needed to decorate the home. The Collection is meant to be, in the words of Lauren's publicists, a total home environment. You can now put on a Lauren dressing gown, slip on a pair of Lauren slippers, shower with Lauren soap, dry with a Lauren towel, walk across a Lauren rug, glance at the Lauren wallpaper, and slip between Lauren sheets, beneath a Lauren comforter, to sip warm milk from a Lauren glass. You can now be a part of the ad.

It is doubtful, however, that this is "the next plateau of life-style   11
marketing," as one enthusiastic distributor has called it. For one thing, the Collection will have a limited clientele. The Lauren furnishings, which are not mass-produced, are expensive, and are being sold only in fashionable department stores in major cities like Chicago, Dallas and Los Angeles. For another, despite Lauren's long list of products the Collection is limited and does not include a full range of furniture — thus far only a few wicker pieces are available. Nevertheless, it is worthwhile examining how a corporation whose success is based on understanding the public's taste for clothing interprets popular images of the home.

I go to Bloomingdale's, New York's store for the upper-middle-class   12
consumer, to witness this next plateau. "Fashion is a function of life-style," a voice says as I get off the escalator. Startled, I turn. There he is, the comfortable man, star of his own furnishings video. Across from the television monitor is the entrance to the Ralph Lauren Home Furnishings boutique, which consists of a number of rooms displaying the Lauren products. They remind me of the Shelburne Museum, in Vermont, where furnishings and objects are displayed in actual houses as part of recreated room settings. This gives the historical rooms the impression of being inhabited. In Bloomingdale's, the Lauren rooms are also fully recreated, with walls, ceilings, even windows, and look more like movie sets than store displays.

13   It turns out that the Collection is not one line but four. The four have
names: "Log Cabin," "Thoroughbred," "New England," and "Jamaica."
The walls of the "Log Cabin" are chinked with white plaster, and the
ceiling is supported by rough-hewn beams. Buffalo Check and
Woodsman Plaid blankets cover the massive pegged timber bed. The
bedclothes are soft brushed flannel with matching pillow shams, sheets,
and bedskirts. The rugged furniture is obviously handmade, and goes
nicely with the American Indian hearth rug on the floor. A pair of Bean
boots stands by the bed; on the side table is a copy of everyone's favorite
summer-cottage reading, the *National Geographic* magazine. The
general effect is one of moneyed rusticity, the furnishings equivalent
of designer jeans.

14   "Jamaica" is across the aisle. It is obviously designed for the Sunbelt.
A giant bamboo four-poster bed, draped with what looks like voile but
could be mosquito netting, stands in the center of a cool white room.
The colors of the Italian linens, Swiss embroidery, and chambray com-
forters are feminine — pink and blue. The bedclothes and table linens
are trimmed with ruffles and embroidered with floral bouquet designs.
If the inhabitant of "Log Cabin" is out shooting moose, the owners of
this home must be on the verandah sipping Planter's Punch.

15   The decor of "Thoroughbred" is equally genteel — a country
gentleman's room of dark colors highlighted by the polished brass of
the bedstead and the gleaming mahogany wall paneling. Pheasant and
hunting motifs abound, as do paisley prints and tartans.* Wall cover-
ings are checks, tattersalls, and foulards. The effect is a bit overwhelming, like being caught inside Rex Harrison's closet. At the foot of the
bed are a pair of riding boots. The publicity stills showed two beagle
hounds dozing among the tweeds. I look for them in the cozy setting,
but that must be where Bloomingdale's drew the line. "Thoroughbred"
includes a distinctly anglophile table setting: teapots, egg cups, and a
covered muffin dish, as well as plates ornamented with scenes of mounted
polo players. "A dream England filtered through preppy America," an
uncharitable British journalist called it.

16   "New England" contains staid Early American furniture; this could

*Lauren is certainly unaware, as are most people, of the recent origin of the "traditional"
Scottish tartan. The idea of associating specific tartans with different families occurred during
the first part of the nineteenth century — not in the mists of Celtic antiquity — and, like the
kilt itself, was a modern invention. The introduction of tartans was the result of Queen Victoria's cult of the Highlands, as evidenced at Balmoral Castle, her Scottish country home, and
of a sales campaign by cloth manufacturers who were seeking to develop larger markets for
their products.

be the bedroom of a restored Vermont country inn. The colors are muted, the wall fabrics are solid and candy-striped to match the Oxford-cloth bedclothes. It is the least theatrical of the four; Yankee sobriety doesn't lend itself to dramatization.

17   The four themes have a lot in common. They are inspired by Lauren's own homes — the Jamaican hideaway, the ranch, the New England farm. They are aimed at the growing number of people who have second, and even third homes — by the lake, next to the ski slope, or on the beach — and so they follow rural models. At the same time, the comfortable informality of these furnishings is likely to be just as appropriate to apartments and townhouses as to weekend retreats. The furnishings are also an extension of Lauren's clothing designs, which have been called "western and outdoorsy or conservative and tweedy." In that sense these are settings, for which the costumes have already been designed. This tendency to coordinate clothes and furnishings is to be continued in two other themes not featured in Bloomingdale's — "Mariner" and "Safari." The former is to establish an appropriately yachtsmanlike setting; the latter will convey, according to the designer, the feeling "of a hunter getting out of his Range Rover and aiming his elephant gun."

18   The settings have something else in common, something which has become the hallmark of the Lauren look. One of his early and more extravagant outfits for men consisted of a Donegal tweed jacket with black belt and bellows pockets, worn with white flannel trousers, and complete with collar pin and English shoes of saddle leather. "You just know that the gentleman wearing it belongs to a private club and drives a Rolls-Royce, or at least wants to give that impression," wrote a fashion reporter, who dubbed this the "Vanderbilt look." In much of his recent clothing designs, Lauren has managed to restrain a tendency to evoke the symbols and the style of turn-of-the-century wealth, but the major influence on the treatment of the furnishing themes continues to be what an associate calls the look of "old money."* Old, in most cases, means falling between 1890 and 1930. The log cabin setting, for instance, has the affected, cedar-stump rusticity that used to characterize rich men's hunting lodges at the end of the last century — although Lauren, a supporter of wildlife preservation, has carefully omitted the stuffed animal heads mounted on the wall. The "old world elegance and refinement" of the Jamaican furnishings brings to mind the relaxed pace

*The friction between new and old money took a bizarre turn recently, when it was reported that Lauren had brought legal action for infringing on "his" corporate symbol against an organization that had the temerity to use the figure of a man on a horse swinging a mallet as its insignia. The object of his suit was the United States Polo Association, founded in 1900.

of life in the white porticoed homes of the island during its colonial period. The country gentleman's retreat evoked by "Thoroughbred" could be Lord Sebastian Flyte's room in Evelyn Waugh's *Brideshead Revisited.* But this is not period decor in the conventional sense — it lacks the consistent and specific details of neo-Georgian or French Antique, to name two popular styles. Lauren is not so much interested in recalling the authentic appearance of a historical period as he is in evoking the atmosphere of traditional hominess and solid domesticity that is associated with the past.

19   This acute awareness of tradition is a modern phenomenon that reflects a desire for custom and routine in a world characterized by constant change and innovation. Reverence for the past has become so strong that when traditions do not exist, they are frequently invented. There are other examples than the Scottish tartan. After England adopted a national anthem in the mid-eighteenth century, most European nations quickly followed suit. The results were sometimes curious. Denmark and Germany, for instance, simply set their own words to the English music. Switzerland still sings "Ruft die, mein Vaterland" to the strains of "God Save the King," and until Congress adopted an official national anthem — in 1931 — Americans sang "My Country 'Tis of Thee" to the same regal music. The "Marseillaise" is original, and authentic; it was written during the French Revolution. But Bastille Day was first celebrated in 1880, a hundred years after the actual event.

20   Another example of invented tradition is the popular fashion for so-called Early American or Colonial furniture. In most people's imagination it represents a link to the values of the Founding Fathers, the Spirit of '76, an integral part of the national heritage. The truth is that the Colonial style owes its existence not to an unbroken continuity passed from colonial father to republican son, but to the much more recent Centennial celebrations of 1876. The Centennial encouraged the founding of many so-called patriotic societies, such as the Sons (now defunct) and the Daughters (still active) of the American Revolution, the Colonial Dames of America, and the Society of Mayflower Descendants. This new interest in genealogy was due partly to the Centennial itself, and partly to efforts by the established middle class to distance itself from the increasing number of new, predominantly non-British immigrants. This process of cultural authentification was fortified by furnishing homes in the so-called Colonial style, thus underlining the link to the past. Like most invented traditions, the Colonial revival was also a reflection of its own time — the nineteenth century. Its visual

taste was influenced by the then current English architectural fashion — Queen Anne — which had nothing to do with the Pilgrim Fathers, but whose cozy hominess appealed to a public sated by the extravagances of the Gilded Age.

Lauren's invented traditions are derived from the literary and cinematic 21 imagination. The English country life suggested by "Thoroughbred" was already in decline when Waugh wrote about it, forty years ago. Today, where fox-hunting still exists, it is practiced almost in secret, to avoid the attacks of various environmental and animal-welfare groups. "Mariner" conjures up the Newport of F. Scott Fitzgerald, but although his blazer-clad sailors lolled about on sixty-foot teak-decked ketches — crewed by hired help — most of us have to be content with a car-topped fiberglass dinghy. "Safari" recalls a time when wealthy Americans and Europeans could go to Africa and shoot their hearts out; today, if they go they are less likely to be carrying a Mannlicher — as Hemingway did — than a Minolta. The real postindependence Jamaica is less old-world charm than packaged tours, dope, and threatening Rastafarians. As for the simple fireside pleasures implicit in "Log Cabin," these have been replaced, or at least augmented, by hang gliders and mountain bikes.

What is also striking about these handsome interiors is the absence 22 of so many of the things that characterize modern life. We look in vain for clock-radios, electric hair dryers, or video games. There are pipe racks and humidors in the bedrooms, but no cordless telephones, no televisions. There may be snowshoes hanging on the cabin wall, but there are no snowmobile boots by the door. In the tropical setting we glimpse an overhead fan instead of an air-conditioning unit. The mechanical paraphernalia of contemporary living has been put away, and replaced by brass-cornered gun boxes, silver bedside water carafes, and leather-bound books.

Admittedly, these tableaux are not real interiors but only backdrops 23 designed to set off the fabrics, tableware, and bedclothes that form the Furnishings Collection; it is unlikely that anyone would ever furnish his or her home to look like the Lauren publicity brochures. But that is beside the point; advertisements often represent a not altogether real, stylized world, but one which does reflect society's view of how things *ought* to be. These themes have been chosen to evoke popular images that are informal and comfortable, reminiscent of wealth, stability, and tradition. What they leave out is as revealing as what they include.

There is little doubt that these carefully arranged rooms would be 24

compromised by the introduction of modern objects. Like a director
filming a costume epic who blanks out the telephone wires and the drone
of the overhead jet, Lauren has kept the twentieth century at bay. There
is no polypropylene thermal underwear drying in front of the stone
fireplace, no electric toaster on the table, to intrude on the traditional
coziness of "Log Cabin," just as there is no personal computer on the
desk in "Thoroughbred." How do we fit reality into this dream world?
One way is to not even try. The headquarters of Estée Lauder Incor-
porated, a large cosmetics corporation, are located in the General Motors
Building in New York. The main offices are conventional; the chairman's office is not − it resembles the small drawing room of a Loire
château. Estée Lauder's desk is Louis XVI, as are two of the side chairs.
The two wing chairs are Second Empire, the couch is Belle Epoque,
and the lamp holder is French Bouillotte (obviously, the candles have
been replaced by electrical bulbs). The only modern objects are two
telephones.   The office of Malcolm S. Forbes, owner of *Forbes*
magazine, does not make even that compromise with modernity. No
telephones disturb the top of his elegant Georgian partner's desk, which
is flanked by a pair of Queen Anne corner chairs and a fine Chippendale-
style wing chair. A chandelier hangs from the ceiling and illuminates
the mahogany-paneled room, originally built in the nineteenth century
and free from any reminders of the twentieth. This is as much a place
for drinking a glass of vintage port as for transacting business.

25   This sort of historical verisimilitude is difficult to achieve, and obviously expensive. In any case, outside Mr. Forbes's and Mrs. Lauder's
offices are the telex machines, flickering word processors, ergonomically
designed stenographer's chairs, steel file cabinets, and fluorescent strip
lighting that are necessary for the proper functioning of a modern corporation. One reason that all this equipment is outside is that it is not
easy to integrate it into a Louis XVI salon or a Georgian study. Only
a few modern devices lend themselves to being camouflaged in period
clothing. A Baume & Mercier carriage clock, for instance, has an oc-
tagonal case of pearwood with brass fittings, that contains a quartz movement. A strictly modern device like a photocopier, on the other hand,
has no precedents, it can only be disguised, and were this ever attempted the result would be about as satisfying as when television sets are
made up to look like Colonial credenzas.

26   So the modern world is kept at bay. These office interiors, like the
settings of the Lauren Collection, present the appearance of a way of
life that no longer exists. Their reality is no deeper than the flocked

covering on the wall; a cynic would point out that the lady in the Louis XVI office was actually born in Queens, and Mr. Forbes in Brooklyn (Lauren, that other anglophile, grew up in the Bronx). But whether the way of life is remembered, or simply imagined, it nevertheless signifies a widely held nostalgia. Is it simply a curious anachronism, this desire for tradition, or is it a reflection of a deeper dissatisfaction with the surroundings that our modern world has created? What are we missing that we look so hard for in the past?

(1986)

The Writer's Subject

1. Why does Rybczynski call Ralph Lauren a "total fashion designer"? (para. 3)

2. What is distinctly American about the look of Lauren's clothes? (para. 4)

3. In what respects, according to Rybczynski, does Lauren differ from such famous couturiers as Yves St. Laurent or Pierre Cardin? (paras. 5-8)

4. What does Rybczynski mean by calling the relationship between clothing and interior decoration "venerable"? (para. 9)

5. What do the different rooms in Lauren's "Collection" in Bloomingdale's have in common? What is the nature of their appeal, according to Rybczynski? (paras. 17-18)

6. What, according to Rybczynski, is Lauren's goal in making use of "period" designs? (paras. 18-23)

7. To what does Rybczynski attribute the modern awareness of and desire for tradition? (para. 19) What does he mean by "invented" traditions? (paras. 19-21)

8 What has been left out of Lauren's interiors? (paras. 22-24)

The Writer's Style and Strategy

1. Why does Rybczynski begin by describing Ralph Lauren as he appears in magazine advertisements?

2. What is Rybczynski's purpose in the repetition of "comfort" and "comfortable" in the first two paragraphs?

3. Discuss the meaning and the intended effect of the following statements, in their respective contexts:
   a) "Now perfumes, soaps, cosmetics, shoes, luggage, belts, wallets, and eyeglasses all bear his imprimatur" (para. 3);
   b) "The feeling of déjà vu is intentional: Lauren is an orchestrator of images" (para. 4);
   c) "You can now be a part of the ad" (para. 10).

4. Rybczynski gives detailed descriptions of the four Lauren rooms in Bloomingdale's. (paras. 12-18) What elements of diction or phrasing suggest the writer's attitude to those rooms?

5. What are the main stages of Rybczynski's discussion? How does he effect transitions from one stage to the next?

6. How does Rybczynski use contrast to drive home his point about "invented traditions" in paragraph 21?

7. Examine the last three paragraphs of the essay. Why does Rybczynski move away from a study of Ralph Lauren? Does the conclusion present us with a change of focus, or is another strategy involved?

8. While this essay is complete in itself, it is also the first chapter in Rybczynski's book, *Home: A Short History of an Idea*. What features of the essay suggest such a relationship? In this regard, look particularly at the last paragraph.

Suggested Topics for Writing and Discussion

1. Rybczynski says that Lauren's designs follow rural models. What, in your view, accounts for the appeal of the rural model, especially what Rybczynski calls "moneyed rusticity"?

2. Rybczynski says that "acute awareness of tradition is a modern phenomenon that reflects a desire for custom and routine in a world characterized by constant change and innovation" (para. 19). How important is tradition in your own family or community? Give examples to illustrate your view.

3. Rybczynski's essay is concerned with nostalgia as it is expressed in home furnishings. Write an essay in which you focus on two or three things that have nostalgic value for you and explain, if you can, the basis of their significance.

4. Analyze an ad for fashion — either in clothing or home furnishings — and discuss what the ad suggests to the audience. Give attention to background as well as foreground details in the ad.

5. Analyze the current trends in fashion evident in the clothes of a particular group (e.g., college students, business executives, teenagers), and suggest what image the wearers seek to project.

Courtship Through the Ages

by James Thurber

1   Surely nothing in the astonishing scheme of life can have nonplussed
Nature so much as the fact that none of the females of any of the species
she created really cared very much for the male, as such. For the past
ten million years Nature has been busily inventing ways to make the
male attractive to the female, but the whole business of courtship, from
the marine annelids up to man, still lumbers heavily along, like a complicated musical comedy. I have been reading the sad and absorbing
story in Volume 6 (Cole to Dama) of the *Encyclopaedia Britannica*.
In this volume you can learn all about cricket, cotton, costume design-
ing, crocodiles, crown jewels, and Coleridge, but none of these subjects is so interesting as the Courtship of Animals, which recounts the
sorrowful lengths to which all males must go to arouse the interest of
a lady.

2   We all know, I think, that Nature gave man whiskers and a mustache
with the quaint idea in mind that these would prove attractive to the
female. We all know that, far from attracting her, whiskers and
mustaches only made her nervous and gloomy, so that man had to go
in for somersaults, tilting and lances, and performing feats of parlor
magic to win her attention; he also had to bring her candy, flowers,
and the furs of animals. It is common knowledge that in spite of all
these "love displays" the male is constantly being turned down, insulted,
or thrown out of the house. It is rather comforting, then, to discover
that the peacock, for all his gorgeous plumage, does not have a particularly easy time in courtship; none of the males in the world do. The
first peahen, it turned out, was only faintly stirred by her suitor's beautiful

train. She would often go quietly to sleep while he was whisking it around. The *Britannica* tells us that the peacock actually had to learn a certain little trick to wake her up and revive her interest: he had to learn to vibrate his quills so as to make a rustling sound. In ancient times man himself, observing the ways of the peacock, probably tried vibrating his whiskers to make a rustling sound; if so, it didn't get him anywhere. He had to go in for something else; so, among other things, he went in for gifts. It is not unlikely that he got this idea from certain flies and birds who were making no headway at all with rustling sounds.

One of the flies of the family Empidae, who had tried everything, 3 finally hit on something pretty special. He contrived to make a glistening transparent balloon which was even larger than himself. Into this he would put sweetmeats and tidbits and he would carry the whole elaborate envelope through the air to the lady of his choice. This amused her for a time, but she finally got bored with it. She demanded silly little colorful presents, something that you couldn't eat but that would look nice around the house. So the male Empis had to go around gathering flower petals and pieces of bright paper to put into his balloon. On a courtship flight a male Empis cuts quite a figure now, but he can hardly be said to be happy. He never knows how soon the female will demand heavier presents, such as Roman coins and gold collar buttons. It seems probable that one day the courtship of the Empidae will fall down, as man's occasionally does, of its own weight.

The bowerbird is another creature that spends so much time courting 4 the female that he never gets any work done. If all the male bowerbirds became nervous wrecks within the next ten or fifteen years, it would not surprise me. The female bowerbird insists that a playground be built for her with a specially constructed bower at the entrance. This bower is much more elaborate than an ordinary nest and is harder to build; it costs a lot more, too. The female will not come to the playground until the male has filled it up with a great many gifts: silvery leaves, red leaves, rose petals, shells, beads, berries, bones, dice, buttons, cigar bands, Christmas seals, and the Lord knows what else. When the female finally condescends to visit the playground, she is in a coy and silly mood and has to be chased in and out of the bower and up and down the playground before she will quit giggling and stand still long enough even to shake hands. The male bird is, of course, pretty well done in before the chase starts, because he has worn himself out hunting for eyeglass lenses and begonia blossoms. I imagine that many a bowerbird, after chasing a female for two or three hours, says the hell with it and goes home to bed. Next day, of course, he telephones someone else and the same trying ritual is gone through with again. A male bower-bird is as exhausted as a night-club habitué before he is out of his twenties.

5   The male fiddler crab has a somewhat easier time, but it can hardly be said that he is sitting pretty. He has one enormously large and powerful claw, usually brilliantly colored, and you might suppose that all he had to do was reach out and grab some passing cutie. The very earliest fiddler crabs may have tried this, but, if so, they got slapped for their pains. A female fiddler crab will not tolerate any caveman stuff; she never has and she doesn't intend to start now. To attract a female, a fiddler crab has to stand on tiptoe and brandish his claw in the air. If any female in the neighborhood is interested - and you'd be surprised how many are not — she comes over and engages in light badinage, for which he is not in the mood. As many as a hundred females may pass the time of day with him and go on about their business. By night-fall of an average courting day, a fiddler crab who has been standing on tip-toe for eight or ten hours waving a heavy claw in the air is in pretty sad shape. As in the case of the males of all species, however, he gets out of bed next morning, dashes some water on his face, and tries again.

6   The next time you encounter a male web-spinning spider, stop and reflect that he is too busy worrying about his love life to have any desire to bite you. Male web-spinning spiders have a tougher life than any other males in the animal kingdom. This is because the female web-spinning spiders have very poor eyesight. If a male lands on a female's web, she kills him before he has time to lay down his cane and gloves, mistaking him for a fly or a bumblebee who has tumbled into her trap. Before the species figured out what to do about this, millions of males were murdered by ladies they called on. It is the nature of spiders to perform a little dance in front of the female, but before a male spinner could get near enough for the female to see who he was and what he was up to, she would lash out at him with a flat-iron or a pair of garden shears. One night, nobody knows when, a very bright male spinner lay awake worrying about calling on a lady who had been killing suitors right and left. It came to him that this business of dancing as a love display wasn't getting anybody anywhere except the grave. He decided to go in for web-twitching, or strand-vibrating. The next day he tried it on one of the nearsighted girls. Instead of dropping in on her sudden-ly, he stayed outside the web and began monkeying with one of its strands. He twitched it up and down and in and out with such a lilting

rhythm that the female was charmed. The serenade worked beautifully; the female let him live. The *Britannica*'s spider-watchers, however,
report that this system is not always successful. Once in a while, even
now, a female will fire three bullets into a suitor or run him through
with a kitchen knife. She keeps threatening him from the moment he
strikes the first low notes on the outside strings, but usually by the time
he has got up to the high notes played around the center of the web,
he is going to town and she spares his life.

Even the butterfly, as handsome a fellow as he is, can't always win   7
a mate merely by fluttering around and showing off. Many butterflies
have to have scent scales on their wings. Hepialus carries a powder
puff in a perfumed pouch. He throws perfume at the ladies when they
pass. The male tree cricket, Oecanthus, goes Hepialus one better by
carrying a tiny bottle of wine with him and giving drinks to such doxies
as he has designs on. One of the male snails throws darts to entertain
the girls. So it goes, through the long list of animals, from the bristle
worm and his rudimentary dance steps to man and his gift of diamonds
and sapphires. The golden-eye drake raises a jet of water with his feet
as he flies over a lake; Hepialus has his powder puff, Oecanthus his
wine bottle, man his etchings. It is a bright and melancholy story, the
age-old desire of the male for the female, the age-old desire of the female
to be amused and entertained. Of all the creatures on earth, the only
males who could be figured as putting any irony into their courtship
are the grebes and certain other diving birds. Every now and then a
courting grebe slips quietly down to the bottom of a lake and then, with
a mighty "Whoosh!," pops out suddenly a few feet from his girl friend,
splashing water all over her. She seems to be persuaded that this is a
purely loving display, but I like to think that the grebe always has a
faint hope of drowning her or scaring her to death.

I will close this investigation into the mournful burdens of the male   8
with the *Britannica*'s story about a certain Argus pheasant. It appears
that the Argus displays himself in front of a female who stands perfectly still without moving a feather....The male Argus the *Britannica* tells
about was confined in a cage with a female of another species, a female
who kept moving around, emptying ashtrays and fussing with lamp-
shades all the time the male was showing off his talents. Finally, in
disgust, he stalked away and began displaying in front of his water
trough. He reminds me of a certain male (Homo sapiens) of my acquaintance who one night after dinner asked his wife to put down her
detective magazine so that he could read a poem of which he was very

fond. She sat quietly enough until he was well into the middle of the thing, intoning with great ardor and intensity. Then suddenly there came a sharp, disconcerting slap! It turned out that all during the male's display, the female had been intent on a circling mosquito and had finally trapped it between the palms of her hands. The male in this case did not stalk away and display in front of a water trough; he went over to Tim's and had a flock of drinks and recited the poem to the fellas. I am sure they all told bitter stories of their own about how their displays had been interrupted by females. I am also sure that they all ended up singing "Honey, Honey, Bless Your Heart."

(1939)

The Writer's Subject

1. What is Thurber's thesis? (para. 1)

2. Why did the male have to resort to various activities in order to attract the attention of the female? (para. 2) What means did he adopt to win attention?

3. What are the characteristic approaches to the female employed by the male Empis? the bowerbird? the fiddler crab? the web-spinning spider, the butterfly? the tree cricket? (paras. 3-7) What equivalents in human behavior are suggested by Thurber's discussion of these species?

4. Why does Thurber refer to *Britannica* at several points in his essay?

5. What incongruities are particularly striking in the story of the Argus pheasant? (para. 8)

6. What is Thurber's point in ending his essay with the statement that he is sure that his friend's companions "all ended up singing 'Honey, Honey, Bless your Heart.'" (para. 8)?

7. What features in Thurber's essay suggest that this account is, like the story of courtship he tells, "bright and melancholy" (para. 7)?

The Writer's Style and Strategy

1. What in the introductory paragraph suggests that Thurber is taking a humorous approach to his subject?

2. What is the implied audience for this essay?

3. What is Thurber's strategy in using "I," "we," and "you" throughout this essay? What is his particular purpose in beginning the first two sentences of paragraph 2 with "We all know . . ."?

4. What means does Thurber use to develop his thesis?

5. How does Thurber effect transitions between paragraphs?

6. How does it become clear that Thurber, in his description of courtship displays, is as concerned with man as with animals?

7. Choose two or three examples of ways in which Thurber surprises the reader and creates humour.

8. Although Thurber uses "female," "lady," and "ladies," he never uses "woman." Why not?

9. How does Thurber create an informal, conversational tone?

10. Comment on Thurber's title.

Suggested Topics for Writing and Discussion

1. Thurber remarks humorously that the male had "to go in for somersaults, tilting with lances, and performing feats of parlour magic to win [the female's] attention; he also had to bring her candy, flowers, and the furs of animals." Discuss current "courting" practices of young men.

2. Thurber suggests that the female of the species expects the male "to display" in order to gain her interest. Do you think that women are, in fact, brought up to expect these activities from men?

3. Thurber talks about the ways in which males try to win the attention of females. Write an essay in which you discuss the ways in which women attempt to get the attentions of men.

4. Thurber uses a number of examples from the animal kingdom to illustrate the human activity of courtship. Choose another animal or insect and write a humorous account of its mating activities, following Thurber's approach.

5. Although Thurber could safely assume in 1942 that his audience would generally be amused, this assumption might not be so certain today. Discuss the possible responses of a feminist audience to Thurber's essay.

Feeding, Feasts, and Females

by Margaret Visser

It has for most of history been common for men and women to eat apart, 1
especially in public. Often taboos ensure that they eat different foods,
women typically being forbidden various edible substances judged
dangerous either to their morality or to their reproductive powers. Eating
together in private often both entails and "means" marriage: it involves
sharing the same house. Ceasing to eat together is tantamount to divorce
– or ceasing to "sleep together," as we still put it. Our euphemism is not
merely coy; it contains the suggestion of sharing the same private space.
Cooking, like digesting, is a common metaphor for pregnancy. The woman
offers cooking in exchange for sex; the man offers sex in exchange for cooking. It follows that women "receive" sex as men "are fed" food. Eating can
be spoken of as synonymous with the sex act itself. In the languages of the
Ghanaian LoDagaa and Gonja, the verb "to eat" is frequently used for sex,
covering a semantic field very similar to that of the English word "enjoy."

   The conjunction of the opposite poles of femaleness and maleness in the 2
married couple is very commonly made to stand for socially and culturally
vital oppositions, including one or more of the following: private and
public, inside and outside, domesticity and "work," down and up, left and
right, dark and light, cold and hot, back and front, curved and straight, soft
and hard, still (female) and moving (male), and so forth. Being made to
"stand for" these in turn enforces conformity with the expectations. If "a
woman's place is in the home," her place implies all the "female"
characteristics: interiority, quietness, a longing to nurture, unwillingness
to stand forth, and renunciation of the "male" claims to authority, publicity,
loudness, brightness, sharpness. These qualities have a multitude of prac-

tical applications; for example, they either make a woman altogether unfit and unwilling to attend feasts, or they influence the way she behaves while participating in them.

3   An ancient Greek wife would not have been seen dead at a symposium. She was thought — and considered herself to be — the embodiment of purity in the family. Her honour was, and had at all costs to remain, unassailable: the legitimacy of her offspring, and the honour of her menfolk, depended upon it. It was all right for *betairai* (courtesans) to mix with revelling and orgiastic males; they were shameless women, outrageous in their freedom and lack of *tenue*. A dining room was called an *andron,* "a room for men": a woman eating there was a woman out of place, marginalized and unworthy of respect. Unphilosophically minded ancient Greeks apparently thought, as many people nowadays still do, that important ideas should never be discussed at table. Plutarch has one such symposiast put it like this: "Philosophy should no more have a part in conversation over wine than should the matron of the house." According to this view, the Persians got it right when they drank and danced with their mistresses, but never with their wives. Wives were serious, but *betairai* and mistresses could be taken lightly. When men, therefore, were asked to a party, they left their wives at home. But a wedding feast was a crowded affair, Plutarch makes his sympotic conversationalists say elsewhere, because women were responsible for a lot of the activities at a wedding — and an invited woman must invariably come accompanied by her husband.

4   Formality at public events is almost invariably a male affair, because it involves social rank (which has often been denied to all but the very top women) and publicity. Formality has always been contrasted with relaxation and intimacy, which are enjoyed at home, where the women have their place. (Men inhabit both spheres, public and private, whereas women have rarely done so; this one-sided overlap is one of the important inconsistencies in the scheme.) It follows that at a banquet in many traditional societies, men observe rank and precedence at table, while women serve the diners, or sit and eat in a separate place where far less ceremony is observed; they might sit in a crowd in the middle of the room, for example, while the men are ranged in order round the walls. At a Winnebago Indian feast, the men sat observing strict precedence round the periphery of the meeting house, with plenty of room between them; the women and children crowded together in a tiny space behind a screen at the back. The women have generally cooked such feasts, though occasionally men will have insisted on handling the meat (a prestigious, "masculine" food) themselves. The women may even think of being permitted to serve the food as a tremendous, and jealously guarded, privilege. Women, say the

Javanese who practise the *slametan* feast, are *mburi*, "behind" (that is, in the kitchen; during the feast they peep through the bamboo partitions at the men as they eat), whereas men are *ngarepan*, "in front," consuming the food prepared by the women.

In nineteenth-century Japan, women were seldom invited to dinner, but 5 if they were they were expected to sit apart, in one corner of the room. In China, they feasted separately from the men, as women do in societies where there is a very strong division between the sexes. In the Ming period, the imperial women, dowagers, wives, daughters, and sisters of their men would host the wives of ministers and officials in the Inner Quarters of the Palace of Female Tranquillity. Their banquets were accompanied by female musicians. Hostesses were required, however, to offer fewer courses at dinner than the men, and to offer wine less often. It is assumed that in private, on ordinary occasions, male and female members of the imperial family ate together, as the commoners did. In the United Arab Emirates today, as in other Arab countries, women often meet and dine together, with complex and sophisticated civility.

It is with a great sense of superiority that a male host may "feed" his guests 6 but not himself partake of the meal; and a woman who cooks and serves a dinner without eating much of it herself may do so with a real sense of the power conferred by the bestowal of food. (Guests always feel uncomfortable eating in front of an abstemious host.) But it is necessary for the giver to be present during the meal to enjoy this particular kind of ego enhancement, for prestige is personal: it is non-existent where there is no knowledge of the person being honoured. As late as the nineteenth century in French peasant households, the women would serve the men at table, but themselves eat standing, or draw up stools by the fire and hold their dishes on their laps; the old and the children might be expected to join them there. It is possible, but unlikely, that such an arrangement expressed appreciation and respect for women.

Young boys in strictly sex-segregated societies must one day make the 7 transition from living as children with the women to joining the men. The initiation, whether accompanied or not by ceremonial rites, is effected in large part by the young male taking his predestined place in public life, among the men at dinner. Girls do not take this step; they remain, in this sense, children. (To "stay where you are," even metaphorically, is of course to cleave to the principle of stillness and centrality which has hitherto been so important in the symbolism of being female.) A man often prefers a woman to keep the status of dependent child: he may reward her for accepting this position by finding her sexually attractive if she does so.

A woman maintains her role as mother by feeding her family; some 8

African societies are said to think of the wife as "mother of her husband" for this reason. Food is a female concern, and often one of the main sources of a woman's power in the household. Women gather food, shop, choose what is to be eaten, and cook it. Social anthropologists have long called women the "gatekeepers" of food supplies in the house. However, since they choose food which they know their husbands and children like and demand, the "gatekeeper" role is often merely executive. Women are reported to make their cooking expressive of their feelings: they "reward" men by producing a special dish, with particular care; they show disapproval by not having dinner ready on time, or by refusing to put effort into the meal. Gertrude Stein tells the story of her French cook Hélène, who disapproved of Matisse because a Frenchman "should not stay unexpectedly to a meal particularly if he asked the servant beforehand what there was for dinner." One could expect such behaviour from foreigners, but in a Frenchman it was unacceptable. When Matisse was invited to dinner she would, for example, serve him fried eggs, never an omelette. "It takes the same number of eggs," she coldly asserted, "and the same amount of butter, but it shows less respect," Monsieur Matisse would understand.

9   If an African wife refuses to cook at all, her husband cannot make her do it; men are often not only incapable of cooking but forbidden to cook. In some Nigerian tribes they are not allowed even to discuss food or express directly a desire to eat: a Jukun male will say, "I am going to eat," when he means he is thirsty, and use a phrase like "I shall go into my hut" (the *kunguni,* where Jukun males eat alone) for "I want some dinner." Eating, for him, requires the kind of euphemism which in our society is reserved for sex or excretion. This attitude towards eating is part of the allocation of roles, and again it goes back to the sexual model: "giving food" for women corresponds to "giving sex" for men; it would be extremely confusing to do things the other way round. It is fairly common for a man to refuse to eat what his wife has cooked, as a sign of his displeasure; he is protected, of course, from having to do without food altogether if he has several wives. A further connection between food and sex is suggested by the fact that a polygamous male usually eats food prepared by the wife he is currently sleeping with.

10   Brewing beer is an ancient female preserve; and where beer is central to the economy and nutrition of a society — as it often still is in Africa, among South American Indians, and elsewhere — control over it naturally becomes a source of female power. It may link up with another commonly traditional female skill and responsibility: that of making and controlling the use of clay pots. (The ancient Greek god Dionysus — feminine is so much of his nature — had power both over wine and over the area of

Athens called Ceramicus, where pots were made.) The Newar women of Nepal must personally serve the beer they have made, even at a public feast. Among the LoDagaa of Ghana, a woman's good beer can turn her home into a beer house, a place where people gather to exchange news and gossip. She sells her product, and pours it out for her clients, always setting aside a calabash of it for herself to show she has not poisoned the batch. She plays a role rather like that of European society hostesses who used to keep "open house" or a "salon" on certain days of the week where people could collect together and socialize. The hostess of a tea party, like the LoDagaa breweress, must pour the tea.

Because food and drink usually reach the family through the women's 11 hands, fear of women frequently translates into suspicion that they are poisoners. Knives, in the traditional view, are "male" weapons. They are wielded aggressively, and they pertain to the masculine realm of fighting, war, and the hunt; they are essential for carving meat. From a symbolic point of view, knives are phallic. We have seen how in medieval Europe, men were supposed to cut for their womenfolk at table. Poison, on the other hand, is a secretive, sneaky way of killing anyone, in addition to which it is often liquid, and administered in food — all of which makes poison a peculiarly "female" weapon, certainly in the folklore and mythology of all races, and possibly in fact as well. Fear of poison can strengthen the pressure upon men not to rove, but stay with their families: they might eat only what is prepared for them by their wives or mothers, or by women otherwise in their control.

Alcoholic drinks, like knives, have always been thought especially 12 dangerous in the hands of women, and men have taken great care to prevent their own partiality for alcohol from infecting "the fair sex." Their solicitude has, until recently, been effective: the percentage of female heavy drinkers has usually been comparatively very low. (It is now rising alarmingly, according to Noel and McCrady for example.) Women must take responsibility for their unborn children, and it is certain that heavy drinking during pregnancy can have ill effects. In any case, what was disgraceful behaviour in a man was always far worse if seen in a woman. During the nineteenth century in Europe, women at table were not to ask for wine; the men were expected to keep them supplied. A man would serve himself and his female partner simultaneously: he would bow, then drink with her. Women were expected not to accept wine every time they were offered it. In France it was correct for a man to offer a woman water at the same time as wine, for a woman, says the Baronne Staffe, never drinks wine neat except at the dessert: she always insists that it be *trempé,* mixed with water.

Women in the Mediterranean countries, from the sixteenth century until 13 recent times, appear to have astonished visitors by their sobriety. In France, in particular, men "cut" their wine with water, but "honourable" French women, if they touched wine at all, "used it merely to redden their water slightly." Wine, these days, has become an object of awe and reverence; the only people who add water to it are those who can obtain it cheaply and drink it regularly, and who pay comparatively little regard to its quality. Women drink it at table as much as men do — but even the most recent of etiquette manuals cling to the idea that men should really serve women with the dangerous liquid, "regardless of the symbolism," as Miss Manners puts it. If the host (not the hostess) does not get up and refill glasses when necessary, then "each man should pour wine for the woman on his left."

14   "Young ladies do not eat cheese, nor game, nor savouries," states a late Victorian etiquette book. The reason was almost certainly the same as that occasionally suggested for women not drinking: their breath would cease to be pleasing to men. Women still conform to expectations about eating less than men do, and preferring lighter, paler foods — chicken and lettuce, for example, over beef and potatoes. In Japan, women were actually given smaller rice bowls and shorter, slimmer chopsticks. In the Kagoro tribe of northern Nigeria, men use spoons, but women are not allowed this privilege. Among the Pedi of South Africa, in the 1950s, women and children used the special men's porridge dishes, but only when they were cracked and "no longer sufficiently respectable" for male use. Cooking and serving food to the men as they do, women are accustomed all over the world to eating what is left over from dinner; they are often able, of course, to look out for themselves while preparing the meal. In Assam, where pollution rules mean that lower castes may accept food from higher castes but not the other way round, a woman eats from the same plates as her husband, after the men have finished their meal: nothing could make the pair more intimate, and nothing could more clearly demonstrate that she is lower than he.

15   In Europe, families have often eaten all together at home, though where several families lived in one dwelling and dinners fed a lot of people, it was probably most common for the men to be fed first, served by the women. It was the nobility who took part in most of the formal banquets, and among them women were sometimes admitted, sometimes allowed on sufferance, and sometimes excluded altogether. During the Middle Ages, women might sit in a gallery or balcony especially provided so that they could watch the men at dinner. But noblemen could at certain places and times sit each with a female partner beside him — "promiscuous seating," as the Victorians were to call this arrangement. Another possibility was for all the women to sit at one end of the table, apparently as meticulously ranked

as were the men at their end. At very big banquets there might be ladies' tables, apart from the men's. We are told that Louis XIV would invite particular women whose company he fancied to join him at high table, or have the noblest and most beautiful women seated at his table for him; his wife the queen, who might be present, or obliged to preside over a separate, all-female dinner elsewhere, did not have the equivalent privilege.

From Elizabethan times women seem to have carved meat at British **16** tables; this is a marked departure from the outlook which insisted that knives were the perquisites of males. In the early eighteenth century the hostess often did all the carving and serving of meat at table. Lady Mary Wortley Montagu as a young girl took carving lessons; on the days when she presided over her widowed father's table, "she ate her own dinner earlier in order to perform without distraction." As the century progressed, men would offer to help their wives or daughters in this task. But by the end of the eighteenth century, servants increasingly carved for the diners; and with the arrival of dinner *à la russe* in the mid-nineteenth century, carving at formal meals was invariably done by servants, away from the dining table itself. At family dinners, the tradition has survived in Britain of the chief male portioning out the roast before the assembled group.

At the end of dinner, wrote Emily Post in 1922, the hostess, having **17** decided that the moment has come, "looks across the table, and catching the eye of one of the ladies, slowly stands up. The one who happens to be observing also stands up, and in a moment everybody is standing." The choreography is strict: the gentlemen give their partners their arms and conduct them out of the dining room into the drawing room. They bow slightly, then follow the host to the smoking room for coffee, cigars, and liqueurs. If there is no smoking room, the women leave the dining room alone. The host sits at his place at the table, and the men all move up towards his end.

Where port is served, the bottle on its coaster stands before the host, the **18** tablecloth having been removed before the ritual begins. He pours for whoever is on his right — to save this person, seated in the honourable place, from having to wait until last to be served. Then the bottle is slid reverently along the polished wooden tabletop (originally so that the dregs might be disturbed as little as possible, though all good ports should be decanted before they are drunk); or it is rolled along in a wheeled silver chariot; or it is handed with special ceremonial gestures from male to male, as drinking cups were handed at ancient Greek symposia. But port is passed clockwise (to the left), not as drinks circulated in ancient Greece, to the right. "Beg your pardon, sir," says Jingle in *The Pickwick Papers,* after the waiter has left the men to themselves, "bottle stands — pass it round

— way of the sun — through the button-hole [both these expressions are ways of saying "to the left": men's buttonholes are traditionally placed on the left] — no heeltaps [meaning "leave no wine at the bottom of the glass"]." At the British Factory House dinners in Oporto, the men move into a second dining room in order to enjoy vintage port, for fear of any smell of food interfering with the drink's aroma.

19   The men discuss politics, and sit with whomever they like; hierarchical seating is often suspended at this time. It is even correct for a man "to talk to any other who happens to be sitting near him, whether he knows him or not," wrote Emily Post in 1922: the men are at last among themselves, and rules can be relaxed. The women, meanwhile, are served coffee, cigarettes, and liqueurs in the library or the drawing room. The hostess sees to it that no one is left out of the conversations which take place. By the 1920s, all of this lasted no longer than fifteen to twenty minutes. The host "takes the opportunity of the first lull in the conversation" to shepherd the men to "join the ladies" in the drawing room. When the men arrive, they must cease talking to each other and find a woman with whom to converse.

20   This ritual performance was commonly carried out at formal dinner parties in Britain at least into the 1960s; it probably still occurs. Americans were told by Emily Post exactly how it was done into the middle of this century, even though at least one American etiquette book a hundred years earlier had professed disgust for the idea. Several foreign visitors to Britain in the eighteenth century had found the custom exotic and distasteful. On the Continent, the company and conversation of women had become essential to the makings of a good dinner party; there was no question of doing without them at any point in the proceedings. Men of polished manners were not supposed to hanker after the kind of behaviour, associated with male company, which could not stand the scrutiny of women.

21   For the point of the ceremony of women "leaving the table" and men being left alone until they "joined the ladies" was not only that men wanted to discuss matters which could not be expected to interest their wives or be understood by them. The origin of it lay in the heavy drinking and toasting, the coarse jokes and laughter among men which the presence of women might inhibit. The ladies would leave the men to it, and perhaps eventually have to go home alone, as drinking and roistering continued into the night. In eighteenth-century Scotland, according to Lord Cockburn's *Memorials*, "saving the ladies" meant that the men would take their womenfolk home, then return to the scene of the dinner party to drink competitive healths to them. They paired off to see who could imbibe more in honour of his true love, "each combatant persisting till one of the two fell upon the floor…. These drinking competitions were regarded with interest by gentlewomen,

who next morning inquired as to the prowess of their champions."

Heavy toasting died out during the nineteenth century, but a new reason 22 for the men staying on alone came in with the advent of smoking, which at first respectable women would not dream of trying. By the time the ceremony of the ladies' withdrawal was described by Emily Post, it had been firmly contained within constricted time limits. There had been significant changes: for example, it had previously been necessary for the women to send a servant in to call the men to them — in Thomas Love Peacock's novel *Headlong Hall* (1816), "the little butler now waddled in with a summons from the ladies to tea and coffee." At a later date, coffee would be sent in to the men to remind them soon to adjourn. Later still, the men were expected to curtail their own gathering and show at least ritual eagerness to rejoin the women. Both men and women, Post is careful to insist in 1922, now smoked; women must be supplied with cigarettes too, and the thought of anyone getting drunk does not even arise.

Another idea behind the ceremony was that when men and women were 23 together, they felt constrained to behave very formally; only when the sexes were segregated could they relax and "be themselves." The dinner party, with its newly necessary "promiscuous" seating (men and women alternating at the table), had been an exhausting performance; it had actually been quite difficult, because of the seating, to speak to people of the same sex as oneself. The after-dinner time among men at the table or women in the drawing room was conceived as a relief from having too strictly to "behave." English nineteenth-century novelists often use the separation of the sexes after dinner as a chance to further the plot by means of free conversation, and a male character's arrival from the dining room, his choice of a female partner for conversation, became dramatic expressions of the women's interest in him, and of his preferences.

All through history, women have been segregated from men and from 24 public power, and "shielded" from the public view; they have been put down, put upon, and put "in their place" — a place defined by males. Yet this is not the whole story; and in the long run it may not be the most important story. For women — and men have very often admitted it, in their behaviour if not always in words or in kindness — have been an enormous civilizing influence in the history of humankind. It is not only that the way women are treated in any specific society is an infallible test of the health of that society. Women have also played the role — and it has been with the connivance of men — of consciousness-raisers in the domain of manners, comfort, and consideration for others. And the more men prized civilized manners, the more they "behaved" in the presence of women. The ideal claimed by Americans in the nineteenth century, when the custom of the ladies leaving the men after dinner was found distasteful, was in fact a sign that grown men were ready to think it normal to behave decently even when there were no women present.

25   Women certainly felt more immediately the advantages of courtesy — *"la courtoisie généreuse,"* the Baronne Staffe called it — and accepted the ceremonial artificiality which saw them as "weaker" than men, but also "finer." Women had to be bowed to, have hats lifted to them, doors opened for them, seats offered to them; they were served first at dinner. Theirs was, ritually speaking, the higher place, in spite of the underlying realities of their social and economic position. Women in "polite society" consequently became sticklers for etiquette — conservative perhaps, but also protective of the gains conquered. The etiquette manuals, many of them written by women in the nineteenth century, are filled with comments about male difficulties with correct behaviour, and bristling with advice about how men might improve themselves. They always assume that women find it far easier to manage all the skills and nuances required.

26   And in fact it has come to pass that in many important respects women have won. Men who succeed and are admired in our culture must demonstrate that they have opted for finesse, sympathetic awareness, and self-control. "Male" vices which men forbade in women, such as alcohol abuse and smoking, have become disreputable in men also — although many women are now claiming the "right" at last to indulge in them. Fighting, swaggering, overeating have all gone out of style; one result of the technological revolution has been to remove the requirement that "real men" should show themselves to be rough, and overbearing: one does not need to be physically powerful in order to control the instruments of technology. The gap between the sexes has closed not only because women have increasingly entered what has until now been the men's public sphere of operations, but because men have gradually been made to feel that they should attain the level of behaviour which previously they expected only from the opposite sex. In short, they have become more like women.

(1991)

The Writer's Subject

1. What connection does Visser draw between gender and eating customs?

2. Why would a married woman in ancient Greece not wish to be present at a public banquet? (para. 3)

3. In what ways, according to Visser, is food "one of the main sources of a woman's power in the household"? (para. 8)

4. Why has poison been viewed as a singularly "female" weapon? (para. 11)

5. Why, according to Visser, have women traditionally eaten and drunk less than men? (paras. 12-14)

6. Why, until quite recently, have men and women separated at the conclusion of a meal? (paras. 17-23)

7. In what ways, in Visser's view, have women exerted a great civilizing influence in society? (paras. 24-26)

The Writer's Style and Strategy

1. At what points does Visser's essay move beyond a historical survey of customs and rituals associated with eating?

2. Discuss Visser's use of contrast as a means of structuring her paragraphs.

3. Discuss Visser's use of examples to support her general observations, and comment on the range of her references.

4. Why does Visser refer on a number of occasions to Emily Post?

5. Explain the relevance to Visser's argument of her anecdote about Gertrude Stein's cook, Hélène. (para. 8)

Suggested Topics for Writing and Discussion

1. Visser argues that women have traditionally attained a higher level of social behaviour than men, and that men, in becoming more socially adept, "have become more like women." Do you agree?

2. Visser's essay deals extensively with the rituals of dining in different societies through history, and with the roles of women in those rituals. To what extent do women still perform the roles traditionally assigned to them in matters relating to food?

3. Visser maintains that "the way women are treated in any specific society is an infallible test of the health of that society" (para. 24). Test this assertion by comparing the way women are treated in two or three different nations or cultures.

4. Do you think that the concept of "courtesy," whereby men treat women with special politeness, still has any place in our society?

The Tyranny of the Clock
by George Woodcock

In no characteristic is existing society in the West so sharply distinguished   1
from the earlier societies, whether of Europe or of the East, as in its
conception of time. To the ancient Chinese or Greek, to the Arab herds-
man or the Mexican peon of today, time is represented by the cyclic
processes of nature, the alternation of day and night, the passage from
season to season. The nomads and the farmers measured and still measure
their day from sunrise to sunset, and their year in terms of seed-time
and harvest, of the falling leaf and ice thawing on the lakes and rivers.
The farmer worked according to the elements, the craftsman for as long
as he felt it necessary to perfect his product. Time was seen as a process of natural change, and men were not concerned in its exact measurement. For this reason civilizations highly developed in other respects
had the most primitive means of measuring time: the hourglass with
its trickling sand or dripping water, the sundial, useless on a dull day,
and the candle or lamp whose unburnt remnant of oil or wax indicated
the hours. All these devices were approximate and inexact, and were
often rendered unreliable by the weather or the personal laziness of the
tender. Nowhere in the ancient or the mediaeval world were more than
a tiny minority of men concerned with time in the terms of mathematical
exactitude.

Modern, western man, however, lives in a world which runs accord-   2
ing to the mechanical and mathematical symbols of clock time. The
clock dictates his movements and inhibits his actions. The clock turns
time from a process of nature into a commodity that can be measured
and bought and sold like soap or sultanas. And because, without some

means of exact timekeeping, industrial capitalism could never have developed and could not continue to exploit the workers, the clock represents an element of mechanical tyranny in the lives of modern men more potent than any individual exploiter or than any other machine. It is therefore valuable to trace the historical process by which the clock influenced the social development of modern European civilization.

3   It is a frequent circumstance of history that a culture or a civilization develops the device that will later be used for its destruction. The ancient Chinese, for example, invented gunpowder, which was developed by the military experts of the West and eventually led to the Chinese civilization itself being destroyed by the high explosives of modern warfare. Similarly, the super achievement of the craftsmen of the mediaeval cities of Europe was the invention of the clock, which, with its revolutionary alteration of the concept of time, materially assisted the growth of the Middle Ages.

4   There is a tradition that the clock appeared in the eleventh century, as a device for ringing bells at regular intervals in the monasteries, which, with the regimented life they imposed on their inmates, were the closest social approximation in the Middle Ages to the factory of today. The first authenticated clock, however, appeared in the thirteenth century, and it was not until the fourteenth century that clocks became common as ornaments of the public building in German cities.

5   These early clocks, operated by weights, were not particularly accurate, and it was not until the sixteenth century that any great reliability was attained. In England, for instance, the clock at Hampton Court, made in 1540, is said to have been the first accurate clock in the country. And even the accuracy of the sixteenth-century clocks is relative, for they were equipped only with hour-hands. The idea of measuring time in minutes and seconds had been thought out by the early mathematicians as far back as the fourteenth century, but it was not until the invention of the pendulum in 1657 that sufficient accuracy was attained to permit the addition of a minute-hand, and the second-hand did not appear until the eighteenth century. These two centuries, it should be observed, were those in which capitalism grew to such an extent that it was able to take advantage of the techniques of the Industrial Revolution to establish its economic domination over society.

6   The clock, as Lewis Mumford has pointed out, is the key machine of the machine age, both for its influence on technics and for its influence on the habits of men. Technically, the clock was the first really automatic machine that attained any importance in the life of man.

Previous to its invention, the common machines were of such nature that their operation depended on some external and unreliable force, such as human or animal muscles, water, or wind. It is true that the Greeks had invented a number of primitive automatic machines, but these were used, like Hero's steam engine, either for obtaining "supernatural" effects in the temples or for amusing the tyrants of Levantine cities. But the clock was the first automatic machine that attained public importance and a social function. Clock-making became the industry from which men learnt the elements of machine-making and gained the technical skill that was to produce the complicated machinery of the Industrial Revolution.

Socially the clock had a more radical influence than any other machine, 7 in that it was the means by which the regularization and regimentation of life necessary for an exploiting system of industry could be best assured. The clock provided a means by which time – a category so elusive that no philosophy has yet determined its nature – could be measured concretely in the more tangible terms of space provided by the circumference of a clock dial. Time as duration became disregarded, and men began to talk and think always of "lengths" of time, just as if they were talking of lengths of calico. And time, being now measurable in mathematical symbols, was regarded as a commodity that could be bought and sold in the same way as any other commodity.

The new capitalists, in particular, became rabidly time-conscious. 8 Time, here symbolizing the labour of the workers, was regarded by them almost as if it were the chief raw material of industry. "Time is money" was one of the key slogans of capitalist ideology, and the timekeeper was the most significant of the new types of official introduced by the capitalist dispensation.

In the early factories the employers went so far as to manipulate their 9 clocks or sound their factory whistles at the wrong times in order to defraud the workers of a little of this valuable new commodity. Later such practices became less frequent, but the influence of the clock imposed a regularity on the lives of the majority of men that had previously been known only in the monasteries. Men actually became like clocks, acting with a repetitive regularity which had no resemblance to the rhythmic life of a natural being. They became, as the Victorian phrase put it, "as regular as clockwork." Only in the country districts where the natural lives of animals and plants and the elements still dominated existence did any large proportion of the population fail to succumb to the deadly tick of monotony.

10   At first this new attitude to time, this new regularity of life, was imposed by the clock-owning masters on the unwilling poor. The factory slave reacted in his spare time by living with a chaotic irregularity which characterized the gin-sodden slums of early-nineteenth-century industrialism. Men fled to the timeless worlds of drink or Methodist inspiration. But gradually the idea of regularity spread downwards and among the workers. Nineteenth-century religion and morality played their part by proclaiming the sin of "wasting time." The introduction of mass-produced watches and clocks in the 1850s spread time-consciousness among those who had previously merely reacted to the stimulus of the knocker-up or the factory whistle. In the church and the school, in the office and the workshop, punctuality was held up as the greatest of the virtues.

11   Out of this slavish dependence on mechanical time which spread insidiously into every class in the nineteenth century, there grew up the demoralizing regimentation which today still characterizes factory life. The man who fails to conform faces social disapproval and economic ruin − unless he drops out into a non-conformist way of life in which time ceases to be of prime importance. Hurried meals, the regular morning and evening scramble for trains or buses, the strain of having to work to time schedules, all contribute, by digestive and nervous disturbance, to ruin health and shorten life.

12   Nor does the financial imposition of regularity tend, in the long run, to greater efficiency. Indeed, the quality of the product is usually much poorer, because the employer, regarding time as a commodity which he has to pay for, forces the operative to maintain such a speed that his work must necessarily be skimped. Quantity rather than quality becoming the criterion, the enjoyment is taken out of the work itself, and the worker in his turn becomes a "clock-watcher," concerned only with when he will be able to escape to the scanty and monotonous leisure of industrial society, in which he "kills time" by cramming in as much time-scheduled and mechanical enjoyment of cinema, radio, and newspaper as his wage packet and his tiredness will allow. Only if he is willing to accept the hazard of living by his faith or his wits can the man without money avoid living as a slave to the clock.

13   The problem of the clock is, in general, similar to that of the machine. Mechanized time is valuable as a means of co-ordinating activities in a highly developed society, just as the machine is valuable as a means of reducing unnecessary labour to a minimum. Both are valuable for the contribution they make to the smooth running of society, and should

be used in so far as they assist men to co-operate efficiently and to eliminate monotonous toil and social confusion. But neither should be allowed to dominate men's lives as they do today.

Now the movement of the clock sets the tempo of men's lives — they **14** become the servants of the concept of time which they themselves have made, and are held in fear, like Frankenstein by his own monster. In a sane and free society such an arbitrary domination of man's functions by either clock or machine would obviously be out of the question. The domination of man by man-made machines is even more ridiculous than the domination of man by man. Mechanical time would be relegated to its true function of a means of reference and co-ordination, and men would return again to a balanced view of life no longer dominated by time-regulation and the worship of the clock. Complete liberty implies freedom from the tyranny of abstractions as well as from the rule of men.

(1939)

The Writer's Subject

1. How did the concept of time in older societies differ from that of modern Western society? (para. 1)

2. How, according to Woodcock, did the development of the clock make possible the rise of industrial capitalism? (paras. 6-8)

3. What impact has the development of clock time had on the life of the modern worker, in Woodcock's view? (paras. 9-12)

4. At several points Woodcock uses the word "commodity" to describe the modern concept of time. What are the implications of this term, and how does its use further Woodcock's thesis?

5. What comparison does Woodcock make between the clock and the machine? (paras. 13-14)

The Writer's Style and Strategy

1. Discuss the appropriateness of Woodcock's choice of title.

2. Is there a rhetorical as well as an expository purpose behind Woodcock's explanation in paragraph 1 of how time was recorded by older societies?

3. Examine Woodcock's description of modern Western concepts of time in paragraph 2. How does his choice of words convey his attitude here? Does the diction seem "slanted" in any way?

4. Woodcock proposes to "trace the historical process by which the clock influenced the social development of modern European civilization" (para. 2). What principle seems to determine his choice of historical evidence? How does he use the history of the Industrial Revolution to further his argumentative purposes?

5. Discuss the ways in which Woodcock describes employers and workers throughout the essay. How does he make clear where his sympathies lie?

6. What use does Woodcock make of such clichés as "Time is money" or "as regular as clockwork" to further his argument?

7. Trace the stages by which Woodcock's argument moves from past to present, and from specific to general.

Suggested Topics for Writing and Discussion

1. Do you agree with Woodcock's view that we have become slaves to "mechanical time"? Draw on your own daily life to support your point of view.

2. Woodcock describes factory workers in the eighteenth and nineteenth centuries as slaves who were brutally exploited by ruthless capitalists. Find out what you can about conditions in factories, mills, or mines in the nineteenth century; using one or two particular examples, show whether or not Woodcock's assertions are justified.

3. Although Woodcock's essay is largely devoted to attacking "the tyranny of the clock," in paragraph 13 he acknowledges the importance of mechanical time in the smooth running of society. Write an essay on the beneficial aspects of mechanical time, illustrating your argument with specific examples.

4. Woodcock and Mumford argue that the clock is "the key machine of the machine age . . . for its influence on the habits of men" (para. 6). Discuss the effects of one other machine upon our daily lives.

Politics and Morality

On Party-Lying
by Joseph Addison

Defendit numerus, junctaeque umbone phalanges.[1]
Juvenal

There is something very Sublime, tho' very Fanciful, in *Plato's* Descrip- 1
tion of the Supreme Being, that *Truth is his Body, and Light his
Shadow.* According to his Definition, there is nothing so contradic-
tory to his Nature as Error and Falshood. The Platonists have so just
a Notion of the Almighty's Aversion to every thing which is false and
erroneous, that they looked upon *Truth* as no less necessary than *Virtue,* to qualifie an Human Soul for the Enjoyment of a separate State.
For this Reason, as they recommended Moral Duties to qualifie and
season the Will for a future Life, so they prescribed several Contempla-
tions and Sciences to rectifie the Understanding. Thus *Plato* has called
Mathematical Demonstrations the Catharticks or Purgatives of the Soul,
as being the most proper Means to cleanse it from Error, and to give
it a Relish of Truth, which is the natural Food and Nourishment of the
Understanding, as Virtue is the Perfection and Happiness of the Will.

There are many Authors who have shewn wherein the Malignity of 2
a *Lie* consists, and set forth, in proper Colours, the Heinousness of the
Offence. I shall here consider one Particular Kind of this Crime, which
has not been so much spoken to: I mean, that abominable Practice of
Party-lying. This Vice is so very predominant among us at present,
that a Man is thought of no Principles, who does not propagate a certain
System of Lies. The Coffee-Houses are supported by them, the Press
is choaked with them, eminent Authors live upon them. Our Bottle-
Conversation is so infected with them, that a Party-Lie is grown as

1. *Motto.* Juvenal, *Satires,* 2. 46: They are protected by their numbers and the close shields
of their phalanx.

fashionable an Entertainment, as a lively Catch or a merry Story: The Truth of it is, half the great Talkers in the Nation would be struck dumb, were this Fountain of Discourse dryed up. There is, however, one Advantage resulting from this detestable Practice; the very Appearances of Truth are so little regarded, that Lies are at present discharged in the Air, and begin to hurt no Body. When we hear a Party-story from a Stranger, we consider whether he is a Whig or a Tory that relates it, and immediately conclude they are Words of Course, in which the honest Gentleman designs to recommend his Zeal, without any Concern for his Veracity. A Man is looked upon as bereft of common Sense, that gives Credit to the Relations of Party-Writers, nay his own Friends shake their Heads at him, and consider him in no other Light than as an officious Tool or a well-meaning Ideot. When it was formerly the Fashion to husband a Lie, and trump it up in some extraordinary Emergency, it generally did Execution, and was not a little serviceable to the Faction that made use of it; but at present every Man is upon his Guard; the Artifice has been too often repeated to take Effect.

3   I have frequently wondered to see Men of Probity, who would scorn to utter a Falshood for their own particular Advantage, give so readily into a Lie when it is become the Voice of their Faction, notwithstanding they are thoroughly sensible of it as such. How is it possible for those, who are Men of Honour in their Persons, thus to become Notorious Liars in their Party? If we look into the Bottom of this Matter, we may find, I think, three Reasons for it, and at the same time discover the Insufficiency of these Reasons to justifie so Criminal a Practice.

4   In the first place, Men are apt to think that the Guilt of a Lie, and consequently the Punishment, may be very much diminished, if not wholly worn out, by the Multitudes of those who partake in it. Though the Weight of a Falshood would be too heavy for *one* to bear, it grows light in their Imaginations, when it is shared among *many*. But in this Case a Man very much deceives himself; Guilt, when it spreads through Numbers, is not so properly divided as multiplied: Every one is criminal in proportion to the Offence which he commits, not to the Number of those who are his Companions in it. Both the Crime and the Penalty lie as heavy upon every Individual of an offending Multitude, as they would upon any single Person, had none shared with him in the Offence. In a Word, the Division of Guilt is like that of Matter; though it may be separated into infinite Portions, every Portion shall have the whole Essence of Matter in it, and consist of as many Parts as the whole did afore it was divided.

But in the second place, though Multitudes, who join in a Lie, can- 5
not exempt themselves from the Guilt, they may from the Shame of
it. The Scandal of a Lie is in a manner lost and annihilated, when dif-
fused among several Thousands; as a Drop of the blackest Tincture wears
away and vanishes, when mixed and confused in a considerable Body
of Water: The Blot is still in it, but is not able to discover it self. This
is certainly a very great Motive to several Party-Offenders, who avoid
Crimes, not as they are prejudicial to their Virtue, but to their Reputation. It is enough to show the Weakness of this Reason, which palliates
Guilt without removing it, that every Man, who is influenced by it,
declares himself in effect an infamous Hypocrite, prefers the Appearance
of Virtue to its Reality, and is determined in his Conduct neither by
the Dictates of his own Conscience, the Suggestions of true Honour,
nor the Principles of Religion.

The third and last great Motive for Mens joining in a popular Falshood, 6
or, as I have hitherto called it, a Party-Lie, notwithstanding they are
convinced of it as such, is the doing Good to a Cause which every Party
may be supposed to look upon as the most meritorious. The Unsound-
ness of this Principle has been so often exposed, and is so universally
acknowledged, that a Man must be an utter Stranger to the Principles,
either of natural Religion or Christianity, who suffers himself to be
guided by it. If a Man might promote the supposed Good of his Country by the blackest Calumnies and Falshoods, our Nation abounds more
in Patriots than any other of the Christian World. When *Pompey* was
desired not to set Sail in a Tempest that would hazard his Life, *It is*
necessary for me, says he, *to Sail, but it is not necessary for me to*
Live: Every Man should say to himself, with the same Spirit, It is my
Duty to speak Truth, tho' it is not my Duty to be in an Office. One of
the Fathers has carried this Point so high, as to declare *he would not*
tell a Lie though he were sure to gain Heaven by it: However extravagant
such a Protestation may appear, every one will own, that a Man may
say very reasonably *he would not tell a Lie, if he were sure to gain*
Hell by it; or, if you have a mind to soften the Expression, that he would
not tell a Lie to gain any Temporal Reward by it, when he should run
the hazard of losing much more than it was possible for him to gain.

(1712)

The Writer's Subject

1. Comment on the appropriateness of the epigraph to the content of the essay.

2. While lamenting the prevalence of lying, Addison sees one advantage in its general acceptance; what is this advantage? (para. 2)

3. What are the reasons which Addison gives for the acceptance of party-lying by "Men of Probity"? (paras. 3-6)

4. What is Addison's own attitude to party-lying, and to lying in general? Where is this attitude given most explicit expression?

The Writer's Style and Strategy

1. What is the function of the opening paragraph? How does Addison effect a transition from this paragraph to his principal subject, party-lying?

2. In paragraph 2, Addison says ". . . a Man is thought of no Principles, who does not propagate a certain System of Lies." What is the figure of speech used here?

3. What is meant by the phrase "Our Bottle-Conversation" in paragraph 2?

4. Find an example of metaphor in paragraph 2 and explain its usefulness in emphasizing Addison's point.

5. Discuss the organization of paragraphs 3 through 6, and show how Addison deals with the arguments of those he is attacking.

6. Explain the analogy in the second sentence of paragraph 5, and discuss its effectiveness.

7. "If a Man might promote the supposed Good of his Country by the blackest Calumnies and Falshoods, our Nation abounds more in Patriots than any other of the Christian World" (para. 6). What is the tone of this statement?

Suggested Topics for Writing and Discussion

1. In what respects are Addison's views on politics similar to those expressed by George Orwell in his essay "Politics and the English Language"?

2. "Party-lying" is as common in our own time as in Addison's. The most notorious recent examples are the "Watergate Affair" during Richard Nixon's presidency and the "Iran arms deal" during that of Ronald Reagan. Find out what you can about one of these episodes in American politics, and offer your views about what the incident revealed concerning the morality of the political scene at the time.

3. Addison attacks those who lie for what they believe to be a good cause (para. 6). Do you believe that there may in fact be any cause worth lying for? (You may wish to look at what Bronowski has to say in "The Real Responsibilities of the Scientist" concerning scientists who lie for what they consider to be good reasons.)

The Writer's Responsibility

by Margaret Atwood

1   The subject we have come together to address is one which increases
in importance as the giants of this world move closer and closer to violent
and fatal confrontation. Broadly put, it is: what is the writer's responsibility, if any, to the society in which he or she lives? The question
is not a new one; it's been with us at least since the time of Plato; but
more and more the answers of the world's governments have taken the
form of amputation: of the tongue, of the soul, of the head.

2   We in Canada are ill-equipped to come to grips even with the problem, let alone the solution. We live in a society in which the main
consensus seems to be that the artist's duty is to entertain and divert,
nothing more. Occasionally our critics get a little heavy and start talking about the human condition, but on the whole the audience prefers
art not to be a mirror held up to life but a Disneyland of the soul, containing Romanceland, Spyland, Pornoland and all the other Escapelands
which are so much more agreeable than the complex truth. When we
take an author seriously, we prefer to believe that her vision derives
from her individual and subjective and neurotic tortured soul — we like
artists to have tortured souls — not from the world she is looking at.
Sometimes our artists believe this version too, and the ego takes over.
I, me and *mine* are our favourite pronouns; *we, us* and *ours* are low
on the list. The artist is not seen as a lens for focusing the world but
as a solipsism. We are good at measuring an author's production in terms
of his craft. We are not good at analyzing it in terms of his politics,

and by and large we do not do so.

By "politics" I do not mean how you voted in the last election, although
that is included. I mean who is entitled to do what to whom, with impunity; who profits by it; and who therefore eats what. Such material
enters a writer's work not because the writer is or is not consciously
political but because a writer is an observer, a witness, and such observations are the air he breathes. They are the air all of us breathe; the
only difference is that the author looks, and then writes down what he
sees. What he sees will depend on how closely he looks and at what,
but look he must.

In some countries, an author is censored not only for what he says
but for how he says it, and an unconventional style is therefore a declaration of artistic freedom. Here we are eclectic; we don't mind experimental
styles, in fact we devote learned journals to their analysis; but our critics
sneer somewhat at anything they consider "heavy social commentary"
or − a worse word − "message." Stylistic heavy guns are dandy, as
long as they aren't pointed anywhere in particular. We like the human
condition as long as it is seen as personal and individual. Placing politics
and poetics in two watertight compartments is a luxury, just as specialization of any kind is a luxury, and it is possible only in a society where
luxuries abound. Most countries in the world cannot afford such luxuries,
and this North American way of thinking is alien to them. It was even
alien in North America, not long ago. We've already forgotten that in
the 1950's many artists, both in the United States and here, were
persecuted solely on the grounds of their presumed politics. Which leads
us to another mistaken Canadian belief: the belief that it can't happen
here.

It has happened here, many times. Although our country is one of
the most peaceful and prosperous on earth, although we do not shoot
artists here, although we do not execute political opponents and although
this is one of the few remaining countries in which we can have a gathering like this without expecting to be arrested or blown up, we should
not overlook the fact that Canada's record on civil rights issues is less
than pristine. Our treatment of our native peoples has been shameful.
This is the country in which citizens of Japanese origin were interned
during the Second World War and had their property stolen (when a
government steals property it is called "confiscation"); it is also the country in which thousands of citizens were arrested, jailed and held without
warrant or explanation, during the time of the War Measures Act, a
scant eleven years ago. There was no general outcry in either case. Worse

things have not happened not because we are genetically exempt but because we lead pampered lives.

6   Our methods of controlling artists are not violent, but they do exist. We control through the marketplace and through critical opinion. We are also controlled by the economics of culture, which in Canada still happen to be those of a colonial branch-plant. In 1960 the number of Canadian books published here was minute, and the numbers sold pathetic. Things have changed very much in twenty years, but Canadian books still account for a mere 25 percent of the overall book trade and paperback books for under 5 percent. Talking about this situation is still considered nationalistic chauvinism. Nevertheless, looked at in the context of the wider picture, I suppose we are lucky to have any percent at all; they haven't yet sent in the Marines and if they do it won't be over books, but over oil.

7   We in this country should use our privileged position not as a shelter from the world's realities but as a platform from which to speak. Many are denied their voices; we are not. A voice is a gift; it should be cherished and used, to utter fully human speech if possible. Powerlessness and silence go together; one of the first efforts made in any totalitarian takeover is to suppress the writers, the singers the journalists, those who are the collective voice. Get rid of the union leaders and pervert the legal system and what you are left with is a reign of terror.

8   As we read the newspapers, we learn we are existing right now in a state of war. The individual wars may not be large and they are being fought far from here, but there is really only one war, that between those who would like the future to be, in the words of George Orwell, a boot grinding forever into a human face, and those who would like it to be a state of something we still dream of as freedom. The battle shifts according to the ground occupied by the enemy. Greek myth tells of a man called Procrustes, who was a great equalizer. He had a system for making all human beings the same size: if they were too small he stretched them, if they were too tall he cut off their feet or their heads. The Procrustes today are international operators, not confined to any one ideology or religion. The world is full of perversions of the notion of equality, just as it is full of perversions of the notion of freedom. True freedom is not being able to do whatever you like to whomever you want to do it to. Freedom that exists as a result of the servitude of others is not true freedom.

9   The most lethal weapon in the world's arsenals is not the neutron bomb or chemical warfare; but the human mind that devises such things and

puts them to use. But it is the human mind also that can summon up the power to resist, that can imagine a better world than the one before it, that can retain memory and courage in the face of unspeakable suffering. Oppression involves a failure of the imagination: the failure to imagine the full humanity of other human beings. If the imagination were a negligible thing and the act of writing a mere frill, as many in this society would like to believe, regimes all over the world would not be at such pains to exterminate them. The ultimate desire of Procrustes is a population of lobotomized zombies. The writer, unless he is a mere word processor, retains three attributes that power-mad regimes cannot tolerate: a human imagination, in the many forms it may take; the power to communicate; and hope. It may seem odd for me to speak of hope in the midst of what many of my fellow Canadians will call a bleak vision, but as the American writer Flannery O'Connor once said, people without hope do not write novels.

(1981)

The Writer's Subject

1. Why is Atwood so critical of the attitudes of Canadians to art and artists?

2. What are the implications of the phrase "a Disneyland of the soul" (para. 2)?

3. What is Atwood's definition of "politics," and how does it bear on her view of the writer's responsibility? (para. 3)

4. Why does Atwood regard the separation of politics and poetics as a "luxury"? (para. 4)

5. After giving examples of Canadian violations of civil rights (para. 5), Atwood concludes that "Worse things have not happened not because we are genetically exempt but because we lead pampered lives." Discuss what Atwood means by this observation.

6. What does Atwood mean by describing the economics of Canadian culture as "those of a colonial branch-plant" (para. 6)?

7. Atwood asserts that "we are existing right now in a state of war" (para. 8). Who are the opponents in this war?

8. What answer does Atwood give to the question she raises in paragraph 1, "what is the writer's responsibility, if any, to the society in which he or she lives? What qualities must the writer possess to fulfil that responsibility?"

The Writer's Style and Strategy

1. Explain the significance of Atwood's use of "amputation" in the opening paragraph.

2. Is there any evidence in style, diction, or tone to indicate that this essay was originally prepared as a spoken address?

3. Why does Atwood first refer to the writer as "she" (para. 2), then shift to a masculine pronoun in subsequent paragraphs?

4. At several points Atwood uses irony as a means of underscoring her point of view. Pick out one or two examples of effective irony.

5. Examine the organization of paragraph 5. What means of development does Atwood employ? Why does she begin the second sentence with four subordinate clauses, each introduced by "although"?

6. Atwood defines "true freedom" negatively rather than positively in paragraph 8. Why does she employ this strategy of definition?

Suggested Topics for Writing and Discussion

1. Atwood provides several examples of the violations of civil rights in Canada. Investigate one of these and explain what climate of opinion or historical events led to the occurrence.

2. Atwood says that our society expects artists "to entertain and divert, nothing more." Is it possible, in your view, for artists to perform the duties which Atwood discusses and, at the same time, entertain and divert? Provide clear examples to support your view.

3. We regard our society as free. We are still subject, however, to various forms of censorship in the arts and in communication. Find and discuss one or two examples of censorship in any medium (books, movies, television, radio, newspapers, exhibitions, advertisements, etc.).

Shooting an Elephant
by George Orwell

In Moulmein, in Lower Burma, I was hated by large numbers of people 1
– the only time I have been important enough for this to happen to
me. I was subdivisional police officer of the town, and in an aimless,
petty kind of way anti-European feeling was very bitter. No one had
the guts to raise a riot, but if a European woman went through the bazaars
alone somebody would probably spit betel juice over her dress. As a
police officer I was an obvious target and was baited whenever it seemed
safe to do so. When a nimble Burman tripped me up on the football
field and the referee (another Burman) looked the other way, the crowd
yelled with hideous laughter. This happened more than once. In the
end the sneering yellow faces of young men that met me everywhere,
the insults hooted after me when I was at a safe distance, got badly
on my nerves. The young Buddhist priests were the worst of all. There
were several thousands of them in the town and none of them seemed
to have anything to do except stand on street corners and jeer at
Europeans.

All this was perplexing and upsetting. For at that time I had already 2
made up my mind that imperialism was an evil thing and the sooner
I chucked up my job and got out of it the better. Theoretically – and
secretly, of course – I was all for the Burmese and all against their
oppressors, the British. As for the job I was doing, I hated it more bitterly
than I can perhaps make clear. In a job like that you see the dirty work
of Empire at close quarters. The wretched prisoners huddling in the
stinking cages of the lock-ups, the grey, cowed faces of the long-term
convicts, the scarred buttocks of the men who had been flogged with

bamboos — all these oppressed me with an intolerable sense of guilt. But I could get nothing into perspective. I was young and ill-educated and I had had to think out my problems in the utter silence that is imposed on every Englishman in the East. I did not even know that the British Empire is dying, still less did I know that it is a great deal better than the younger empires that are going to supplant it. All I knew was that I was stuck between my hatred of the empire I served and my rage against the evil-spirited little beasts who tried to make my job impossible. With one part of my mind I thought of the British Raj as an unbreakable tyranny, as something clamped down, in *saecula saeculorum,*[1] upon the will of prostrate peoples; with another part I thought that the greatest joy in the world would be to drive a bayonet into a Buddhist priest's guts. Feelings like these are the normal by-products of imperialism; ask any Anglo-Indian official, if you can catch him off duty.

3   One day something happened which in a roundabout way was enlightening. It was a tiny incident in itself, but it gave me a better glimpse than I had had before of the real nature of imperialism — the real motives for which despotic governments act. Early one morning the sub-inspector at a police station the other end of the town rang me up on the 'phone and said that an elephant was ravaging the bazaar. Would I please come and do something about it? I did not know what I could do, but I wanted to see what was happening and I got on to a pony and started out. I took my rifle, an old .44 Winchester and much too small to kill an elephant, but I thought the noise might be useful *in terrorem.* Various Burmans stopped me on the way and told me about the elephant's doings. It was not, of course, a wild elephant, but a tame one which had gone "must". It had been chained up, as tame elephants always are when their attack of "must" is due, but on the previous night it had broken its chain and escaped. Its mahout, the only person who could manage it when it was in that state, had set out in pursuit, but had taken the wrong direction and was now twelve hours' journey away, and in the morning the elephant had suddenly reappeared in the town. The Burmese population had no weapons and were quite helpless against it. It had already destroyed somebody's bamboo hut, killed a cow and raided some fruit-stalls and devoured the stock; also it had met the municipal rubbish van, and, when the driver jumped out and took to his heels, had turned the van over and inflicted violences upon it.

4   The Burmese sub-inspector and some Indian constables were waiting for me in the quarter where the elephant had been seen. It was a very poor quarter, a labyrinth of squalid bamboo huts, thatched with palm-

---

1. Forever and ever.

leaf, winding all over a steep hillside. I remember that it was a cloudy, stuffy morning at the beginning of the rains. We began questioning the people as to where the elephant had gone, and, as usual, failed to get any definite information. That is invariably the case in the East; a story always sounds clear enough at a distance, but the nearer you get to the scene of events the vaguer it becomes. Some of the people said that the elephant had gone in one direction, some said that he had gone in another, some professed not even to have heard of any elephant. I had almost made up my mind that the whole story was a pack of lies, when we heard yells a little distance away. There was a loud, scandalized cry of "Go away, child! Go away this instant!" and an old woman with a switch in her hand came round the corner of a hut, violently shooing away a crowd of naked children. Some more women followed, clicking their tongues and exclaiming; evidently there was something that the children ought not to have seen. I rounded the hut and saw a man's dead body sprawling in the mud. He was an Indian, a black Dravidian coolie, almost naked, and he could not have been dead many minutes. The people said that the elephant had come suddenly upon him round the corner of the hut, caught him with its trunk, put its foot on his back and ground him into the earth. This was the rainy season and the ground was soft, and his face had scored a trench a foot deep and a couple of yards long. He was lying on his belly with arms crucified and head sharply twisted to one side. His face was coated with mud, the eyes wide open, the teeth bared and grinning with an expression of unendurable agony. (Never tell me, by the way, that the dead look peaceful. Most of the corpses I have seen looked devilish.) The friction of the great beast's foot had stripped the skin from his back as neatly as one skins a rabbit. As soon as I saw the dead man I sent an orderly to a friend's house nearby to borrow an elephant rifle. I had already sent back the pony, not wanting it to go mad with fright and throw me if it smelt the elephant.

The orderly came back in a few minutes with a rifle and five cartridges, and meanwhile some Burmans had arrived and told us that the elephant was in the paddy fields below, only a few hundred yards away. As I started forward practically the whole population of the quarter flocked out of the houses and followed me. They had seen the rifle and were all shouting excitedly that I was going to shoot the elephant. They had not shown much interest in the elephant when he was merely ravaging their homes, but it was different now that he was going to be shot. It was a bit of fun to them, as it would be to an English crowd; besides they wanted the meat. It made me vaguely uneasy. I had no intention of shooting the elephant — I had merely sent for the rifle to defend myself if necessary — and it is always unnerving to have a crowd following you. I marched down the hill, looking and feeling a fool, with the rifle over my shoulder and an ever-growing army of people jostling at my heels. At the bottom, when you got away from the huts, there was a metalled road and beyond that a miry waste of paddy fields a thousand yards across, not yet ploughed but soggy from the first rains and dotted with coarse grass. The elephant was standing eight yards from the road, his left side towards us. He took not the slightest notice of the crowd's approach. He was tearing up bunches of grass, beating them against his knees to clean them and stuffing them into his mouth.

6   I had halted on the road. As soon as I saw the elephant I knew with perfect certainty that I ought not to shoot him. It is a serious matter to shoot a working elephant — it is comparable to destroying a huge and costly piece of machinery — and obviously one ought not to do it if it can possibly be avoided. And at that distance, peacefully eating, the elephant looked no more dangerous than a cow. I thought then and I think now that his attack of "must" was already passing off; in which case he would merely wander harmlessly about until the mahout came back and caught him. Moreover, I did not in the least want to shoot him. I decided that I would watch him for a little while to make sure that he did not turn savage again, and then go home.

7   But at that moment I glanced round at the crowd that had followed me. It was an immense crowd, two thousand at the least and growing every minute. It blocked the road for a long distance on either side. I looked at the sea of yellow faces above the garish clothes — faces all happy and excited over this bit of fun, all certain that the elephant was going to be shot. They were watching me as they would watch a conjurer about to perform a trick. They did not like me, but with the magical rifle in my hands I was momentarily worth watching. And suddenly I realized that I should have to shoot the elephant after all. The people expected it of me and I had got to do it; I could feel their two thousand wills pressing me forward, irresistibly. And it was at this moment, as I stood there with the rifle in my hands, that I first grasped the hollowness, the futility of the white man's dominion in the East. Here was I, the white man with his gun, standing in front of the unarmed native crowd — seemingly the leading actor of the piece; but in reality I was only an absurd puppet pushed to and fro by the will of those yellow faces behind. I perceived in this moment that when the white man turns

tyrant it is his own freedom that he destroys. He becomes a sort of hollow, posing dummy, the conventionalized figure of a sahib. For it is the condition of his rule that he shall spend his life in trying to impress the "natives", and so in every crisis he has got to do what the "natives" expect of him. He wears a mask, and his face grows to fit it. I had got to shoot the elephant. I had committed myself to doing it when I sent for the rifle. A sahib has got to act like a sahib; he has got to appear resolute, to know his own mind and do definite things. To come all that way, rifle in hand, with two thousand people marching at my heels, and then to trail feebly away, having done nothing — no, that was impossible. The crowd would laugh at me. And my whole life, every white man's life in the East, was one long struggle not to be laughed at.

But I did not want to shoot the elephant. I watched him beating his **8** bunch of grass against his knees, with that preoccupied grandmotherly air that elephants have. It seemed to me that it would be murder to shoot him. At that age I was not squeamish about killing animals, but I had never shot an elephant and never wanted to. (Somehow it always seems worse to kill a large animal.) Besides, there was the beast's owner to be considered. Alive, the elephant was worth at least a hundred pounds; dead, he would only be worth the value of his tusks, five pounds, possibly. But I had got to act quickly. I turned to some experienced-looking Burmans who had been there when we arrived, and asked them how the elephant had been behaving. They all said the same thing: he took no notice of you if you left him alone, but he might charge if you went too close to him.

It was perfectly clear to me what I ought to do. I ought to walk up **9** to within, say, twenty-five yards of the elephant and test his behaviour. If he charged I could shoot, if he took no notice of me it would be safe to leave him until the mahout came back. But also I knew that I was going to do no such thing. I was a poor shot with a rifle and the ground was soft mud into which one would sink at every step. If the elephant charged and I missed him, I should have about as much chance as a toad under a steam-roller. But even then I was not thinking particularly of my own skin, only of the watchful yellow faces behind. For at that moment, with the crowd watching me, I was not afraid in the ordinary sense, as I would have been if I had been alone. A white man mustn't be frightened in front of "natives"; and so, in general, he isn't frightened. The sole thought in my mind was that if anything went wrong those two thousand Burmans would see me pursued, caught, trampled on and reduced to a grinning corpse like that Indian up the hill. And if that happened it was quite probable that some of them would laugh. That would never do. There was only one alternative. I shoved the cartridges into the magazine and lay down on the road to get a better aim.

10   The crowd grew very still, and a deep, low, happy sigh, as of people who see the theatre curtain go up at last, breathed from innumerable throats. They were going to have their bit of fun after all. The rifle was a beautiful German thing with cross-hair sights. I did not then know that in shooting an elephant one would shoot to cut an imaginary bar running from ear-hole to ear-hole. I ought, therefore, as the elephant was sideways on, to have aimed straight at his ear-hole; actually I aimed several inches in front of this, thinking the brain would be further forward.

11   When I pulled the trigger I did not hear the bang or feel the kick — one never does when a shot goes home — but I heard the devilish roar of glee that went up from the crowd. In that instant, in too short a time, one would have thought, even for the bullet to get there, a mysterious, terrible change had come over the elephant. He neither stirred nor fell, but every line of his body had altered. He looked suddenly stricken, shrunken, immensely old, as though the frightful impact of the bullet had paralysed him without knocking him down. At last, after what seemed a long time — it might have been five seconds, I dare say — he sagged flabbily to his knees. His mouth slobbered. An enormous senility seemed to have settled upon him. One could have imagined him thousands of years old. I fired again into the same spot. At the second shot he did not collapse but climbed with desperate slowness to his feet and stood weakly upright, with legs sagging and head drooping. I fired a third time. That was the shot that did for him. You could see the agony of it jolt his whole body and knock the last remnant of strength from his legs. But in falling he seemed for a moment to rise, for as his hind legs collapsed beneath him he seemed to tower upwards like a huge rock toppling, his trunk reaching skywards like a tree. He trumpeted, for the first and only time. And then down he came, his belly towards

12 me, with a crash that seemed to shake the ground even where I lay.

I got up. The Burmans were already racing past me across the mud. It was obvious that the elephant would never rise again, but he was not dead. He was breathing very rhythmically with long rattling gasps, his great mound of a side painfully rising and falling. His mouth was wide open — I could see far down into caverns of pale pink throat. I waited a long time for him to die, but his breathing did not weaken.

Finally I fired my two remaining shots into the spot where I thought his heart must be. The thick blood welled out of him like red velvet, but still he did not die. His body did not even jerk when the shots hit him, the tortured breathing continued without a pause. He was dying, very slowly and in great agony, but in some world remote from me where not even a bullet could damage him further. I felt that I had got to put an end to that dreadful noise. It seemed dreadful to see the great beast lying there, powerless to move and yet powerless to die, and not even to be able to finish him. I sent back for my small rifle and poured shot after shot into his heart and down his throat. They seemed to make no impression. The tortured gasps continued as steadily as the ticking of a clock.

In the end I could not stand it any longer and went away. I heard 13 later that it took him half an hour to die. Burmans were bringing dahs and baskets even before I left, and I was told they had stripped his body almost to the bones by the afternoon.

Afterwards, of course, there were endless discussions about the 14 shooting of the elephant. The owner was furious, but he was only an Indian and could do nothing. Besides, legally I had done the right thing, for a mad elephant has to be killed, like a mad dog, if its owner fails to control it. Among the Europeans opinion was divided. The older men said I was right, the younger men said it was a damn shame to shoot an elephant for killing a coolie, because an elephant was worth more than any damn Coringhee coolie. And afterwards I was very glad that the coolie had been killed; it put me legally in the right and it gave me a sufficient pretext for shooting the elephant. I often wondered whether any of the others grasped that I had done it solely to avoid looking a fool.

(1936)

The Writer's Subject

1. What were Orwell's feelings about his role as a representative of British imperialism in Burma? (paras. 1-2)

2. Orwell received his education at Eton, one of the finest schools in England; why, then, does he refer to himself as "ill-educated"? (para. 2)

3. What is Orwell's point in telling us at length about his initial difficulty in finding the elephant? (paras. 3-4)

4. Why did Orwell first take a rifle that he knew was too small to kill an elephant? What does this detail suggest about his state of mind at that point? (para. 3)

5. Why at first did Orwell not want to shoot the elephant? What considerations led him to change his mind? (paras. 6-9)

6. Why was Orwell concerned at the thought that the crowd might laugh if he were trampled to death? (para. 9)

7. Why did Orwell fail to kill the elephant with his first shot? Why did he leave the scene before the elephant finally expired? (paras. 10-13)

8. How does the final paragraph demonstrate Orwell's earlier statement, "I had had to think out my problems in the utter silence that is imposed on every Englishman in the East"? (para. 2)

The Writer's Style and Strategy

1. What is Orwell's purpose in this essay?

2. Why does Orwell choose the form of autobiographical narrative to carry out his purpose?

3. Orwell provides many details of physical setting. Choose some of these and explain their importance in the narrative.

4. Besides setting the scene, how do the details in paragraph 1 prepare the reader for the central events in the narrative?

5. How does Orwell use concrete images to convey his inner conflict in paragraph 2?

6. Why does Orwell provide so many details about the elephant's destructiveness and the appearance of the dead Indian? (paras. 3-4) What relation do these details bear to the essay's conclusion?

7. How does Orwell convey the mood of the Burmans who witness his conduct in dealing with the elephant? Why does he place such emphasis on their forming a huge crowd? (paras. 5, 7, 9-10)

8. How does the final paragraph reinforce Orwell's earlier statement, "I had had to think out my problems in the utter silence that is imposed on every Englishman in the East" (para. 2)?

9. What is Orwell's purpose in providing such a vivid and detailed description of the elephant's death? (paras. 11-13)

10. How does Orwell's conclusion sum up and re-state the moral issues dramatized in the narrative?

Suggested Topics for Writing and Discussion

1. Orwell recounts a personal experience in "Shooting an Elephant." He begins his account of the experience by saying, "One day something happened which in a roundabout way was enlightening. It was a tiny incident in itself, but it gave me a better glimpse that I had had before of the real nature of. . . ." Using Orwell's introduction, write a narrative in which you discuss an enlightening personal experience and show how that experience has given you greater insight.

2. Orwell's essay demonstrates the powerful influence of social pressures on the individual. Have you ever found yourself in a situation in which you had to go against your own feelings or convictions in order to satisfy the rules or expectations of society? Recount this experience.

3. In our daily lives, we encounter many different kinds of authority. Choose one example of authority, describe the form it takes, and examine your own response to it.

Another Accolade for Charter Arms Corp.

by Mike Royko

1 I was pleased to see that the stories reporting the death of John Lennon were specific and accurate about the kind of gun that was used to murder the world-renowned musician.

2 It was a .38 calibre pistol made by Charter Arms Corp. of Bridgeport, Conn.

3 You might ask: What difference does it make what kind of gun was used?

4 It makes a great deal of difference. Especially to Charter Arms Corp.

5 There are guns and then there are guns. Cheap guns, ordinary guns, and finely crafted guns.

6 And when people become emotional about guns, as many do when somebody famous is killed, they tend to lump all guns together. They don't show proper respect for an excellent gun, such as the Charter .38.

7 It happens this is not the first time a famous person has been shot by this make of weapon., When former Alabama Gov. George C. Wallace was shot and paralyzed for life by another deranged person in 1974, the bullet that tore into his spine came from a Charter .38.

8 If I'm not mistaken, that makes the Charter .38 the first gun in modern times to have two famous people to its credit. The weapons used to blast President Kennedy, the Rev. Dr. Martin Luther King, Jr., and Sen. Robert F. Kennedy were all of different manufacture.

9 When Wallace was shot, a CBS reporter made it obvious that he didn't know a fine gun from a cheap gun.

10 The reporter went on network TV and said that Wallace had been wounded by a "cheap handgun." He obviously had in mind the kind

of Saturday Night Special that is so popular among the criminal riffraff who have no respect for quality and workmanship.

When the proud executives of Charter Arms Corp. heard the reporter, 11 they became indignant.

They contacted the CBS and demanded an apology. The incident was 12 described in an editorial in the company magazine of the Charter Corp.

The editorial, which was headlined "An Apology from CBS," said: 13

"We are too dedicated to high quality in American-made handguns and have poured too much of ourselves into our products to have one of them even casually referred to as a 'cheap handgun'.

"That was exactly the phrase used in a broadcast description of the handgun used by Arthur Bremer in his assassination attempt on Gov. Wallace, which happened to be one of our Undercover .38 Specials.

"The broadcast emanated from CBS . . . and our public relations people were immediately instructed to bring the error to their attention."

The editorial went on to say that an apology was indeed received from 14 CBS network vice-president, who contritely told Charter Arms Corp., "I am sending a copy of your letter to all our TV producers. In the event that we make reference to the Undercover .38 special used by Arthur Bremer, we will certainly avoid characterizing it as a 'Saturday Night Special' or any other term which labels it as a 'cheap weapon'."

Presumably that soothed the wounded pride of the gunmakers at 15 Charter Arms Corp., since no further public protests were heard.

And you can't blame them for having felt hurt at such a slur on their 16 product. When Wallace was shot, a Charter .38 cost $105. Today, with rising prices, the gun costs about $180 or $190, depending on where you do your gun shopping.

That is not a cheap gun, especially when compared to the trashy 17 weapons that some gunmen, to whom quality is unimportant, arm themselves with.

Now I don't know if it was mere coincidence that both Bremer, who 18 shot Wallace, and Mark David Chapman, who apparently shot Lennon, used the same weapon. Or if it was that they both recognized quality when they saw it, and were willing to spend money to get the best.

But the fact is, both opted for quality and they got what they paid 19 for. There was no misfiring, no jamming, no bullet flying off line, and no gun exploding in their hands — all of which can happen when one uses a cheap gun.

True, Wallace wasn't killed. That was the fault of Bremer, not the 20 Charter gun. Bremer shot Wallace in the stomach, which isn't the best place to shoot a person if you want to kill him.

21   But even in that case, the gun did its job — blowing a terrible hole in Wallace's gut and putting him into a wheelchair for good.

22   In the case of Lennon, you couldn't ask for a better performance from a gun. Lennon was shot several times, but according to the doctor who pronounced him dead, the first bullet hit him in the chest and killed him on the spot. The other shots weren't even necessary.

23   You can never be sure of getting those kinds of results from a Saturday Night Special.

24   Now the Charter Arms Corp. has the unique distinction of having two famous people shot by one of their products, I wonder if they have considered using it in their advertising. Something simple and tasteful like: "The .38 that got George Wallace AND John Lennon. See it at your gun dealer now."

25   If so, they shouldn't wait. With so many handguns — both cheap and of high quality — easily available to Americans, it could be just a matter of time until another manufacturer moves into the lead in the famous-person derby. All it would take would be a few pop-pop-pops from say, a Colt — maybe a politician or two and another rock star or two — and they would have the lead.

26   On the other hand, maybe Charter Arms Corp. doesn't want recognition — just the kind of pride one feels in a job of fine craftsmanship.

27   If so, they have a right to feel proud.

28   Once again, your product really did the job, gents.

(1980)

The Writer's Subject

1. What precisely is Royko's target for satire here?

2. What concerns appear to be missing in Royko's references to the various victims of assassination? How do these omissions fit his purpose in the essay?

3. How does Royko apply the idea of quality and craftsmanship to the subject of guns?

4. Royko first describes the gunmen as "deranged." How does he subsequently treat them? How does this treatment fit his satiric purposes?

5. What is Royko's attitude to the Charter Arms Corp.? What does he imply about the company's values — and possibly those of business in general?

6. What is Royko's attitude to handguns?

The Writer's Style and Strategy

1. What indications does the essay give that it was originally written for a newspaper audience?

2. What is the tone of Royko's essay? How is it established in the opening paragraph?

3. What persona does Royko create for the speaker of this essay?

4. Why does Royko constantly use "Corp." instead of "corporation" in referring to the gun company?

5. A method frequently employed by satirists is to reverse praise and blame, thus creating an ironic effect. Point out some specific examples of the praise/blame inversion and suggest Royko's real intent.

6. What use does Royko make of the editorial and the "Apology from CBS" published in the Charter Arms Corp. company magazine?

7. Why does Royko say that "Bremer shot Wallace in the stomach" but speak in the next paragraph of "blowing a hole in Wallace's gut"?

8. Discuss the intended effect of the last three sentences.

Suggested Topics for Writing and Discussion

1. Write an argument for or against the view that the individual citizen should have the right to possess a handgun.

2. Find some reports concerning the murder or attempted murder of a well-known public figure. Compare accounts of the incident and show how the attitudes and emphases of the reporters differ in their coverage of two or three particulars.

3. Write an essay in which you attack something you believe is wrong by ironically praising what you wish to criticize.

4. One target in Royko's essay is the marketing of guns. Choose another product with potential for harm (such as cigarettes, diet pills, instant formula for babies), and discuss the ways in which the product's manufacturer attempts to persuade consumers to buy it, despite its dangers.

Sport and Nationalism

by Alan Sillitoe

1 Sometime during February 1969 a certain person wrote to me from Munich — I forget his name, because I destroyed the letter — asking for my views on sport. His request was short, and put in rather general terms, yet my mind immediately understood it in a particular way, as it was meant to do, perhaps. For some reason I copied the body of my reply into my notebook at the time, and this is what I told him:

2   'I have never practised any kind of sport. It has always seemed to me that sport only serves to enslave the mind and to enslave the body. It is the main "civilising" weapon of the western world ethos, a way of enforcing collective discipline which no self-respecting savage like myself could ever take to . Society was built on "competition", and "sport" is a preliminary to this society and an accompaniment to it. It is a sort of training ground for entering into the war of life. The Olympic torch is a flame of enslavement — run from it as fast as you can , and that in itself will give you plenty of exercise.'

3   In olden days sport was the king's pastime. Now, it can be everybody's. By sport I mean competitive sport, when one man or woman matches himself or herself against another, either for so-called glory, or for cash gain.

4   Even as late as the end of the nineteenth century a particularly vicious sport existed in a certain area of south-east England. Its name was 'kickshins' — which is as good a description of it as any. Two men would stand facing, arms on each other's shoulders, and take it in turns to give a kick at each other's shins. Matches were arranged between the kickshin champions of various villages, and the local squires would bet on their favourites.

Just as universal literacy was necessary to get people into the modern   5
age, so mass competitve sport was used as further cement to enslave
them. Like every such distraction offered to the people, the people reached out to it with alacrity.

Why was this?   6

First of all, sport of big business and big propaganda was allied to   7
nationalism. If England lost a football match against Germany the people were made to feel as if the Battle of the Somme had just been refought
(and that maybe it would have been a better result if they'd played
cricket). If England won the game of football the Union Jack was in
blatant evidence, as a symbol of a national victory. It is no accident
that the English say (a false claim in any case), that 'the Battle of Waterloo
was won on the playing fields of Eton.'

One might easily think that sport has taken the place of war. Not at   8
all. Sport is a means of keeping the national spirit alive during a time
of so-called peace. It prepares the national spirit for the eventuality of ∤
war.

The ceremony of the Olympic Games is initiated by shields and flags,   9
artillery salutes and fanfares of trumpets. The honour of each nation
is invoked and put at stake immediately the runner sets out with his
flaming torch.

It is almost as if sport is diplomacy carried on by other means. Sport   10
is encouraged in schools so that young boys won't masturbate. It is encouraged among the grown-ups, as participants or spectators, to take
their minds off urgent social problems, and the need to rebel when they
are not resolved quickly enough.

If England wins an international football match, or clears twenty gold- ·11
plated tin medals at some games or other, then production goes up in
England's factories. Likewise when England lost at football in Mexico
in 1970, Mr. Harold Wilson, the Labour Party Prime Minister of the
day, lost the following general election to his Conservative opponent
Mr. Edward Heath.

Perhaps Mr. Heath is even looking for victories at the present Olym- 12
pic Games to increase his chances at the next election! Woe betide him
if England loses against Poland, or Brazil!

You might almost think that England's sporting prowess was linked 13
to the floating of the pound. One lost goal, and a few more cents are
chipped off it in the world's financial arenas. A few centimetres off the
high jump, and a left wing demonstration gets too close to the American
Embassy in Grosvenor Square.

14   If England loses, faces are long for a week. Or they might be, if radio
and television had its way, for those media too pander to the lowest
common denominator of nationalism when it comes to sport. They ex-
ult in what is known as victory, but hide as best they can so-called defeat.

15   True sport — I'm not sure that there is such a thing — but true sport,
as I see it, is not to set people competing against each other both in
deed and thought, but to work together as a team perhaps, against some
arduous enterprise or obstacle. If a dozen people set out on foot to cross
South America gathering scientific information on the way — that is
good. But if two such groups set out in order to see who can do it
quickest, or who can get to know most — that is demoralising.

16   If one man can jump sixteen feet, and another tries to jump seven-
teen in order to get a piece of gold with his name stamped on it — in
smaller letters though than the name of his country — and so that he
will become a national hero for a few weeks as well, that is both ludicrous
and sinister.

17   He is surrounded by flags and partisan spectators while he performs
his act, his national ritual, and all those people are getting some semi-
sexual power-drive from the fact that his jump would be their jump
if only they had trained for it, and hadn't eaten such big meals during
their recent lives.

18   His power is their power. They see him or her, for a moment, as
them, and them as him. And if at that moment a government minister
or national general came into the stands and ordered them to jump to
their feet, and then to jump sixteen feet the same as he — or she —
they would no doubt all stand up fully confident that they could do it
— or something close.

19   If some mechanism were fitted into every television set which, immediately after the big jump, put out a voice which said to all the wat-
chers: 'Now YOU jump — for the good of your country, because those
in every other country are doing the same to compete with you, and
the honour of your country is at stake' — the nation would jump as one
person. The nation in armchairs would become the nation in arms. y

20   The Olympic Games cannot, therefore, be considered as anything other
than a mass rally. Under the guise of international friendly competition the same old nationalist values and rivalries are fostered. It is not
the thing to engender real friendship between countries, or between the
people of these countries.

21   As soon as a man participates, either in body or spirit, either at the
actual place or vicariously through the medium of the television set,

or the radio, or the newspapers, he loses his individuality, and becomes part of his nation — with unreasonable yearning in his heart.

We all know that in the totalitarian state sport is used to drill and 22 make the individual subservient to the totalitarian system. In a so-called democratic state, competitive sport is used for the same ends, in the same way, but so that the participants appear to be competing primarily for themselves and not their country. But as soon as they enter that stadium or arena they are just as much representatives of their country as are those who belong to a totalitarian system. The media sees to that and so do the people who take up the message of the media.

When that Olympic torch is lit we must see it for what it is. It is a ,23 symbol of the oppression of the free human spirit. That flame is a burning torch being carried along the highway, and all sensible people would get out ot its way, flee from it and take to the hills. When it gets to the stadium and the crowd roars, you know that that is the place to keep away from.

Gladitorial combats in Ancient Rome, chariot races in Constantino- 24 ple, bull-fights in modern Spain, and the Olympic Games in whatever place they are held — it means that the true and human spirit of man is being killed there, the body wrecked and abused, and the heart broken. '25

Just as all war supposes human weakness, and is directed against that weakness, so all sport is a human way of arranging the survival of the fittest. Thus the arena is a sort of jungle concocted by so-called civilisation, wherein the fittest people are made to be the human measurement of nationalist aspirations.

It is a thing that the truly civilised must instinctively abominate, and 26 then with reason protest against. We must somehow make our sane voices heard — even while the crowd roars.

The voice of civilisation is not measured by the loudness of the roar- 27 ing. And civilisation itself must not be jeopardised by the contests in the arena. The Olympic torch lights up the hollow eyes of the dictator, and turns all eyes toward the national flag.

After the death of the Israelis the voices of commentators from the 28 Olympic Games in Munich have taken on tones of vile obscenity — real obscenity, the deepest obscenity of the spirit which henceforth will be represented by the Olympic Games.

The resumption of these so-called games in such indecent haste only 29 emphasised their true spirit — that of a host country unwilling to give up its pride, its financial investments; and of athletes who are in the grip of their physical investment at the expense of all human feeling.

30   That the 'games' should go on after the black-hearted murder of eleven
participants shows that true sporting spirit is so dead that one must doubt
whether it ever existed. The continuation of the games is a victory for
the Arab terrorists, for it is the quickest and most effective way of drawing a curtain on this atrocity.

                                                                    (1972)

The Writer's Subject

1. Why does Sillitoe refer to himself in paragraph 2 as a "savage"?

2. What parallel does Sillitoe draw between the rise of literacy and the growth
    of competitive sport? (para. 5)

3. What is the connection, in Sillitoe's view, between sport and the spirit
    of nationalism? (paras. 7-9)

4. According to Sillitoe, what impact does sport have on the social or political
    climate of a nation? (paras. 10-14)

5. What contrast does Sillitoe draw between competitive sport and what he
    calls "true sport"? (para. 15)

6. How, in Sillitoe's opinion, are both athletes and spectators affected by com-
    petitive sport? What sinister influence does he imagine might be exerted
    over a television audience? (paras. 16-19)

7. On what grounds does Sillitoe maintain that the Olympic torch is "a sym-
    bol of the oppression of the free human spirit" (para. 23)? What parallels
    does he draw between the Olympics and totalitarianism?

8. This essay was written after the murder of eleven Israeli athletes at the
    Munich Olympics in 1972. Why is Sillitoe so outraged that the Games
    should have been resumed after this event? (paras. 28-30) How does that
    resumption seem to him a confirmation of his views on competitive sport?

The Writer's Style and Strategy

1. What is Sillitoe's strategy in beginning an essay written in 1972 with a brief anecdote and an excerpt from a notebook, both dating from 1969?

2. Sillitoe offers an argument against competitive sport based on assertion and appeals to emotion rather than on factual evidence and logical reasoning. Pick out passages in which you feel that the appeal to emotion is particularly evident.

3. Note the use of "loaded" language (e.g., "so-called glory," "gold-plated tin medals," "his national ritual"). Choose some examples of such language, and discuss the intended effect.

4. What is the purpose of the description in paragraph 4 of the game called "kickshins"? Does it add anything to Sillitoe's thesis?

5. On what does Sillitoe base his argument that there is a correlation between victory or defeat in sport and events on the English political scene? (paras. 11-13) How convincing is this argument?

6. Discuss how Sillitoe's paragraph structures, sentence lengths, and word choice suit his purpose. How do they serve it convey his tone?

7. How would you characterize the tone of this essay? Does the tone change as the essay progresses?

Suggested Topics for Writing and Discussion

1. At several points, Sillitoe attacks the media for helping to foster the spirit of nationalism in competitive sport. Argue for or against Sillitoe's position, bringing supporting evidence from radio, T.V., or the print media.

2. Sillitoe maintains that the Olympic Games promote an unhealthy, warlike nationalism among competitors. Do you agree? What elements of the Games, if any, do you think should be changed?

3. Like Ken Dryden, in his essay "The Game," Sillitoe sees sport as a function of "big business." To what extent, in your view, has commercialism helped or hindered the development of sport?

4. Sillitoe concludes his essay by asserting that "true sporting spirit" is dead. Write an essay in which you explain what you mean by "true sporting spirit," and indicate whether you agree with Sillitoe.

5. Does competition build a strong character? Explain your view.

A Modest Proposal
For Preventing The Children of Poor People in Ireland, From Being a Burden to Their Parents or Country; and for Making Them Beneficial to the Public

by Jonathan Swift

1 It is a melancholy object to those who walk through this great town or travel in the country, when they see the streets, the roads and cabin doors crowded with beggars of the female sex, followed by three, four, or six children, all in rags and importuning every passenger for an alms. These mothers, instead of being able to work for their honest livelihood, are forced to employ all their time in strolling to beg sustenance for their helpless infants; who as they grow up either turn thieves for want of work, or leave their dear native country to fight for the Pretender in Spain, or sell themselves to the Barbadoes.

2 I think it is agreed by all parties that this prodigious number of children in the arms, or on the backs, or at the heels of their mothers, and frequently of their fathers, is in the present deplorable state of the kingdom a very great additional grievance; and, therefore, whoever could find out a fair, cheap, and easy method of making these children sound and useful members of the Commonwealth, would deserve so well of the public as to have his statue set up for a preserver of the nation.

3 But my intention is very far from being confined to provide only for the children of professed beggars; it is of a much greater extent, and shall take in the whole number of infants at a certain age who are born of parents in effect as little able to support them as those who demand our charity in the streets.

4 As to my own part, having turned my thoughts for many years upon this important subject, and maturely weighed the several schemes of other projectors, I have always found them grossly mistaken in their computation. It is true a child, just dropped from its dam, may be sup-

ported by her milk for a solar year, with little other nourishment; at
most not above the value of two shillings, which the mother may certainly get, or the value in scraps, by her lawful occupation of begging;
and it is exactly at one year old that I propose to provide for them in
such a manner as instead of being a charge upon their parents or the
parish, or wanting food and raiment for the rest of their lives, they shall
on the contrary contribute to the feeding, and partly to the clothing,
of many thousands.

There is likewise another great advantage in my scheme, that it will 5
prevent those voluntary abortions, and that horrid practice of women
murdering their bastard children, alas! too frequent among us, sacrificing
the poor innocent babes, I doubt, more to avoid the expense than the
shame, which would move tears and pity in the most savage and inhuman breast.

The number of souls in Ireland being usually reckoned one million 6
and a half, of these I calculate there may be about two hundred thousand couples whose wives are breeders; from which number I subtract
thirty thousand couples who are able to maintain their own children
(although I apprehend there cannot be so many, under the present
distresses of the kingdom); but this being granted, there will remain
an hundred and seventy thousand breeders. I again subtract fifty thousand for those women who miscarry, or whose children die by accident or disease within the year. There only remain an hundred and twenty
thousand children of poor parents annually born. The question therefore
is, how this number shall be reared and provided for? which, as I have
already said, under the present situation of affairs, is utterly impossible by all the methods hitherto proposed. For we can neither employ
them in handicraft or agriculture; we neither build houses (I mean in
the country) nor cultivate land; they can very seldom pick up a livelihood
by stealing, till they arrive at six years old, except where they are of
towardly parts; although I confess they learn the rudiments much earlier;
during which time they can, however, be properly looked upon only
as probationers; as I have been informed by a principal gentleman in
the county of Cavan, who protested to me that he never knew above
one or two instances under the age of six, even in a part of the kingdom
so renowned for the quickest proficiency in that art.

I am assured by our merchants, that a boy or a girl before twelve 7
years old is no saleable commodity; and even when they come to this
age they will not yield above three pounds or three pounds and half
a crown at most on the Exchange; which cannot turn to account either

to the parents or the kingdom, the charge of nutriment and rags having been at least four times that value.

8   I shall now therefore humbly propose my own thoughts, which I hope will not be liable to the least objection.

9   I have been assured by a very knowing American of my acquaintance in London, that a young healthy child well nursed is, at year old, a most delicious, nourishing, and wholesome food, whether stewed, roasted, baked, or boiled; and I make no doubt that it will equally serve in a fricassee or a ragout.

10   I do therefore humbly offer it to public consideration that of the hundred and twenty thousand children already computed, twenty thousand may be reserved for breed, whereof only one-fourth part to be males; which is more than we allow to sheep, black cattle, or swine; and my reason is, that these children are seldom the fruits of marriage, a circumstance not much regarded by our savages; therefore one male will be sufficient to serve four females. That the remaining hundred thousand may, at a year old, be offered in sale to the persons of quality and fortune through the kingdom; always advising the mother to let them suck plentifully in the last month, so as to render them plump and fat for a good table. A child will make two dishes at an entertainment for friends; and when the family dines alone, the fore or hind quarter will make a reasonable dish, and seasoned with a little pepper or salt will be very good boiled on the fourth day, especially in winter.

11   I have reckoned upon a medium that a child just born will weigh twelve pounds, and in a solar year, if tolerably nursed, will increase to twenty-eight pounds.

12   I grant this food will be somewhat dear, and therefore very proper for landlords, who, as they have already devoured most of the parents, seem to have the best title to the children.

13   Infant's flesh will be in season throughout the year, but more plentiful in March, and a little before and after: for we are told by a grave author, an eminent French physician, that fish being a prolific diet, there are more children born in Roman Catholic countries about nine months after Lent than at any other season; therefore reckoning a year after Lent, the markets will be more glutted than usual, because the number of popish infants is at least three to one in this kingdom: and therefore it will have one other collateral advantage, by lessening the number of Papists among us.

14   I have already computed the charge of nursing a beggar's child (in which list I reckon all cottagers, laborers, and four-fifths of the farmers)

to be about two shillings per annum, rags included; and I believe no gentleman would repine to give ten shillings for the carcass of a good fat child, which, as I have said, will make four dishes of excellent nutritive meat, when he has only some particular friend or his own family to dine with him. Thus the squire will learn to be a good landlord, and grow popular among his tenants; the mother will have eight shillings net profit, and be fit for work till she produces another child.

Those who are more thrifty (as I must confess the times require) may flay the carcass; the skin of which artifically dressed will make admirable gloves for ladies, and summer boots for fine gentlemen.

As to our city of Dublin, shambles may be appointed for this purpose 16 in the most convenient parts of it, and butchers we may be assured will not be wanting: although I rather recommend buying the children alive, and dressing them hot from the knife as we do roasting pigs.

A very worthy person, a true lover of his country, and whose virtues 17 I highly esteem, was lately pleased in discoursing on this matter to offer a refinement upon my scheme. He said that many gentlemen of this kingdom, having of late destroyed their deer, he conceived that the want of venison might be well supplied by the bodies of young lads and maidens, not exceeding fourteen years of age nor under twelve; so great a number of both sexes in every county being now ready to starve for want of work and service; and these to be disposed of by their parents, if alive, or otherwise by their nearest relations. But with due deference to so excellent a friend and so deserving a patriot, I cannot be altogether in his sentiments. For as to the males, my American acquaintance assured me from frequent experience that their flesh was generally tough and lean, like that of our schoolboys by continual exercise, and their taste disagreeable; and to fatten them would not answer the charge. Then as to the females, it would, I think, with humble submission be a loss to the public, because they soon would become breeders themselves: and besides, it is not improbable that some scrupulous people might be apt to censure such a practice (although indeed very unjustly) as a little bordering upon cruelty; which, I confess, has always been with me the strongest objection against any project, how well soever intended.

But in order to justify my friend, he confessed that this expedient 18 was put into his head by the famous Salmanaazor, a native of the island Formosa, who came from thence to London above twenty years ago: and in conversation told my friend, that in his country when any young person happened to be put to death, the executioner sold the carcass to persons of quality as a prime dainty; and that in his time the body of a plump girl of fifteen, who was crucified for an attempt to poison the emperor, was sold to his imperial majesty's prime minister of state, and other great mandarins of the court, in joints from the gibbet, at four hundred crowns. Neither indeed can I deny, that if the same use were made of several plump young girls in this town, who without one single groat to their fortunes cannot stir abroad without a chair, and appear at the playhouse and assemblies in foreign fineries which they never will pay for, the kingdom would not be the worse.

19   Some persons of a desponding spirit are in great concern about that vast number of poor people, who are aged, diseased, or maimed, and I have been desired to employ my thoughts what cause may be taken to ease the nation of so grievous an encumbrance. But I am not in the least pain upon that matter, because it is very well known that they are every day dying and rotting by cold and famine, and filth and vermin, as fast as can be reasonably expected. And as to the young, labourers, they are now in as hopeful a condition: they cannot get work, and consequently pine away for want of nourishment, to a degree that if at any time they are accidentally hired to common labour, they have not strength to perform it; and thus the country and themselves are in a fair way of being soon delivered from the evils to come.

20   I have too long digressed, and therefore shall return to my subject. I think the advantages by the proposal which I have made are obvious and many, as well as of the highest importance.

21   For first, as I have already observed, it would greatly lessen the number of Papists, with whom we are yearly overrun, being the principal breeders of the nation as well as our most dangerous enemies; and who stay at home on purpose with a design to deliver the kingdom to the Pretender, hoping to take their advantage by the absence of so many good Protestants, who have chosen rather to leave their country than stay at home and pay tithes against their conscience to an idolatrous Episcopal curate.

22   Secondly, the poor tenants will have something valuable of their own, which by law may be made liable to distress and help to pay their landlord's rent, their corn and cattle being already seized, and money a thing unknown.

23   Thirdly, whereas the maintenance of an hundred thousand children from two years old and upwards, cannot be computed at less than ten shillings apiece per annum, the nation's stock will be thereby increased fifty thousand pounds per annum, beside the profit of a new dish introduced to the tables of all gentlemen of fortune in the kingdom who

have any refinement in taste. And the money will circulate among ourselves, the goods being entirely of our own growth and manufacture.

Fourthly, the constant breeders besides the gain of eight shillings sterling per annum by the sale of their children, will be rid of the charge of maintaining them after the first year. 24

Fifthly, this food would likewise bring great custom to taverns, where the vintners will certainly be so prudent as to procure the best receipts for dressing it to perfection, and consequently have their houses frequented by all the fine gentlemen, who justly value themselves upon their knowledge in good eating; and a skilful cook who understands how to oblige his guests, will contrive to make it as expensive as they please. 25

Sixthly, this would be a great inducement to marriage, which all wise nations have either encouraged by rewards or enforced by laws and penalties. It would increase the care and tenderness of mothers towards their children, when they were sure of a settlement for life to the poor babes, provided in some sort by the public, to their annual profit instead of expense. We should soon see an honest emulation among the married women, which of them could bring the fattest child to the market. Men would become as fond of their wives during the time of their pregnancy as they are now of their mares in foal, their cows in calf, their sows when they are ready to farrow; nor offer to beat or kick them (as is too frequent a practice) for fear of a miscarriage. 26

Many other advantages might be enumerated. For instance, the addition of some thousand carcasses in our exportation of barreled beef, the propagation of swine's flesh, and improvement in the art of making good bacon, so much wanted among us by the great destruction of pigs, too frequent at our tables, and which are no way comparable in taste or magnificence to a well-grown, fat, yearling child, which roasted whole will make a considerable figure at a Lord Mayor's feast or any other public entertainment. But this and many others I omit, being studious of brevity. 27

Supposing that one thousand families in this city would be constant customers for infant's flesh, besides others who might have it at merry meetings, particularly weddings and christenings, I compute that Dublin would take off annually about twenty thousand carcasses; and the rest of the kingdom (where probably they will be sold somewhat cheaper) the remaining eighty thousand. 28

I can think of no one objection that will possibly be raised against this proposal, unless it should be urged that the number of people will 29 be thereby much lessened in the kingdom. This I freely own, and it was indeed one principal design in offering it to the world. I desire the reader will observe, that I calculate my remedy for this one individual kingdom of Ireland and for no other that ever was, is, or I think ever can be upon earth. Therefore let no man talk to me of other expedients: of taxing our absentees at five shillings a pound: of using neither clothes nor household furniture except what is of our own growth and manufacture: of utterly rejecting the materials and instruments that promote foreign luxury: of curing the expensiveness of pride, vanity, idleness, and gaming in our women: of introducing a vein of parsimony, prudence, and temperance: of learning to love our country, wherein we differ even from Laplanders and the inhabitants of Topinamboo: of quitting our animosities and factions, nor act any longer like the Jews, who were murdering one another at the very moment their city was taken: of being a little cautious not to sell our country and conscience for nothing: of teaching landlords to have at least one degree of mercy towards their tenants. Lastly, of putting a spirit of honesty, industry, and skill into our shopkeepers; who, if a resolution could now be taken to buy only our native goods, would immediately unite to cheat and exact upon us in the price, the measure, and the goodness, nor could ever yet be brought to make one fair proposal of just dealing, though often and earnestly invited to it.

30   Therefore, I repeat, let no man talk to me of these and the like expedients, till he has at least a glimpse of hope that there will ever be some hearty and sincere attempt to put them in practice.

31   But as to myself, having been wearied out for many years with offering vain, idle, visionary thoughts, and at length utterly despairing of success, I fortunately fell upon this proposal; which, as it is wholly new, so it has something solid and real, of no expense and little trouble, full in our own power, and whereby we can incur no danger in disobliging England. For this kind of commodity will not bear exportation, the flesh being of too tender a consistence to admit a long continuance in salt, although perhaps I could name a country which would be glad to eat up our whole nation without it.

32   After all, I am not so violently bent upon my own opinion as to reject any offer proposed by wise men, which shall be found equally innocent, cheap, easy, and effectual. But before something of that kind shall be advanced in contradiction to my scheme, and offering a better, I desire the author or authors will be pleased maturely to consider two points. First, as things now stand, how they will be able to find food

and raiment for a hundred thousand useless mouths and backs? And secondly, there being a round million of creatures in human figure throughout this kingdom, whose whole subsistence put into a common stock would leave them in debt two millions of pounds sterling, adding those who are beggars by profession to the bulk of farmers, cottagers, and labourers, with the wives and children who are beggars in effect; I desire those politicians who dislike my overture, and may perhaps be so bold to attempt an answer, that they will first ask the parents of these mortals, whether they would not at this day think it a great happiness to have been sold for food at a year old in the manner I prescribe, and thereby have avoided such a perpetual scene of misfortunes as they have since gone through by the oppression of landlords, the impossibility of paying rent without money or trade, the want of common sustenance, with neither house nor clothes to cover them from the inclemencies of weather, and the most inevitable prospect of entailing the like or greater miseries upon their breed for ever.

I profess, in the sincerity of my heart, that I have not the least per- 33 sonal interest in endeavouring to promote this necessary work, having no other motive than the public good of my country, by advancing our trade, providing for infants, relieving the poor, and giving some pleasure to the rich. I have no children by which I can propose to get a single penny; the youngest being nine years old, and my wife past child-bearing.

(1729)

The Writer's Subject

1. How does the speaker demonstrate that the problems of poverty in Ireland have reached crisis proportions? (paras. 1-6)

2. What image of himself does the speaker project in the first six paragraphs of his Proposal? What clues are contained in the early paragraphs that might contradict that image?

3. What are the real values of the speaker, as revealed in paragraphs 7-9?

4. Why does the speaker propose to preserve only one male child to every four female children? (para. 10). How does this fit in with the speaker's general attitude to the poor of Ireland?

5. Who might be the speaker's "very knowing American acquaintance" in paragraph 9, and where is his identity made clearer?

6. At what points is the speaker's inhumanity most extreme?

7. What religious, economic, and social advantages does the speaker maintain would accrue to Ireland if his Proposal were to be implemented? (paras. 21-26)

8. What are the realities of life in Ireland, as these emerge from the Proposal? How are conditions in Ireland determined by its relation to England?

9. What is the function of the concluding paragraph? How does the final sentence undercut the speaker's intention?

The Writer's Style and Strategy

1. Why does Swift create a persona as the author of this Proposal? Would his intentions have been better served by a more direct attack on English policies in Ireland?

2. To what audience does the speaker address his Proposal, and what are its supposed values?

3. What effect is gained by delaying the revelation of the Proposal, with its details, until paragraph 10?

4. Discuss the speaker's use of statistics and his reference to authorities as ways of supporting his argument.

5. At what points in the essay does Swift's own voice seem to emerge from behind the mask? Why does Swift allow this to happen?

6. Irony consists in the reader's perception of a discrepancy between the appearance of things and their reality. Discuss the operation of irony in paragraph 17. What makes the speaker's references to his friend in that paragraph ironic?

7. How does Swift make the reader recognize that the inhumanity of the supposed writer is not so far removed from the real attitudes of the English rulers of Ireland?

8. Discuss the speaker's tone in this essay. Does the tone remain the same throughout, or does it change? Account for any shifts in tone.

Suggested Topics for Writing and Discussion

1. Choose an issue about which there has been some controversy (e.g. apartheid, the treatment of the indigenous peoples of North America, abortion, pornography) and offer a "Modest Proposal" to solve the problem.

2. Swift would have been horrified to see that the attitudes he burlesques through the speaker of "A Modest Proposal" have found grim expression in the twentieth century (e.g., Hitler's "final solution," Stalin's "purges," South Africa's apartheid policy). Describe to Swift one or more of the horrors of modern history and the attitudes which gave rise to them.

3. Find one or two examples of writing that uses satire and/or humour in dealing with serious subjects. Do you think that humour is an appropriate means of dealing with topics of an horrific or disturbing nature? Are there any topics which you would consider a taboo subject, too sensitive to be treated in a humorous way?

Society and the Individual

The Game

by Ken Dryden

Once I used to wait in line like everyone else. Then one day a bank 1
teller motioned me out of the line, and I haven't been back in one since.
I feel no small guilt each time; nonetheless I continue to accept such
favours. For the tellers and me, it has become normal and routine. They
treat me the way they think people like me expect to be treated. And
I accept.

It is the kind of special treatment professional athletes have grown 2
accustomed to, and enjoy. It began with hockey, with teenage names
and faces in local papers, with hockey jackets that only the best players
on the best teams wore, with parents who competed not so quietly on
the side; and it will end with hockey. In between, the longer and better
we play the more all-encompassing the treatment becomes. People give,
easily and naturally. And we accept. Slippers, sweaters, plant holders,
mitts, baby blankets, baby clothes sent in the mail. Paintings, carv-
ings, etchings, sculptures in clay, metal, papier-mâché. Shirts, slacks,
coats, suits, ties, underwear; cars, carpets, sofas, chairs, refrigerators,
beds, washers, dryers, stoves, TVs, stereos, at cost or no cost at all.
After all, a special person deserves a special price. A hundred letters
a week, more than 3,000 a year — "You're the best," all but a few of
them say. On the street, in restaurants and theatres, we're pointed at,
talked about like the weather. "There he is, the famous hockey player,"
your own kids announce to their friends. In other homes, your picture
is on a boy's bedroom wall. Magazines, newspapers, radio, TV; hockey
cards, posters, T-shirts, and curios, anywhere, everywhere, name, face,
thousands of times.

3   And we love it. We say we don't, but we do. We hate the nuisance
and inconvenience, the bother of untimely, unending autographs, hand-
shakes, and smiles, living out an image of ourselves that isn't quite real,
abused if we fail to, feeling encircled and trapped, never able to get
away. But we also feel special — head-turning, chin-dropping, forget-
your-name special. What others buy Rolls-Royces and votes and hockey
teams for, what others take off their clothes for, what others kill for,
we have. All we have to do is play.

4   If exposure is the vehicle of celebrity, attention is what separates one
celebrity from another. Guy Lafleur and Yvon Lambert are both
celebrities, yet on the same ice, the same screen, Lafleur is noticed,
Lambert is not. Lambert, methodical and unspectacular, has nothing
readily distinctive about him. His image is passed over, his name
unheard. Lafleur *is* distinctive. The way he skates, the sound of the
crowd he carries with him, the goals he scores.

5   And so, too, others, for other reasons. Mario Tremblay, for his fiery,
untamed spirit; Bob Gainey, for his relentless, almost palpable will;
Tiger Williams, Eddie Shack, Ron Duguay, each colourful and exciting;
and Dave Schultz, once king of the mountain. As sports coverage pro-
liferates beyond games, as it becomes entertainment and moves to prime
time, as we look for the story behind the story, off-ice performance
becomes important. And so personas are born, and sometimes made,
and cameras and microphones are there as it happens. The crazies, the
clowns, the "sports intellectuals," the anti-jock rebels (Jim Bouton, Bill
"Spaceman" Lee), the playboys (Joe Namath, Derek Sanderson), each
a distinctive personality, each a bigger celebrity because of what he
does away from the game.

6   TV has given us a new minimum off-ice standard. The modern player
must be articulate (or engagingly inarticulate, especially southern style).
It's not enough to score a goal and have it picked apart by the all-seeing
eyes of replay cameras. A player must be able to put it in his own eloquent words. How did you do it? How did you feel? Live, on-camera
words that cannot be edited for the morning paper.

7   Celebrity is a full, integrated life, earned on-ice, performed, sustained,
strengthened, re-earned off-ice. As Roger Angell once put it, we want
our athletes to be "good at life." Role models for children, people we
want to believe earned what they have, every bit as good at things off
the ice as on. If they're inarticulate, harsh and pejorative, they're suddenly just jocks. Merely lucky, less likable, less good at life, less
celebrated; finally, they even seem less good *on* the ice.

At its extreme, the process creates the category of professional cele-   8
brity, people "famous for being famous," so accomplished at being
celebrities that their original source of deity is forgotten. At the least,
it encourages all celebrities to learn the *skills* of the public person. How
to look good, how to sound modest and intelligent, funny and self-
deprecatory, anything you want. It's a celebrity's short-cut to the real
thing, but it works. Walter Cronkite *looks* trustworthy, Ronald Reagan
seems like a nice guy, Denis Potvin *sounds* intelligent; or is he only
articulate? Good enough at something to be a public person, or simply
a good public person? You'll never get close enough long enough to
know.

All around us are people anxious to help us look better. Not just flacks   9
and PR types but a whole industry of journalists, commentators,
biographers, award-givers. Ghost-writers who put well-paid words under
our names, then disappear; charity organizers, volunteers who give time
and effort so that "honorary presidents," and "honorary directors" may
look even better. Children in hospitals, old folks in old folks' homes
— we autograph their casts, shake their hands, make them props to our
generosity and compassion. And never far away, photographers and
cameramen record the event. It is the bandwagon momentum of
celebrityhood.

In the end, for us, is an image. After thousands of confused messages,   10
we cut through what is complex and render it simple. One image, concrete and disembodied. What agents call "Ken Dryden."

Recently, I asked an executive at an advertising agency to pretend   11
he was trying to persuade a client to use me as a commercial spokesman
for his company. We'd met two or three times, several years before,
so he knew me mostly as others do. He wrote the following memo to
his client: "Historically I know you have had some concerns about using
an athlete . . . either because of potential problems developing out of
their careers and public life, or due to simply their lack of availability.
I think Ken is quite different from the rest. He is known as a thoughtful,
articulate and concerned individual. I think it would go without saying
he would not participate in any endorsation unless he was fully committed to and satisfied with the product. (His Ralph Nader exposures
would assure that.) He is serious, respected and appears to be very much
his own man. I don't think we could ever consider using him in humorous
or light approaches (like Eddie Shack) unless it would be by juxtaposition with another . . . actor or player. He has good media presence. . . .

His physical presence is also commanding. He is quite tall and impressive. . . . Other encouraging things would be his intelligence and educational background. He would be more in tune with our target audience with his credentials as a college graduate (Cornell) and a fledgling professional person (law). Also, during production, I think this intelligence and coolness would help in case of commercial production as well as helping to keep costs under control due to mental errors. . . ."

12 So that's my image. Is it accurate? It doesn't matter. It's what people think, it presupposes how they'll react to me. And for the ad man and his client, how people will react is what matters.

13 If I don't like my image, I can do something about it. I can do things that are "good for my image." I can stop doing things that are "bad for my image." As actors remind us casually and often, I can do things to change my image. Is it too serious? If I run around the dressing room throwing water at the right moment, someone is bound to notice. A journalist with a deadline to meet and space to fill, a new angle, news — "Dryden misunderstood."

14 Want to be known as an antique collector? Collect an antique. A theatre-goer? Go. Once is enough. Tell a journalist, sound enthusiastic, and, above all, play well. Then stand back and watch what happens. Clipped and filed, the news spreads like a chain letter, to other journalists who don't have time to check it out. Presto, it's part of your standard bio. And your image.

15 If you substitute the word "reputation" for "image," as you might have done a few years ago, you'd have something quite different. A reputation is nothing so trifling or cynical. Like an old barge, it takes time to get going. It's slow and relentless, difficult to manoeuvre, even harder to stop. An image is nothing so solemn. It is merely a commercial asset, a package of all the rights and good-will associated with "Ken Dryden" — something I can sell to whomever I want.

16 But it's a sticky matter. For the image I'm selling is *your* image of me. The good-will, though it relates to me, is your good-will. Whatever commercial value there is in my name, my image, it's you who puts it there. You like me or trust me, and any prospective buyer of my image, anxious to put my name alongside his product, knows that and counts on it to make you buy his product. And you might, even though it may not be in your best interest. So by selling my name, I have perhaps taken your trust and turned it against you.

17 I did a commercial once, six years ago. I'd decided I never would,

but this one was different enough to start a web of rationalizations until I forgot the point and accepted. A fast-food chain was looking for a winter promotion; Hockey Canada, the advisory and promotional body, wanted a fundraiser and a way to deliver the message to kids and their parents that minor hockey can be approached and played differently. The idea was a mini-book done by Hockey Canada, then sold through the restaurant chain. I was to be a collaborator on the book, and its public spokesman. But after doing the TV and radio ads (for the book, but with a corporate jingle at the end), and seeing the point-of-purchase cardboard likenesses of me in the restaurant, I realized my mistake.

Since then, I have turned down endorsements for, among other things, 18 a candy bar ("The way I see it, a full body shot of you in the net, mask up, talking, then we draw in tight on your catching glove, you open it, the bar's inside. . . ."), a credit card company ("You may not know me without my mask, but. . . ."), and a roll-on deodorant that would also be promoted by several other people whose names begin with the sound "dry."

It's a game — an ad game, an image game, a celebrity game — that 19 no one really loses. Everyone needs someone to talk about — why not about us? Everyone needs heroes and villains. We earn a little money, get some exposure. The commercials are going to be done anyway. Besides, it doesn't last long. A few years and images change, celebrity cools, it's over. It all evens out.

But it doesn't. We all lose, at least a little. We lose because you think 20 I'm better than I am. Brighter than I am, kinder, more compassionate, capable of more things, as good at life as I am at the game. I'm not. Off the ice I struggle as you do, but off the ice you never see me, even when you think you do. I appear good at other things because I'm good at being a goalie; because I'm a celebrity; because there's always someone around to say I'm good. Because in the cozy glow of success, of good news, you want me to be good. It's my angle, and so long as I play well the angle won't change. I appear bright and articulate because I'm an athlete, and many athletes are not bright and articulate. "Like a dog's walking on his hind legs," as Dr. Johnson once put it, "it is not done well; but you are surprised to find it done at all."

But you don't believe that, just as I don't believe it about celebrities 21 I don't know. They're taller, more talented, more compassionate. They glitter into cameras and microphones, give each other awards for talent and compassion, "great human beings" every one. Wet-eyed I applaud, and believe. And all of us lose. You, because you feel less worthy than you are. Me, because once, when I was twenty-three years old and trying to learn about myself, I wanted to believe I was, or soon would be, everything others said I was. Instead, having learned much and grown older, I feel co-conspirator to a fraud.

22   Professional athletes do exciting, sometimes courageous, sometimes ennobling things, as heroes do, but no more than you do. Blown up on a TV screen or a page, hyped by distance and imagination, we seem more heroic, but we're not. Our achievement seems grander, but it isn't. Our cause, our commitment, is no different from yours. We are no more than examples, metaphors, because we enter every home; we're models for the young because their world is small and we do what they do.

23   A few years ago, Joe McGinniss, author of *The Selling of the President, 1968*, wrote a book called *Heroes*. It sketches McGinniss's own tormented trail from being *the youngest*, to *the highly acclaimed*, to *the former* — all before he was thirty. At the same time, he ostensibly searches for the vanished American hero. He talks to George McGovern and Teddy Kennedy, General William Westmoreland, John Glenn, Eugene McCarthy, author William Styron, playwright Arthur Miller — some of them heroes of his, all of them heroes to many.

24   But it's like chasing a rainbow. He finds that, as he gets closer, his heroes disappear. In homes and bars, on campaign trails, they're distinctly, disappointingly normal. Not wonderfully, triumphantly, down-to-earth normal, but up-close, drinking-too-much, sweating, stinking, unheroically normal. And for heroes, normal isn't enough. We are allowed one image; everything must fit.

25   The Greeks gave their gods human imperfections. In the modern hero, however, every flaw is a fatal flaw. It has only to be found, and it *will* be. Moving from celebrity to hero is like moving from a city to a small town. In a city, the camera's eye, though always present, is distant. In a small town, there isn't that distance. There's no place to hide.

26   "Whom the gods would destroy," Wilfrid Sheed wrote in *Transatlantic Blues*, "they first oversell." Superficially created, superficially destroyed — for the hero, for the celebrity, it all evens out. Except a heavy price is paid along the way. We all lose again. You, because, saddened and hurt by heroes who turn out not to be heroes at all, you become cynical and stop believing. Me, because I'm in a box. What is my responsibility? Is it, as I'm often told, to be the hero that children think I am? Or is it to live what is real, to be something else.

27   Recently, a friend asked me to speak to his college seminar. Near the end of two hours, we began to talk about many of these questions.

A girl raised her hand. She said that a year or two earlier, on the Academy Awards, she had seen Charlton Heston receive an award for his "humanitarian" work. Heston had made the point, the girl said, that thousands of volunteers had done far more than he, that they deserved the award.

I asked the class what that story told them about Charlton Heston. 28 That he's even modest, they decided. A few of the students laughed; then, one by one, several others joined in.

(1983)

The Writer's Subject

1. In the opening paragraph Dryden describes the guilt he feels in accepting favours. What is the source of this feeling, and where is it most explicitly discussed in this essay?

2. Why, according to Dryden, is an athlete's "off-ice performance" so important if he achieves celebrity status? (paras. 5-7)

3. Dryden argues that "celebrity" is really an image, "one image, concrete and disembodied." Who or what creates this image, and for what reasons? Is the presumed reader involved in this process in any way? (paras. 8-10)

4. According to Dryden, how difficult is it for celebrities to change their images? (paras. 13-15)

5. Why, after making one commercial, did Dryden decline to be further involved in the advertising of products? (paras. 17-18)

6. What loss is involved in accepting the "image" of the celebrity at face value? (paras. 20-26)

7. What does Dryden mean when he says "In the modern hero . . . every flaw is a fatal flaw" (para. 25)?

8. What is the dilemma of the professional athlete who attains celebrity? (para. 26)

9. What point is Dryden making with his concluding anecdote about Charlton Heston?

The Writer's Style and Strategy

1. How does Dryden's opening sentence prepare the reader for what is to follow?

2. What method of development does Dryden employ in paragraph 2 to demonstrate his assertion that professional athletes have grown accustomed to special treatment?

3. What effect does Dryden achieve by italicising "looks," "seems," and "sounds" in paragraph 8? By putting his own name, "Ken Dryden," in quotation marks in paragraph 10?

4. Why does Dryden provide actual excerpts from the advertising agency's description of him? (para. 11)

5. Why does Dryden use so many short sentences and fragments in paragraph 14? How does this particular paragraph contribute to the overall tone of the essay?

6. What figure of speech does Dryden use to illustrate the difference between "reputation" and "image"? (para. 15)

7. Why does Dryden repeat "game" so many times in the opening sentence of paragraph 19?

8. How would you characterize Dryden's attitude to his own celebrity? How is this attitude revealed throughout the essay?

Suggested Topics for Writing and Discussion

1. Discuss the distinctions Dryden perceives between "jocks," sports celebrities, and professional celebrities, providing your own examples. Can you think of any professional athlete who might fit into all of these categories?

2. Examine Dryden's discussion of the modern hero (note especially paragraphs 23-26). He says, ". . . for heroes, normal isn't enough"; do you agree with this view? What is the role of the hero in our society? Is heroism possible in modern times?

3. Choose an advertisement in print or on television that makes use of a celebrity from the worlds of sport or entertainment. What is the image of the celebrity that the advertisement conveys? How is that image intended to influence our view of the product? Indicate whether, in your opinion, the advertisement affirms Dryden's views about "the ad game."

Dangerous Determination

by Moira Farr

*"When I found so astonishing a power placed within my hands,
I hesitated a long time concerning the manner in which I should employ it. "*

Doctor Victor Frankenstein, from *Frankenstein,* by Mary Shelley

In an Angus Reid poll on new reproductive technologies conducted last 1
June, Canadians were asked, "Are you aware of anything that can be done
to human sperm in a lab to improve the chances of having a boy or a girl?"
Seventy-two percent answered no.

The pollsters stated in their report that "Canadians are not yet aware of 2
the application of new reproductive technologies in the area of genetic
screening. During the focus groups, it was discussion of sex preselection
and genetic engineering that produced the most future shock in the minds
of participants."

I hate to break it to 72 percent of Canadians, but future shock is not an 3
appropriate response to something that has been around for a long time
now. While we weren't paying much attention, sex determination (followed
by abortion of the wrong-sex fetus) and sex preselection — through new
reproductive technologies such as sperm separation, ultrasound, amniocentesis and chorionic villi sampling — have moved steadily from the realm
of sci-fi imagining to concrete reality. That makes it harder to deal with,
and more crucial that we do; the way old ideology allies with, and
thoroughly informs, new technology is nowhere more evident than in the
practice of gender preselection and determination, which has mostly been
advanced through strong cultural biases against females and, in the name
of population control, by way of eliminating them.

It's easy and obvious to express repugnance, and apparently most Cana- 4
dians do, at the thought of any technology being used to rid the population
of people with traits society happens to devalue, now or in the future

(femaleness, red hair, myopia, where would it end?). But the question of how to stop this from happening once we've said "Isn't it awful?" seems so fraught with ethical dilemmas that until recently, most of us, including feminists, haven't wanted to touch it with a ten-foot speculum.

5   Discussion of sex selection within the National Action Committee on the Status of Women (NAC) proved so contentious, only a passing reference to it appeared in the initial draft brief to the Royal Commission on New Reproductive Technologies (though the final document states that NAC is against sex selection and the licencing of clinics offering sex determination and preselection services). The brief presented by the Ontario Advisory Council on Women's Issues had 38 recommendations on new reproductive technologies, but not one of them dealt specifically with sex selection. The Toronto Women's Health Network, which also presented a brief, was under the impression that NAC would address it. In a newsletter, the network admitted it "heaved a mighty sigh of relief that someone else was including this issue in their written submission."

6   As NAC ultimately recognized, it is time for Canadian feminists to face the unpleasant and paradoxical aspects of this issue: is there a way to regulate sex-selection technology without infringing on abortion rights? Do laws emanating from patriarchal governments have any place in the realm of women's health? Some feminists would answer no to both those questions, opting in the case of sex selection for an ignore/disapprove-in-theory strategy. "No encouragement should be given to the uses of [sex selection] while recognizing that there is no way of enforcing a prohibition," argues sociologist Thelma McCormack in her 1988 article, "Public Policies and Reproductive Technology: A Feminist Critique."

7   Banning the technologies outright may not be the answer — they are capable of use for less sinister purposes than weeding out women, such as giving couples the choice of whether to bear children with sex-linked disorders, or allowing families to "balance" the sexes of their offspring — though ethical arguments against both of these uses have been advanced by disabled activists and feminists; and it should also be noted that these uses have never been, and aren't now, the chief focus for research and development of sex-selection techniques.

8   Nor can we stop people who want to determine the sex of their children from employing methods that include everything from intercourse positions to vaginal douches. But we can start to examine the implications of the whole concept as it gains ground in Canada; a completely hands-off approach, in my view, amounts to encouragement. At the very least, restrictions on the proliferation of high-tech commercial clinics offering sex preselection and determination services should be considered. India

and Denmark have enacted legislation that limits the use of sex-selection techniques. Germany, understandably sensitive about the eugenic capabilities of new reproductive technologies, is working on such legislation. One thing is certain; ignoring the problem won't make it go away. And misogyny, in the service of a patriarchal status quo, has a banal way of insinuating itself until we accept it as just part of life.

I first became aware of the notion of sex selection a couple of years ago, **9** through a television documentary about the uses of ultrasound and amniocentesis in India for determining gender and, in virtually all cases, aborting fetuses that show up female. After swearing loudly at the TV (an ineffective form of protest that is nevertheless therapeutic in the short-term), I did what I usually do when confronted with horrible things happening *out there*; felt gloomy and helpless, discussed it with a few friends and gradually let it slip from my consciousness.

But last July, I was reactivated while perusing, of all things, Rosemary **10** Sexton's society column in *The Globe and Mail*. Covering a benefit ball in aid of The Canadian Hemophilia Society, Sexton quoted a Toronto woman named Susan Bernstein, the mother of a hemophiliac boy (the disorder affects only males), who had gone to a gender preselection clinic in order to better the chances that her second child would be female. Of those using the clinic, Bernstein said, "I'm one of the few who wants a girl."

I called Bernstein. Yes, she had contacted a Toronto clinic (there is also **11** one in Calgary), a franchise of a U.S. outfit, operated by urologist Alan Abramovitch. Susan Cole wrote an article in the Toronto weekly *NOW* when this clinic opened in 1987. She reported in detail on the sex-preselection techniques offered: the Ericsson method, perfected and patented by American biologist Ronald Ericsson, involves separating sperm into those containing male and those containing female chromosomes (when being inseminated with female sperm, the woman must take the fertility drug Clomid); and for selecting girls, the Sephadex method (by now gathering cobwebs), which filters female sperm through a tube.

Bernstein hadn't decided whether to go through with the procedure, **12** which would cost about $1,800; she wasn't yet sure if the increased odds claimed for having the gender of choice were accurate. She was discussing her concerns with a geneticist at North York Hospital (in the end, she concluded that the clinic wasn't for her). She said that clients had to sign a consent form saying they would accept either gender, but she also came away with the impression that the majority of Abramovitch's clients wanted boys. (Unfortunately, I was unable to verify this with Abramovitch, who did not return repeated phone calls. However, I subsequently learned that

Ericsson's clinics operate in 46 countries in Europe, the U.S., Asia and Latin America; Ericsson himself has stated that in one study, 248 of 263 couples selected boys.)

13   I began doing further research, and found that feminists throughout the world have done their homework on this one. In articles with titles like "Sex Selection: From Here to Fraternity," and "The Endangered Sex," they point to the overwhelming preference for sons evident in the folklore and customs of virtually all cultures. They show how the new sex-selection technologies researched and developed in the past three decades have served that preference, in the most dramatic cases (in some areas of China, for instance), very clearly being seen as a "humane" alternative to female infanticide and neglect (sort of like the difference between public hanging and the electric chair, I guess).

14   Even in Europe and North America, where son preference is generally less pronounced than in some Third World countries, study after study indicates that the majority of people who use sex-preselection and determination techniques do so to ensure the birth of males — if not exclusively, then at least as their first child, which leads feminists to speculate on the psychological and social ramifications of entire nations filled with first-born sons and second-born daughters. In India, where sex selection has been so rampant that males have begun outnumbering females in the population, women have rallied and won (as of 1989) acts of parliament that seek to control prenatal sex determination.

15   Feminists have also revealed the repulsive ideas about global population control that have driven research into sex selection and other new reproductive technologies: Gena Corea, in *The Mother Machine,* outlines the ideas of a doctor in the seventies who gained widespread coverage for his proposal that a "boy-pill" be developed; no less a personage than Clare Booth Luce endorsed this notion in the *Washington Star.* Corea also writes about an organization called The Good Parents Group of Nutley, New Jersey (I don't make these things up, I just report them), which "supports the practice of aborting the female fetuses of the poor in India (it calls this 'Therabort') and has offered to help finance a model therapeutic termination clinic. Women found to be carrying male fetuses would not be permitted abortions at the clinics unless the fetus were defective."

16   Rationales for the development of artificial wombs have also been based on ideas about the expendability of women. A man named Edward Grossman argued in a 1971 article entitled "The Obsolescent Mother," that with this technology "geneticists could program-in some superior trait; sex preselection would be simple; women could be permanently sterilized." When this astonishing article was cited by Robin Rowland, in a chapter

she wrote in the book *Man-Made Women,* I thought at first, why highlight loony ideas from some grimy, marginal tract? Then I looked up the bibliography: Grossman's piece had appeared in *The Atlantic.* It's no wonder feminist writers have begun speaking about the unspeakable: femicide.

Absorbing all this stuff about the threat of female extermination, I thought 17 I might perhaps be getting a little overwrought; other feminists I spoke to didn't seem that concerned. And when I polled several hospitals, I was heartened to find that most Canadian doctors, such as Philip Wyatt, head of the clinical genetics centre at North York General Hospital, find the idea of gender selection "extremely distasteful." In other words, if you were to present yourself at a hospital ultrasound clinic today, and say "tell me the sex of my fetus so I can abort it if it's female," you probably would not be accommodated.

But that "distaste," Wyatt makes clear, isn't part of some formal, written 18 code of ethics. It's just a matter of how most individual Canadian doctors happen to feel. And one night last October, I heard an item on *As It Happens,* in which Dale Goldhawk interviewed a doctor, John Stevens of California, who had patented an ultrasound technique he said could determine the sex of a fetus at nine weeks. Stevens spoke obnoxiously about protecting his "intellectual property;" he whined about unfair treatment in Canada. He had advertised his services in the Vancouver community newspaper, *The Link,* aimed at the South Asian community in that city. There had been an uproar; Goldhawk also interviewed a member of a South Asian women's group, whose protest to the newspaper had caused the ads to be withdrawn by the publisher. And a doctor from Vancouver's Grace Hospital expressed disapproval and skepticism about Stevens' technique, and said that the American doctor had not been granted hospital privileges (he wouldn't reveal why) and so would not be able to set up a clinic in Vancouver.

I tuned in the next night, wondering if the "Talk Back" segment of the 19 show, where listeners phone in responses to what they've heard, would include some reaction to the Stevens item. It did, but not of the kind I'd anticipated. No outraged female voices that night. Both callers featured were men; one basically said: So what if this guy wants to operate in Canada, let him. The other seemed to have totally missed the point, harshly criticizing the piece for being biased because it didn't include an interview with a male member of the South Asian community.

Stevens got a lot of ink and air-time across Canada after that initial *As* 20 *It Happens* item. He thought it "authoritarian" of Canadians not to welcome him with open arms; it wasn't his responsibility, he argued, if clients went on to abort female fetuses his ultrasound technique revealed. In fact, he presented himself as a kind of hero, saving South Asian women from the shame of bearing daughters, which could result in violent reactions from angry husbands.

21   Charges of racist stereotyping ensued, and I wanted to find out what the situation really was in Canada's South Asian communities. I phoned Aruna Papp, director of a Toronto organization called South Asian Family Services, and asked her if it was true that some South Asian women were so pressured to bear sons that they would seek out sex-preselection and determination services, and abort female fetuses. "Yes!" She replied as though she'd been waiting a long time for someone to ask her that question. Could she cite examples? "Well, I've lived with it," she replied, with a mirthless laugh, and proceeded to tell me some very painful details of her life.

22   She was born in Pakistan, the first of six daughters in her family. (Her parents finally got a boy on try number seven.) "All my life, I tried to be the son I wasn't," she says, explaining that Hindu cultural and religious beliefs hinge salvation on the birth of sons. "It's only in middle age that I've been able to feel it's okay to be a woman." Now divorced, she says some South Asian women in Canada do suffer abuse at the hands of their husbands when they bear daughters. (She herself had two daughters, then "eventually" a son.) According to Papp, pregnant women in these communities in Canada often go "for a holiday" to India and Pakistan, where despite legislation, it is still easier to obtain access to sex-determination services and subsequent abortions, and return to Canada, female-fetus free.

23   Some feminists and doctors I've interviewed (including Philip Wyatt, who has referred people to the Abramovitch clinic, and says he has witnessed an East Indian woman having a "complete mental breakdown" when told she was carrying a female fetus) have argued that the pressure on South Asian women in Canada to bear sons, and the abuse that can result when they don't, is reason enough to allow, however warily, sex-preselection clinics to operate here.

24   But Aruna Papp is not the only woman of South Asian descent who doesn't want to see these clinics, or the kind Stevens proposes, starting up in Canada. Sharmini Peries, a board member of the South Asian Women's Group in Toronto, argues strongly against them. While she makes it clear that not *all* South Asian families value sons above daughters (she herself was never so pressured, and she and her husband have "two beautiful daughters"), she doesn't deny the existence of such bias. But she is adamant in her denunciation of Stevens and his ilk. "Doctor Stevens has a gun to our heads as surely as Marc Lepine did," she states, in no uncertain terms. The same position is held by South Asian women's groups in Vancouver.

John Stevens may for now be thwarted from coming to Canada to "make   25
a buck," as he puts it (though he is setting up a clinic in Buffalo, in hopes
that residents of southern Ontario will make the trip across the border).
But it isn't any law, or even the cry of outrage from South Asian women's
groups that is keeping him out; he simply hasn't yet been able to persuade
a Canadian hospital, for reasons that haven't been made public, to affiliate
with him (a licensing requirement of provincial colleges of physicians and
surgeons).

Are the medical profession's rules, regulations and codes of moral   26
conduct enough to safeguard against the future use of technologies in ways
that are injurious to the status of women? Medical licensing bodies in
Alberta and Ontario have apparently had no problem giving the go-ahead
to clinics offering sex-preselection services. Wouldn't it have been more
appropriate to have had some form of public debate about whether commercial operators of American franchises should be allowed to offer such
services in Canada *before* they were up and running? (I realize this is a time-
honoured approach to women's health matters: barrel ahead, then say
"oops, we goofed" when the casualties roll in.)

The Canadian Medical Association has stated to the commission that it   27
does not consider gender preselection or determination an ethical practice,
except in cases where there is a family history of a sex-linked disorder, and
CMA ethics-committee director Eike Kluge told me he'd like to see gender
clinics shut down. But the CMA is not a regulating body; it provides
guidelines, but can't enforce them.

I'm dismayed when feminists downplay the current availability and   28
appeal of sex-selection techniques in Canada, and make statements like
"This isn't India," as CARAL did in its brief to the royal commission. What
exactly is that supposed to mean? Regardless of their ethnic origin, the
people using sex-preselection clinics here are Canadians, availing themselves of services open to all in the great, free capitalist marketplace.

Beyond the issue of whether we should support the commercialization   29
of reproductive health services, we are dealing with a trend primarily
fuelled by the insidious power of hate-filled ideas; in this case, a patriarchal bias that utterly negates the value of daughters, blames females giving
birth to females for overpopulation, and suggests that beyond their reproductive capacities — which we may soon be able to wholly duplicate in labs
anyway — women have nothing of worth to contribute to the world. It
shouldn't matter what group such ideas are aimed at, or how widespread
we perceive their present influence to be. When James Keegstra taught high
school students that the world was run by a Jewish conspiracy, did we say
"What's the big deal? This isn't Nazi Germany. And it's only a few kids in

rural Alberta anyway." No. Media klieg lights shone on Keegstra until he was brought before a human-rights commission and then lost his job. When Philippe Rushton of the University of Western Ontario came forward with claims of a connection between race and intelligence, did we say, "Oh well, he's just one professor. Who cares?" No. People like David Suzuki denounced Rushton in public; CBC Radio's *Quirks and Quarks* won at least one award for a show that completely discredited his research.

30   As far as I know, neither Keegstra nor Rushton ever secured a platform for their views on the op/ed page of *The Globe and Mail*; but a Vancouver freelance writer named Graeme Matheson did, to argue in favour of eliminating women. In case you missed "What's Wrong With Choosing Your Baby's Sex?" here's one highlight: "Following the laws of supply and demand, as the numbers of available women fell, their value would go up ... grooms [in India] could eventually expect to pay for brides, raising the value of girls...."

31   Fortunately, a rebuttal to both the racism and sexism of Matheson's Nutleyite views appeared four days later, written jointly by NAC president Judy Rebick, Sharmini Peries, and Judy Vashti Persad of Women Working With Immigrant Women. Their response was stinging and eloquent, but I couldn't help thinking that if feminists had been more vigilant on this issue, it would have been their view that appeared first, and Matheson who would have been forced, if so moved, to write a letter to the editor.

32   In wading through the ethical dilemmas posed by sex selection, I've been torn between the stance of feminists such as Thelma McCormack who, though personally offended by the notion of sex selection, do not support *ad hoc* legislation on this or any other technology and the more interventionist approach favoured by some members of NAC and South Asian women's groups, who feel most threatened by sex-selection technology right now. Ultimately, all feminists want the same thing: holistic, woman-centred, woman-run health centres accessible to all, where care does not revolve around drugs and high-tech gizmos. We are a long way from such Utopian setups right now, but my feeling (and just like a woman, I'm trusting my intuition on this one) is that the existence of boy factories in Canada does nothing to further such a goal, especially when they appear to be aiding and abetting the victimization of women of a particular cultural group. At the very least, we should stand alongside these women and denounce such practices; call for government support services (shelters, education) to be channelled towards women who are physically and emotionally abused when they give birth to daughters (ditto for the daughters themselves); monitor and study legislation in other countries

(which regulates the use of sex-selection techniques, *not* access to abortion) and think about how it might be applied in Canada; finally, seriously consider the virulently sexist legacy of this use of technology, and its potential contribution to the future of humanity, before standing aside in good liberal fashion and watching it flourish.

It beats swearing at the TV. 33

(1991)

The Writer's Subject

1. Discuss the relevance to the essay of the epigraph from *Frankenstein*.

2. What evidence does Farr bring in support of her contention that the practice of gender preselection and determination "has mostly been advanced through strong cultural biases against females"? (para. 3)

3. What dilemmas face feminist groups in dealing with the issue of sex selection? (paras. 4-6)

4. What controls on sex preselection presently exist? Does Farr believe such controls should be introduced in Canada?

5. How, according to Farr, is research into reproductive technologies linked to "repulsive ideas about global population control"? (para. 15)

6. Farr observes that women of South Asian descent in Canada face certain pressures created by gender bias. What are these pressures?

7. What measures does Farr believe are needed to counter the threat to women posed by current sex-selection technology?

The Writer's Style and Strategy

1. Why does Farr begin her essay with an account of an opinion poll on new reproductive technologies?

2. Where does Farr make her own position on sex selection clear? How does her choice of language indicate her attitude to this technology and its advocates?

3. In the course of her essay Farr mentions James Keegstra and Philippe Rushton, neither of whom has anything to do with reproductive technology (paras. 29-30). What effect does she hope to create by alluding to these men?

4. Who is Farr addressing in her article? Point out details of diction and tone that suggest the kind of audience she has in mind.

5. How effective is the essay's closing sentence?

Suggestions for Writing and Discussion

1. In 1990 the Canadian government established a federal Royal Commission on New Reproductive Technologies. Find out what you can about the goals of the Commission, and about its reception by feminist groups.

2. Farr argues for regulation and control of sex-selection technology, and calls for the study of legislation governing such technology in other countries. Do you think that sex selection should be subject to government regulation?

3. What is your response to Farr's accusations of misogyny in current official handling of women's health issues?

My Wood

by E.M. Forster

A few years ago I wrote a book which dealt in part with the difficulties 1
of the English in India. Feeling that they would have had no difficulties
in India themselves, the Americans read the book freely. The more they
read it the better it made them feel, and a cheque to the author was
the result. I bought a wood with the cheque. It is not a large wood —
it contains scarcely any trees, and it is intersected, blast it, by a public
footpath. Still, it is the first property that I have owned, so it is right
that other people should participate in my shame, and should ask
themselves, in accents that will vary in horror, this very important question: What is the effect of property upon the character? Don't let's touch
economics; the effect of private ownership upon the community as a
whole is another question — a more important question, perhaps, but
another one. Let's keep to psychology. If you own things, what's their
effect on you? What's the effect on me of my wood?

In the first place, it makes me feel heavy. Property does have this 2
effect. Property produces men of weight, and it was a man of weight
who failed to get into the Kingdom of Heaven. He was not wicked,
that unfortunate millionaire in the parable, he was only stout; he stuck
out in front, not to mention behind, and as he wedged himself this way
and that in the crystalline entrance and bruised his well-fed flanks, he
saw beneath him a comparatively slim camel passing through the eye
of a needle and being woven into the robe of God. The Gospels all
through couple stoutness and slowness. They point out what is perfectly obvious, yet seldom realized: that if you have a lot of things you
cannot move about a lot, that furniture requires dusting, dusters require

servants, servants require insurance stamps, and the whole tangle of
them makes you think twice before you accept an invitation to dinner
or go for a bathe in the Jordan. Sometimes the Gospels proceed further
and say with Tolstoy that property is sinful; they approach the difficult
ground of asceticism here, where I cannot follow them. But as to the
immediate effects of property on people, they just show straightforward
logic. It produces men of weight. Men of weight cannot, by definition,
move like the lightning from the East unto the West, and the ascent
of a fourteen-stone bishop into a pulpit is thus the exact antithesis of
the coming of the Son of Man. My wood makes me feel heavy.

3   In the second place, it makes me feel it ought to be larger.

4   The other day I heard a twig snap in it. I was annoyed at first, for
I thought that someone was blackberrying, and depreciating the value
of the undergrowth. On coming nearer, I saw it was not a man who
had trodden on the twig and snapped it, but a bird, and I felt pleased.
My bird. The bird was not equally pleased. Ignoring the relation between us, it took fright as soon as it saw the shape of my face, and
flew straight over the boundary hedge into a field, the property of Mrs.
Henessy, where it sat down with a loud squawk. It had become Mrs.
Henessy's bird. Something seemed grossly amiss here, something that
would not have occurred had the wood been larger. I could not afford
to buy Mrs. Henessy out, I dared not murder her, and limitations of
this sort beset me on every side. Ahab did not want that vineyard –
he only needed it to round off his property, preparatory to plotting a
new curve – and all the land around my wood has become necessary
to me in order to round off the wood. A boundary protects. But – poor
little thing – the boundary ought in its turn to be protected. Noises
on the edge of it. Children throw stones. A little more, and then a little
more, until we reach the sea. Happy Canute! Happier Alexander! And
after all, why should even the world be the limit of possession? A rocket
containing a Union Jack, will, it is hoped, be shortly fired at the moon.
Mars. Sirius. Beyond which. . . . But these immensities ended by sad-
dening me. I could not suppose that my wood was the destined nucleus
of universal dominion – it is so very small and contains no mineral
wealth beyond the blackberries. Nor was I comforted when Mrs.
Henessy's bird took alarm for the second time and flew clean away from
us all, under the belief that it belonged to itself.

5   In the third place, property makes its owner feel that he ought to do
something to it. Yet he isn't sure what. A restlessness comes over him,

a vague sense that he has a personality to express — the same sense which, without any vagueness, leads the artist to an act of creation. Sometimes I think I will cut down such trees as remain in the wood, at other times I want to fill up the gaps between them with new trees. Both impulses are pretentious and empty. They are not honest movements towards money-making or beauty. They spring from a foolish desire to express myself and from an inability to enjoy what I have got. Creation, property, enjoyment form a sinister trinity in the human mind. Creation and enjoyment are both very very good, yet they are often unattainable without a material basis, and at such moments property pushes itself in as a substitute, saying, 'Accept me instead — I'm good enough for all three.' It is not enough. It is, as Shakespeare said of lust, 'The expense of spirit in a waste of shame': it is 'Before a joy proposed; behind, a dream.' Yet we don't know how to shun it. It is forced on us by our economic system as the alternative to starvation. It is also forced on us by an internal defect in the soul, by the feeling that in property may lie the germs of self-development and of exquisite or heroic deeds. Our life on earth is, and ought to be, material and carnal. But we have not yet learned to manage our materialism and carnality properly; they are still entangled with the desire for ownership, where (in the words of Dante) 'Possession is one with loss'.

And this brings us to our fourth and final point: the blackberries. 6

Blackberries are not plentiful in this meagre grove, but they are easily 7 seen from the public footpath which traverses it, and all too easily gathered. Foxgloves, too — people will pull up the foxgloves, and ladies of an educational tendency even grub for toadstools to show them on the Monday in class. Other ladies, less educated, roll down the bracken in the arms of their gentlemen friends. There is paper, there are tins. Pray, does my wood belong to me or doesn't it? And, if it does, should I not own it best by allowing no one else to walk there? There is a wood near Lyme Regis, also cursed by a public footpath, where the owner has not hesitated on this point. He has built high stone walls each side of the path, and has spanned it by bridges, so that the public circulate like termites while he gorges on the blackberries unseen. He really does own his wood, this able chap. Dives in Hell did pretty well, but the gulf dividing him from Lazarus could be traversed by vision, and nothing traverses it here. And perhaps I shall come to this in time. I shall wall in and fence out until I really taste the sweets of property. Enormously stout, endlessly avaricious, pseudo-creative, intensely selfish, I shall weave upon my forehead the quadruple crown of possession until those nasty Bolshies come and take it off again and thrust me aside into the outer darkness.

(1926)

The Writer's Subject

1. Why does Forster begin his essay with an oblique reference to his novel *Passage to India?*

2. What does Forster mean by the phrase "men of weight" (para. 2)?

3. Summarize the four points which Forster makes about the effect of property. Are these points all of the same kind?

4. How does Forster demonstrate the absurdity of the property owner's attempt to lay claim to property, and of his desire for expansion? (para. 4)

5. Why, according to Forster, are the desires to chop down or to plant trees "not honest movements towards money-making or beauty" (para. 5)?

6. Explain what Forster means by saying "creation, property, enjoyment form a sinister trinity in the human mind" (para. 5).

7. Why does Forster give such prominence to the public footpath in Lyme Regis? (para. 7)

8. Who are the "nasty Bolshies" that Forster refers to in his closing sentence? Why does he say that they will throw him "into the outer darkness"?

9. While Forster restricts his discussion to his wood, he may be commenting on broader issues. What might these be?

The Writer's Style and Strategy

1. What is Forster's tone in the opening paragraph, and how does he establish it? Is it maintained throughout the essay? Discuss the appropriateness of Forster's tone to his topic.

2. How does Forster narrow his discussion of the very large topic of property?

3. Forster uses many allusions in this brief essay. What use does he make of the allusions to the Gospels (to the Rich Man in *Matthew* 19:24; to the story of Dives and Lazarus in *Luke* 16:19-31)? To the story of Ahab (in *I Kings* 21:17-29)? To Canute and Alexander? To Tolstoy and Dante?

4. Trace Forster's references to the blackberries. What purpose do these references serve? Comment on his use of a single-sentence paragraph to introduce the subject of the blackberries.

5. Comment on Forster's final sentence, its meaning, structure and tone.

Suggested Topics for Writing and Discussion

1. What is the effect of ownership on you?

2. Forster says that he may one day "wall in and fence out." Discuss one or two examples of walls used to bound international "properties" (e.g., the Great Wall of China, Hadrian's Wall, the Berlin Wall), and say what the makers of the walls were hoping to wall in and fence out.

3. Forster uses very specific, concrete, and personal details to write on a highly abstract subject. Using Forster's method, write an essay on an abstraction which interests you (e.g., identity, loyalty, education, community, faith).

Life & Death in Ontario County
by Hugh Graham

*A profile of John Beedon, farm labourer,
of the Township of Reach*

1   I was seven in the winter of 1959 when my parents and I went to look at a farm house near Greenbank, about twenty-five miles north of Whitby, Ontario. It was occupied by a ferretish old man with faded blue eyes and his wife and their sixty-year-old son. They lived in one large room and my mother discovered that they slept under coats upstairs. Everything they had was old and worn out. The ceiling was low and buckled, the blistered wallpaper was from the twenties, and the air thick and dry with stove heat. Puzzles of Scottish castles had been framed and hung on the wall. Everything that could be saved was stacked in another room behind a door closed and stuffed with rags.

2   We returned several times that winter, sometimes after dark, and entering that house was to cross into a warm and dim place that was otherworldly and unsettling. The son, a lumbering giant of a man, shaved in front of us beside the stove in his undervest and suspenders using a cracked mirror, a straight razor, and a basin with steaming water from a blackened kettle. The old man sat idly in a rocking chair among other chairs around the stove with flattened torn cushions. The old woman was the only one who was moving, large and bird-like, giving me and my friends candy and pictures. Out in the back, on the unfinished planks of the woodshed wall there was a tattered collage of pasted-up magazine illustrations that included a painted thirties advertisement of an old countryman in a suit playing the violin. The evening light in the picture seemed to be like the light in their house, the night sky was the colour of his suit, and for a long time I was certain that the fictional fiddler was the old man. Beyond the woodshed a track through

the snow led to a hand pump. In the depths of that hard winter when they were snow-bound, food had to be brought to them from the village. I had never seen such people. My mother explained to me that it was poverty. They maintained the land for a beef farmer, their name was Beedon, and I later realized they were the forgotten; tenants of a type commonly associated with the American south.

When we took possession and began work on the farm house, they had   3 moved down two concession lines to a solid ancient fieldstone house on high and bald melancholy farm land. The old man, John Beedon, and his son Alf put in our garden, built livestock fencing, and taught us how to manage our woodlot and sixty acres of pasture. And now we seemed to be visiting in the new place, where they had brought the same heavy smell of mildew and stove heat, just as we had visited the old. Mrs. Beedon still had a miniature museum she had created in an aquarium that displayed a growing and changing collection of postcards, dolls, doll furniture, miniature flags, and buttons, which she called her "funny box."

I had been afraid of them at first. They were crude, spoke with "don't"   4 and "ain't." Beedon was slight, bantam-like, testy, and irascible, and the son, haunted and moronic, towered over his parents. The three looked alike, with sharp eyes and big noses and thin flat mouths and the two men had abscess scars in the right cheek, which gave them a look of wild inhaling. One winter Mrs. Beedon was talking to my mother, when, in a moment of womanly confidence, steadying her thick glasses, she pulled down a black stocking and then pulled up a leg of long underwear and showed a faint blue mark where the old man had given her a kick.   5

The son, Alf, as Beedon told us outright, was dim, subnormal, while Alf himself, with his monumental craggy face and deepset grey eyes seemed to agree with equanimity. All his life he had held menial jobs and worked with his father in labouring or picking up highway tree-trimmings in a horse and wagon for Ontario Hydro. Alf spoke with a solemn nodding expertise about cutting post tops to a slant to keep out rot and expounded with an air of grave foreboding on the common details of maintaining the property. He had a high hearse-like black '48 Dodge and at every opportunity he opened the hood to display the engine with my father listening and nodding politely while trying to get on with things. But when his father was discussing the plans for the day with mine, and Alf attempted to add a detail, the old man snapped, "There, we heard enough from you," with a swift short kick in the shin.

On weekends Alf drove home from a cleaning job in Milton and spent   6 the time with a case of twenty-four in front of the television mildly sloshed; the program, which he highly recommended, was *Popeye*. "I've courted every girl in Reach Township," he told us, with the implication he'd turned them all down, but it was when my mother hired him to drive her into Port Perry to do shopping that he talked. My mother, who was easily bored, was impressed with his skill as a raconteur as he told his stories with reverence and amazement, saying he'd been overseas during the war and that an English girl had slapped him for proposing they go to Petticoat Lane. His father told us flatly that Alf had never been out of the country and had been turned down for the service "because of bad nerves." My mother later gathered that Alf had taken stories he'd heard from braggarts, farmers, and servicemen, and honed them into his own imaginary past.

7   In the summers when I got to know the old man, he was eighty and cycling six miles a day to our place over hilly gravel concession roads. I recall him always in indigo twill trousers with suspenders, a light-coloured fedora he never took off, hawk-like without teeth and with alert pale eyes that never seemed to change; an expression of amused, open-mouthed, almost delectable outrage, as if he had caught you doing something he had predicted you would do. In those summers I was a city kid with no friends in the country and I spent my days with the old man. He taught me how to build livestock fencing, to use an axe and a scythe, to cut and trim timber and till a garden. He worked slowly and with certainty and economy. He used an axe gently and perfectly, everything he had was immaculate and shopworn, his tools white with wear, fastidiously sharp and clean. He had nothing new, but rather items that seemed to be part of the derelict inside of our barn; rags, pegs, bottles, wire, and a jealously guarded enamel drinking ladle. For stretches of summers running, my only life was his, as we replaced rods of fencing in hot dry pasture ringing with crickets. He stretched fence wire by hand, strand by strand with a crowbar, set posts in straight, dugout stones four feet in the ground, planted solid anchor posts, and cut exact and tightly notching brace poles. With a pale wild eye he could line up posts so that lengthwise they appeared as one from here to the horizon. I stayed with him while he ate his gum-soft lunch out of the same old Wonderbread bag and drank Pepsi (Coca-Cola was "poison") in the noon shade of the driving shed.

8   He and his family had lived dirt poor with no plumbing in the same kinds of houses for close to sixty years. He had visited no city since he'd been to Toronto in 1908. He had gone to see the Exhibition, then a celebrated agricultural fair, disliked the city, condemned the fair, which was nowhere near as good as the one in Lindsay, and went home quickly never to return. His time was that of teams and traces; he operated no machinery, would not even touch a tractor. He had no use for television, found football ridiculous, could just read headlines and sign his name, and kept their

money in cash at the post office. But all his life seemed to have been lived in a struggle to prove he was, or had been, right. He argued tooth and nail with my mother about putting in the garden and was always vindicated; when my father's car arrived on weekends, Beedon looked up with a smile, ready to show him his errors. The old man's tales were of cleverness and cheating, triumphant accounts of meanness and dishonesty and in these he seemed to stand alone in a world of rural propriety. Where the conversation of the farm wives and close-mouthed farmers that we knew was filled with righteous anodynes, tact, and caution, Beedon's eyes lit up at recollections of incompetence and shabbiness. Perhaps he had nothing to lose by such stories; he seemed to have fought with every employer he had ever had; he walked out on fence-building jobs because the farmer insisted on hanging the wire upside down. His suspicions of malice were often senseless and extravagant, for example, that a shovel of ours found in the pond had been thrown there by a man we hardly knew, for spite.

We on the other hand were city middle-class, devoid of the natural suspi-   9
cion of farmers, and since we had the money to pay him what he wanted without welshing, he seemed, for that practical reason, to respect us — even if he always told us we were wrong, or was amused by our ignorance and capriciousness. After my father hung a stark contemporary conceptual piece over the mantle, the old man smiled toothlessly and said, "What you doing with a picture of a shovel?" His affections were indeed practical and determined his loyalty, and yet when local painters accidentally set our house on fire, he ran in alone through dense smoke and tried to drag out the furniture before he was pulled out by firemen.

He had lived and worked longer in the county than almost anyone and   10
yet for all his stories almost no one seemed to know him. In turn, the world he described seemed to have passed, a spectral place devoid of witnesses where he fought two men to court a woman, where he had been able single-handedly to lift a full-grown heifer into the back of a wagon. When he'd dart in laughing and jab at the tail of my pony just to make him kick, he seemed very much of another age. Likewise, his entertainment was in talking: in denials, claims, and tales; the brush with death riding the famous long slope at Sandy Hook after his bicycle chain broke; a renowned giant elm near Goodwood, which he said had yielded seventy-odd cords of wood in its death, and then regretted, "I never did get down to see that tree."

The stories he told were redolent of the abandoned farm houses that were   11
scattered around Greenbank, of suicide, fraud, and arson, of vandalized, trashed, melancholy places where frozen overalls still hung by the door over boots ghosted with dust and among the mites and mildew of a medicine cabinet where you could find a dusky tin of brilliantine, still viscous and

marked by the scoop of fingers; where the son of a man whose farm had
a broken dam decorated with a cow skull had died drinking strychnine.
Those very places that smelled of mildew and damp plaster but hadn't fallen
to dereliction were the places lived in by Beedon and his family. In a house
rented in Uxbridge the attic had been closed and several nights running he
heard a heavy chain dragged the length of the house across the floor above.
In the daytime he investigated and found nothing; it was bare and completely sealed, but a few days later he learned that two years before, the butcher
who lived there had hanged himself. There was a story of the thirties that
began with a column of smoke he had seen over near Uxbridge and ended
with the owner of a blazing house tearing out of the front door with a baby
carriage draped for protection with heavy blankets. And what made Beedon
look at you as if he dared you to believe anyone could be courageous or
honest, was the fact that the carriage had concealed no baby but four
expensive folded suits. The implication, of course, was insurance fraud.

12   After five years I could scarcely remember the time when I had been
afraid of him and now he was the first person the prospect of whose death
made me sad. By then I knew he didn't mind me, and his gone world, which
seemed to live on in the stillness before thunderstorms and the dry decay
of barns, had become mine as well, a ghost world of Reach Township which
followed me back to the city and to school. He had become a major figure
in my life and in my imagination.

13   When my father hired an old farm couple from Quebec to live and run
a mechanized operation on our place, it now seems we were pushing
Beedon on as the world was pushing him. While he was still working for
us, I remember the two old men talking in lawn chairs and my mother's
remark that they were rivals and fundamentally disliked each other. Indeed,
he moved on but even the riot of the sixties and what appeared to be relentless and ineluctable change were well on their way before I saw the last
of him, and one spring when he didn't come round to the farm, it seemed
only inevitable. We visited him and I saw him pale as parchment, small
and hatless in his rocker. Then they were gone from that house too; the
world seemed determined to move them on.

14   About eighty-five years ago, John Beedon, the eleventh or twelfth son
of a Wiltshire game warden, came to Canada as a Barnardo Boy; one of
the thousands of orphans sponsored by the Barnardo homes in England to
populate the Empire from a pool of unskilled labour that Great Britain
couldn't feed. This was how he had made his way to his first job turning
over vegetable gardens with a horse and plough in Uxbridge, Ontario, in
1906. He also did the ornamental flower-bed that spelled C.N.R. at the
Uxbridge railway station. But it was in the network of walking and wagon-

hopping itinerant farm labour that he met and courted and married a hawk-faced woman, his female doppelganger, a farmer's daughter from a remote hamlet at the end of the Marsh Hill road. Even when Beedon was old, you could see from his arms and hands, elongated and burly for his small frame, that his life had been the eternity of ploughing, pitching hay, managing horses and cattle, and all the other endless and thankless work of a time now unknown to us.

Two daughters who disappeared seemed to us long gone and mythical. 15 "Oh, she was wayward," they had spoken in gruff euphemism of one who had run off with a variety of men, perhaps in the twenties or thirties, and whom they had never seen since. Cannier, perhaps more worldly than the first, the other had married a lawyer in Whitby and, apart from meager financial help, refused to acknowledge her parents, having risen into a middle-class town world where such people as her parents supposedly didn't exist. So the Beedons and their son lived on in a world without clan or extension, where the old woman noted, remembered, and honoured every birthday in every neighbourhood they moved to. With the mechanization of farms and the reduction of country labour after the war, the old man took to his bicycle and travelled the same circuits tending gardens, and in that quiet time when we first went to Port Perry, many of the handsome gardens around the commodious Victorian villas would have been his work.

In the summer of 1970 I was nineteen, they were long gone, and with 16 education and travel, childhood had become remote, when I heard somewhere that they were still alive and living on in another old house, inevitably in Ontario County — this time in the village of Kinsale. It would be their last. I went down with a couple of friends and we found a listing frame peaked Victorian farm house covered in insulbrick and we knocked. The old woman, vague and almost blind now, told us to come in and again there was the hot odour of old plaster and stove heat I had smelled twelve years before. She had no idea who any of us were and told us to sit down and began without comment to give us tea. I asked her where Beedon was, and she waved a massive work-hardened hand dismissively in front of her face and croaked, "They killed him. He's gone. They took him away two months ago." She couldn't explain more than that. She couldn't remember either of the farms where we had known them, and apologized and directly began to recall her youth in Marsh Hill at the turn of the century. We spoke to a neighbour who confirmed that Beedon had died in hospital two years before, and not two months, and if we wanted to know more we should wait till Alf came home.

Alf came by and Mrs. Beedon offered us dinner with her son. Close to 17 seventy, he was just as massive, still a bachelor but had whitened and was a different man. He jobbed at country fairs and came home irregularly with money for his mother. He ate a corn cob with giant forearms on the oilcloth and spoke with a sober hardness as if finally wakened by the death of his father. "We always lived in the houses like this, old houses, every damn one built the same way, four-square, mortise and tenon joints, the same roof joists." But he remembered me and even my best friend who was with me: "the little yellow-haired fella." Our place, which had remained in my mind their original place, he remembered tersely as "the place with the pond" — turning out to be but one of myriad tenancies. I asked him about his father and he said, "They said he died, but they took him in the hospital and cut off his leg, they killed him." As we left, I saw him watching us leave, shadowed and headless behind a drawn blind.

18   In a year I came back to that house in the winter, the insulbrick had been half stripped off and the door was answered by downtrodden people I had never seen. A young and toothless woman told me the old woman and her son were gone. Mrs. Beedon had died, and he had been committed to a mental hospital, but they believed the gravestone of Beedon and his wife had been erected in the cemetery at the next concession road. In blowing snow that formed wells around the monuments I found no stone, not even an unmarked plot.

19   When they disappeared, the Beedons had lived in twenty-two houses in a single county since he had arrived in 1906. Unmarked in death, John Beedon, his wife, and son left almost no impression either among those who knew them or had hired the old man; few could recall them well, fewer could really distinguish him in their memories of the gone world into which he had dissolved like a footprint in pasture.

(1990)

The Writer's Subject

1. Mr. Beedon does not seem a friendly or likeable figure; yet the writer says that "he was the first person the prospect of whose death made me sad" (para. 12). Why should Graham as a child have been so drawn to the old man?

2. Why does Graham describe the Beedons' home in such detail? (paras. 1-2)

3. What does Graham mean by calling the Beedons "tenants of a type commonly associated with the American south"? (para. 2)

4. What are the most noticeable features of Mr. Beedon's character? What qualities or characteristics are given particular emphasis?

5. In what ways is Beedon shown to be a man very much of another age?

6. What does Graham mean by calling Beedon's wife "his female doppelganger"? (para. 14)

7. What kind of man is Beedon's son Alf? How does he change as he grows older?

The Writer's Style and Strategy

1. Early in the essay Graham observes that no one seemed to know the Beedons — "they were the forgotten." Where in the essay is this idea given most effective expression?

2. What use does Graham make of physical description in his portrait of the Beedons? Which details does he emphasize?

3. It is clear that Graham himself has sympathy for the Beedons. In what ways does he seek to awaken the reader's sympathy also?

4. Why does the writer draw attention at several points in the essay to his own age?

5. What is the importance of the stories told by Alf (para. 6) and by his father (para. 11)? What do these stories contribute to our understanding of the kind of people they are?

Suggested Topics for Writing and Discussion

1. To Graham the Beedons represent a way of life driven out by change and progress. Offer your own experience of this kind of awareness, perhaps in the form of a portrait of an elderly relative or acquaintance.

2. Graham shows the intimate connection between the Beedons and their dwellings. Using the home of someone you know well, describe how that home reflects the character of its occupant.

3. Graham describes how Beedon "came to Canada as a Barnardo boy" (para. 14). Find out what you can about the Barnardo homes, and about the "home children" who were brought to Canada from Britain in large numbers at the end of the 19th century and the beginning of the 20th.

Thoughts on a Shirtless Cyclist, Robin Hood and One or Two Other Things

by Russell Hoban

1   The other day when I was going to my office in the morning I saw a man without a shirt riding a bicycle in circles at a traffic light and shouting unintelligibly. It was a chilly morning, so he must have been uncomfortable without a shirt on, and he wasn't a hippy. He looked like a workman, and he didn't look drunk. So it seemed to me that he must be having a mental breakdown of some sort.

2   I thought about it for a while, and then it occurred to me that maybe the man's mind wasn't breaking down. Maybe what had broken down was the system of restraints and conventions inside him that ordinarily made him keep his shirt on and not shout. That system, I think, is part of what could be called an inner society. The inner society has its ballrooms and bedrooms and kitchens, its shops and offices, its narrow alleys and its open places, its figures of authority and rebellion, of usage and surprise, love and hate, should and should not, is and isn't. As in the outer society, some things are done and some are not.

3   When I had thought that far, my next thought was that on that particular day man's inner society was rioting. The windows of the shops were being smashed, the offices were being deserted, and he was doing what he was doing.

4   My next thought was that the previous thought had been wrong: he was doing what he was doing because there were no rioters and no provision for riot in his inner society, and so there was no one for the job but him. His trouble, perhaps, was that his inner society was not suffi-

ciently different from the outer one: too many of the same things were done and not done. And having no interior colleague to whom he could assign the task or delegate the responsibility, he himself had to take off his shirt and ride in circles at a traffic light and shout. And it must have taken something out of him to do it.

Now my inner society, on the other hand, has always had that shirtless 5 shouting cyclist in it. I know him of old as I know myself, even though I hadn't given him much thought until I actually saw him in the outer world. So it isn't likely that I shall ever have to go out into the street and do that myself; he's always there to take care of it for me. There may, of course, come a day when I shall riotously put on a bowler hat and a neat black suit, buy a tightly furled umbrella, and mingle in wild silence with brokers in the city. One never knows what will come up.

Which brings me, by cobweb bridges perhaps invisible to the naked 6 eye, to a book I threw into an incinerator.

The book was *Robin Hood*. My edition, an American one, was bound 7 in what I think was Lincoln Green. I don't remember who it was that wrote that particular version of the story, but it had large black type and was illustrated by an artist named Edwin John Prittie with line drawings and paintings in full colour. I used to read that book up in an old wild-cherry tree, and it was the cosiest reading I can remember.

But there came a time when I got to be eighteen years old, and there 8 was a war, and I was going off to be a soldier, and it seemed to me that I had better stop being a child and be a man altogether. So I took *Robin Hood* and pitched it into the incinerator. It's a crime that I am driven to confess from time to time, as I do now.

When I came home from the war and found myself, surprisingly, 9 alive and having to go on with the business of growing up, I looked for that same edition that I had thrown away. Years later I found a copy. I haven't it with me now; it is gone again, lost in a removal. But I remember how it was when I held it in my hands again. There were all the pictures looking just as good as ever, and that whole dappled word-world of sun and shade with nothing lost whatever — Little John and Robin fighting on the plank bridge with their quarterstaves; the hateful Sheriff of Nottingham in his arrogance and his scarlet cloak; the beautiful Maid Marian and all the merry men in Lincoln Green; Robin in the *capul hide*, standing over the corpse of Guy of Gisborne. I've always liked the sound of the words *capul hide*: the skin of a horse, with the eyes of a man looking out through the eyeholes in the head — the skin of a dead beast hiding a live man, magical and murderous.

10   Obviously Robin Hood is a part of my inner society and has never stopped being in my thoughts, but it's only recently that I've become fully aware of how much he is to me, of how far the theme of that child's book has gone beyond childhood. Now as I think about him Robin Hood grows deeper and darker and stronger. Constantly he takes on new shadowy identities, and in his *capul hide* he sometimes evokes the dancing *Shaman* in the drawing on the cave wall at Les Trois Frères, sometimes Frazer's *Rex Nemorensis*, doomed King of the Wood, the killer waiting for his killer' who will be next king.

11   In the absence of my found-and-lost-again edition I bought Roger Lancelyn Green's Puffin *Robin Hood*. On the title page was a stanza from the Alfred Noyes poem, *Sherwood*, and it gave me gooseflesh when I read it:

Robin Hood is here again: all his merry thieves
Hear a ghostly bugle-note shivering through the leaves. . .
The dead are coming back again, the years are rolled away
In Sherwood, in Sherwood, about the break of day.

12   I wanted it to be Sherwood again, about the break of day. I turned the pages, reading with impatience. But it wasn't the same. This book started with Robin Hood's birth, and I didn't want that, I wanted the opening that had been in the cherry-tree book of childhood, and it wasn't there and I couldn't remember it.

13   Then, on page 19 I found it — the incident in which the Sheriff of Nottingham and his men capture a serf who had killed a royal deer. The beginning of my book came back to me then, just like Proust's Combray — all at once and clear and vivid. 'Saxon hind' was what my book called the serf, and I could see the scene again as it first came to me through the passing leaves, the prisoner trussed up on the sledge like meat, helpless, rolling his eyes in terror as the Sheriff's foresters drag him to his death. Robert Fitzooth, not yet Robin Hood the outlaw, encounters the group and questions the Sheriff's men. The Chief Forester taunts him about the power of the bow he carries, doubts that such a stripling can wield such a weapon. Fitzooth shows his strength and skill with a long shot that brings down one of the King's deer. And with that he has fallen into the forester's trap — like the prisoner, he has forfeited his life with that shot. The Sheriff's men attempt to take him, but he kills some of them and frees the 'Saxon hind.' They escape into the greenwood, and the outlaw life of Robin Hood begins.

14   The light and the air of that first encounter have never left my mind,

and the sounds of the forest, the hissing of the sledge runners over the grass, the rattle of weapons, the shouts, the whizzing arrows. It is the metaphorical value of that action that has made it so memorable for me: the free and active wild self of the forest, armed and strong, freed the bound and helpless captive self and so became the outlaw self I recognized within me — the self indwelling always, sometimes kept faith with, sometimes betrayed.

Free and savage, the Robin Hood who has always walked the pathways 15 of my inner society has been exemplary — a standard and a reminder to the unfree and unsavage boy that I was, who lusted for that green-wood world: excellence was the price of Robin Hood's freedom, his untamedness, and his power. He was able to be what he was only because of his matchless skill; he was the archer who could shoot farther and truer than any other; he was a hero and a winner who had a thing that he could do better than anybody else.

Heroes who can do something well are still considered necessary for 16 children. And if many of today's books for grownups offer us a selection of the infirm and the awkward, the losers who lap up defeat like chicken soup ladled out by a Jewish-mother kind of fate, we need those too: the composite hero of the collective, cumulative, juvenile-adult imagination has got to have some antiheroism about him in order to be complete. Certainly anything that closes the gap between the real and the ideal makes the hero more useful for everyday reference — and here I can't help thinking about the god Krishna, who disported himself with fifty or sixty cowgirls at a wonderful party out on the meadow that lasted many nights, during which he made all the cowgirls think he was making love with each of them. But despite his divine powers — or because of them — he did it all with his mind, which I think is charming. A hero no better than the reader, however, will scarcely last a lifetime. And I think that heroes who excel and win all kinds of good things are the best kind. Myself, I can't use a mythology in which there is nothing to win and consequently nothing to lose. I have to have something to try for, and the more excellence I can manage the better I feel. In that respect Robin Hood has been a great help to me all my life.

Reading the Roger Lancelyn Green version, I realize that there was 17 a great deal more to the story and the archetypes than I had thought before. In my edition Marian was simply called Maid Marian, and nothing more was said about it. Once or twice as I grew older and more cynical I may have questioned the validity of her title. She was, after all, presumably sleeping rough like everyone else in the outlaw band, and Robin being her lover, what could have been more natural than for them to sleep together? But Green spells it out and no mistake: Marian *was* a maid; she kept her virginity the whole time that she and Robin lived together in the forest. Although she had pledged herself to him the marriage was not to be consummated until the return of Richard the Lion-Hearted, the true and lawful king.

18   Robin Hood has no other woman that I ever heard of in any of the stories. So I have to think of him as celibate, as putting off the assumption of a full male role, as being less than a complete, grown-up man. He is asexual and pure, mercurial, airy almost, Ariel -like – a natural innocent, murderous but sweet-natured, light and quick. And he shares with Marian that mystical virtue that chastity confers, so useful for catching unicorns. The male and the female elements, the *yang* and the *yin* of this legend, are allied but not conjoined at the peak of their vigour, and when later a legitimate union is formed, they decline.

19   Robin Hood is more often with Little John than with Maid Marian. He and his giant companion are like a clean-cut, somewhat prim ego and id. They continually test and prove themselves, tempting fate, daring all comers, looking for trouble, never content with safety and boredom. They fight with quarterstaves at their first meeting; they quarrel from time to time; they rescue each other from capture; they compete with each other against the terrible strong beggar with potent quarterstaff and the bag meal that blinds the usually cunning Robin. And so they stay young and jolly until King Richard, the lawful ruler, the inevitable mature authority, returns.

20   And with that return Robin Hood is absorbed into grownupness and legitimacy. He is pardoned, and no more an outlaw; he is married, and no more a child-man. His best men are called into the service of King Richard. Robin Hood's power is drained off into the lawful self; the puissant youth becomes the waning man.

21   I'm no scholar, and I have no idea of the origin of the legend that is Robin Hood. What is inescapable is that the stone of the legend is worn into shape by the sea of human perception and need that continually washes over it. Legends, myth and fantasy both ask and tell us how life is, and there seems to be a strong need in us to think about the theme that is in *Robin Hood*: the absorption into law and order of that mysterious, chthonic, demiurgic power that we vitally need but cannot socially tolerate. We regret the loss of it and we rationalize the necessity

of that loss. We say to it, 'Yes, be there. But lose yourself in us at the proper time. Grow up.' But I wonder what the proper time is, and I wonder if the loss is necessary. And I wonder what growing up is. And I wonder whether young people now are not validly reconsidering and reshaping that theme, reclassifying it as well, so that the values assigned are no longer the same as those agreed upon until now. Maybe what we've always called growing up is sometimes growing down. It bears thinking about.

Robin Hood is only one development of that theme; there must be 22
many others. In *Great Expectations*, for instance, Magwitch, the outlaw self, is content to subsidize anonymously Pip, the lawful self. And it is Magwitch the outlaw who refines what is base and shallow in the respectable youth. Pip thinks that Miss Havisham is financing him, but the money that makes it possible for him to cut a dash as a young gentleman does not come from her decaying beauty, wealth and gentility, but from the starveling and tenacious humanity of what in us is violent, inchoate, unshapen and fit only to be put in prison.

Again, in Conrad's *Secret Sharer*, a young captain, a young lawful 23
authority in his first command, is appealed to by a young man who closely resembles him, a fugitive fleeing trial for killing a mate on another vessel. With characteristic genius Conrad opens his story with the unfledged captain taking the anchor watch alone at night on his ship that is still unfamiliar to him. He looks over the side and sees looking up at him from the water a face like his own, the face of a desperate swimmer. The captain shelters his criminal *doppelganger* aboard his ship during a period of self doubt before putting to sea. But when the barque leaves port the fugitive must be put ashore to take his chances alone. A wide-brimmed hat, given him by the captain as protection against the sun, falls into the water and becomes a sea mark by which the young master gauges the current while negotiating a difficult offing under sail in light and baffling airs.

The fugitive's hat gets the lawful master safely out to sea, but the 24
fugitive cannot go with the ship. Magwitch gives Pip what he can and dies. Robin Hood is killed by the establishment that has no use for him. The predatory church that he has always fought will take him in, ailing and ageing, will bleed him to death at the end by the hand of the treacherous Prioress of Kirkleys Nunnery. Robin Hood, supported by Little John, will loose his last arrow from his deathbed and be buried where it falls. Marian, first magical maid and then magicless woman, will

become a nun and Prioress in her turn. Robin in the earth and she in the nunnery will both regain their innocence and power.

25   After the first reading of the book, the death and the last arrow were always there waiting for Robin Hood and me; he carried that death with him, carried that last arrow in his quiver always. He seems such a year-king! He seems, in his green and lightsome strength, always to hasten toward his sacrificial death that will bring forth from the winter earth another spring. And like a year-king, he must be given up, cannot be kept.

26   But I cannot give him up entirely. I think that we need our outlaw strength alive and brother to our lawful vigour. The one is not healthy without the other. I keep calling the elements outlaw self and lawful self, but that is unfair, really, to the essence of the thing. Society defines the terms of lawful and unlawful, because society makes the laws. And society is a retarded child with a loaded gun in its hands; I don't completely accept society's terms. Something in us makes us retell that myth; some drive there is in us to find and name the demon in us that is more real than laws and conventions that tell us what is right and what is wrong. And that demon is, I think, the radical spirit of life: it is the dark and unseen root system of our human tree whose visible branches are so carefully labelled and scientifically pruned by us. Maybe we think we don't need to know more about that nameless creative chaos, but we do, because in it we must find all real order. Polite gentlemen wearing suits and ties and with neat haircuts sit around tables with the death of the world in their briefcases, and they do not hesitate to tell us what is order. But to me it seems disorder. Other polite gentlemen some years ago sent up human smoke signals from the chimneys of crematoria, and they too defined order with great clarity. I think that fewer definitive definitions and many more tentative ones are needed now.

27   The fantasy of our legends, myths and stories helps with those definitions. It is as close as we can get to noumena through phenomena, as close as we can get to the thingness of things through the appearances of things. Fantasy isn't separate from reality; it is a vital approach to the essence of it. As to its importance, it is simply a matter of life and death. If we don't find out more about the truly essential thingness of things, then some future generation, if not this one, won't have anything left to find out about. So we must have fantasy constructed as scaffolding from which to work on actualities. And to work with fantasy is a risky business for the writer: it can change his whole world of actualities.

28   Which brings me back to the man on the bicycle, shirtless and

shouting. I was sorry for that man. I know how he felt. I wish he had been able to do something better with the baffled demon in him. I think he might have found something better to do if he had had more workable material in his mind, more useful people in his inner society. Robin Hood would have helped him, perhaps Captain Ahab too, and Lord Jim and Raskolnikov and goodness knows who else, functioning as surrogate actors-out of extreme and exaggerated degrees of the human condition. They might have taken on for him certain time-consuming and self-defeating tasks. They might have shown him other ways to be, might have freed him to do something more effective than what he was doing, might have helped him to find an identity in that wild surge of random creation that vanished into silence on the indulgent and indifferent air.

Well, you may say, perhaps that man wasn't a reader, and whatever is in books won't help him. But books permeate both the outer and inner societies, moving through readers to non-readers with definitions and provision for societal roles, expectations and probabilities. Always more figures are needed to people our inner societies – personifications of all the subtly different modes of being, *avatars* of the sequential and often warring selves within us. Books in nameless categories are needed – books for children and adults together, books that can stand in an existential nowhere and find a centre that will hold.

(1971)

The Writer's Subject

1. What is the relevance of the opening anecdote of the shirtless cyclist to the essay as a whole?

2. Hoban gives prominence to the story of Robin Hood and his outlaws. What personal significance does he derive from the story? What meanings does he attach to it?

3. What connection is there between the outcome of the Robin Hood story and the growth of a child to adulthood? (paras. 19-21)

4. Why, according to Hoban, do we need a "composite hero" with anti-heroic as well as heroic qualities? (para. 16)

5. Why does Hoban think that "we need our outlaw strength alive and brother to our lawful vigour" (para. 26)?

6. Why does Hoban believe that fantasy is so important? (paras. 27-28)

7. Why does Hoban think that the shirtless cyclist might have done "something better with the baffled demon in him" if he had more experience of books? What importance does Hoban attach to books for the well-being of children and adults generally? (paras. 28-29)

The Writer's Style and Strategy

1. How does Hoban's title reflect the pattern of development of the essay?

2. Comment on Hoban's use of "riotously" in his statement, "There may, of course, come a day when I shall riotously put on a bowler hat and a neat black suit, buy a tightly furled umbrella, and mingle in wild silence with brokers in the City" (para. 5).

3. How does Hoban signal the shift from the introductory material to the main body of his essay?

4. Hoban alludes to a number of examples from literature in addition to *Robin Hood*. How does he use these to advance his thesis?

5. What figure of speech is Hoban employing when he says, "Maybe we think we don't need to know more about that nameless creative chaos, but we do, because in it we must find all real order" (para. 26)?

6. What is the dominant tone of this essay and how does Hoban create it? Identify places where the tone seems to shift, and account for the shifts.

Suggested Topics for Writing and Discussion

1. Discuss a book that was important to you in your childhood.

2. Hoban says that Robin Hood, as a symbol of excellence, has been a great help to him all his life. Choose another literary hero or heroine. Identify and discuss those qualities that you think make the character a helpful model.

3. Hoban says, "we must have fantasy constructed as scaffolding from which to work on actualities." Choose a work of fantasy in any genre (film, drama, literature, painting) and discuss the ways in which the work helps us to a better understanding of reality. Make clear your definition of fantasy at the outset.

4. "Maybe what we've always called growing up is sometimes growing down" (para. 21). Apply Hoban's comment to your own experience; do you think that your growth into adulthood has involved losses as well as gains? (You may wish to read Wordsworth's poem "Ode: Intimations of Immortality" for another view of this subject.)

Bella Coola
by Edith Iglauer

1   This piece about Bella Coola was originally part of my book, *Fishing with John*. My editor for the whole book was Bill Shawn, who had just resigned from *The New Yorker*. It was a wonderful experience to work with him so directly.

2   You can tell the difference right away between great editors and the rest of them, because the great ones don't rewrite; they leave your thoughts and phrasing intact, and just clean up around them so that everything is very clear. Bill thought, and I agreed with him, that the Bella Coola chapter carried a story of its own, but it broke the thread of the narrative, so we removed it.

3   John and I went to Bella Coola because we had the time and were more than halfway there when the 1975 fishermen's strike began. We wanted to see whether we would like to move there. John believed Pender Harbour, with its scenic beauty and proximity to Vancouver, was about to become a tourist mecca and a place where retired people would want to come to live, which is what has happened. He felt that many people would be far more concerned with so-called "development" and the value of their land, than with the quality of the life here. Areas of Pender Harbour could already be mistaken for a city suburb, houses side by side with manicured lawns.

4   Fortunately for me, it rained almost the whole week we were in Bella Coola: all kinds of rain, from cold drizzles to pelting rainstorms, and once, a hailstorm. I say fortunately for me, because after I drove partway up the only road into or out of Bella Coola, I knew I wasn't going to live there. There are two other ways to depart from Bella Coola: by air, and the weather can make it impossible to fly in or out for weeks; and by boat, and

the Trudeau government eliminated the scheduled coastal passenger service that stopped regularly at Bella Coola.

I said to John, "If you want to live in Bella Coola, I will visit you from 5 time to time, but I can't live here." After that week of rain, rain, rain, I never heard another word about moving there.

Our fishing life was put on hold while we were in Bella Coola, but our 6 visit there was quite an experience. I was glad afterward that I had been there. Howard White liked what I wrote as an entity by itself, especially about the Bella Coola Road, and thought it should be part of *Raincoast Chronicles.*

Bella Coola. The name caught my eye on a map of Canada long before 7 I ever dreamed of moving to British Columbia. I saw BELLA COOLA at the end of one section of a jagged waterway called North Bentinck Arm, part of a fjord that made a deep cut in the coastline. The words stood out because they were, I mistakenly thought, so Spanish, so romantic, in among a lot of Indian and Anglo-Saxon place names. I longed, for no logical reason, to go there some day.

When I came to British Columbia for the first time in 1969 with my two 8 young sons, Jay and Richard, we flew out from New York, where we were living, and camped in provincial parks, following a route marked in heavy black ink on a worn road map that I clutched like a security blanket. Bella Coola was not one of the marked stops, but I figured we would make a side trip there if we possibly could.

Our route took us north on Vancouver Island, by ferry boat to Prince 9 Rupert, along the Skeena River and down into the Chilcotin, to Williams Lake. At a crossroads there I saw a sign pointing west that said, BELLA COOLA.

We turned down a bumpy, dusty dirt road and stopped for gas. "How 10 far is it to Bella Coola?" I asked.

The man selling the gas looked us up and down, stopped chewing tobacco 11 long enough to spit accurately into a trash can and said, "How long you got?"

"Only today," I said. "I thought we'd go and take a look." 12

He shook his head. "It's a couple of hours just to get to the road," he said. 13 "The Bella Coola Road. You driving?"

I said I was, and he shook his head again. "That's pretty rough road. You 14 better come back when you got more time. Plenty of time."

In 1973 I met my second husband John Daly, a commercial salmon 15 fisherman, and went fishing with him on his forty-one-foot troller, the *MoreKelp.* One season we had to stop work suddenly for a whole month because the fishermen went on strike. We were in Namu, where B.C.

Packers has an upcoast fish-buying installation in summer, when the strike started, so we decided to go on our boat to Eucott Bay and visit two elderly gentlemen, Frenchy and Simpson, who lived there on a rotting fish-camp float. On the way in I looked at the map and saw that we were now inside the same fjord-like waterway system as Bella Coola and said, "I wish we could go there!"

16   By coincidence, on our way out of Eucott we met Al Perkins, a big man with a large black moustache, who was an old friend of John's. We stopped to admire his handsome new white troller, the *Salmon Stalker,* and he remarked, "I've just been to Bella Coola, where I've been looking for land. I live in Duncan, and that place is getting too crowded for me."

17   "I know what you mean," John replied. "I've been thinking of doing the same thing myself."

18   The next morning John said, "I think we ought to explore the idea of moving to Bella Coola ourselves," as he started the boat's motor. We were soon moving along back down from where we had come, and part way he turned left, and right, into new territory; I lost track of our direction in the winding passages. The channel had high rock borders, and as we proceeded, mile after mile, twisting and turning through a steep-sided corridor, snow-capped mountains appeared ahead, above and around us. We must have gone at least fifty miles, deeper and deeper into the fjord, until we were in the narrow reach of North Bentinck Arm.

19   While we were running, I plucked our reference book, *British Columbia Coast Names,* out from under the mattress on John's bunk and looked up Bella Coola. Spanish origin indeed! According to the book's author, Captain John Walbran, the name Bella Coola is "an adaptation of the name of a tribe of Indians residing in the neighbourhood," and Bella Coola is "the local spelling used by the postal authorities," and only one of several ways of spelling it; the others being Bela Kula; Bellaghchoolas; and Bel-houla. So much for Spain and romance!

20   After eight miles, we arrived at an area of mudflats and swamp grass swathed in mist. Low red buildings marked CANADIAN FISH COMPANY were on our left, and to our right were a mass of floats crowded with the boats of other commercial fishermen on strike; plus the usual mix of sailboats and pleasure cruisers. Behind this picturesque jumble were the highest mountains I had yet seen on the maintainous B.C. coast, with snowy tips and the white streaks of glaciers on their slopes. "It's like Switzerland here," I said. "These mountains have that same lofty beauty." I looked at the chart to reassure myself. "Bella Coola! What a surprise!" I exclaimed. "I didn't know it would be so lovely. I guess I didn't know anything about it at all."

John was busy looking for a place on the floats to tie up. He stopped 21 beside a troller about the size of ours, the *Jan-Jac-Ann*. When our ropes were securely fastened to it, he came in and said, "Bella Coola has a big fishing fleet, and a strong union group. I've *always* thought I'd like to live in Bella Coola some day. When Al Perkins talked about moving here, I decided we'd take a look too. I don't know how much longer I can stand the noise of those airplanes flying in and out of Garden Bay, and the crowds. All the things I came to Pender Harbour to get away from are catching up with us. What I like about the people in Port Hardy and the Bella Coolaites is they don't want to increase the gross national product, they want to garden, and stay as they are. They do get tourists who fly in to hunt or fish, and a few drive in, but coming over that road is a long and hairy trip. I don't think Bella Coola is likely to get the hordes of tourists we get. At least, that's how it seems to me."

It had been raining, but now, at the end of the day, the sun took a notion 22 to shine. I stood on our deck, dazzled by the scenery; fading rays of sun lit up the mountains, their glaciers and their valleys. "Is *this* Bella Coola?" I asked. "I don't see any houses."

"Oh, it's a two-mile walk to 'downtown' Bella Coola," John said. "I hope 23 the telephone on the dock works. Last time I was here, the rain was *pouring* when I went up to phone you in New York, and most of the glass in the kiosk was smashed. All I got was a recorded voice, and I lost the money I had put in, besides. I walked into Bella Coola three or four times and tried to telephone. I reported the phone the first day, and when it wasn't fixed the second night, I put my foot through the last whole piece of glass and you know why? Because I kept getting that bloody recorded voice that said, 'The number you have reached is not in service.' It just enraged me. If I had a human answer I would have been far less mad. Those fiendish recorded voices are an atrocity against all who cannot afford a phone in their own houses; a non-humanity that causes real angry frustration. I certainly understand the violent vandalism that occurs in an inarticulate 'won't answer back' phone booth." With that, he turned and marched up the ramp to telephone.

The telephone must have worked, because he was back shortly to say 24 we had been invited for supper by the local game warden, Tony Karup. He arrived shortly in a yellow government truck; a greying, bald man in a khaki uniform. He drove us along a road bordered by the grassy flats of a river estuary that appeared to be a dumping ground for dilapidated and abandoned boats; and then we were in the main part of the town of Bella Coola. It consisted of a few rectangular streets, a United Church hospital, a library, several churches and stores. He pointed out a large store, famous for its excellent stock of books and handicrafts, that was owned and run by a local author, Cliff Kopas, whose book, *Bella Coola,* has become a standard historical reference. Driving along, it was clear that most of the Indian population in town lived on one side of the main intersection and the white people on the other.

25   We spent a pleasant evening at the neat, official house of the game warden and his good-looking Danish wife, but our meal was interrupted several times by telephoned reports about a grizzly bear in the area. "It's been killing cattle right in town, and I don't want any vigilante action," Tony said, returning to the table looking concerned. "Everybody's complaining now about all kinds of bears since they heard about this one; about bears that show up at their back doors, or claw marks on the windows, or garbage bags ripped apart. I was talking to one of our best Indian guides this morning, and he said, 'If I want to attract a bear for my clients, I buy new bread and they can smell it for miles around.' He also told me, 'I was at the garbage dump yesterday and I felt the wind of a paw on the back of my neck, and I sure jumped into the cab of my truck in a hurry!'"

26   The next morning, John and I walked the two miles into town in drizzling rain that shortly turned into a downpour. When we were wandering around in the Cliff Kopas store, a tall, cheerful man greeted John. He was walking with the aid of two canes, and his name was Tom Gee. John called to me several counters away and I arrived in time to hear that Gee had jumped off a roof and landed on his heels, breaking them both. The last time John had seen him he was gillnetting.

27   Tom hustled us into his truck and for the several more days we stayed in Bella Coola he was our guide and transportation. That was fortunate because it never stopped raining. The rain in Bella Coola had a special wetness that gave everything a damp aura, and soaked through my fairly waterproof red windbreaker. Even now, when I am asked my impression of Bella Coola, all I can remember is the rain — and the friendliness of the people.

28   One morning when Tom arrived to pick us up he said, "I thought we'd go up the Bella Coola Road, oh, just for an hour or so." He explained as we drove away that the local inhabitants had built the road themselves. It was a tremendous effort, over the mountain range that separated Bella Coola by land from any other community. It connected over the top of the range to the town of Anahim Lake, where my sons and I would have landed if we had been foolish enough to keep on driving from Williams Lake.

29   John said, "I've never been on that road. It's the only land route in and out of Bella Coola. The only other way to go is by boat or plane, and often the weather's so bad planes can't fly. The government wouldn't do anything

about a road, so the Bella Coola people built their own. I think they got a
little grant for dynamite. Constructing that road over that mountain range
was an extraordinary achievement."

"What's the road like?" I asked.   30

John replied, "I once met the man in charge of roads for the government   31
and he said to me, 'It's really embarrassing. When I make road inspections
my wife and daughter sometimes come with me, but when I start down the
Bella Coola road, they either insist on staying at Anahim or they drive in
with me with a rug over their heads.'"

We turned and started up a gravel road through a valley. Tom stopped   32
once to show us an old water wheel, and again to let cattle cross in front
of us. We drove past Indian smokehouses, sheds with rows of deep red
salmon hanging on lines, then a federal fisheries counting hut that looked
like an outhouse perched over a stream, and then a house shaped like an
ark. "Here's hippieville in Noah's Ark," Tom said, and then we were crossing a bridge over rushing water. "A truck went through here when the
bridge collapsed, and a little boy drowned," he said. "The fellow driving
found the boy pinned under a bunker." We passed a handsome farm. "That
belongs to the biggest farmer around here; he also has a house in town,"
Tom said.

Somewhere along the way, near where Tom said the Bella Coola River   33
joined with the white water of another river, I saw a sign that said, "Closed
to bear hunting. Do not feed, tease or molest bears." The road was becoming steeper and below us was spread a vista of beautiful bare green hills
and snow slides. Tom was driving in first gear now, very, very slowly.
Rocks slid down, rolling around the fenders of the truck.

I saw Tom put his elbows on the wheel, steering with them while he lit   34
a cigarette. It was a horrifying sight. "You'd be surprised at the number
of people who come in and don't drive out again," he said casually. "They
put their cars on a barge instead and fly home. The road was just a goat trail
when I came over it in 1956, and pretty tough here in the beginning; not
the way it is now, with lots of turnbacks and turnarounds. Hello there!"
he exclaimed, as a boulder hit the truck and rolled over the embankment.

I was sitting between the two men, so I had to stretch my neck to see   35
where the rock had gone. The boulder bounced along down until it disappeared into what looked to me like a bottomless chasm, at least two
thousand feet down.

We stopped suddenly. A large truck was just ahead, which shocked me.   36
We could see such a short distance in front of us that I thought we had the
road to ourselves. We sat and waited while the truck backed up over the
edge. Its rear end hung out over space while it made the sharp turn in the

road to go forward again.

37   Gee said, "Someone asked a trucker friend of mine how he did this in winter, when it's a sheet of ice and he said, 'Nothin' to it. I just drink a gallon of goof at the top of the hill and it smoothes out like a prairie.'"

38   There was a general chuckle, which I joined in weakly. Then we went through the same manoeuvre we had watched the truck make: backing over the edge in a switchback, to go forward. I tried not to think about the back end of our truck hanging out into space while we sat in the front end.

39   "There's never been a fatal accident on this road," Tom continued cheerfully. "A fellow went over in a Toyota station wagon with a load of sewing machines 'way up past here, and dropped sixty feet onto a switchback below, hit a tree and hung up there. It wrecked the tree, and he was in the hospital for two or three days. That's all. People drive this road at a crawl because they know they have to, even if they are drunk."

40   We were grinding our way up the road again, catching up to the truck ahead of us, then falling back to wait. We continued to stop and back up at each hairpin turn on what I now viewed as an insane road, admirable as the effort must have been to build it. I was not put at ease by Gee's steering with his elbows again as he lit another cigarette. John was silent, but I must have stirred nervously in my seat between them, because to ease the tension Gee said, "There were four bears on Main Street last night. One about four hundred pounds was seen in the telephone booth, probably phoning to find out where the garbage dump is, and when he came out someone saw him pick up a garbage can and walk off with it. A bear scattered a garbage pail on the back porch of the hotel, and another bear was seen by the beer hall, looking in store windows. I guess they're taking the path of least resistance and not picking berries any more. Tony finally shot one last night."

41   I was beyond conversation; just hoping, well praying, that Tom wouldn't light another cigarette. When I thought I couldn't stand looking over one more thousand or two thousand or whatever thousand-foot drop on another hairpin switchback turn, I saw a turn-around ahead. John glanced at his watch and cleared his throat. Tom said, "Do you think we'd better go back now? We're having supper with the matron of the hospital, who wants to meet you, and we shouldn't be late."

42   "I think we'd better," John said. We turned around and headed back. My relief was short-lived. Going down was worse. Looking through the windshield, the short span of road ahead extended only a few feet and disappeared in the vertical drop. Then, over the edge and down we went, to another vanishing point and another steep drop, prefaced by a switchback that left us teetering over the side of the mountain. I tried looking ahead. Glancing over the side, across John, was not a pleasing view either — just

emptiness, nothing below as far as I could see from where I sat, except on the switchbacks, where I could unfortunately see exactly how far down it was into the canyons beneath us. I thought about the mother and daughter who drove with a blanket over their heads. I wished I had brought one with me. I would have used it, without shame.

John put his hand over mine. He said, "Tom, I heard you had some sort 43 of an accident with your gillnetter. What happened?"

"It was off Egg Island, and the engine started to miss," Tom said, throw- 44 ing his cigarette out the window. I took a stick of gum out of my purse and started chewing, bracing myself for the moment when he would light another cigarette. Mercifully, he didn't. "As soon as I turned off the switch she blew, and blew me right out over the drum into the water," he continued. "I think the fire caught in the fuel pump. I didn't have a skiff along, so I swam away from the boat and got mixed up in some kelp. Then I swam back to the boat, got a grip on the tail end of the net, and made a hand hold. With the stabilizer and poles and the mast coming down, I felt pretty small, I can tell you. Everything burning and no skiff; and a hundred and twenty dollars in my pocket that I couldn't use. I was sure I'd be picked up because I had seen the Air Rescue on Egg Island. Somebody finally *did* pick me up, but I've always taken a skiff with me since then. I don't know when I'll get back fishing though. Breaking all those little bones in your heels is *really* painful, and they take a long time to heal."

We were down in the woods, in the valley now, driving through lovely 45 green forests. I sat back with an audible sigh of relief. "If we had gone the whole way to Anahim, how long is that road?" I asked.

"Two hundred and fifty miles," Tom said. 46

"And that's the *only* way out of Bella Coola by land?" I asked. 47

"That's right," John said. 48

Back on the boat that night I said to John, "If you move to Bella Coola, 49 I'll come and visit you. Maybe." He laughed and turned on the news. A few minutes later, the fisherman on the *Jan-Jac-Ann* told us that a strike vote had been called for the next day in Namu.

It was time to leave anyway. The continual rasp of our boat rocking 50 against its neighbour, the rumble of the Gardner being run to prevent the chilly damp from overwhelming us, particularly in my quarters below, and the endless patter of raindrops on the pilothouse roof were getting on our nerves. For the first and only time on the *MoreKelp*, we began to snap at one another.

I packed for travelling; stowing loose items in the sink, ramming a knife 51 in the cupboard door to keep it shut. The sun came out, casting a lovely yellow-white light on the mountains as we moved slowly away from the dock. I had seen Bella Coola, at last. It was beautiful, just as I had imagined, but I had no regrets about leaving.

(1991)

The Writer's Subject

1. What drew the writer to Bella Coola in the first place?

2. What kind of community is Bella Coola, as drawn by Iglauer?

3. What do we learn about the way of life of the people Iglauer meets in Bella Coola?

4. What kind of man is Tom Gee?

The Writer's Style and Strategy

1. The essay, though obviously about Bella Coola and its infamous road, is also a piece of autobiography. What does Edith Iglauer tell us about herself, directly or indirectly?

2. What use does Iglauer make of dialogue?

3. What details does Iglauer select to emphasize the hazardous nature of the Bella Coola Road? How does she convey her own feelings during the drive?

4. How does Iglauer give the reader an insight into the character of her husband?

5. Discuss the last two paragraphs of the essay. Do they form an appropriate conclusion?

Suggestions for Writing and Discussion

1. Describe an occasion on which you were subjected to great stress (e.g., your acting debut; a mountain-climbing adventure; an athletic competition). Choose details that will help the reader understand your feelings on that occasion.

2. Describe a trip that turned out differently from your expectations, and convey your feelings about the experience.

3. Present a portrait of someone you know who seems unusual or special in some way. Focus on those details of character, appearance, or behaviour that bring out the particular qualities of the person you are describing.

The Shadow of Captain Bligh
by Hugh MacLennan

Not long ago, in the same evening, I listened to my gramophone re- 1
cording of Haydn's *Mass for St. Cecilia* and then went upstairs and began
rereading the account of the mutiny on H.M.S. *Bounty* as written by
Nordhoff and Hall. The grand cadences of the Mass kept sounding
through my mind, and every now and then I stopped reading to let them
swell and subside. I was rereading the book for a purpose and I didn't
feel I could put it down. But the counterpoint made me realize with
a sensation of shock that Joseph Haydn and Captain Bligh were contemporaries, that the society that had produced and honoured the one
was the same society that had employed and respected the other.

Haydn's *Mass for St. Cecilia,* which was partially lost until Dr. Brand 2
recovered it little more than a decade ago, and which hardly anyone
had heard performed until it appeared recently in a recording of the
Haydn Society, is certainly one of the most sublime works the human
spirit has ever created. It seems to me worth all the music composed
since the death of Beethoven. Beethoven himself was never able to sustain
the power that is manifest here, for his struggle with himself and his
medium was too great. Haydn's Mass, like the greatest work of
Shakespeare, is at once majestic and intimate. Above all it seems ef-
fortless, and its joy and triumph are so breath-taking that no one who
is moved by music can easily listen to it without reflecting that our
modern world has produced no creative genius with his originality, his
joyousness, or his power.

Yet Haydn was not unique in his time. His career overlapped those 3
of Bach, Handel, Mozart, and Beethoven. Though his age acclaimed

him a master, it occurred to nobody in the eighteenth century to think it miraculous that he was able to compose those immensely complex works, some of great length, in so short a time. The best of his contemporaries were equally prolific and worked with equal speed. Handel composed *The Messiah* in a few weeks and Mozart wrote one of his most famous symphonies in a few days. Compared to these eighteenth-century masters, a modern creative artist moves at a snail's pace. Our most famous poets will die leaving behind only a slim body of published verse. The average modern novelist takes from two to three years to write a single good novel. Our musicians — men like Sibelius, Stravinsky, and Vaughan Williams — have together, in their long lives, equalled only a fraction of Haydn's output.

4   How lucky Haydn was to have lived before the radio and the telephone, before civic societies which would have made exorbitant and unavoidable demands on his time and energy, before publicity and interviewers and income tax and traffic horns and metropolitan dailies — to have lived, in short, before the age of distraction.

5   But *Mutiny on the Bounty* reminded me of the other side of the eighteenth century. The very fact of Captain Bligh implies that the forces which have made ours an age of distraction are far subtler and less avoidable than technical innovations like the telephone and the radio. *Mutiny on the Bounty* should be required reading for anyone who is apt, like myself, to be romantic about past ages and to decry his own. For Captain Bligh was just as typical of the eighteenth century as Haydn was. When I bow before Haydn I must remember that Haydn accepted without question and apparently without remorse the fact that he lived in a world that contained Captain Bligh.

6   Nothing Mickey Spillane has ever written can be compared in horror to some of the factual scenes in *Mutiny on the Bounty*. Few passages in literature describe more revolting episodes than those of the *Bounty* sailors being seized in the gangway and flogged until the flesh hung in strips from their backs. With our modern knowledge of neurology, we know that the agonies of these poor creatures did not end when the boatswain's mate ceased swinging the cat. Such beating damaged the nerve roots along the spine and condemned the victims to permanent suffering. What makes those scenes of torture so unbearable to think about is the added realization that they were not sporadic, were not the offshoots of a psychopathic movement like Nazism, but were standard practice in one of the most stable and reflective societies that ever existed. Captain Bligh's cruelty had the weight and approval of his entire soci-

ety behind it. When the mutineers were later court-martialled, the court had no interest in determining whether Bligh had been cruel or not. It was interested solely in whether the accused had obeyed to the letter the harsh laws of the British Navy.

Haydn, Bach, Handel, and Mozart, sublime spirits full of mercy, with 7 sensibilities exquisitely delicate, knew that men like Bligh were the mainstays of the societies they inhabited. Yet this knowledge, which to us would be a shame, felt personally, seldom if ever troubled their dreams or ruffled their serenity. The humanitarianism that disturbed Beethoven a generation later had not dawned when Haydn wrote the *Mass for St. Cecilia.*

Haydn reached his prime in the last moments when it was possible 8 for a creative artist to mind his own business in the sense that his conscience could remain untroubled by the suffering of the unfortunate. If sailors were flogged to death and peasants had no rights, if a neighbouring country was ruined by famine or pestilence, if laws were unjust or princes cruel, none of it was Haydn's affair. He was compelled to no empathy in the suffering of others as modern artists are.

It is this awareness of personal responsibility for the welfare of 9 strangers that makes uneasy all men of imagination today, that troubles their work and makes much of it seem tortured, that frustrates it, too, for seldom can a modern man of creative imagination do anything concrete to change the world he lives in.

Responsible only to himself, to his family, and to his God, Haydn 10 enjoyed a freedom few artists have known since. The result was as glorious as it is inimitable. It is on most of his successors that the shadow of Captain Bligh has fallen and remained.

As Haydn represents the spiritual grandeur of the eighteenth-century 11 imagination, Bligh represents its irresponsibility. In Bligh's own words, it was only through fear and cruelty that the stupid, the weak, the incompetent, the ignorant, and the unfortunate could be ruled and compelled to do what their masters considered to be their duty. Unless they were so compelled, the supporters of the system argued, there could be no fineness, no spiritual grandeur, no great literature or beautiful buildings, no masses for St. Cecilia. Civilization, as men of Haydn's day conceived it, could not exist if it yielded to the prompting of a social conscience.

When we realize this it becomes easier to reconcile ourselves to the 12 fact that the world we live in is producing no more Haydns or Mozarts. In the nineteenth century men of imagination turned their attention to the miseries of the world they saw about them, accepted responsibility for it, and forever lost the peace and concentration of spirit which enabled the Haydns and Mozarts to devote the full force of their genius to the realization of the gifts God had given them.

13   Could a modern artist witness a public flogging and then go home and compose exquisite music? Could he even live quietly under a régime that permitted such atrocities and retain his own respect and that of others?

14   Merely to ask such questions is to answer them. Musicians who took no more active part in the Hitler régime than perform for a Nazi audience have had to spend years as outcasts before western society would accept them again. The social conscience of today demands the service of every artist alive, and does not forgive him if he refuses it.

15   On the other hand western society did not make outcasts of the physicists, chemists, and engineers who served Hitler. Until very recently science reserved for itself the same mental freedom that art enjoyed in Haydn's day. If politicians or monsters used the work of science for evil purposes, the scientists felt no personal responsibility. Enjoying such peace of mind, physicists and chemists have been able to devote the full force of their intellects to their work, and so their work has been more impressive than that of the artists who were their contemporaries. No wonder our age, when it looks for a genius to match Bach or Haydn, does not even stop to search among the ranks of the artists. It picks Einstein.

16   But when the atomic bomb fell on Hiroshima any number of scientists succumbed to a social conscience as the artists had done long ago. Einstein, Oppenheimer, and hundreds of others were overcome with a Hamlet-like self-questioning. If our world lasts long enough it will be interesting to see whether science in the next generation will be as original and productive as it has been in the last three. For a conscience, as Shakespeare knew when he created Hamlet, inhibits action and beclouds genius. Our collective conscience may not have made the modern artist a coward, but it has certainly made him a prisoner.

17   Consider in contrast to Haydn the life of Albert Schweitzer. Schweitzer began as a musician, and had he lived in the eighteenth century there is no knowing what masterpieces he might have composed. But his conscience would not permit him to devote his entire life to music, so he studied theology and became a minister of the Gospel. Then his conscience told him that preaching was not enough, so he studied medicine and became a doctor. His conscience then informed him that it was self-

indulgent to practise medicine in a comfortable European city while there were millions in the world without medical care of any kind. So Schweitzer took his gifts to one of the most primitive parts of Africa. There he has lived and worked ever since, among men so elemental that they can know nothing of Bach or Haydn and cannot even guess at the greatness of the strange healer who came to help them.

Albert Schweitzer will die leaving behind him no tangible or audible **18** monument, no record of objective achievement beyond a few books which are mere by-products of his life and interests. His enormous powers have been spread so widely in the service of others that neither as a musician, nor as a theologian, nor as a doctor-scientist, has his work, in itself, been such as to ensure his immortality. An earlier age would have said that Schweitzer had squandered his gifts on savages. But our age, rightly or wrongly, acclaims him as one of its noblest representatives because his life has translated into action, as hardly any other life has done, the highest aspirations of our social conscience.

No other modern artist I know of has made the total sacrifice of his **19** talents that Schweitzer made; yet no modern artist (musician or poet or even the great individualist, Picasso) has been undisturbed by the social conscience of our day.

Critics who argue that the subject-matter of modern art is proof of **20** the decadence of modern society don't really understand what they are talking about. Art has always been a reflection of the aspirations and obsessions of its time and the art of today is no exception. If it is haunted and distracted, if it is often ugly and even horrifying, it does not mean that the artists themselves are worse men than Haydn was. It means only that they have not refused, as Haydn did, to accept responsibility for Captain Bligh. For all its horrors, the twentieth century is better than the eighteenth; no politician or dictator who has tried to defy its conscience has been able, in the end, to succeed.

Some time in the future art may reflect the tranquillity that Haydn **21** knew. If it does so, it will not be because those artists of the future are likely to be abler men than artists of today. It will happen because, after this age of transition, the shadow of Captain Bligh has been removed from the whole world.

(1953)

The Writer's Subject

1. Why did MacLennan feel shock at the realization that the same society had produced both Haydn and Captain Bligh? (paras. 1-7)

2. What contrast does MacLennan draw between the productivity of eighteenth-century artists and that of modern artists? (para. 3)

3. What does MacLennan find most disturbing about the treatment of the sailors on the *Bounty*? (para. 6)

4. Why, in MacLennan's view, were artists such as Haydn not disturbed by the savagery of the world around them? What does MacLennan mean when he says that the shadow of Captain Bligh has fallen not on Haydn but on his successors? (para. 7-11)

5. Why does MacLennan think it is no longer possible for the world to produce any more Haydns or Mozarts? (paras. 12-14)

6. What contrast does MacLennan draw between the achievements of modern artists and those of modern scientists? (para. 15)

7. MacLennan says that today scientists, like artists, have become prisoners of conscience. How does he demonstrate this point? (para. 16)

8. What is MacLennan's attitude to Haydn?

The Writer's Style and Strategy

1. Explain the meaning of "counterpoint" as MacLennan uses it in the first paragraph.

2. How does MacLennan establish the contrast between the two sides of eighteenth-century life? How does MacLennan signal the shift in his discussion from the one to the other?

3. MacLennan's essay works, in part, on the principle of cause and effect. That is, because Haydn was not distracted by his society he could produce great works. What other instances of cause and effect are evident in this essay?

4. Despite the extensive use of detail and supporting examples, this essay relies heavily upon assertions or generalizations to convey a very personal impression of the relationship between art and life. Find one or two examples of such assertions or generalizations; examine the assumptions that underlie them; and comment on their persuasiveness, or lack of it.

Suggested Topics for Writing and Discussion

1. MacLennan suggests that modern artists can seldom do anything concrete to change the world they live in. Do you agree?

2. MacLennan chooses Haydn as representative of the great artists of the eighteenth century. Choose another artist (e.g., painter, writer, architect, composer) either from a past age or from our own time, and show why, in your view, this artist represents his or her age.

3. Do you agree with MacLennan's view that the development of a social conscience in modern times has made the production of great art an impossibility?

4. "Art has always been a reflection of the aspirations and obsessions of its time and the art of today is no exception." Choose a well-known work of twentieth-century art in any medium and explain how the work reflects the concerns of its time.

5. MacLennan uses Captain Bligh as a symbol of evil in the eighteenth century. Write an essay about the dark side of the twentieth century and focus on one individual as a symbol of the evil of the age.

St John's

by Jan Morris

1   *Of all the cities I have written about, anywhere in the world, none has given me more enjoyment than St John's, Newfoundland, the most entertaining town in North America.*

2   *It was as a historian of the British Empire that I first went there, thirty-odd years ago, Newfoundland having occupied a unique place in the imperial scheme of things, and St. John's having remained until recent times an anachronistic curiosity among imperial towns. By the time I came to write this essay the Empire's effects had long faded, and there were different excitements that beguiled me, but I remembered with particular affection an incident from my original visit, in 1956, that said a lot about the continuing character of St John's.*

3   *In the Newfoundland of those days it was necessary to find a local guarantor before one could cash foreign money orders. Knowing nobody in town, and discovering that the public library had a copy of a book of mine about Venice, I introduced myself to the librarian and asked her to endorse a traveler's cheque. How could she confirm, she sensibly demanded, that I was who I said I was? By a simple literary test, said I; surely nobody else on earth could recite by heart the last line of my Venetian book, which she had upon her own shelves.*

4   *Solemnly she reached for the volume. Nervously I stood at her desk while she turned to the final page, and ran her eye down the paragraphs to the end of it. Well? she said. I cleared my throat. The concluding words of my book were not very stately. "No wonder," I mumbled them, feeling distinctly*

*disadvantaged, "no wonder George Eliot's husband fell into the Grand
Canal." Without a flicker that librarian of old St John's closed the book,
returned it to the shelf and authorized my money.*

Thwack! Despite it all, the personality of St John's, Newfoundland, hits 5
you like a smack in the face with a dried cod, enthusiastically administered
by its citizenry.

The moment you arrive they take you up Signal Hill, high above the 6
harbour, where winds howl, superannuated artillery lies morose in its
emplacements, and far below the ships come and go through the rock gap
of the Narrows. Within an hour or two they are feeding you seal-flipper
pie, roast caribou, partridgeberries, or salt cod lubricated with pork fat.
They introduce you to the mayor, John "Rags" Murphy. They show you
the grave of the last Beothuk Indian and the carcass of the final Newfoundland wolf. They remind you that they, alone in continental North
America, live three and a half hours behind Greenwich Mean Time.

They chill you with tales of the corpses lying in Deadman's Pond. They 7
warm you up with Cabot Tower rum. They take you to the site of the city's
first (hand-operated) traffic signal. They show you the house into which
the prime minister of Newfoundland escaped from a lynch mob in 1932,
and the field from which the aviators Harry G. Hawker and Kenneth
Mackenzie-Grieve unfortunately failed to cross the Atlantic in 1919. They
guide you down higgledy-piggledy streets of grey, green, yellow, and
purple clapboard. They explain to you in detail the inequities of the 1948
Confederation referendums. They tell you repeatedly about their cousins
in Boston, and involve you in spontaneous and often incomprehensible
conversations on street corners.

Such is the nature of this city; windy, fishy, anecdotal, proud, weather- 8
beaten, quirky, obliging, ornery, and fun.

I start with "despite it all" because St John's is undeniably a knocked-about 9
sort of town. Economic slumps and political hammerings, tragedies at sea,
sectarian bigotries, riots, fires, poverty, and unemployment − all have
taken their toll, and make the little city feel a trifle punch-drunk.

The very look of it is bruised. The outskirts of St John's are much like 10
the purlieus of many another North American city − malls, car dealers,
airport, duplexes, a big modern university − but its downtown is bumpily
unique. Set around the dramatically fjord-like harbour, overlooked by oil
tanks and fort-crowned heights but dominated by the twin towers of the
Catholic basilica, its chunky wooden streets clamber up and down the civic
hills with a kind of throwaway picturesqueness, suggesting to me sometimes a primitive San Francisco, sometimes Bergen in Norway, occasional-

ly China, and often an Ireland of long ago.

11   "Either it's the Fountain of Youth," said a dockyard worker when I asked him about a peculiarly bubbling sort of whirlpool in the harbour, "or it's the sewage outlet." St John's is nothing if not down-to-earth. The shambled slums I remember from twenty-five years ago have been miraculously abolished, but the best efforts of the conservationists have not deprived the town of its innate fishermen's fustian. The most enlightened restoration of its streets has not managed to make it self-conscious. The first dread fancy lampposts and ornamental bollards, the first whiff of novelty-shop sachets, the arrival on the waterfront of that most ludicrously architectural cliché, mirror-glass – even the presence of Peek-a-Boutique in the premises of the former Murray fishery depot – have so far failed to make St John's feel in the least chichi. It remains that rarity of the Age of Collectibles, an ancient seaport that seems more or less real.

12   I hear some expostulations, nevertheless. "Fishermen's fustian," indeed! For all their hospitality, I get the sensation that the inhabitants of St John's may prove prickly people to write about, and there is a prejudice I am told among some of the grander St John's persons (we can no longer, I suppose, call them St John'smen) against the city's association with the fish trade.

13   Yet even the loftiest burghers' wives could hardly claim that this is a very sophisticated place. It is like a family city, meshed with internecine plot, but still somewhat reluctantly united by blood, history, and common experience. It is the poorest of the Canadian capitals; it has little industry and few great monuments; its responses are those of a permanently beleaguered seaport on a North Atlantic island – which is to say, responses altogether its own.

14   Actually within the city limits of St John's there are pockets of the probably spurious Arcadianism that Newfoundland picture postcards so love to show. Small wooden houses speckle seabluffs, dogs lie insensate in the middle of steep lanes, and here and there one may still see the fish stretched out to dry, as they have been stretched for 400 years, on the wooden flakes of tradition. Almost within sight of Peek-a-Boutique I met a hunter going off to the hills in search of partridge, buckling his cartridge belt around him, hoisting his gun on his shoulder, just like a pioneer in an old print. And immediately outside the windows of one of the city's fancier restaurants ("Step Back in Tyme to Dine") one may contemplate over one's cods' tongues the whole rickety, stilted, bobbing, seabooted, genial muddle that is the classic image of maritime Newfoundland.

15   It really is a community of cousins, too. I happened to notice on a monument one day that the now defunct police force called the Newfoundland Rangers numbered, among its Guzzwells, Stucklesses, and Snelgroves,

a disproportionate number of Noseworthys. So I looked up that clan in the St John's telephone book: 305 are listed, by my count, including Randy Noseworthy, Ethel Noseworthy, Dwayne Noseworthy, Franklin Noseworthy, Major H. Noseworthy, and Noseworthy, Keating, Howard and Kung, Accountants — their names constituting in themselves, I thought, a proper register of St John's social consciousness.

It happened that while I was in town St John's was celebrating its **16** centenary as a municipality with what it called a Soiree — generally pronounced swarr-ee — and recalling a favourite old Newfoundland song:

There was a birch rine, tar twine,
Cherry wine and turpentine,
Jowls and cavalances, ginger beer and tea,
Pig's feet, cat's meat, dumplings boiled in a sheet,
Dandelion and crackies' teeth at the
Kelligrews's Soiree....

The festivities closed with a public party at the St John's Memorial Stadium that powerfully reinforced the family illusion, and suggested to me indeed an enormous country wedding — everyone someone else's in-law, everyone ready to talk, with no pretence and no pretension either. Noseworthys were numerous, I do not doubt, and Kelligrews were certainly there in force, though content no longer with ginger beer and tea. Jigs and folk songs sounded from the stage, miscellaneous bigwigs sat stared-at in the middle like rich out-of-town relatives, and when people seemed slow to dance, jolly Mayor Murphy took the floor alone, offering free booze coupons to any who would join him — "You have to get them half-tight," he remarked to me as he handed out these inducements, jigging the while himself.

The pubs of St John's are mostly less than trendy. The downtown corner **17** store flourishes. The St John's *Telegram* carries not merely death announcements but long and sometimes extremely gloomy poems to go with them, such as:

He's gone, oh gone for ever,
The one we loved the best.
Our days of joy are ended
As the sun sets in the west.

"Your mouths are so big they could fit in a zoo," a member of the city council told his colleagues in plenary session during my stay. "You're a sook," responded the deputy mayor.

I puzzled, as every stranger must, about the mingled origins of this **18** pungent civic character, and the first strain I identified was undoubtedly the Irish. The simplicity of St John's is streaked, I came to sense, with a particularly Irish reproach, wit, and irony — sometimes I felt that Ireland itself was only just out of sight through that harbour entrance. The prickly pensioners and layabouts who hang around on Water Street, "The Oldest Continuously Occupied Street in North America," look pure Cork or Wexford. The instant response that one gets from nearly everyone is Ireland all over. And the complex of buildings that surrounds the Basilica of St John the Baptist, episcopal, conventual, didactic, societal buildings, is a reminder that here Irish values and memories, however dominant the British colonial establishment of the place, proved always inextinguishable.

19   But that establishment too still flies its flags — literally, for at city hall they flaunt not only the ensigns of the city, the province, and the Confederation but actually the Union Jack too, for reasons defined for me as "purely sentimental." This was a self-governing British possession within my own lifetime, after all (no school stamp collection of my childhood was complete without the 1¢ Caribou of our oldest colony), and within the city centre it is still easy enough to descry the old power structure of the Pax Britannica. The governor's mansion is recognizably the social fulcrum that it was in every British colony. The garrison church is spick-and-span. The Anglican cathedral is authentically unfinished, like all the best Anglican cathedrals of the Empire. The old colonial legislature is properly pillared and stately, and down the hill is the Supreme Court building, smelling of warm wood and depositions in triplicate, which once also housed the prime minister's office, responsible directly to the Crown in London.

20   Indeed, as a sign reminds us on the waterfront, The British Empire Began Here — when Sir Humphrey Gilbert established the first permanent settlement of New Founde Land in 1583. The city is appropriately rich in heroic memorials, commemorative plaques, royally planted trees or dukely laid foundation stones (though as a matter of fact, St John's being St John's, the stone laid by the Duke of Connaught in Bowring Park in 1914 turns out to be the thriftily recycled headstone of a dog's grave). Kipling himself worded the plaque at the site of Gilbert's landing, Field Marshal Earl Haig unveiled the Water Street war memorial. Nor are the imperial loyalties merely lapidary: one devoted monarchist drives around town with British flags stuck on her trunk and flying from her radio aerial, and another was not much pleased, I fear, when I suggested that in Britain itself royalism, like cigarette smoking, was primarily a lower-middle-class enthusiasm....

21   "Not that the British," even these zealots are quite likely to say, "ever did much for Newfoundland." On the contrary, the general view seems to be that London behaved as negligently towards its oldest colony as

Ottawa does to its youngest province. Most people I asked said that emotionally at least they would prefer to enjoy the independence signed away to Canada in 1949, but a good many told me that if they had the choice they would opt for union with the U.S.

This did not surprise me. In some ways St John's is very American. It 22 does not feel to me in the least like Canada, being altogether too uninhibited, but I can conceive of it as a half-Irish, half-Empire Loyalist backwater of New England. A century ago the Newfoundlanders were all for free trade with the Americans, at least, and would have got it if the British government had not intervened; today half the people I met seemed to have American connections of some kind or another, mostly in Boston. When I suggested to one elderly lady that closer links with the United States might in the end mean more corruption, exploitation, and general degradation, she seemed quite affronted. "That's only the *fringe* of things down there," she said.

But I looked her in the face as she said this, and I rather think I detected 23 in it, through the patina of the years, the bright eager features of a GI groupie of long ago. I know of nowhere in the world where the American soldiers of the Second World War are remembered with such affection, or where, perhaps as a result, the equivocal colossus of the south seems to be given the benefit of so many doubts. "I can assure you that at heart the Americans are very good people," my informant firmly added, and as we parted I swear I heard, as in historic echo, a giggle in the shadows of McMurdo's Lane, and a distant beat of "In the Mood."

These varied inheritances and associations save St John's from any sug- 24 gestion of provincialism. History does it, one might say. The fateful gap of the Narrows is like a door upon a world far wider than Canada itself, while the city's particular kinds of expertise, to do with ships, and fish, and ice, and seals, and perilous navigations, make it a place beyond condescension. Memorial University of Newfoundland has a formidable reputation, the Marine Institute is world-famous, and ships of many nations and many kinds, perpetually coming and going through the harbour, give the town a cosmopolitan strength — rust-streaked fishing vessels from the deep Atlantic grounds, hulking coastguard ships, coastal freighters, ocean research vessels, container ships and warships and ships bringing salt for the winter roads — ships in such ceaseless progress that each morning of my stay, when I walked down to the waterfront before breakfast, I found that some new craft had come out of the night like a messenger while I slept.

The historical continuity of St John's, too, allows it a status beyond its 25 size. The Grand Banks, which brought the first Europeans to these parts, still figure inescapably in its affairs, and the matter of the 200-mile fishing limit profoundly affects not only the economy of the port but its very style. Gone, like enemy aliens from a land at war, are the Iberian fishermen who used to bring a Latin emollient of wine and lantern light to this northern waterfront, but the statue of Our Lady of Fatima in the basilica, presented by grateful Portuguese mariners in 1955, pointedly remembers still the long Romance connection.

26 Then the matter of St Pierre-Miquelon, St John's own foreign-relations issue, is really a last irritant from the Seven Years' War, which ended in this very city 227 years ago. Though the islands are familiar enough to St John's people (university students go there for French-language immersion courses), their presence somewhere over the southern horizon queerly haunted my thoughts in the city — so resolutely foreign still out there, so utterly separate, a department of France behaving, so close to Mayor Murphy's homely bailiwick, with such absolute damned Frenchness.

27 The world has been passing through St John's certainly for a longer time, and perhaps with a greater intensity, than through any other Canadian city — from the Basques, Dutch, French, and English of the early years to the GIs of the Second World War and the Russian and Japanese seamen who are familiars of the place today. All their influences have been absorbed, in one degree or another, into the city's persona. To take two oppositely alcoholic examples (for St John's loves its drink): the rum called Newfoundland Screech, born out of the eighteenth-century Caribbean saltfish trade, is bottled in St John's to this day, while Newman's Celebrated Port Wine, originally sent here to mature because the long sea voyage from Europe was said to have a beneficial effect upon it, is offered still under the antiseptic auspices of the Liquor Corporation.

28 Such range, for a city of 100,000 souls, longitude 52.43 W, latitude 47.34 N! No wonder St John's, though long reduced to the condition of a provincial capital, remains so defiantly itself. There is no false modesty here. "You're right, but it isn't true of St John's," a man told me when I remarked that the citizens of most Canadian cities wanted to talk about nothing but themselves — and he went on to rehearse in loving and elaborate detail all other superiorities of the civic character.

29 In fact the people of St John's are irresistible talkers about themselves, and their peculiar accent, which strikes me as a cross between Irish, Devonian, and Atlantic Seal, makes the flow of their infatuation all the more unguent. Since everyone seems to know nearly everyone else, throughout my stay I felt myself encompassed within a web of overlapping reminiscence, amusement, and complaint. Gossip flows lively in St John's; images of scandal, joke, and mischief passed before me like figures on a wide and gaudy screen. The moneyed dynasties of the town, the Ayres,

the Jobs, the Harveys, the Outerbridges, were dissected for me in richest idiom whether living or extinct; politicians suffered the sharp sting of Newfoundland iconoclasm; as I was guided around the streets one by one the pedigrees and peccadillos of their structures stood revealed. Here was the store which was all that was left of the Xs' fortunes, here the mansion where the wildly successful Ys resided. One of the less estimable of the lieutenant governors lived in this house, a whiz-kid entrepreneur had lately installed eight bathrooms in that, and down by the waterfront was the not very upmarket department store whose ownership had given Mayor Murphy his affectionate nickname.

All this makes life in the city feel remarkably *immediate*. There is no lag, **30** it seems, between introduction and confidence. By my second day in town I was being given under-the-counter comments on the local judiciary by a well-known politician. By my third day I was being treated to the lowdown about some spectacular financial goings-on. Hardly had I been introduced to a member of one of St John's oldest families, who has one house in town and another on its outskirts, in a kind of Newfoundland version of the trans-humance system — hardly had I met this distinguished citizen and his wife before they were explaining why their cat is named after — well, I had better not say who it's named after, let alone why.

I was walking along a city street one day when a man sweeping leaves **31** launched upon me without warning an obviously political statement in such advanced Newfoundlandese that I can only reproduce it impressionistical-ly, so to speak, with the help of a glossary of the dialect. It sounded something like: "Sish yarkin trapse John Murphy, tacker snarbucklerawny yok John Crosbie, glutch aninst Suzanne Duff." He looked at me expec-tantly for a response, so I simultaneously shook my head and nodded, to be on the safe side.

1 Extend Arm (*says a notice at a pedestrian crossing outside city hall*)
2 Place Foot on Street
3 Wait Until Cars Stop
4 Thank Driver

It struck me as a quintessentially St John's announcement, with its blend of the amiable, the unexpected, and the tongue-in-cheek. If reading this essay makes you too feel rather as though you are being slapped in the face with a dried codfish, that is because I was beguiled by almost everything about the city and its inhabitants (almost, because I do wish they wouldn't smoke so much…). I dare say that if the long-promised oil bonanza ever happens the town will ruin itself with affluence, but I rather think not: it is too rooted in the satisfaction of being utterly unlike anywhere else.

32   The standard history of St John's is a monumental two-volume work by
Paul O'Neill. One might expect such a labour of municipal devotion to be
heavy going; in fact it is one of the most consistently entertaining history
books I have ever read, full of excellent stories, gamy characters, and
surprising historical allusions. Similarly, every corner of old St John's
offers its own intriguing details. At 100 Water Street there is the sweetly
old-school china shop that the Steele family has run for more than a century,
while not far away the Neyle-Soper Hardware Store displays in its
windows, like *objets d'art* in a museum, grandly Newfoundland things like
paraffin lamps, hatchets, scythes, and mousetraps that catch four mice at
a time. There is a shop that sells nothing costing more than three dollars,
and a shop that sells Young Seal Carcass at forty-nine cents a pound, and
Kim Lee's Tailor Shop with tailoring visibly taking place inside. Above
the old lovers' steps of McMurdo's Lane the starlings roost in their noisy
thousands.

33   See that object on the rooftop there? That's the periscope of a German
U-boat, mounted triumphantly above the Crow's Nest Club, which was
a famous haven of the convoy captains in the Second World War. See those
wagons beyond the dockyard? That's the rolling stock of the narrow-gauge
Newfoundland Railway, forlornly immobilized here because the railroad
no longer exists. Hear that bang? That's the gun on Signal Hill, fired each
day at noon as it was in the days of the redcoats.

34   As for the concrete city hall, it is a very repository of the civic self-
esteem. Such banners and plaques and portraits and statues and old
municipal photographs! Such ship models and armorial bearings and frater-
nal messages from admirals, mayors, and societies of merchant venturers!
When I remarked how proper it was that the mayor's own office should
look directly down upon the historic waterfront, somebody said yes, and
directly down upon his own store, too — such is the organic frankness of
this close-hauled sceptic town.

35   I was conscious always all the same, as I wandered so enjoyably through
the city, that life and history have never been easy here. Beneath the charm
there lies a bitterness. St John's is full of disappointment, and is an exposed
and isolated place in more senses than one. One afternoon, by driving the
few miles out to Cape Spear, I made myself for a moment the easternmost
person in North America, and was chilled to think, as I stood there in the
wind, that while at my back there was nothing but the ocean, before me
there extended, almost as far as the imagination could conceive, the awful
immensity of Canadian rock, forest, prairie, and mountain. St John's is
the edge of everywhere, the end and start of everything. The sign for Mile
"O" of the Trans-Canada Highway stands immediately outside city hall;

it was on Signal Hill that Marconi received the very first radio communication from across the ocean. Hawker and Grieve failed indeed to fly across the Atlantic from St John's, but Alcock and Brown succeeded, and here one evening in 1927 people hearing the drone of an aircraft ran outside to see Lindbergh's *Spirit of St Louis* disappear into the twilight for Paris.

And to this day, though much of the activity of St John's has moved 36 inland, everything in this city looks down, if only metaphorically, to the Narrows. Even the stolid Confederation Building, erected with a becoming diffidence well back from the bloody-minded seaport, peers cautiously from its distance towards that dramatic fissure. I found myself bewitched by it: repeatedly driving up to its headlands, or around the southern shore to the lighthouse at the end, or waving goodbye to the ships as they trod carefully between the buoys towards the open sea – a distant slow wave of an arm, from wheelhouse or forecastle, returning my farewell as seamen must have responded down all the centuries of Atlantic navigation.

Once I was contemplating that hypnotic view from the bar of the Hotel 37 Newfoundland, which looks immediately out to the Narrows and the Atlantic beyond. It was evening, and the prospect was confused by the reflection, in the plate-glass windows, of the people, plants, and ever-shifting patterns of hotel life behind me. Beyond this insubstantial scene, though, I could see the stern outline of the cliffs, the floodlit Cabot Tower on Signal Hill, the white tossing of the ocean breakers, and the slowly moving masthead light of a ship sliding out to sea.

The hotel pianist was playing Chopin – and as he played, with the re- 38 condite inflections of Newfoundland conversation rising and falling around me, mingled with laughter and the clink of glasses, somehow the riding light of that ship, moving planet-like through the mirror images, brought home to me with a *frisson* the grand poignancy that lies beneath the vivacity of St John's. I thought it sad but exciting, there in the air-conditioned bar.

(1990)

The Writer's Subject

1. Given that the writer finds St. John's "knocked about," poor, and unsophisticated, why does she appear to like it so much?

2. Why does the city strike Morris as "a half-Irish, half-Empire Loyalist backwater of New England"? (para. 22) What attitudes does she detect among the citizens towards Britain and the U.S.?

3. What in Morris's view saves the city from the charge of provincialism? (para. 24)

4. In what ways, according to Morris, is St. John's a memorial to the British Empire? (paras. 19-20)

5. Why, according to Morris, is the "Narrows" such an important feature of St. John's? (para. 36)

6. What does Morris mean by "the grand poignancy that lies beneath the vivacity of St. John's"? (para. 38)

The Writer's Style and Strategy

1. Discuss the relevance of the introductory anecdote about the librarian in St. John's.

2. Why does Morris begin the main part of her essay with the word "Thwack!" (para. 5)? What is the point of her reference to dried cod?

3. Examine some of the terms with which Morris describes St. John's in the first six or seven paragraphs (e.g., "fishy," "quirky," "knocked-about," "punch-drunk," "bruised"), and discuss their appropriateness.

4. What sense does Morris give the reader of what the inhabitants of St. John's are like?

5. Discuss some of the methods that Morris employs to describe the city of St. John's. How does she avoid making her account a dull recital of facts and figures?

6. There is a marked shift in the mood of the essay over the last four paragraphs. Identify the nature of this change, and discuss the possible reasons behind it.

7. The essay sets out to describe a Canadian city. What, directly or indirectly, does it tell us about the writer herself?

Suggested Topics for Writing and Discussion

1. Morris introduces her description of St. John's with a personal anecdote about an encounter with one of the city's inhabitants. Construct your own version of this: write a brief personal account of an incident in which you meet someone who typifies the town or city in which you were brought up or in which you now live.

2. Point out those features (e.g., architecture, history, social institutions) that give the community or neighbourhood in which you live its distinctive character.

3. Choose one notable event in the history of your town or city, and prepare a ten-minute talk for a high school audience.

4. The writer speaks of the peculiarities of Newfoundland dialect. Are there any distinctive features in the vocabulary or idioms of your region?

Specifications for a Hero
by Wallace Stegner

1   In our town, as in most towns, everybody had two names — the one his parents had given him and the one the community chose to call him by. Our nicknames were an expression of the folk culture, and they were more descriptive than honorific. If you were underweight, you were called Skinny or Slim or Sliver; if overweight, Fat or Chubby; if left-handed, Lefty; if spectacled, Four Eyes. If your father was the minister, your name was Preacher Kid, and according to the condition and color of your hair you were Whitey, Blacky, Red, Rusty, Baldy, Fuzzy, or Pinky. If you had a habit of walking girls in the brush after dusk, you were known as Town Bull or T.B. If you were small for your age, as I was, your name was Runt or Peewee. The revelation of your shape at the town swimming hole by the footbridge could tag you for life with the label Birdlegs. The man who for a while ran one of our two grocery stores was universally known as Jew Meyer.

2   Like the lingo we spoke, our nicknames were at odds with the traditional and educational formalisms; along with them went a set of standard frontier attitudes. What was appropriate for Jimmy Craig in his home or in church or in school would have been shameful to Preacher Kid Craig down at the bare-naked hole. When we were digging a cave in the cutbank back of my house, and someone for a joke climbed up on top and jumped up and down, and the roof caved in on P.K. and he had to be dug out and revived by artificial respiration, even P.K. thought the hullabaloo excessive. He did not blame us, and he did not tattle on anyone. His notions of fortitude and propriety — which were at the other end of the scale from those of his parents — would not have let him.

When we first arrived in Whitemud the Lazy-S was still a working 3
ranch, with corrals, and calves, and a bunkhouse inhabited by heroes
named Big Horn, Little Horn, Slivers, Rusty, and Slippers. There was
a Chinese cook named Mah Li, who had been abused in imaginative
ways ever since he had arrived back at the turn of the century. In the
first district poll for a territorial election, in 1902, someone had taken
Mah Li to the polls and enfranchised him on the ground that, having
been born in Hong Kong, he could swear that he was a British subject
and was not an Indian, and was hence eligible to vote. When I knew
him, he was a jabbering, good-natured soul with a pigtail and a loose
blue blouse, and I don't suppose a single day of his life went by that
he was not victimized somehow. He couldn't pass anybody, indoors
or out, without having his pigtail yanked or his shirt tails set on fire.
Once I saw the cowboys talk him into licking a frosty doorknob when
the temperature was fifteen or twenty below, and I saw the tears in his
eyes, too, after he tore himself loose. Another time a couple of Scandinavians tried to get him onto a pair of skis on the North Bench hill.
They demonstrated how easy it was, climbed up and came zipping by,
and then offered to help his toes into the straps. But Mah Li was too
many for them that time. "Sssssssssss!" he said in scorn. "Walkee half
a mile back!" When I was ten or eleven Mah Li was a friend of mine.
I gave him suckers I caught in the river, and once he made me a present of a magpie he had taught to talk. The only thing it could say was
our laundry mark, the number O Five, but it was more than any other
magpie in town could say, and I had a special feeling for Mah Li because
of it. Nevertheless I would have been ashamed not to take part in the
teasing, baiting, and candy-stealing that made his life miserable after
the Lazy-S closed up and Mah Li opened a restaurant. I helped tip over
his backhouse on Hallowe'en; I was part of a war party that sneaked
to the crest of a knoll and with .22 rifles potted two of his white ducks
as they rode a mud puddle near his shack in the east bend.

The folk culture sponsored every sort of crude practical joke, as it 4
permitted the cruelest and ugliest prejudices and persecutions. Any visible
difference was enough to get an individual picked on. Impartially and
systematically we persecuted Mah Li and his brother Mah Jim, Jew
Meyer and his family, any Indians who came down into the valley in
their wobble-wheeled buckboards, anyone with a pronounced English
accent or fancy clothes or affected manners, any crybaby, any woman
who kept a poodle dog and put on airs, any child with glasses, anyone
afflicted with crossed eyes, St. Vitus's dance, feeble-mindedness, or

a game leg. Systematically the strong bullied the weak, and the weak did their best to persuade their persecutors, by feats of courage or endurance or by picking on someone still weaker, that they were tough and strong.

5   Immune, because they conformed to what the folk culture valued, were people with Texas or Montana or merely Canadian accents, people who wore overalls and worked with their hands, people who snickered at Englishmen or joined the bedevilment of Chinamen, women who let their children grow up wild and unwashed. Indignation swept the school one fall day when the Carpenter kids were sent home by the new teacher from Ontario. She sent a note along with them saying they had pediculosis and should not return to school until they were cured. Their mother in bewildered alarm brought them in to the doctor, and when she discovered that pediculosis meant only the condition of being lousy, she had to be restrained from going over and pulling the smart-alec teacher's hair out. We sympathized completely. That teacher never did get our confidence, for she had convicted herself of being both over-cleanly and pompous.

6   Honored and imitated among us were those with special skills, so long as the skills were not too civilized. We admired good shots, good riders, tough fighters, dirty talkers, stoical endurers of pain. My mother won the whole town because once, riding our flighty mare Daisy up Main Street, she got piled hard in front of Christenson's pool hall with half a dozen men watching, and before they could recover from laughing and go to help her, had caught the mare and remounted and ridden off, tightly smiling. The fact that her hair was red did not hurt: among us, red hair was the sign of a sassy temper.

7   She was one of the immune, and so was my father, for both had been brought up on midwestern farms, had lived on the Dakota frontier, and accepted without question — though my mother would have supplemented it — the code of the stiff upper lip. She had sympathy for anyone's weakness except her own; he went strictly by the code.

8   I remember one Victoria Day when there was a baseball game between our town and Shaunavon. Alfie Carpenter, from a riverbottom ranch just west of town, was catching for the Whitemud team. He was a boy who had abused me and my kind for years, shoving us off the footbridge, tripping us unexpectedly, giving us the hip, breaking up our hideouts in the brush, stampeding the town herd that was in our charge, and generally making himself lovable. This day I looked up from something just in time to see the batter swing and a foul tip catch

Alfie full in the face. For a second he stayed bent over with a hand over his mouth; I saw the blood start in a quick stream through his fingers. My feelings were very badly mixed, for I had dreamed often enough of doing just that to Alfie Carpenter's face, but I was somewhat squeamish about human pain and I couldn't enjoy seeing the dream come true. Moreover I knew with a cold certainty that the ball had hit Alfie at least four times as hard as I had ever imagined hitting him, and there he stood, still on his feet and obviously conscious. A couple of players came up and took his arms and he shook them off, straightened up, spat out a splatter of blood and teeth and picked up his mitt as if to go on with the game. Of course they would not let him — but what a gesture! said my envious and appalled soul. There was a two-tooth hole when Alfie said something; he freed his elbows and swaggered to the side of the field. Watching him, my father broke out in a short, incredulous laugh. "Tough kid!" he said to the man next, and the tone of his voice goose-pimpled me like a breeze on a sweaty skin, for in all my life he had never spoken either to or of me in that voice of approval. Alfie Carpenter, with his broken nose and bloody mouth, was a boy I hated and feared, but most of all I envied his competence to be what his masculine and semi-barbarous world said a man should be.

As for me, I was a crybaby. My circulation was poor and my hands ⁹ always got blue and white in the cold. I always had a runny nose. I was skinny and small, so that my mother anxiously doctored me with Scott's Emulsion, sulphur and molasses, calomel, and other doses. To compound my frail health, I was always getting hurt. Once I lost both big-toe nails in the same week, and from characteristically incompatible causes. The first one turned black and came off because I had accidentally shot myself through the big toe with a .22 short; the second because, sickly thing that I was, I had dropped a ten-pound bottle of Scott's Emulsion on it.

I grew up hating my weakness and despising my cowardice and trying to pretend that neither existed. The usual result of that kind of condition is bragging. I bragged, and sometimes I got called. Once in Sunday School I said that I was not afraid to jump off the high diving board that the editor of the Leader had projected out over the highest cutbank. The editor, who had been a soldier and a hero, was the only person in town who dared use it. It did not matter that the boys who called my bluff would not have dared to jump off it themselves. I was the one who had bragged, and so after Sunday School I found myself out on that thing, a mile above the water, with the wind very cold around my knees. The tea-brown whirlpools went spinning slowly around the deep water of the bend, looking as impossible to jump into as if they had been whorls in cement. A half dozen times I sucked in my breath and grabbed my courage with both hands and inched out to the burlap pad on the end of the board. Every time, the vibrations of the board started such sympathetic vibrations in my knees that I had to creep back for fear of falling off. The crowd on the bank got scornful, and then ribald, and then insulting; I could not rouse even the courage to answer back, but went on creeping out, quaking back, creeping out again, until they finally all got tired and left for their Sunday dinners. Then at once I walked out to the end and jumped.

11   I think I must have come down through thirty or forty feet of air, bent over toward the water, with my eyes out on stems like a lobster's, and I hit the water just so, with my face and chest, a tremendous belly-flopper that drove my eyes out through the back of my head and flattened me out on the water to the thickness of an oil film. The air was full of colored lights; I came to enough to realize I was strangling on weed-tasting river water, and moved my arms and legs feebly toward shore. About four hours and twenty deaths later, I grounded on the mud and lay there gasping and retching, sick for the hero I was not, for the humiliation I had endured, for the mess I had made of the jump when I finally made it — even for the fact that no one had been around to see me, and that I would never be able to convince any of them that I really had, at the risk of drowning, done what I had bragged I would do.

12   Contempt is a hard thing to bear, especially one's own. Because I was what I was, and because the town went by the code it went by, I was never quite out of sight of self-contempt or the contempt of my father or Alfie Carpenter or some other whose right to contempt I had to grant. School, and success therein, never fully compensated for the lacks I felt in myself. I found early that I could shine in class, and I always had a piece to speak in school entertainments, and teachers found me reliable at cleaning blackboards, but teachers were women, and school was a woman's world, the booby prize for those not capable of being men. The worst of it was that I liked school, and liked a good many things about the womanish world, but I wouldn't have dared admit it, and I could not respect the praise of my teachers any more than I could that of my music teacher or my mother.

13   "He has the arteestic tempera*ment*," said Madame Dujardin while collecting her pay for my piano lessons. "He's *sensitive*," my mother would tell her friends, afternoons when they sat around drinking coffee and

eating Norwegian coffee cake, and I hung around inside, partly for the sake of coffee cake and partly to hear them talk about me. The moment they did talk about me, I was enraged. *Women* speaking up for me, noticing my "sensitivity," observing me with that appraising female stare and remarking that I seemed to like songs such as "Sweet and Low" better than "Men of Harlech," which was *their* sons' favorite — my mother interpolating half with pride and half with worry that sometimes she had to drive me out to play, I'd rather stay in and read Ridpath's *History of the World*. Women giving me the praise I would have liked to get from my father or Slivers or the Assiniboine halfbreed down at the Lazy-S. I wanted to be made of whang leather.

Little as I want to acknowledge them, the effects of those years re- 14 main in me like the beach terraces of a dead lake. Having been weak, and having hated my weakness, I am as impatient with the weakness of others as my father ever was. Pity embarrasses me for the person I am pitying, for I know how it feels to be pitied. Incompetence ex- asperates me, a big show of pain or grief or any other feeling makes me uneasy, affectations still inspire in me a mirth I have grown too mannerly to show. I cannot sympathize with the self-pitiers, for I have been there, or with the braggarts, for I have been there too. I even at times find myself reacting against conversation, that highest test of the civilized man, because where I came from it was unfashionable to be "mouthy."

An inhumane and limited code, the value system of a life more limited 15 and cruder than in fact ours was. We got most of it by inheritance from the harsher frontiers that had preceded ours-got it, I suppose, mainly from our contacts with what was left of the cattle industry.

So far as the Cypress Hills were concerned, that industry began with 16 the Mounted Police beef herd at Fort Walsh, and was later amplified by herds brought in to feed treaty Indians during the starving winters after 1879. In practice, the Indians ate a good deal of beef that hadn't been intended tor them; it took a while to teach them that the white man's spotted buffalo were not fair game when a man was hungry. The raiding of cattle and horse herds was never controlled until the Cana- dian Indians were moved to reservations far north of the Line after 1882. Nevertheless it was the Indians who first stimulated the raising of cat- tle on that range, and the departure of the Indians which left the Whitemud River country open to become the last great cattle country.

In some ways, the overlapping of the cattle and homesteading phases 17 of the plains frontier was similar to the overlapping of the horse and gun cultures earlier, and in each case the overlapping occurred latest around the Cypress Hills. Cattle came in from the south, homesteaders from the east and southeast. Among the homesteaders — Ontario men, Scandinavians and Americans working up from the Dakotas, and Englishmen, Scots, and Ukrainians straight off the immigrant boats — there was a heavy percentage of greenhorns and city men. Even the experienced dryland farmers from the States were a prosaic and law-abiding lot by comparison with the cowboys they displaced. As it turned out, the homesteaders, by appropriating and fencing and plowing the range, squeezed out a way of life that was better adapted to the country than their own, and came close to ruining both the cattlemen and themselves in the process, but that is a later story. What succeeded the meeting and overlapping of the two cultures was a long and difficult period of adaptation in which each would modify the other until a sort of amalgamation could result. But while the adaptations were taking place, during the years of uneasy meeting and mixture, it was the cowboy tradition, the horseback culture, that impressed itself as image, as romance, and as ethical system upon boys like me. There were both good and bad reasons why that should have been true.

18   Read the history of the northern cattle ranges in such an anti-American historian as John Peter Turner and you hear that the "Texas men" who brought the cattle industry to Canada were all bravos, rustlers, murderers, gamblers, thugs, and highwaymen; that their life was divided among monte, poker, six-guns, and dancehall girls; and that their law was the gun-law that they made for themselves and enforced by hand. Allow sixty or seventy per cent of error for patriotic fervor, and Mr. Turner's generalizations may be accepted. But it is likewise true that American cow outfits left their gun-law cheerfully behind them when they found the country north of the Line well policed, that they cheer-fully cooperated with the Mounted Police, took out Canadian brands, paid for grazing leases, and generally conformed to the customs of the country. They were indistinguishable from Canadian ranchers, to whom they taught the whole business. Many Canadian ranches, among them the 76, the Matador, the Turkey Track, and the T-Down-Bar, were simp-ly Canadian extensions of cattle empires below the border.

19   So was the culture, in the anthropological sense, that accompanied the cattle. It was an adaptation to the arid Plains that had begun along the Rio Grande and had spread north, like gas expanding to fill a vacuum, as the buffalo and Indians were destroyed or driven out in the years following the Civil War. Like the patterns of hunting and war that had

been adopted by every plains tribe as soon as it acquired the horse, the cowboy culture made itself at home all the way from the Rio Grande to the North Saskatchewan. The outfit, the costume, the practices, the terminology, the state of mind, came into Canada ready-made, and nothing they encountered on the northern Plains enforced any real modifications. The Texas men made it certain that nobody would ever be thrown from a horse in Saskatchewan; he would be piled. They made it sure that no Canadian steer would ever be angry or stubborn; he would be o'nery or ringy or on the prod. Bull Durham was as native to the Whitemud range as to the Pecos, and it was used for the same purposes: smoking, eating, and spitting in the eye of a ringy steer. The Stetson was as useful north as south, could be used to fan the fire or dip up a drink from a stream, could shade a man's eyes or be clapped over the eyes of a bronc to gentle him down. Boots, bandanna, stock saddle, rope, the ways of busting broncs, the institution of the spring and fall roundup, the bowlegs in batwing or goatskin chaps — they all came north intact. About the only thing that changed was the name for the cowboy's favorite diversion, which down south they would have called a rodeo but which we called a stampede.

It was a nearly womanless culture, nomadic, harsh, dangerous, essen-   20
tially romantic. It had the same contempt for the dirtgrubbers that Scythian and Cossack had, and Canadian tillers of the soil tended to look upon it with the same suspicion and fear and envy that tillers of the soil have always expressed toward the herdsmen. As we knew it, it had a lot of Confederate prejudices left in it, and it had the callousness and recklessness that a masculine life full of activity and adventure is sure to produce. I got it in my eyes like stardust almost as soon as we arrived in Whitemud, when the town staged its first stampede down in the western bend. Reno Dodds, known as Slivers, won the saddle bronc competition and set me up a model for my life. I would grow up to be about five feet six and weigh about a hundred and thirty pounds. I would be bowlegged and taciturn, with deep creases in my cheeks and a hide like stained saddle leather. I would be the quietest and most dangerous man around, best rider, best shot, the one who couldn't be buffaloed. Men twice my size, beginning some brag or other, would catch my cold eye and begin to wilt, and when I had stared them into impotence I would turn my back contemptuous, hook onto my pony in one bowlegged arc, and ride off. I thought it tremendous that anyone as small and skinny as Slivers could be a top hand and a champion rider. I don't think I could have survived without his example, and he was

still on my mind years later when, sixteen years old and six feet tall
and weighing a hundred and twenty-five pounds, I went every afternoon to the university gym and worked out on the weights for an hour
and ran wind sprints around the track. If I couldn't be big I could be *hard*.

21   We hung around the Lazy-S corrals a good deal that first year or two,
and the cowpunchers, when they had no one else to pester, would egg
us into what they called shit-fights, with green cow manure for snowballs;
or they would put a surcingle around a calf and set us aboard. After
my try I concluded that I would not do any more of it just at that time,
and I limped to the fence and sat on the top rail nursing my sprains
and bruises and smiling to keep from bawling out loud. From there I
watched Spot Orullian, a Syrian boy a couple of years older than I,
ride a wildly pitching whiteface calf clear around the corral and halfway
around again, and get piled hard, and come up wiping the cow dung
off himself, swearing like a pirate. They cheered him, he was a favorite
at once, perhaps all the more because he had a big brown birthmark
on his nose and so could be kidded. And I sat on the corral rail hunch-
ing my winglike shoulder-blades, smiling and smiling and smiling to
conceal the black envy that I knew was just under the skin of my face.
It was always boys like Spot Orullian who managed to be and do what
I wanted to do and be.

22   Many things that those cowboys represented I would have done well
to get over quickly, or never catch: the prejudice, the callousness, the
destructive practical joking, the tendency to judge everyone by the same
raw standard. Nevertheless, what they themselves most respected, and
what as a boy I most yearned to grow up to, was as noble as it was
limited. They honored courage, competence, self-reliance, and they
honored them tacitly. They took them for granted. It was their absence,
not their presence, that was cause for remark. Practising comradeship
in a rough and dangerous job, they lived a life calculated to make a
man careless of everything except the few things he really valued.

23   In the fall of 1906 it must have seemed that the cowboy life was certain to last a good while, for the Canadian range still lay wide open,
and stockmen from the western states had prospected it and laid large
plans for moving bigger herds across the Line to escape the nesters and
sheepmen who had already broken up the Montana ranges. Probably
the entire country from Wood Mountain to the Alberta line would have
been leased for grazing, at the favorable Canadian rate of a few cents
an acre, if the winter of 1906-07 had not happened.

24   That winter has remained ever since, in the minds of all who went

through it, as the true measure of catastrophe. Some might cite the winter of 1886-87, the year of the Big Die-Up on the American range, but that winter did not affect the Whitemud country, where cattle came in numbers only after 1887. Some who had punched cows in Alberta in the early days might cast a vote for the fatal Cochran drive of 1881, when 8,000 out of 12,000 cattle died over by Lethbridge; and some would certainly, just as weather, mention the April blizzard of 1892, or the winter that followed it, or the big May blizzard of 1903. But after 1907 no one would seriously value those earlier disasters. The winter of 1906-07 was the real one, the year of the blue snow. After it, the leases that might have been taken up were allowed to lapse, the herds that might have been augmented were sold for what they would bring — fifteen to twenty dollars a head with suckling calves thrown in. Old cattlemen who had ridden every range from Texas north took a good long look around in the spring and decided to retire.

The ranches that survived were primarily the hill ranches with shelter 25 plus an access to bench or prairie hay land where winter feed could be cut. The net effect of the winter of 1906-07 was to make stock farmers out of ranchers. Almost as suddenly as the disappearance of the buffalo, it changed the way of life of the region. A great event, it had the force in the history of the Cypress Hills country that a defeat in war has upon a nation. When it was over, the protected Hills might harbor a few cowboys, and one or two of the big ranches such as the 76 might go on, but most of the prairie would be laid open to homesteading and another sort of frontier.

That new frontier, of which my family was a part, very soon squeezed 26 out the Lazy-S. The hay lands in the bottoms were broken up into town lots, my father was growing potatoes where whitefaces had used to graze, the punchers were drifting off to Alberta. But while we had them around, we made the most of them, imitating their talk and their walk and their songs and their rough-handed jokes; admiring them for the way they tormented Mah Li; hanging around in the shade of the bunkhouse listening to Rusty, who was supposed to be the second son of an earl, play the mouth organ; watching the halfbreed Assiniboine braid leather or horsehair into halter ropes and hackamores. I heard some stories about the winter of 1906-07, but I never heard enough. Long afterward, digging in the middens where historians customarily dig, I found and read some more, some of them the reminiscences of men I knew. What they record is an ordeal by weather. The manner of recording is laconic, deceptively matter of fact. It does not give much idea of how it feels to ride sixty or eighty miles on a freezing and exhausted pony, or how cold thirty below is when a fifty-mile wind is driving it into your face, or how demoralizing it is to be lost in a freezing fog where north, south, east, west, even up and down, swim and shift before the slitted and frost-stuck eyes.

27   They do not tell their stories in Technicolor; they would not want to seem to adorn a tale or brag themselves up. The calluses of a life of hardship blunt their sensibilities to their own experience. If we want to know what it was like on the Whitemud River range during that winter when the hopes of a cattle empire died, we had better see it through the eyes of some tenderfoot, perhaps someone fresh from the old country, a boy without the wonder rubbed off him and with something to prove about himself. If in inventing this individual I put into him a little of Corky Jones, and some of the boy Rusty whose mouth organ used to sweeten the dusty summer shade of the Lazy-S bunkhouse, let it be admitted that I have also put into him something of myself, the me who sat on a corral bar wetting with spit my smarting skinned places, and wishing I was as tough as Spot Orullian.

(1955)

The Writer's Subject

1. On what principle were nicknames bestowed on the inhabitants of Stegner's town? (para. 1)

2. What does Stegner mean by "the standard frontier attitudes" shown by his companions? (para. 2)

3. Stegner says that the Chinese cook Mah Li was a friend of his, yet he still took part in the "persecution" of Mah Li; why did he do so? (paras. 3 and 4) Which of Stegner's townsfolk were immune from such persecution, and why? (paras. 5-7)

4. What is meant by "the code of the stiff upper lip"? (para. 7) How is this code related to the stories of Alfie Carpenter's accident (para. 8) and Spot Orullian's calf riding? (para. 21) Account for Stegner's feelings of envy.

5. What is the importance of Stegner's anecdote of his dive from the high diving board into the river? (paras. 10-11)

6. Why did the young Stegner find no satisfaction in his success at school, or in the praise of his mother's friends? (paras. 12-13)

7. What were the values of the "horseback culture" that impressed themselves so strongly on Stegner and boys like him? Which of these values does Stegner see as having been potentially damaging? (paras. 17-22)

8. What were the particularly romantic elements of the cattle culture? (para. 20)

9. Why did Stegner see Reno Dodds ("Slivers") as a model? (para. 20)

10. What was the impact of the winter of 1906-07 on the Cypress Hills country and the cattle culture? (paras. 23-26)

The Writer's Style and Strategy

1. Stegner's account forms a chapter of his book *Wolf Willow: A History, a Story and a Memory of the Last Plains Frontier.* What elements of this chapter reflect the book's subtitle?

2. Stegner is writing as an adult recalling his childhood. Choose one or two paragraphs which focus on Stegner's childhood experiences (e.g., paras. 10-11, or 21), and show how he manages to convey a sense of how he felt as a child.

3. How would you characterize the adult Stegner's attitude to the code of the frontier that he admired so much as a child? Where, and how, is that attitude revealed?

4. What function is performed by paragraph 14? How is it related to the preceding paragraphs?

5. What function is performed by paragraph 15?

6. What differences in diction are apparent in paragraphs 21 and 22? How does the style of each paragraph reflect its substance and purpose?

7. Stegner provides portraits of a number of characters, including Mah Li, Alfie Carpenter, Reno Dodds, and Spot Orullian. Choose one of these characters and explain how Stegner's description throws light on Stegner's childhood and the society he grew up in.

Suggested Topics for Writing and Discussion

1. Stegner describes a major change in the region of his childhood, from cattle-ranching and the cowboy culture to "homesteading and another sort of frontier." Find out what you can about the significant changes that have taken place in the neighbourhood or region in which you grew up. What gains or losses have the changes brought, in your view?

2. Stegner specifies the qualities that were demonstrated by the heroes of his childhood. Write an essay in which you use anecdote to describe the childhood heroes of your neighbourhood or region. In what ways are your "specifications" similar to or different from Stegner's?

3. Stegner describes at length his mortifying experience on the diving board. Re-create an event in your own childhood which caused you extreme embarrassment, fear, or humiliation. What feelings about the event do you have now as you look back on it?

4. What, in your view, are the qualities that constitute true heroism? What model would you offer for the admiration of children today?

Marilyn Monroe: The Woman Who Died Too Soon

by Gloria Steinem

Saturday afternoon movies — no matter how poorly made or incred- 1
ible the plot, they were a refuge from my neighborhood and all my
teenage miseries. Serials that never ended, Doris Day, who never
capitulated, cheap travelogues, sci-fi features with zippers in the monster
suits: I loved them all, believed them all, and never dreamed of leaving until the screen went sickeningly blank.

But I walked out on Marilyn Monroe. I remember her on the screen, 2
huge as a colossus doll, mincing and whispering and simply hoping her
way into total vulnerability. Watching her, I felt angry, even humiliated,
but I didn't understand why.

After all, Jane Russell was in the movie, too (a very bad-taste ver- 3
sion of *Gentlemen Prefer Blondes*), so it wasn't just the vulnerability
that all big-breasted women seem to share. (If women viewers prefer
actresses who are smaller, neater — the Audrey Hepburns of the world
— it is not because we're jealous of the *zoftig* ones as men suppose. It's
just that we would rather identify with a woman we don't have to worry
about, someone who doesn't seem in constant danger.) Compared to
Marilyn, Jane Russell seemed in control of her body and even of the
absurd situations in this movie.

Perhaps it was the uncertainty in the eyes of this big, blond child- 4
woman; the terrible desire for approval that made her different from
Jane Russell. How dare she express the neediness that so many women
feel, but try so hard to hide? How dare she, a movie star, be just as
unconfident as I was?

So I disliked her and avoided her movies, as we avoid that which 5
reflects our fears about ourselves. If there were jokes made on her name

and image when I was around, I joined in. I contributed to the laughing, the ridicule, the put-downs, thus proving that I was nothing like her. Nothing at all.

6   I, too, got out of my neighborhood in later years, just as she had escaped from a much worse life of lovelessness, child abuse, and foster homes. I didn't do it, as she did, through nude calendar photographs and starlet bits. (Even had there been such opportunities for mildly pretty girls in Toledo, Ohio, I would never have had the courage to make myself so vulnerable.) Yes, I was American enough to have show-business dreams. The boys in my neighborhood hoped to get out of a lifetime in the factories through sports; the girls, if we imagined anything other than marrying a few steps up in the world, always dreamed of show-business careers. But after high-school years as a dancer on the Toledo show-business circuit, or what passed for show business there, it seemed hopeless even to me. In the end, it was luck and an encouraging mother and a facility with words that got me out; a facility that helped me fake my way through the college entrance exams for which I was totally unprepared.

7   But there's not much more confidence in girls who scrape past college boards than there is in those who, like Marilyn, parade past beauty-contest judges. By the time I saw her again, I was a respectful student watching the celebrated members of the Actors Studio do scenes from what seemed to me very impressive and highbrow plays (Arthur Miller and Eugene O'Neill were to be served up that day). She was a student, too, a pupil of Lee Strasberg, leader of the Actors Studio and American guru of the Stanislavski method, but her status as a movie star and sex symbol seemed to keep her from being taken seriously even there. She was allowed to observe, but not to do scenes with her colleagues.

8   So the two of us sat there, mutually awed, I think, in the presence of such theater people as Ben Gazzara and Rip Torn, mutually insecure in the masculine world of High Culture, mutually trying to fade into the woodwork.

9   I remember thinking that Strasberg and his actors seemed to take positive pleasure in their power to ignore this great and powerful movie star who had come to learn. Their greetings to her were a little too studiously casual, their whispers to each other about her being there a little too self-conscious and condescending. Though she stayed in the back of the room, her blond head swathed in a black scarf and her body hidden in a shapeless black sweater and slacks, she gradually became a presence, if only because the group was trying so hard *not* to look,

to remain oblivious and cool.

As we filed slowly out of the shabby room after the session was over, 10
Marilyn listened eagerly to the professional postmortem being carried
on by Ben Gazzara and others who walked ahead of us, her fingers
nervously tracing a face that was luminous and without makeup, as if
she were trying to hide herself, to apologize for being there. I was suddenly glad she hadn't participated and hadn't been subjected to the
criticisms of this rather vulturous group. (Perhaps it was an unschooled
reaction, but I hadn't enjoyed watching Strasberg encourage an initimate
love scene between an actor and actress, and then pick them apart with
humiliating authority.) Summoning my nerve, I did ask the shy, blond
woman in front of me if she could imagine playing a scene for this group.

"Oh, no," Marilyn said, her voice childish, but much less whispery 11
than on the screen, "I admire all these people so much. I'm just not
good enough." Then, after a few beats of silence: "Lee Strasberg is a
genius, you know. I plan to do what he says."

Her marriage to Arthur Miller seemed quite understandable to me 12
and to other women, even those who were threatened by Miller's casting
off of a middle-aged wife to take a younger, far more glamorous one.
If you can't be taken seriously in your work, if you have an emotional
and intellectual insecurity complex, then marry a man who has the
seriousness you've been denied. It's a traditional female option — far
more acceptable than trying to achieve that identity on one's own.

Of course, Marilyn's image didn't really gain seriousness and intellec- 13
tuality. Women don't gain serious status by sexual association any more
easily than they do by hard work. (At least, not unless the serious man
dies and we confine ourselves to being keepers of the flame. As Margaret
Mead has pointed out, widows are almost the only women this country
honors in authority.) Even Marilyn's brave refusal to be intimidated
by threats that she would never work in films again if she married Miller,
who was then a "subversive" called to testify before the House Un-
American Activities Committee, was considered less brave than Miller's
refusal to testify. Indeed, it was barely reported at all.

Perhaps she didn't take her own bravery seriously either. She might 14
be giving up her livelihood, the work that meant so much to her, but
she was about to give that up for marriage anyway. As Mrs. Arthur
Miller, she retired to a Connecticut farm and tried to limit her life to
his solitary work habits, his friends, and his two children. Only when
they badly needed money did she come out of retirement again, and
that was to act in *The Misfits*, a film written by her husband.

15   On the other hand, the public interpretation was very different. She was an egocentric actress forcing one of America's most important playwrights to tailor a screenplay to her inferior talents: that was the gossip-column story here and in Europe. But her own pattern argues the case for her. In two previous marriages, to an aircraft factory worker at the age of sixteen and later to Joe Di Maggio, she had cut herself off from the world and put all her energies into being a housewife. When it didn't work out, she blamed herself, not the role, and added one more failure to her list of insecurities. "I have too many fantasies to be a housewife," she told a woman friend sadly. And finally, to an interviewer: "I guess I *am* a fantasy."

16   *The Misfits* seemed to convey some facets of the real Marilyn: honesty, an innocence and belief that survived all experience to the contrary, kindness toward other women, a respect for the life of plants and animals. Because for the first time she wasn't only a sex object and victim, I also was unembarrassed enough to notice her acting ability. I began to see her earlier movies – those in which, unlike *Gentlemen Prefer Blondes*, she wasn't called upon to act the female impersonator.

17   For me as for so many people, she was a presence in the world, a life force.

18   Over the years, I heard other clues to her character. When Ella Fitzgerald, a black artist and perhaps the greatest singer of popular songs, hadn't been able to get a booking at an important Los Angeles nightclub in the fifties, it was Marilyn who called the owner and promised to sit at a front table every night while she sang. The owner hired Ella, Marilyn was faithful to her promise each night, the press went wild, and, as Ella remembers with gratitude, "After that, I never had to play a small jazz club again."

19   Even more movingly, there was her last interview. She pleaded with the reporter to end with "What I really want to say: That what the world really needs is a real feeling of kinship. Everybody: stars, laborers, Negroes, Jews, Arabs. We are all brothers. . . . Please don't make me a joke. End the interview with what I believe."

20   And then she was gone. I remember being told, in the middle of a chaotic student meeting in Europe, that she was dead. I remember that precise moment on August 5, 1962 – the people around me, what the room looked like – and I've discovered that many other people remember that moment of hearing the news, too. It's a phenomenon usually reserved for the death of family and presidents.

21   She was an actress, a person on whom no one's fate depended, and

yet her energy and terrible openness to life had made a connection to strangers. Within days after her body was discovered, eight young and beautiful women took their lives in individual incidents clearly patterned after Marilyn Monroe's death. Some of them left notes to make that connection clear.

Two years later, Arthur Miller's autobiographical play, *After the Fall*,   22
brought Marilyn back to life in the character of Maggie. But somehow that Maggie didn't seem the same. She had Marilyn's pathetic insecurity, the same need to use her sexual self as her only way of getting recognition and feeling alive. But, perhaps naturally, the play was about Miller's suffering, not Marilyn's. He seemed honestly to include some of his own destructive acts. (He had kept a writer's diary of his movie-star wife, for instance, and Marilyn's discovery of it was an emotional blow, the beginning of the end for that marriage. It made her wonder: Was her husband exploiting her, as most men had done, but in a more intellectual way?) Nonetheless, the message of the play was mostly Miller's view of his attempts to shore up a creature of almost endless insecurities; someone doomed beyond his helping by a mysterious lack of confidence.

To women, that lack was less mysterious. Writer Diana Trilling, who   23
had never met Marilyn, wrote an essay just after her death that some of Marilyn's friends praised as a more accurate portrayal than Miller's. She described the public's "mockery of [Marilyn's] wish to be educated"; the sexual awareness that came only from outside, from men's reactions, "leaving a great emptiness where a true sexuality would have supplied her with a sense of herself as a person with connection and content." She questioned whether Marilyn had really wanted to die, or only to be asleep, not to be conscious through the loneliness of that particular Saturday night.

Trilling also recorded that feeling of connection to Marilyn's loneliness   24
felt by so many strangers ("especially women to whose protectiveness her extreme vulnerability spoke so directly"), so much so that we fantasized our ability to save her, if only we had been there. "But we were the friends," as Trilling wrote sadly, "of whom she knew nothing."

"She was an unusual woman — a little ahead of her times," said Ella   25
Fitzgerald. "And she didn't know it."

Now that women's self-vision is changing, we are thinking again about   26
the life of Marilyn Monroe. Might our new confidence in women's existence with or without the approval of men have helped a thirty-six-year-old woman of talent to stand on her own? To resist the insecurity

and ridicule? To stop depending on sexual attractiveness as the only proof that she was alive - and therefore to face aging with confidence? Because the ability to bear a child was denied to her, could these new ideas have helped her to know that being a woman included much more? Could she have challenged the Freudian analysts to whom she turned in her suffering?

27   Most of all, we wonder if the support and friendship of other women could have helped. Her early experiences of men were not good. She was the illegitimate daughter of a man who would not even contribute for her baby clothes; her mother's earliest memory of her own father, Marilyn's grandfather, was his smashing a pet kitten against the fireplace in a fit of anger; Marilyn herself said she was sexually attacked by a foster father while still a child; and she was married off at sixteen because another foster family could not take care of her. Yet she was forced always to depend for her security on the goodwill and recognition of men; even to be interpreted by them in writing because she feared that sexual competition made women dislike her. Even if they had wanted to, the women in her life did not have the power to protect her. In films, photographs, and books, even after her death as well as before, she has been mainly seen through men's eyes.

28   We are too late. We cannot know whether we could have helped Norma Jean Baker or the Marilyn Monroe she became. But we are not too late to do as she asked. At last, we can take her seriously.

(1972)

The Writer's Subject

1. Why was Steinem's first response to Marilyn Monroe one of anger and humiliation? (paras. 2-5)

2. In what ways was Steinem's early life like Monroe's? (para. 6)

3. How was Monroe treated by members of the Actors Studio? How did this episode affect Steinem's view of Monroe? (paras. 7-10)

4. Why, according to Steinem, did Monroe marry the celebrated American playwright, Arthur Miller? (para. 12)

5. What qualities in Monroe's character does Steinem find admirable? How are those qualities illustrated?

6. What is the importance of Marilyn's last interview described in paragraph 19?

7. Why, according to Steinem, did the news of Monroe's death have an impact on so many people? (paras. 20-21, 24)

8. Steinem suggests that Miller may have exploited his marriage to Monroe. How? (para. 22)

9. What, according to Steinem's account, was missing in Monroe's life?

10. Why, in Steinem's view, was Marilyn Monroe "the woman who died too soon"? (paras. 25-28)

The Writer's Style and Strategy

1. Steinem's essay presents an initially hostile view which is re-evaluated and then altered. Analyze the stages of the essay to show how Steinem presents this shift in view.

2. What use does Steinem make of her own experiences in her attempt to explain the mysterious appeal of Marilyn Monroe?

3. What tone does Steinem create by means of the transition from paragraph 5 into paragraph 6?

4. What is Steinem's purpose in repeating "mutually" in paragraph 8?

5. What use does Steinem make of the Actors Studio anecdote to illustrate Monroe's character? Why does she quote directly Monroe's comments about Lee Strasberg? (para. 11)

6. This essay was originally published in *Ms.* magazine. What features of Steinem's style or approach suggest that she was writing specifically for a feminist audience?

Suggested Topics for Writing and Discussion

1. Marilyn Monroe achieved considerable fame as the sex symbol for her generation. Who in your view, among today's male and female stars, has attained the status of a sex symbol? Explain this person's appeal for the present generation.

2. Steinem alludes to the American dreams of escape from an ordinary life to fame and fortune, chiefly through sports for the boys and show business for the girls. Are these, in your view, still the stuff of escape dreams for American – and Canadian – youth?

3. Steinem says that a traditional option for a woman has been to marry a man in order to gain an identity rather than achieve that identity on her own. Do you think that is still the case?

Ethnicity and Culture

"I'm Not Racist But ..."
by Neil Bissoondath

Someone recently said that racism is as Canadian as maple syrup. I have 1
no argument with that. History provides us with ample proof. But, for
proper perspective, let us remember that it is also as American as apple
pie, as French as croissants, as Jamaican as ackee, as Indian as aloo, as
Chinese as chow mein, as .... Well, there's an entire menu to be written.
This is not by way of excusing it. Murder and rape, too, are international,
multicultural, as innate to the darker side of the human experience. But
we must be careful that the inevitable rage evoked does not blind us to the
larger context.

The word "racism" is a discomforting one: It is so vulnerable to manipula- 2
tion. We can, if we so wish, apply it to any incident involving people of
different colour. And therein lies the danger. During the heat of altercation,
we seize, as terms of abuse, on whatever is most obvious about the other
person. It is, often, a question of unfortunate convenience. A woman,
because of her sex, easily becomes a female dog or an intimate part of her
anatomy. A large person might be dubbed "a stupid ox," a small person
"a little" whatever. And so a black might become "a nigger," a white "a
honky," an Asian "a paki," a Chinese "a chink," an Italian "a wop," a French-
Canadian "a frog."

There is nothing pleasant about these terms; they assault every decent 3
sensibility. Even so, I once met someone who, in a stunning surge of
naiveté, used them as simple descriptives and not as terms of racial abuse.
She was horrified to learn the truth. While this may have been an extreme
case, the point is that the use of such patently abusive words may not always

indicate racial or cultural distaste. They may indicate ignorance or stupidity or insensitivity, but pure racial hatred — such as the Nazis held for Jews, or the Ku Klux Klan for blacks — is a thankfully rare commodity.

4   Ignorance, not the willful kind but that which comes from lack of experience, is often indicated by that wonderful phrase, "I'm not racist but...." I think of the mover, a friendly man, who said, "I'm not racist, but the Chinese are the worst drivers on the road." He was convinced this was so because the shape of their eyes, as far as he could surmise, denied them peripheral vision.

5   Or the oil company executive, an equally warm and friendly man, who, looking for an apartment in Toronto, rejected buildings with East Indian tenants not because of their race — he was telling me this, after all — but because he was given to understand that cockroaches were symbols of good luck in their culture and that, when they moved into a new home, friends came by with gift-wrapped roaches.

6   Neither of these men thought of himself as racist, and I believe they were not, deep down. (The oil company executive made it clear he would not hesitate to have me as a neighbour; my East Indian descent was of no consequence to him, my horror of cockroaches was.) Yet their comments, so innocently delivered, would open them to the accusation, justifiably so if this were all one knew about them. But it is a charge which would undoubtedly be wounding to them. It is difficult to recognize one's own misconceptions.

7   True racism is based, more often than not, on willful ignorance, and an acceptance of — and comfort with — stereotype. We like to think, in this country, that our multicultural mosaic will help nudge us into a greater openness. But multiculturalism as we know it indulges in stereotype, depends on it for a dash of colour and the flash of dance. It fails to address the most basic questions people have about each other: Do those men doing the Dragon Dance really all belong to secret criminal societies? Do those women dressed in saris really coddle cockroaches for luck? Do those people in dreadlocks all smoke marijuana and live on welfare? Such questions do not seem to be the concern of the government's multicultural programs, superficial and exhibitionistic as they have become.

8   So the struggle against stereotype, the basis of all racism, becomes a purely personal one. We must beware of the impressions we create. A friend of mine once commented that, from talking to West Indians, she has the impression that their one great cultural contribution to the world is in the oft-repeated boast that "We (unlike everyone else) know how to party."

9   There are dangers, too, in community response. We must be wary of the self-appointed activists who seem to pop up in the media at every given

opportunity spouting the rhetoric of retribution, mining distress for personal, political and professional gain. We must be skeptical about those who depend on conflict for their sense of self, the non-whites who need to feel themselves victims of racism, the whites who need to feel themselves purveyors of it. And we must be sure that, in addressing the problem, we do not end up creating it. Does the *Miss Black Canada Beauty Contest* still exist? I hope not. Not only do I find beauty contests offensive, but a racially segregated one even more so. What would the public reaction be, I wonder, if every year CTV broadcast the *Miss White Canada Beauty Pageant*? We give community-service awards only to blacks: Would we be comfortable with such awards only for whites? In Quebec, there are The Association of Black Nurses, The Association of Black Artists, The Congress of Black Jurists. Play tit for tat: The Associations of White Nurses, White Artists, White Jurists: visions of apartheid. Let us be frank, racism for one is racism for others.

Finally, and perhaps most important, let us beware of abusing the word 10 itself.

(1989)

The Writer's Subject

1. What does Bissoondath mean by saying that the word "racism" is "so vulnerable to manipulation"? (para. 2)

2. What is the connection that the writer perceives between racism and the acceptance of stereotypes?

3. What, according to Bissoondath, are the possible dangers that lie in multi-culturalism?

4. What are the dangers that Bissoondath sees in community responses to racism? (para. 9)

The Writer's Style and Strategy

1. What is the intended effect of the comparison in the opening sentence of the essay?

2. Explain the relevance of the title to Bissoondath's purpose.

3. Discuss Bissoondath's use of personal anecdote as a means of supporting his thesis.

Suggested Topics for Writing and Discussion

1. In paragraph 2, Bissoondath instances examples of frequently-used derogatory terms. Discuss the origins of these words or of other racist terms.

2. Bissoondath asserts that Canadian multicultural programmes have become "superficial and exhibitionistic." In your view, have government policies encouraging multiculturalism been a success or a failure?

3. In discussions about the integration of immigrants, American society is sometimes called a "melting-pot," while Canada is imaged as a "mosaic." Compare these two concepts.

Taking the Missionary Position

by Susan Crean

When *Into the Heart of Africa* opened at the Royal Ontario Museum in   1
November 1989, it was with a dull, deceptive thump. The controversy that
shattered the museum's polite facade, earning it the title Racist Ontario
Museum, simmered in private for almost three months before it erupted;
but, by the end of the exhibition's nine-month run, both curator and institution had been thoroughly discredited.

I had been aware that an exhibition of the African collection was in the   2
offing for some time, as someone from the museum had contacted my father
about displaying Great Uncle John's pith helmet, a family relic he'd donated
to the museum to accompany the small collection of African artifacts Great
Uncle had himself deposited with the Royal Military Institute before he
died in 1907. Born in 1858, this older brother of my grandfather became
a professional soldier at 18, fought with the Queen's Own Rifles and, by
the mid-eighteen-nineties, was in west Africa with the British forces of
occupation in what is now Ghana, leading a battalion of Hausa men of the
Gold Coast Regiment with whom he would fight in the fabled Asante wars
of 1900.

To be blunt about it, Great Uncle John spent his entire adult life in one   3
part or another of the globe killing native people on behalf of God, Queen
and Empire. His job was to provide the brute force necessary to keep *"Pax"*
Britannica operating in the interests of the British merchant class. In Africa
this involved participating in the vainglorious "cause" of bringing European civilization, Christianity and commerce to the continent, though it
was, of course, experienced by the African people as the hostile aggression by a race of foreigners it actually was.

4   It is easy enough to grasp the political and ideological dynamics of the world that produced Captain Crean and put him in Africa. What his presence does in the here and now — specifically his presence in *Into the Heart of Africa* — is provoke the ultimate (and unanswerable) question about his personal role in the imperial scheme. Did he pillage and loot? Did he rape women or brutalize children? Did he kill in anger or just in the line of duty? We are talking here of the ugly macho underside of the war; the secret part we are never asked to remember on Remembrance Day, the part veterans and generals keep to themselves.

5   The truth is, though, that none of us get to choose our ancestors, and none of us can claim any singular moral authority for condemning their exploits. Even if they can individually be a source of eternal shame, it's a shame that ultimately has to be shared; in Great Uncle's case, by the white community as a whole. Still, it must be said that it is one thing to have an ancestor who took part in deplorable events a century ago and quite another to have a major cultural institution use his story in your own time to perpetuate misunderstanding.

6   Which brings me back to the ROM show. Because of Great Uncle I had some inkling about its origin and, indeed, guest curator Jeanne Cannizzo has said the project grew around her desire to exhibit the African collection that had been languishing in storerooms for almost a century. Even the exhibition brochure introduces it as "an historical journey through the world of sub-Saharan Africa, illustrated by the ROM's outstanding collections."

7   So I wasn't at all prepared for what I found: Great Uncle elevated to the status of a quaint Canadian Rambo dressed in original Tilley Endurables. He is treated as a historical figure; an entire case of "his" collection of Hausa weaponry and Asante objects (drum, quran pouch, stool and tobacco pipe) is displayed, his life is illustrated with newspaper accounts from the battle-front and his 1902 photograph of the Hausa battalion is mounted on a wall nearby.

8   Most disconcerting, however, is the appearance of the old pith helmet, reverently displayed in the very first room, in hushed lighting and a glass box of its own. Spruced up with a new red band and brass spike atop, it floats in timelessness, reminding me, curiously, of a similar sight I saw years ago at Saint Joseph's Oratory in Montreal on my first visit there in 1957, age 12. I'd never been inside a Roman Catholic church before, and I was astonished by the make-believe setting of that enormous stone basilica, the inside walls festooned with the discarded crutches and braces of the cured, the heavy scent of incense combined with the sounds of Latin.

9   And then I saw it, something I had never seen in my life before — a real

human heart. In this case, the preserved heart of the sainted Brother André. It was all quite fantastic to me, but most fantastic of all was that pickled heart, which I approached with a mixture of horror and wonder, my own heart thumping.

Thirty years later I am assaulted by the same combination of revulsion 10 and fascination in front of Great Uncle's bloody dress helmet. Only the embalming fluid is missing.

The official guide explains that *Into the Heart of Africa* is divided 11 thematically into four areas; the Imperial Connection, the Military Hall, the Missionary Hall and the Africa Room. The first three of these and more than half the exhibition space, then, is devoted to the history of a small band of white Canadians, missionaries and militia men, who brought artifacts back with them as souvenirs and trophies.

As I walk along I find myself growing increasingly disturbed by the roll- 12 call of former owners, the detailed label explanations of whose estate gave what and how it passed along from one person to another and eventually to the museum. The names parade along like a nagging subtext, casting the artifacts as misappropriated byproducts of all that religious and military fervour. The lives of the white folks are featured, their stories personalized and connected to the larger stream of history while beside them, in photos and in absentia, the Africans with whom they lived remain silent. And, with a couple of rare exceptions, nameless.

The imbalance bothers me, as does the presentation of the objects as the 13 possessions of people who in reality traded, seized and otherwise made off with them as spoils of war. It strikes me as bad karma not to mention bad form. And a good example of how contemporary art history and ethnography, ruled as they are by linear academic techniques, are at the mercy of whatever documentation is available.

As I go along I am also thinking of the headlines I am going to read, taking 14 off on the title — *Into the Heart of Controversy, Into the Heart of Racist Canada, Into the Belly of Bigotry*. Take your pick. I say this not because the exhibition denies Canada's colonialist past (although I think it more accurate to call it imperialist past, as the activity of British colonials was very unambiguous as to who were the colonizers and who was being colonized in Africa), nor because it whitewashes the role of Canadians in it. Nor is it because the curator and organizers condone the white supremacist rhetoric the exhibit depicts. But they are awfully quiet and oblique in their disapproval, never directly condemning or examining its legacy.

There is a sense that it all happened so long ago, explanations aren't 15 necessary. Says the brochure: "The rich cultural heritage of African religious, social and economic life is celebrated through objects brought back by Canadian missionaries and military men over one hundred years ago. The exhibition examines this turbulent but little-known period in history when Canadians participated in Britain's efforts to colonize and convert the African nations." For whom, I wonder, was this period merely turbulent, and to whom is the period so little-known?

16   And there I think, lies the error. By presenting the African collection through the history of its donors, by giving pride of place to the personal stories of the white Canadians who happened to bring them to Canada, Cannizzo creates a context in which that history is claimed rather than criticized and rejected, showcased even while she tut-tuts from between the lines. "Well, Great Uncle certainly was a scoundrel, and who knows what he got up to in Africa; but, well, you can't blame the old boy for being a product of his time." That seems to be the sentiment.

17   Cannizzo does try to dissociate herself by putting ironic quotes around phrases like "barbarous people" and "savage customs." But such subtle irony is not only lost on those who can't (or don't) read the explanatory texts, it is also a pretty limp way to examine a subject as grave as racially motivated genocide. And, occasionally, she slips up, for example on one plaque: "Canadian missionaries were often inspired by the exploits of the British hero, missionary explorer Dr. David Livingstone. They followed him into the heart of Africa." The absence of ironic quotes around the word hero beside "Livingstone" is telling, implying that unlike "savage customs" it is not an idea under suspicion, much less one up for retirement.

18   The most curious of all the curatorial decisions that undermined Cannizzo's good intentions was undoubtedly the audio-visual lantern slide show called, "In Livingstone's Footsteps." This was a re-creation of the kind of fundraising lecture missionaries would have given in church halls in the early part of this century to awe-struck Torontonians. At the beginning and end of the presentation (and in writing on a panel at the entrance to the viewing room) is the disclaimer, "The sense of cultural superiority and paternalism that you will hear in this fictional narrative was characteristic of the missionary world view at the time. So was the genuine spirit of adventure and the sincere belief that missionaries were bringing 'light' to the 'Dark Continent.'" Now, if you have ever watched people in a museum you'll know the vast majority tend to drift in and out of such presentations; relatively few pay strict attention all the way through. To make matters worse, the day I was there, the soundtrack could be heard throughout the first part of the exhibition, and detached phrases kept wafting through my consciousness. The unctuous voice delivering highly derogatory commentary could have been that of the ROM's director on the

intercom for all I knew. By the time I reached the end of the section and realized the voice was an actor's and the opinions not those of anyone living (presumably), I had been assailed with this semi-subliminal commentary for over an hour.

With a similar weird disregard for the sensibilities of visitors, especially 19 black children, the installation made use of some extremely graphic and violent images. At the end of the first set of rooms a wall-sized sketch from the *Illustrated London News* shows a British soldier on horseback plunging his sword into the chest of a Zulu warrior. Further on, in the missionary section a photograph shows four African women kneeling on the ground doing laundry in tubs while a white woman in voluminous skirts looks on, smiling approvingly. This, the caption tells us, is "Mrs. Thomas Titcombe offering 'a lesson in how to wash clothes' to Yagba women in Northern Nigeria in 1915." (Tell me this is how you would explain the cultural bias and racial arrogance of that image to school children.)

And whatever is one to make of the old-fashioned decorative display of 20 captured spears and shields arranged with gemsbok and hartebeest horn, a typical "trophy-wall" of a Toronto home circa 1900? Why this compulsion to humanize the white experience of imperialism, I wonder. And likewise, why the decision to let the soundtrack of the slide show dominate the environment when African music (which is piped into headsets in the last room) could have been?

I left the show feeling nervous and slightly ill. The final section, featuring 21 a glorious display of textiles and musical instruments where, at last, the African pieces were left to speak on their own behalf, was worth the wait. And it seemed to me they stole the show. But they couldn't save the show from itself or prevent the unintended response some people had to it. (I can't help thinking of the anonymous visitor who wrote in the comment book at the exhibit exit, "A good display of life in primitive Africa.") By last February, members of the black community had begun to organize. The Coalition for the Truth about Africa, some 30 community groups strong, was formed and charges were levelled that the show was conceptually and structurally racist.

This, incidentally, was not the first hint there were going to be people 22 who did not see *Into the Heart of Africa* the way the ROM or the curator did; people who were going to be offended, even angered by it. Six months before the exhibit opened, initial contact with the community brought back complaints about the brochure, which described the show in tired, stereotypical language. Under pressure, it was withdrawn and another produced. A consultant was also hired to hold focus groups and smooth community relations.

23   In June 1989, an informal reception for members of the black community
was held. But this preview may have done more harm than good, as several
of those invited left with the distinct impression they were being presented
with a *fait accompli*, their views not seriously solicited, only their support.
In curator Hazel A. da Breo's interview for *Fuse* magazine, Cannizzo said
as much herself. "There is not a large number of Black Canadians who are
specialists in art," she said. "There is a wider issue in how museums choose
curators but that's a policy thing.... I also think that the generation of
scholarly aspects of the exhibition must be done by experts, however those
experts are defined. For me it's not a race issue, it's a question of expertise. Scholarly issues should be left in the hands of scholars."

24   Admittedly Cannizzo does flash occasional warnings to visitors that
everything is relative and objects change their meaning with context. One
text says "The context in which an object is used, found, or viewed can
significantly alter its meaning and function. What was once an African
spear or shield became a trophy when collected by a Canadian soldier
campaigning in Africa. It then appeared as a piece of decorative art when
displayed in that soldier's home. Later in a museum collection it was
catalogued as an ethnographic object. Now when viewed by you it takes
on another meaning as a museum exhibit." And again: "[I]t is impossible
actually to reconstruct another cultural reality in a museum. The artifacts
you see here are displayed according to their 'function' or 'form' in a way
that would be quite familiar to late nineteenth century museum-goers, but
not the people who made them. The things are theirs, the arrangement
is not."

25   That says a lot, actually, and Cannizzo is right. The traditions of the
institution and its constituent "departments" (academic disciplines) are
derived from European, not African, culture. The coalition was making
roughly the same point when it reminded the museum that the white point
of view was still telling the story and presenting the information while
African voices and interpretations were absent or invisible. As the show's
nine-month run progressed, the coalition pressed the case that the exhibition
was biased and misleading. "The exhibit depicts a colonialist, imperialist,
racist interpretation of Africa's historical past," it stated in a letter to
Contrast magazine in May of that year. "The curators have effectively
disguised the destruction that was brought upon African society and have
deliberately neglected the tremendous contribution Africans made to World
Science, Technology and Culture."

26   There were criticisms of some facts and interpretations and several
writers, teachers and scholars – notably Molefe Kete Asante, chairman
of African Studies at Temple University in the U.S. – denounced the show

in its entirety. After viewing the exhibition, Asante told reporters, "They have reinforced that same kind of arrogance the missionaries had. The presentation of Africa this way is not only fragmentary, it is limited and gives a very, very negative impression."

Indeed, young children were reported to have had nightmares after 27 seeing the show, and the Toronto Board of Education commissioned a review, which recommended the exhibition was unsuitable for elementary school children and suitable for high school students only if significant classroom preparation was provided beforehand. Poet Ayanna Black gives this analysis of what went wrong. "They used the propaganda of the period without proper explanation or preamble. [The curator] did not want to manipulate the material, but she ended up implanting racist images because the critique of 'intellectual arrogance' did not come through. People missed it. I watched when they came upon that picture of the Zulu warrior. It was such a shock, some just froze and couldn't go on."

For others — writer and broadcaster Robert Payne, for instance — the 28 disclaimers were adequate. In a *Share* editorial, he wrote, "In so many words they tell us that *Into the Heart of Africa* is very narrow in its perspective. So I look at the various stringed instruments on display, and tell myself that they are the great grandfathers and great grandmothers of today's guitar. I see colourful, intricately woven fabric, and they hint at the great contribution which Africans have made to today's fashions.... The links are obvious — or should be to anyone in touch with history." All the same, Payne allows that the ROM was insensitive and probably stupid to mount such an exhibit, "because the glorification of colonialism in so multicultural a city as Toronto is colossally bad judgement."

Too true. In her various calculations about context and the shifting 29 meanings of things, Cannizzo would seem to have missed something; namely the context in which her own creation was going to happen, in which it was, in fact, transformed from an academic event into a *cause célèbre*. While she could never have predicted the exhibit would coincide with the bloodiest year on record for the shooting of black youths by Toronto police, much less with the release of Nelson Mandela, she might still have thought about how African descendants would feel about reliving those brutal nineteenth century attitudes. As Payne put it, "Given our druthers, most of us are a touch reluctant to celebrate the men who raped our grandmothers." (Ditto, I'd say, about celebrating our grandfathers who were rapists.) But if Cannizzo's research was closed to present time (she did not consider consulting with contemporary artists and teachers relevant), one still might have expected the ROM to bring a little savvy and street-smarts to the party.

For example, in anthropological circles, cultural appropriation is a very 30 live and exceedingly touchy issue at the moment. More than one anthropologist has been asked to leave town and more than one museum has found itself confronted by native people contesting its use of collections that are part of their heritage. (I think of the Lubicon in Calgary three years ago protesting *The Spirit Sings*.) And more than once white artists, ethnologists and writers have been asked to respect native ownership of images and not to usurp their right to tell their own stories. Although this has been raised primarily in connection with native communities, the same sensitivities clearly come into play with an exhibition like *Into the Heart of Africa*.

31 So why did the ROM stand so resolute and inflexible behind the terse assertion that the show was historically accurate? "It's a historical examination of Canada's involvement in Africa," said the museum's director, Cuyler Young, in response to Asante's remarks. "It has to tell a story that's historically true. The essence of this exhibition was to demonstrate what was wrong with Canadians' attitudes as missionaries." (And even on that score, the ROM managed to outrage people. An irate William Samarin, professor of linguistic anthropology at the University of Toronto, wrote in *Christian Week,* "It is deplorable ... that a public institution should exploit what should be a tribute to Africans as an opportunity to reinforce the stereotype of the missionary as an ethnocentric, bigoted and insensitive person.")

32 The shame of it is that the ROM dug in its heels and refused to take any criticism whatsoever. In this they were helped by white journalists like Michael Valpy in *The Globe & Mail* and Christopher Hume in the *Toronto Star*, who declared that negative responses to the exhibition were simply unfounded and suggested, by implication, that the protestors were disingenuous.

33 Yet, surely the point is not whether those who missed the cues and were offended by the show had any right to be, or whether they ought to have had the grace to give the ROM benefit of their doubt. (Concludes Hume in a tone of insufferable superiority, "If Coalition members were better informed, they would have realized that the organizers of *Into the Heart of Africa* are on their side. There may be plenty of instances of racism in Canadian museums, but this isn't one of them.") The ROM is, after all, in the business of education and communication, and whatever else you want to say about the rights and wrongs of *Into the Heart of Africa,* the museum has to assume some responsibility for the fact people felt demeaned and misrepresented by it. It doesn't do to claim purity of purpose for yourself while casting aspersions on all objections, especially when they come in such number and with such unanimity from the very community whose past you are displaying. It begins to sound like arrogance, like an invoca-

tion of a divine right of expertise. But the ROM persisted and, instead listening or learning why and how it was that the exhibit had such a negati impact, took the position that the show was historically accurate and th was all that mattered.

With no room to maneuver, the coalition began insisting that the exhibi be closed. A mini Oka developed as the two sides failed to meet, and in the end, the museum let the worst of all possible situations happen. Groups of mostly black protestors gathered outside on the sidewalk voicing their objection to an exhibition representing their own cultural heritage while inside, mostly white staff busied themselves calling the police. Predictably, there were arrests, and the museum went to court to get an injunction to keep the protestors at bay, threatening them with lawsuits. A dreadfully symbolic replay of the clash of attitudes depicted inside in *Into the Heart of Africa.*

Ironically and very unexpectedly, the last word came from two other 35 Canadian museums that had booked the show. Both announced early last September they were cancelling out. Sylvie Morel, director of exhibitions for the Museum of Civilization, says the decision was made in the face of evidence the exhibit was failing to communicate what it had set out to. The Vancouver Art Gallery took a look at the Toronto troubles and read the same message. (And eventually, in November, the two American museums that had also taken the show followed suit.)

Even while we can enjoy the sight of the ROM being forced to eat crow, 36 questions remain. Such as, how well was Jeanne Cannizzo served by her partner in the project? Sure museum officials came to her defence — by standing up behind her and saying nothing. But did they improve matters or provoke them by resorting to the old routine of pulling rank on critics and depicting them as extremists? Why could they not move an inch or two to meet what were perfectly legitimate complaints? Was there really no way to introduce an authentic African voice in the exhibition; no better way to deconstruct toxic images from the past; no way of accommodating a different perspective or of redesigning the show so the collection could remain on view instead of being hustled back into storage?

Into the Heart of Africa was above all a spoiled opportunity. The ROM walked straight into the controversy with its eyes open and its heart closed; a classic case of a cultural institution unable to see its own bias and unprepared to examine its own cultural assumptions. What the situation called for was some generosity and a bit of ordinary humility; what we got was a stone wall and that, in my book, was adding insult to the original injury.

(1991)

The Writer's Subject

1. What was the "Pax Britannica"? (para. 3) Why does Crean put extra emphasis on the word "Pax"?

2. Why does Crean compare her great-uncle's "old pith helmet" to the preserved heart of a saint in Montreal? (paras. 8-10)

3. What exactly is the "imbalance" that Crean finds disturbing? (para. 13)

4. What in Crean's view was the prime error committed by the exhibition's curator, Jeanne Cannizzo, and how was this error reflected in the selection and presentation of the objects in the exhibition?

5. What efforts did the Royal Ontario Museum make to distance itself from the colonialist and racist attitudes shown by the British in Africa in the 19th century?

The Writer's Style and Subject

1. Discuss the implications of Crean's title.

2. Why does Crean begin her essay with the story of her great-uncle John?

3. Discuss Crean's description of her great-uncle as "a quaint Canadian Rambo dressed in original Tilley Endurables." (para. 7)

4. Where does Crean first make her personal views apparent? In what ways, in your opinion, do those views affect Crean's account of the exhibition she describes?

5. In what ways does Crean convey public reaction to the ROM exhibition?

6. Do you think that Crean is fair in her presentation of Jeanne Cannizzo (curator of the exhibition) and the Royal Ontario Museum?

Suggested Topics for Writing and Discussion

1. In what respects did the exhibition "Into the Heart of Africa" raise the issue of "cultural appropriation"? (para. 30) For other discussions of this issue, see the essays by Awiakta, Giangrande, and Keeshig-Tobias elsewhere in this anthology.

2. Crean points out that removing objects from their usual context and placing them in a museum changes their meaning and function, so that we look at them in a new way. Imagine a museum exhibition a hundred years from now, the

and moved on to the next listing. But there was something different now about the Canadian atmosphere, and about me. I found out quickly and easily from an embarrassed clerk that Queen City had a "whites only" rental policy. My reaction was interesting — not anger, or fear, or shame. Rather it was a welcome opportunity to right a wrong, summed up simply as "You can't do that in this country." Any more. Saskatchewan had passed a bill of rights, and "The Queen vs. Queen City Real Estate" was the first case of discrimination tried under the legislation. The attorney general insisted that the crown, not the complainant, lay the charge; and with little fanfare, Queen City was found guilty and fined. It offered me an apartment, which I declined.

I met John Diefenbaker in the early 1960s, mainstreeting in Prince **14** Albert. How easily politicians moved about in those days! Dief, full of righteous vitality, was out for a walk down a road that was really called Main Street, shaking hands and talking to the people with no entourage and no bodyguards. When he shook my hand I felt genuine warmth, which I returned. As a reporter, I had covered the 1958 election for radio station CFCF in Montreal with appropriate cynicism, nearly getting punched by George Hees when I asked him about the Diefenbaker-Duplessis axis which delivered the Tory landslide in Quebec.

But I felt that Diefenbaker's 1960 Canadian Bill of Rights had been a mile- **15** stone for Canada. It redeemed him in my mind for the alliance with Duplessis, who these days is being given a revised place in history as a defender of Quebec autonomy. But in my time in Montreal he was known, among other things, as the author of the Padlock Law, used as a legal bludgeon against Jehovah's Witnesses in Quebec under the guise of fighting communism.

I had argued in favour of the Bill of Rights, with all its limitations. It was **16** not entrenched in the constitution and it applied only to federal law. It could be dismissed, as it was by J.D. Morton in *Saturday Night* in September, 1960, as "a lawyer's tool." I remember well the arguments that the bill would limit rather than enlarge human rights already, opponents said, effectively guaranteed under British common law. The bill would open loopholes, it was full of escape clauses. It could even be superseded by the War Measures Act. And so on. With the passage of the bill, Canadians, for the first time, could not be discriminated against on the basis of race, colour, or creed. The bill moved individual rights out of British common law and into hard legislation.

The Royal Commission on Bilingualism and Biculturalism came official- **17** ly face to face, for the first time in our history, with the fact that there was an important minority in Canada of neither British nor French descent. In the commission's report the term "multiculturalism" first assumed the status of hard currency. The other day I came across a brochure I had saved announcing a conference on multiculturalism for Canada in August 1970, at the University of Alberta. The conference was opened by Senator Paul Yuzyk, and I, wearing as one of my hats the programme directorship of Canada's first educational television station, got a half-hour to talk about multiculturalism in broadcasting. The back of the programme listed the sixteen recommendations in book four of the B & B Commission, "The Cultural Contribution of the Other Ethnic Groups."

18   Jean Lesage's clarion call to an awakening French Canada did much more than give Francophones a new sense of themselves. It stirred the aspirations of minorities in other provinces. If Francophones in Quebec could get out from under the British hegemony, what about Ukrainians in Alberta, Italians in Toronto, Chinese in Vancouver, and Indians everywhere?

19   And there were the thousands who, when they encountered discrimination, began slowly to realize, as I did, that "You can't do that in this country, any more" – and found the laws backed them up. Many who had come in waves of postwar immigration – from Hungary and Czechoslovakia and Poland, from Bangladesh and Uganda, from the United States during the Vietnam war, from the East and West Indies, and later from southeast Asia – didn't come here to be second-class citizens or part of a melting pot. They came to what they perceived as a compassionate country. Few other nations had opened their doors as Canada did. And the remnant of racism and discrimination they found, now with no legal, institutional, or moral base, was ripe for attack.

20   In many parts of Canada the attack is now in full flood. But even though the outcome of the war seems inevitable, no one should believe that all the battles have been won. While those of us who have been here for a generation or more usually find a comfortable niche, it's still tough to be a new immigrant in Canada. And while there are some who see a future in which we double our present population with new immigration, there are also those who continue to fight the rearguard action. For all the usual reasons: they'll take our jobs – they won't adapt to our system – they'll only bring another country's problems to our shores – they'll spoil our way of life.

21   In a series of articles under the heading "A Minority Report," the *Toronto Star* illustrated "the Metro mosaic." More than 100 minority groups, who make up a majority of the population, still face prejudice, hidden and un-hidden. Some kids today, as I did in the 1930s and 1940s, have to fight their way home from school. Still, we've come a long way from the days when immigrants were greeted with signs that proclaimed "no dogs or Jews allowed."

In 1986 the minister of justice, John Crosbie, told the House of Commons   22
that the government was committed to ending discrimination that keeps
individuals in Canada from fully realizing their potential, and embraced
its duty to take the lead in making sure that federal laws and policies met
the high standards of the charter and that individuals were not forced un-
necessarily into court.

In a speech last April in Toronto, the then minister of state for multi-   23
culturalism, Otto Jelinek, was able to say, "Our society has become *irrever-
sibly* multicultural and multiracial," even though he has still not resolved
the question of an apology and honourable compensation for the wartime
insult to Japanese Canadians. And the prime minister, speaking to the same
gathering, issued what might well have been the slogan for multiculturalism
in the 1980s. "Tokenism is over," he said. "Fairness is in."

Our record, in the years after World War II, stands in stark contrast to   24
a long and shameful series of events culminating with the internment of
Japanese and German Canadians in the 1940s. In 1903 the government of
Canada raised the head tax on Chinese immigrants originally established
at $50 in 1885, to $500. In 1914, a boatload of 376 Indian refugees was
refused permission to land in Vancouver, and suffered incredible priva-
tion because we were stingy, to put it kindly, about giving them food and
water. In 1939, 907 Jews escaping Nazi Germany aboard the *St. Louis* were
refused entry to Canada. At the time, Hitler's attempted genocide was in
full flood.

Canada's postwar immigrants landed with a painful awareness of war   25
and racism. After they found their feet in this new land, they weren't about
to put up with more. There was little to be done about private prejudice
but, as the law developed, in provincial and federal jurisdictions it said that
public services were equally available to all.

It was, ironically, Pierre Trudeau who finished the legal transformation   26
that John Diefenbaker, for whom he had only disdain, had started. The full-
bodied reverberations from the act of patriation and the enshrinement of
the charter in the Canadian constitution will be felt beyond the next generation. Canada's first ombudsman, George McClelland, a former commis-
sioner of the RCMP, was appointed by the government of Alberta in 1967.
By 1986 all provinces except Prince Edward Island had established such
an office. Now, not only did human-rights legislation have teeth, but a
publicly funded defender. Individual rights in Canada no longer depend
upon some vaguely defined and unevenly interpreted "common law." Our
most "uncommon" laws (if you look around the world) are meeting the tests
of the courts, as precedent upon precedent builds a legal and moral base.

It's somehow typical that we Canadians have difficulty recognizing our   27 uniqueness. We see ourselves as a not very powerful, not very innovative, not very exciting land that is nevertheless safe. We look to other countries with envy, wishing we had·their strength, their depth of culture and character, their creativity.

28   But look more closely. Our first motherland, France, is culturally stagnant, lurching from political to economic to social crisis. Britain, once the home of empire, is in danger of losing its role as leader of the Commonwealth. Its immigration policy is a shambles; its class society still flourishes; its problems with Ireland defy solution. And when we look, nervously, at our continental neighbour, our desire to buy into the American dream becomes highly selective. The melting pot never really worked — yet in the United States multiculturalism is a very recent notion. Everyone — the Puerto Ricans, the Indians, the Mexicans, the various other Latinos — is "American," whether they like it or not.

29   In the Middle East, the cradle of civilization, even brothers can't get along. Beirut, once one of the world's most sophisticated cities, is a war zone. In Israel, Jews attack Jews, desecrating synagogues. India is still trying to grapple with racial and religious strife, even though untouchability is officially dead. China is working at being homogeneous. In the Soviet Union some are more equal than others. The Swiss are multicultural, but only for the four official groups. Most of the world's countries are either unicultural, uniracial, and religiously homogeneous, or else caught up in internal strife.

30   It's not hard to understand why the notion of multiculturalism is so difficult, and why so few countries have contemplated adopting the ideal as policy. It is, first of all, risky. When you allow people to emigrate from other countries and keep their cultures, their ties to former countries, you invite ancient rivalries and hatreds to settle into the land. The hope is that old hurts and fears will mellow as those people find a measure of security in a benign environment — and the Canadian experience has, by and large, borne this out.

31   But multiculturalism, with its implicit ties to other cultures, also obviates narrow nationalism. In a way, you ride the fine line between being an open, free, and tolerant society, and not really being a country at all, at least in the "My country right or wrong" sense. The gamble is that in the end there is pride in tolerance; that a new kind of nationhood, safer in a tinderbox world, can be built on the open international communication that comes with multiculturalism. As Eric Hoffer noted of the "true believer," those who most loudly protest, defend, and propagate the faith are those who are the least secure in it. Nations that feel threatened, uncertain of their morality, become aggressive and dangerous.

How then to explain Canada's behaviour? Does the moral authority 32 flowing from our compassionate immigration policy, from our record in foreign aid, from Pearson's Nobel Peace Prize or Trudeau's international stardom, give a kind of courage? Is there some special serenity, some security that stems from knowing that multiculturalism, while not easy, works? Not only are we comfortable with the extraordinary diversity of our peoples, we plan expansion on the same basis. Major political parties are now arguing not about where new immigrants will come from, or what their colour or creed will be, but about how many we can absorb, and how soon.

Canadians have yet to discover the creativity of their social order. If we 33 can solve the problems of making it possible for people of every kind to live together in reasonable harmony, we have a message for the world. The problems of this shrinking planet are problems we're solving in Canada.

When I was invited to a mainstream event in the 1950s it was because 34 I was exotic. In the sixties and seventies I was often the token black. But in the eighties when they call, I know it's really me they want. Not bad for a kid who grew up in east-end Montreal thinking someone had put him on the wrong planet.

(1987)

The Writer's Subject

1. What differences does Fraser perceive between racist attitudes in Canada and those in the U.S.A.?

2. How were immigrants and members of minorities treated in Canada in the first half of the 20th century?

3. What changes came about to improve the situation of minorities in Canada, starting in the 1960s?

4. Why does Fraser consider himself to be "as typically Canadian as anyone"? (para. 11)

5. How does Fraser back up his claim that Canada is "the only truly open, multi-cultural country in the world"? (para. 10)

6. What does Fraser mean by stating that "multiculturalism, with its implicit ties to other cultures ... obviates narrow nationalism"? (para. 31)

The Writer's Style and Strategy

1. Discuss Fraser's choice of title.

2. How does Fraser make use of personal experience to strengthen his argument?

3. What does Fraser mean by the statement "We are officially, and by degrees viscerally, a multicultural country"? (para. 9)

4. Though this is a short essay, Fraser makes many specific references to Canadian politics and history. Where do you find the use of such details particularly effective?

Suggested Topics for Writing and Discussion

1. Find out what you can about some of the political figures mentioned by Fraser, such as Mackenzie King, Camillien Houde, John Diefenbaker, Jean Lesage, or Tommy Douglas. What part did they play, directly or indirectly, in the development of multicultural policies in Canada?

2. Fraser states that, despite many improvements in the area of human rights, "it's still tough to be a new immigrant in Canada" (para. 20). Do you agree with this opinion?

3. Would you agree with Fraser's claim that the Canadian experience has shown that multiculturalism works? Compare his view with the view expressed by Neil Bissoondath.

4. Find out what you can about one or two of the racist incidents alluded to by Fraser in paragraph 24.

Matata

by Kildare Dobbs

Although his face was not less brown than other faces of his tribe, it 1
had a sort of pallor, as if the blood under the skin were thinner, less
warm and confident as it moved in his veins than that of his fellows.
Yet you didn't feel any repellent coldness about him. You felt he had
been sadly hurt, outraged in some catastrophic way which had caused
him to withdraw into himself, to close the damper upon his vital fires.
He was now plainly at the nadir of his life, like a tree in the depth of
winter from whose twigs and branches the sap has retreated, so that it
seems dead beyond all hope of recovery. I saw that he walked with
a limp, but that alone did not account for the weariness of his movements.
And though there were a few white hairs tangled in his wooly poll,
I could see that he was not an old man.

He had come to ask for a job as a clerk; he told me his name was 2
Matata. We talked in English, which he spoke very well — I sensed
that it helped his self-esteem to address me in my own language. I asked what experience he had. After a momentary pause he said in a flat
tone, 'For fifteen years I was treasury clerk of this district.' I looked
up in surprise. The post was one of considerable responsibility involving the management of large sums of money, and I had not seen Matata
before. I had prided myself on knowing all the better-educated men in
the tribe.

'But where have you been since you left?' 3

'In prison,' said Matata. 4

It was not hard to find him a job. Men of his ability were too rare 5
in the territory to be discarded merely because of a criminal record,

and I was able to give Matata a desk in my own office where he could
not have offended even if he had wanted to. The arrangement suited
both of us. He had a measure of privacy which he needed and could
not otherwise have found. I for my part was able to answer for his good
conduct without having to make tedious enquiries. Moreover, I was
able to draw on his experience and have the benefit of his advice in
many affairs where a knowledge of tribal custom and local history was
useful. In time we came to trust one another, and even to be friends.
At first his confidences came reluctantly (I never pressed for them),
but as the months went by he began to put forth his leaves and be himself
again without fear, to tell what he had hoped for from his life, how
he had pursued it, and how come to grief. Like most colonial relations,
ours was imperfect. I became Matata's patron, and we both knew it.
But if he sought my favour (and so, in a sense, was degraded) and sometimes resorted to guile, I myself, for less obvious and even more devious
reasons, needed and invited his confidence. The proof of my corruptness is that I am now coldly moralizing upon our relation, whereas true
friendship, like true love, is a secret we hug to ourselves and do not
speak of aloud, even to hidden listeners.

6   Matata had been convicted of stealing about four hundred shillings
from the funds for which he was responsible. His story was that he
had borrowed it to meet the needs of some relatives he was bound by
custom to support. He had intended to replace the cash and had not
falsified his accounts in any way. Unfortunately his books were checked before he had a chance to put the matter straight. The District Com-
missioner immediately had him arrested and charged, and in due course
he was tried in the High Court and sentenced by an impartial judge to
three years' imprisonment. 'You have abused a position of public trust,'
said the judge. 'It is men like you who hold your country back in its
progress towards self-government. There has been too much of this sort
of thing recently, and I propose to make an example of you. I take into
account your long service and previous good character.' Poor Matata
heard all this twice over, once in English and again in his own tongue
from the interpreter. He thought over it in prison.

7   Though he had been educated at government schools and so touched
with Western knowledge and ideas, his upbringing had been little different from that of his fellow tribesmen. He had been born into a large
family. While yet a small child he had learnt to address them all correctly, to distinguish between those with whom he could speak freely
and those with whom his relations were governed by tabu. He learnt

to call his father *Dada* and his mother *Yuva*. That was simple enough. But he had to call all his father's brothers *Dada* too, and all his mother's sisters *Yuva*. So he had six fathers and four mothers to start with. But that was not all, for his proper father had two other wives who were also called *Yuva*, and not only they, but their sisters as well. The daughters of all these so-called mothers and fathers were considered his sisters, and their sons his brothers. This army of siblings all had claims on him.

It was not surprising that Matata's first confused thoughts in the early 8 months of his imprisonment were to believe himself completely innocent. This is commonly the reaction of a normally law-abiding man who finds himself convicted of a crime. The impersonality of the legal machine which crushes him in its cogs, the remoteness of formal evidence form the inner realities of motive and intention, the brusque efficiency of police and clerks, the patient obtuseness of judges — all these combine to put the whole situation from him as utterly unreal. At the same time the ground of his faith in himself and in other people is sprung like the trap from under the condemned. He has thought of himself as a middling decent person. Now it seems he was mistaken. He is a monster so dangerous that he must be locked away for years.

Matata felt all this and more. For the better part of his adult life he 9 had been working hard at the business of civilizing himself and his people. He believed in civilization. He believed in roads and schools and penicillin and septic tanks. He was not bored, as I was, by the apostles of hygiene, the health officer and his team of sanitary inspectors. It is true that he, like the rest of his tribe, always referred to the health officer as Bwana Mavi, or Mister Excrement, but he intended no disrespect. Mr. Excrement was as much a limb of civilization as Matata's gold watch, which he loved very much and at which, in idle moments, he used to stare raptly like a man in a trance. Since Matata loved civilization so well, it went very hard with him to discover that he was not loved equally in return. In his heart, too, he looked at the world as a man of his tribe. Working with the white men in the days of their power was like working with powerful spirits; it conferred wealth and prestige. But these spirits exacted a price. So long as you walked carefully they smiled on you and showed you their secrets. The moment you made a mistake they turned on you without mercy and tore out your heart.

It was the prison superintendent, a severe but good-hearted Afrikaner, 10 who helped Matata recover some of his faith in himself. He gave him a responsible job and cheered him when he felt sorry for himself. Matata was grateful to this rough good man.

11   Though Matata became once more a useful and happy member of his tribe, I could not console myself with any notion that his sufferings had turned out for the best, or that others would profit by his example. Failure teaches a man nothing except compassion for the failure of others. I am still haunted, shall perhaps always be haunted, by the image of Matata as I first saw him, halting towards my desk, his dark eyes full of a pain I did not then understand, but which is now as familiar as a guilty secret.

(1962)

The Writer's Subject

1. Why was Matata a man of rare ability in the territory? (paras. 2-5)

2. What benefits accrued to both Dobbs and Matata through their working together in the same office? (para. 5)

3. Why does Dobbs accuse himself of deviousness and corruptness? (para. 5)

4. How does Matata's theft of money throw light on the clash between his own culture and that of the white man he served?

5. What are Matata's reactions to his arrest and subsequent imprisonment?

6. What did civilization mean to Matata? (para. 9)

7. Why does Dobbs say that he is still haunted by the image of Matata as he first saw him? (para. 11)

The Writer's Style and Strategy

1. Why does Dobbs devote the first paragraph to a physical description of Matata? How does this prepare us for the essay's conclusion?

2. Discuss the use Dobbs makes of the metaphor of the tree in paragraphs 1 and 5.

3. Why does Dobbs give the words of the "impartial" judge in direct speech rather than merely reporting his judgment? (para. 6)

4. What does Dobbs's reference to the health officer and his team as "the apostles of hygiene" convey of his attitude to them? (para. 9)

Suggested Topics for Writing and Discussion

1. Compare this essay with Orwell's "Shooting an Elephant." In what respects did the writers react in similar fashion to their experiences as colonial administrators?

2. To Matata his gold watch is a symbol of civilization. Choose this or some other object or artifact and discuss it as a symbol of civilization (i.e., civilizations in general, or a particular civilization).

3. Describe a person from a culture other than your own and indicate what you have learned about this person's culture and cultural values. What has this contact taught you about your *own* culture and its values?

Allowing the Mind to Wander

by Carole Giangrande

1 A few years ago, I travelled through a cluster of isolated hamlets in north-western Saskatchewan, home to Cree and Metis trappers, some of whom I was lucky enough to interview. A timid but curious big-city writer, I drove, trudged and flew my way through this huge expanse of bush and snow with notebooks, tape recorder and absolutely no first-hand experience of either wilderness life or native issues.

2   Through the introductions of a local Cree (who was kind enough to act as interpreter), I had come to document the loss of trapping lands that the federal government had expropriated in the late 1950s for the Air Weapons Testing Range that straddles the provinces of Alberta and Saskatchewan.

3   One of the trappers, a lively talker who spoke in Cree, told his story with such immediacy that it felt as if it had been only the day before that he was tricked out of his trapping lands for small change and false promises that the land would be returned. As he spoke he grew more animated and he took the pen out of my hand and marked an X on my pad to show me how he — lacking English but not trust — innocently signed the deal.

4   Without his language or his particular experience, I had only the jour-nalist's sense of the person before me who gave the story meaning, a vital and sympathetic individual whose suffering and forbearance were as evi-dent as his unexplainable good nature in the face of so much injustice. Even more remarkable was the fact that the man still had it in him to trust another stranger, this time one who promised to tell his story. His faith felt mysterious to me, the kind of small, unnoticed gift that so often slips

between words as easily as light through the slats of a blind. It was not something a writer with conscience would dismiss lightly, let alone betray.

Anyone who works with the one-on-one intimacy of print and radio has   5
to start by assuming that such revelations are possible, and that the experiences of a single human being have the power to resonate with all the silent emotions of those who are reading or listening. Never mind that the trapper grew up a native in the bush while I, a Canadian of Italian descent, lived my early years in New York City's Bronx. Common humanity is supposed to turn a babble of voices into a dialogue whatever our race or culture, a fact as fundamental to an interviewer as tapes and mikes and recording gear.

Or so I thought. My old perceptions of common ground appear almost   6
simple-minded these days, a smokescreen hiding the differences between privileged and oppressed of all races, a way of denying the power relationship that exists between those of my (white) race and every other. At the annual meeting of the Writers' Union in Kingston, Ontario, last spring, a number of writers, shamed by the complaint of white dominance over native culture, promised to abstain from handling native subject matter of any kind.

However well-intentioned, their pledge left me grateful to have published   7
my work back in 1983. It also left me wondering how many publishers today would touch an account of that same native trapper's experience as perceived, however insightfully, by a non-native. Without forgetting that "cultural appropriation" is a painful and sensitive issue for many, we're also in real danger of denying what is most human in us by cluttering our psychic landscape with "No Trespassing" signs.

Glutted as we are with politics, we keep forgetting that there are other,   8
equally profound dimensions of human understanding and reality. Telling writers and artists of one culture that they are no longer welcome to imagine and enter into the heart of another is a denial of the miraculous and the unexpected, of the hope we place in new insight and its power to reach out and heal old wounds. We end up saying that there is little more to life than the particulars: nation, gender, politics, ethnic group and the color of our mortal human skin.

What we are really talking about is our lack of belief in capital-H   9
Humanity, that very old idea now getting a rough ride through the byways of the global village. Common human ground is out of fashion politically. Some see it as a crude form of Western dominance, a euphemism for a world-view imposed by white, male humanity. Instead, we're moving into a New Babel of what theologian Gregory Baum calls "a multitude of

small narratives," a cluster of exclusively cultural and racial understandings of the world, empty of any "larger story" of collective human purpose or destiny.

10 This new form of tribalism has some good things to offer; a sense of heritage and place is far better than the emptiness of life on a bland, "globalized" MacPlanet where the only "big picture" gets bounced off a satellite dish. Yet we Canadians, dispossessed and alienated, "distinct" and "sovereign," have been pushing our luck. Right about now we could do with a Gandhi or a Martin Luther King to speak to ideals that are universal and above the tribe before our near-violent obsession with cultural differences puts an end to us as a country.

11 And those of us who write can have faith in the power of the imagination where we transcend ourselves, where we enter into and become the people of all races – real or fictitious – that we write. In this way we understand and cherish them as deeply and with as much courtesy as we would our loved ones.

12 Rather than avoid writing outside our cultural experience, our hope of defying the curse of racism lies in doing just the opposite. The gift of words and language then becomes our common ground, symbolic of the human mystery that defies race and includes us all. For such creative acts, the appropriate metaphor is not "theft" but love. Simplistic? No more so than guns or the rhetoric of death.

(1990)

The Writer's Subject

1. What did Giangrande learn from her interview with a Cree trapper in northwestern Saskatchewan?

2. What has led the writer to view her earlier perceptions as "almost simpleminded these days"? (para. 6)

3. Explain the meaning of Giangrande's statement that we are "in real danger of denying what is most human in us by cluttering our psychic landscape with 'No Trespassing' signs." (para. 7)

4. What does the writer mean by the phrase "our lack of belief in capital-H Humanity"? (para. 9)

5. What, as Giangrande sees it, are the advantages and the disadvantages of what she calls a "new form of tribalism"? (para. 10)

6. What in Giangrande's view is the importance of the imagination in countering racism?

The Writer's Style and Strategy

1. Why does the writer give such prominence to the anecdote about her interview with the Cree trapper?

2. What does Giangrande choose to tell us about herself? Is it relevant to her purpose in the essay?

3. Why does the writer invoke the names of Gandhi and Martin Luther King? (para. 10)

4. Comment on Giangrande's phrase, "the emptiness of life on a bland, 'globalized,' MacPlanet." (para. 10)

5. What is the tone of the concluding paragraph? How does the writer's choice of words help to create that tone?

Suggested Topics for Writing and Discussion

1. Giangrande remarks that "'cultural appropriation' is a painful and sensitive issue for many" (para. 7). Explain what she means, and compare the position she takes on this issue with the views of Lenore Keeshig-Tobias.

2. Do you agree or disagree with the writer's contention that one need not have been born into a culture in order to write about it?

3. Giangrande fears that "our near-violent obsession with cultural differences" may put an end to Canada as a country. What are your views on this subject?

Is That All There Is?
Tribal Literature
by Basil H. Johnston

1   In the early 60's Kahn-Tineta Horn, a young Mohawk model, got the attention of the Canadian press (media) not only by her beauty but by her articulation of Indian grievances and her demands for justice. Soon after Red Power was organized threatening to use force. Academics and scholars, anxious and curious to know what provoked the Indians, organized a series of conferences and teach-ins to explore the issues. Even children wanted to know. So for their enlightenment experts wrote dozens of books. Universities and colleges began native studies courses. Ministries of Education, advised by a battery of consultants, adjusted their Curriculum Guidelines to allow units of study on the native peoples of this continent. And school projects were conducted for the benefit of children between ten and thirteen years of age.

2   One such project at the Churchill Avenue Public School in North York, Ontario lasted six weeks and the staff and students who had taken part mounted a display as a grand finale to their studies. And a fine display it was in the school's library.

3   In front of a canvas tent that looked like a teepee stood a grim chief, face painted in war-like colours and arms folded. On his head he wore a head-dress made of construction paper. A label pinned to his vest bore the name, Blackfoot. I made straight for the chief.

4   "How!" I greeted the chief, holding up my hand at the same time as a gesture of friendship.

Instead of returning the greeting, the chief looked at me quizzically.   5
"How come you look so unhappy?" I asked him.   6
"Sir! I'm bored," the chief replied.   7
"How so, chief?"   8
"Sir, don't tell anybody, but I'm bored. I'm tired of Indians. That's all   9
we've studied for six weeks. I thought they'd be interesting when we started,
because I always thought that Indians were neat. At the start of the course
we had to choose to do a special project from food preparation, transportation, dwellings, social organization, clothing, and hunting and fishing.
I chose dwellings" and here the chief exhaled in exasperation "... and that's
all me and my team studied for six weeks; teepees, wigwams, longhouses,
igloos. We read books, encyclopedias, went to the library to do research,
looked at pictures, drew pictures. Then we had to make one. Sir, I'm
bored."

"Didn't you learn anything else about Indians, chief?"   10
"No sir, there was nothing else ... Sir? ... Is that all there is to Indians?"   11
Little has changed since that evening in 1973. Books still present native   12
peoples in terms of their physical existence as if Indians were incapable
of meditating upon or grasping the abstract. Courses of study in the public
school system, without other sources of information, had to adhere to the
format, pattern, and content set down in books. Students studied Kaw-lijas,
wooden Indians, who were incapable of love or laughter; or Tontos, if you
will, whose sole skill was to make fires and to perform other servile duties
for the Lone Ranger; an inarticulate Tonto, his speech limited to "Ugh!,"
"Kimo Sabi," and "How."

Despite all the research and the field work conducted by anthropologists,   13
ethnologists and linguists, Indians remain "The Unknown Peoples" as
Professor George E. Tait of the University of Toronto so aptly titled his
book written in 1973.

Not even Indians Affairs of Canada, with its more than two centuries   14
of experience with natives, with its array of experts and consultants, with
its unlimited funds, seems to have learned anything about its constituents,
if we are to assess their latest publication titled *The Canadian Indian*. One
would think that the Honourable William McKnight, then Minister of
Indian and Northern Affairs, under whose authority the book was published
in 1986 should know by now the Indians who often come to Ottawa, do
not arrive on horseback, do not slay one of the RCMP mounts and cook
it on the steps of the Parliament Buildings. Moreover, most Indians he has
seen and met were not dressed in loincloths, nor did they sleep in teepees.
Yet he authorized the publication of a book bereft of any originality or
imagination, a book that perpetuated the notion and the image that the

Indians had not advanced one step since contact, but are still living as they had one hundred and fifty, even three hundred years ago. There was not a word about native thought, literature, institutions, contributions in music, art, theatre. But that's to be expected of Indian Affairs; to know next to nothing of their constituents.

15   Where did the author or authors of this latest publication by Indian Affairs get their information? The selected readings listed at the back of the book provide a clue; Frances Densmore, Harold Driver, Philip Drucker, Frederick W. Hodge, Diamond Jenness, Reginald and Gladys Laubin, Frank G. Speck, Bruce G. Trigger, George Woodcock, Harold A. Innis, Calvin Martin, E. Palmer Patterson, eminent scholars, none of whom spoke or attempted to learn the language of any of the Indian nations about whom they were writing. Modern scholars because they are not required by their universities to learn, are no more proficient in a native language than were their predecessors.

16   Herein, I submit, is the nub and the rub. Without the benefit of knowing the language of the Indian nation that they are investigating, scholars can never get into their mind, the heart and soul and the spirit and still understand the native's perceptions and interpretations. The scholar must confine his research and studies to the material, physical culture, subsistence patterns and family relationships.

17   Without knowing the spiritual and the intellectual, aesthetic side of Indian culture, the scholar cannot furnish what that little grade five youngster and others like him wanted to know about Indians.

18   Admitting his boredom was that grade five youngster's way of expressing his disappointment with the substance of the course that he and his colleagues had been made to endure. In another sense, it was a plea for other knowledge that would quench his curiosity and challenge his intellect.

19   Students such as he, as well as adults, are interested in the character, intellect, soul, spirit, heart of people of other races and cultures. They want to know what other people believe in, what they understand, what they expect and hope for in this life and in the next, how they keep law and order and harmony within the family and community, how and why they celebrated ceremonies, what made them proud, ashamed, what made them happy, what sad. Whether the young understand what they want to know and learn does not matter much, they still want to know in order to enrich their own insights and broaden their outlooks.

20   But unless scholars and writers know the literature of the peoples that they are studying or writing about they cannot provide what their students and readers are seeking and deserving of.

21   There is, fortunately, enough literature, both oral and written, available

for scholarly study, but it has for the most part been neglected. Myths, legends, and songs have not been regenerated and set in modern terms to earn immortalization in poetry, dramatization in plays, or romanticization in novels.

What has prevented the acceptance of Indian literature as a serious and 22
legitimate expression of native thought and experience has been indifferent and inferior translation, a lack of understanding and interest in the culture and a notion that it has little of importance to offer to the larger white culture.

In offering you a brief sketch, no more than a glimpse, as it were, of my 23
tribe's culture, I am doing no more than what anyone of you would do were you to be asked "What is your culture? Would you explain it?" I would expect you to reply, "Read my literature, and you will get to know something of my thoughts, my convictions, my aspirations, my feelings, sentiments, expectations, whatever I cherish or abominate."

First, let me offer you an observation about my language for the simple 24
reason that language and literature are inseparable, though they are too often taught as separate entities. They belong together.

In my tribal language, all words have three levels of meaning; there is 25
the surface meaning that everyone instantly understands. Beneath this meaning is a more fundamental meaning derived from the prefixes and their combinations with other terms. Underlying both is the philosophical meaning.

Take the word "Anishinaubae." That is what the members of the nation, 26
now known as Chippewa in the United States or Ojibway in Canada, called themselves. It referred to a member of the tribe. It was given to the question "What are you?" But it was more than just a term of identification. It meant, "I am a person of good intent, a person of worth" and it reflected what the people thought of themselves, and of human nature; that all humans are essentially, fundamentally good. Let's separate that one word into its two terms The first, "Onishishih" meaning good, fine, beautiful, excellent: and the second "naubae" meaning being, male, human species. Even together they do not yield the meaning "good intention." It is only by examining the stories of Nanabush, the tribes' central and principal mythical figure who represents all men and all women, that the term Anishinaubae begins to make sense. Nanabush was always full of good intentions, ergo the people of the tribe. The Anishinaubae perceive themselves as people who intended good and therefore of merit and worth. From this perception they drew a strong sense of pride as well as a firm sense of place in the community. This influenced their notion of independence.

Let's take another word, the word for truth. When we say "w'daeb-awae" 27 we mean he or she is telling the truth, is correct, is right. But the expression is not merely an affirmation of a speaker's veracity. It is as well a philosophical proposition that in saying a speaker casts his words and his voice as far as his perception and his vocabulary will enable him or her, it is a denial that there is such a thing as absolute truth; that the best and most the speaker can achieve and a listener expect is the highest degree of accuracy. Somehow that one expression, "w'daeb-awae," sets the limits to a single statement as well as setting limits to truth and the scope and exercise of speech.

28   One other word: "to know." We say "w'kikaendaun" to convey the idea that he or she "knows." Without going into the etymological derivations, suffice it to say that when the speaker assures someone that he knows it, that person is saying that the notion, image, idea, fact that that person has in mind corresponds and is similar to what he or she has already seen, heard, touched, tasted or smelled. That person's knowledge may not be exact, but similar to that which has been instilled and impressed in his or her mind and recalled from memory.

29   The stories that make up our tribal literature are no different from the words in our language. Both have many meanings and applications, as well as bearing tribal perceptions, values and outlooks.

30   Let us begin at the beginning with the tribe's story of creation which precedes all other stories in the natural order. Creation stories provide insights into what races and nations understand of human nature; ours is no different in this respect.

31   This is our creation story. Kitchi-manitou beheld a vision. From this vision, The Great Mystery, for that is the essential and fundamental meaning of Kitchimanitou and not spirit as is often understood, were created the sun and the stars, the land and the waters, and all the creatures and beings, seen and unseen, that inhabit the earth, the seas and the skies. The creation was desolated by a flood. Only the manitous, creatures and beings who dwelt in the waters were spared. All others perished.

32   In the heavens dwelt a manitou, Geezhigo-quae (Sky-woman). During the cataclysm upon the earth, Geezhigo-quae became pregnant. The creatures adrift upon the seas prevailed upon the giant turtle to offer his back as a haven for Geezhigo-quae. They then invited her to come down.

33   Resting on the giant turtle's back Geezhigo-quae asked for soil.

34   One after another water creatures dove into the depths to retrieve a morsel of soil. Not one returned with a particle of soil. They all offered an excuse; too deep, too dark, too cold, there are evil manitous keeping watch. Last to descend was the muskrat. He returned with a small knot of earth.

35   With the particle of mud retrieved by the muskrat Geezhigo-quae

recreated an island and the world as we know it. On the island she created over the giant turtle's shell, Geezhigo-quae gave birth to twins who begot the tribe called the Anishinaubaeg.

Millenia later the tribe dreamed Nanabush into being. Nanabush 36 represented themselves and what they understood of human nature. One day his world too was flooded. Like Geezhigo-quae, Nanabush recreated his world from a morsel of soil retrieved from the depths of the sea.

As a factual account of the origin of the world and of being, the story 37 has no more basis than the biblical story of creation and the flood. But the story represents a belief in God, the creator, a Kitchi-manitou, the Great Mystery. It also represents a belief that Kitchi-manitou sought within himself, his own being, a vision. Or perhaps it came from within his being and that Kitchi-manitou created what was beheld and set it into motion. Even the lesser manitous, such as Geezhigo-quae and Nanabush, must seek a morsel of soil with which to create and recreate their world, their spheres. So men and women must seek within themselves the talent or the potential and afterward create their own worlds and their own spheres and a purpose to give meaning to their lives.

The people begotten by Geezhigo-quae on that mythological island called 38 themselves Anishinaubaeg, the good beings who meant well and were human beings, therefore fundamentally good. But they also knew that men and women were often deflected from fulfilling their good intentions and prevented from living up to their dreams and visions, not out of any inherent evil, but rather from something outside of themselves. Nanabush also represented this aspect of human nature. Many times Nanabush or the Anishinaubaeg fail to carry out a noble purpose. Despite this, he is not rendered evil or wicked but remains fundamentally and essentially good.

Men and women intend what is good, but they forget. The story called 39 "The Man, The Snake and The Fox" exemplifies this aspect of human nature.

In its abbreviated form the story is as follows. The hunter leaves his lodge 40 and his family at daybreak to go in search of game to feed his wife and his children. As he proceeds through the forest, the hunter sees deer, but each time they are out of range of his weapon.

Late in the afternoon, discouraged and weary, he hears faint cries in the 41 distance. Forgetting his low spirits and fatigue he sets out with renewed optimism and vigour in the direction of the cries. Yet the nearer he draws to the source of the cries, the more daunted is the hunter by the dreadful screams. Only the thought of his family's needs drove him forward, otherwise he might have turned away.

At last he came to a glade. The screams came from a thicket on the 42 opposite side. The hunter, bow and arrow drawn and ready, made his way forward cautiously.

43 To his horror, the hunter saw an immense serpent tangled fast in a thicket as a fish is caught in the webbing of a net. The monster writhed and roared and twisted. He struggled to break free.

44 The man recoiled in horror. Before he could back away, the snake saw him.

45 "Friend!" the snake addressed the man.

46 The man fell in a heap on the ground the moment that the snake spoke. When he came to much later the snake pleaded with the man to set him free. For some time the man refused but eventually he relented. He was persuaded by the monster's plea that he too, though a serpent, had no less right to life than did the man. And the serpent promised not to injure the man on his release. The hunter was convinced.

47 The snake sprang on his deliverer the moment the last vine was cut away.

48 It was like thunder as the man and the snake struggled. Nearby a little fox heard the uproar. Never having seen such a spectacle the fox settled down to watch. Immediately he realized that the man was about to be killed.

49 Why were the snake and the man locked in mortal struggle? The little fox shouted for an explanation. The man and the snake stopped.

50 The hunter gasped out his story, then the snake gave his version. Pretending not to understand the snake's explanation the fox beguiled the aggressor into returning to the thicket to act out his side of the story.

51 The snake entangled himself once more.

52 Realizing that he had been delivered from the edge of death by the fox, the man was greatly moved. He felt bound to show his gratitude in some tangible way. The fox assured him that no requital was required. Nevertheless the hunter persisted. How might he, the hunter, perform some favour on behalf of the fox?

53 Not only was there no need, the fox explained, there was nothing that the man could do for the fox; there was not a thing that the fox needed or desired of human beings. However, if it would make the man happier, the fox suggested that the man might feed him should he ever have need.

54 Nothing would please the man more than to perform some good for his deliverer; it was the least that he could do for a friend who had done so much.

55 Some years later the hunter shot a little fox who had been helping himself to the family storage. As the man drew his knife to finish off the thief, the little fox gasped, "Don't you remember?"

56 That no snakes as monstrous as the one in the story are to be found on this continent makes no difference to the youngsters' sense of outrage over

the treachery of the snake and the forgetfulness of the man; nor does the exercise of speech which enables the snake and the fox to communicate with the hunter and each other prevent the young from being moved to compassion for the fox. Their sense of justice and fairness bears them over the anomalies in the story.

Before the last words "Don't you remember?" have echoed away, the 57 young begin to ask questions. "Why? Why did the man not recognize the fox? Why did he forget? How did the man feel afterwards? Why did the snake attack the man? Why did the snake break his promise? Why didn't the man leave the snake where he was? Do animals really have as much right to live as human beings do?"

Indians cared, loved as passionately as other people. 58

The story called "The Weeping Pine" raises the same questions about 59 love and marriage and the span of either that have been asked by philosophers, poets, and lovers of every race and generation. It does not pretend to give answers to these age old questions beyond suggesting that love may bloom even in circumstances where it is least expected to flower and endure. But owing to shoddy translation, the story has been presented as an explanation for the origin of pine trees.

According to the story, the elders of a village came to a certain young 60 woman's home where she lived with her parents, brothers and sisters. They had come to let her family know that they had chosen her to be the new wife to an old man. This particular man had been without a friend since the death of his first wife some years before. The old man was described as good-natured and kind. As one who had done much to benefit the tribe in his youth, the old man deserved something in return from his neighbours. In the opinion of the elders the most fitting reward the old man could have was a wife. In their judgement the young woman they had chosen would be a suitable companion for the old man.

They assured her that the tribe would see to it that they never had need. 61

Because this sort of marriage was a matter that the young woman had 62 not considered, it was unexpected. The delegation understood this. They did not demand an immediate answer but allowed the young woman a few days in which to make up her mind.

The young woman cried when the delegation left. She didn't want to 63 marry that man. That old man whose days were all but over and who could never look after her. She had, like every young girl her age, hoped to marry someone young, full of promise, someone she would love and who would love her in return. Besides, it was too soon. How could she, not yet eighteen, be a companion to an old man of seventy or more? The disparity was too great.

64   At first her parents too were aggrieved. But soon after they prevailed upon her to defer to the wishes of the elders, and her father delivered word of their daughter's consent to the elders.

65   But neither the disparity in age nor the disposition of the young girl to enter into a loveless marriage was too great; in the years that followed she came to love this old man. And they had many children.

66   Thirty years later the old man died.

67   On the final day of the four-day watch, the mourners went home but the widow made no move to rise. She continued to keen and rock back and forth in great sorrow.

68   "Come mother, let us go home," her children urged, offering to assist her to her feet and to support her on their way home.

69   "No! No! Leave me. Go," she said.

70   "Mother! Please. Come home with us," her children pleaded. Nothing they said could persuade their mother to leave.

71   "No. You go home. This is where I belong. Leave me."

72   Her children prayed she would relent; give in to the cold and hunger. They went home, but they did not leave their mother alone. During the next few days a son or daughter was always at her side, watching with her and entreating her to come home. They tried to comfort her with their own love and care, assuring her that her wound would pass and heal. They even brought her food and drink to sustain her. She refused everything.

73   As their mother grew weaker with each passing day, the children besought the elders to intercede on their behalf. Perhaps the elders could prevail on their mother.

74   But the elders shook their heads and said, "If that is what she wants, there is nothing that you can do to change her mind. Leave her be. She wants to be with him. Leave her. It's better that way."

75   And so the family ceased to press their mother to come home, though they still kept watch with her. They watched until she too died by the grave-side of her husband, their father.

76   Using the term "grandchild" that all elders used in referring to the young, the elder who presided over the woman's wake said, "Our granddaughter's love did not cease with death, but continues into the next life."

77   The next spring a small plant grew out of the grave of the woman. Many years later, as the sons, daughters and grandchildren gathered at the grave-side of their parents, they felt a mist fall upon their faces and their arms. "It is mother shedding tears of love for dad," cried her daughter.

78   And it is so. On certain days, spruces and pines shed a mist of tears of love.

By remaining at her husband's graveside until she too died, the woman   **79**
fulfilled the implied promise, "whither thou goest, there too will I go"
contained in the term "weedjeewaugun," companion in life, our word
for spouse.

As she wept for her love she must have wept for the love of her children.   **80**
Their love threatened to break that bond that held her to her husband. No!
She would not let even death part her from the man to whom she had given
her heart, her soul, her spirit forever.

It is unlikely that the woman ever uttered more than "K'zaugin" (I love   **81**
you) during her marriage. In this respect she was no different from most
other women, or men for that matter, who are not endowed with the poetic
gift, though they feel and love with equal passion and depth. K'zaugin said
everything. I love you, today, tomorrow, forever. It expressed everything
that the finest poets ever wrote and everything that the unpoetic ever thought
and felt but could not put into rhyme or rhythm.

(1991)

The Writer's Subject

1. What is the point of the anecdote about the school project Johnston describes in the first section of the essay?

2. Why is Johnston so critical of the book entitled *The Canadian Indian*, published in 1986 by the Department of Indian Affairs? (para. 14)

3. What, in Johnston's view, is lacking in scholarly studies of Indian life and culture?

4. Why does Johnston attach such significance to tribal language?

5. Johnston states that creation stories "provide insights into what races and nations understand of human nature" (para. 30). What insight is embodied in the creation story that Johnston then presents in paragraphs 31-38?

6. What do the other stories related by Johnston tell us about the beliefs or values of North American Indians?

The Writer's Style and Strategy

1. Discuss the way Johnston organizes the essay. Why is the larger part devoted to tribal narratives?

2. What relation does the title bear to Johnston's thesis?

3. What is the writer's attitude towards the school display he describes in paragraphs 2-11? How does he make this attitude plain?

4. What is the point Johnston wishes to emphasize by his allusion to the figure of Tonto in paragraph 12?

5. Johnston observes that "language and literature are inseparable" (para. 24). How is this illustrated in his retelling of Indian stories?

Suggested Topics for Writing and Discussion

1. Johnston is highly critical of modern scholars for their inadequate understanding of Native Indian languages and culture. Examine one of the books or articles on Canadian Indians by any of the writers listed by Johnston in paragraph 15, and discuss the work's strengths and/or weaknesses. Provide specific examples to support your view.

2. According to Johnston, "Creation stories provide insights into what races and nations understand of human nature" (para. 30). Find examples of creation myths from other cultures, and discuss how these stories reflect a particular understanding of human nature.

3. What aspects of First Nations' literature and culture do you think should be included in the high-school curriculum?

Stop Stealing Native Stories
by Lenore Keeshig-Tobias

AAA-IIII-EEE Y-Aah!
Clear the way.
In a sacred manner I come.
The stories are mine!
- Ojibway war song

Critics of non-native writers who borrow from the native experience have 1
been dismissed as advocates of censorship and accused of trying to shackle
artistic imagination, but their objections are prompted by something much
more.

Where The Spirit Lives may be a bad film. *Bone Bird* by Calgary novelist 2
Darlene Barry Quaife may oversimplify native spirituality. W.P.
Kinsella's Hobbema stories may be insulting. But the real problem is that
they amount to culture theft, the theft of voice.

Canada's Francophones have a strong and unique voice in North 3
America. Why? Because they have fought to ensure that their language
remains intact. Language is the conveyor of culture. It carries the ideas
by which a nation defines itself as a people. It gives voice to a nation's
stories, its *mythos*.

How do Canadians feel about the U.S. mythos defining them and their 4
country? This is quickly becoming a reality, I fear, because Canadians have
been too quick to hand over their voice and their stories to Americans.

Stories, you see, are not just entertainment. Stories are power. They 5
reflect the deepest, the most intimate perceptions, relationships and
attitudes of a people. Stories show how a people, a culture, thinks. Such
wonderful offerings are seldom reproduced by outsiders.

This is the root of the problem with *Where The Spirit Lives*, which deals 6
with the treatment of native students in government-sponsored residential schools during the 1930s. The film has been shown on the CBC and

TVOntario and as part of Canada Day at the recent festival in Palm Springs, California.

7   So what is it all about, anyway? In the end, a little Indian girl and her brother ride off into the vast, uninhabited wilderness. (Anne Shirley goes west?) They ride right out of the sentimentalized Canadian consciousness — stoic child warriors noble in defeat, marching home with Bible in hand. (A book of truth, perhaps, but whose?)

8   Native people were not involved in any creative aspect of the film. Their voice was heard only through cultural consultants hired to provide the nuances and insights lacked by the movie's writer and producers.

9   Cultural insight, nuance, metaphor and symbols give a book or film the ring of truth, but their essence — the thing that gives stories universal appeal, that allows true empathy and shared emotion — is missing from *Where The Spirit Lives,* as it is from most "native" writing by non-natives.

10   Canadians all too often use native stories, symbols and history to sell things — cars, tobacco or movies. But why hasn't Basil Johnston's *Indian School Days* become a best-seller? Why hasn't *Half Breed* by Marie Campbell been reprinted? (Why, for that matter, has Ms. Campbell, as one of Canada's "celebrated" authors, never received a writer's grant?)

11   *Where The Spirit Lives,* after having squeezed out the native version of what happened in the residential schools, turns around and tells natives to make their own movies. How can we? Even if we had access to financial backers, they would say: "Residential schools? It's been done."

12   With native people struggling for justice with land claims and in education, what makes Canadians think they have equality in the film industry? In publishing? With agencies that make arts grants? In the arts themselves?

13   Instead, the Canadian cultural industry is stealing — unconsciously, perhaps, but with the same devastating results — native stories as surely as the missionaries stole our religion and the politicians stole our land and the residential schools stole our language. As Leslie Marmon Silko writes in *Ceremony,* stories "are all we have, you see — all we have to fight off illness and death." As a storyteller I was once advised by an elder that there is a season for storytelling — winter. "Blackflies, mosquitoes and other creatures like those stories," she cautioned.

14   How quaint, I thought. Nonetheless, I respected her advice and as time went on, I began to understand it. If storytellers sit around all summer telling stories, then surely they'll become the feast of blackflies and mosquitoes. My elder was telling me that these stories are meant for certain ears only — and native ears.

15   So potent are stories that, in native culture, one storyteller cannot tell another's story without permission.

But why are Canadians so obsessed with native stories anyway? Why **16**
the urge to "write Indian?" Have Canadians run out of stories of their own?
Or are their renderings just nostalgia for a simpler, more "at one with
nature" stage of human development? There's a cliché for you.

Maybe Canadian stories about native people are some form of exorcism. **17**
Are they trying to atone for the horrible reality of native-Canadian relations? Or maybe they just know a good story when they find one and are
willing to take it, without permission, just as archaeologists used to rob
our graves for museums.

What about the quest for native spirituality? It is mostly escapist, and **18**
people such as Quaife would rather look to an ideal native living in never-
never land than confront the reality of what being native means in Canadian
society.

For example, residential-school survivors tell of children being forced **19**
to eat their own vomit when their stomachs could no longer hold down the
sour porridge. They tell of broken knuckles from fingers being rapped.
Some even tell of having pins stuck through their tongues as punishment
for speaking their own language. (Now, that's censorship.)

And what about the teacher who was removed from one residential **20**
school for abusing children? He was simply sent to another, more remote
school.

It's not that these stories have never been told; Canadians just haven't **21**
heard them. Nor does it mean that writers and storytellers are incompetent and inexperienced, as Mr. Kinsella seemed to suggest.

It means our voices have been marginalized. Imagine, Canadians tell- **22**
ing native stories because their government outlawed native languages,
native culture.

However, as Ms. Campbell said on CBC radio's Morningside, "If you **23**
want to write our stories, then be prepared to live with us." And not just
for a few months.

Hear the voices of the wilderness. Be there with the Lubicon, the Innu. **24**
Be there with Teme-Augama Anishnabai on the Red Squirrel Road. The
Saugeen Ojibway. If you like these stories, fight for them. I dare you.

(1990)

The Writer's Subject

1. What does the writer mean by "the theft of voice"? (para. 2)

2. What is the relevance of the writer's observations about French and English Canada in paragraphs 3 and 4?

3. What are Keeshig-Tobias's objections to *Where The Spirit Lives,* a film about the treatment of Native students in residential schools? How do these objections fit into the argument as a whole?

4. Why, according to Keeshig-Tobias, are Canadians "obsessed" with Native stories? (para. 16)

5. Why does the writer object to non-Native Canadians telling stories about Native people?

6. According to the writer, how has Native experience been dealt with in stories by non-Natives?

The Writer's Style and Strategy

1. What is the prevailing tone of this essay?

2. Examine paragraph 7. What details convey the writer's attitude to the story she is describing?

3. Discuss the references in this essay to particular Native and non-Native writers. How does Keeshig-Tobias use such references to advance her argument?

4. The writer frequently asks questions (see, for example, paragraphs 10, 12, 16). What is the effect she is aiming at through this technique?

5. Discuss the effectiveness of the essay's ending.

Suggested Topics for Writing and Discussion

1. Keeshig-Tobias argues that non-Natives have "marginalized" Native voices and stolen Native stories. Compare her view with the position taken by Carole Giangrande in her essay "Allowing the Mind to Wander."

2. What is your view of the argument that a people's mythos, the stories that embody their history and culture, should not be appropriated by outsiders?

3. Do you think that Canadians are, as the writer argues in paragraph 16, nostalgic for "a simpler, more 'at one with nature' stage of human development"?

4. Find out what you can about the Native Indian residential schools described in the books referred to in paragraph 10 of the essay.

Westward Oh!

by Martin Walker

The American Western artist Irving Couse painted *The Captive* in 1892, 1
when he was in Paris. It depicts an event which had taken place nearly 50
years earlier, and which became a highly symbolic archetype for the perils
inherent in the white man's thrusting advance across Indian country.

The capture of 17-year-old Lorinda Bewly by the Cayuse chief, Five 2
Crows, in 1847 became a celebrated "atrocity," a key moment in the process
which changed American perceptions of the Indians who stood in the way
of their expansion; the transformation from noble Red Man to murderous
savage within a single generation. The painting has now become once more
a highly-charged political symbol in an extraordinary row which is
convulsing the American art establishment.

"Couse's lurid treatment unconsciously expresses his culture's fears of 3
miscegenation," says the catalogue commentary on *The Captive*. "This is
evident first in the network of intimations that thinly repress an actual sexual
encounter. Bewly's skewed and foreshortened body suggests as much as
the blood on her wrist a violent physical confrontation with Five Crows.
The array of phallic objects pointing in her direction, together with the
tepee's open entry, further imply a sexual encounter.

"Yet at odds with its violent racial drama, the picture develops another, 4
quieter erotic relationship. If Bewly's body is skewed and foreshortened,
cut and cutoff, it is at the same time almost gently displayed for the viewer.
Against the logic of the narrative, Bewly's figure is oriented more to the
picture plane than to her Indian captor. It is the viewer who sees her face,
hair, and covering gesture. Through the fiction of the scene, what is denied
to Five Crows becomes available to the (white) audience who would see

Couse's painting."

5   Grand and formal exhibitions of art in a national gallery occasionally and sometimes deliberately provoke an aesthetic furore. But an entirely political row over a retrospective of 19th century American painting, in a city dedicated to the U.S. Constitution and its inalienable right to free speech, is something remarkable.

6   Senators are threatening budgetary retaliation against the Smithsonian, the complex of national museums which receives some $300 million a year in public funds. The public is flocking to the show, and engaging in furious debate in the large comment books thoughtfully provided for the purpose. Galleries in the Western cities of St. Louis and Denver have now cancelled their plans to show the exhibition. And angry editorials in the national press are trumpeting accusations of something close to treason. "Only in the land of the free is it possible to mount an entirely hostile ideological assault on the nation's founding and history; to re-cast that history in the most distorted terms — and have the taxpayers foot the bill," says the *Wall Street Journal.*

7   On this occasion, the usually more liberal *Washington Post* led the charge with a political commentary disguised as an art review: "With the sort of tortured revisionism now so stridently de rigueur in academia, it effectively trashes not only the integrity of the art it presents but most of our national history as well, reducing the saga of America's Western pioneers to little more than victimization, disillusion and environmental rape."

8   The exhibition — *The West As America: Reinterpreting Images Of The Frontier* — contains 164 paintings, sculptures and engravings of the way American artists between 1820 and 1920 portrayed the nation's expansion across the prairies and to the Pacific. The fuss has arisen because of the interpretation placed on their vision by the exhibition's curator and organizer, William Treuttner, and the scholars he recruited.

9   "Images from Christopher Columbus to Kit Carson show the discovery and settlement of the West as a heroic undertaking," says the plaque at the exhibition's entrance. "A more recent approach argues that these images are carefully staged fiction, constructed from both supposition and fact. Their role was to justify the hardship and conflict of nation-building. Western scenes extolled progress, but rarely noted damaging social and environmental change. Looking beneath the surface of these images gives us a better understanding of why national problems created during the westward expansion still affect us today."

10   The exhibition begins with a photograph, taken on the rooftop of a building just across the river from bustling New York in 1903. The Western artist Charles Schreyvogel, who painted the famous *Defending The Stockade,* stands at his easel, painting from life a fully dressed U.S.

cavalryman who is kneeling and aiming his revolver at some Indian attacker who is at least 2,000 miles and probably 40 years away.

Defending The Stockade, or an event very like it, is a scene that almost 11 certainly did take place in the brutal decade after the end of the U.S. Civil War when the Army was despatched to win and hold the frontier for settlers, railroads and Western civilization. And the exhibition documents the way the railroad companies became patrons of the painters they sent out to record the West in a suitable way. The point the exhibition seeks to make is that by the time Schreyvogel painted it, the Indians were history, and his art has a more contemporary cultural resonance, as a metaphor of patriotic and Anglo-Saxon America holding the gates against a flood of immigrants from southern and eastern Europe. "The paintings reveal far more about the urban culture in which they were made and showed. For it was according to the culture's attitudes — about race, class and history — that artists such as Schreyvogel and Remington created the place we know as the 'Old West'," says the plaque.

Just across the hall is the photograph, taken at about the same time, of 12 another U.S. cavalryman who is riding a wooden horse and managing to look extremely heroic. He is a model for Frederic Remington, most famous of the artists of the Old West. Remington's classic *Fight For The Water Hole* depicts five cowboys, their horses huddled in the hollow around the dwindling pond, grimly fighting off the encircling Indians in an implacable desert heat.

"This painting is about fear of the impending industrial era. These 'last 13 stand' paintings were popular with the wealthy patrons who bought them. They had a lot to lose with social change," says the exhibition organizer, William Treuttner, in an interpretation which has infuriated the press, the politicians and much of the American public who were flooding into Washington for their Desert Storm victory parade. But Treuttner quotes Remington himself to sustain his argument that the 20th century creators of the myth of the Old West were working within a political context attuned to their own times. The unashamedly racist Remington himself was deeply opposed to more immigration and diluting the Anglo-Saxon stock, and thoroughly disapproving of the new politicized working class which the immigrants manned.

"You can't glorify a Jew — coin-lovin' puds — nasty humans," Remington 14 wrote to a publisher friend. "I've got some Winchesters and when the massacring begins which you speak of, I can get my share of 'em and what's more I will." He went on to attack "Jews, injuns, Chinamen, Italians, Huns, the rubbish of the earth I hate."

Sent to Chicago by *Harpers' Weekly* to cover and illustrate the famous 15

Pullman strike, Remington described the strikers as "a malodorous crowd
of anarchistic foreign trash ... vicious wretches with no blood circulating
above the ears ... will follow readily any demagogue with revolutionary
tendencies."

16   One of his illustrations is called *Giving The Butt,* and portrays a squad
of clean-cut soldiers smashing their rifle butts into the faces of brutish
strikers armed with sticks and their bare hands. For Remington, the soldiers
were "pure and simple of speech, honest and no man can be one who can't
pass the most rigid physical examination imaginable."

17   Remington was aware of the gap between the reality of the West during
the Indian wars and his own much later painting. "I sometimes feel that I
am trying to do the impossible in my pictures in not having a chance to work
direct but as there are no people such as I paint, it's 'studio' or nothing,"
Remington wrote. And he was conscious of the wider artistic movement,
which he defined as "we fellows who are doing the 'Old America' which
is so fast passing."

18   In this carefully documented context, the deconstruction of the icons of
the American frontier myth becomes more plausible. The commentary on
the plaque alongside *Fight For The Water Hole* says the painting is a
metaphor for "the plight of an embattled capitalist elite in an era of strikes,
violence and widespread immigration.... Does it borrow its imagery —
a group of outnumbered whites desperately defending against the 'strike'
of a racial enemy — from the urban world where Remington lived?"

19   Reading the catalogue and knowing what Remington wrote and thought,
the commentary makes sense. But many of the attacks upon this exhibition have been made on a more casual basis. Senator Ted Stevens of Alaska,
who has warned the gallery's administrators that when they next apply for
government funds, "You're in for a battle," had not at that point visited the
exhibition at all.

20   And yet the senator went on to demand of the curators, in an inquisition
which reminded *Newsweek* magazine of McCarthy's Un-American
Activities Committee witch-hunting in the 1950s: "Why should people
come to your institution and see a history that is so perverted? I don't think
the Smithsonian has any business, or has ever had any business, developing
a political agenda."

21   The senators perceive a political agenda in the way the exhibition argues
that the Western artists were "propagandists for the dominant and aggressive white culture." And they have been infuriated by the commentaries on the gallery's walls which set each group of paintings in context.
The one they cite most reads: "Artistic representation of Indians developed
simultaneously with white interest in taking their lands. At first, Indians

Carson's Men, Charles Russel, 1913

Defending the Stockade, Charles Schreyvogle, 1905

Fight for the Waterhole, Frederic Remington, 1903

The Captive, Irving Couse, 1892

were seen as possessing a natural nobility and innocence. This assessment gave way gradually to a far more violent view that stressed hostile savagery."

The attack by Senator Stevens has been taken up by other Western 22 senators, their regional patriotism excited by his charge that "We from the West live here in the East really under attack all the time — to see that exhibit, I'll tell you, it really set me off."

Remember, he had not seen it. But Senator Alan Simpson of Wyoming 23 has been twice, and professes himself "shocked." Senator Slade Gorton of Washington State toured the show and was "appalled."

The attendance of the Chief Justice of the Supreme Court, and Vice- 24 President Dan Quayle (who are both by virtue of office on the gallery's Board of Regents) has been demanded to see "what abuse is being perpetrated in the nation's name."

This would be so much knockabout for a quiet month in politics except 25 for two things. The first is that America's intellectual great and good have entered the debate. The renowned historian and former Librarian of Congress, Daniel Boorstin, visited the exhibition and wrote in the Commentary book: "Perverse, historically inaccurate, destructive exhibit. No credit to the Smithsonian."

The second striking development is the way this revisionist treatment 26 of the Old West has been taken as symptomatic of an alleged penetration of a broadly leftist ideology into the nation's cultural institutions. The way the exhibition compares the concept of "Manifest Destiny" in America's conquest of the West to its quasi-imperial role in Asia, culminating in the disaster of the Vietnam War, has reopened old wounds.

"Ever since the 1960s, the one-time campus radicals of the Baby Boom 27 generation have sought repeatedly and noisily to rewrite the rules of American society in ways large and small," ran a furious denunciation of the exhibition in the Washington Post.

"On the campuses they seized by force in the 1960s and 1970s they have 28 moved from early demands as students for such things as black studies programmes to efforts as tenured professors to reshape not only the core curriculum of American higher education but its value system as well ... aging radicals now as teachers and curators increasingly in charge of the nation's cultural patrimony," it went on.

The curators have tried to fend off the attacks by toning down the 29 commentaries alongside the paintings, removing phrases like: "This pre-dominance of violent and negative views was a manifestation of Indian-hating, a largely manufactured, calculated reversal of the basic facts of white encroachment and deceit."

30   But the fuss goes on, a new round in the war of attrition between politicians and the art establishment which follows the decision last year by Washington's Corcoran Gallery to withdraw an exhibition of Robert Mapplethorpe's homo-erotic photographs. This year's debate has been heightened by the success of the movie *Dances With Wolves,* Kevin Costner's Oscar-winning portrayal of the Oglala Sioux Indians and their fate at the hands of the white settlers and the U.S. Army.

31   But the America that flocked to see the Costner movie is also an America newly invigorated by the simplistic flag-waving patriotism of George Bush's election campaign, by the war against Iraq and "the end of the Vietnam syndrome." In this context, an artistic and academic reinterpretation of the myth of the frontier becomes a subversive attack upon the quasi-divine American mission of winning the West.

32   Take Charles Russell's *Carson's Men,* which the exhibition argues to be a powerful religious allegory, from the Golgotha-like skull of the dead cow at Kit Carson's feet to the cross made by his figure and the rifle across his saddle-bow.

33   "Other details, the halo-like hats, the twilight sky that recalls the time of day of the Deposition (from the Cross), and above all the remarkably symmetical arrangement of Carson and the two men, with the centralized Carson higher against the sky and closer to the viewer, intensify the picture's allusions to the Crucifixion," suggests the catalogue.

34   It is an argument which portrays the visceral and mystic power of the Western myth which the exhibition has set out to challenge. And in the process, it has exposed the raw nerves beneath the fragile new patriotism, and the old guilts about the price the Indians paid for the imposition of the new white empire upon the West.

(1991)

The Writer's Subject

1. Walker's essay focuses on an exhibition entitled "The West As America," held in Washington, D.C. in 1991. According to the exhibition catalogue cited by Walker, what does Couse's painting "The Captive" reveal about the fears of America in the late 19th century?

2. What evidence did the exhibition provide that many images of the heroic settlement of the West were "carefully staged fiction"? (para. 9)

3. Walker cites the attacks made on the exhibition by a number of Western senators. What appear to be the chief grounds of their criticism?

4. What connection do the exhibition's critics see between "this revisionist treatment of the Old West" and current developments in American cultural institutions? (paras. 26-28)

5. Why does it seem to Walker that the America that "flocked" to see *Dances With Wolves* may be offended by the attitudes conveyed in the Washington exhibition? (paras. 30-31)

6. In what ways, according to Walker, did the racism of the artist Frederick Remington inform his paintings? (paras. 13-18)

The Writer's Style and Strategy

1. How does Walker present the conflicting viewpoints in the "furious debate" created by the Washington exhibition? Is he fair to both sides of the argument?

2. Where does Walker allow his own views to be seen? Pick out words or phrases which may indicate the writer's position.

3. Why does Walker begin his account of the exhibition with a discussion of Couse's painting "The Captive," rather than with a general description of the exhibition as a whole?

4. Discuss the last three paragraphs. Do they provide a satisfactory conclusion to the article?

5. What do such matters as level of diction, allusion, or historical or political reference tell us about the kind of audience Walker is addressing here?

Suggested Topics for Writing and Discussion

1. Walker sees the furore concerning "The West As America" exhibition as part of a broader conflict between art and the state. What are some of the issues in this conflict, as stated or implied in Walker's article?

2. Walker describes the angry reaction of some Western senators to the "revisionist" interpretation of the old West presented by the Washington exhibition. Political hostility to the arts is not uncommon, whether at the local or the national level; find one or two other examples of attacks on artists or writers by political figures, and identify the issues in contention.

3. Walker cites a number of passages from the exhibition catalogue and plaques that "deconstruct" the American frontier myth and its icons. Choose an image that makes a statement about Canada's past and offer your own interpretation of what that image reveals. Examples might include the famous photograph of "The Last Spike," Benjamin West's painting of the death of General Wolfe, or the painting of the Fathers of Confederation.

4. Choose a well-known painter or photographer, and find out what you can about the artist's work as a whole. Then select a representative work by that artist, and say what it tells us about the time (and place) in which it was created. What does it reveal about the cultural or political assumptions of the artist or of the artist's time?

5. Do you think that public funding of museums or art galleries should depend on public approval of the kinds of works collected and exhibited?

The World of Science

The body of Tolund Man

The Body in the Bog
by Geoffrey Bibby

The business of the archaeologist is the digging up of the past, the   1
reconstruction of remote history. He does his best to find out what our
remote ancestors did and thought and felt from the material remains
they left in the ground. A distinguished archaeologist has unflattering-
ly described himself and his colleagues as surgeons probing into the
workings of the human brain with picks, shovels, and builders' trowels.
"Fortunately," he adds "our patients are already dead."

This comparison must not be taken too literally. When Sir Mortimer   2
Wheeler describes the archaeologist as investigating people who are
dead, he means, I am afraid, that we are trying to find out about these
dead-and-gone people by studying the things they left behind them, their
implements and weapons and coins and pots and pans. The nearest we
normally get to the people themselves is their skeletons, and there is
a limit to what can be deduced from dry bones.

I wish to tell an archaeological detective story that is different – a   3
detective story that begins with a body and no artifacts.

My part in the story began on Monday, April 28, 1952, when I ar-   4
rived at the Prehistoric Museum of Aarhus, in mid- Denmark, to find
a dead body on the floor of my office. On an iron sheet stood a large
block of peat, and at one end of it the head and right arm of a man
protruded, while one leg and foot stuck out from the other end. His
skin was dark brown, almost chocolate colored, and his hair was a
brownish red.

He had been found on Saturday afternoon by workers cutting peat   5
in a little bog near Grauballe, about twenty miles away. He lay a yard

below the surface, but peat had been dug for generations there so that the "surface" had lain much higher, even within living memory. The finders had informed the local doctor of their discovery, not so much because he was a doctor but because he was known to be an antiquary of repute. And he had informed Professor Peter Glob, who was the director of our museum.

6   This was not Professor Glob's first "bog body"; he knew what to expect and made preparations accordingly. The next day he drove out to the bog, cut a section through the peat exposing the lie of the body, drew and photographed that section, took samples of the peat surrounding the body, and then cut out the whole block in which the body lay and brought it in to the museum in a truck.

7   That Monday we carefully dug away the peat covering the body, taking samples every two inches. The body lay face down, with one leg drawn up and the arms twisted somewhat behind it. It was completely naked. When we removed the peat from below the body (after turning it over in a plaster cast to preserve its original position), we still found nothing, no trace of clothing, no artifacts – nothing except the naked body.

8   At this point we turned for help to the professor of forensic medicine at Aarhus University, who carried out a thorough autopsy and presented us with a lengthy and detailed report:

9   "This most unusually well-preserved body has, as a result of the particular composition of the earth in which it has lain, undergone a process of conservation which appears to resemble most closely a tanning. This has made the skin firm and resistant, and has to a high degree counteracted the various processes of decay which normally commence soon after death . . . the subject is an adult male, and the condition of the teeth suggests that he was of somewhat advanced age. . . . On the front of the throat was found a large wound stretching from ear to ear. . . . This wound may with certainty be interpreted as an incised lesion, probably caused by several cuts inflicted by a second person. The direction of the wound and its general appearance make it unlikely that it could be self-inflicted or accidentally inflicted after death. . . . The investigation of the hair suggests that the subject was dark-haired. The reddish coloration is presumably accounted for by the body having lain in peat."

10   So the man from Grauballe had had his throat cut, and we had a murder mystery on our hands.

11   The investigation went on. The police expert reported: "There is nothing unusual about the fingerprints obtained. I myself possess the

same type of pattern on the right thumb and middle finger – without 12
therefore claiming any direct descent from Grauballe Man. Among the
present-day Danish population the two patterns occur with a frequency
of, respectively, 11.2 and 68.3 per cent."

More important were the results we got from the peat samples and 13
from a portion of the liver region that we had excised and sent to the
radioactive-carbon laboratory.

It happens that the botanists of Scandinavia have worked out in great 14
detail the changing composition of the vegetation of the region since
the last ice age ended more than ten thousand years ago. They do this
by means of the thousands of infinitesimal grains of pollen to be found
in any cubic centimeter of peat. The time within this sequence when
any particular specimen of peat was formed is shown by the proportion
of certain types of pollen grains, particularly of tree pollen. And the
pollen analysts could tell us that the peat immediately below Grauballe
Man had been formed early in the period the Danes call the Roman
Iron Age, a period extending from the beginning of the Christian Era
to about A.D. 300.

But they could tell us more. The peat *above* the body was of *earlier* 15
date than that directly below and around the body, and the peat at a
little distance to either side of the body was earlier still. The body had
clearly been buried in a hole cut in the peat – but not in a hole cut
to receive it. The only explanation to fit the facts was that a hole had
been cut, probably to obtain peat for fuel, had stood open for some
years (long enough for new peat to form in the water at the bottom of
the hole), and then Grauballe Man had been thrown into this new peat
and the hole had been filled in with peat from the surface layers.

The radio-carbon laboratory – which determines the age of organic 16
substances by measuring the residual carbon-14 in the specimen – could
tell us that this had occurred and that Grauballe Man had died in A.D.
310, with a possible error of a hundred years in either direction. This
did not surprise us; for, though local newspapers and gossip had made
much of a certain "Red Christian," a drunkard farmhand who was said
to have disappeared one night some sixty years before, not far from
the Grauballe peat bog, we should have been very surprised indeed if
the pollen laboratory and the radio-carbon laboratory had *not* given us
a date in the region of 100 B.C.-A.D. 300.

For Grauballe Man was far from being an isolated example. Bodies 17
have always been turning up in the peat bogs of Denmark – and not
only in Denmark. They are frequently found in northwest Germany and

even as far south as Holland. In that area there are records of something like two hundred bog bodies. Since the earlier records are not very detailed, sometimes merely an entry in a parish registry of the "body of a poor man drowned in such and such a bog," the statistics are far from exact. The earliest doubtful record of this nature is from 1450, at Bonstorf in Germany. And the first detailed report is from 1773, when a completely preserved body of a man was found three feet deep in the peat at Ravnholt on the Danish island of Fünen. The body lay on its back with its arms crossed behind it — "as though they had been bound," says the parish clerk. Apart from a sheepskin around the head, it was naked. When the sheepskin was removed, it could be seen that the man had had his throat cut.

18   In 1797, in southwest Jutland, another well-preserved male body was found, naked save for one oxhide moccasin but covered with two calfskin cloaks. The cause of death is not recorded, and the body was hurriedly buried in a nearby churchyard when it began to dry out and decompose.

And so it went. Every few years a body would be found, would be a nine-day wonder in its immediate locality because of its surprising state of preservation, and would be buried again when it began to smell.

19   A few of the bodies achieved more than local fame. In 1853, about fifty miles south of Copenhagen a body was found, probably that of a woman, though there was little left besides the skeleton and the long, fair hair. The body was noteworthy because it was accompanied by a bronze brooch and seven glass beads, which even then could be dated to the Iron Age and which we can now date to about A.D. 300.

20   Eight years earlier a much more complete female body had been found at Haraldskaer, in south Jutland, not far from the burial mounds of Gorm, the last heathen king of Denmark and his queen, nor from the site of the first Christian church in Denmark, built about A.D. 950 by Gorm's son, Harald Bluetooth. The body lay in the peat with its hands and feet held down by forked sticks, and it achieved some notoriety in Denmark because some learned antiquaries claimed that it was Queen Gunhild of Norway, who, according to legend, had been enticed to Denmark by Harald Bluetooth and drowned by him in a morass. Even at the time of discovery, though, the evidence for this identification was regarded as too slender.

21   The first photograph of a peat-bog body dates from 1873 and is of a body found near Kiel. It was a man's body with a triangular hole in the forehead. He was naked except for a piece of leather bound around the left shin, but his head was covered with a large square woollen blanket

and a sewn skin cape. An attempt was made to preserve him for exhibition by smoking, and several photographs were taken, some extravagantly posed. The first photograph of a body *in situ* was taken in 1892. The body was found not many miles away from the place where Grauballe Man was discovered sixty years later, and very close indeed to another recent find, the Tollund Man.

The list could be continued almost indefinitely. But it is only within 22 recent years that pollen analysis has been developed to a stage where the bodies can be accurately dated. And all the bodies found since have proved to date to the same restricted period of Danish prehistory, the first three centuries of the Christian Era. This fact makes it possible-indeed essential – to regard them as a single "case."

Apart from Grauballe Man, four bodies have been found in the peat 23 bogs of Denmark since World War II, and all have been subjected to the same thorough analysis that we gave Grauballe Man. Three came from the same bog, the large peat area of Borremose in north Jutland. The first was a man, naked like so many of the others but with two cloaks of skin beside him. Around his neck was a rope noose, which may have been the cause of death, although the body was too badly preserved to be certain. There were odd features about the noose; it had been knotted at the neck, and both of the fairly short ends had been bent over and lashed with leather thongs to prevent them from unraveling, surely an unduly elaborate treatment for an ordinary hangman's noose.

The second body was that of a woman, again poorly preserved. The 24 upper part of the body appeared to have been naked, while the lower part was covered with a blanket, a shawl, and other bits of clothing. There was a leather cord around the neck, but the cause of death was apparently a crushing blow on the skull.

The third body was also a woman's, a rather stout lady who lay face 25 downward in the peat with only a blanket wrapped around her middle and held in place by a leather strap. She was no sight for squeamish archaeologists – she had been scalped and her face battered to pieces, though perhaps after death.

It is with quite unjustified relief that one turns from the rather macabre 26 Borremose bodies to the well-known Tollund Man whose portrait has been in the press of the world and who has had the honor of appearing on British television. Tollund Man was discovered in 1950, two years before Grauballe Man and under the same circumstances, by farmers cutting peat. The discovery was reported to the police, and they called in Professor Glob, who described what he saw:

27   "In the peat cut, nearly seven feet down, lay a human figure in a crouched position, still half-buried. A foot and a shoulder protruded, perfectly preserved but dark-brown in color like the surrounding peat which had dyed the skin. Carefully we removed more peat, and a bowed head came into view.

28   "As dusk fell, we saw in the fading light a man take shape before us. He was curled up, with legs drawn under him and arms bent, resting on his side as if asleep. His eyes were peacefully shut; his brows were furrowed, and his mouth showed a slightly irritated quirk as if he were not overpleased by this unexpected disturbance. . . ."

Tollund Man was found to be naked except for a leather belt around his waist and a leather cap upon his head, a cap made of eight triangular gussets of leather sewn togeter. There was one other item. Around his neck was the elaborately braided leather rope with which they had hanged him.

29   It is clear, I think, that we have a case of mass murder. There are too many points of similarity between the killings for it to be possible to consider each independently of the others. I should point out, though, that their generally fantastic state of preservation is not one of these points of similarity. It is merely our good fortune. The preservation is due the fact that the peat bogs contain sufficient humic acid and tannic acid to halt the processes of decay and start a tanning process that can preserve the body. (This process, incidentally, we have carried to its logical conclusion with Grauballe Man. Eighteen months in an oak vat in a concentrated solution based on oak shavings has completed the tanning process that nature commenced some eighteen hundred years ago. Grauballe Man, on exhibition at the Prehistoric Museum in Aarhus, needs only a little linseed oil now and then in order to last indefinitely.)

30   There is one condition for preservation, however, for otherwise the peat bogs would be full of the bodies of every animal that falls into them. The body must be *buried* in the peat, deep enough down to be below the oxygen-containing surface levels. And this − the fact that all these bodies were disposed of in old cuttings in the peat − *is* one of the common factors that cause us to regard all the killings as a single phenomenon.

31   Another is the fact that all the bodies are naked. Though it is the rule rather than the exception for articles of clothing to be found with the bodies, and sometimes wrapped around the bodies, they are never regularly clothed in the garments. But the most obvious similarity is

that all have died violent deaths and that all are found in bogs.
And that leads to the next step in the inquiry: the question of motive.   32
Why are these bodies there at all?

These are not ordinary burials. Archaeologists are very well acquainted   33
with the burials of this period of Danish prehistory. They were elaborate,
clearly showing evidence of belief in an afterlife in which the dead would
have need of material things. The graves are large and edged with stones.
The body lies carefully arranged on its side, together with a whole set
of pottery vessels, or in the case of the wealthy, with glass and silver
ware imported from the Roman Empire. The vessels must have held
provisions for the journey to the afterworld, for there is often a leg of
pork or of mutton with the rest of the provisions, and even a knife to
carve the joint.

It is clear that whatever it was that resulted in the deaths of the bodies   34
in the bogs also deprived them of regular, ritual burial.

We must dismiss the most obvious explanation − that the bodies were   35
victims of robbery with violence. All are dated to the comparatively
short period of three hundred years at the beginning of our era. It may
have been a lawless time − though farther south it is the period of the
Pax Romana − but certainly it was no more lawless than many other
periods: the period before, of the great Celtic and Germanic wander-
ings; or the period after, when the Roman Empire was breaking up and
all the vultures flocked to the kill; or the Viking period; or much of
the Middle Ages. We should expect a much greater spread in date if
the bodies are to be explained as the victims of robber bands.

We must widen our scope and look not so much at the bodies as at   36
the bogs. What do we find there?

Any Danish archaeologist can answer that question at length. And   37
he can illustrate his answer at the Danish National Museum in
Copenhagen, where room after room is full of things found in bogs.
More than half of the best treasures of Danish prehistory have been
found in bogs, and the archaeologist will tell you that these treasures
were offerings to the gods.

Now, archaeologists have often been accused of calling in hypothetical   38
gods and cult practices whenever they find anything they cannot explain by obvious mundane means. A theory of offerings in the peat bogs
must not be accepted uncritically. But how else is one to explain why
a Stone Age farmer, some four thousand years ago, very carefully laid
seven large, new, unused stone axes side by side in a row in a peat
bog? How is one to explain why several pairs of the big bronze trumpets

known as lurs, the finest known products of the Danish Bronze Age, have been found in the bogs in good working order?

39   It begins to look as though anything of prehistoric date found in the bogs of Denmark is a priori likely to be an offering to the gods. If we move forward to the actual period of the bog bodies, we find the offerings in the bogs getting more numerous and more varied and richer. In the early 1950's I spent three years a few miles south of our museum, helping to dig out an immense offering of weapons — several thousand iron swords and spearheads and arrowheads and shield bosses — all of them burned, bent, hacked to pieces, and then deposited in a lake in the middle of a peat bog. They had been deposited at various times — it was a regular place of offering — but all during the period A.D. 150-300. Among the weapons lay the skeletons of two horses — and here perhaps we approach quite close in spirit to the bog bodies, for the horses had been beheaded before they were offered, and marks on the bones showed quite clearly where spears had been stuck into the carcasses, before or after death.

40   We are entering a dark region. Our probings into the minds of our distant ancestors are lifting a corner of a veil that seems to cover an area of deep superstition, a time when the peat bogs were the abodes of gods and spirits, who demanded sacrifice. When we look now at the bodies in the bogs it seems by no means impossible that they, too, were offerings; that the sacrifices to the gods also included human sacrifices.

41   We must ask ourselves what we know about the gods and goddesses of this period.

42   At the northern end of that very bog at Borremose in which three of the bodies were found, there was discovered in 1897 a large caldron of solid silver. In itself the Gundestrup caldron is far and away the most intrinsically valuable of all the bog offerings. But it is more than that; it is a picture book of European religion around the beginning of the Christian Era. Its sides are decorated, inside and out, with a series of panels bearing pictures, in relief, of gods and goddesses, of mythical animals, and of ritual scenes. Admittedly the caldron is believed to have been manufactured in southeast Europe and to have been brought to Denmark as booty, but the deities portrayed are like the native Danish gods of the period.

43   It is particularly noteworthy that each one of these deities, although otherwise naked, bears a torque, or broad necklet, at the throat, which appears to have been a symbol of kingship and of divinity. It has even been suggested – perhaps not entirely fancifully – that the oddly elaborate nooses around the necks of Tollund and Borremose Man in some way set them apart as consecrated to the gods. We know from the sagas, not many hundreds of years later, that in Viking times hanged men were sacred to Odin, the chief god of the Viking pantheon.

One of the interior caldron panels shows clearly that the idea of human 44 sacrifice was not alien to the religion of the time. It is admittedly a different ceremony of sacrifice, with the victim dropped headfirst into, or perhaps slaughtered above, a caldron, perhaps the Gundestrup caldron itself. The cutting of the throats of animal victims and the draining of their blood into a caldron was not unknown even among the civilized Greeks and Romans – and Grauballe Man, like many of the victims in the Danish bogs, had had his throat cut.

Speculation concerning details of ritual, though fascinating, can hardly 45 be justified by the slender evidence at our disposal. But the general picture cannot be questioned: the Danes of the early Christian centuries worshipped torque-bearing gods and goddesses; they were not averse to human sacrifice; and the holy places of the divinities were the peat bogs.

There is one source of information that we have not yet tapped. The 46 historians and geographers of the Roman Empire wrote books, some of which describe the manners and customs of peoples beyond the imperial frontiers. The books must be used with caution; few of the authors had visited the regions they describe, and their accounts may well be as full of misunderstandings and fanciful explanations as anything the modern archaeologist can invent to explain what he finds.

But there is a passage in Tacitus's *Germania,* an account of the peoples 47 beyond the Rhine written in A.D. 98, that bears on our study of the Danish bog bodies. Tacitus names seven tribes to the north of Germany, including the Angles, who are known to have lived in south Jutland before they invaded England in the fifth century together with the Saxons and Jutes. And he says: "these people . . . are distinguished by a common worship of Nerthus, or Mother Earth. They believe that she interests herself in human affairs and rides through their peoples. In an island of Ocean stands a sacred grove, and in the grove stands a car draped with a cloth which none but the priest may touch. The priest can feel the presence of the goddess in this holy of holies, and attends her, in deepest reverence, as her car is drawn by oxen. Then follow days of rejoicing and merrymaking in every place that she honors with her advent and stay. No-one goes to war, no-one takes up arms; every object of iron is locked away; then, and only then, are peace and quiet known and prized, until the goddess is again restored to her temple by the priest, when she has had her fill of the society of men. After that, the car, the cloth and, believe it if you will, the goddess herself are washed clean in a secluded lake. This service is performed by slaves who are immediately afterwards drowned in the lake. Thus mystery begets terror and a pious reluctance to ask what that sight can be which is allowed only to dying eyes. "

48   Here we may be getting close to an answer. Nerthus — Mother Earth — is clearly a goddess of fertility; she may be the "goddess with the torque." And the time of peace and rejoicing when the goddess is driven around the countryside in her draped carriage wiil be the time of sowing, the vernal equinox. Pagan survivals of this spring festival still exist in many parts of Europe, in mummers' plays and Maypole dancing and Queens of the May. And in the National Museum in Copenhagen may be seen one of the ox-drawn carriages that almost certainly was used to carry the image of the fertility goddess around the fields. It was found — inevitably — in a peat bog, Dejbjerg in east Jutland, in the 1880's. Richly carved and decorated with ornaments of bronze, it is far too fine a wagon to have been used for mundane purposes. Upon it stands a palanquin, a carrying chair with a canopy, within which the image of the goddess must have rested.

49   A final point brings the evidence full circle to the bodies in the bogs. Microscopic examination of the stomach contents of the men from Borremose, Tollund, and Grauballe shows that their food for several days before death had been vegetarian. It seems to have consisted of some sort of porridge or mash composed of various kinds of corn, or sorrel and heart's ease (both cultivated during the Iron Age), and of the seeds of such weeds as were accidentally harvested along with the corn. It has been suggested that this was a ritual diet, part of the ceremony needed to make the corn grow. Be that as it may, it is significant that there was no trace of any of the edible plants or fruits of summer in the stomach contents. So whatever our uncertainty about the precise year of death, we can say with confidence that the season of the year was winter or early spring.

50   Further we cannot go. We have been probing, with our picks and shovels and builders' trowels, not merely into the brains but perhaps also into the souls of men, and we must be content if our diagnosis is imprecise and inconclusive. But it does take us a little way beyond the conventional archaeological picture of the material lives of the simple

peasants of barbarian Europe. Behind the material life, interleaved with it and perhaps dominating it, was the world of taboos and magic and superstition, the spirits of the earth and of the heavens, who had to be bribed or placated or bought off. One of the occupational risks of Iron Age Europe, right up to the end of the Viking period scarcely a thousand years ago, was that of being chosen as victim, as the price to be paid for prosperity in the next harvest or victory in the next war. It was only with the coming of Christianity that human sacrifice ceased in Europe; looking on the bodies from the Danish bogs we should do well to realize that there, but for the grace of God, lie we.

(1968)

The Writer's Subject

1. How did Bibby and his colleagues first come to realize that they had a murder mystery on their hands?

2. What part did the Scandinavian botanists play in the investigation? (paras. 12-15)

3. Bibby describes the characteristics of a number of bog bodies. What features did these have in common that led him to conclude that these bodies represented "a case of mass murder"? (para. 29)

4. Why did the archaeologists dismiss "the most obvious explanation – that the bodies were victims of robbery with violence"? (para. 35)

5. What led Bibby and his colleagues to conclude that these bodies were ritual offerings?

6. What was the signficance of the Gundestrup cauldron in the unravelling of the mystery of the bog bodies? (paras. 42-44)

7. How does Tacitus's account of the goddess Nerthus throw light on the cir-cumstances of the ritual murders? (paras. 47-48)

8. How does Bibby's conclusion demonstrate that the archaeologist's interests are not restricted to a study of material remains?

The Writer's Style and Strategy

1. Bibby speaks of his intention to tell "an archaeological detective story." In what ways does the essay follow the pattern implied by such a description?

2. Is this essay intended for a specialist or a generalist audience? Pick out details of content, style, or diction that support your opinion.

3. Was the reasoning employed in Bibby's investigation primarily deductive or inductive?

4. Discuss the uses that Bibby makes of paragraphs of one or two sentences.

5. What features of Bibby's approach lead the reader to have confidence in the plausibility of his conclusions?

Suggestions for Writing and Discussion

1. Find out what you can about archaeological excavations in your region or community. What conclusions have been reached about the history of your region through such investigations? (A good place to begin your study is your local museum.)

2. Bibby speaks of the part played by scientific experts in his investigation (e.g., pollen analysis, carbon dating). With the help of a librarian, locate an account of a fairly recent archaeological "dig" or underwater expedition (e.g., in the Mediterranean, in China). Show what part science and technology have played in helping the archaeologists understand their finds.

3. Bibby points to the importance of ritual in pre-Christian Danish society. Though we no longer subscribe to rituals of the kind Bibby describes, we do practise other kinds of rituals. Discuss one or two rituals still practised in your community in connection with such occasions as births, deaths, marriages, harvest, etc.

The Real Responsibilities
of the Scientist

by Jacob Bronowski

We live in times of very difficult decisions for scientists, for statesmen,   1
and for the lay public. Many of these decisions are forced on us by
new scientific discoveries, and the difficulties in making them are created
by the distance between the scientist and the public. (Indeed, there is
a frightening distance even between scientists in one field and those
in another.) This sense of distance is, I think, a grave threat to the survival of the kind of society in which science can flourish at all.

People hate scientists. There is no use in beating about the bush here.   2
The scientist is in danger of becoming the scapegoat for the helplessness
which the public feels. And if an immense revulsion of public feeling
does lead to the destruction of the scientific tradition, then the world may
again enter a dark age as it did after the Goths destroyed Rome. It is
not impossible that the whole mechanical and intellectual society which
we know could be abolished by a great wave of fanaticism.

That is the danger which faces us, because people hate scientists. But   3
even if this danger does not materialize, something as terrible can happen — and is happening. This is that the scientist is forced, by the hatred
of public opinion, to side with established authority and government.
He becomes a prisoner of the hatred of the lay public, and by that
becomes the tool of authority.

My purpose is not to underline these obvious dangers, which we may   4
hide from ourselves but which in our hearts we all know to exist. My purpose is to try to give a picture, as I see it, of the real responsibilities
of scientists, government, and public, in order that, beginning from this
diagnosis, we may begin to cure the great and threatening division
between them.

The Abuse of Science

5   What the lay public does when it hates the scientist is what it does also when it hates policemen and ministers of state and all symbols of authority. It tries to shift the responsibility for decisions from its own shoulders to the shoulders of other people. "They have done this," it says. And "They" is always the law, the government − or in this case, the scientist.

6   You must allow me here to make a digression which is not strictly part of my theme, but which I think needs saying. It is this: that we must not forget that scientists do bear a heavy responsibility. I am of course about to explain that really the public and governments bear the main responsibility. But this does not shift from us, the scientists, the grave onus of having acquiesced in the abuse of science. We have contrived weapons and policies with our public conscience, which each of us individually would never have undertaken with his private conscience. Men are only murderers in large groups. They do not individually go out and strangle their neighbor. And scientists are only murderers in large groups − collectively. For scientists are very ordinary human beings. Any collection of people in any laboratory contains good and bad, people with consciences and without, and what we have allowed to happen is the conquest of science by the minority without conscience which exists in every group.

7   It is sad that scientists have been exceptionally corruptible. Look into your own experience. Most of us have come from poor parents. We have worked our own way up. The practice of science has enabled us to earn salaries which would be unthinkable to us if we had stayed peddling whatever our fathers peddled. Quite suddenly, the possession of a special skill has opened to us a blue door in the antechambers of prime ministers. We sit at conference tables, we have become important people, because we happen to be able to be murderers. And therefore scientists have been bought with large salaries and fellowships and rewards quite inappropriate to their merits, because a policy was furthered by their techniques. The scientist has proved to be the easiest of all men to blind with the attractions of public life.

8   Having said this I now propose to stop abusing the scientist. I think it is right that we should all make this confession of guilt − I have been as guilty as anyone else − but this is all spilt milk, this is all water over the dam. We must now look toward what we can do to remedy what has happened. And it cannot be remedied by a gigantic strike of

scientists, who will suddenly refuse to have anything to do with commercial or war research, because the society of scientists contains too many fallible human beings to make this practicable.

When the public dreams of such a strike, when it says: "scientists 9 ought not to have invented this or disclosed that secret," it is already demanding something of the individual scientist which lies beyond his personal responsibility.

The voters of Great Britain elect for the purpose of making their policy 10 six hundred and thirty members of Parliament. They do not elect the people who go to Harwell or the people who go to my own research laboratory. That is: we have already deputed to those whom we elect the responsibility for framing policy in peace and war, and it is quite wrong to ask a body of professional experts like the scientists to take this responsibility from the men whom our society has named.

The individual scientist is not the keeper of the public conscience, 11 because that is not what he was chosen for. The population at large, through its deputed ministers, has chosen scientists to execute certain public orders which are thought to represent the public will. And you cannot ask the scientist to be executioner of this will, and judge as well. If you have given a body of scientists this particular hangman's task, you cannot ask them also to form a collective opposition to it. The collective responsibility belongs to the lay public and through that, to those who were elected by that public to carry it out.

Thus when Einstein on August 2, 1939, wrote a letter to President 12 Roosevelt in order to draw his attention to the possibility of an atomic bomb, he was acting with exemplary correctness. He was disclosing to the elected head of government a matter of public importance on which the decision was not his, the writer's, but was the President's to make.

We must explain to people that they are asking of scientists quite the 13 wrong collective decision when they say, "you should not have invented this," or "you should not have disclosed that." This is asking us all to betray the public in the same way as Dr. Klaus Fuchs did, by asking scientists to make decisions which are for the nation to make. The only man who ever, on his own responsibility, was willing to shoulder public responsibility in this way, was Dr. Fuchs. But so far from being hailed as the only sane scientist, he was treated as quite the opposite – as of course he was, since scientists have no right to betray the will of the nation. Yet Fuchs did just what the public asks of every scientist – he decided what to do with a scientific invention.

The Private Conscience

14   Very well. We will agree that the scientist is not the keeper of the nation's policy. Then what is he the keeper of? He is the keeper of his own private conscience. His responsibility is not to be seduced as a person. He has the right to act individually as a conscientious objector. Indeed, I believe he has the duty to act as a conscientious objector. I would like to repeat this point. It is in this country an offense to betray the armed forces or to seduce their members from their allegiance. It is not an offense to refuse to be a soldier. And I believe that this is exactly like the position of the scientist. He has no business to act as if he commands the army, but he has a business to settle with his own conscience: the serious business whether he personally will engage in forms of research of which he does not morally approve.

15   My claim then is that the individual scientist should exercise his own personal conscience. This is his duty. What is the duty of governments in this respect? It is to make it possible for him to exercise his conscience. The responsibility of governments in this is to create the conditions in which a scientist can say: No! to projects in which he does not want to take part. He must even be able to give advice which is distasteful to those in authority, and still must not be hounded out of public life or prevented from making a living.

16   In all countries the serious threat to scientists who have once touched the fringes of secret subjects is that they are then caught in something from which they can never escape again. They do not get a passport, in case somebody captures them. They cannot get a job because, if they do not want to do this, then they are too dangerous or awkward to be trusted with anything else. This is what we must prevent governments from doing, and this can only be prevented by the opinion of quite ordinary citizens. This is the duty which citizens owe to scientists, to insist that governments shall make it possible for scientists to be conscientious objectors if they wish.

17   I have explored this subject in general terms, and I would now like to be specific. I would like to tell you precisely what I think is the responsibility of the public, of the scientists, and of governments.

18   The responsibility of the public is to make the decisions of policy on which their future depends, and to make them themselves. And in a democracy the apparatus for this is to elect those people in whose judgment you have confidence — and to elect them on the issues which in fact face the world. Now you can only elect such people, you can

only put pressure on them about public issues, if you are well informed. The greatest lack of public opinion today is lack of information about what is possible and not possible in science. This sets my teeth on edge every time I read a scientific newsflash. I will quote one of many instances which I find distasteful: the use of the phrase "cobalt bomb." This is a technical term for a piece of medical equipment, but has suddenly become transformed into something to describe how a hydrogen bomb might be clothed. As a result, of the fifty million people in this country, forty-nine million and nine hundred odd thousand have heard the words "cobalt bomb," but are helplessly confused between radioactive treatment and something that you blow people up with. The public must be well informed; and the public gets not only the government it deserves, but the newspapers it deserves.

If this is once granted, the next step I think is simple. If it is once 19 granted that we believe in democratic election, and that in our generation this can only be carried out by a public informed on the scientific issues on which the fate of nations hangs, then the duty of the scientist is clear. The duty of the scientist is to create the public opinion for right policies, and this he can only create if the public shares his knowledge.

My generation has a heavy task here, because it ought to spend the 20 bulk of its time — alas — not in laboratories at all, but in explaining to the voting public what is going on in the laboratories. What are the choices which face us? What could be done with antibiotics, with new materials, with coal (if you like), and with alternative forms of energy? These are urgent questions and yet, however many times we raise them, the layman still does not understand the scale of the changes which our work is making, and on which the answers must hang.

There is a slightly irreverent story about this. At the time the Smyth 21 Report was published in America there was published in this country a White Paper on the British contribution to atomic energy. One of the documents in it is the directive which Mr. Winston Churchill, as he then was, gave about the setting up of an atomic energy project. This directive begins with the words, "Though personally satisfied with the power of existing explosives. . . ." This bland phrase is a monument to a nonscientific education. For it could only have been written by a man, an intelligent man, who simply does not understand how big a million is. The difference between atomic explosives and ordinary explosives is the difference between the length of a nuclear bond and a molecular bond; and this is a factor of more than a million. To suppose somehow that in multiplying the energy of an explosive by a million, you are doing nothing very different from multiplying it by two, or five, or ten — this is simply not to grasp the scale of the world.

22   And the public does not grasp it. To say "ten to the sixth" to anybody, however educated, is still to invite the reproof today that one is stressing mere numerical details. One of our tasks, as scientists, must be to educate people in the scale of things.

23   While I am telling improper stories — improper only in the amusing sense — I will tell you that everybody who works in industrial research has this trouble all the time, when he discusses the economics of new processes. We put forward the result of research, or we simply estimate what would happen if a piece of research proved successful. And at once we get back a balance sheet from the finance department which says: The current process makes a profit of 2/2d a ton, and what you have in mind might make a loss of 8d a ton; it is therefore not worth pursuing. This, if you please, is the comment on a piece of research which, if it works on the full scale, might cut costs by a factor of five. But no accountant understands a factor of five; he budgets in shillings and pence, and what is liable to loss is to him as good as lost. One cannot explain a factor of five, or a factor of a million, to people who have not been brought up in a scientific tradition. This is what I mean when I say that the scientist has a duty to become a teacher to the public in understanding the pace, the nature, the scale of the changes which are possible in our lifetime.

Government and Opportunity

24   I have detailed the duties of the public and of the scientist. What are the duties of government? The duties of government are to give its public the opportunity to learn, and therefore to give scientists the opportunity to teach. And I have already suggested that these duties are twofold. One is to give scientists freedom to live their own lives if they do not want to go on with research projects which seem to them without conscience. The other is the duty to allow scientists to speak freely on subjects of world importance.

25   As for the second, everyone who has ever been connected with the atomic energy projects knows how it is met today. We spend our time waiting for some American journalist to publish some piece of information which we know to be accurate, so that we may then quote it as being the opinion of the *New York Times*. I am being frank about this: I do it all the time. I read what the greatest indiscreet senator said to the small indiscreet reporters, and I know that nine statements are

nonsense and one statement is accurate. Then I quote the one that is accurate — but not as my opinion.

Of course it is natural that governments resist the explosive opinions 26 of scientists. All governments, all societies are resistant to change. Rather over two thousand years ago, Plato was anxious to exile poets from his society; and in our lifetime, for the same reason, governments are, in effect, anxious to exile or at least silence scientists. They are anxious to exile all dissidents, because dissidents are the people who will change society.

There is a simple difference between governments and scientists. 27 Governments believe that society ought to stay the way it is for good — and particularly, that there ought to be no more elections. Scientists believe that society ought to be stable, but this does not mean the same thing to them as being static. We scientists want to see an *evolving* society, because when the physical world is evolving (and we are helping to evolve it) the forms of society and government cannot be kept the same.

The Moral Contract

Having described the duties of the public, of scientists, and of govern- 28 ments, let me now underline what I have said by describing what happens in all three cases if these duties are not kept. If governments do not allow scientists freedom of conscience, to work at what they like and to refuse to work at what they do not like, and to speak freely about why they do so, then you get the gravest of all disasters — the disaster of state intolerance. This is a disaster because it saps both sides of the moral contract. For there is a moral contract between society and its individuals which allows the individual to be a dissident; and if the state breaks this moral contract, then it leaves the individual no alternative but to become a terrorist. I do not know whether the great state trials in Russia were just or were false. But I know that if they were just, if men like Radek and Trotsky and Zinoviev really committed those enormities, then this in itself condemns the system of government which does not allow any other form of protest than such a form. The grave danger to our society too is that this becomes the only choice which is left open to scientists, if state intolerance imprisons them and tries to turn them into a secret Egyptian priestcraft.

The great sin of the public is acquiescence in this secrecy. I am hor- 29 rified by the feeling that I get, from such trifling things as American advertisements, that people really enjoy the sense that they are not to be trusted. There is an advertisement running in the *New Yorker* at the moment (I think for a clothing firm) which shows a man who has just got out of an airplane. He has a face like a prizefighter, he is well-dressed and wears what in New York is called a sharp hat, and he carries a bag in one hand which is chained to his wrist. He is carrying secret documents. This is the holy of holies. This is what we are to admire — the man with his mouth shut tight who is not trusting you and me, because of course you and I are not to be trusted. When people come to believe this, when they themselves believe that it is better for them not to know, then totalitarianism is on the doorstep. Then you are ready for Hitler to get up and say: "I am the man who will take your communal responsibilities. I will make your decisions for you."

3(And the third in our scheme, the scientist, must preserve the tradition of quarrelling, of questioning, and of dissent on which science (and I believe all post-Renaissance civilization) has been built. He must do this for two reasons. First, there is the mundane reason which is obvious in the failure of German research after Hitler took power. It is this: that you do not get good science as soon as you have reduced the scientists to yes-men. It is the nature of scientists to be thoroughly contrary people — let us own up to that. It is the nature of science as an activity to doubt your word and mine. As soon as you get a science, such as atomic energy research in totalitarian Germany, in which the young men are no longer allowed to question what the great men have said, then that science is dead. You can find in the files of the German Atomic Energy Commission that several young men made what I suppose must be called very good suggestions, but they were not followed because (such is the influence of totalitarianism) Heisenberg already knew the answers already.

31 This does not happen in English laboratories yet. Mr. Churchill begins by saying that he is satisfied with existing explosives, but after the comma he does give scientists the opportunity to be dissatisfied. This tradition, this independence and tolerance, is I believe the base of all our values; and this is what we as scientists must preserve.

The Duty of Heresy

32 I have given you the simple practical grounds for allowing scientists to be awkward, but I believe also that imaginatively and intellectually this is equally important. The sense of intellectual heresy is the lifeblood of our civilization. And the heresy of scientists cannot be confined to their science. Newton was thoroughly and rightly contrary in science,

and he was also a thorough heretic in religious matters. For the same reason, people like Oppenheimer and Einstein are found to associate with such unreliable characters. You cannot say to scientists: "When you get into the laboratory at nine in the morning you are going to become a dissenter; and when you go out at five-thirty you are going to become a citizen who touches his cap and who is politically sound. The intellect is not divided into these simple categories.

I have said that the duty of the scientist is today publicly to become 33 a teacher. Let me end by saying something of what he is to teach. There is, of course, the scientific method. There are things about the scale and order of size, of which I have spoken. There are the possibilities which are open to us in controlling nature and ourselves. Above all, he can teach men to ask whether the distance between promise and achievement in our age need be quite so large; whether there must be such a gap between what society is capable of doing and what it does. All this, every scientist can teach.

But every scientist can also teach something deeper. He can teach 34 men to resist all forms of acquiescence, of indifference, and all imposition of secrecy and denial. We must resist the attitude of officials, that there ought to be a good reason why something should be published before you allow it. We must teach even officials that there will have to be a very good reason indeed before anyone is silenced by secrecy.

Mr. Gordon Dean, former chairman of the American Atomic Energy 35 Commission, has just been complaining against secrecy on practical grounds. He says that the commercial reactors which are being built in America are still on the secret list and that this is handicapping American business in its competition with English business for world reactor markets. God works in a mysterious way and it may be that by this anxiety to sell atomic power, science will be liberated. At any rate, let us not look askance at any ally in the drive against silence. My message, in this and in all else, has been the scientist's duty to speak. There is one thing above all others that the scientist has a duty to teach to the public and to governments: it is the duty of heresy.

(1956)

The Writer's Subject

1. What is the chief responsibility of the scientist, as Bronowski sees it?

2. Why, according to Bronowski, do people regard scientists in the same way that they regard other symbols of authority? (para. 5)

3. How, in Bronowski's view, have scientists contributed to the abuse of science? (para. 7)

4. How does Bronowski answer those who think that scientists should oppose government policy on such matters as war research? (paras. 8-13)

5. How does Bronowski illustrate the danger of allowing a scientist rather than a government to make the decision about what to do with a scientific invention? (para. 13)

6. Why does Bronowski say the scientist "has the duty to act as a conscientious objector"? (para. 14)

7. Why is it so important for the public to be well informed, and what are the responsibilities of the scientist in this regard? (paras. 18-22)

8. What are the consequences of governments' not allowing scientists freedom of conscience? (para. 28)

The Writer's Style and Strategy

1. How does Bronowski make clear that his audience is made up of scientists?

2. What evidence in the style of this essay indicates that it was also intended to reach a wider audience?

3. "The Real Responsibilities of the Scientist" is a good example of a public address. Bronowski skilfully identifies himself with his audience and employs direct appeals to his listeners, anecdotes, clear transitions between the stages of his argument, and restatements of central ideas for clarity. Find examples of these and other techniques which demonstrate Bronowski's command as a public speaker.

4. What use does Bronowski make of anecdote and historical example?

Suggested Topics for Writing and Discussion

1. Bronowski is opposed to "all imposition of secrecy and denial." Do you think there are ever circumstances in which a scientist should observe total secrecy in connection with his or her research?

2. Bronowski speaks of the importance of educating the public on matters of science. What does an educated citizen need to know about science in order to perform his or her duties as a responsible member of a democratic society?

3. In recent times several fields of science have led to controversy (e.g., *in vitro* fertilization, organ transplants, genetic engineering, irradiation of food, nuclear energy). Focusing on one area of scientific research, discuss the extent to which you think governmental controls should be exercised.

4. Should governments continue to supply power needs through the development of atomic energy, or should they make greater use of other resources, such as fossil fuels, hydro-electric power, or solar energy?

Posture Maketh the Man

by Stephen Jay Gould

1   No event did more to establish the fame and prestige of The American Museum of Natural History than the Gobi Desert expeditions of the 1920s. The discoveries, including the first dinosaur eggs, were exciting and abundant, and the sheer romance fit Hollywood's most heroic mold. It is still hard to find a better adventure story than Roy Chapman Andrews's book (with its chauvinistic title): *The New Conquest of Central Asia*. Nonetheless, the expeditions utterly failed to achieve their stated purpose: to find in Central Asia the ancestors of man. And they failed for the most elementary of reasons — we evolved in Africa, as Darwin had surmised fifty years earlier.

2   Our African ancestors (or at least our nearest cousins) were discovered in cave deposits during the 1920s. But these australopithecines failed to fit preconceived notions of what a "missing link" should look like, and many scientists refused to accept them as bona fide members of our lineage. Most anthropologists had imagined a fairly harmonious transformation from ape to human, propelled by increasing intelligence. A missing link should be intermediate in both body and brain — Alley Oop or the old (and false) representations of stoopshouldered Neanderthals. But the australopithecines refused to conform. To be sure, their brains were bigger than those of any ape with comparable body size, but not much bigger. Most of our evolutionary increase in brain size occurred after we reached the australopithecine level. Yet these small-brained australopithecines walked as erect as you or I. How could this be? If our evolution was propelled by an enlarging brain, how could upright posture — another "hallmark of hominization," not just an in-

cidental feature — originate first? In a 1963 essay, George Gaylord Simpson used this dilemma to illustrate

> the sometimes spectacular failure to predict discoveries even when there is a sound basis for such prediction. An evolutionary example is the failure to predict discovery of a "missing link," now known [*Australopithecus*], that was upright and tool-making but had the physiognomy and cranial capacity of an ape.

We must ascribe this "spectacular failure" primarily to a subtle pre-   3
judice that led to the following, invalid extrapolation: We dominate other animals by brain power (and little else); therefore, an increasing brain must have propelled our own evolution at all stages. The tradition for subordinating upright posture to an enlarging brain can be traced throughout the history of anthropology. Karl Ernst von Baer, the greatest embryologist of the nineteenth century (and second only to Darwin in my personal pantheon of scientific heroes) wrote in 1828: "Upright posture is only the consequence of the higher development of the brain . . . all differences between men and other animals depend upon construction of the brain." One hundred years later, the English anthropologist G. E. Smith wrote: "It was not the adoption of the erect attitude or the invention of articulate language that made man from an ape, but the gradual perfecting of a brain and the slow building of the mental structure, of which erectness of carriage and speech are some of the incidental manifestations."

Against this chorus of emphasis upon the brain, a very few scientists   4
upheld the primacy of upright posture. Sigmund Freud based much of his highly idiosyncratic theory for the origin of civilization upon it. Beginning in his letters to Wilhelm Fliess in the 1890s and culminating in his 1930 essay on *Civilization and Its Discontents*, Freud argued that our assumption of upright posture had reoriented our primary sensation from smell to vision. This devaluation of olfaction shifted the object of sexual stimulation in males from cyclic odors of estrus to the continual visibility of female genitalia. Continual desire of males led to the evolution of continual receptivity in females. Most mammals copulate only around periods of ovulation; humans are sexually active at all times (a favorite theme of writers on sexuality). Continual sexuality has cemented the human family and made civilization possible; animals with strongly cyclic copulation have no strong impetus for stable family structure." The fateful process of civilization," Freud concludes, "would thus have set in with man's adoption of an erect posture."

5   Although Freud's ideas gained no following among anthropologists, another minor tradition did arise to stress the primacy of upright posture. (It is, by the way, the argument we tend to accept today in explaining the morphology of australopithecines and the path of human evolution.) The brain cannot begin to increase in a vacuum. A primary impetus must be provided by an altered mode of life that would place a strong, selective premium upon intelligence. Upright posture frees the hands from locomotion and for manipulation (literally, from *manus* = "hand"). For the first time, tools and weapons can be fashioned and used with ease. Increased intelligence is largely a response to the enormous potential inherent in free hands for manufacture — again, literally. (Needless to say, no anthropologist has ever been so naive as to argue that brain and posture are completely independent in evolution, that one reached its fully human status before the other began to change at all. We are dealing with interaction and mutual reinforcement. Nevertheless, our early evolution did involve a more rapid change in posture than in brain size; complete freeing of our hands for using tools preceded most of the evolutionary enlargement of our brain.)

6   In another proof that sobriety does not make right, von Baer's mystical and oracular colleague Lorenz Oken hit upon the "correct" argument in 1809, while von Baer was led astray a few years later. "Man by the upright walk obtains his character," writes Oken, "the hands become free and can achieve all other offices. . . . With the freedom of the body has been granted also the freedom of the mind." But the champion of upright posture during the nineteenth century was Darwin's German bulldog Ernst Haeckel. Without a scrap of direct evidence, Haeckel reconstructed our ancestor and even gave it a scientific name, *Pithecanthropus alalus,* the upright, speechless, small-brained ape-man. (*Pithecanthropus*, by the way, is probably the only scientific name ever given to an animal before it was discovered. When Du Bois discovered Java Man in the 1890s, he adopted Haeckel's generic name but he gave it the new specific designation *Pithecanthropus erectus.* We now usually include this creature in our own genus as *Homo erectus.*)

7   But why, despite Oken and Haeckel's demurral, did the idea of cerebral primacy become so strongly entrenched? One thing is sure; it had nothing to do with direct evidence — for there was none for any position. With the exception of Neanderthal (a geographic variant of our own species according to most anthropologists), no fossil humans were discovered until the closing years of the nineteenth century, long after the dogma of cerebral primacy was established. But debates based on no evidence

are among the most revealing in the history of science, for in the absence of factual constraints, the cultural biases that affect all thought (and which scientists try so assiduously to deny) lie nakedly exposed.

Indeed, the nineteenth century produced a brilliant exposé from a 8 source that will no doubt surprise most readers — Friedrich Engels. (A bit of reflection should diminish surprise. Engels had a keen interest in the natural sciences and sought to base his general philosophy of dialectical materialism upon a "positive" foundation. He did not live to complete his "dialectics of nature," but he included long commentaries on science in such treatises as the *Anti-Dühring*.) In 1876, Engels wrote an essay entitled, *The Part Played by Labor in the Transition from Ape to Man*. It was published posthumously in 1896 and, unfortunately, had no visible impact upon Western science.

Engels considers three essential features of human evolution: speech, 9 a large brain, and upright posture. He argues that the first step must have been a descent from the trees with subsequent evolution to upright posture by our ground-dwelling ancestors. "These apes when moving on level ground began to drop the habit of using their hands and to adopt a more and more erect gait. This was the decisive step in the transition from ape to man." Upright posture freed the hand for using tools (labor, in Engels's terminology); increased intelligence and speech came later.

Thus the hand is not only the organ of labor, it is also the product of labor. Only by labor, by adaptation to ever new operations . . . by the ever-renewed employment of these inherited improvements in new, more and more complicated operations, has the human hand attained the high degree of perfection that has enabled it to conjure into being the pictures of Raphael, the statues of Thorwaldsen, the music of Paganini.

Engels presents his conclusions as though they followed deductively 10 from the premises of his materialist philosophy, but I am confident that he cribbed them from Haeckel. The two formulations are almost identical, and Engels cites the relevant pages of Haeckel's work for other purposes in an earlier essay written in 1874. But no matter. The importance of Engels's essay lies, not in its substantive conclusions, but in its trenchant political analysis of why Western science was so hung up on the a priori assertion of cerebral primacy.

As humans learned to master their material surroundings, Engels 11 argues, other skills were added to primitive hunting — agriculture, spinning, pottery, navigation, arts and sciences, law and politics, and finally, "the fantastic reflection of human things in the human mind: religion." As wealth accumulated, small groups of men seized power and forced others to work for them. Labor, the source of all wealth and the primary impetus for human evolution, assumed the same low status of those who labored for the rulers. Since rulers governed by their will (that is, by feats of mind), actions of the brain appeared to have a motive power of their own. The profession of philosophy followed no unsullied ideal of truth. Philosophers relied on state or religious patronage. Even if Plato did not consciously conspire to bolster the privileges of rulers with a supposedly abstract philosophy, his own class position encouraged an emphasis on thought as primary, dominating, and altogether more noble and important than the labor it supervised. This idealistic tradition dominated philosophy right through to Darwin's day. Its influence was so subtle and pervasive that even scientific, but apolitical, materialists like Darwin fell under its sway. A bias must be recognized before it can be challenged. Cerebral primacy seemed so obvious and natural that it was accepted as given, rather than recognized as a deep-seated social prejudice related to the class position of professional thinkers and their patrons. Engels writes:

> All merit for the swift advance of civilization was ascribed to the mind, to the development and activity of the brain. Men became accustomed to explain their actions from their thoughts, instead of from their needs. . . . And so there arose in the course of time that idealistic outlook on the world which, especially since the downfall of the ancient world, has dominated men's minds. It still rules them to such a degree that even the most materialistic natural scientists of the Darwinian school are still unable to form any clear idea of the origin of man, because under that ideological influence they do not recognize the part that has been played therein by labor.

12   The importance of Engels's essay does not lie in the happy result that *Australopithecus* confirmed a specific theory proposed by him — via Haeckel — but rather in his perceptive analysis of the political role of science and of the social biases that must affect all thought.

13   Indeed, Engels's theme of the separation of head and hand has done much to set and limit the course of science throughout history. Academic science, in particular, has been constrained by an ideal of "pure" research, which in former days barred a scientist from extensive experimentation and empirical testing. Ancient Greek science labored under the restriction that patrician thinkers could not perform the manual work

of plebeian artisans. Medieval barber-surgeons who had to deal with battlefield casualties did more to advance the practice of medicine than academic physicians who rarely examined patients and who based their treatment on a knowledge of Galen and other learned texts. Even today, "pure" researchers tend to disparage the practical, and terms such as "aggie school" and "cow college" are heard with distressing frequency in academic circles. If we took Engels's message to heart and recognized our belief in the inherent superiority of pure research for what it is — namely social prejudice — then we might forge among scientists the union between theory and practice that a world teetering dangerously near the brink so desperately needs.

(1973)

The Writer's Subject

1. Why did anthropologists formerly believe that growth of the brain must have preceded upright posture in the evolution of man? (para. 3)

2. What effect did the discovery of australopithecine man have upon older theories of the brain in the evolution of man?

3. What is the modern view regarding the relationship between brain size and posture as summarized by Gould in paragraph 5?

4. Why does Gould give so much prominence to the essay on evolution by the nineteenth-century political philosopher Engels, when, as Gould himself says, the scientific aspects of the essay were probably derived from the work of Ernst Haeckel? (paras. 8-13)

5. What is the particular class bias which Gould cites as operative in western society (i.e., from Plato's time onward)? How has this bias affected attitudes towards scientific research? (para. 11)

6. What is Gould's concluding plea concerning attitudes towards scientific research? (para. 13)

The Writer's Style and Strategy

1. What is the function of the opening paragraph of the essay?

2. Much of Gould's argument is conducted by reference to nineteenth and twentieth century authorities. How does Gould use these authorities to develop his thesis?

3. What use does Gould make of asides and parenthetical comments?

4. Why does Gould put the word "pure" in quotations in paragraph 13?

5. Gould is a scientist writing for non-scientists. What features of his style reflect his awareness of his intended audience? Where might he be addressing his arguments to his fellow scientists, too?

6. Comment on Gould's title. What phrase is it meant to echo?

Suggested Topics for Writing and Discussion

1. Gould says, "Debates based on no evidence are among the most revealing in the history of science, for in the absence of factual constraints, the cultural biases that affect all thought . . . lie nakedly exposed." Consider one controversial topic (e.g., creationism vs. Darwinism, whether life exists on other planets, whether God exists, at what moment human life begins), and discuss the "cultural biases" that seem to underlie one side or other of the debate.

2. Gould is critical of what he calls "pure" research and implies an irresponsibility on the part of the scientific community. What do you think are the primary considerations that should govern scientific research? (Compare Gould's comments about the scientist's relationship to the society to those made by Bronowski in "The Real Responsibilities of the Scientist.")

3. Gould speaks of the class attitude, which he says prevailed until Darwin's day, that thought was "more noble and important than the labour it supervised." What attitudes does our own society have toward labour today?

Some Enemies of Science

by J.B.S. Haldane

Last week my wife successfully poisoned a number of rats. They were   1
eating the food of our chickens, and would have eaten the smaller of
the birds if they had got the chance. Owing to the failure of a more
humane poison she found herself compelled to use phosphorous; which
is a slow and, to judge from the experience of the human beings who
commit suicide by eating matches, often rather painful means of death.

During the same period I killed two rats in the course of experimen-   2
tal work intended to advance medical science. One of them, if we can
judge from human experience (and we have no more direct means of
evaluating the consciousness of animals), died after a period of rather
pleasant delirium like that of alcoholic intoxication. The other had con-
vulsions, and may have been in pain for three or four minutes. I should
be very thankful if I knew that I should suffer no more than it did before
my death. It therefore seems to me somewhat ridiculous that, whereas
my wife is encouraged by the Government and the Press, I should be
compelled to apply to the President of the Royal Society and another
eminent man of science for signatures to an application to the already
overworked Home Secretary, before I can even kill a mouse in a slightly
novel manner.

It is probably right that some control should be kept over experiments 3
likely to involve severe and prolonged pain to animals; but it is monstrous
that with regard to wholly or nearly painless procedures the scientific
man should be worse treated than any other member of the community.

Under the present law, or, at any rate, under the law as at present   4
interpreted, a license is required for a large number of absolutely painless

experiments, and, what is more serious, they can only be performed in a limited number of laboratories. In consequence, the isolated amateur worker, who has played so great a part in the development of British science, is debarred from wide fields of physiology. The sportsman may go out and shoot as many rabbits as he pleases; and if some of them are wounded and escape to die a lingering death in their holes, no blame attaches to him. But if he anaesthetizes one of his own rabbits at home, and opens its abdomen to observe the effect of a drug on its intestines, killing it before it recovers consciousness, he will be lucky if he escapes with a fine.

5   Nor may the doctor, after his day's shooting of unanaesthetized partridges, acquire surgical skill by an operation on an anaesthetized animal, even in a licensed laboratory. He has to practise on human patients. There are, of course, a few operations of human surgery for which animals would furnish relatively little guidance. In the majority of cases, however, they would be of very real value, and have been proved to be so in America. Not only is medical science already greatly hampered by the law, but a constant fight has to be kept up to preserve what possibilities are left it. It is worth while enquiring into the reasons which have led to this state of affairs.

6   There are a few honest anti-vivisectionists. They are, of course, vegetarians; for the painless killing of animals for physiology is no more reprehensible than their killing for meat. They wear canvas shoes, cotton or woollen gloves, and artificial pearls if any. They refuse to sit on leather-covered chairs, or to wear horn-rimmed spectacles. They do not spray their roses, or employ Keating's powder even under the gravest provocation. I have not met any of them, but I am quite prepared to believe that they exist. No one who does not come up to this rather exacting standard can logically demand the total abolition of vivisection. But logic is not the strongest point of the enemies of science.

7   All others who demand the prohibition of experiments on anaesthetized animals are quite definitely hypocrites, engaged in the familiar pursuit of

'Compounding sins they are inclined to
By damning those they have no mind to.'

There are few more disgusting spectacles in our public life than that of the two or three sporting peers who habitually introduce or support Bills to prohibit such experiments. Each of them has caused more pain to animals in a single day's sport than the average physiologist inflicts in a lifetime, and usually for no end except his personal pleasure. For it seems to me that from the ethical point of view a fairly sharp distinction can be drawn between the killing of animals bred for this purpose at considerable expense, which would produce far more food if applied to agriculture; and that of rabbits, hares, and pigeons which must be kept down in the interest of crops and livestock. Personally, since I have realized from my own experience with shell splinters that it is no fun to carry bits of metal about one's person, I would no more shoot a rabbit than kill my bacon for breakfast. But I certainly do not condemn those who do so.

We must next consider the relatively small number of anti-vivisection- **8** ists who would merely prohibit all painful or possibly painful experiments. Now, the world is so constituted that we cannot avoid inflicting pain on others. I cannot dig in my garden without bisecting a number of earthworms, or drive a car for any time without running over a few of the various animals whose flattened corpses decorate our country roads. But it is our duty, as far as possible, to diminish the amount of pain in the world. The question therefore is whether medical research does this or not.

Now, anti-vivisectionist literature distorts both sides of the account. **9** It states that a great deal of severe suffering is inflicted on animals in the name of science, and that there is little or no return for this in the diminution of human and animal suffering. With regard to the first of these assertions I can speak with a certain degree of experience. I have seen numerous experiments on animals, but I have never seen an animal undergoing pain which I would not have been willing to undergo myself for the same object. Why, then, it may be asked, should not all painful experiments be done on human volunteers?

There are several reasons why not. One is the very simple fact that **10** many of these experiments possibly or necessarily involve the death of the animal. For example, rats are frequently inoculated under the skin of their sides with transplantable cancers. These are not painful, for the rat does not wince or squeak when the lump is pressed. If it were allowed to die of cancer it would often suffer; for the original tumour or its metastases elsewhere would press on nerves, and one of them would probably start to ulcerate. But before either of these events occurs, all such rats in the laboratory in which I work are killed, and the tumours used for chemical study of inoculation. A man, even if he could legally be used for such a purpose and chloroformed before pain began, would presumably suffer from the anticipation of an early death.

Just the same applies to deformity. A rickety child suffers mainly **11** because it cannot take part in the activities of its comrades and is made to realize that it is deformed. A rickety rat has none of these disadvantages, not only because it is probably not self-conscious, but because under laboratory conditions all its acquaintances are rickety too. Finally, there is the question of expense. Human beings cost a lot in board and lodging, and must be compensated for loss of time. If, as in experiments on the effects of small changes in the diet, hundreds of individuals and years of time are needed, this consideration is generally final.

12   However, if we are to believe anti-vivisectionists, animals constantly undergo tortures which no human being would voluntarily endure. I recently received an illustrated pamphlet, which I should think is fairly typical, describing the sufferings of laboratory animals. There was a picture of an oven in which dogs were slowly heated till they died, while a physiologist watched their agonies through a window. The thought of such cruelty would have made my blood boil, if it had not already been partially boiled in such a chamber on several occasions. Under such circumstances one becomes dizzy long before there is any definite pain, and death, if it occurs, is from heat stroke, not from burning. Personally, I prefer being overheated in a bath. Immersion of all but the head in water kept hot enough just not to be painful, causes loss of consciousness, after a good deal of panting, in about twenty minutes. Hence there is reason to think that a lobster, if put into cold water and heated fairly slowly, feels no pain, which it must certainly do if dropped into boiling water. Probably, however, it would suffer still less if about 2½ per cent of salt were added to the cold water.

13   Then came a picture of a dog's mouth held open by a somewhat brutal-looking contrivance. This was said to be taken from a scientific periodical called the 'Transactions of the Physiological Society.' There is, unfortunately, no such journal, nor could I find the picture in the Proceedings of that body for the date given. Perhaps, therefore, it was the anti-visectionist's idea of what an instrument of scientific torture ought to look like. But if I had been a maiden lady with a pet dog and no knowledge either of the facts or the literature of physiology, I might have sent a cheque to one of the ladies and gentlemen who make a living by compiling documents of this kind.

14   In some cases experiments are supposed to be painful out of ignorance rather than malice. A group of experiments by Sir John Bradford, in which parts of the kidneys of dogs were removed under an anaesthetic, are constantly described in parliament as torture. Some of these dogs

recovered completely, others died with the symptoms of chronic kidney disease, which in human beings seldom causes any pain worse than a headache. Stone in the kidney can, of course, be very painful, but the dogs were not so treated as to cause them pain of this type, nor did they show any signs of suffering it. As a matter of fact, too, dogs can stand a good deal of wounding without much suffering, so far as one can judge. I know this, not from laboratory experience, but because I have owned a dog whose courage and love affairs constantly led him into fights with larger dogs.

A large part of the unhappiness of dogs in English laboratories is direct- **15** ly due to the anti-vivisectionists. In the laboratory where I work there are a number of dogs, each of which, for two or three months in the year, eats certain organic compounds which it transforms in its body. The newly formed compounds are excreted in the urine. To facilitate the collection of urine an operation has been performed on them analogous to circumcision, and not nearly so severe as tail-docking. Of course, an anaesthetic was used. But because the operation has been performed in the cause of science rather than fashion, these dogs are forbidden by law to leave the laboratory. They are exercised in the grounds twice daily, but may not go into the street, and must lead a rather dull life. This regulation is typical of the present law, which is designed quite as much to hamper research as to protect animals.

While the large majority of experiments performed annually are nearly **16** painless, a few dozen, which attempt to reproduce a painful human disease, and thus to discover its cause or cure, are as painful as the disease which they imitate, except that when the animal's condition is clearly hopeless it can be killed.

I do not think it will be necessary to convince any reader of this book **17** of the value of medical research. It has been the principal cause which renders the worst slum of to-day healthier than the palace of a century ago. If that result had been reached by the infliction of appalling torture on millions of animals the ethical justification of this torture would certainly be a matter for discussion. Actually the fate of experimental rats, for example, is no worse than that of pet rats, which generally die from deficient diet or epidemic disease.

It remains to consider the psychology of anti-vivisectionists. I think **18** that their most important motive is a hatred of science, which they attack at its weakest point. They hate science partly because they do not understand it, and will not take the trouble to; partly because it is ethically neutral. Many of them feel that disease must be a punishment for sin,

and that it could be avoided if we lived according to their own particular prejudices. This view has been taken by most religions, though,
of course, Jesus did not share it (John, chap. 9,v.3). Almost all believe
that there is some short cut to health. So a great many simple-lifers,
vegetarians, faith-healers, Christian scientists, and so forth, are opposed
to medical research, and say that its results are worthless.

19   In some cases anti-vivisection goes with pacifism. The fallacy involved
in this association is rather interesting. Non-resistance of human evil
is sometimes effective. A certain percentage of human smiters are
seriously disconcerted if one turns the other cheek to them. But this
kind of method does not work on bacteria, which have no finer feelings. We cannot find out how they behave, and thus acquire power over
them, except by experiments on men or animals. This is a very unfortunate fact, but then the universe differs in a great many ways from
what we should wish it to be. Medicine continued on non-experimental
lines (with a very few exceptions) from the dawn of history till the seventeenth century. And in consequence it remained stationary during
thousands of years. If its enemies get their way it will begin to stagnate
again.

20   But there is a less respectable side to the anti-vivisectionist mind.
During the recent agitation aginst experiments on dogs I made an offer
of £100 (published in the *Daily Mail*) to the National Canine Defence
League, if they would produce any evidence for certain libels on the
medical profession which they were circulating in order to obtain
signatures for a petition. I got no answer from the League, but a number
of abusive and most instructive letters.

21   One of them, from E. Hough of Hammersmith, objected to experiments 'on the dear, faithful doggies for the benefit of worthless human
beings.' 'I like to think,' she wrote (for I picture the writer as an elderly
and soured spinster) 'that God will torture physiologists in a future life.
I would not lift a finger to save one of them if he were writhing in agony.'
There is, then, a group of anti-vivisectionists who like to think about
torture. As they can no longer attend the burning of atheists and wit-
ches, they gloat over imaginary stories of animal torture till their blood
boils; and then cool it with the thought of physiologists in hell fire.
Thanks largely to the psychological mutilation to which our society subjects adults, and more particularly children, the world is over-full of

'Ceux dont le rêve obscur salit tout ce qu'il touche,'[1]

and I suspect that a fair number of them become anti-vivisectionists.

1. "Those whose dark dream dirties all that it touches."

Those who have benefited by the results of medical research and wish 22
it to continue might do worse than support the Research Defence Society,
which carries on a lonely fight against a vast flood of lies. And they
should urge the following alterations in the law, none of which would
increase animal suffering in the faintest degree. Stray dogs impounded
by the police should be used for experiment. This would abolish dog
stealing for laboratories, and save the lives of some thousand dogs per
year. No licence should be required for experiments on fully anaesthetized animals which are killed under the anaesthetic. Surgeons should
be allowed to practise their art under the same conditions. Animals should
not be condemned to imprisonment for life because an experiment has
been done on them. And in the interests of national economy the number
of officials and of Government forms used in the supervision of research
should be cut down.

At present biological and medical research workers are enormously 23
handicapped by the law and by public opinion. Several hospitals, out
of deference to subscribers, do not allow animal experiments. They thus
render the rapid diagnosis of various diseases impossible, and kill a
certain number of patients annually. And medical teaching is seriously
handicapped in the same way. These are some of the reasons why
England is less healthy than a number of other European countries. Anti-
vivisectionists are responsible for far more deaths per year in England
than motor vehicles, smallpox, or typhoid fever.

(1928)

The Writer's Subject

1. What is Haldane's point in contrasting his wife's use of rat poison and
   his own experiments? (paras. 1-2)

2. What, in Haldane's view, distinguishes the "honest anti-vivisectionists" from
   those he calls hypocrites? (paras. 6-7)

3. What are Haldane's reasons for rejecting the idea that all painful experiments should be carried out on human volunteers? (paras. 9-11)

4. On what grounds does Haldane blame the anti-vivisectionists for "a large
   part of the unhappiness of dogs in English laboratories" (para. 15)?

5. What motives does Haldane attribute to the anti-vivisectionists? (paras.
   18-19)

6. What does he fear may happen to medical research if the anti-vivisectionists get their way? (para. 19)

7. Why, according to Haldane, is England "less healthy than a number of European countries" (para. 23)?

The Writer's Style and Strategy

1. How does Haldane seek to convince his reader that animals used in experiments suffer little or no pain? (paras. 10, 12, 14)

2. What picture does Haldane draw of his opponents, the anti-vivisectionists? What tone does he generally adopt in his description of them? Does he make use of any loaded terms in his references to them? (See, for example, paras. 6, 7 and 18.)

3. For what reason does Haldane allude to his own experience with shell splinters? (para. 7)

4. How does Haldane deal with the charges in the anti-vivisectionists' pamphlet described in paragraphs 12 and 13? What does he imply about its authors at the end of paragraph 13?

5. How does Haldane make use of irony to answer his opponents in paragraph 19?

6. Why does Haldane give prominence to the letter from E. Hough in paragraph 21? Why does he picture the writer as "an elderly and soured spinster"?

7. Explain the function of paragraph 22.

Suggested Topics for Writing and Discussion

1. Haldane argues against the restrictions placed on scientists who wish to use animals for medical research. What is your view of this issue? Do you believe that scientists should be free to experiment with animals in the interests of reducing human suffering? Are there any restrictions which you think should be imposed?

2. Haldane complains that a hunter, unlike the scientist, may kill or maim animals without penalty. Write an argument for or against recreational hunting, addressing your argument to an audience opposed to your own views.

3. Choose one area of modern medical research (e.g., artificial organs or limbs, drug therapy, disease control, plastic surgery) and show the con-

tribution it has made to the quality of life, either of the individual or of the society at large.

4. Haldane's essay originally appeared in 1928, but the issue which he addresses is still widely discussed. The present-day spokesman for those opposing the use of animals in experiments is Peter Singer, the author of *Animal Liberation.* Consult Singer's work and shape a response to Haldane's arguments.

5. Compare Haldane's views on the scientific use of animals with the views expressed by David Suzuki in "The Pain of Animals".

The Science of Walking

by Jay Ingram

1 Walking is one of those things that we do automatically, like eating or breathing. There's nothing more commonplace or everyday, but that shouldn't delude you into thinking it's simple. Walking on two legs is an extremely complicated way of getting around, and even though we adopted this method millions of years ago, we're still feeling the effects of having done it.

2 Each stride of normal walking involves a cascade of little tricks that we perform quite unconsciously. Are you even aware of what you do to break into a stride from a standing start? When you're standing still, you're perfectly balanced, and you can't move forward unless you upset that balance. So your first movement is to relax your calf muscles, which immediately causes you to start toppling over. As you lurch forward, you quickly throw one leg forward to break your fall, and you are now walking. Once the heel of that lead leg hits the ground, you're actually in quite a stable position, one leg forward and one leg back, but only momentarily, because the rear leg pushes off, the foot rolling from back to front until, at the last moment, all the remaining weight is squarely on your big toe.[1]

3 Once your rear leg is off the ground, you swing it right through underneath your body (with surprisingly little muscular effort) and out in front, keeping the knee and ankle slightly bent so the leg doesn't hit the ground

---

[1] If we were much heavier the big toe couldn't handle that weight, and our pattern of walking would have to be different. Interestingly, whoever has faked (I guess I should say, *if* they're faked) the thousands of Sasquatch footprints in the Rockies has taken this into account and designed a foot that appears – from the prints – to push off with all the toes at once, something you'd have to do if you weighed as much as a Sasquatch.

on its way through. Then that leg breaks the fall, with the heel absorbing most of the impact, and the other begins pushing off, starting the cycle all over again.

Averaged-sized adults can walk at most between two and a half and three 4 metres per second, about five or six miles per hour. That speed is limited not by muscle power but by the length of the legs. Mathematical models of walking show that the longer the legs, the smaller the up-and-down movement of the torso as you walk, and the greater the maximum speed. This is why little children have to break into a run to keep up with their parents, and why people on crutches can walk surprisingly fast — their "legs" extend from their armpits to the ground. This also explains why the peculiar swaying, waddling gait used by race walkers allows them to walk about 25 percent faster than the rest of us. Their secret? They minimize the bobbing up and down of the torso, not by having longer legs, but by bending their backs and tilting their hips with each stride. That's why they can go four metres per second instead of three.

You consume the least energy per metre walked if you average about 5 100 steps per minute — any faster and you're putting too much energy into accelerating each foot from a standing start, then stopping it as it hits the ground again. However, studies of city pedestrians show that men take about 110, and women 118 steps per minute. Obviously the pressures of the big city force you to sacrifice efficiency for speed.

The remarkable thing about all this is just how precarious walking is. 6 You spend three-quarters of your time balanced on only one leg — more if you're walking faster — and while you do manage to move forward, you're also bobbing up and down (obvious in film scenes of oncoming pedestrians), swaying dangerously forward, and at the same time nearly toppling over sideways. You're not aware of this happening yourself, and it's not even evident when you watch someone else walk, because you're distracted by swinging arms and legs. But if you could somehow focus just on a pedestrian's torso, you'd see it rocking and rolling, up and down and side to side. It's curious that your head, even at its highest point, is never quite as high when you are walking as when you're standing still. You could walk through a tunnel that's exactly your height and never bump your head.

Even your forward motion is irregular, alternately slowing and acceler- 7 ating. If you don't believe it, remember what happens when you try walking and holding a shallow pan full of water: it slops back and forth because your forward speed isn't constant. When either of your legs is out front, it's actually slowing you down; it only contributes to accelerating you when it's behind and pushing down on the ground. The thing that keeps us upright through all this up-and-down and to-and-fro motion is the subtle contraction and relaxation of the right muscles at the right time.

8   For instance, the moment one leg leaves the ground to swing through, your body wants to fall to the unsupported side, and is only prevented from doing so because of the action of two members of the gluteus family of muscles. The gluteus minimus and medius on your left side contract when your right leg is off the ground, thus tightening up your left side and preventing you from falling to the right. At the same time, the pelvis rotates a little, increasing the length of the stride. Females have to rotate their pelvis slightly more to achieve a longer stride, because their hips don't have the same forward range as males. This, of course, leads to a distinctive female walking style, of interest particularly to experts in biomechanics and manufacturers of blue jeans.

9   The most famous gluteus muscle of all, the gluteus maximus, not only gives the buttocks whatever shape they have, but also prevents us from pitching forward by contracting and pulling us upright, especially as we climb stairs or run uphill. That tendency to jack-knife forward is much reduced on level ground, and in that situation the gluteus maximus is surprisingly unimportant — you can walk nearly normally even if it's paralyzed. The gluteus maximus is the biggest muscle in our bodies, and is a perfect illustration of how complicated the transition was from four legs to two. Chimps and gorillas, our closest living relatives, have gluteus maximus muscles too, but they're relatively insignificant because these animals are quadrupeds and have no need to stabilize an upright torso balanced on two legs. (Blue jean manufacturers have no interest in chimpanzees and gorillas.)

10   Despite the fact that so many alterations are necessary to change a quadruped into a biped, it's clear that the process began a long time ago. The oldest signs come from Africa. The skeleton of the little hominid called "Lucy," found in Ethiopia, is about three million years old and already shows all the skeletal adaptations necessary for a little woman-ape to walk upright. She isn't completely modern yet — some anthropologists see in her curved toes signs that she might still have been adept at climbing — but there's no doubt she's on her way. In 1977 Mary Leakey, wife of the famed anthropologist Louis Leakey, mother of the famed anthropologist Richard Leakey, and a famed anthropologist herself, announced the discovery of two sets of footprints in volcanic ash in Tanzania that are three and three-quarter million years old and have all the features of footprints made by upright-walking creatures.

11   Why walking upright came at all is still an open question, but most theories these days are predicated on the idea that freeing the hands was

the most important reason. There are many variations on this theme: two-legged hominids could carry their offspring and so become nomadic and exploit new food sources; or two-legged males could bring food back to a female, who, thus freed from the responsibility of gathering food herself, could spend more time having babies. But these aren't the only explanations for our two-leggedness — one recent theory even suggests that our ancestors stood up to cool off. By doing so, they would have presented less surface area to the overhead sun and absorbed 60 percent less heat.

Regardless of why our ancestors stood up, we are still paying the price for that move, at least three and three-quarter million years later. The problem is that we're walking upright using a skeleton built for four-legged travel. You don't have to go to Olduvai Gorge to dig up evidence of the shift from four legs to two: just check out your own body as you sit slumped in the living-room chair. Bothered by flat feet or fallen arches? That's what happens when you try to bear the entire weight of the body on two feet. Sore back? Four-legged creatures have no such problems, built as they are with their weight distributed evenly along the backbone. But tilt that backbone on end, and you've got discs being squeezed out of place, and a torso sitting on pelvic bones that never had to support any weight before. Suffering from a hernia? You wouldn't be if you were still on all fours, with your internal organs suspended from and supported by a horizontal backbone. Hemorrhoids? Blame those congested blood vessels on the fact that they were upended in the move from four legs to two. 12

It's funny that after millions of years of walking, we still haven't got it quite right. We sway and rock and lurch our way forward, punishing bodies that never really were designed to be upright. In that same time span our brains have trebled or even quadrupled in size, allowing us to develop language, culture and civilization. Upright walking came first (Lucy has a brain the size of a chimpanzee's, yet she's practically modern in her walking) and probably played an important role by allowing the hands to manipulate objects and work with a brain that was capable of incredible growth. Maybe walking was a kind of an off-the-shelf evolutionary solution to the problem of freeing the hands, which, once accomplished, was never fine-tuned. It's something to think about the next time you take a stroll — you probably owe your big brain to that imperfect, but unique, mode of transport. 13

(1990)

The Writer's Subject

1. What is Ingram's explanation for the varying speeds at which people walk?

2. When did our ancestors first begin to walk upright?

3. What theories account for the development of two-legged hominids?

4. Why, according to Ingram, are we "still paying the price" for having learned to walk upright? (para. 12)

5. Why does Ingram regard our walking as "imperfect"? (para. 13)

The Writer's Style and Strategy

1. How does Ingram's opening paragraph reflect or anticipate the development of his essay as a whole?

2. How does Ingram organize his explanation of the mechanics of walking?

3. Who is the intended audience for this essay? Is the writer's tone appropriate for that audience?

4. As Ingram observes, "walking on two legs is an extremely complicated way of getting around." How does he try to make this complex subject accessible to the reader?

Suggested Topics for Writing and Discussion

1. Jay Ingram points out that walking is an activity that we take for granted, yet it is far from simple. Choose another common physical action or motion, such as scratching, smiling, or whistling, and describe it as clearly as possible.

2. Choose a scientific or a technological topic (e.g., the computer chip, the workings of a carburetor, the making of beer), and provide a clear explanation in everyday language for a non-technical audience.

3. Find out what you can about the skeleton of "Lucy," the hominid referred to in paragraph 10, and explain the importance of this discovery for theories of evolution and the "missing link."

The Discus Thrower
by Richard Selzer

"Do not go gentle"

I spy on my patients. Ought not a doctor to observe his patients by any means and from any stance, that he might the more fully assemble evidence? So I stand in the doorways of hospital rooms and gaze. Oh, it is not all that furtive an act. Those in bed need only look up to discover me. But they never do.

From the doorway of Room 542 the man in the bed seems deeply tanned. Blue eyes and close-cropped white hair give him the appearance of vigor and good health. But I know that his skin is not brown from the sun. It is rusted, rather, in the last stage of containing the vile repose within. And the blue eyes are frosted, looking inward like the windows of a snowbound cottage. This man is blind. This man is also legless — the right leg missing from midthigh down, the left from just below the knee. It gives him the look of a bonsai, roots and branches pruned into the dwarfed facsimile of a great tree.

Propped on pillows, he cups his right thigh in both hands. Now and then he shakes his head as though acknowledging the intensity of his suffering. In all of this he makes no sound. Is he mute as well as blind?

The room in which he dwells is empty of all possessions — no get-well cards, small, private caches of food, day-old flowers, slippers, all the usual kickshaws of a sickroom. There is only the bed, a chair, a nightstand, and a tray on wheels that can be swung across his lap for meals.

"What time is it?" he asks.

"Three o'clock."

"Morning or afternoon?"

"Afternoon."
He is silent. There is nothing else he wants to know.
"How are you?" I say.
"Who is it?" he asks.
"It's the doctor. How do you feel?"
He does not answer right away.
"Feel?" he says.
"I hope you feel better," I say.
I press the button at the side of the bed.
"Down you go," I say.
"Yes, down," he says.
He falls back upon the bed awkwardly. His stumps, unweighted by
legs and feet, rise in the air, presenting themselves. I unwrap the ban-
dages from the stumps, and begin to cut away the black scabs and the
dead, glazed fat with scissors and forceps. A shard of white bone comes
loose. I pick it away. I wash the wounds with disinfectant and redress
the stumps. All this while, he does not speak. What is he thinking behind
those lids that do not blink? Is he remembering a time when he was
whole? Does he dream of feet? Of when his body was not a rotting log?
He lies solid and inert. In spite of everything, he remains impressive,
as though he were a sailor standing athwart a slanting deck.
"Anything more I can do for you?" I ask.
For a long moment he is silent.
"Yes," he says at last and without the least irony. "You can bring
me a pair of shoes."
In the corridor, the head nurse is waiting for me.
"We have to do something about him," she says. "Every morning he
orders scrambled eggs for breakfast and, instead of eating them, he picks
up the plate and throws it against the wall."
"Throws his plate?"
"Nasty. That's what he is. No wonder his family doesn't come to visit.
They probably can't stand him any more than we can."
She is waiting for me to do something.
"Well?"
"We'll see," I say.
The next morning I am waiting in the corridor when the kitchen
delivers his breakfast. I watch the aide place the tray on the stand and
swing it across his lap. She presses the button to raise the head of the
bed. Then she leaves.
In time the man reaches to find the rim of the tray, then on to find

the dome of the covered dish. He lifts off the cover and places it on the stand. He fingers across the plate until he probes the eggs. He lifts the plate in both hands, sets it on the palm of his right hand, centers it, balances it. He hefts it up and down slightly, getting the feel of it. Abruptly, he draws back his right arm as far as he can.

There is the crack of the plate breaking against the wall at the foot of his bed and the small wet sound of the scrambled eggs dropping to the floor.

And then he laughs. It is a sound you have never heard. It is something new under the sun. It could cure cancer.

Out in the corridor, the eyes of the head nurse narrow.

"Laughed, did he?"

She writes something down on her clipboard.

A second aide arrives, brings a second breakfast tray, puts it on the nightstand, out of his reach. She looks over at me shaking her head and making her mouth go. I see that we are to be accomplices.

"I've got to feed you," she says to the man.

"Oh, no you don't" the man says.

"Oh, yes I do," the aide says, "after the way you just did. Nurse says so."

"Get me my shoes," the man says.

"Here's oatmeal," the aide says. "Open." And she touches the spoon to his lower lip.

"I ordered scrambled eggs," says the man.

"That's right," the aide says.

I step forward.

"Is there anything I can do?" I say.

"Who are you?" the man asks.

In the evening I go once more to that ward to make my rounds. The head nurse reports to me that Room 542 is deceased. She has discovered this quite by accident, she says. No, there has been no sound. Nothing. It's a blessing, she says.

I go into his room, a spy looking for secrets. He is still there in his bed. His face is relaxed, grave, dignified. After a while, I turn to leave. My gaze sweeps the wall at the foot of the bed, and I see the place where it has been repeatedly washed, where the wall looks very clean and very white.

(1977)

The Writer's Subject

1. This essay takes the form of narration, with the usual elements of a story: character, plot, setting. The focus is on the central action, and there is no "thesis" in the sense of an explicit statement of meaning or intention. What, then, is the point of the essay? What meaning, or meanings, may be derived from the story Selzer tells?

2. Why does the doctor compare himself to a spy in the first and last paragraphs?

3. What is suggested about the doctor's patients by the last two sentences of the first paragraph?

4. What details reveal the doctor's feelings about the patient in Room 542? In what ways are the nurses' feelings different from the doctor's?

5. Suggest why the patient laughs as he breaks the plate of eggs. Why does it seem to the doctor that this laugh is "something new under the sun. It could cure cancer"?

6. Why does the patient ask for his shoes? What is Selzer's point in noting that the patient does so "without the least irony"?

The Writer's Style and Strategy

1. Discuss the purpose and the effectiveness of the comparisons of the patient to a snowbound cottage and a bonsai.

2. What is the effect of the phrase "vile repose"?

3. Discuss Selzer's use of dialogue as a means of revealing elements of character in the patient, the doctor, and the two nurses.

4. Why does Selzer choose not to give names to any of the people in his narrative?

5. How does Selzer use details of setting to enhance the mood of his narrative?

6. What is the effect of the phrase "Room 542 is deceased" in the conclusion?

7. How has the reader been prepared for the ending? How is it related to the essay's opening?

8. What are the connotations of the phrase, "The Discus Thrower"? Why is this title so effective (as compared with "The Plate Thrower," "A Difficult Patient," "The Dying Man," or some such title)?

Suggested Topics for Writing and Discussion

1. Offer an argument for or against the view that the terminally ill should be cared for, and allowed to die, at home rather than in a hospital.

2. Write a narrative describing an experience in which you have found yourself an involved observer (e.g., visiting a hospital patient, witnessing an accident).

3. Read Dylan Thomas's poem "Do not go gentle into that good night," and discuss Selzer's reasons for alluding to that poem in the epigraph to his essay. How does your reading of the poem enrich your understanding of Selzer's essay?

The Pain of Animals

by David Suzuki

1   Medical technology has taken us beyond the normal barriers of life and death and thereby created unprecedented choices in *human* lives. Until recently, we have taken for granted our right to use other species in any way we see fit. Food, clothing, muscle power have been a few of the benefits we've derived from this exploitation. This tradition has continued into scientific research where animals are studied and "sacrificed" for human benefit. Now serious questions are being asked about our right to do this.

2   Modern biological research is based on a shared evolutionary history of organisms that enables us to extrapolate from one organism to another. Thus, most fundamental concepts in heredity were first shown in fruit flies, molecular genetics began using bacteria and viruses and much of physiology and psychology has been based on studies in mice and rats. But today, as extinction rates have multiplied as a result of human activity, we have begun to ask what right we have to use all other animate forms simply to increase human knowledge or for profit or entertainment. Underlying the "animal rights" movement is the troubling question of where we fit in the rest of the natural world.

3   When I was young, one of my prized possessions was a BB gun. Dad taught me how to use it safely and I spent many hours wandering through the woods in search of prey. It's not easy to get close enough to a wild animal to kill it with a BB gun, but I did hit a few pigeons and starlings. I ate everything I shot. Then as a teenager, I graduated to a .22 rifle and with it, I killed rabbits and even shot a pheasant once.

One year I saw an ad for a metal slingshot in a comic book. I ordered 4 it, and when it arrived, I practised for weeks shooting marbles at a target. I got to be a pretty good shot and decided to go after something live. Off I went to the woods and soon spotted a squirrel minding its own business doing whatever squirrels do. I gave chase and began peppering marbles at it until finally it jumped onto a tree, ran to the top and found itself trapped. I kept blasting away and grazed it a couple of times so it was only a matter of time before I would knock it down. Suddenly, the squirrel began to cry — a piercing shriek of terror and anguish. That animal's wail shook me to the core and I was overwhelmed with horror and shame at what I was doing — for no other reason than conceit with my prowess with a slingshot, I was going to *kill* another being. I threw away the slingshot and my guns and have never hunted again.

All my life, I have been an avid fisherman. Fish have always been the 5 main source of meat protein in my family, and I have never considered fishing a sport. But there is no denying that it is exciting to reel in a struggling fish. We call it "playing" the fish, as if the wild animal's desperate struggle for survival is some kind of game.

I did "pleasure-fish" once while filming for a television report on the 6 science of fly fishing. We fished a famous trout stream in the Catskill Mountains of New York state where all fish had to be caught and released. The fish I caught had mouths gouged and pocked by previous encounters with hooks. I found no pleasure in it because to me fish are to be caught for consumption. Today, I continue to fish for food, but I do so with a profound awareness that I am a predator of animals possessing well-developed nervous systems that detect pain. Fishing and hunting have forced me to confront the way we exploit other animals.

I studied the genetics of fruit flies for twenty-five years and during that 7 time probably raised and killed tens of millions of them without a thought. In the early seventies, my lab discovered a series of mutations affecting behaviour of flies, and this find led us into an investigation of nerves and muscles. I applied for and received research funds to study behaviour in flies on the basis of the *similarity* of their neuromuscular systems to ours. In fact, psychologists and neurobiologists analyse behaviour, physiology and neuroanatomy of guinea pigs, rats, mice and other animals as *models* for human behaviour. So our nervous systems must closely resemble those of other mammals.

These personal anecdotes raise uncomfortable questions. What gives 8 us the right to exploit other living organisms as we see fit? How do we know that these other creatures don't feel pain or anguish just as we do? Perhaps there's no problem with fruit flies, but where do we draw the line? I used to rationalize angling because fish are cold-blooded, as if warm-bloodedness indicates some kind of demarcation of brain development or greater sensitivity to pain. But anyone who has watched a fish's frantic fight to escape knows that it exhibits all the manifestations of pain and fear.

9   I've been thinking about these questions again after spending a weekend in the Queen Charlotte Islands watching grey whales close up. The majesty and freedom of these magnificent mammals contrasted strikingly with the appearance of whales imprisoned in aquariums. Currently, the Vancouver Public Aquarium is building a bigger pool for some of its whales. In a radio interview, an aquarium representative was asked whether even the biggest pool can be adequate for animals that normally have the entire ocean to rove. Part of her answer was that if we watched porpoises in the pool, we'd see that "they are quite happy."

10   That woman was projecting human perceptions and emotions on the porpoises. Our ability to empathize with other people and living things is one of our endearing qualities. Just watch someone with a beloved pet, an avid gardener with plants or, for that matter, even an owner of a new car and you will see how readily we can personalize and identify with another living organism or an object. But are we justified in our inferences about captive animals in their cages?

11   Most wild animals have evolved with a built-in need to move freely over vast distances, fly in the air or swim through the ocean. Can a wild animal imprisoned in a small cage or pool, removed from its habitat and forced to conform to the impositions of our demands, ever be considered "happy"?

12   Animal rights activists are questioning our right to exploit animals, especially in scientific research. Scientists are understandably defensive, especially after labs have been broken into, experiments ruined and animals "liberated." But just as I have had to question my hunting and fishing, scientists cannot avoid confronting the issues raised, especially in relation to our closest relatives, the primates.

13   People love to watch monkeys in a circus or zoo and a great deal of the amusement comes from the recognition of ourselves in them. But our relationship with them is closer than just superficial similarities. When doctors at Loma Linda hospital in California implanted the heart of a baboon into the chest of Baby Fae, they were exploiting our close *biological* relationship.

14   Any reports on experimentation with familiar mammals like cats and dogs are sure to raise alarm among the lay public. But the use of primates is most controversial. In September 1987, at the Wildlife Film Festival in Bath, England, I watched a film shot on December 7, 1986, by a group of animal liberationists who had broken into SEMA, a biomedical research

facility in Maryland. It was such a horrifying document that many in the audience rushed out after a few minutes. There were many scenes that I could not watch. As the intruders entered the facility, the camera followed to peer past cage doors, opened to reveal the animals inside. I am not ashamed to admit that I wept as baby monkeys deprived of any contact with other animals seized the fingers of their liberators and clung to them as our babies would to us. Older animals cowered in their tiny prisons, shaking from fear at the sudden appearance of people.

The famous chimpanzee expert, Jane Goodall, also screened the same   15
film and as a result asked for permission to visit the SEMA facility. This is what she saw (*American Scientist,* November-December 1987):

Room after room was lined with small, bare cages, stacked one above   16
the other, in which monkeys circled round and round and chimpanzees sat huddled, far gone in depression and despair.

Young chimpanzees, three or four years old, were crammed, two   17
together into tiny cages measuring 57 cm by 57 cm and only 61 cm high. They could hardly turn around. Not yet part of any experiment, they had been confined to these cages for more than three months.

The chimps had each other for comfort, but they would not remain   18
together for long. Once they are infected, probably with hepatitis, they will be separated and placed in another cage. And there they will remain, living in conditions of severe sensory deprivation, for the next several years. During that time they will become insane.

Goodall's horror sprang from an intimate knowledge of chimpanzees   19
in their native habitat. There, she has learned, chimps are nothing like the captive animals that we know. In the wild, they are highly social, requiring constant interaction and physical contact. They travel long distances, and they rest in soft beds they make in the trees. Laboratory cages do not provide the conditions needed to fulfill the needs of these social, emotional and highly intelligent animals.

Ian Redmond (*BBC Wildlife,* April 1988) gives us a way to understand   20
the horror of what lab conditions do to chimps:

Imagine locking a two- or three-year-old child in a metal box the size   21
of an isolette — solid walls, floor and ceiling, and a glass door that clamps shut, blotting out most external sounds — and then leaving him or her for months, the only contact, apart from feeding, being when the door swings open and masked figures reach in and take samples of blood or tissue before shoving him back and clamping the door shut

again. Over the past 10 years, 94 young chimps at SEMA have endured this procedure.

22   Chimpanzees, along with the gorilla, are our closest relatives, sharing ninety-nine per cent of our genes. And it's that biological proximity that makes them so useful for research — we can try out experiments, study infections and test vaccines on them as models for people. And although there are only about 40,000 chimps left in the wild, compared to millions a few decades ago, the scientific demand for more has increased with the discovery of AIDS.

23   No chimpanzee has ever contracted AIDS, but the virus grows in them, so scientists argue that chimps will be invaluable for testing vaccines. On February 19, 1988, the National Institute of Health in the U.S. co-sponsored a meeting to discuss the use of chimpanzees in research. Dr. Maurice Hilleman, Director of the Merck Institute for Therapeutic Research, reported:

24   We need more chimps.... The chimpanzee is certainly a threatened species and there have been bans on importing the animal into the United States and into other countries, even though ... the chimpanzee is considered to be an agricultural pest in many parts of the world where it exists. And secondly, it's being destroyed by virtue of environmental encroachment — that is, destroying the natural habitat. So these chimpanzees are being eliminated by virtue of their being an agricultural pest and by the fact that their habitat is being destroyed. So why not rescue them? The number of chimpanzees for AIDS research in the United States [is] somewhere in the hundreds and certainly, we need thousands.

25   Our capacity to rationalize our behaviour and needs is remarkable. Chimpanzees have occupied their niche over tens of millennia of biological evolution. We are newcomers who have encroached on their territory, yet by defining them as pests we render them expendable. As Redmond says, "The fact that the chimpanzee is our nearest zoological relative makes it perhaps the unluckiest animal on earth, because what the kinship has come to mean is that we feel free to do most of the things to a chimp that we mercifully refrain from doing to each other."

26   And so the impending epidemic of AIDS confronts us not only with our inhumanity to each other but to other species.

(1989)

The Writer's Subject

1. Why has modern biological research depended so heavily on the use of animals?

2. Why did the squirrel-hunting experience described in paragraph 4 have such an effect on the young Suzuki?

3. Suzuki, himself a geneticist of note, is troubled by thoughts of the work he did on fruit flies (paras. 7-8). Why?

4. Why is Suzuki critical of the practice of keeping whales in aquariums?

5. Why, according to Suzuki, is the use of primates in research so controversial?

6. What role do chimpanzees play in the research on AIDS?

The Writer's Style and Strategy

1. How does Suzuki draw on personal experience to advance his argument?

2. Discuss the ways in which Suzuki appeals to the reader's emotions.

3. What use does Suzuki make of quotations from other sources?

4. How does Suzuki convey his own horror at some of the practices of research on animals? In this regard, comment on his use of connotative language, particularly in paragraphs 4 and 14.

Suggested Topics for Writing and Discussion

1. What are the arguments for and against keeping wild animals in zoos or aquariums?

2. Should scientists be permitted to make unrestricted use of animals in biological research?

3. Is it fair to animals to keep them as household pets for our own pleasure?

4. Suzuki gives particular prominence to the work of the chimpanzee expert Jane Goodall. Find out what you can about the significance of her studies of chimpanzee behaviour in the wild.

Humanities and Science

by Lewis Thomas

1 Lord Kelvin was one of the great British physicists of the late nineteenth century, an extraordinarily influential figure in his time, and in some ways a paradigm of conventional, established scientific leadership. He did a lot of good and useful things, but once or twice he, like Homer, nodded. The instances are worth recalling today, for we have nodders among our scientific eminences still, from time to time, needing to have their elbows shaken.

2 On one occasion, Kelvin made a speech on the overarching importance of numbers. He maintained that no observation of nature was worth paying serious attention to unless it could be stated in precisely quantitative terms. The numbers were the final and only test, not only of truth but about meaning as well. He said, "When you can measure what you are speaking about, and express it in numbers, you know something about it. But when you cannot – your knowledge is of a meagre and unsatisfactory kind."

3 But, as at least one subsequent event showed, Kelvin may have had things exactly the wrong way round. The task of converting observations into numbers is the hardest of all, the last task rather than the first thing to be done, and it can be done only when you have learned, beforehand, a great deal about the observations themselves. You can, to be sure, achieve a very deep understanding of nature by quantitative measurement, but you must know what you are talking about before you can begin applying the numbers for making predictions. In Kelvin's case, the problem at hand was the age of the earth and solar system. Using what was then known about the sources of energy and the loss

of energy from the physics of that day, he calculated that neither the earth nor the sun were older than several hundred million years. This caused a considerable stir in biological and geological circles, especially among the evolutionists. Darwin himself was distressed by the numbers; the time was much too short for the theory of evolution. Kelvin's figures were described by Darwin as one of his "sorest troubles."

T.H. Huxley had long been aware of the risks involved in premature   4
extrapolations from mathematical treatment of biological problems. He said, in an 1869 speech to the Geological Society concerning numbers, "This seems to be one of the many cases in which the admitted accuracy of mathematical processes is allowed to throw a wholly inadmissible appearance of authority over the results obtained by them. . . . As the grandest mill in the world will not extract wheat flour from peascods, so pages of formulas will not get a definite result out of loose data."

The trouble was that the world of physics had not moved fast enough 5
to allow for Kelvin's assumptions. Nuclear fusion and fission had not yet been dreamed of, and the true age of the earth could not even be guessed from the data in hand. It was not yet the time for mathematics in this subject.

There have been other examples, since those days, of the folly of   6
using numbers and calculations uncritically. Kelvin's own strong con- viction that science could not be genuine science without measuring things was catching. People in other fields of endeavor, hankering to turn their disciplines into exact sciences, beset by what has since been called "physics envy," set about converting whatever they knew into numbers and thence into equations with predictive pretensions. We have it with us still, in economics, sociology, psychology, history, even, I fear, in English-literature criticism and linguistics, and it frequently works, when it works at all, with indifferent success. The risks of un- toward social consequences in work of this kind are considerable. It is as important – and as hard – to learn when to use mathematics as how to use it, and this matter should remain high on the agenda of con- sideration for education in the social and behavioral sciences.

Of course, Kelvin's difficulty with the age of the earth was an excep- 7
tional, almost isolated instance of failure in quantitative measurement in nineteenth-century physics. The instruments devised for approaching nature by way of physics became increasingly precise and powerful, carrying the field through electromagnetic theory, triumph after triumph, and setting the stage for the great revolution of twentieth-century physics. There is no doubt about it: measurement works when the instruments

work, and when you have a fairly clear idea of what it is that is being measured, and when you know what to do with the numbers when they tumble out. The system for gaining information and comprehension about nature works so well, indeed, that it carries another hazard: the risk of convincing yourself that you know everything.

8   Kelvin himself fell into this trap toward the end of the century. (I don't mean to keep picking on Kelvin, who was a very great scientist; it is just that he happened to say a couple of things I find useful for this discussion.) He stated, in a summary of the achievements of nineteenth-century physics, that it was an almost completed science; virtually everything that needed knowing about the material universe had been learned; there were still a few anomalies and inconsistencies in electromagnetic theory, a few loose ends to be tidied up, but this would be done within the next several years. Physics, in these terms, was not a field any longer likely to attract, as it previously had, the brightest and most imaginative young brains. The most interesting part of the work had already been done. Then, within the next decade, came radiation, Planck, the quantum, Einstein, Rutherford, Bohr, and all the rest — quantum mechanics — and the whole field turned over and became a brand new sort of human endeavor, still now, in the view of many physicists, almost a full century later, a field only at its beginnings.

9   But even today, despite the amazements that are turning up in physics each year, despite the jumps taken from the smallest parts of nature — particle physics — to the largest of all — the cosmos itself — the impression of science that the public gains is rather like the impression left in the nineteenth-century public mind by Kelvin. Science, in this view, is first of all a matter of simply getting all the numbers together. The numbers are sitting out there in nature, waiting to be found, sorted and totted up. If only they had enough robots and enough computers, the scientists could go off to the beach and wait for their papers to be written for them. Second of all, what we know about nature today is pretty much the whole story: we are very nearly home and dry. From here on, it is largely a problem of tying up loose ends, tidying nature up, getting the files in order. The only real surprises for the future — and it is about those that the public is becoming more concerned and apprehensive — are the technological applications that the scientists may be cooking up from today's knowledge.

10   I suggest that the scientific community is to blame. If there are disagreements between the world of the humanities and the scientific enterprise as to the place and importance of science in a liberal-arts

education, and the role of science in twentieth-century culture, I believe that the scientists are themselves responsible for a general misunderstanding of what they are really up to.

Over the past half century, we have been teaching the sciences as 11 though they were the same academic collection of cut-and-dried subjects as always, and — here is what has really gone wrong — as though they would always be the same. The teaching of today's biology, for example, is pretty much the same kind of exercise as the teaching of Latin was when I was in high school long ago. First of all, the fundamentals, the underlying laws, the essential grammar, and then the reading of texts. Once mastered, that is that: Latin is Latin and forever after will be Latin. And biology is precisely biology, a vast array of hard facts to be learned as fundamentals, followed by a reading of the texts.

Moreover, we have been teaching science as though its facts were 12 somehow superior to the facts in all other scholarly disciplines, more fundamental, more solid, less subject to subjectivism, immutable. English literature is not just one way of thinking, it is all sorts of ways. Poetry is a moving target. The facts that underlie art, architecture, and music are not really hard facts, and you can change them any way you like by arguing about them, but science is treated as an altogether different kind of learning: an unambiguous, unalterable, and endlessly useful display of data needing only to be packaged and installed somewhere in one's temporal lobe in order to achieve a full understanding of the natural world.

And it is, of course, not like this at all. In real life, every field of 13 science that I can think of is incomplete, and most of them — whatever the record of accomplishment over the past two hundred years — are still in the earliest stage of their starting point. In the fields I know best, among the life sciences, it is required that the most expert and sophisticated minds be capable of changing those minds, often with a great lurch, every few years. In some branches of biology the mind-changing is occurring with accelerating velocities. The next week's issue of any scientific journal can turn a whole field upside down, shaking out any number of immutable ideas and installing new bodies of dogma, and this is happening all the time. It is an almost everyday event in physics, in chemistry, in materials research, in neurobiology, in genetics, in immunology. The hard facts tend to soften overnight, melt away, and vanish under the pressure of new hard facts, and the interpretations of what appear to be the most solid aspects of nature are subject to change, now more than at any other time in history. The conclusions reached in science are always, when looked at closely, far more provisional and tentative than are most of the assumptions arrived at by our colleagues in the humanities.

14   The running battle now in progress between the sociobiologists and the antisociobiologists is a marvel for students to behold, close up. To observe, in open-mouthed astonishment, the polarized extremes, one group of highly intelligent, beautifully trained, knowledgeable, and imaginative scientists maintaining that all sorts of behavior, animal and human, are governed exclusively by genes, and another group of equally talented scientists saying precisely the opposite and asserting that all behavior is set and determined by the environment, or by culture, and both sides brawling in the pages of periodicals such as *The New York Review of Books*, is an educational experience that no college student should be allowed to miss. The essential lesson to be learned has nothing to do with the relative validity of the facts underlying the argument, it is the argument itself that is the education: we do not yet know enough to settle such questions.

15   It is true that at any given moment there is the appearance of satisfaction, even self-satisfaction, within every scientific discipline. On any Tuesday morning, if asked, a good working scientist will gladly tell you that the affairs of the field are nicely in order, that things are finally looking clear and making sense, and all is well. But come back again, on another Tuesday, and he may let you know that the roof has just fallen in on his life's work, that all the old ideas – last week's ideas in some cases – are no longer good ideas, that something strange has happened.

16   It is the very strangeness of nature that makes science engrossing. That ought to be at the center of science teaching. There are more than seven-times-seven types of ambiguity in science, awaiting analysis. The poetry of Wallace Stevens is crystal-clear alongside the genetic code.

17   I prefer to turn things around in order to make precisely the opposite case. Science, especially twentieth-century science, has provided us with a glimpse of something we never really knew before, the revelation of human ignorance. We have been used to the belief, down one century after another, that we more or less comprehend everything bar one or two mysteries like the mental processes of our gods. Every age, not just the eighteenth century, regarded itself as the Age of Reason, and we have never lacked for explanations of the world and its ways. Now, we are being brought up short, and this has been the work of science.

We have a wilderness of mystery to make our way through in the centuries ahead, and we will need science for this but not science alone. Science will, in its own time, produce the data and some of the meaning in the data, but never the full meaning. For getting a full grasp, for perceiving real significance when significance is at hand, we shall need minds at work from all sorts of brains outside the fields of science, most of all the brains of poets, of course, but also those of artists, musicians, philosophers, historians, writers in general.

It is primarily because of this need that I would press for changes **18** in the way science is taught. There is a need to teach the young people who will be doing the science themselves, but this will always be a small minority among us. There is a deeper need to teach science to those who will be needed for thinking about it, and this means pretty nearly everyone else, in hopes that a few of these people — a much smaller minority than the scientific community and probably a lot harder to find — will, in the thinking, be able to imagine new levels of meaning that are likely to be lost on the rest of us.

In addition, it is time to develop a new group of professional thinkers, **19** perhaps a somewhat larger group than the working scientists, who can create a discipline of scientific criticism. We have had good luck so far in the emergence of a few people ranking as philosophers of science and historians and journalists of science, and I hope more of these will be coming along, but we have not yet seen a Ruskin or a Leavis or an Edmund Wilson. Science needs critics of this sort, but the public at large needs them more urgently.

I suggest that the introductory courses in science, at all levels from **20** grade school through college, be radically revised. Leave the fundamentals, the so-called basics, aside for a while, and concentrate the attention of all students on the things that are *not* known. You cannot possibly teach quantum mechanics without mathematics, to be sure, but you can describe the strangeness of the world opened up by quantum theory. Let it be known, early on, that there are deep mysteries, and profound paradoxes, revealed in their distant outlines, by the quantum. Let it be known that these can be approached more closely, and puzzled over, once the language of mathematics has been sufficiently mastered.

Teach at the outset, before any of the fundamentals, the still im- **21** ponderable puzzles of cosmology. Let it be known, as clearly as possible, by the youngest minds, that there are some things going on in the universe that lie beyond comprehension, and make it plain how little is known.

22   Do not teach that biology is a useful and perhaps profitable science; that can come later. Teach instead that there are structures squirming inside all our cells, providing all the energy for living, that are essentially foreign creatures, brought in for symbiotic living a billion or so years ago, the lineal descendants of bacteria. Teach that we do not have the ghost of an idea how they got there, where they came from, or how they evolved to their present structure and function. The details of oxidative phosphorylation and photosynthesis can come later.

23   Teach ecology early on. Let it be understood that the earth's life is a system of interliving, interdependent creatures, and that we do not understand at all how it works. The earth's environment, from the range of atmospheric gases to the chemical constituents of the sea, has been held in an almost unbelievably improbable state of regulated balance since life began, and the regulation of stability and balance is accomplished solely by the life itself, like the internal environment of an immense organism, and we do not know how that one works, even less what it means. Teach that.

24   Go easy, I suggest, on the promises sometimes freely offered by science. Technology relies and depends on science these days, more than ever before, but technology is nothing like the first justification for doing research, nor is it necessarily an essential product to be expected from science. Public decisions about what to have in the way of technology are totally different problems from decisions about science, and the two enterprises should not be tangled together. The central task of science is to arrive, stage by stage, at a clearer comprehension of nature, but this does not mean, as it is sometimes claimed to mean, a search for mastery over nature. Science may provide us, one day, with a better understanding of ourselves, but never, I hope, with a set of technologies for doing something or other to improve ourselves. I am made nervous by assertions that human consciousness will someday be unraveled by research, laid out for close scrutiny like the workings of a computer, and then, *and then!* I hope with some fervor that we can learn a lot more than we now know about the human mind, and I see no reason why this strange puzzle should remain forever and entirely beyond us. But I would be deeply disturbed by any prospect that we might use the new knowledge in order to begin doing something about it, to improve it, say. This is a different matter from searching for information to use against schizophrenia or dementia, where we are badly in need of technologies, indeed likely one day to be sunk without them. But the ordinary, everyday, more or less normal human mind

is too marvelous an instrument ever to be tampered with by anyone, science or no science.

The education of humanists cannot be regarded as complete, or even 25 adequate, without exposure in some depth to where things stand in the various branches of science, and particularly, as I have said, in the areas of our ignorance. This does not mean that I know how to go about doing it, nor am I unaware of the difficulties involved. Physics professors, most of them, look with revulsion on assignments to teach their subject to poets. Biologists, caught up by the enchantment of their new power, armed with flawless instruments to tell the nucleotide sequences of the entire human genome, nearly matching the physicists in the precision of their measurements of living processes, will resist the prospect of broad survey courses; each biology professor will demand that any student in his path must master every fine detail within that professor's research program. The liberal-arts faculties, for their part, will continue to view the scientists with suspicion and apprehension. "What do the scientists want?" asked a Cambridge professor in Francis Cornford's wonderful *Microcosmographia Academica*. "Everything that's going," was the quick answer. That was back in 1912, and universities haven't much changed.

The worst thing that has happened to science education is that the 26 great fun has gone out of it. A very large number of good students look at it as slogging work to be got through on the way to medical school. Others look closely at the premedical students themselves, embattled and bleeding for grades and class standing, and are turned off. Very few see science as the high adventure it really is, the wildest of all explorations ever undertaken by human beings, the chance to catch close views of things never seen before, the shrewdest maneuver for discovering how the world works. Instead, they become baffled early on, and they are misled into thinking that bafflement is simply the result of not having learned all the facts. They are not told, as they should be told, that everyone else — from the professor in his endowed chair down to the platoons of post doctoral students in the laboratory all night — is baffled as well. Every important scientific advance that has come in looking like an answer has turned, sooner or later — usually sooner — into a question. And the game is just beginning.

An appreciation of what is happening in science today, and of how 27 great a distance lies ahead for exploring, ought to be one of the rewards of a liberal-arts education. It ought to be a good in itself, not something to be acquired on the way to a professional career but part of the cast of thought needed for getting into the kind of century that is now just down the road. Part of the intellectual equipment of an educated person, however his or her time is to be spent, ought to be a feel for the queernesses of nature, the inexplicable things.

28 And maybe, just maybe, a new set of courses dealing systematically with ignorance in science might take hold. The scientists might discover in it a new and subversive technique for catching the attention of students driven by curiosity, delighted and surprised to learn that science is exactly as Bush described it: an "endless frontier." The humanists, for their part, might take considerable satisfaction watching their scientific colleagues confess openly to not knowing everything about everything. And the poets, on whose shoulders the future rests, might, late nights, thinking things over, begin to see some meanings that elude the rest of us. It is worth a try.

(1983)

The Writer's Subject

1. What, according to Thomas, was the nineteenth-century view of the importance of numbers and quantitative measurement? What showed the limitations of this view? (paras. 1-5)

2. How does the uncritical use of numbers and calculations persist into our own day? (para. 6)

3. What "trap" did Lord Kelvin fall into? (paras. 7-8)

4. According to Thomas, what is the impression of science held by the general public? Who does he maintain is primarily responsible for creating this impression? (paras. 9-10)

5. What point is Thomas making when he compares the current teaching of science with the teaching of Latin? (para. 11)

6. How does Thomas counter the view that scientific facts are "more solid, less subject to subjectivism" than facts in other disciplines? (paras. 12-13)

7. What "essential lesson" is to be learned from following the public controversy between sociobiologists and their opponents? (para. 14)

8. What does Thomas mean by his assertion that "The poetry of Wallace Stevens is crystal-clear alongside the genetic code"? (para. 16)

9. Why does Thomas attach importance to the scientific education of non-scientists? What role does he foresee for poets, historians, and philosophers? (paras. 17-19)

10. What changes does Thomas suggest in the teaching of science? What does he think such teaching should emphasize? (paras. 20-24)

11. What are Thomas's objections to specialization in education? (para. 25)

The Writer's Style and Strategy

1. What is Thomas's purpose?

2. What kind of audience does Thomas have in mind for this essay? Support your view with specific references.

3. What are the general characteristics of Thomas's diction and sentence style? How appropriate are they to his purpose and audience?

4. Why does Thomas begin his essay by recounting the errors of the famous nineteenth-century English scientist, Lord Kelvin?

5. At what point does Thomas shift from an attack on erroneous ways of thinking about science to proposals for change? How is this shift signalled?

6. What patterns of diction and sentence structure does Thomas employ to add force to his arguments in paragraphs 20-23?

Suggested Topics for Writing and Discussion

1. Thomas argues that a knowledge of science should be "part of the intellectual equipment of an educated person, however his or her time is spent." What aspects of modern science do you think an educated person should know something about? Provide examples to support your view.

2. Thomas believes that it is vital for humanists to acquire some understanding of science. Discuss the corollary of this view: that courses in the humanities should be included in the education of scientists.

3. In the course of his essay, Thomas rejects the view that the task of science is to seek "mastery over nature," and expresses concern at the possibility that technology may be misapplied to achieve such a goal. Is there any evidence that Thomas's fears may be justified? What developments in modern science or medicine do you think should be regarded with concern?

4. Thomas says, "The worst thing that has happened to science education is that the great fun has gone out of it." Do you agree? To support your view, use examples from a particular area of science education (e.g., a programme in college or university, the curriculum for children in a particular stage of school).

5. Lewis Thomas, Rachel Carson, and David Suzuki all point to the dangers and problems of living in, as Carson says, "an era of specialists, each of whom sees his own problem and is unaware of the larger frame into which it fits." Argue for or against the training of specialists in our society.

Unexpected Vistas

by James Trefil

One of the great rewards of hiking or backpacking is to follow a trail   1
and, suddenly and without warning, top a hill or come to a break in
the trees and see the panorama of the coutryside laid out before you.
The view of the distant waterfall or rolling hills is often remembered
as the high point of the entire excursion.

   Such experiences occur in intellectual life, too. The moment of the   2
"Aha!" — which cartoonists usually render by showing a light bulb coming on above someone's head — is an analogous happening. So too is
the unexpected discovery that two things seemingly unconnected with
each other are in fact intimately related. But while every hiker on a
given trail will see the same view, the intellectual vista has the property that each person who comes to it can see something entirely
different.

   For example, imagine a line of motorists at a traffic light. Each of   3
them is looking at the same thing, a rectangular yellow box with three
colored lights in it. But it is possible, even likely, that each of them
sees something very different from the others. Suppose that the first
person in line is an electrical engineer. To him, the traffic light is just
one appendage of a large computer-operated grid that regulates the movement of vehicles throughout the downtown area. If you pressed him
to go on — to describe the far reaches of his view — he might start
musing about the light as one example of control systems and eventually wind up talking about the best-designed control system of them
all, the human brain.

   The driver of the second car in line is the representative of a large   4 manufacturing firm. He sees the traffic light as an item that is built in a factory and sold to the city. After thinking for a while, he might go on to talk about the vast interconnecting web of economic activity, from mining to maintenance work, that has to be in place before something like a traffic signal is possible. He might even end with some general speculations about human beings as tool-making animals.

5   In the third car is an attorney. To him the traffic light might symbolize the set of laws human beings have developed. The mechanical or economic aspect of the device would be much less important than the rules of conduct it symbolizes. After all, at any given moment there are thousands of cars being driven in a city, and almost every driver obeys the traffic signals. Behind this display of mass obedience, our attorney may see the vast structure of the modern legal system, from legislators to courts to police officers. If pressed, he might go on to speculate about those aspects of the human character that require such a system to allow large groups of people to live together in relative harmony.

6   Each of our motorists sees the traffic light as part of a large interconnected network. The simple apparatus is seen to be just one aspect of an important system that governs some aspect of our lives. In a sense, the traffic light is like an object in the foreground of some marvelous medieval landscape painting, a device the artist uses to induce us to look further and see the rich tapestry of nature and civilization that lies behind it. I will call each driver's view of the traffic light a vista, a term that carries with it the connotation of wide-ranging view.

7   So the traffic light teaches us several important lessons. It tells us that the breadth and scope of the vista really have very little to do with the object that starts us looking. Whether the traffic light is seen as just a self-contained mechanical device or as part of a much larger system is primarily a function of the individual looking at it, and, more importantly, of that individual's training and habits of thought.

8   The traffic light also teaches us that two individuals looking at the same thing need not see the same vista. It's almost as if two hikers reach the same point in a trail, from which one sees a waterfall while the other sees a shady forest. We can often get an entirely different view of the world just by talking to people whose backgrounds lead them to see vistas different from our own.

9   Like other professionals, scientists have their unique vistas. It would be a mistake, however, to assume that all scientists share a common view of things. I was frequently surprised during the several years I

spent as part of an interdisciplinary team in cancer research by just how much the training of the other team members affected the way they looked at our work. To a biologist a cell is part of an evolving, growing, living system; to a physicist it is a "black box" that processes energy and produces an ordered system; to a statistician it is one more bit of data to put into a computer program. Clearly, there is no such thing as a single, monolithic "scientific" vista.

(1983)

The Writer's Subject

1. How does Trefil's use of the word "vista" unite the ideas in paragraphs 1 and 2?

2. Trefil says in paragraph 2 that "every hiker on a given trail will see the same view," but he goes on to say in paragraph 8 that "two individuals looking at the same thing need not see the same vista." Is this simply a contradiction?

3. What principle is Trefil demonstrating by his example of the motorists and the traffic light?

4. Why does Trefil state that "there is no such thing as a single, monolithic 'scientific' vista" (para. 9)?

The Writer's Style and Strategy

1. In discussing the nature of perception and the "intellectual vista," Trefil is dealing with abstract, intangible ideas. How does he help the reader to grasp these ideas?

2. What is Trefil's general pattern of reasoning: inductive or deductive?

3. Examine the concluding paragraph. How does its development reflect the pattern of discussion that precedes it?

Suggested Topics for Writing and Discussion

1. Trefil makes the point that "two individuals looking at the same thing need not see the same vista." With this in mind, put yourself into the place of two different persons and write brief descriptions on one of the topics below. Or, choose two "vistas" of another subject which interests you.
   (a) A prison, from the viewpoint of an inmate and of a guard.
   (b) A college or university from the viewpoint of a student and of a worker in the campus cafeteria.
   (c) An alpine meadow from the point of view of a hiker and of a real estate developer.
   (d) A funeral from the point of view of a child and of an adult.

2. Choose a process or concept which you have recently been introduced to in one of the subjects which you are studying. Put yourself in the position of a tutor and use an extended analogy to explain the matter in everyday, simple, or familiar terms.

3. Write a well-developed paragraph using an analogy. You may wish to use one of the topics which follow.
   (a) A university or college education as a savings account.
   (b) A selling technique as a method for catching fish.
   (c) A freshman at registration as a mouse in a maze.
   (d) The university or college curriculum as a smorgasbord.

4. Using one of the following topics as a starting point, develop an essay of explanation by means of an analogy.
   (a) Falling in love.
   (b) Writing an essay.
   (c) Stopping trade in drugs.
   (d) Listening to music.

Biographical Notes

ADDISON, Joseph (1672-1719)
English playwright, essayist, and critic; celebrated for his style, particularly in his contributions to the periodicals *The Spectator, Tatler,* and *The Guardian.*

ALLEN, Woody (b. 1935)
Pseudonym of Heywood Allen Konigsberg; American film director, writer, actor, and comedian; widely acclaimed for such films as *Annie Hall* (1977; Academy Award) and *Hannah and Her Sisters* (1986); author of *Getting Even* (1971), *Without Feathers* (1975), and *Side Effects* (1981), and *Three Films: Broadway Danny Rose, Zelig, and The Purple Rose of Cairo* (1987).

ATWOOD, Margaret (b. 1939)
Canadian poet, critic, novelist; winner of Governor General's awards for poetry (*The Circle Game,* 1966), and for fiction (*The Handmaid's Tale,* 1985). Her most recent work of fiction is the short story collection *Wilderness Tips* (1991).

AVIS, Walter (b. 1919)
Lexicographer and historian of language; editor of *A Dictionary of Canadianisms on Historical Principles* (1967).

AWIAKTA, Marilou
A Cherokee/Appalachian poet and writer, winner of the 1989 Distinguished Tennessee Writer Award, and author of *Selu: Spirit of Survival* (1991).

BACON, Francis (1561-1626)
English statesman and philosopher; writer on learning and scientific method (*The Advancement of Learning,* 1605; *Novum Organum,* 1620).

BAKER, Russell (b. 1925)
American journalist and humourist; columnist for the *New York Times* since 1962; winner of two Pulitzer Prizes. His most recent book is *There's a Country in My Cellar* (1990).

BETTELHEIM, Bruno (1903-1990)
Austrian-born American professor of educational psychology, author of studies on emotionally-disturbed children and child rearing, including *The Empty Fortress* (1967), *The Children of the Dream* (1969), and *The Uses of Enchantment: The Meaning and Importance of Fairy Tales* (1976).

BIBBY, Geoffrey (b. 1917)
British archaeologist, author of *Testimony of the Spade* (1956) and *Four Thousand Years Ago: A World Panorama of Life in the Second Millenium B.C.* (1961).

BISSOONDATH, Neil (b. 1955)
Canadian novelist and short story writer, born in Trinidad. Author of *Digging Up the Mountains: Selected Stories* (1985), *A Casual Brutality* (1988), and *Uncertain Tomorrows* (1990).

BRODY, Hugh (b. 1943)
British anthropologist; participant in research on Inuit and Indian language and customs in Canada, and author of a number of studies, including *The People's Land* (1975) and *Maps and Dreams: Indians and the British Columbia Frontier* (1981), and *The Living Arctic* (1987).

BRONOWSKI, Jacob (1903-1974)
Polish-born English scientist, critic, essayist; concerned for much of his life with the relationship between art, science, and human values, examined in such books as *The Common Sense of Science* (1951), *Science and Human Values* (1956), *The Ascent of Man* (1973).

CARSON, Rachel (1907-1964)
Biologist for U.S. Fish and Wildlife Service from 1936-1952; author of *The Sea Around Us* (1951), *The Edge of the Sea* (1955), *Silent Spring* (1962).

CASTILLO, Edward D.
Chair of Native American Studies at Sonoma State University; a California Cahuilla Indian.

COLLIER, Simone
Canadian journalist; editor of the *Ryerson Review of Journalism*.

COWLEY, Malcolm (1898-1990)
Literary historian and critic; long-time literary advisor to Viking Press; author of *Exile's Return* (1934), a celebrated account of literary life in the 1920's.

CREAN, Susan (b. 1945)
Art critic and observer of Canadian culture. She is the author of *Who's Afraid of Canadian Culture?* (1973), *Two Nations: An Essay on the Culture and Politics of Canada and Quebec* (1983), and *Newsworthy: The Lives of Media Women* (1985).

DOBBS, Kildare (b. 1923)
Canadian journalist; born in India, served in British colonial service in Tanganyika 1948-52; author of *Running to Paradise* (1962; Governor General's Award).

DRYDEN, Ken (b. 1947)
Canadian lawyer, formerly star goaltender for the Montreal Canadiens; author of *The Game* (1984), a study of professional hockey.

EISELEY, Loren (1907-1977)
Anthropologist, historian, and philosopher of science, author of many books and articles explaining science to the lay reader (*Darwin's Century*, 1958; *Firmament of Time*, 1960; *The Star Thrower*, 1978).

FARR, Moira
A Canadian freelance writer based in Toronto. An editor of *This Magazine*.

FLANNER, Janet (1892-1978)
Regular contributor to the *New Yorker* from 1925-75, with her "Letter from Paris," under the pseudonym "Genet."

FORSTER, E.M. (1879-1970)
Novelist, essayist, writer of short stories; best known for *A Room with a View* (1908), *Howard's End* (1910), and *A Passage to India* (1924).

FRASER, Fil
A journalist born and raised in Montreal's East End; employed by ACCESS, Alberta's educational television network.

FRYE, Northrop (1912-1991)
Critic, editor, professor of English at University of Toronto; one of the most influential literary theorists of his time; author of many books, including *Anatomy of Criticism* (1957); *The Bush Garden: Essays on the Canadian Imagination* (1971); *The Great Code: The Bible and Literature* (1982), and *The Double Vision: Language and Meaning in Religion* (1991).

FULFORD, Robert (b. 1932)
Canadian journalist, film reviewer, contributor to CBC Radio and Television; editor, for many years, of *Saturday Night* magazine.

GIANGRANDE, Carole (b. 1945)
Canadian author of *The Nuclear North: The People, the Regions and the Arms Race* (1983) and *Down to Earth: The Crisis in Canadian Farming* (1985).

GILLMOR, Don
Canadian journalist, contributing editor of *Saturday Night,* and author of *I Swear By Apollo: Dr. Ewen Cameron and the CIA-brainwashing Experiments* (1987).

GOULD, Glenn (1932-1982)
Renowned Canadian pianist and musical prodigy; retired from concert performance in 1964 to devote himself to recording; writer and editor of documentaries for CBC Radio, of notes for his own recordings, and of articles for music magazines.

GOULD, Stephen J.
Harvard paleontologist and geology professor, author of award-winning books on evolution and biological determinism, including *Ever Since Darwin* (1977), *The Mismeasure of Man* (1981) and *The Flamingo's Smile: Reflections in Natural History* (1985), *Wonderful Life: The Burgess Shale and the Nature of History* (1990), and *Bully for Brontosaurus* (1991).

GRAHAM, Hugh
A Toronto writer whose plays and skits have often been performed on CBC radio; in recent years he has turned increasingly to writing non-fiction.

HALDANE, J.B.S. (1892-1964)
Controversial English geneticist and biochemist, known for his eccentric scientific methods, and for his work on heredity; author of many books and essays on science and society.

HOBAN, Russell (b. 1925)
American author of books for children, including *The Mouse and His Child* (1967) and for adults, including *Turtle Diary* (1975) and *Riddley Walker* (1980).

HOGGART, Richard (b. 1918)
British academic, critic, and educator. Contributor to many collections of critical essays; author of the influential study *The Uses of Literacy* (1957) and numerous other books, including *Only Connect* (The Reith Lectures, 1972) and *The Future of Broadcasting* (1982).

IGLAUER, Edith
American-born writer who has written about Canada's North in such books as *Denison's Ice Road* (1975) and *Inuit Journey* (1979); married commercial fisherman John Daly, about whom she wrote in *Fishing with John* (1988); a frequent contributor to major national magazines such as the *New Yorker* and *Maclean's*. Her most recent book is *The Strangers Next Door* (1991).

INGRAM, Jay
Canadian broadcaster and writer on science; host of CBC's science program *Quirks and Quarks* for many years. He has written non-fiction for children (*Twins: An Amazing Investigation*, (1988) as well as adults (*The Science of Everyday Life*, 1990).

JOHNSON, Samuel (1709-1784)
English essayist, poet, critic, editor, and lexicographer (*A Dictionary of the English Language*, 1755).

JOHNSTON, Basil (b. 1929)
An Ojibway writer born on Parry Island Indian Reserve, Ontario; member of the Ethnology Department at the Royal Ontario Museum; author of many short stories, essays and books on First Nations' culture and history, including *Ojibway Heritage* (1976), *How the Birds Got Their Colours* (1978), and *Indian School Days* (1988).

KAEL, Pauline (b. 1919)
Controversial film critic for the *New Yorker* from 1968-1991; many of her reviews are collected in book form (*Kiss Kiss, Bang Bang*, 1968; *Deeper into the Movies*, 1973; *When the Lights Go Down*, 1980; *Movie Love*, 1991). Received a National Book Award in 1974 for *Deeper into the Movies*.

KEESHIG-TOBIAS, Lenore
Toronto-based Ojibway poet, storyteller and cultural activist; past editor of *Ontario Indian*; editor of the *Magazine to Re-establish the Trickster*; writer of a number of tales for children.

KENNEDY, X.J. (b. 1929)
Pseudonym of Joseph Charles Kennedy, poet, professor of English, editor of literary anthologies.

LAURENCE, Margaret W. (1926-1987)
Canadian writer best known for her novels of prairie life, including *A Jest of God* (1966) and *The Diviners* (1974), both of which received a Governor General's Award. Her memoir, *Dance on the Earth*, appeared posthumously in 1989.

LEACOCK, Stephen (1869-1944)
Economics professor at McGill, and a prolific writer of humorous books, including *Literary Lapses* (1910), *Sunshine Sketches of a Little Town* (1912), and *Arcadian Adventures with the Idle Rich* (1914).

LURIE, Alison (b. 1926)
Cornell English professor and novelist; Pulitzer Prize in fiction for *Foreign Affairs* (1984). Her most recent works include *Don't Tell the Grown-ups: Subversive Children's Literature* (1990) and a novel, *The Truth about Lorin Jones* (1988).

MacLENNAN, Hugh (b. 1907)
Canadian novelist, essayist, and former English professor at McGill University; winner of five Governor General's Awards; his novels include *Two Solitudes* (1945), *The Watch That Ends the Night* (1959), and *Voices in Time* (1980).

MORRIS, Jan (b. 1926)
British writer, born James Morris, name changed to Jan after sex change in 1972. A distinguished journalist for the London *Times* and the *Manchester Guardian*; fellow of the Royal Society of Literature; author of many books on travel and history, including *Venice* (1960, 1974), *Oxford* (1965, 1978), *Among the Cities* (1985), and *City to City* (1990).

MOWAT, Farley (b. 1921)
Born in Ontario; a fierce and controversial defender of life in the Canadian Arctic (*People of the Deer*, 1952) and of animals threatened by man (*Never Cry Wolf*, 1963, *A Whale for the Killing*, 1972, and *Sea of Slaughter* 1982).

O'CONNOR, (Mary) Flannery (1925-1964)
American author of short stories and novels, including *Wise Blood* (1952), and *Everything That Rises Must Converge* (stories, 1965).

ORWELL, George (1903-1950)
Pseudonym of English political journalist and satirist Eric Blair; served with the Indian Imperial Police in Burma, 1922-27; fought with the Republicans in Spain, describing the experience in *Homage to Catalonia* (1938); author of *Animal Farm* (1945) and *Nineteen Eighty-Four* (1949).

PLUMB, John Harold (b. 1911)
Cambridge historian, broadcaster, contributor to journals; author of many books on cultural and political history, and of a work on the nature of history, *The Death of the Past* (1969).

RAFFERTY, Terrence
Film critic for the *New Yorker* magazine.

RICHLER, Mordecai (b. 1931)
Canadian satirist, author of essays and novels, including The *Apprenticeship of Duddy Kravitz* (1959) and *St. Urbain's Horseman* (1971; Governor General's Award), and *Solomon Gursky Was Here* (1990). His most recent work of non-fiction is *Oh Canada! Oh Quebec!* (1992).

ROYKO, Mike (b. 1932)
Reporter and columnist for Chicago newspapers since 1959, winner of Pulitzer Prize in 1972.

RYBCZYNSKI, Witold Marian (b. 1943)
Scottish-born architect and planner, professor at McGill University in Montreal. Author of several books, including *Home: A Short History of an Idea* (1986), *The Most Beautiful House in the World* (1989), and *Waiting for the Weekend* (1991).

SALUTIN, Rick (b. 1942)
A critic, playwright, novelist, journalist, and an editor of *This Magazine*. His works include the plays *1837: The Farmer's Revolt* (1976) and *Les Canadiens* (1977), the novel *A Man of Little Faith* (1988), and two works of non-fiction, *Waiting for Democracy: A Citizen's Journal* (1989) and *Living in a Dark Age* (1992).

SELZER, Richard (b. 1928)
Surgeon, essayist, writer of short stories. Collections of his essays include *Confessions of a Knife* (1979) and *Rituals of Surgery* (1987).

SILLITOE, Alan (b. 1928)
Self-educated English novelist and short-story writer, author of such anti-establishment works as *Saturday Night and Sunday Morning* (1958) and *The Loneliness of the Long-Distance Runner* (1959).

STEGNER, Wallace (b. 1909)
Formerly professor of English at Stanford; writer about the American and Canadian West (*The American West as Living Space,* 1987); writer of short stories and novels, winning a Pulitzer Prize for *Angle of Repose* (1971), and author of *On the Teaching of Creative Writing* (1988).

STEINEM, Gloria (b. 1934)
Journalist; a leading figure in the American feminist movement; founded *Ms* magazine in 1972. Author of *Marilyn* (1986), a book on Marilyn Monroe, and an autobiographical work, *Revolution from Within* (1992).

SUZUKI, David (b. 1936)
Canadian scientist, academic, and broadcaster, renowned for his work in genetics; the host of the CBC television programme *The Nature of Things*. Two recent books, co-authored with Peter Knudtson, are *Genethics: The Clash Between the New Genetics and Human Values* (1989), and *The Wisdom of the Elders* (1992).

SWIFT, Jonathan (1667-1745)
Irish satirist and pamphleteer; dean of St. Patrick's in Dublin; critic of English policy in Ireland; author of *Gulliver's Travels* (1726).

THOMAS, Lewis (b. 1913)
Formerly professor of pathology; head of Sloan-Kettering Cancer Center; contributor of many articles to medical and scientific journals, some collected in the National Book Award-winning *Lives of a Cell: Notes of a Biology Watcher* (1974) and in *Late Night Thoughts on Listening to Mahler's Ninth Symphony* (1983). His most recent work is *Et Cetera, Et Cetera: Notes of a Language Watcher* (1990).

THURBER, James (1894-1961)
Journalist and humorist, long-time contributor to the *New Yorker*; collaborated with E.B. White on *Is Sex Necessary?* (1929). Collections of his essays and drawings include *The Thurber Carnival* (1945).

TREFIL, James (b. 1938)
Professor of physics at University of Virginia; author of works explaining developments in science to the general public (From *Atoms to Quarks*, 1980; *The Unexpected Vista*, 1983). His other works include *Space, Time, Infinity: The Smithsonian Views the Universe* (1985), and *Science Matters: Achieving Scientific Literacy*, co-authored with Robert M. Hazen (1991).

TUCHMAN, Barbara (b. 1912)
Journalist, historian, winner of Pulitzer Prizes for *The Guns of August* (1962) and *Stillwell and the American Experience in China, 1911-1945* (1971). Her most recent work is *The First Salute* (1988).

TWAIN, Mark (1835-1910)
Pseudonym of Samuel Langhorne Clemens, steamboat pilot, prospector, journalist; celebrated as a lecturer and humorist; author of *The Adventures of Tom Sawyer* (1876), *Life on the Mississippi* (1883), *The Adventures of Huckleberry Finn* (1884).

VANDERHAEGHE, Guy (b. 1951)
Canadian novelist and short story writer; author of collection *Man Descending* (1982; Governor General's Award). His most recent novels are *My Present Age* (1984) and *Homesick* (1989).

VISSER, Margaret (b. 1940)
South-African born professor of Classics at York University in Toronto; author of *Much Depends on Dinner: The Extraordinary History and Mythology, Allure and Obsessions, Perils and Taboos, of an Ordinary Meal* (1986) and *The Rituals of Dinner* (1991).

WALKER, Martin (b. 1947)
English journalist, novelist, and social commentator who has reported on international affairs for the *Manchester Guardian* for many years. Books include *The National Front* (1977), *Daily Sketches* (a history of political cartoons) (1978), and *The Waking Giant: The Soviet Union under Gorbachev* (1986).

WHITE, E.B. (1899-1985)
Journalist, essayist, contributor to the *New Yorker* for over half a century; author of renowned children's books *Stuart Little* (1945) and *Charlotte's Web* (1952).

WILSON, Edward O. (b. 1929)
Harvard professor of zoology, one of the world's leading experts on the insect world. whose book *Sociobiology: The New Synthesis* (1975) put forward controversial theories about genetic determinism and human behaviour. His book *On Human Nature* (1978) was awarded the 1979 Pulitzer Prize in general non-fiction.

WOODCOCK, George (b. 1912)
Canadian critic; friend and biographer of George Orwell (*The Crystal Spirit*, 1966); prolific writer of travel books, critical studies, literary and social histories. In 1959 founded *Canadian Literature,* which he edited until 1977.

WOOLF, Virginia (1882-1941)
Innovative and influential English novelist (*To the Lighthouse,* 1927; *The Waves,* 1931), a literary critic, and an early advocate of feminism (*A Room of One's Own,* 1929).

Glossary

Abstract This is used in two ways: first, to mean general as opposed to specific or particular; second, to mean general as distinguished from **concrete**, a physical embodiment (e.g., *home* is abstract; a *wooden-frame house* is concrete). While writers may rely upon abstractions to some extent, they usually introduce **concrete** or specific details to give the abstraction matter, body, and meaning.

Allusion A fleeting or casual reference to a well known person, place, thing, event, or phrase. These may be real or fictional. Allusions are generally drawn from history, literature, mythology, the *Bible,* or other such sources. Examples: Cleopatra, the shot heard around the world (the assassination of the Archduke Ferdinand), Tom Sawyer, Athena, Eve. Allusions are an economical way for writers to enlarge upon a statement.

Analogy A comparison of some length; analogy is usually employed to explain something new in terms of something familiar, something unknown in terms of the known. (See Trefil's "Unexpected Vistas.") Analogy is frequently employed in argument, usually to dramatize the writer's position, but it is often open to question because the two things compared, though they may be alike in many points, may not be alike in all essential points.

Analysis A method of exposition which employs logical division. The writer uses analysis to break the topic into component parts as a means of organizing the discussion.

Argument A prose form which, in presenting a particular view, assumes that there are two sides to the issue under discussion; the writer of argument aims to influence readers to see the matter from the writer's point of view, to change their beliefs and opinions. The writer usually employs one or more of the other prose forms — exposition, narration, description — to present an argument. In trying to prove a point, the argumentative writer employs **logic** by appealing to reason with various kinds of proofs. The writer of argument usually defines terms and explains facts and ideas. Logical argument usually proceeds by **inductive reasoning** (from specific examples to a general conclusion) or **deductive reasoning** (from premises to a logical conclusion).

Another element of argument which has some importance is the demonstration of the speaker's good character in the establishing of the line of argument. Look, for example, at the closing paragraphs of Swift's "Modest Proposal" to see how the speaker seeks to demonstrate his disinterestedness in the cause he advances.

A distinction is usually made between **argument** and **persuasion.** The argumentative writer employs *logic* to appeal to the reader's intellect with the aim to change the reader's mind whereas the persuasive writer employs various devices of *pathos* to appeal to the reader's feelings or emotions with the aim to instigate action. While the proof in argument rests upon the presentation of objective evidence, that in persuasion derives in large part from the writer's use of controlled language, particularly **diction** with powerful connotations. Whatever the technique used, the writer aims to convince readers to share the writer's own values and opinions (and, in the case of persuasion, possibly to take action to change a situation). Whether an author chooses to emphasize logic or pathos depends on the subject and the audience.

Assumption   That part of an argument which is not stated because the writer takes for granted the clarity of the position or the sympathy of the audience. (A good example is the belief of the Proposer in Swift's "A Modest Proposal" that his audience will share his view that any solution proposed for Ireland's problems will be acceptable.)

Burlesque   A form of comedy in which people, actions, or literary works are made ridiculous by incongruous imitation and by exaggeration. The sublime may be made ridiculous, a serious subject approached with considerable silliness, or a frivolous subject treated with high seriousness. Style is important (e.g., a style which is usually reserved for serious matters is used to treat trivial matters, or the reverse). **Parody** and **caricature** are species of burlesque. Generally, burlesque makes fun of a literary *form,* whereas **parody** makes fun of a particular *work.* (See Woody Allen's "Slang Origins.")

Caricature   A type of portrait which makes its subject ridiculous by exaggerating or distorting prominent features without losing the general likeness. In visual art, the cartoon — especially the political cartoon — is the commonest form.

Classification   A strategy of expository writing used to break a subject into categories or classes. Once the subject is placed in classes, the writer discusses the characteristics which distinguish the members of the class one from another.

Cliché   An over-used expression that has lost its original power. Clichés are entirely predictable (e.g., "as old as the hills," "as innocent as a newborn babe," "as fresh as a daisy").

Coherence   Logical connection or congruity of thought within writing. When the various parts of an essay fit together and the flow of thought from section to section is clear and easy to follow, the essay has coherence. This quality is also achieved when the essay develops a single, central idea, since it is difficult to separate coherence from **unity.**

Colloquialism   A word used chiefly in conversation. Appropriate to informal writing, but not to formal writing.

Comparison and Contrast   A strategy of expository writing used to explore similarities and differences between two subjects. In strict terms, **comparison** is used to present a subject by means of showing similarities between two or more things. To be comparable, the components of the comparison should be members of the same class. In common practice, however, comparison often includes differences or elements of **contrast** as well, for the writer may be striving to emphasize only general similarities rather than point-by-point similarities (as, for example, the strict comparisons required for effective **analogy**).

Conclusion   The closing of an essay, that part which gives the reader a sense of resolution of ideas, and a sense of an ending. The conclusion may be brief — a line or two — or it may be a section of the essay on its own. There are many strategies for conclusions, from the signals of transitional phrases such as "finally" and "in conclusion" to a reiteration of the opening stance with a variation. Writers may conclude with such techniques as an answer to an opening question, with echoes of the instruction, with a plea for action, with an allusion, a quotation, an ironic statement, or an illustrative anecdote.

Concrete   Definite, particular, capable of being seen and understood directly; the opposite of **abstract.** *Rain* and *Tokyo* are concrete, *weather* and *city* are abstract.

Connotation   The associative meanings of a word; implications and overtones that may be added to the dictionary meaning of a word. While the denotation of "mother" is "a female who has borne offspring," its connotation is emotionally charged with associations of love, security, nurture, protection, warmth, etc. Connotations of "mother" are so powerful, for example, that we speak of issues which are not readily open to attack as "motherhood" issues.

Contrast   The presentation of a subject by means of showing differences between two or more things. To be contrasted, the subjects discussed should be members of the same class. See **comparison.**

Deductive Reasoning   The process of reasoning from premises to a logical conclusion. Deduction is often presented in the form of a logical syllogism. The classic example is: "All men are mortal; Socrates is a man; therefore, Socrates is mortal" (inference or conclusion). If the syllogism is correctly constructed, then the inference is *logically* valid. Logical *fallacies* occur when the conclusion does not follow from the premises (e.g., "Some students are radical; John is a student; therefore, John is a radical"). Even if the logic is sound, however, the conclusion will not be true if one of the premises is false (e.g., "All students are radicals; John is a student; therefore, John is a radical").

Definition The act of stating what a word, term, phrase or set of terms signifies, usually by means of placing it in a class and demonstrating how it differs from other members of the class. The essay of definition generally extends a definition by means of details, anecdotes, examples, and metaphorical language (e.g., Forster employs definition in part to answer the central question of his essay, "My Wood"; Allen parodies the essay of definition in "Slang Origins").

Denotation The dictionary meaning of a word. "Mother," for example, denotes "a female who has borne offspring; a female parent." (See also **connotation**.)

Description A type of writing which uses details or images appealing to the five senses to create a mental picture. A descriptive essay or passage of description in an essay employs specific details and concrete diction to explain a person, place, scene, thing, or sensory experience.

Diction Choice of words. Diction will depend upon the writer's intended audience, purpose, and the stylistic effect aimed at. The writer may choose many different levels of diction: simple or colloquial rather than Latinate diction in order to address a school-aged audience; words with strong connotations rather than words relatively free of associations in order to persuade; archaic or foreign words and phrases in order to impress, or to give a false seriousness to the topic. A writer may draw from formal or standard language, informal or colloquial language, slang, or dialect (e.g., old man, old coot, eighty-year-old, octogenarian).

Emphasis The arrangement of the components of a composition to ensure that the important points are prominent (in an essay as a whole, in an argument, in a paragraph, in a sentence). Emphasis may be achieved through order of increasing importance, proportion of evidence, repetition of elements, transitional markers (e.g., "the single most important factor is. . . ."), metaphorical language, rhetorical questions, and mechanical devices such as underlinings, exclamation marks, or the highlighting of material in obvious ways (headings, indentations).

Epigraph A quotation or motto which prefaces a work. Epigraphs are often in foreign languages. (See Addison's "On Party-lying," Selzer's "The Discus Thrower.")

Euphemism The substitution of a mild or roundabout expression for another felt to be distasteful, blunt, or painful (e.g., "pass away" for "die").

Exposition A prose form which explains or informs. Definition, classification, illustration and example, analysis, and comparison and contrast are some of the common means of developing an expository piece.

Figures of Speech A form of expression in which the usual, literal meanings of words are extended. Figures of speech are based upon comparisons of unlike things which have some point of similarity. See this glossary for some of the common figures of speech: **metaphor, simile, personification, allusion, analogy, irony, paradox.**

Inductive Reasoning The process of reasoning from specific examples or illustrations to a general principle. Inductive reasoning, the method of the scientist, is generally more common in argumentation than deductive reasoning. A writer may, in practice, state the conclusion first and then proceed to show the specifics which lead to the general principle. An inductive argument is only as valid as its supporting evidence; this evidence must be relevant, representative, accurate, and complete; the writer who employs induction must be certain that the evidence will bear close scrutiny.

Introduction The opening of an essay. Introductions are remarkably variable, but they do have some functions in common: they establish the **tone** of the essay; and they often show the plan of the essay as a whole. A writer may try to "grab" readers by means of rhetorical questions, surprising statements or statistics, engaging anecdotes, allusions, paradoxes, quotations, or a particular claim about the importance of the subject.

Irony A reality that differs significantly from appearance. In its broadest terms, *verbal irony* is a sarcastic or humorous means of discourse in which what is expressed literally means the opposite, as for example, when "I had an absolutely great day" means "I had a terrible day." *Irony of situation* presents a discrepancy between what is expected to happen and what actually does happen (e.g., see Thurber's "Courtship Through the Ages"). To sustain irony, authors often employ a naive narrator or expositor; the well-intentioned but simplistic Proposer in Swift's "A Modest Proposal" is a striking example (see also **Persona**).

Jargon A specialized vocabulary used by a particular group; the language of "insiders" intended for a particular audience within a profession or special-interest group (pilots, psychoanalysts, skiers, motorcycle gangs). (See Cowley's "Sociological Habit Patterns in Linguistic Transmogrification.")

Metaphor A figure of speech which compares two unlike things without using "like" or "as," and which asserts the identity of the two terms of comparison: e.g., "The road was a ribbon of light." (See also **simile.**) A metaphor's effectiveness is dependent upon its power of association. Dead metaphors are those in such frequent use that their metaphorical nature is hardly ever thought of (e.g., "a head of state" or "the hands of a clock" no longer recall the parts of the body they refer to). See Orwell's "Politics and the English Language" for a discussion of dying metaphors.

Narration The telling of a story which may be real or fictional. When a story is told for the sake of the story itself, it may be said to be "pure" narration. Narration is, however, commonly employed to support an argument or to illustrate an exposition.

Objective The detached way in which a writer sees the material, characterized by an impersonal, fact-based and unbiased approach. In contrast,

subjective writing is characterized by an individual, opinion-based, and judgmental approach (e.g., "The douglas fir is a conifer" is a fact; "the douglas fir is the noblest of the conifers" is an opinion.) Totally objectivity is not possible, of course, since the writer is an individual with individual perceptions and a unique consciousness. (See also **Point of view.**)

Paradox A statement that seems self-contradictory or absurd but which actually contains some truth in it. This rhetorical device is used to attract attention. An example taken from Wordsworth: "The child is father of the man."

Parallel Structures or Constructions Elements with similar rhetorical importance (e.g., words, phrases, clauses) used in similar patterns. A writer will use two or more words from the same grammatical category, and relate them in the same way in order to achieve a particular effect. Virginia Woolf's "How Should One Read a Book?" has many examples: "It may be one letter — but what a vision it gives! It may be a few sentences — but what vistas they suggest!" See also Samuel Johnson, an author celebrated for his use of parallel structures.

Parody A composition which mimics the language and style of another work. Parody is generally intended to ridicule an author or a particular work — one which is usually serious. The parody has been used as a powerful means of satire by authors from ancient Greece to modern times. (See also **Burlesque.**)

Persona The Latin word for the mask worn by actors in classical drama. A persona is a character, "second self," or voice created by an author for a specific audience. An author might, for various reasons, be able to speak more freely through a persona than in his own voice. Often, a persona is used for satiric purposes as, for example, in Swift's "A Modest Proposal" and Royko's "Another Accolade for Charter Arms Corp."

Personification A figure of speech which endows an inanimate object or abstraction with human qualities (e.g., "the heavens wept").

Persuasion A writing approach used to convince an audience to do something or to share the writer's beliefs. The writer employs various devices of *pathos* to move the reader to action. An important part of persuasive writing is the establishment of the author's credibility or *ethos* — the writer's ethical stance, fairness, knowledge, honesty. (See **Argument.**)

Point of View Literally, the point from which something is seen, the angle from which a writer tells a story. Writers use the first-person point of view (characterized by "I") to establish a familiar tone and to emphasize personal involvement; the third-person point of view (characterized by "he," "she," and "it") to maintain distance; and the second-person point of view (characterized by "you") to establish an immediate one-to-one relationship with the reader. Writers often shift point of view for a particular purpose. (See Thurber's "Courtship Through the Ages" and Gloria Steinem's "Marilyn Monroe: The Woman Who Died Too Soon.") In a loose way, point of view may refer to the writer's closeness to or distance from the subject. (See also **objective/subjective**.)

Pun A humorous play on the meaning of words, or on their sound (e.g., "How big is this bookstore?" "Oh — about two stories"). An author may also pun upon a well known phrase (e.g., Lewis Thomas's "physics envy," a pun on "penis envy").

Refutation A technique in argument in which the writer recognizes and then counters the arguments or objections of those opposed him; sometimes called rebuttal. (See Gould's "Let's Ban Applause!")

Rhetorical Question Often used to suggest only questions which do not require an answer. In practice, a rhetorical question may also be the starting point for a discussion which does, in fact, provide the answer (e.g., Virginia Woolf's "How Should One Read a Book?")

Rhythm Patterned emphasis in language through the use of light and heavy stresses, long or short syllables, or repetitions of phrase or clause. Rhythm is a characteristic feature of good prose, but it does not have the regularity of rhythm in poetry.

Sarcasm The blatant and caustic use of apparent praise for actual disapproval or criticism. It is the commonest form of irony.

Satire The literary art of diminishing a subject by making it ridiculous and creating in the reader attitudes of amusement, contempt, or scorn. The laughter arising from satire is not laughter for the fun of laughter; rather, the laughter is a weapon, usually directed against a particular target (e.g., a particular individual, a character type, an institution, a class, a nation, or perhaps mankind itself). Satire is usually employed with the aim of correcting human vice and folly.

Simile A figure of speech which, using "like" or "as," compares two distinctly different things or actions (e.g., Orwell's "The friction of the great beast's foot had stripped the skin from his back as neatly as one skins a rabbit").

Slang A level of language associated with conversation and informal writing. It is characterized by liveliness of expression employed for effect, and it is considered to be at the "low" end of colloquial expression. Slang tends to date quickly (e.g., "tin lizzie" for automobile). In general, it should be avoided, but an isolated example or two may create a special effect.

Style The appropriate use of language or, in the words of Swift, "proper words in proper places." But style is more than the fitting of language with context, for it is highly individualistic — as the old adage "the style is the man" suggests; style is *how* the writer says what he says. Writers establish a personal style and create a sense of life in written work by many different means. Among these are choice of diction, figures of speech, sentence structure (length and variety), particular rhetorical patterns, tonal variations, and rhythm.

Subjective   An attitude of personal involvement with the topic discussed. The writer clearly reveals personal feelings and opinions about the topic discussed. (See **Objective**.)

Syllogism   An argument which takes two premises and joins them to produce a logical conclusion. See **deductive reasoning**.

Symbol   A person, place, or thing that exists in itself but which also stands for something else, something abstract or intangible (e.g., a flag, a tangible piece of cloth, may symbolize a nation or a political movement; an object such as a cross or a menorah may symbolize a particular religion).

Thesis or thesis statement   That part of the essay which states most clearly the writer's position or attitude. It is what the writer has to say — the chief idea or proposition advanced — about the subject. In brief essays the thesis is usually, though not always, expressed in a single sentence, and placed in the opening paragraph or paragraphs.

Tone   A writer's attitude toward the subject. A writer's involvement with the subject and attitude towards the audience determines tone. In speech, a speaker's attitude may be conveyed through tone of voice; in writing, tone is expressed chiefly through style, especially diction and sentence structure. The tone may be **objective,** appealing chiefly to the reader's intellect; or it may be **subjective,** appealing chiefly to the reader's emotions. Tone has many shades (cool, amused, mocking, cynical, bitter, joyful).

Topic sentence   The sentence in the paragraph that carries the main idea. While the thesis statement directs the development of an essay, the topic sentence directs the development of a paragraph.

Transition   The linking of parts of an essay. Depending upon the length of the essay, the transition may be a word, phrase, sentence or paragraph (e.g., "consequently," "another factor to consider," "And this brings us to our fourth and final point: the blackberries"). Transitions contribute to the smooth flow of ideas within a paragraph and between paragraphs. (See also **coherence**.)

Understatement   A form of **irony** which creates its effect by deliberately representing something as much less than it is in fact. In general, the speaker's emotional response is less than the response normally expected as, for example, when a speaker describes a movie star thought to be outstandingly beautiful or handsome as "not bad looking."

Unity   Oneness, the relevance of all the materials contained in an essay to its **thesis** or central idea. Within the paragraph, unity is achieved when all the materials relate to the **topic sentence** of the paragraph. (See also **coherence**.)

Index of Authors and Titles

Printed in Canada